The Congressional Club
Cook Book

The Congressional Club

Cook Book

A Collection of
National and International Recipes

Twelfth Edition

Compiled and Published by

The Congressional Club
Washington, D.C.

1993

MRS. TRENT LOTT, MISSISSIPPI
President

The year 1927 was a wonderful year in our nation's history. The first "talkie", *The Jazz Singer*, starring Al Jolsen, was released; Charles Lindburgh flew the "Spirit of St. Louis" from New York to Paris; Babe Ruth hit 60 homeruns; and The Congressional Club introduced their first cookbook.

Sixty six years have passed since that first edition cookbook was published. We are now extremely delighted to present the Twelfth Edition. This beautifully bound book is proudly dedicated to all the First Ladies and it is as regal as each First Lady herself.

The tradition of producing a lovely cookbook—one to be read, consulted, passed down from generation to generation, given as a gift, or simply displayed on the bookshelf—belongs to the Cookbook Committee. This challenging project requires countless hours of collecting, proofing and editing recipes. These appetizing contributions are generously submitted by members of The Congressional Club, Congress, The Cabinet, The White House, state Governors, and Ambassadors.

Under the capable leadership of Mrs. Jay (Annie) Rhodes of Arizona, and Mrs. John (Janet) Bryant of Texas, the committee has produced a collection of recipes representing every section of our country, including recipes from our diplomatic community posted in Washington, D.C. These recipes represent a country that has always been rich in ethnic heritage, history, and family tradition!

Deep appreciation to Mrs. Jim (Mary) Bunning of Kentucky and Mrs. Peter (Sally) Smith of Vermont for their beautiful illustrations that make this edition even more special.

The Cookbook Committee and the members of The Congressional Club hope you will enjoy this lovely book for years to come.

Tricia Lott

Additional copies of this book are available at:

The Congressional Club
2001 New Hamsphire Avenue, N.W.
Washington, D.C. 20009
Telephone—202-332-1155
Fax Number—202-797-0698

ACKNOWLEDGMENTS

The Congressional Club wishes to thank all those individuals whose contributions have made this, The Twelfth Edition of our cookbook, possible. We extend our special thanks to the Cook Book Committee, whose time, diligence and commitment made it all possible. We have tried to thank each one individually and acknowledge them here publicly. To those whom we may have inadvertently overlooked our sincere apologies and thanks.

Editors

Mrs. John Bryant, Texas

Mrs. Jay Rhodes, Arizona

Committee Members

Mrs. Bill Barrett, Nebraska
Mrs. Herbert Bateman, Virginia
Mrs. John Breaux, Louisiana
Mrs. Jim Chapman, Texas
Mrs. Dan Donovan, Washington
Mrs. Dale Kildee, Michigan

Mrs. Trent Lott, Mississippi
Mrs. Ralph Regula, Ohio
Mrs. Martin Sabo, Minnesota
Mrs. Richard Schulze, Pennsylvania
Mrs. Mick Staton, West Virginia
Mrs. Al Swift, Washington

Mrs. William Zeliff, New Hampshire

Art Work

Mrs. Jim Bunning, Kentucky

Mrs. Peter Smith, Vermont

Special Thanks

Affiliated Graphics
Dan Bradley
Gloria Chavez
Heather Cronrath
Decorating Den Systems, Inc.
Alice Duvall
Mrs. Robert Filner, California
Lydia de La Vina de Foley
Rodolfo Franco
General Electric

Mrs. Jimmy Hayes, Louisiana
Judy Hum
Pat Hutchens
Susan Keenan
Meyers and Associates
Choi Lin Phua
Peggy Rubach
Mrs. George Sangmeister, Illinois
Mrs. Ray Thornton, Arkansas

History of
The Congressional Club

The Congressional Club is celebrating its eighty fifth anniversary. In May 1908, during the Sixtieth Congress, the Bill H.R. 22029 was passed by both the House and the Senate. This Bill incorporated The Congressional Club, the only club in the world to be incorporated by an Act of Congress.

Active membership includes the spouses of Members and former Members of Congress, spouses of Supreme Court Justices and spouses of the Members of the President's Cabinet. Honorary membership is conferred upon the wives of the President, the Vice President and the Speaker of the House. Many members retain their membership upon leaving Washington.

The Club House, 2001 New Hampshire Avenue, N.W., was dedicated in 1914, with a formal reception at which time President Wilson was the guest of honor. The mortgage for all indebtedness was burned at a 40th Anniversary Breakfast for the First Lady when Mrs. Truman was present and did the burning. From the Club's membership comes eight First Ladies—Mrs. Harding, Mrs. Hoover, Mrs. Truman, Mrs. Kennedy, Mrs. Johnson, Mrs. Nixon, Mrs. Ford, and Mrs. Bush.

Since 1927, the Club has been self-sustaining through the sale of The Congressional Club Cook Book, which can be purchased only through the Club.

Table of Contents

This volume is dedicated
with love to
all those women who
have graced our country
as First Lady of the Land

Martha Dandridge Custis Washington
1789–1797

CHESS CAKES

1 cup butter
1 cup sugar
6 egg yolks, beaten
⅓ cup dry white wine
1 tablespoon lemon juice and grated rind of 1 lemon
¼ teaspoon salt
pastry for 1 9″ pie or 12 tarts (made in muffin tins or fluted patty pan)

Cream butter and beat into it slowly ½ cup sugar, reserving the rest of the sugar. Beat egg yolks with salt until light and lemon colored, then slowly beat in the remaining ½ cup sugar; with a whisk fold in the lemon juice and grated lemon rind. Combine with the creamed mixture, stirring in the wine.

Pour into pie shell or tart shells, and bake at 350 degrees for 50 to 60 minutes until set.

Abigail Smith Adams
1797–1801

BAKED SALMON

salmon
skinned eel
1 pint oysters
2 tablespoons oyster
  liquid (reserved)
4 cups bread crumbs
3 tablespoons melted butter
3 eggs, beaten whole
1 tablespoon chopped
  parlsey
1 teaspoon thyme
dash of pepper
salt
dash of cloves
dash of nutmeg
pint of claret

Clean the salmon; wash and dry it. Lard it with a skinned eel. Combine a pint of oysters (reserve liquid), 4 cups bread crumbs, 3 tablespoons melted butter, 3 whole eggs, beaten, chopped parsley, thyme, pepper and salt, cloves, nutmeg, and 1 tablespoon oyster liquid. Fill the salmon with stuffing. Baste well with butter, lay salmon on a rack in a roasting pan, pour over it a pint of claret, and cover salmon with buttered paper. Bake in a preheated oven (550 degrees) for 10 minutes; then reduce the heat to 425 degrees, and bake 20–35 minutes longer. Allow 10 minutes per pound for the first 4 pounds and 5 minutes for each additional pound.

Baste several times. Ten minutes before the baking is done, uncover and bake until done.

Sauce:

drippings from the salmon
some shrimp
pickled mushrooms
2 anchovies

Sauce:
Boil ingredients together for sauce.

PLUM PUDDING

2 lbs. seedless raisins
1 lb. currants
1 lb. sultana raisins
1 qt. grated bread crumbs
1 qt. beef suet, chopped fine
½ lb. citron, cut fine
2 ozs. candied orange peel,
   cut fine
2 ozs. candied lemon peel,
   cut fine
1 grated nutmeg
1 teaspoon salt
1 teaspoon ginger
12 eggs, beaten whole
1 cup brandy
  milk
  spray of holly for decoration

Hard Sauce
⅓ cup butter
1 cup granulated sugar
   (sugar may be powdered,
   brown or maple)
1 teaspoon flavoring (vanilla,
   almond, or rum)

Mix the dry ingredients together well. Beat the eggs, and stir in the dry mixture. Add 1 cup brandy; if not moist enough, add as much milk as will make it cling together.

Put into closed tin forms, making sure that the cover is on tight. Put into boiling water, and boil 4 or 5 hours. The water must be boiling when the pudding is put in. When the water boils away, add boiling water, to keep the tin forms covered. Before turning out the pudding, plunge the closed pudding form into cold water for a few minutes. Serve with hard sauce in a separate dish. Decorate with a sprig of holly.

Sauce:
Cream the butter until it is very soft, then stir in the desired kind of sugar, and the desired flavoring. Set in a cool place until required for use. May be put into a star tube and squeezed out in rosette form.

Dorothea "Dolley" Payne Todd Madison
1809–1817

MADISON CAKES

2 medium-size potatoes
1 yeast cake crumbled over 1
   tablespoon granulated
   sugar
4 tablespoons butter
2 teaspoons salt
1 tablespoon sugar
2 eggs, beaten whole
6 cups flour

Boil potatoes well in 1¼ cups boiling water, until tender. Strain, and save 1 cup of the potato water. Mash potatoes into a bowl, add butter, sugar, and salt. When potato-water and potato are cooled to lukewarm, mix dissolved yeast cake in potato-water, and then combine with mashed potato mixture. Beat well. Sift in flour, beating continuously. Knead until smooth and spongy; then return to a well-greased bowl. Cover with a damp tea towel and place away from draft. Let double in bulk for about 3 hours, depending on heat and humidity.

Turn out on a floured board and roll 1-inch thick. Cut into rounds with a biscuit cutter. Place on buttered cookie sheets placed far apart. Let rise until light. Bake at 350°F in moderate oven until golden brown. Brush tops lightly with butter, and serve at once.

Elizabeth Kortright Monroe
1817–1825

GUMBO

2 spring fryers, cup up (about 4 pounds)

1½ pounds of fresh or frozen, sliced okra

1 large onion, chopped

5 tablespoons bacon drippings, or half butter and half lard

2 No. 2 cans solid-packed tomatoes or 5 cups, peeled, diced, fresh tomatoes

1 teaspoon salt
coarse black pepper

2 to 3 pounds flour

2 cups water

3 stalks celery with tops

1 bay leaf

½ teaspoon basil

1 cup rice

Put chicken giblets in cold water with celery, bay leaf, basil, salt and pepper to taste, and add backs and necks. Simmer gently while preparing the gumbo. In a paper or plastic bag, put flour, salt, and coarse black pepper. Shake the chicken pieces, a few at a time, until each piece is well covered with the flour and seasoning mixture. Fry in fat in heavy skillet until brown and transfer to a soup kettle; do not use iron, as the okra will discolor the entire dish and turn into an unappetizing gray. Next add the onions to the fat and brown until clear over low heat. Add several tablespoons flour to make a roux. Strain the broth from the giblets over this, stir well, and pour over chicken. Add tomatoes and okra, and simmer over low heat for about 2 hours. Correct seasonings to taste. Serve over fluffy rice. Serves 8–10.

Louisa Catherine Johnson Adams
1825–1829

CHICKEN CROQUETTES

3 tablespoons butter
⅓ cup flour
1½ cups minced cooked
   chicken
1 tablespoon minced scal-
   lions
1 tablespoon chopped
   parsley
2 eggs
2 tablespoons sherry
   salt and pepper to taste
1 tablespoon water
   Fine bread crumbs
   oil for frying

Melt butter, blend in flour and the milk. Cook, stirring with a wire whisk, until the mixture thickens and boils.

Add the chicken, onion, parsley and one egg, the sherry, salt and pepper. Cook, until thickened. Chill.

Use ¼ cup of the mixture to shape a croquette. Continue until mixture is used. Beat the remaining egg with the water. Coat the croquettes with crumbs, then with beaten egg, and again with crumbs. Dry on a rack for 20–30 minutes.

Fry in oil heated to 380 degrees F. Drain and serve. 9–10 croquettes

Rachel Donelson Robards Jackson
1829–1837

STRAWBERRY MOUSSE

2 pints strawberries, hulled,
sliced
¾ cup sugar
2 envelopes unflavored
gelatin
½ cup water
1 teaspoon almond extract
1 cup whipping cream
¼ cup rum

Put 2 cups of the strawberries in blender, process until smooth. Transfer to bowl. Mix ½ cup of the sugar and the gelatin in small saucepan: stir in water. Let stand 1 minute. Heat stirring constantly, over low heat until gelatin dissolves.

Add gelatin mixture and almond extract to strawberry puree and mix well. Refrigerate covered, until mixture mounds slightly when dropped from spoon, about one hour.

Beat cream in small mixing bowl until stiff and fold into gelatin mixture. Pour into 1 quart mold; refrigerate covered until firm, about three hours. Mix remaining strawberries, remaining ¼ cup sugar and rum in medium bowl, let stand 1 hour. Blend until smooth, 1 cup strawberries and rum. Mix with remaining strawberries and rum.

To serve, dip mold into hot water, invert and unmold onto serving dish. Serve with strawberry-rum sauce. Makes 8 servings.

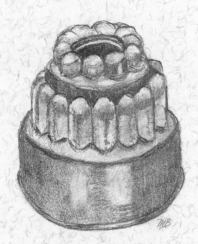

Angelica Singleton Van Buren
Daughter-in-Law and Official Hostess
of the Widower President, Martin Van Buren
1837–1841

CHICKEN AND GREEN GRAPE SALAD

6 chicken breasts, cooked
   and skinned
4 celery stalks, chopped
½ cup green onions
   dash cayenne
2 cups whole seedless grapes
   bottled French dressing
½ cup mayonnaise
1 cup heavy cream, whipped
1 cup toasted slivered
   almonds

Slice chicken into bite-sized pieces. Place in large bowl. Add celery, onion, cayenne and grapes. Mix. Add French dressing to cover chicken. Refrigerate overnight.

Return to room temperature and drain French dressing from chicken. Combine mayonnaise and whipped cream, add to salad. To serve, add almonds and toss. 8–10 servings.

Anna Tuthill Symmes Harrison
1841

MALLARD DUCK

5 mallard ducks
   salt and pepper to taste
¼ cup lemon juice
10 tart apples
1 bunch watercress
1 cup red wine

Clean and rinse ducks. Remove fat from inside. Rub with salt, pepper and lemon juice inside and out.

Core and quarter apples. Put apples and watercress in each duck. Close openings and place in roasting pans.

Roast at 450° degrees for 15 minutes to brown and bring out fat. Pour off fat. Roast at 350 degrees basting with red wine until tender. 1 to 1½ hours. Serves 10.

Letitia Christian Tyler
1841–1842

Julia Gardiner Tyler
1844–1845

SALLY LUNN

1 yeast cake
1 cup milk, warm
½ cup butter
⅓ cup sugar
3 eggs, beaten
4 cups flour

Put yeast cake in one cup of warm milk. Cream together ½ cup of butter and ⅓ cup sugar, add the 3 beaten eggs and mix well. Sift in flour alternately with the milk and yeast. Let rise in a warm place; then beat well. Pour into one well-buttered Sally Lunn mold, and two smaller molds. Let rise again before baking in a 325 degree oven until light brown.

Decorate with glacé cherries, glacé orange and lemon rind.

Sarah Childress Polk
1845–1849

HICKORY NUT CAKE

1 cup butter
2 cups sugar
4 eggs, separated
1 teaspoon lemon juice
3 cups flour, sifted
2 teaspoons baking powder
½ teaspoon salt
1 cup milk
1 cup chopped hickory nuts
1 teaspoon almond flavoring

Grease an 8¼" tube cake pan and flour well. Cream butter with 1 cup sugar. Beat egg yolks until light, beating in the remaining cup of sugar until light and lemon-colored. Then fold in lemon juice and combine with the creamed mixture. Sift in dry ingredients with the milk. Stir in nuts and flavoring. Beat the egg whites until light, but not dry. Fold in lightly. Pour into cake pan, bake at 350 degrees for 1 hour.

Icing
1 cup sugar
½ cup cold water
2 egg whites
1 teaspoon vanilla
1 cup chopped nuts

Icing:
Make a syrup of the sugar and water, cooking to 238 degrees F, the soft-ball stage. Allow to cool, while you beat egg whites. Pour the syrup in a thin steady stream onto the beaten egg whites, beating the mixture until it is thick enough to spread over the top and sides of the cake. Add flavoring before spreading. Sprinkle with nuts on top and around the cake. Makes 8 servings.

Mary Elizabeth "Betty" Taylor Bliss
Daughter and Official Hostess
of President Zachary Taylor
1849–1850

CRAB MEAT WITH HERBS

4 tablespoons butter
1½ lbs. crab meat, remove cartilage and shell
salt and pepper to taste
juice of ½ lemon
1 tablespoon chopped chives
1 tablespoon chopped
  parsley
1 tablespoon chopped tar-
  ragon

Heat the butter until it bubbles and cook the crab meat until heated through. Season the crab with salt, pepper, lemon juice and herbs. Serve on noodles or pasta. Four servings.

Abigail Powers Fillmore
1850–1853

ROAST CHICKEN

1 4 lb. roasting chicken
½ lemon
    salt and pepper to taste
1 small onion, peeled
½ teaspoon thyme
1 sprig tarragon
2 to 4 tablespoons butter,
    softened

Garnish:
parlsey sprigs
whole mushrooms, cut
into rosettes

Preheat the oven to 350 degrees. Clean the inside of the chicken and rub with lemon juice, and sprinkle with salt and pepper. Add onion and herbs to the cavity. Truss chicken and place in a roasting pan. Rub softened butter over the skin. Bake 20 minutes per pound. Baste as it roasts with its own juices. Chicken is done when leg moves up and down easily. Add garnish. Serves 4.

Jane Means Appleton Pierce
1853–1857

BOILED LIVE LOBSTER

1 small lobster per serving

Plunge the lobster, head first, into a large pot of rapidly boiling salted water. Cover, return to boil and boil 12-15 minutes for a 1½ to 2 pound lobster. When done, remove from water with tongs and place the lobster on its back. Slit the undershell lengthwise with a sharp knife or scissors. Remove and discard the dark vein, the sac near the head and spongy tissue. Serve hot with melted butter. Garnish with parsley and lemon wedges.

Harriet Lane Johnston
Niece and Official Hostess
of the Bachelor President, James Buchanan
1857–1861

APPLESAUCE

2½ pounds tart green apples
½ cup water
¼ cup sugar

Core and peel the apples. Cut into thin pieces, there should be about 6 cups. Put them in a heavy saucepan. Add water and sugar, bring to a boil. Cover over low heat until the apples disintegrate, stirring often. Pour the mixture into food processor or blender and puree until fine, Serves 8.

Mary Todd Lincoln
1861–1865

CORN ON THE COB

Ears of corn
Salt
Pepper

Bring enough water to boil to more than cover the corn when it is added to the kettle. Add one tablespoon of salt for each quart of water. Remove the husks from the corn and trim the ends. Drop the corn into the boiling water and return to a boil. Turn off the heat immediately and let the corn stand in the water for exactly five minutes. Serve with butter. 1–2 ears per person.

LINCOLN'S HOME IN SPRINGFIELD

Eliza McCardle Johnson
1865–1869

BAKED EGGPLANT PARMIGIANA

1½ to 2-pound eggplant
4 tablespoons butter (room temperature)
3 tablespoons grated Parmesan cheese
salt and pepper to taste
chopped parsley for garnish

Preheat oven to 400 degrees. Peel the eggplant and trim the ends. Cut the eggplant into half inch thick slices. There should be six to eight slices. Blend the butter and cheese and spread the eggplant slices on both sides. Sprinkle with salt and pepper. Arrange the slices on a baking sheet. Bake 15 to 20 minutes until eggplant is tender. Sprinkle with parsley and serve. Makes 4 servings.

Julia Dent Grant
1869–1877

LEMON CHAMPAGNE PUNCH

1 quart lemon sherbet
1 cup light rum
1 split of chilled champagne
  mint leaves

Place lemon sherbet in a chilled punch bowl. Slowly add rum and then quickly add the chilled champagne. Serve in sherbet glasses. Garnish with a mint leaf. Serves 10.

Lucy Ware Webb Hayes
1877–1881

OYSTERS ON THE HALF SHELL

6 to 12 oysters per person
lemon juice
fresh lemons, sliced
pepper to taste

Wash and scrub the oyster shells. Pry them open. Leave them in the shell or place them on oyster plates. Sprinkle with lemon juice and coarsely ground pepper. Serve with lemon wedges and if desired your favorite seafood sauce.

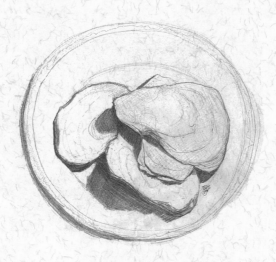

Lucretia Rudolph Garfield
1881

POPOVERS

1 cup flour
½ teaspoon salt
2 eggs
1 cup milk
1 tablespoon vegetable oil

Heat the oven to 425 degrees. Grease aluminum popover pans and set aside. Measure all ingredients into a bowl and beat with a rotary beater until smooth. Fill cups a little less than half full and bake in preheated oven for 35 minutes. Do not open the door—they might fall. Makes 6–8 popovers.

Ellen Lewis Herndon Arthur
1881–1885

BUTTERED ASPARAGUS

12 to 16 fresh asparagus
    spears
  salt to taste
2 tablespoons melted butter

Cut off the ends of the asparagus, about one inch from the bottom. Place the asparagus in a skillet and add water to cover and salt to taste. Bring to a boil and simmer until tender, about 2 to 5 minutes. Drain and add the melted butter. Serve hot. Makes 4 servings.

Frances Folsom Cleveland
1885–1889
1893–1897

GRILLED QUAIL

4 quails, boned
2 tablespoons Dijon mustard
2 tablespoons vegetable oil
1 teaspoon minced garlic
1 teaspoon chopped thyme
4 teaspoons pepper
salt to taste

Place the quails skin side up and press so they lie flat. Combine all other ingredients in a bowl, mix and rub on the birds. Preheat charcoal grill. Arrange the quails skin side down and flat on the grill. Cook 5 minutes on one side and turn. Cook 5 minutes longer. Makes 2 to 4 servings.

Caroline Lavinia Scott Harrison
1889–1893

SAUSAGE BALLS

1 pound pork sausage
1 egg, lightly beaten
⅓ cup dried bread crumbs
½ teaspoon ground sage

In a bowl, mix sausage, egg, bread crumbs and sage. Shape into bite-sized meatballs. Brown slowly on all sides, drain excess grease. Pour sauce over meatballs. Cover and simmer 30 minutes, stirring to coat evenly. Serve in a chafing dish with toothpicks.

Sauce:
½ cup catsup
2 tablespoon brown sugar
1 tablespoon vinegar
1 tablespoon soy sauce

Sauce:
Combine ingredients and mix well. 12 Servings

Ida Saxton McKinley
1897–1901

COLD TOMATO SOUP

4 cups canned tomatoes,
   drained
2 celery stalks, sliced
1 bay leaf
2 tablespoons minute tapioca
¼ teaspoon ground ginger
⅛ teaspoon allspice
   salt to taste
   sour cream, and cucum-
   bers to garnish

Boil the tomatoes with the celery, onion and bay leaf for ½ hour. Strain and return to a boil. Add the tapioca and cook until clear. Add the seasonings and chill. To serve, garnish each serving with slice of cucumber and dollop of sour cream. Serves 6.

Edith Kermit Carow Roosevelt
1901–1909

MY GRANDMOTHER'S INDIAN PUDDING
(E. Carow)

3 pints of scalded milk
7 tablespoonfuls of Indian
    Meal

Stir ingredients well together while hot. When it is cold, add 5 eggs, ½ pound raisins, 4 ounces butter. Spice and sugar to your taste.

Mrs. Theodore Roosevelt, Sr., Widow of the late President Roosevelt. Reprinted from the 1927 Congressional Club Cookbook. First edition.

Helen Herron Taft
1909–1913

With kind regards,
Helen H. Taft

A DESSERT

1 cup of powdered sugar
6 eggs, beaten
2 teaspoons cocoa
1 teaspoon prepared coffee
1 teaspoon of vanilla
6 whites of eggs, beaten very
   light.

Mix all together. Bake in one thin pan in a moderate oven for ten minutes. Then beat cream very light, and put it on the cake. Roll up cake and cream. Put chocolate icing over it and put whipped cream in stripes at the end.

Mrs. Wm. H. Taft, Wife of the Chief Justice and former President of the United States Reprinted from the 1927 Congressional Club Cookbook. First edition.

Ellen Louise Axson Wilson
1913–1914

Edith Bolling Galt Wilson
1915–1921

Edith Bolling Wilson

PINEAPPLE KIWI FRUIT SALAD

½ cup orange juice
½ cup water
¼ cup sugar
½ teaspoon ground cinnamon
1 tablespoon lime juice
½ small pineapple, peeled,
   cored
1 pint strawberries
2 bananas, sliced
1 kiwi fruit, peeled, sliced
1 cup toasted pinenuts

Heat the orange juice, water, sugar and cinnamon in small saucepan to boiling; reduce heat. Simmer uncovered for 5 minutes. Let cool; stir in lime juice. Cut pineapple lengthwise into 3 wedges and then cut crosswise into slices. Combine fruit in large bowl, and toss lightly. Pour warm syrup over fruit and stir. Refrigerate, covered until cold. To serve sprinkle with nuts. Serves 6.

Florence Kling De Wolfe Harding
1921–1923

Mrs Harding
Presented by
Carolyn Harding Votaw

TUNA NOODLE CASSEROLE

1 7 oz can tuna
½ package egg noodles
   Water
   Pads of butter
   parsley for garnish

White Cheese Sauce:
 2 tablespoons butter
1½ cups milk
 ¼ teaspoon salt
1½ tablespoons flour
 ¼ teaspoon pepper
 ¼ lb. sharp grated cheddar
    cheese

Boil the noodles according to package directions. Drain well. Drain the tuna, and flake with a fork. Make the cheese sauce as follows: Over low heat melt the butter and blend in the flour stirring until smooth. Slowly add the milk, stirring constantly. Add the cheese and seasonings. Reduce heat and cook 5 minutes longer. Place alternate layers of tuna and noodles into well greased casserole, cover with sauce and bake in moderate 375 degree oven for 30 minutes. Garnish with parsley. Serves 4.

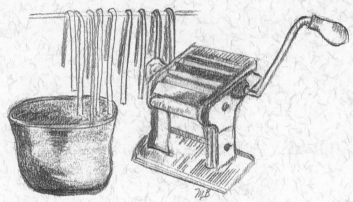

Grace Anna Goodhue Coolidge
1923–1929

*To the Members of the Congressional Club of Washington D.C.
with friendly greetings and best wishes*
March 1928.
            Grace Coolidge

CORNMEAL MUFFINS

2 cups cornmeal
1 cup flour
1 cup sweet milk
2 eggs, well beaten
½ cup sugar
2 tablespoonsful baking
    powder

This quantity will make 14 muffins.

Mrs. Calvin Coolidge, Wife of the President of the United States.
Reprinted from the 1927 Congressional Club Cookbook. First Edition

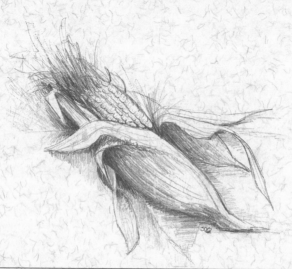

Lou Henry Hoover
1929–1933

To the Congressional Club with grateful appreciation of being any included in its membership

Lou Henry Hoover

MARY RATTLEY'S MUSHROOM SOUP

1 pound of mushrooms, chopped fine
1 pint cold water

Let this stand for 2 hours then put on a slow fire, cook about 30 minutes. Strain the juice.

1 pint of chicken stock, well seasoned
1 pint of thin cream
Salt to taste
Dash of paprika

Add one tablespoonful of flour mixed in cold milk to the soup. When perfectly smooth run through a fine strainer. Just before serving add 2 table-spoonfuls of whipped cream.

Mrs. Herbert Hoover, Wife of Secretary of Commerce (Cal.).
Reprinted from the 1927 Congressional Club Cookbook. First edition.

Anna Eleanor Roosevelt
1933–1945

With good wishes
Eleanor Roosevelt

KEDGEREE

1 cup any boiled white fish
   (flaked)
1 cup boiled rice
2 hard boiled eggs
   Seasoning to taste

Mix all ingredients together. Heat again and serve hot. (The hard boiled eggs are, of course, chopped and added. If one likes the mixture a little moist, milk may be added.)
Can be served with a tomato sauce.

Mrs. Franklin D. Roosevelt, Wife of former President of the United States. Reprinted from the 1945 Congressional Club Cookbook. Third Edition.

Elizabeth "Bess" Virginia Wallace Truman
1945–1953

With best wishes to The Congressional Club
from
June 1947.
Bess W. Truman

HERMITS

½ cup shortening (generous)
1 cup brown sugar
2 eggs
2½ cups flour, sifted three
     times
1 scant cup buttermilk, in
     which dissolve 1 scant
     teaspoon of soda.
½ cup nuts chopped
½ lb. raisins
1 large teaspoon allspice
1 large teaspoon cinnamon
½ teaspoon cloves

Drop on cookie sheet and bake about twenty five minutes at 350-375 degrees.
Makes 30-35.

Bess W. Truman

Mrs. Harry S. Truman, Wife of the President of the United States.
Reprinted from the 1945 Congressional Club Cookbook. Third edition.

Mary "Mamie" Geneva Doud Eisenhower
1953–1961

In the Congressional Club
Mamie Doud Eisenhower

PUMPKIN CHIFFON PIE

3 beaten egg yolks
¾ cup brown sugar
1½ cups cooked pumpkin
½ cup milk
½ teaspoon salt
1 teaspoon cinnamon
½ teaspoon nutmeg
1 envelope Knox gelatin
¼ cup cold water
3 stiffly beaten egg whites
¼ cup granulated sugar

Combine egg yolks, brown sugar, pumpkin, milk, salt and spice. Cook in double boiler until thick, stirring constantly. Soak gelatin in cold water, stir into hot mixture. Chill until partly set. Beat egg whites, add granulated sugar, and beat stiff. Fold into gelatin mixture. Pour into pie shell and chill until set. Garnish with whipped cream.

Makes one big pie or 8 individual pies.

Mamie Doud Eisenhower

Mrs. Dwight D. Eisenhower, Wife of the President of the United States. Reprinted from the 1955 Congressional Club Cookbook. Fifth edition.

Patricia Ryan Nixon
1969–1974

To the members of the Congressional Club with best wishes always,

Patricia Nixon

HAM MOUSSE

½ cup cooked ham (finely
    ground)
1 cup tomato juice
1 cup beef consomme
½ teaspoon paprika
4 tablespoons cold water
1 envelope gelatin
2 cups cream, whipped
salt to taste
mayonnaise
few drops lemon juice
a little heavy cream
finely chopped chives

Mix first four ingredients and bring to a boil. Dissolve gelatin in water, add to ham mixture. Put into refrigerator to cool, stirring occasionally. When it begins to slightly congeal, fold in the whipped cream. Add salt to taste. Pour into one large mold or smaller individual molds. Let set in refrigerator until firm. Unmold, garnish with watercress. Serve with mayonnaise thinned with a few drops of lemon juice and a little heavy cream, adding finely chopped chives. Serves 4 to 6.

Patricia Nixon

Mrs. Richard M. Nixon, Wife of the President of the United States.
Reprinted from The 1970 Congressional Club Cook Book. Eighth Edition.

The White House

The White House

The White House is a symbol of American history and government. John and Abigail Adams were the first residents, and since that time, babies have been born, brides married and Presidents have lain in state in this house which belongs to the American people.

More than a million people tour this museum each year and throughout history it has been a home to the First Family, all of whom have left their own personal legacy.

APPETIZERS
AND
BEVERAGES

"PLAINS SPECIAL" CHEESE RING
A Carter Family Favorite

1 pound grated sharp ched-
    dar cheese
1 cup mayonnaise
1 cup chopped nuts
1 small onion, grated
    black pepper to taste
    dash of cayenne

Mix; mold with hands into desired shape. (We mold into a ring); refrigerate until chilled. To serve, fill center with strawberry preserves. Can be served as a complement to a main meal or as an hors d'oeuvre with crackers.

Rosalynn Carter

Mrs. Jimmy Carter, Wife of former President of the United States

SAUMON FUMÉ POUR LE CHAMPAGNE

⅛ pound of smoked salmon
¼ cup of cream cheese
1 medium-size onion (prefera-
    bly Vidalia, Maui or Red
    Onion)
20 Triscuit crackers

Spread cream cheese over crackers. Add a small amount of smoked salmon on each cracker. Top with a small amount of chopped onion. Serve cold. Best enjoyed with champagne. Makes 4 servings.

Theana Yatron Kastens

Mrs. Royal Kastens, Daughter of former Representative Gus Yatron (Pennsylvania)

MARINATED MUSHROOMS FILLED WITH SMITHFIELD HAM

2 ozs. fresh mushrooms
1 pkg. Good Seasons Italian Dressing
1 cup ground or shredded Smithfield Ham (or North Carolina Country Ham)
1 8 oz. pkg. cream cheese (at room temperature)
2 spring onions minced
1/4 teaspoon crushed garlic
1 teaspoon Worcestershire sauce
1 teaspoon lemon juice
1 tablespoon mayonnaise
1 tablespoon Dijon mustard

Wipe mushrooms with damp cloth and remove stems. Make Good Seasons dressing according to package instructions. Marinate mushrooms at least 4 hours or overnight in salad dressing. Drain well when ready to fill. Combine all other ingredients and fill mushroom caps with this mixture. Refrigerate until ready to serve. Just before serving, sprinkle tops with chopped chives or parsley. (Ham/cream mixture may be made the day before and refrigerated). Makes 20 servings.

Mrs. Alex McMillan, Wife of Representative (North Carolina)

APPETIZER QUESADILLAS

6 flour tortillas (6 or 7 inches in diameter)
4 ozs. reduced-fat goat cheese, crumbled or reduced-fat cheddar or longhorn cheese, shredded (about 1 cup)
4 ozs. reduced-fat Monterey Jack cheese, shredded (about 1 cup)
freshly ground black pepper to taste
1 cup salsa

Preheat oven to 350°. Spray baking sheet with vegetable cooking spray. Cover with single layer of tortillas. Toss the cheeses together in a small bowl and sprinkle them evenly over the tortillas. Season with pepper. Bake 5 minutes or until the cheeses are melted. Remove the baking sheet from the oven and immediately fold the tortillas in half. Cut each folded tortilla into 3 triangles. Serve warm, with a bowl of salsa for dipping. Makes 6 servings.

Mrs. Cece Zorinsky-White, Wife of former Senator Edward Zorinsky (Nebraska)

LINDA'S CAVIAR PIE

9 Inch Pie Plate:
- 8 eggs
- 1 small chopped onion
- 1/4 pound butter
- 1 1/2 pints sour cream
- 1/2 pound caviar

or

Quiche Pan/10 Inch Plate:
- 12 eggs
- 1 medium chopped onion
- 3/4 cup butter
- 2 pints sour cream
- 3/4 pound caviar

Red lumpfish caviar is normally used but Black caviar can be used if it doesn't run or use a combination of both. Hard boil eggs and peel and chop in Cuisinart using the metal blade until very fine. (If food processor is unavailable, put the eggs through a fine sieve). Chop onion and add to the eggs. Melt butter, mix with eggs and onion. Make a shell in the pie plate or quiche pan from this mixture. Pour in the sour cream. Spread caviar on top in a design of your choice. Decorate with slices of egg and parsley. Refrigerate. Makes 16 or 24 servings.

Mrs. Clarence Brown, Wife of former Representative (Ohio)

CINNAMON SUGARED NUTS

- 1/4 cup sugar
- 1/2 teaspoon cinnamon
- 2 tablespoons margarine
- 2 cups pecans

Mix together sugar and cinnamon. Place butter in a 10-inch ceramic skillet. Melt in microwave for 1 minute. Combine nuts with butter. Microwave for 5 minutes until toasted. Stir every 1 1/2 minutes. Remove nuts from microwave and quickly stir in cinnamon-sugar mixture, coating nuts evenly. Spread mixture in a baking dish. Cool and store in tightly covered container. These are great for bridge. Makes 2 cups.

Mrs. Scotty Baesler, Wife of Representative (Kentucky)

DOROTHY'S CHEERIO NUGGETS

1 cup packed brown sugar
½ cup margarine
¼ cup light syrup
½ teaspoon salt
½ teaspoon baking soda
6 cups Cheerios
1 cup salted peanuts
1 cup raisins

Heat oven to 250°. Grease two 13″×9″×2″ pans. Heat brown sugar, margarine, corn syrup and salt in two quart saucepan over medium heat, stirring constantly until bubbly around edges. Cook uncovered, stirring occasionally two minutes longer. Remove from heat, stir in baking soda until foamy and light colored. Pour over nuts, cereal and raisins in greased 4 quart bowl. Stir well. Spread in pans and bake 15 minutes, stir. Let stand until cool, for about 10 minutes. Loosen with spatula. Let stand until firm, for about 30 minutes, then break into pieces. Store in a cool place. Makes 10 servings.

Liz McEwen

Mrs. Bob McEwen, Wife of former Representative (Ohio)

GRANDMOTHER CARSWELL'S MARINATED VIDALIA ONIONS

4 or 5 Vidalia onions, sliced
   very thin
½ cup vinegar
1 cup sugar
2 cups ice water
½ cup mayonnaise
1 tablespoon celery salt
1 tablespoon celery seeds
crackers

Mix onions, vinegar, sugar and ice water. Soak overnight in refrigerator. Drain onions. Mix onions with mayonnaise, celery salt and celery seeds. Serve on crackers. Keeps for several weeks in ice box. Makes 20 servings.

Libby Kingston

Mrs. Jack Kingston, Wife of Representative (Georgia)

PESTO-STUFFED CHERRY TOMATOES

⅓ cup freshly grated Parmesan
10 small, or 5 large, garlic cloves
½ teaspoon salt
⅓ cup chopped pecans
20 good sized basil leaves or 1 bunch, leaves picked off
1 stalk parsley
olive oil
1 cup cottage cheese
2 dozen cherry tomatoes

Place the Parmesan, garlic, salt, pecans, basil leaves and parsley in the bowl of a Cuisinart. Pulse until everything is finely chopped. Add olive oil in a slow drizzle until pesto is the consistency of mayonnaise. Mix 1 cup of pesto with 1 cup of cottage cheese. Hollow out 2 dozen cherry tomatoes. Fill with pesto and cottage cheese mixture. Chill and serve. Makes a yummy, spicy, hot weather hors d'oeuvres. 2 cups pesto makes several dozen.

Hints for serving: Pesto can be used on pasta.

Sally Smith

Mrs. Peter Smith, Wife of former Representative (Vermont)

COSTINI WITH TOMATO

1½ pounds plum tomatoes
1 teaspoon salt
1 clove garlic
1 tablespoon fresh basil
2 tablespoons flat parsley
¼ cup olive oil
1 loaf day old Italian bread

Slice bread and lightly toast in broiler. Chop tomatoes, add salt and drain one hour. Whisk garlic, basil and parsley into tomatoes. Add olive oil. Serve on toast. Makes 24 toasts.

Sally J Patterson

Mrs. Jerry Patterson, Wife of former Representative (California)

TORTILLA-CREAM CHEESE APPETIZER

1 pkg. flour tortillas
1 8 oz. pkg. cream cheese
1 small can green chilies
  garlic powder (to taste)
1 jar picante sauce

Soften cream cheese. Add garlic powder and green chilies. Mix well. Spread cream cheese mixture on tortillas, roll up tortillas and cut into slices. Serve with picante sauce for dipping. Makes 4 to 6 servings. May be frozen.

Laurie Kirby

Mrs. Laurie Kirby, Wife of Representative Earl Pomeroy (North Dakota)

MARINATED BROCCOLI

1⅓ cup oil, vegetable
 ½ cup white wine vinegar
  2 tablespoons garlic salt
  2 tablespoons Accent
  1 tablespoon dill weed
  1 stalk of fresh broccoli flo-
    rettes

Marinate overnight in covered bowl. Drain and serve. Serves 6.

Marilyn Burnside Weaver

Mrs. George Weaver, Daughter of former Representative M. G. Burnside (West Virginia)

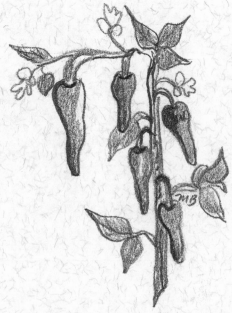

TORTILLA WHEELS

1 dozen 12″ flour tortillas
2 pkgs. 8 oz. cream cheese
   or neufchatel cheese
2 6 oz. cans diced green
   chilis (mild or hot)
1 small can black olives,
   chopped (10 to 15
   olives)
1 small jar pimentos (op-
   tional)

Optional Recipe:
1 jar chunky salsa (hot or mild)

Soften cream cheese in microwave 2–3 minutes on 70% (medium high) power. Stir. Mix cream cheese with green chilis and olives. Spread mixture over each tortilla and roll up, (soften tortillas in microwave for 10–15 seconds if necessary). Wrap in plastic wrap or waxed paper and chill in refrigerator until firm, about 1 hour. Slice into ¼–½ inch slices and if desired garnish each slice with pimento. These are also excellent prepared with salsa replacing the green chilis and olives. Use approximately ¾–1 cup chunky salsa and mix with softened cream cheese. Cream cheese mixture can be slightly chilled and used for a dip for tortilla chips or as a spread for crackers as well. Can be made well in advance. Uncut, will keep in the refrigerator for several days. Makes 80 to 100.

Martha Regula, Daughter of Representative Ralph Regula (Ohio)

HAM-RICE PINWHEELS

2 pkgs. (3 ozs. each) cream
   cheese (room temper-
   ature)
1 cup cooked rice
6 tablespoons chopped green
   or ripe olives
3 tablespoons grated onions
1½ tablespoons horseradish
1 tablespoon pickle relish
1 teaspoon Worcestershire
   sauce
6 to 8 thin slices baked or
   boiled ham

Cream cheese until fluffy. Add rice, olives, onion, horseradish, pickle relish and Worcestershire sauce. Blend well. Spread meat slices with rice mixture and roll tightly. Skewer with toothpicks. Cover and chill several hours. At serving time, cut into 1 inch slices. Makes 3 dozen.

Mrs. Kika de la Garza, Wife of Representative (Texas)

KATHRYN'S CHEESE ROLL

1 pound Velveeta cheese
1 six oz. pkg. cream cheese
1 clove of garlic (finely
   chopped)
   Worcestershire sauce to
   taste (about one tablespoon)
1 pkg. chopped walnuts
   chili powder
   Ritz crackers

Mix cream cheese and Velveeta cheese together (with hands) until well blended. Add garlic, Worcestershire sauce and walnuts. Mix well and make into two rolls. Roll in chili powder that has been placed on wax paper. Wrap in waxpaper and refrigerate overnight. Slice and serve on Ritz crackers. Makes 10 servings. May be frozen.

Mrs. Evan Howell, Wife of former Representative (Illinois)

AUNT JAN'S OYSTER CRACKER SNACKS

1 12 oz. box of oyster
   crackers
1 pkg. Hidden Valley Ranch
   dressing mix
½ teaspoon dill weed
¼ teaspoon lemon pepper
¼ teaspoon garlic powder
¼ cup salad oil

Mix dry ingredients, then add oil. Stir gradually. Slowly add oyster crackers. Stir until all are coated. Bake on cookie sheet 15 to 20 minutes at 250°. Stir occasionally. Store in airtight container. Makes 8 servings.

Bob McEwen, former Representative (Ohio)

SPINACH ROLL WITH MUSHROOMS

3 10 oz. pkgs. frozen spinach
¼ cup bread crumbs
2 teaspoons salt
½ teaspoon pepper
  pinch of ground nutmeg
4 tablespoons grated Parmesan cheese
6 tablespoons melted butter
4 eggs, separated (I use egg substitute instead of yolks)
⅛ teaspoon cream of tartar
1½ pounds mushrooms, sliced
¼ cup butter
1½ tablespoons flour
1 cup Hollandaise sauce

Thaw spinach, squeeze out all excess moisture. Chop. Butter a 5 × 10 × 1 inch jelly roll pan, line with wax paper. Place spinach and bread crumbs in bowl, add 1 teaspoon salt, ¼ teaspoon pepper, nutmeg and melted butter. Beat in egg yolks one at a time. Beat egg whites in a small bowl until they hold soft peaks—not using a copper bowl. Add cream of tartar when egg whites reach foamy stage. Fold into spinach mixture. Spoon mixture into prepared pan and smooth the top evenly with a spatula. Sprinkle with Parmesan cheese. Bake at 350° for 15 minutes or until center feels barely firm when touched. While the spinach roll is baking, saute mushrooms quickly in ¼ cup butter. Sprinkle mushrooms with flour, remaining 1 teaspoon salt and ¼ teaspoon pepper. When roll is done baking, place a sheet of buttered wax paper or foil, butter side down, over the roll and invert onto a warm cookie sheet. Carefully remove bottom paper. Spread mushroom mixture over hot spinach roll. Roll up, jelly roll fashion, then ease roll onto warm platter. Spread Hollandaise sauce over top. Serve immediately. Makes 6 to 8 servings.

Note: This can be made ahead up to the point when you spread Hollandaise sauce over the top. Cover with foil and heat until warmed through, then spread sauce.

Barbara Vucanovich, Representative (Nevada)

DOLMA BY MEHMET AND NAZILE
(STUFFED GRAPE LEAVES)

2	cups rice (uncooked)
4	medium onions chopped
¾	cup oil
¼	cup pinenuts
¼	cup mint leaves chopped
¼	cup allspice
1½	teaspoons black pepper
¼	cup black raisins
1	quart jar grape leaves (rinsed)
2	cups water
3	fresh lemons

In saucepan, add oil and onion. Saute onion until brown. Add dry rice and continue to saute. Add pinenuts, mint, allspice, pepper and raisins. Saute for 2-3 minutes. Be careful not to scorch. Add 1 cup water and the juice of 2 lemons. Slowly boil for about 45 minutes. Remove from heat and roll mixture in grape leaves. Place stuffed grape leaves in a circular fashion in a large boiler. When finished, add 1 cup of water and the juice of ½ lemon and cover with a plate directly lying on the grape leaves to maintain shape. Simmer until tender. Serve cold. Makes 8 servings. May be frozen.

Ms. Shelly Hefner, Daughter of Representative Bill Hefner (North Carolina)

> *If your guests will be standing—serve finger food—not, hard to eat hors d'oeuvre's. Heavier appetizers require a small plate, fork and napkin.*

TORTELLINI IN HERB GARLIC DRESSING

1 pound tortellini
$\frac{1}{4}$ cup red wine vinegar
$\frac{3}{4}$ cup olive oil
1 clove garlic, minced
1 tablespoon Dijon mustard
 salt and pepper
8 fresh basil leaves, finely
 chopped
2 tablespoons chopped fresh
 parsley
4 green onions, finely
 chopped
 cherry tomatoes or red bell
 peppers
$\frac{1}{2}$ cup freshly grated Parmesan cheese

Cook tortellini al dente. Drain and rinse with cold water. Place in a bowl. Whisk the vinegar and oil together until well blended. Whisk in the garlic, mustard, salt and pepper. Pour the mixture over the tortellini. Add the basil, parsley, green onions and toss gently. Serve on skewers alternating with red pepper squares or cherry tomatoes. Top with Parmesan cheese. Makes 10–12 servings.

Sharon Archer

Mrs. Bill Archer, Wife of Representative (Texas)

CHEDDAR CAROUSEL

1 pound sharp cheddar
 cheese, grated
$\frac{3}{4}$ cup mayonnaise
1 medium onion, finely
 chopped
1 clove garlic, pressed
$\frac{1}{2}$ teaspoon Tabasco sauce
1 cup chopped pecans
1 cup strawberry preserves
 crackers or pumpernickel
 bread slices

Combine all ingredients except strawberry preserves and crackers/bread and mix well. Put in ring mold. Chill thoroughly. (Mixture will form together when chilled.) Unmold and fill center with preserves. Serve with crackers or pumpernickel bread slices.

Chris M. Rhodes

Mrs. Thomas Rhodes, Daughter-in-law of former Representative John J. Rhodes (Arizona)

JARLSBERG CHEESE SPREAD

3/4 pound Jarlsberg swiss
    cheese, grated
1/2 medium size red onion,
    chopped
    Hellmann's mayonnaise,
    enough to keep together
Triscuits

Don't be fooled—this is wonderful! Grate cheese in food processor. Chop the onion in the food processor. Mix the two together and add Hellmann's until they stick together. The amount depends on you and how much you want to make. Serve on Triscuits.

Aardie Knollenberg

Mrs. Joe Knollenberg, Wife of Representative (Michigan)

HOLIDAY CHEESE BALLS

2 8 oz. pkgs. cream cheese
2 5 oz. jars Old English ched-
    dar cheese
1 5 oz. jar bleu cheese
3 tablespoons wine vinegar
    dash of garlic salt
1 cup chopped nuts

Allow cheese spread to soften at room temperature. Combine with remaining ingredients; blend until smooth. Refrigerate about 30 minutes. Shape into 3 balls. Roll in chopped nuts. Wrap in wax paper and return to the refrigerator until ready to serve. Makes 3 balls.

Whitney R. Williams

Miss Whitney Williams, Daughter of Representative Pat Williams (Montana)

MARVELOUS CHEESE SPREAD

1 pound sharp cheese, grated
12 scallions chopped
1 cup slivered almonds;
   toasted
1 pound bacon, cooked crisp
2 cups mayonnaise

Mix ingredients together well. Cover and chill. Serve with your favorite crackers. This makes a marvelous gift in a pretty crock or bowl. May be frozen.

Mrs. Michael Castle, Wife of Representative (Delaware)

OLIVE NUT CHEESE SPREAD

1 8 oz. pkg. softened cream
   cheese
½ cup mayonnaise
½ cup chopped pecans
1 cup chopped salad olives
2 tablespoons olive juice

Put all ingredients in bowl and blend well. Store in covered container in refrigerator.

Mrs. John Hammerschmidt, Wife of former Representative (Arkansas)

PARTY BREAD SPREAD

1 cup finely chopped pecans
2 hard-cooked eggs, finely
   chopped
1 small onion, minced
½ cup mayonnaise
1 3 oz. jar pimento-stuffed
   olives, drained and finely
   chopped
Additional pimento-stuffed
   olives, sliced (optional)

Combine first 5 ingredients. (I use the food processor to chop pecans, eggs, onion, and olives separately instead of by hand.) Stir well. Serve spread on party ryebread or crackers. Garnish with olive slices, if desired. May also use as sandwich filling. People think it is chicken salad. Makes 20 servings, or two cups.

Mrs. Tom Bevill, Wife of Representative (Alabama)

LIPTAUER CHEESE

1 8 oz. pkg. cream cheese
¼ cup butter or margarine
1 teaspoon capers
2 rolled anchovies, finely
   chopped
½ teaspoon caraway seed
1 teaspoon paprika
1 slice onion, minced

Cream cheese and butter. Add remaining ingredients.

Mrs. Thomas Bliley, Jr., Wife of Representative (Virginia)

ACCENT THE POSITIVE

1 2 oz. can black olives
2 bundles green onions
1 small jar Armour chipped
   beef
1 4 oz. can chopped mushrooms
3 8 oz. pkgs. cream cheese
3 teaspoons Accent

Drain and mince ripe olives. Chop onions (use green tops only). Put olives, onions, chipped beef and mushrooms into food processor. Stir in softened cream cheese and add Accent. Make into one large cheese ball or two small balls. Refrigerate at least one day—however, two days is better.

Penny Ichord

Mrs. Richard Ichord, Wife of former Representative (Missouri)

CHIPPED BEEF SPREAD

½ cup pecans, chopped
2 tablespoons butter
¼ teaspoon salt
1 8 oz. pkg. cream cheese
2 tablespoons milk
4 ozs. chipped beef
½ cup sour cream
¼ cup chopped green pepper
2 tablespoons chopped
   onion
¼ teaspoon black pepper
¼ teaspoon garlic powder

Saute pecans in butter and salt. Mix other ingredients together and place in small casserole or oven-proof crock and top with the pecans. Bake in 350° oven 20 minutes. Serve with crackers. Easily doubled, just bake about 5 minutes more.

Louise R. Brotzman

Mrs. Donald Brotzman, Wife of former Representative (Colorado)

SOMBRERO SPREAD

1 pound ground beef
1/2 cup chopped onion
1/2 cup extra hot ketchup
3 teaspoons chili powder
1 teaspoon salt
1 15 oz. can kidney beans
  (with liquid)
1 cup shredded cheddar
  cheese
1/2 cup chopped stuffed green
  olives
1/2 cup chopped onion

Brown meat and 1/2 cup onion. Stir in ketchup, chili powder and salt. Mash in beans. Heat through. Pour in chafing dish. Garnish with cheese, olives and second 1/2 cup of onion. Serve with tortilla chips. (This can be multiplied many times over, but I don't always multiply the amount of salt and chili powder as much as the other ingredients.) Makes 3 cups.

Katie Lowery

Mrs. Bill Lowery, Wife of former Representative (California)

HOT PASTRAMI SPREAD

2 8 oz. pkgs. cream cheese
1 1/2 cups sour cream
2 tablespoons minced fresh
  onion
1 teaspoon Worcestershire
  sauce
1/4 teaspoon garlic powder
1 dash Tabasco
6 ozs. pastrami—cut up fine
  small package slivered almonds

Mix cream cheese and sour cream until smooth. Add other ingredients, except pastrami and almonds, and mix until smooth. Add pastrami. Put in lightly greased casserole. Cover with almonds. Bake 30 minutes at 350°. Serve with rye crackers. Can be made ahead of time. Sprinkle on almonds just before baking.

Diane Nelson

Mrs. E. Benjamin Nelson, Wife of Governor (Nebraska)

WILD GAME PATÉ

1 pound deer, elk or buffalo
  liver
½ pound chicken liver (not
  needed with buffalo)
2 softened sticks butter or
  oleo
  wine
2 to 3 tablespoons cognac,
  brandy or bourbon
½ teaspoon salt
¼ teaspoon pepper
¼ cup dry green peppercorns
  (soak in hot water 5
  minutes)

Slice game liver, saute with chicken livers in lightly buttered pan. Cover with white or red wine, cook slowly until tender. Cool. Cut into small pieces, blend in blender or Cuisinart (best method). Add brandy, cognac or bourbon, salt and pepper. Fold peppercorns into paté. Pack in lightly buttered pan (loaf pan or round bowl so it can be easily removed). Cover with something heavy (brick for loaf pan) after covering with foil. Unmold by using table knife or rubber spatula around edges. May need to place pan in hot water for a few seconds to loosen. Trim platter with parsley. Place crackers or small, thinly sliced french bread (a baquette is best). A squeeze of fresh lemon juice adds zing. Makes 30 to 40 servings. May be frozen.

Ann Simpson

Mrs. Alan Simpson, Wife of Senator (Wyoming)

KELLY'S CHICKEN SPREAD

1 cup cooked white chunk
  chicken
1 8 oz. pkg. lite cream
  cheese
1 tablespoon Worcestershire
  sauce
¼ cup minced onion
1 teaspoon Italian seasoning

Mix all ingredients well. Place in mold or form into a ball. Chill for 30 minutes. May be topped with almonds or pecans. Serve as a spread for crackers or party rye bread.

Faye Flippo

Mrs. Ronnie Flippo, Wife of former Representative (Alabama)

CHOPPED CHICKEN LIVER

1 pound chicken livers
1 cube butter or margarine
1 large onion, chopped

Saute the chicken livers with the cube of butter and the onion. When done, process in a food processor until smooth. Chill and serve with crackers. Makes 2 cups. May be frozen.

June Miller

Mrs. John Miller, Wife of former Representative (Washington)

WILD DUCK PATÉ

Gelatin Topping:
  1 package gelatin
  1 cups beef bouillon
  1 tablespoon Worcestershire sauce
  3/4 tablespoon lemon juice
  2 dashes Tabasco

Gelatin Topping: Sprinkle gelatin over 1/4 cup bouillon and let stand 5 minutes. In the top of a double boiler over hot water, dissolve the gelatin. Add remaining bouillon, Worcestershire, lemon juice, and hot pepper sauce. Spray a 1 1/2 quart mold with cooking spray, add bouillon mixture and chill until set.

Ducks:
  4 Mallard ducks
    salt, black pepper
    Tony's Creole Seasoning
  2 onions chopped
  2 stalks celery, chopped
  1 bell pepper, chopped
    red wine, water

Ducks: Season ducks with salt, pepper, and Creole seasoning, and rub into skin. Put ducks in roasting pan and cover with onion, celery and bell pepper. Put a combination of red wine and water in roaster to almost cover the ducks. Cover and bake at 350° for about 2 hours until the ducks are tender. Skin, debone ducks, and put meat in bowl of food processor and process until fine. Strain and reserve 3/4 cup duck liquor.

Pate:
  3/4 cup reserved duck liquor
  2 envelopes gelatin
  5 hard boiled eggs, grated
  2 small onions, grated
  3 stalks celery, finely chopped
  1 1/2 cups mayonnaise (I use Kraft Free)

Pate: Sprinkle gelatin over 1/4 cup reserved duck liquor and let stand 5 minutes. In top of a double boiler over hot water, dissolve gelatin. Add remaining duck liquor and set aside. In a large bowl combine eggs, onion, celery, mayonnaise, and gelatin mixture. Add duck meat and mix well. Pour over congealed bouillon and chill several hours or overnight to set. 30–50 servings. Serve with a variety of dark breads.

Variety of dark breads

Lois Breaux

Mrs. John Breaux, Wife of Senator (Louisiana)

HAM BALL

1 8 oz. pkg. cream cheese
1 cup ham (Hormel chunk ham)
1 tablespoon horseradish
1 tablespoon mustard
1 tablespoon grated onion
½ cup chopped walnuts or pecans
2 tablespoons parsley flakes

Soften cream cheese; chop ham very fine. Mix cream cheese, ham, horseradish, mustard, and onion. Form into a ball. Mix nuts and parsley together and roll ball until well covered with nuts and parsley. Place ball on serving platter with crackers for appetizer. Makes 20 servings. May be frozen.

Mrs. John Marsh, Wife of former Representative (Virginia)

MOLDED CRAB

1 pkg. (6 oz.) Wakefield's frozen King Crab meat, thawed, drained and cut stringy
1 envelope Knox gelatin
3 tablespoons cold water
1 6 oz. pkg. cream cheese, softened
1 can cream of mushroom soup
1 small minced onion
1 cup chopped celery
1 cup mayonnaise

Dissolve gelatin in water over low heat. Heat soup, add gelatin and beat well. Remove from heat. Add sliced softened cream cheese and mayonnaise and beat until smooth. Blend in the onion, celery and crab meat. Pour into 4 cup ring mold. Chill until firm. Remove by placing mold in hot water a few seconds to loosen it. Garnish center of ring with fresh parsley and serve with Triscuits. Note: Mold should be lightly greased or sprayed with vegetable oil. Makes 20 servings.

Mrs. John Linder, Wife of Representative (Georgia)

SALMON MOUSSE

2 envelopes unflavored
    gelatin
1½ cups cold tomato juice
1 cup mayonnaise
1 cup sour cream
1 pound can salmon, drained
    and flaked
1 cup chopped cucumber
¼ cup chopped green olives
1 teaspoon grated onion
1 teaspoon dillweed
    lettuce
    party crackers

Soften gelatin in the cold tomato juice. Stir over low heat until dissolved. Cool. Combine mayonnaise and sour cream, then stir into gelatin. Chill until slightly thickened. Fold in flaked salmon. Add cucumber, green olives, onion and dillweed. Pour into mold sprayed with Pam (fish mold is great) and chill until firm. Unmold onto bed of lettuce and serve with crackers for spreading.

Suzanne Johnson

Mrs. Don Johnson, Wife of Representative (Georgia)

SHRIMP PASTE

1 pound shrimp
½ cup butter, softened
½ teaspoon nutmeg
    cayenne pepper to taste
    Carr's Table Water Crackers, or toasts

Boil shrimp until pink. Peel and devein. In a blender or food processor fitted with a steel blade, grind prepared shrimp to a fine consistency. Transfer to a bowl and blend in butter and spices. Pack the paste into a buttered 2-cup baking dish and bake it in a preheated oven at 350° for 30 minutes, or until it pulls away from the dish and the top is lightly browned. Chill the paste. If the dish is attractive, serve it on a tray with crackers or toast or turn it out onto a serving plate whole, or slice and spread it before hand. Makes 8 to 10 servings.

Bethine Church

Mrs. Frank Church, Wife of former Senator (Idaho)

SALMON SPREAD

2 cups cooked or canned
    salmon
½ cup mayonnaise
1 tablespoon mustard
1 tablespoon coarse ground
    horseradish

Combine, mix and chill. Serve on pumpernickel or rye rounds or great on bagel chips. Makes 32 servings.

Barbara Burlison

Mrs. Barbara Burlison, Member of The Congressional Club

JANET'S SHRIMP MOLD

8 oz. softened cream
    cheese
1½ envelopes unflavored
    gelatin
½ cup cold water
¾ cup finely chopped celery
1 tablespoon chopped
    parsley
1 cup mayonnaise
2 teaspoons chopped green
    onions
2 cups minced cooked
    shrimp
1 tablespoon lemon juice
    salt (to taste)
    white pepper (to taste)
    seasoned salt (to taste)
    dash of Worcestershire
    sauce

Beat cream cheese with mixer until smooth. Soften gelatin with water. Dissolve on low heat. Fold in cream cheese. Fold in remaining ingredients. Pour into lightly oiled mold. Refrigerate until firm. Unmold. Serve with crackers. Makes 20 servings.

Libby Kingston

Mrs. Jack Kingston, Wife of Representative (Georgia)

ARTICHOKE SPREAD

1 can artichoke hearts
1 cup mayonnaise (I use low
    fat)
1 cup grated Parmesan
    cheese
2 tablespoons grated onion
1 clove garlic, chopped
1 tablespoon lemon juice
    salt and pepper to taste
    French bread rounds or
    toasted pita triangles

Drain artichokes well. Chop artichokes. Mix artichokes with all remaining ingredients, except bread. Turn mixture into casserole and bake for 20 minutes (or until lightly browned) at 350°. Serve hot with French bread rounds or toasted pita triangles. Makes 6 to 8 servings. May be frozen.

Carol Laxalt

Mrs. Paul Laxalt, Wife of former Senator (Nevada)

RADISH BALL

½ cup butter
    8 oz. pkg. cream cheese
½ to ¼ cup beer
½ bottle chopped capers
3 cut up green onions
1 teaspoon caraway seeds
1 bunch radishes

Mix butter, cream cheese and beer. Add capers and onions. Shape into ball. Press diced radishes on cheese ball. Chill and serve with small slices of rye bread. Makes 12 servings.

Fran Symms

Ms. Fran Symms, Member of The Congressional Club

SONNY'S SAUCE

1 18 oz. jar pineapple preserves
1 18 oz. jar apple jelly
1 small can dry mustard
1 small jar horseradish

Combine all ingredients. Blend well. Put in jelly jars and refrigerate. Sauce will keep indefinitely. Serve with pork or roast beef. Also delicious spread over cream cheese served with crackers.

Karen Callahan

Mrs. Sonny Callahan, Wife of Representative (Alabama)

GREEN ONION AND CHEESE SQUARES

2 bunches green onion,
  chopped
2 tablespoons butter
1 pound spinach, finely
  chopped
3 tablespoons chopped
  parsley
6 eggs
¼ cup sour cream
½ cup soft bread crumbs
¾ cup shredded Swiss cheese
  (3 oz.)
½ cup shredded Parmesan
  cheese (2 oz.)

Saute onions in butter. Add spinach and saute one minute. Remove from heat and add parsley. Beat eggs until light and add sour cream, bread crumbs, Swiss cheese, ¼ of Parmesan and onion mixture. Pour into buttered nine inch square baking pan. Sprinkle rest of Parmesan cheese on top. Bake in preheated 350° oven for 20 minutes. Cut into 16 squares and serve hot. Makes 16 servings. May be frozen.

Carolyn Hobson

Mrs. David Hobson, Wife of Representative (Ohio)

MARILYN'S CHEESE SQUARES

1 loaf of firm white bread,
    sliced
margarine or butter,
    enough to spread one
    side of slices
1 cup grated cheddar cheese
1/4 teaspoon curry powder
1/4 cup chopped green onion
1/4 cup mayonnaise
    grated Parmesan cheese

Trim crusts from bread and spread one side with margarine or butter. Lightly brown slices in broiler, spread side up. Cut into squares and spread untoasted sides with mix of cheese, curry powder, onion and mayonnaise. Press tops into Parmesan cheese. Arrange squares on cookie sheet and broil until topping bubbles. Serve immediately. Makes 2 dozen. May be frozen.

Marguerite R. Cederberg

Mrs. Elford Cederberg, Wife of former Representative (Michigan)

HOT CHEESE CANAPES

3 cups white cheddar cheese
    or Kraft's coon brand,
    grated
1 cup mayonnaise
1/2 cup chopped green onions
1 cup chopped black olives
1 package pita bread

Mix the ingredients by hand. Split and quarter pita bread. Spread cheese mixture on lightly toasted pita quarters and broil or bake until cheese melts. Serve hot. Makes 8 to 10 servings.

Linda J. Mickelson

Mrs. George Mickelson, Wife of former Governor (South Dakota)

JALAPENO CHEESE BREAD

2 teaspoons sugar
1½ cups cornmeal
1 tablespoon flour
2 teaspoons salt
1 teaspoon soda
1 cup buttermilk
½ cup fried meat grease (or
  vegetable oil)
2 eggs
1 small can creamed corn
2 jalapenos, chopped
½ green pepper, chopped
1 small onion, chopped
2 cups cheddar cheese,
  grated

Mix sugar, cornmeal, flour, salt and soda. Add buttermilk, grease, eggs and corn, beating well. Stir in jalapenos, green pepper and onion. Fold in grated cheese. Pour into a greased 10 × 14 baking dish. Bake at 375° for 30 minutes. Cut into bite sized pieces. Great served with cold beverages. Makes 50 servings. May be frozen.

Jeane Chappell

Mrs. Bill Chappell, Wife of former Representative (Florida)

DOROTHY'S CURRY AND CHEESE HORS D'OEUVRES

24 slices of thinly sliced white
  bread
¼ cup green onions (scal-
  lions) finely chopped—
  green parts too
1 cup grated mild cheddar
  cheese
1 4-oz. can chopped ripe
  olives
½ cup mayonnaise
¼ teaspoon curry powder

Toast two slices of bread in a toaster. Remove and immediately cut them into 2-inch rounds with a biscuit cutter. Repeat until all slices have been toasted and cut into rounds. Set aside. Combine remaining five ingredients in a bowl. Mix well. Spread mixture on toast rounds. Place on a cookie sheet, place under preheated broiler and broil until cheese begins to bubble. Serve immediately. Makes 24 servings.

Jo Zschau

Mrs. Ed Zschau, Wife of former Representative (California)

SPINACH ROLL

½ cup all purpose flour
1 egg yolk
2 tablespoons water
1 teaspoon olive oil
1 bunch fresh spinach
1 small chopped onion
1 beaten egg
⅓ cup ricotta cheese
¼ cup Parmesan cheese
2 cups sliced mushrooms
1 15 oz. can tomato sauce

In a small mixing bowl, combine flour and a pinch of salt. Make a well in center. Combine the yolk, water and oil; add to flour and mix well. Turn dough out on floured surface and knead till dough is smooth and elastic (about 10 minutes). Cover and let rest 10 minutes. On a lightly floured surface, roll dough to a square that is 12 × 12 and about ¹⁄₁₆ inch thick. Let stand 15 minutes. Bring a dutch oven of water to boil. Carefully add pasta and cook 1 to 2 minutes. Rinse in colander with cold water and drain well. Wash and chop spinach. Steam or saute till wilted. Saute onion. Add spinach, egg, ricotta cheese, Parmesan cheese and, if you'd like, a dash of nutmeg. Set aside.

To assemble spread pasta on a damp cloth. Let stand 15 minutes to dry. Spread with filling and roll up like a jelly roll and place in rectangular baking dish sprayed with Pam. In a saucepan, saute mushrooms in a little butter until tender. Add tomato sauce and season as desired (sugar, oregano and basil are nice). Bring to boil and cook for 5 minutes. Pour over pasta roll and bake in 375° oven for 20 to 25 minutes. Makes 6 servings.

Mrs. David Levy, Wife of Representative (New York)

SPINACH BALLS

2 10 oz. pkg. cooked,
 chopped spinach
1½ cups Pepperidge Farm
 stuffing
1 cup grated Parmesan
 cheese
3 beaten eggs
¾ cup sweet butter

Combine all ingredients. Roll into bite size balls, freeze. Place on cookie sheet and bake for 15 minutes at 350°. Good approach to get children to eat spinach. Makes 60 servings. May be frozen.

Mrs. John Boehner, Wife of Representative (Ohio)

POTATO CROQUETTES

4 servings of instant mashed
 potatoes (prepared)
½ cup Parmesan cheese
 chopped fresh parsley (a
 bit)
salt and pepper to taste

Make instant mashed potatoes; add ½ cup Parmesan cheese, parsley, salt and pepper. Make a consistency to be able to mix by hand. Scoop a large spoonful, roll in flour, then shape with hands into a small oblong croquette. Fry at high temperature until golden brown.

Mrs. Wally Herger, Wife of Representative (California)

ENGLISH MUFFIN TREATS

6 whole English muffins,
   split
2 cups grated sharp cheese
1½ cups chopped black olives
1 cup mayonnaise
1 teaspoon salt
1 teaspoon curry powder
½ teaspoon pepper
1 bunch green onions,
   chopped

Mix all ingredients and spread on muffins. Cut each muffin into 6 pieces. Freeze. Thaw and bake at 375° for 15 minutes. Makes 6 servings. May be frozen.

Lee Wampler

Mrs. William Wampler, Wife of former Representative (Virginia)

BACON WRAPPED WATER CHESTNUTS

1 8 oz. can water chestnuts
¼ cup soy sauce
¼ cup sugar
8 slices bacon, cut in half
   crosswise

Marinate chestnuts in soy sauce at least 30 minutes. Drain and roll each in sugar. Wrap each with a piece of bacon, securing with a toothpick. Arrange on a pie rack in a shallow baking pan. Bake at 400° 30 minutes or until golden brown. Drain on paper towels. Keep hot on warming tray. Note: Can be prepared ahead and stored until ready to bake. Makes 16 servings.

Glen Kleppe

Mrs. Thomas Kleppe, Wife of former Representative (North Dakota)

ZUCCHINI WITH SUN-DRIED TOMATO PUREE

2 cloves garlic
½ pound oil-packed sun-dried tomatoes, drained
¼ cup plus 2 teaspoons Parmesan cheese
10 small zucchini

In a blender or food processor, mince garlic and sun-dried tomatoes and add ¼ cup cheese and process until smooth. Cut off ends of the zucchini and slice into 1 inch asymmetrical rounds by alternately cutting straight down, then diagonally across (one side will be flat, the other will slant). Using a melon baller, scoop out a small amount of zucchini flesh, making sure not to scoop through the bottom. Fill each hole with about 1 teaspoon of the tomato mixture. Place on a cookie sheet and sprinkle with remaining cheese. Bake at 400° until heated through and bubbly (5 minutes). They can be made a few hours ahead and refrigerated until ready to heat. Makes 50 servings.

Laura Livingstain

Mrs. Harris Livingstain, Daughter of former Representative Don Fuqua (Florida)

BOURSIN MUSHROOMS

12 medium fresh mushrooms
1 5 oz. package boursin cheese
paprika
melted butter
parsley

Preheat oven to 350°. Remove stems from mushrooms and wipe caps with damp cloth. Brush outside of caps with melted butter. Fill caps with boursin and sprinkle with paprika. Arrange on cookie sheet, bake 15 minutes. Garnish with parsley. (Caps may be refrigerated overnight *before* baking). Makes 4 servings.

Suzanne Johnson

Mrs. Don Johnson, Wife of Representative (Georgia)

MUSHROOM PASTRY TURNOVERS

Pastry:
- ½ cup butter at room temperature
- 3 3 oz. packages cream cheese at room temperature
- 1½ cups flour

Pastry: Mix softened butter and cream cheese. Add flour and work dough with fingers until smooth. Place ball of pastry in wax paper. Refrigerate while preparing filling.

Mushroom Onion Filling:
- 1 large onion, finely chopped (Cuisinart is fine)
- 3 tablespoons butter
- ½ pound mushrooms, finely chopped (Cuisinart is fine)
- ¼ teaspoon dried thyme
- ½ teaspoon salt
  some freshly ground pepper
- 2 tablespoons flour
- ¼ cup sour cream

Mushroom Onion Filling: Saute onion in butter until just transparent. Add mushrooms and cook slowly on medium heat. Add seasonings. Sprinkle flour on to mixture and stir. Add sour cream. Cook until mixture thickens.

Roll pastry out on floured board to ⅛ inch thick. Cut into 3 inch rounds (biscuit cutter). Place ¼ to ½ teaspoon filling on each round. Fold over to make turnover. Press edges securely with fingers and press edges with tines of fork. Prick tops of turnovers with fork. If cooking right away, bake at 425° (ungreased cookie sheet) for 15 minutes until nicely puffed and browned. Watch carefully. (Freeze in freezer bags before cooking. Bring out as needed.) Makes 4 dozen. May be frozen.

Nini Horn

Mrs. Steve Horn, Wife of Representative (California)

APPATEASER BASKETS

12 round wonton wrappers
½ cup salad oil
½ cup thick chili (cooked)
    taco seasoning to taste
¾ cup chopped lettuce
¾ cup chopped fresh
    tomatoes
½ cup grated cheddar cheese
    salt and pepper to taste

Spread each wonton wrapper on both sides with oil using pastry brush. Press each into greased muffin tin to form small serving bowls. Bake in hot oven (400°) for eight to ten minutes until just tips of cups are brown. Watch carefully. Remove, cool. Fill cups with one tablespoon hot chili flavored with taco seasoning. Add chopped lettuce and tomatoes. Sprinkle top with grated cheese. Broil only until cheese melts. (Filling can vary to your choice of chicken, fish or chopped ham.) Makes 6 servings.

Olga Esch

Mrs. Marvin Esch, Wife of former Representative (Michigan)

SAVED AGAIN-HOT HORS D'OEUVRES

bread, any kind, cut into
    bite-sized rounds
mayonnaise
onion, diced
Parmesan cheese

Combine mayonnaise and onions. Place dollup of mayonnaise/onion mixture on each bread round. Top with Parmesan cheese. Place under broiler. Broil until hot and cheese melts. Serve immediately. So easy—so quick—so yummy! Makes as many as you want.

Suzie Dicks

Mrs. Norm Dicks, Wife of Representative (Washington)

SPRING ROLLS

½ pound ground pork
½ pound ground beef
¾ cup chopped water
    chestnuts
4 pieces dried mushrooms,
    soaked and chopped
½ cup chopped spring onions
½ cup shredded cabbage
    (optional)
1 egg
1 teaspoon salt
¼ teaspoon pepper
1 tablespoon soy sauce
30 to 35 lumpia wrappers

In bowl, combine first 5 ingredients. Add egg and mix thoroughly. Season with salt and pepper and soy sauce. At one end, spoon a tablespoon of mixture onto lumpia wrapper and roll tightly. Brush other end with water to seal. Deep fry until golden brown. Serve with warm sweet and sour sauce. Makes 10 servings.

Debbie Dingell

Mrs. John Dingell, Wife of Representative (Michigan)

ANN'S CRAB DIP

8 oz. canned or fresh crab
    meat
1 8 oz. pkg. cream cheese
1 small onion, diced
2 tablespoons butter
1 box wheat crackers
    (Wheatsworth)
    sprig of parsley

Drain crab meat. Mix crab and cream cheese together making a ball. Chop onion into small diced pieces, add to crab mixture. Use 2 tablespoons of butter to heavily grease baking dish. Place crab ball into center of dish. Bake at 375° for 15–20 minutes. Stir after removing to further mix ingredients. Garnish with parsley. Makes 8 servings. May be frozen.

Ann Santini

Mrs. Jim Santini, Wife of former Representative (Nevada)

68

CRAB DIP

1 pound lump crab meat
3 8 oz. packages cream
   cheese
2 tablespoons prepared
   mustard
1 tablespoon powdered
   sugar
½ cup mayonnaise
½ cup white wine
1 tablespoon onion juice
1 tablespoon lemon juice

Melt cream cheese in double boiler. Add remaining ingredients. Stir, serve with toast cups. Keep warm in chafing dish. Makes 30 servings.

Alice M. Lancaster

Mrs. Martin Lancaster, Wife of Representative (North Carolina)

DEVILED CRAB APPETIZER

1¼ cups dry bread crumbs
½ cup milk
1 cup sour cream
1 tablespoon Worcestershire
   sauce
1 tablespoon minced onion
½ teaspoon salt
¼ teaspoon dry mustard
6 drops Tabasco sauce
¼ cup olive oil
¼ pound fresh mushrooms,
   sliced
2 cups fresh crabmeat
2 teaspoons butter

Butter 6 ramekins. Soak 1 cup of the crumbs in milk for 10 minutes. Add sour cream, Worcestershire sauce, onion, salt, mustard, Tabasco sauce, olive oil, and mushrooms. Mix well. Gently fold in the crab. Divide the mixture into prepared ramekins. Refrigerate, covered, overnight. Preheat oven to 400°. Sprinkle crab mixture with remaining crumbs and dot with butter. Bake 15 minutes; serve immediately. Makes 6 servings.

Joyce Chandler

Mrs. Rod Chandler, Wife of former Representative (Washington)

MIMI'S EGGROLLS

Filling:
- 1 cup cooked beef or chicken, cut in small pieces
- 1 cup cooked shrimp
- 1 cup celery, diced
- ½ cup water chestnuts, chopped
- ½ cup green onions, chopped
- 2 teaspoons salt
- 1 teaspoon sugar
- 1 teaspoon soy sauce
- ⅛ teaspoon black pepper
- 1 tablespoon butter, melted
- 1 tablespoon peanut butter, melted

Wrappers:
- 8 Chinese noodle squares
  peanut oil
- 2 eggs, beaten

  Chinese hot mustard
  duck sauce

Saute the cooked shrimp briefly in some peanut oil, cool and chop into small pieces. Then combine all the filling ingredients and stir until blended. Refrigerate until ready to use. To assemble, divide each Chinese noodle square into 4 sections, and brush each section with beaten egg. Take 1 tablespoon of the filling per noodle square, roll up, and turn in the edges. Fry lightly in peanut oil and drain. Eggrolls can be frozen at this point. When ready to eat, fry in hot peanut oil until lightly browned (about 5 minutes). Drain and serve with hot mustard and duck sauce. Note: Chinese noodle squares, mustard and duck sauce are available in the international section of most grocery stores. Makes 12 servings. (32 small eggrolls).

Rhoda J Glickman

Mrs. Dan Glickman, Wife of Representative (Kansas)

To get people to circulate, serve different courses of a buffet or a variety of appetizers in various rooms.

GOLDEN CRAB PUFFS

7 oz. can crab or 6 oz.
  frozen crab
½ cup Bisquick
¼ cup grated Parmesan
  cheese
2 tablespoons green onion,
  chopped
1 egg, beaten
⅓ cup water
½ teaspoon Worcestershire
  sauce

Mustard Sauce:
½ cup Miracle Whip
½ teaspoon Worcestershire
  sauce
¼ cup prepared mustard
  few drops of Tabasco

Drain crab. Combine Bisquick, cheese, onions and crab meat. Combine egg, water and sauce. Add to crab mixture and stir until well blended. Drop by teaspoonful into ½ inch of oil, heated to 375°. Fry until golden brown, turning once. Drain. Serve warm with mustard sauce.

Cindy Daub

Mrs. Hal Daub, Wife of former Representative (Nebraska)

KATHY'S CRAB APPETIZERS

1 stick softened butter or
  margarine
1 jar (5 ounces) Old English
  Sharp Cheese Spread
1½ teaspoons mayonnaise
½ teaspoon garlic salt
½ teaspoon salt
8 ozs. lump crabmeat (fresh
  or frozen)
6 English muffins—split

Combine all ingredients except muffin halves. Mix well and spread mixture on untoasted muffin halves. Freeze (at least overnight) in airtight container. Remove from freezer several hours before serving. Cut each muffin into bite-size pieces (about 6 pieces per muffin half). Bake on cookie sheets at 350° for 15-20 minutes, or until hot and bubbly. Makes 96 pieces.

Jo Kleppe McClelland

Mrs. Scott McClelland, Daughter of former Representative Thomas Kleppe (North Dakota)

HOT CLAM DIP

2 cans minced or chopped
   clams with juice
1 cup seasoned bread
   crumbs
2 cups shredded mozzarella
   cheese
5 tablespoons melted oleo
1 clove crushed garlic
1 teaspoon oregano
   pepper to taste
   Parmesan cheese

Mix all ingredients. Pour in casserole. Sprinkle with Parmesan cheese and bake for 30 minutes at 350°. Serve warm with crackers or bread. Makes 4 cups. 8 to 10 servings.

June Miller

Mrs. John Miller, Wife of former Representative (Washington)

ESCALLOPED OYSTERS

1 pint oysters
1 cup cracker crumbs, me-
   dium coarse
½ cup melted butter or oleo
½ teaspoon salt
   dash pepper
¾ cup cream
¼ cup oyster liquid
¼ teaspoon Worcestershire
   sauce

Drain oysters, save liquid. Combine crumbs, butter, salt and pepper. Spread ⅓ of buttered crumbs in greased 8 inch square pan or baking dish. Cover with ½ of the oysters. Using another ⅓ crumbs, spread a second layer. Cover with remaining oysters. Combine cream, oyster liquid and sauce. Pour over oysters. Top with last of crumbs. Bake at 350° for 40 minutes. Serves 8.

Betty J. Applegate

Mrs. Doug Applegate, Wife of Representative (Ohio)

ROGERS' OYSTERS

oysters on the half shell
lemon juice
white wine
small bits of freshly fried
 bacon
chopped onion
Ritz cracker crumbs
butter

Serve as an hors d'oeuvres or a first course. Select fresh oysters on the half shell—the number depending on how many oysters per person you wish to serve. On each oyster, put 1/4 teaspoon of lemon juice; 1/2 teaspoon white wine; small bits of freshly fried bacon; about 1/4 teaspoon finely chopped onion; 1/2 teaspoon Ritz cracker crumbs and 1/4 teaspoon butter. Place prepared oysters on a baking dish and put under preheated broiler just long enough to see that the topping is nicely brown and beginning to bubble. Serve immediately.

Paul Rogers, former Representative (Florida)

SAUTÉED SCALLOPS WITH GARLIC AND PARSLEY

1/2 pound tiny bay scallops
2 tablespoons olive oil
1 teaspoon garlic, finely
 chopped
1/8 salt
 freshly ground black
 pepper
1 tablespoon finely chopped
 parsley
1 tablespoon chopped capers
2 tablespoons chopped
 roasted peppers, preferably freshly home-roasted
1 1/2 tablespoons fine, dry unflavored bread crumbs
4 scallop shells or 4 small
 shallow serving bowls

Wash the scallops in cold water, drain, and pat dry with paper towel. Put the olive oil and garlic in a small crepe pan and saute the garlic over medium heat until it turns a pale gold. Add scallops, salt, several liberal grindings of pepper and turn up the heat. Stir briskly and cook for no more than 5 minutes. Turn off the heat, add the parsley, capers, peppers, 1 tablespoon of bread crumbs, and mix thoroughly. Divide the scallop mixture into 4 scallop shells, or small flameproof gratin pans. Sprinkle with the remainder of the bread crumbs. Run the shells or pans under a hot broiler for about 2 minutes or no more than necessary to brown the tops of the scallops very lightly. Serve at once. Makes 4 servings.

Mrs. Ronald Machtley, Wife of Representative (Rhode Island)

CHICKEN APPETIZERS WITH MUSTARD SAUCE

3 whole chicken breasts,
   boned and skinned
½ cup crushed stuffing or
   bread crumbs
½ cup grated Parmesan
   cheese
2 tablespoons of chopped
   parsley
⅓ cup melted butter

Mustard Sauce:
2 tablespoons Dijon mustard
½ cup sour cream
2 teaspoons minced onion
   salt and pepper to taste

Cut chicken into bite size pieces. Combine crumbs, cheese, and parsley. Roll chicken in butter, then the crumb mixture. Place on cookie sheet and bake at 400° for 10-15 minutes. Mix all ingredients for the mustard sauce. Serve hot chicken with toothpicks for dipping in mustard sauce. Chicken may be made ahead and frozen after placing on foil lined cookie sheet. Thaw prior to baking. Makes 20 servings.

June Harvey

Mrs. James Harvey, Wife of former Representative (Michigan)

B & D'S CHICKEN WINGS

36 chicken wings or
   drumettes
½ cup of flour
½ to ¾ cup light olive oil
   salt to taste

Marinade:
1 cup lemon juice (juice of 2
   lemons)
   zest of 1 lemon
2 tablespoons + 1 teaspoon
   of sugar
⅓ cup of water

Marinade: Combine all ingredients and stir until sugar is dissolved. Wash chicken wings, pat dry. Shake in ½ cup of flour. Shake excess flour from each piece. Heat oil in heavy weight frying pan until very hot. Add chicken wings one layer at a time. Cook until golden brown on all sides. Remove to casserole with cover. Place in 225° oven to steam for 30 minutes. Remove from oven. Baste each wing with marinade and bake for 15-20 minutes longer, until the meat is tender. Allow 2 to 3 wings for appetizer, and 4 to 5 wings for entree. Makes 12 servings as an appetizer. May be frozen.

Mrs. Mark Hatfield

Mrs. Mark Hatfield, Wife of Senator (Oregon)

CHICKEN POT STICKERS

3 cups all-purpose flour
½ teaspoon salt
1 cup boiling water
⅓ cup cold water
¼ cup all-purpose flour
chicken-vegetable filling
cooking oil
water
soy-vinegar dripping sauce

Soy-Vinegar Dipping Sauce:
3 tablespoons soy sauce
3 tablespoons rice vinegar
2 tablespoons cilantro
1 thinly sliced green onion

Chicken-Vegetable Filling:
1 pound ground chicken (2 whole chicken breasts)
¼ cup thinly sliced green onion
¼ cup finely chopped carrots
1 cup finely chopped Nappa cabbage
½ cup finely chopped water chestnuts
½ cup finely chopped bean sprouts
4 teaspoons soy sauce
1 tablespoon grated ginger (fresh)

In a large mixing bowl, stir together the 3 cups of flour and salt. Pour the boiling water slowly into flour, stirring constantly. Stir until well blended. Stir in the cold water. When cool enough to handle, knead dough on a well floured surface, kneading in the ¼ cup flour until dough is smooth and elastic (8 to 10 minutes). Shape dough in a ball. Place dough back into bowl; cover with a damp towel. Let stand 15 to 20 minutes. Turn dough out onto a lightly floured surface. Divide dough into four equal portions. Roll each portion to ⅛ inch thickness. With a cookie cutter, cut into 3-inch rounds, making about 45 rounds (reroll as needed). Spoon about 1 tablespoon filling into the center of each dough round. Fold round in half across filling, pleating one edge to smoothly fit against opposite edge; pinch edges to seal. Set sealed edge of dumpling upright; press gently to slightly flatten the bottom. Transfer to a floured baking sheet. Cover with a dry towel. Repeat with remaining filling and rounds. In a 12-inch skillet heat 2 tablespoons oil about 1 minute or until very hot. Set half of the pot stickers upright in skillet (making sure the pot stickers do not touch each other); cook in hot oil about 1 minute or until bottoms are lightly browned. Reduce heat. Add ⅔ cup water to skillet. Cover and cook about 10 minutes. Uncover and cook 2 to 3 minutes or until all water evaporates. Cook, uncovered for 1 more minute. Using a wide spatula, gently remove the pot stickers from the skillet. Keep warm while cooking remaining Pot Stickers. Serve with soy-vinegar dipping sauce. Makes 45 servings.

Chicken-Vegetable Filling: Mix all ingredients in a large bowl. Add salt and pepper to taste. Fill Pot Stickers. Makes four cups.

Judy Hum, The Congressional Club Chef

DUCK FINGERS

2 eggs
salt
pepper
small amount of milk
1 or 2 sticks of butter
filet of duck breast

Allow one duck for 2 or 3 people as an appetizer. Filet a duck breast and cut into thin (¼ inch strips). In a bowl, combine 2 eggs with a little milk and salt and pepper. Whip with a wire whisk. (Create an egg/milk wash). In a paper bag, combine flour, salt and pepper. Melt 1 to 2 sticks of butter in a skillet. (I Can't Believe It's Not Butter seems to work even better.) Make sure butter is very hot, being careful not to burn. Dip the strips in the egg mixture and put into paper bag, shaking to insure that flour adheres. Put into hot butter, quickly and carefully browning on all sides until crispy but not burned. Drain on paper towels and serve immediately with Reeses white wine/coarse ground mustard or similar product. Duck fingers should be served while hot to the touch. Important: Do not make up strips in advance. They should be dipped in egg batter and flour just before cooking. Scrape the pan and add more butter as necessary.

John Dingell, Representative (Michigan)

SAUSAGE-CHEESE BALLS

1⅓ cups Bisquick
1 pound grated cheddar cheese
1 pound ground pork sausage

Combine ingredients until dough sticks together. Roll into 1 inch balls. Bake in a 350° oven for about 25 minutes. Drain on paper towels. Serve warm. Makes 75 balls. May be frozen.

Mrs. Wally Herger, Wife of Representative (California)

SCOTS EGGS

1 pound pork sausage
¼ cup dry bread crumbs
2 egg yolks
2 tablespoons milk
1 teaspoon Worcestershire
   sauce
1 cup all-purpose flour
2 egg whites, beaten
1 cup dry bread crumbs
6 hard cooked eggs
   vegetable oil
   salt
   pepper
   mustard

Mix sausage, ¼ cup bread crumbs, egg yolks, milk and Worcestershire sauce in small bowl. Place flour, egg whites, and 1 cup bread crumbs in separate bowls. Coat each hard cooked egg with flour. Pat ⅙ sausage mixture onto each egg, coat egg in flour again, then egg whites, then bread crumbs. Heat oil (4–5 inches) in deep fat fryer or kettle to 350. Fry eggs, one at a time, turning occasionally, until deep brown, about 5 minutes. Drain on paper toweling. Cut eggs in half. Serve hot or cold with salt, pepper and mustard. Makes 12 servings

Peggy Soderberg

Mrs. William Soderberg, Daughter of former Representative Robert Grant (Indiana)

SAUSAGE BALLS

1 pound sausage (hot or
   mild)
2 cups Bisquick
1 cup sharp cheese, grated

Mix all ingredients together. Roll in very small balls. Bake at 350° for 25 minutes. Makes 90 servings. May be frozen.

Evelyn Burnside

Mrs. Maurice Burnside, Wife of former Representative (West Virginia)

> *Soak bamboo skewers in water to prevent from burning.*

PORK BALLS CANTONESE

2 pounds mild bulk sausage
1 small onion, minced
½ cup milk

1 green pepper, julienned
1 red pepper or 2 tomatoes,
   cut up

Sweet Sour Sauce:
1 can (20 oz.) pineapple bits,
   reserve juice
½ cup vinegar
½ cup sugar
1 tablespoon soy sauce
¼ cup water
3 tablespoons cornstarch
2 tablespoons butter

Combine sausage, onion, and milk. Shape into small balls. Bake in shallow pan at 325° for 40–50 minutes. For sauce, combine pineapple juice, vinegar, sugar and soy sauce. Blend water and cornstarch; add to pineapple juice mixture. Cook on medium until thick and clear. Stir in butter. Mix sauce, vegetables, and meat balls. Serve in chafing dish. (Also may be served over rice as a main dish.) Makes 10 + servings. May be frozen.

Ruth Fawell

Mrs. Harris Fawell, Wife of Representative (Illinois)

UNUSUAL MEATBALLS

1 pound smoked ham
   (ground)
1½ pounds pork sausage
2 cups dry bread crumbs
1 scant cup milk
2 beaten eggs

Syrup:
½ cup vinegar
1½ cups brown sugar
1 teaspoon dry mustard
½ cup water

Mix all ingredients together and roll into 1 inch balls. Place on bottom of large roasting pan. Pour syrup over the meatballs and bake for 2 hours at 300°. Meatballs may be turned once during baking. Syrup: Boil water, vinegar, brown sugar and mustard until it forms a smooth syrup. Makes 20 servings. May be frozen.

Martha Sundquist

Mrs. Don Sundquist, Wife of Representative (Tennessee)

MINI SAUSAGE QUICHES

1 package refrigerator but-
   terflake rolls, cut in half
   and rolled thin
½ pound ground pork sau-
   sage (or ground Italian-
   seasoned sausage)
1½ cups cottage cheese
3 eggs, beaten
1 tablespoon chopped
   parsley
½ cup grated Parmesan
   cheese
   dash of salt and pepper

Press dough into tiny muffin tins. Brown sausage and drain. Crumble and divide among tins. Combine eggs, cheese, parsley, salt, and pepper. Spoon over sausage. Bake for 20 minutes, or until set and lightly browned. Quiches can be frozen after baking. Cool and wrap thoroughly in foil, then in plastic, and freeze. Reheat in a slow oven (375°), 20–25 minutes. Makes 24 servings. May be frozen.

Mrs. David Bradley, Daughter of former Representative James Harvey (Michigan)

REUBEN APPETIZERS

1 can corned beef
1 pound can sauerkraut
   (drained and mashed
   with fork)
3 ounces cream cheese
2 tablespoons minced onion
   flour for rolling
   evaporated milk
   cracker meal for rolling
   oil for cooking

Mix all ingredients and form small balls. Roll in flour. Dip in evaporated milk. Roll in cracker meal. Brown in hot oil. Makes 25 appetizers.

Mrs. Maurice Burnside, Wife of former Representative (West Virginia)

LAMB MEAT BALLS

1 pound ground lamb
1 egg, beaten
1/3 cup fine dry bread crumbs
1/4 cup chopped parsley
1 teaspoon salt
1/4 teaspoon pepper
1/2 teaspoon rosemary
2 tablespoons chopped
   chives
2 tablespoons butter
1/2 cup Madeira wine
1 chicken bouillon cube
1 teaspoon paprika
   lemon slices

Combine lamb, egg, crumbs, parsley, salt, pepper, rosemary, and chives; mix well. Shape into 1 inch balls. Melt butter in skillet. Add lamb balls and cook over low heat until browned on all sides. Drain off fat. Add Madeira, bouillon cube, and paprika; mix well. Cover and cook 20 minutes, stirring frequently. Serve lamb balls in Madeira sauce from chafing dish. Garnish with lemon-slice twists. Makes 4 to 6 servings. May be frozen.

Mrs. Joe Skeen, Wife of Representative (New Mexico)

MEXICAN QUESO DIP

1 pound hamburger (lean)
1 pound sausage (hot or
   mild)
2 cans Ro-tel tomatoes
1 large pkg. Velveeta cheese
   (2 lbs.)
1 small can diced green
   chiles

Brown meat, drain fat and set aside. Melt cheese in microwave. Place melted cheese in chafing dish. Add all other ingredients, including meat, and heat thoroughly. Serve with Tostito chips.

el Hefley, Representative (Colorado)

CURRY DIP FOR VEGGIES

1 cup mayonnaise
2 teaspoons honey
2 teaspoons curry powder
2 teaspoons grated onion
2 teaspoons ketchup
2 teaspoons cognac
1 teaspoon lemon juice
6 or 7 drops of Tabasco
   sauce
pinch of salt

Mix all ingredients well (can be done in blender, but do not overblend). Chill. Serve as dip accompanying raw carrots, cauliflower, broccoli, celery, mushrooms, etc. Note: For less spicy dip, increase mayonnaise to 1½ cups.

Dian Bradley

Mrs. David Bradley, Daughter of former Representative James Harvey (Michigan)

STRAWBERRY AND CHEESE DIP

1 pound sharp cheddar
   cheese, grated
1 cup chopped nuts
1 cup mayonnaise
1 small onion, grated
   dashes of salt, black pepper, red pepper
12 oz. jar of strawberry
   preserves

Mix all ingredients, except preserves. Press into pie pan. Chill for a few hours. Before serving spread preserves evenly over mixture. Serve with crackers. Makes 8 servings.

Marilyn Broyhill Beach

Mrs. Robert Beach, Daughter of former Senator James Broyhill (North Carolina)

> *When preparing a punch, all ingredients should be cold. The ice ring will last longer if the punch is chilled.*

CURRIED DIP

1 cup chutney (in two
    portions)
3 teaspoons curry powder
½ teaspoon dry mustard
16 ozs. cream cheese
½ cup chopped peanuts
2 small chopped scallions
1 chopped hard-boiled egg

In a food processor, mix cream cheese, ½ cup chutney, curry powder and dry mustard until well blended. Place in shallow serving dish and chill. Before serving, top with ½ cup chutney, peanuts, scallions and egg. Serve with crackers. Makes 6 servings.

Anne Burhans

Mrs. Nicholas Burhans, Daughter of former Representative John Mackie (Michigan)

MEXICALI BEAN SPREAD

1 can cooked red kidney
    beans
3 tablespoons water
1 tablespoon tomato paste
1 tablespoon lemon juice
1 teaspoon ground cumin
1 teaspoon oregano
½ teaspoon Tabasco sauce
    pinch ground cinnamon
    (optional)

In a food processor (or blender), whirl all ingredients together until smooth. Serve as a dip with tortilla chips or crackers.

Katharine S. McHugh

Mrs. John McHugh, Wife of Representative (New York)

HOT MEXICAN DIP

8 ozs. soft cream cheese
6 chopped green onions
1 cup sour cream
1 can Frito jalapeno bean
    dip/Tabasco/garlic salt
½ pound grated cheddar
    cheese
½ pound grated Monterey
    Jack cheese
1 jar picante sauce
1 can chopped black olives
    (optional)
    Tostidos, Fritos or Doritos

Mix first five ingredients. Layer this mixture alternately with the two cheeses, i.e., ½ mixture, ½ cheddar, ½ monterey jack, then repeat layers, in a rectangular pyrex dish. Bake 20 minutes at 325° until cheese is bubbly. Spread 1 can picante sauce on top and garnish with chopped black olives (optional). Serve with Tostidos, Doritos or Fritos. (Can be put in chafing dish). Makes 12 to 14 servings.

Don Johnson, Representative (Georgia)

PICO DE GALLO

8 long green chiles, roasted,
    peeled and deveined
2 small yellow chiles,
    roasted, peeled and
    chopped, or 2 jalapeno
    chiles
5 green onions, chopped
    (including tops)
5 medium tomatoes,
    chopped
¼ cup chopped fresh cilantro
    leaves
2 tablespoons vegetable oil
1 teaspoon vinegar
    salt to taste

Combine all ingredients except salt; chill. Salt to taste prior to serving. Serve with warm tostados, meats, chicken, hamburgers, etc. Makes 2 cups.

Mrs. Blaine Purcell, Daughter-in-law of former Representative Graham Purcell (Texas)

CRYSTAL'S HOT SALSA

1 bunch green onions or ½
   regular onion
1 large (28 oz.) can whole tomatoes or 6 fresh tomatoes, cooked and peeled
1 7 oz. can chopped green
   chilies
4 ozs. picante sauce
   salt, pepper, crushed red
   pepper, garlic salt to
   taste
1 teaspoon vinegar
   juice of ½ fresh lime

Mince the green onions in a food processor. Add the tomatoes and chop, being careful not to over process. Transfer to serving bowl and add remaining ingredients. The picante sauce and spices may be varied according to your taste, so have some tortilla chips ready to sample as you go. Makes 20 servings.

Kristy Gavin

Mrs. Stephen Gavin, Daughter of Representative Jon Kyl (Arizona)

TEXAS CAVIAR

2 cans (14 oz.) black eyed
   peas, drained
1 can (15 oz.) white hominy,
   drained
2 medium tomatoes,
   chopped
½ cup parsley, chopped
1 medium onion, chopped
2 cloves garlic, minced
1 red pepper, chopped
1 jalapeno pepper, finely
   chopped
1 8 oz. bottle Italian dressing

Combine all of the above. Mix well. Pour Italian dressing over mixture being sure to coat well. Refrigerate. Let marinate at least two hours. Hint: Make mixture a day ahead, stir two or three times. Use oil based Italian dressing. Seems to cling better. Serve with taco chips. Makes 8 to 12 servings.

Connie Ewing

Mrs. Thomas Ewing, Wife of Representative (Illinois)

AMARETTO DIP

1 3 oz. pkg. instant vanilla
   pudding
1 cup milk
1 container of Cool Whip
½ cup Amaretto

Mix pudding with milk and fold in Cool Whip. Add Amaretto and blend well. Serve with fresh fruit. Makes 12 servings. May be frozen.

Tish Traficant

Mrs. James Traficant, Wife of Representative (Ohio)

SPINACH DIP

½ cup chopped green onions
½ cup minced parsley
1 10 oz. pkg. of frozen
   chopped spinach,
   thawed and squeezed
   free from liquid
½ cup mayonnaise
   salt and ground pepper

Use food processor to chop and mince green onions and parsley if desired. Mix spinach and other ingredients in bowl. Salt and pepper to taste. You may use more or less mayonnaise. Serve with large Fritos for dipping. Makes 8 servings.

Cece Zorinsky-White

Mrs. Cece Zorinsky-White, Wife of former Senator Edward Zorinsky (Nebraska)

Serve sliced meats and dips in a hollowed purple cabbage to add color.

SPINACH DIP

1 10 oz. pkg. frozen spinach
   (drain well)
2 cups Hellman's mayonnaise
½ cup parsley (chopped)
½ onion (chopped)
1 tablespoon lemon juice
½ teaspoon pepper

Mix ingredients and refrigerate at least 4 hours. Serve with vegetables.

Dorothy F. Mathews

Mrs. Patrick Mathews, Daughter of former Representative Claude Fuller (Arkansas)

SPINACH DIP

1 cup mayonnaise
½ pint sour cream
1 pkg. Knorr dried vegetable
   soup mix
1 pkg. frozen chopped spinach, thawed and well
   drained
1 cup finely chopped water
   chestnuts
   small onion, finely
   chopped

Mix all ingredients. Serve in a hollowed out round loaf of bread, unsliced, with cut up vegetables or melba toast. Makes 12 servings.

'Peatsy' Hollings

Mrs. Fritz Hollings, Wife of Senator (South Carolina)

Lemon perks up the flavor of sour cream dips.

GUACAMOLE DIP

1 can jalapeno bean dip
3 ripe avocados, mashed
2 tablespoons lemon juice
1 bunch green onions, finely
    chopped
1 cup sour cream
1 cup mayonnaise
1 package taco seasoning
    mix
1 can ripe olives, drained
    and chopped
1 pound cheddar cheese,
    finely shredded
½ fresh tomato (remove
    seeds, skin and mem-
    brane) and dice

In 9 × 13 glass baking dish place the following layers:
jalapeno bean dip
avocado and lemon juice
green onions
sour cream, mayonnaise and taco seasoning (mixed together)
olives
cheese
tomato

Refrigerate overnight to blend flavors and serve with Tostada chips.

Terry Branstad, Governor (Iowa)

VERMONT GUACAMOLE

1 small onion
2 to 3 Hass avocados,
    depending on size
1 bunch, or fistful of fresh
    cilantro, or lemon grass
    dash of lemon juice
    dash of salt

Place onion in bowl of food processor and chop. Add remaining ingredients and process until smooth, with green flakes. Serve with nachos (corn chips with cheese melted on the top) and salsa. Makes 2 cups.

Mrs. Peter Smith, Wife of former Representative (Vermont)

ARTICHOKE DIP

2 jars of artichokes, drained
8 ozs. of low fat mayonnaise
½ Parmesan cheese
1 pkg. of frozen chopped
   spinach
   white pepper
   garlic salt (optional)

Cook and drain spinach, and set to the side to cool. Cut artichoke into small pieces after draining. Combine artichoke, mayonnaise and Parmesan cheese. Mix well and then add spinach. Again, mix well. Add white pepper to taste. Bake for 30 minutes at 400°. This dip can be served either hot or cold. Makes 12 servings.

Robyn Porter, Daughter of Representative John Porter (Illinois)

EASY ARTICHOKE DIP

1 pound can artichoke hearts
1 cup mayonnaise
1 cup Parmesan cheese
   little lemon juice
   dash or two of garlic
     powder
   dash Worcestershire sauce

Drain can of artichoke hearts and chop artichokes fine. Combine artichoke mixture with mayonnaise and Parmesan cheese. Season with lemon juice, garlic powder and Worcestershire. Top with Parmesan cheese. Bake at 350° for 20–30 minutes, until bubbly and slightly browned. Serve with your favorite cracker. Makes 12 servings.

Mrs. John Dingell, Wife of Representative (Michigan)

HOT ARTICHOKE DIP

14 oz. can artichoke hearts
1 cup Parmesan cheese
²/₃ to ¾ cup mayonnaise
approximately 2 table-
spoons Worcestershire
sauce
approximately 1 to 2 tea-
spoons Tabasco sauce
approximately 1 teaspoon
garlic salt

Drain artichoke hearts well and cut up. Mix all ingredients and bake at 350° for 20 to 30 minutes until slightly brown on top. Makes 6 to 8 servings.

Margaret Morgan

Margaret Morgan, Daughter of former Senator Robert Morgan (North Carolina)

FABULOUS HOT ARTICHOKE CHEESE DIP

2 cans artichoke hearts (or
fresh equivalent)
1 cup mayonnaise
1 cup plain lowfat yogurt
garlic (at least 7–8 cloves)
chopped fine
1½ cups Parmesan cheese or
Parmesan/Romano
cheese
paprika

Mash artichoke hearts in bowl. Add mayonnaise and yogurt. Add Parmesan/Romano cheese. Add garlic and mix well. Turn into deep baking dish. Cover top with liberal sprinkling of paprika. Bake at 400° for 20 minutes. Serve hot with warmed, whole wheat pita bread, or on crackers. (Everyone asks for this recipe!) Makes enough for 12 people.

Ilene Marder

Mrs. Maurice Hinchey, Wife of Representative (New York)

HOT CLAM DIP

½ green pepper (diced)
½ medium onion (diced)
2 tablespoons margarine
½ cup catsup
   several dashes hot sauce
4 slices American cheese
1 cup grated mild cheddar
2 6½ oz. cans minced clams
¼ cup dry sherry

Saute pepper and onion in small coated skillet. Add remaining ingredients in order. The clams should be drained. Cook on low heat until cheeses melt. If this needs to be thickened, dissolve ½ teaspoon corn starch in 2 tablespoons sherry and add to hot mixture. Serve warm with favorite crackers. Makes 12 servings. May be frozen.

Dorothy W. Hungate

Mrs. William Hungate, Wife of former Representative (Missouri)

SHRIMP AND ARTICHOKE DIP

2 cans artichoke hearts,
   drained and chopped
½ pound shrimp, cooked and
   cleaned
1 cup sour cream
1 cup mayonnaise
1 bunch chopped green
   onions
   garlic salt to taste

Mix all ingredients and refrigerate overnight. Serve with crackers. Makes 20 servings.

Suzanne Johnson

Mrs. Don Johnson, Wife of Representative (Georgia)

"GRETTA'S CEDAR KEY HOT CRAB DIP"

1 8 oz. pkg. cream cheese
1 6 oz. can crab meat
1½ teaspoon chopped onion
½ tablespoon horseradish
¼ teaspoon salt
   dash of pepper

Mix all ingredients. Bake at 375° for 15 minutes or until bubbly. Serve on crackers.

Mrs. Cynthia Mitchell-Gingles, Daughter of former Representative Donald Mitchell (New York)

KIT'S CRABMEAT DIP

1 pound lump crabmeat
⅔ pint Hellman's mayonnaise
1 teaspoon minced onion
1 tablespoon or more of
      capers
2 dashes Tabasco sauce
¼ teaspoon Worcestershire
      sauce
¼ cup sherry
   seasoned salt to taste

Mix and chill. Serve with crackers.

Mrs. Jack Edwards, Wife of former Representative (Alabama)

Don't make your cocktail hour more than it should be— you want your guests to enjoy their meal.

CRABMEAT DIP

12 ozs. cream cheese
2 tablespoons Worcestershire
  sauce
1 tablespoon lemon juice
  small chopped onion
1 cup seafood cocktail sauce
2 cans large lump crabmeat
  paprika

Mix first three ingredients and press into dish. Sprinkle onion on top. Chill until hard. Mix cocktail sauce and crabmeat. Spread over cream cheese mixture. Sprinkle paprika. Chill again before serving. Makes 8 servings.

Marilyn Broyhill Beach

Mrs. Robert Beach, Daughter of former Senator James Broyhill (North Carolina)

EASY CRAB DIP

1 large jar Cheez-Whiz
1 pound fresh crab meat
¼ cup sherry
  Fritos or Triscuits

Mix all ingredients and warm to just below a boil in a fondue pot and serve with Fritos or Triscuits for dipping. Makes many servings.

Sydna Zeliff

Mrs. Bill Zeliff, Wife of Representative (New Hampshire)

CRAWFISH DIP

1 pound crawfish
1 small bunch green onions
1 tablespoon parsley
1 pint half and half
1 stick butter or margarine
3 tablespoons sherry
3 scant tablespoons flour
  salt, red pepper, Lea &
    Perrin and Tabasco

Cook onions and parsley in ½ stick butter; mix in flour, but do not brown. Add cream slowly, using wooden spoon. In another skillet, cook crawfish in ½ stick butter, add cream sauce, (to double, add 1 can cream of celery soup after adding half and half to first batch crawfish) add sherry and let stand for 2 hours. Serve warm. Makes 20 servings. May be frozen.

Mary Johnston

Mrs. Bennett Johnston, Wife of Senator (Louisiana)

"DAD'S CEDAR KEY SMOKED OYSTER DIP"

1 4 oz. can smoked oysters
1 8 oz. pkg. cream cheese,
  softened
½ cup chopped black olives
  juice of 1 lemon
2 tablespoons Worcestershire
  sauce
½ cup mayonnaise

Blend ingredients in blender. May be stored in refrigerator. Remove 1 hour before serving. Serve with crackers.

Donald Mitchell, former Representative (New York)

BEEF DIP

1 pound ground beef
1 onion, chopped
1 4 oz. can chopped green
  chilies
½ pound Velveeta cheese
¼ pound Monterey Jack
  cheese
  picante sauce, salt and pepper to taste

Microwave ground beef and onion until meat is gray. Drain excess fat. Melt cheese in microwave or double boiler. Combine all ingredients and heat through. Add small amount of canned milk if dip is too thick. Serve with chips. May be frozen.

Mrs. Thomas Morris, Wife of former Representative (New Mexico)

GUS' GARLIC SAUCE

6 garlic cloves
1 cup olive oil
1 fresh lemon
½ teaspoon salt
2 tablespoons white vinegar
3 cups mashed potatoes

Mash hot potatoes in a large bowl. To blender, add garlic, olive oil, lemon, salt, and vinegar. Blend until very smooth. Add blended mixture to mashed potatoes and mix with electric mixer. For smoother sauce, you may add a little water. If desired, you can return all mixture to blender, a little at a time. Serve with vegetables, seafood, or crusty bread. This sauce may be stored in a closed jar in the refrigerator. Makes 12 servings.

Mike Bilirakis

Michael Bilirakis, Representative (Florida)

SEAFOOD COCKTAIL SAUCE

1 cup ketchup
10 drops Tabasco
1 generous teaspoon Worcestershire sauce
1 teaspoon horseradish
2 teaspoons lemon juice
dash of salt

Mix together. Good for shrimp, lobster, crab.

Katie Lowery

Mrs. Bill Lowery, Wife of former Representative (California)

SPICED TEA

1 cup lemon flavored iced
   tea mix (low calorie)
2 cups Tang
2 teaspoons ground cloves
1 teaspoon ground cinnamon

Mix ingredients well. Store in airtight container. For one serving, mix 2 teaspoons of dry mixture with 6 ounces hot water. Makes 60 servings.

Lynn Staton

Mrs. Mick Staton, Wife of former Representative (West Virginia)

ICED TEA SYRUP

3½ cups water
 ¾ cup loose tea
2½ cups sugar

Boil water; add tea. Steep 8–10 minutes. Strain. Add sugar. Store in glass container (covered) in refrigerator. For one serving, mix 2 tablespoons of syrup with 8 ounces cold water. Add ice. Makes 30+ servings.

Lynn Staton

Mrs. Mick Staton, Wife of former Representative (West Virginia)

VERMONT ICED TEA

3 bags Lipton tea
2 bags lemon herb tea
1 12 oz. can frozen lem-
   onade
  at least 24 leaves fresh
   apple (woolly) mint (or
   other, but apple is best)
sugar or sweetener to taste

Make 6 cups of tea with the 5 tea bags. Sweeten to taste. In a gallon container, add mint leaves and tea and let brew for 10 minutes. Add frozen lemonade and water in the amount it suggests on the can. Let sit for a bit and serve. This is consumed in quantity on our Vermont porch in the summer. Makes 1 gallon.

Sally Smith

Mrs. Peter Smith, Wife of former Representative (Vermont)

MOM'S EGG NOG

12 eggs
1½ cups sugar
1 quart whipping cream
1 quart milk
¼ teaspoon salt

Beat 12 egg whites until stiff. Beat ½ cup of sugar into the egg whites after stiff. In a separate bowl, beat 12 egg yolks until light. Add 1 cup sugar and ¼ teaspoons salt to egg yolk mixture. Combine both egg mixtures and gently stir. In a separate bowl, beat 1 quart of whipping cream until stiff. Add 1 quart milk. Mix all together. Put in large punch bowl. Add 1 cup rum or bourbon if desired. Cover with plastic wrap and store in refrigerator. Makes 15 servings.

Erin Williams, Daughter of Representative Pat Williams (Montana)

CITRUS PUNCH

2 cups sugar
4 cups water
½ cup lemon juice
½ cup lime juice
4½ cups orange juice
2 cups grapefruit juice
2 cups pineapple juice
1 750 milliliter bottle medium-sweet white wine
1 750 milliliter bottle champagne

Boil for 1 minute the sugar, 2 cups water and lemon juice. Stir in remaining water and cool. Stir in lime juice, orange juice and grapefruit juice. Pour over ice. Add pineapple juice, white wine and champagne. Garnish with citrus slices, strawberries, mint, etc. Makes 1½ gallons.

Mrs. Kika de la Garza, Wife of Representative (Texas)

> *Wine adds delicious flavor to all foods. As it cooks, the alcohol evaporates leaving a mellow taste.*

HOT CRANBERRY DRINK

1 pound cranberries
1 quart water
1 cup sugar
½ cup "red hots" cinnamon candies
2 cloves
¼ cup lemon juice
2 cups orange juice

Boil cranberries in water until popped. Turn heat down and simmer about 5 minutes. Strain, using a colander, and save juice. To juice add 1 cup sugar, ½ cup cinnamon candies and 2 cloves. Cook until candy melts. Take off heat and add 2 cups orange juice and ¼ cup lemon juice. Let cool. Put in jar and refrigerate. To serve, add 2 parts water to 1 part mixture or 1 part to 1 part. Serve in clear mug and float lemon slice on top. Makes 20 servings.

Barbara L. Battle

Mrs. L. Hunt Battle, Daughter-in-law of former Representative Laurie C. Battle (Alabama)

SPLUSH PARTY PUNCH

6 cups water
4 cups sugar
5 bananas, medium ripe
1 6 oz. can frozen lemon juice
1 12 oz. can frozen orange juice
1 can pineapple juice (46 ozs.)
3 cups water
3 large bottles ginger ale or Sprite

Combine the sugar and 6 cups of water and boil for 5 minutes, stirring mixture continually until syrup forms. Allow to cool completely. Slice bananas thinly and cover with the fruit juices. Add the can of pineapple juice and the other 3 cups of water. Mix in the cooled sugar mixture. Pour mixture into 3 plastic freezer bags and freeze until ready to use. Thaw for two hours before serving and add 1 bottle of ginger ale or Sprite per bag of mixture. Note: This recipe calls for frozen lemon juice, not frozen lemonade. Makes 38 servings. May be frozen.

Lillian Darden

Mrs. George Darden, Wife of Representative (Georgia)

RHUBARB PUNCH

1 cup grape juice
½ cup sugar
2 cups orange juice
2 cups rhubarb juice
4 cups water

Combine all ingredients. Serve very cold. Makes 8 servings.

Lucille K. Carter

Mrs. Steven V. Carter, Wife of former Representative (Iowa)

"GRASS HOPPER" DEMI-TASSE

1 jigger crème de menthe
1 jigger brandy
1 scoop vanilla ice cream

Put in an electric blender, mix and serve in demi-tasse cups that have been chilled. Use as a dessert with Nabisco chocolate wafers. Makes 2 to 3 servings.

Harold S. Sawyer, former Representative (Michigan)

GEORGIA PEACH

2 ozs. Amaretto
2 ozs. peach schnapps
4 ozs. orange juice
large splash of club soda
ice

Combine ingredients and serve over ice. Makes 2 servings. May be frozen.

Mrs. Jerry Costello, Wife of Representative (Illinois)

CHAMPAGNE PUNCH

champagne (your preference)
cranberry juice
cranapple juice
lemon-lime soda

Use equal amounts of champagne, cranberry juice, cranapple juice, and lemon-lime soda. Freeze additional cranberry or cranapple juice in cubes or ring mold. Chill other ingredients. At serving time, put equal amounts of each into punch bowl over frozen cubes. Serve in cups or crystal glasses.

Miss Keely Burns, Daughter of Senator Conrad Burns (Montana)

Jacqueline Bouvier Kennedy
1961–1963

To The Congressional Club
with best wishes;

Jacqueline Kennedy

Jacqueline Bouvier Kennedy

1961 marked the beginning of one of the most glamorous eras in the White House. The youthful President Kennedy and his beautiful wife represented a new generation filled with hope for the future.

During her tenure as First Lady, Mrs. Kennedy worked tirelessly to restore the decor, furniture and other historic treasures of the White House. To help future administrations continue her efforts, she formed the White House Historical Association, which published the "White House—An Historical Guide." In addition, her love of the arts drew leading performing artists to Washington and helped stimulate enthusiasm for the variety of American culture.

Jacqueline Kennedy Garden at the White House

SOUPS, BREADS,
EGGS AND CHEESE

TORTILLA SOUP GIRAUD

1½ chopped onions
1 chopped bell pepper
2 potatoes, diced
2 carrots, diced
¼ cup celery, diced
3½ quarts chicken stock
¾ cup garbanzo beans
1 pound chicken meat, diced
2 tablespoons chili powder
1 tablespoon comino
1 teaspoon pepper
1 teaspoon granulated garlic
2 tablespoons cilantro,
   chopped

Saute onion and bell pepper for ten seconds; add carrots, celery, potatoes, saute two more minutes. Add hot chicken stock and simmer five to ten minutes. Add seasonings. Finish by adding chicken meat and cilantro. Slow simmering improves flavor. Garnish and serve. Strips of avocado and lime juice are very important.

GARNISH:
fried tortilla strips
lime
avacado

Lady Bird Johnson

Mrs. Lyndon B. Johnson, Wife of former President of the United States

CARROT VICHYSSOISE

2 cups peeled, diced potatoes
1¼ cups peeled, sliced carrots
1 tablespoon chopped onion
3 cups canned chicken broth
white pepper and salt to taste
1 cup sour cream
chopped chives and parsley

Simmer potatoes and carrots in chicken broth with the onion until tender. Season to taste. Cool puree in a blender and chill thoroughly in refrigerator. Approximately 1 hour before serving, fold in 1 cup of sour cream to which has been added 1 heaping teaspoon of chopped chives. Serve with a topping of chopped parsley. Serves 6.

Mrs. Gerald R. Ford

Mrs. Gerald R. Ford, Jr., Wife of former President of the United States Reprinted from the 1970 Congressional Club Cookbook. Eighth Edition.

BARBARA RATCHFORD'S TOMATO BISQUE SOUP

¼ pound butter
1 cup chopped celery
1 cup chopped onion
½ cup chopped carrots
⅓ cup flour
2 1 pound 12 oz. cans whole Italian plum tomatoes, drained and chopped
2 teaspoons sugar
1 teaspoon marjoram or summer savory
1 teaspoon basil
1 bay leaf
4 cups chicken broth
2 cups whipping cream or cream substitute
½ teaspoon curry powder
¼ teaspoon white pepper
½ teaspoon paprika
salt to taste

Melt butter. Saute vegetables until tender. Stir in flour. Cook 2 minutes stirring constantly. Add tomatoes, sugar, marjoram, basil, bay leaf and chicken broth. Simmer, stirring occasionally for 30 minutes. Discard bay leaf. Puree. Add remaining ingredients. Serve warm or cold. Makes 8 servings. May be frozen.

Sylvia Lee Sabo

Mrs. Martin Sabo, Wife of Representative (Minnesota)

CREAM OF TOMATO SOUP

2 tablespoons butter
1 medium-sized onion, chopped
2 carrots, chopped
3 tablespoons flour
1 quart chicken stock
1 small garlic clove
2 leeks, thinly sliced
4 white peppercorns
1 teaspoon salt
1 tablespoon sugar
6 medium-sized ripe tomatoes, roughly chopped
1 cup canned tomatoes
1 cup light cream

Melt butter in medium-sized saucepan. Add the onion and carrots, and cook slowly until the onion is translucent and carrots are firm, but slightly soft. Add the flour and mix. Add the chicken stock, the garlic clove, leeks, white peppercorns, salt, sugar, and tomatoes. Cover and cook over low heat for 1 to 1½ hours, skimming as needed. Using a separate bowl, rub the soup mixture through a finely-meshed strainer. Combine the cream with the strained soup. Add more cream or chicken stock as needed, to obtain the desired consistency. Return the mixture to a pot, and warm over low heat. Serve with finely chopped fresh parsley or touch of heavy cream. Makes 4 to 6 servings.

Valerie Blatnik, Daughter of former Representative John A. Blatnik (Minnesota)

BUTTERNUT AND ACORN SQUASH SOUP

1 medium butternut squash
1 medium acorn squash
½ medium onion, chopped
1 Grannysmith apple, chopped
4 cups chicken stock (canned or fresh made)
1 cup heavy cream
1 tablespoon margarine or butter
salt, pepper, nutmeg, cumin and curry to taste

Split both squashes, remove seeds, and bake at 350°, split side up in a shallow pan with ½ inch water for 45 minutes or until tender. Saute onions and apples in a large heavy pan in margarine or butter until tender. Add chicken stock and boil slowly until soft. Scoop out cooked squash and puree in food processor or blender along with onions and apples and stock. Reheat on low heat and adjust salt to taste. Add ½ teaspoon nutmeg, ½ teaspoon cumin and curry to taste. Add cream and serve with chopped fresh parsley or chives. Makes 6 servings. May be frozen.

Mrs. David King, Wife of former Representative (Utah)

CHEESE SOUP

½ cup grated carrot
½ cup finely chopped celery
1 cup water
2 tablespoons chopped onion
¼ cup butter
6 tablespoons flour
2 cups milk
2 cups chicken broth
1 pound Velveeta

Cook carrots and celery in boiling water until tender. Set aside. Cook onion in butter until tender, not brown. Stir in flour. Add milk and chicken broth. Cook over low heat until thickened, stirring constantly. Add cheese, stir to blend. Stir in vegetables and cooking water. Serve hot. Makes 6 servings. May be frozen.

KARel Ratcliffe

Mrs. Brian Ratcliffe, Daughter of Representative Bill Brewster (Oklahoma)

LIMA BEAN SOUP

1 pkg. dried lima beans
1 ham hock with a lot of meat on it
2 large onions, sliced
1 large can of tomatoes
salt and pepper to taste

Soak beans overnight or bring to a boil according to package directions. Add a sufficient amount of water and the ham bone and meat, sliced onions, salt and pepper. Bring to a boil then reduce and cook slowly until the beans are very soft and the meat very tender. Be sure to remove all fat remaining from the meat and bones. Add the canned tomatoes and resume cooking until they are tender. The more you cook it the better it gets, (at least 1½ hours or more). As the beans absorb, you may need to add more water. Makes 6 servings. May be frozen.

Clay Shaw

E. Clay Shaw, Representative (Florida)

A teaspoon each of cider vinegar and sugar added to salty soup or vegetables will remedy the situation.

WHITE BEAN SOUP

2 teaspoons olive oil
1 medium yellow onion, finely chopped
3 celery stalks, finely chopped
2 carrots, finely chopped
salt and pepper to taste
1 can pureed tomatoes (with juice)
1 can chicken broth
½ teaspoon basil
½ teaspoon crushed fennel seeds
1 can cannellini beans, drained and rinsed

In a large saucepan, heat the oil then add the onion, celery, carrot, salt and pepper and saute. Add the tomatoes, broth, basil and fennel seeds and bring to a boil. Cover, lower the heat and simmer for 10 minutes. Add the beans and simmer until beans are heated through. Makes 4 servings. May be frozen.

John McHugh, Representative (New York)

BEAN SOUP

1 16 oz. pkg. dry beans
1½ teaspoons minced onion
1 teaspoon celery salt
2 teaspoons salt
½ teaspoon nutmeg
½ teaspoon pepper

This soup tastes like it is made with a ham hock, yet it has no fat or cholesterol. Place all ingredients into a large pot with two quarts of water. Bring to a boil, then simmer all day stirring occasionally. Makes 6 servings. May be frozen.

Mrs. Nicholas Burhans, Daughter of former Representative John C. Mackie (Michigan)

LENTIL SOUP

2 quarts water or chicken broth
2 cups lentils
2 slices bacon, cut in small pieces and lightly crisped (ham or sausage may be substituted)
1 can tomatoes (1 pound)
1 medium onion, chopped
1 clove garlic, mashed
2 teaspoons salt
1/2 teaspoon pepper
  few dashes Tabasco may be added
1 teaspoon oregano
1/4 cup carrots, chopped
1/2 cup celery, chopped
3 tablespoons parsley
2 tablespoons wine vinegar

Wash the lentils and place in pan with water, bacon, onion, carrots, celery, parsley, garlic, salt, pepper and oregano. Cover and simmer 1½ hours. Break up tomatoes and add to lentils. Add vinegar and simmer 30 minutes longer. Taste, add salt and pepper, if needed. May be served as is, or puree part of the lentils and return to pan. When serving, try a splash of wine vinegar on each bowl of soup. Makes 10 servings. May be frozen.

Paula J Swift

Mrs. Al Swift, Wife of Representative (Washington)

If you have over salted soup or vegetables, add cut raw potatoes and discard once they have cooked and absorbed the salt.

LENTIL BEAN SOUP

1 pound lentils
  ham hock, optional
6 to 8 cups brown beef
    stock
2 carrots, diced
1 green pepper, diced
2 large onions, diced
2 tablespoons oil
1 large can whole italian to-
    matoes, chopped
  salt and pepper
2 to 4 tablespoons tarragon
    vinegar

Place lentils and optional ham hock in a large pot. Cover with stock, bring to a boil and simmer for 1 hour or until lentils are soft. Stir occasionally to prevent sticking. Saute carrots, green pepper and onion in 2 tablespoons oil until soft. Add to beans. Add tomatoes, salt and pepper to taste, and vinegar. Simmer 1½ to 2 hours.

Mrs. Jim Sasser, Wife of Senator (Tennessee)

GLEN'S BEAN SOUP

 3 cups (1 large pkg.) great
     northern or navy beans,
     dry
 1 large ham bone or 2
     smoked ham hocks
 6 quarts cold water
 1 small can V8 or tomato
     juice
10 or more peppercorns
 1 large onion, cut fine
   celery leaves
 1 large carrot, diced small
 2 stalks celery, cut fine

Pick over beans, removing stones. Cover with cold water 2 inches above beans. Soak several hours or over night. Drain. Bury ham bones or hocks in beans. Add water, V8 juice, peppercorns, onion and celery leaves. Cut carrot and celery may be added then or two hours before serving. Bring to boil and simmer 4 hours or longer. Remove as much fat as possible and celery leaves. Beans and vegetables may be left for clear soup or pureed for a thicker soup. Adjust flavor. Chicken bouillon cubes or salt may be added if needed. Ham meat can be diced and served in soup or served on the side. I like to cook this almost all day. Makes 12 to 15 servings. May be frozen.

Mrs. Thomas S. Kleppe, Wife of former Representative (North Dakota)

BEAN SOUP

¼ cup olive oil
1 onion, chopped
¼ cup fresh dill, chopped
1 carrot, sliced thin
2 stalks celery, sliced thin
1 potato, cubed
1 14 oz. can tomato sauce
16 ozs. water
2 8 oz. cans great northern beans

Use a two quart sauce pan. Saute onions in olive oil. Add remaining vegetables, including potatoes, and saute for a few more minutes. Add tomato sauce and 16 oz. of water. Cook until all vegetables are done, about 20 minutes. Add salt and pepper to taste. Add beans that have been rinsed. Cook for another 15 minutes. Dry beans which have been soaked overnight may also be used, but would require longer cooking. Makes 6 servings.

Evelyn Bilirakis

Mrs. Michael Bilirakis, Wife of Representative (Florida)

POTATO CHOWDER

8 slices bacon
1 cup chopped onion
2 cups cubed potatoes
1 cup water
1 teaspoon salt
⅛ teaspoon pepper
1½ cups milk
1 can cream of chicken soup
1 cup sour cream

Dice bacon and fry until crisp. Remove from pan and drain on paper towel. Add chopped onion and saute until clear, 2 to 3 minutes. Drain off as much grease as possible. Add potatoes and water and cook until tender, (about 15 minutes). Then add salt, pepper, milk, chicken soup and sour cream. Heat through, but do not boil. Add bacon and serve. Makes 5 servings.

Barbara Ann Grassley

Mrs. Charles Grassley, Wife of Senator (Iowa)

The best method for removing fat from soup is to refrigerate until it hardens. If you place wax paper over the top of the soup, it can be peeled right off, along with the hardened fat.

POTATO-CHEESE SOUP

4 tablespoons sweet butter
2 cups finely chopped yellow onions
2 cups peeled and chopped carrots
6 parsley sprigs
5 cups chicken stock
2 large potatoes, about 1½ pounds, peeled and cubed (3 to 4 cups)
1 cup chopped fresh dill
  salt and freshly ground black pepper, to taste
2 to 3 cups grated cheddar cheese

Melt the butter in a soup pot. Add onions and carrots and cook over low heat, covered, until vegetables are tender and lightly colored, about 25 minutes. Add parsley, stock and potatoes, and bring to a boil. Reduce heat, cover and simmer until potatoes are very tender, about 30 minutes. Add dill, remove soup from heat and let it stand, covered for 5 minutes. Pour soup through a strainer and transfer the solids to the bowl of a food processor. Add one cup of the cooking stock and process until smooth. Return pureed soup to the pot and add additional cooking liquid, about 3 to 4 cups, until the soup reaches the desired consistency. Set over low heat, add salt and pepper to taste, and gradually stir in the grated cheese. When all the cheese is incorporated and the soup is not boiling, serve immediately. Makes 6 servings.

Lydia de La Viña de Foley

Mrs. John R. Foley III, Daughter-in-law of former Representative John R. Foley (Maryland)

CREAM OF POTATO SOUP

2 cups diced potatoes
3 cups boiling water
  celery salt or celery
4 cups thin white sauce
1 tablespoon minced onion
  salt, pepper, paprika
    garnish with diced bell pepper

Combine potatoes, water and onion. Cook until vegetables are tender. Mash with potato masher. Add white sauce. Season to taste with salt, pepper, and paprika. Garnish with pieces of bell pepper, after heated to boiling. Makes 8 servings. May be frozen.

Lucille K. Carter

Mrs. Steven Carter, Wife of former Representative (Iowa)

POTATO SOUP

4 medium potatoes
2 celery stalks
1 whole onion
  salt and pepper
  milk
  bread

Peel potatoes and cut up in fourths. Add celery stalks, whole onion, and salt and pepper to taste. Cook on medium heat for 1 to 1½ hours. When potatoes are soft, drain off water and take out the celery and onion. Mash the potatoes and add milk slowly. Add milk to get the right consistency for the soup you want. Beat until the soup is smooth. Serve in bowls and add toasted bread cubes. (Toast some bread, and butter it, cut in cubes). Place cubes on top of soup. It is yummy. Even our children like it. Makes 6 servings.

Mrs. Mike Crapo, Wife of Representative (Idaho)

POTATO SOUP

6 tablespoons margarine
1 large onion, chopped
2 leeks, thinly sliced
4 cups potatoes, diced
4 cups chicken broth
3 cups milk
  instant mashed potatoes
¼ cup minced parsley
  salt and pepper

Melt margarine in 6 quart pan. Add onions and leeks and saute until soft. Add potatoes and broth. Simmer until potatoes are cooked. Coarsely crush potatoes with masher. Stir in milk. Bring back to a simmer. Thicken with instant mashed potatoes to desired consistency—maybe ¼ or ½ cup. Season to taste and sprinkle with parsley when served.

Mrs. John Paul Hammerschmidt, Wife of former Representative (Arkansas)

CHEESE CHOWDER

3 diced potatoes
3 stalks chopped celery
1 medium chopped onion
4 sliced/grated carrots
2 teaspoons salt
½ teaspoon pepper
1 stick butter
½ cup flour
1 quart milk
1 pound sharp cheese
2 cups cubed ham

Cook vegetables in 3 cups water with salt and pepper—don't drain. Melt butter and add flour and milk to make white sauce. Boil for 1 minute to thicken—stir so it doesn't burn. Add cheese, vegetables and cubed ham. Heat until warm, but don't boil. Makes 12 servings.

Mrs. Pat Roberts, Wife of Representative (Kansas)

COUNTRY CHEESE SOUP

¾ cup butter
6 tablespoons flour
3 cups milk
1 cup light cream
1 teaspoon salt
2 cups grated american
    cheese
½ cup chopped celery
½ cup chopped green pepper
½ cup chopped onion
½ cup chopped carrot
1 pint clear chicken broth

Melt ½ cup butter and slowly add flour. Mix well stirring constantly. Add milk, cheese, cream and salt slowly to make a rich sauce. Saute celery, pepper, onion and carrot in ¼ cup butter to the crunchy stage. Add chicken broth and then combine with the cheese sauce. Heat over low heat. Makes 8 servings.

Mrs. John Terry, Wife of former Representative (New York)

ZUCCHINI SOUP

5 medium zucchini (pared or unpared)
1 medium onion
1 potato
2 tablespoons olive oil
¼ teaspoon curry powder
3 chicken bouillon cubes
  LA hot sauce and worcestershire sauce to taste

Chop zucchini, onion and potato. Boil in salted water to cover, with lid on pot, until soft. Drain in colander and transfer to mixing bowl. Add remaining ingredients. Place mixture in blender and blend. Serve hot or cold, garnished with chopped parsley or chopped green onion. Makes 5 servings.

Mrs. Bennett Johnston, Wife of Senator (Louisiana)

CARROT DILL SOUP

4 tablespoons (½ stick) unsalted butter
1 large onion, diced
2½ pounds of carrots, peeled and diced
2 ribs celery, leaves included, diced
8 cups of chicken stock or canned broth
¼ cup plus 2 tablespoons chopped fresh dill
1 teaspoon salt
¼ teaspoon freshly ground black pepper
  pinch of cayenne pepper
6 teaspoons sour cream, for garnish
¼ teaspoon finely diced red bell pepper, for garnish
6 dill sprigs, for garnish

Melt the butter in a soup pot. Add the onion and cook over low heat until wilted, for 10 minutes. Add the carrots, celery, stock, ¼ cup dill, salt, black pepper and cayenne. Bring to a boil, reduce heat and cover. Simmer until the carrots are tender, 40 minutes. Allow to cool for a little while. Puree the soup, in batches, in a food processor or a blender. Return it to the soup pot, stir in the remaining 2 tablespoons dill, and adjust the seasonings. Heat through. Serve each bowl of soup garnished with a dollop of sour cream, the red pepper, and a sprig of dill. Makes 6 servings.

Mrs. John R. Foley III, Daughter-in-law of former Representative John R. Foley (Maryland)

CHILLED CARROT SOUP WITH DILL

1 pound carrots
1 onion
1 tablespoon chopped fresh
   dill
1 tablespoon chopped fresh
   parsley
   salt and pepper
1¾ cups chicken stock or
½   canned broth
½ cup heavy cream
½ cup milk

Peel and chop the carrots. Chop the onion. Combine the carrots, onion, dill, parsley, ½ teaspoon salt, ¼ teaspoon pepper and stock in a large pot. Bring to a boil, reduce heat and simmer until the carrots are soft, about 15 minutes. Puree in a food processor or blender with the cream and milk until smooth. Chill. Thin with stock, cream and milk or water until the soup is the consistency you like. Garnish with extra dill. Makes 4 servings. May be frozen.

Rebecca Rogers

Mrs. Paul Rogers, Wife of former Representative (Florida)

TOO MUCH SQUASH SOUP

   yellow squash (sliced, fill 8
      quart pot)
   onion, chopped into large
      pieces to taste
   garlic salt
   salt/pepper
   cream (or half and half)
   country ham to garnish

Chop squash and onions to fill 8 quart pot. Add water to fill half of pot. Add garlic salt, salt and pepper to taste. Cook on medium heat until tender and much of water evaporated. Cool slightly. Puree in blender until smooth. Put back on stovetop in pot on low heat. Just before serving, add cream, half and half or for dieters, low fat milk—just enough cream to make soup appear smooth (about ½ cup). Put into bowls, garnish with chips of country ham. For freezing, freeze puree, do not add cream until thawed and heated. Makes 6 to 8 servings. May be frozen.

Martie Parris

Mrs. Stan Parris, Wife of former Representative (Virginia)

HATTERAS ISLAND CLAM CHOWDER

2 slices salt pork, cubed
2 dozen medium clams
1 medium onion, chopped
2 medium-sized potatoes,
    cubed (about 1 cup)
2 cups water
½ cup fresh corn
    salt and pepper
⅛ teaspoon ground thyme

Fry the cubed salt pork until crisp. Open the clams, saving the juice, and chop clams. Saute the onion in 2 tablespoons of the meat grease. Add clams, juice, and 2 cups water. Simmer about 15 minutes. Add remaining ingredients and enough water to make chowder the consistency you wish. Simmer until the potatoes are done. Makes 4 to 6 servings.

H. Martin Lancaster, Representative (North Carolina)

LONG ISLAND CLAM CHOWDER

4 tablespoons sweet butter
2 cups finely chopped yel-
    low onions
1 cup chopped celery
5 cups chicken stock (home-
    made or canned)
1⅓ teaspoons thyme
1 bay leaf
    salt and pepper to taste
1 can (28 oz.) peeled Italian
    plum tomatoes with
    juice
1 cup chopped Italian
    parsley
2 medium-size boiling pota-
    toes, peeled and diced
2 pounds chopped fresh
    clams

Melt the butter in a large pot. Add onions and celery and cook over low heat, covered, until vegetables are tender and lightly colored, about 20 minutes. Add remaining ingredients except clams and simmer partially covered for 30 minutes or until potatoes are very tender. Taste the soup and correct the seasoning. Just before serving add the clams. Simmer gently for 5 minutes. Serve with homemade cornbread or crusty rolls. Makes 8 servings. May be frozen.

Mrs. George Hochbrueckner, Wife of Representative (New York)

GAZPACHO

2 cans Campbell's tomato
  bisque soup
1 can water
⅓ cup chopped onion
½ cup chopped pepper
⅓ cup chopped celery
1 teaspoon Worcestershire
  sauce
4 tablespoons olive oil
¼ cup wine vinegar
½ teaspoon salt
  croutons

Place all ingredients in a blender and blend for a short time. Leave chunky. Refrigerate at least 6 hours before serving. Add croutons before serving. Makes 6 servings.

Jean Thompson

Mrs. Richard Thompson, Daughter of former Representative John Terry (New York)

GAZPACHO

4 cups V-8 juice
1 small minced onion
2 cups diced tomatoes
1 cup minced green pepper
1 teaspoon honey
1 diced cucumber
1 teaspoon minced garlic
  juice of 1 lemon
  juice of 1 lime
  tablespoons wine vinegar
2 teaspoon basil
1 cup fresh chopped parsley
¼ tablespoon olive oil
1 salt and pepper to taste

Combine all ingredients and chill for 2 hours. Makes 6 servings.

Jane Sutermeister

Mrs. Richard Sutermeister, Daughter of former Representative Tom Kleppe (North Dakota)

PUMPKIN SOUP

1 large onion, chopped
¼ cup butter
2 cups pumpkin
1½ teaspoons salt
½ teaspoon curry powder
2½ cups chicken broth
2 cups heavy cream

Cook onions in butter until tender. Add all ingredients, except cream, in heavy pan. Simmer 45 minutes. Add cream when ready to serve. May sprinkle with parsley. Makes 6 servings.

Penny Ichord

Mrs. Richard Ichord, Wife of former Representative (Missouri)

WEST INDIAN PUMPKIN SOUP

1½ to 2 pounds pumpkin, peeled and cubed
2 cloves garlic, chopped
1 medium Spanish onion, chopped
herb bundle: parsley, thyme, bay leaf, leek, celery top, marjoram
2 medium tomatoes, peeled, seeded and chopped
3 chicken cubes
5 cups water
3 oz. white wine
1 tablespoon honey
1 teaspoon cinnamon
salt and pepper
1 cup heavy cream

Put all ingredients except salt, pepper and cream into large saucepan. Simmer, covered, until pumpkin falls apart. Remove herbs. Puree soup in blender. Return to saucepan. Add salt and pepper to taste, stir in cream. Heat through. Makes 6 servings. May be frozen.

To serve: For festive effect serve in small, hollowed out pumpkin shells, surrounded by pressed fall leaves.

Christine K. Knuth

Mrs. Charles Knuth, Daughter of former Representative David King (Utah)

HARDWICK HOUSE CHOWDER

1 tablespoon butter
¼ cup chopped red pepper
   or pimento
¼ cup chopped green onion
1 clove garlic, minced
⅛ teaspoon pepper
2 cups milk
2 10 oz. cans cream of potato soup (undiluted)
1 3 oz. pkg. cream cheese
1 pkg. frozen corn
1½ pounds fresh shrimp,
   peeled and deveined
¼ cup sherry or brandy
   (optional)

Melt butter in large pot. Add onion, red pepper, garlic and pepper. Saute over medium heat until garlic is tender, not brown. Stir in soup, milk, cheese and corn. Bring to a boil, stirring frequently. Add raw shrimp, cover, reduce heat and cook 5–7 minutes. May be made ahead and kept in refrigerator the day before serving. To serve, heat and add sherry or brandy if desired. Makes 6 to 8 servings.

Mrs. W. G. (Bill) Hefner, Wife of Representative (North Carolina)

TUNA CHOWDER

¼ cup celery, chopped
1 cup onion, chopped
1 cup potato, diced
4 tablespoons butter
   salt and pepper
½ teaspoon thyme, crumbled
¼ teaspoon dill, crumbled
2 tablespoons flour
1 can stewed tomatoes (8
   oz.)
3 cups milk
1 6½ oz. can of tuna, drained
2 tablespoons parsley,
   minced
1 cup Monterey Jack cheese,
   grated

Cook celery, onion, potato with butter until potato is tender (about 15 min.). Stir in all seasonings, flour and add tomatoes, milk, tuna and parsley. Cook until chowder is thickened and boils. Stir in cheese. Makes 4 servings. May be frozen.

Mrs. Andy Ireland, Wife of former Representative (Florida)

OYSTER STEW

1 pint raw oysters and juice
  from oysters
3 tablespoons butter
1 quart milk
½ cup diced ham
1 tablespoon Worcestershire
  sauce
½ teaspoon salt
  dash of pepper

Cook oysters with oyster liquid and butter in a saucepan over low heat for five minutes. Let stand until cool. Add milk, ham, Worcestershire sauce, salt and pepper. Simmer at low heat for five minutes. Makes 4 servings.

John O. Marsh, Jr., former Representative (Virginia)

Chilling soup often mutes the seasoning. Taste just before serving to test for extra seasoning needed.

Adding a chunk of butter before serving adds a shiny finish to hot pureed soup.

BOUILLABAISSE

2 bay leaves
⅓ cup olive oil
3 green peppers
2 large white onions, sliced
4 or 5 celery ribs, sliced
2 large cloves elephant garlic
1 bunch green onions
6 tomatoes, peeled and chopped or one 18 oz. can whole tomatoes, chopped
2½ quarts of fish or chicken stock
1 lemon cut in half or one orange rind cut into 3 inch strips
2 tablespoons chopped fresh parsley
1 teaspoon saffron threads
¼ teaspoon crushed fennel seeds
1½ teaspoons chopped fresh thyme
1½ teaspoons chopped summer savory
2 pounds red snapper, cod or bass fillet, cut into bite size pieces (heads, bones and tails included)
1½ cups dry white wine
2½ pounds of lobster or shrimp cut into pieces
1 dozen plus 4 cleaned fresh oysters and shells
freshly ground pepper and kosher salt to taste

Place bay leaves, olive oil, peppers, onions, celery, garlic and green onions in a heavy bottomed 4 quart kettle or Dutch oven and saute for 5 minutes. Add tomatoes, fish or chicken stock and lemon or orange rind. Add parsley, saffron threads, fennel seeds, herbs, firm fish and wine to kettle. Cover and bring to boil. Saute lobster or shrimp (or as many kinds of fish or seafood as desired). Instead of sauteing, the fish can be baked. Add the cooked seafood and raw oysters and continue to boil for 8 to 10 minutes. Season to taste and remove lemon before serving. Makes 8 servings.

Ms. Rachel Worby, Wife of Governor Gaston Caperton (West Virginia)

LONG ISLAND F-14 FISH CHOWDER

8 slices of bacon cut in one-
   inch pieces
3 medium-large onions,
   coarsely chopped
2 celery stalks, coarsely
   chopped
4 large Long Island potatoes
   (6 medium); peeled and
   cut into ½ inch cubes
3 cups fish stock (chicken
   stock or clam juice can
   be used)
½ teaspoon dried thyme
3 tablespoons parsley,
   chopped
1½ cups fresh tomatoes,
   skinned and seeded
   (canned tomatoes can be
   used)
½ cup heavy cream
2 cups milk (or more if
   needed)
   salt and pepper to taste
   Tabasco sauce (optional),
   amount determined by
   taste
2 pounds fish (cod, scrod, or
   any other solid white
   fish), cut into 1-inch
   cubes
½ pound bay scallops (sea
   scallops can be used if
   cut into 2 or 3 pieces)

Cook bacon in a large heavy pot over medium heat, stirring frequently until done. Remove bacon and drain on paper towels. Pour fat from the pot, keeping that which coats the pot. Place onions and celery in pot, toss to coat with bacon fat, cover, and cook over low heat, stirring frequently, for about 12 minutes, adding a tablespoon or two of fish stock if vegetables begin to stick. Add potatoes, fish stock, thyme, and parsley. Liquid should cover vegetables; if not, add water. Bring to a boil, lower heat, and simmer until potatoes are barely tender (12 to 15 minutes). Remove half the vegetables and puree them in a food processor. Return them to pot and add tomatoes, cream, milk, salt, pepper, and Tabasco sauce. Bring to a boil, stir frequently until liquid is smooth. If necessary, soup can be thinned with additional milk. Reduce heat, add fish. Cover and simmer gently for two or three minutes. Fold scallops and bacon, being very careful not to break the fish. Check seasoning. Cover and simmer two or three minutes (until fish and scallops are cooked). Serve hot. Makes 6 to 8 servings.

George J. Hochbrueckner, Representative (New York)

LOUISIANA GUMBO

1 cup cooking oil
2 cups flour
2 large onions, chopped
½ cup celery, chopped
½ cup bell peppers, chopped
1 cup parsley, chopped
1 cup green onions, chopped
1 large garlic clove, chopped
2 cans tomatoes (stewed)
3 pounds chicken
3 pounds sausage, sliced
2 pounds crab claws or meat
3 pounds shrimp
  file

Place oil in pot/skillet. Stir in flour and mix well. Stir often as roux changes colors. Cook roux until color is very dark. Add onions, celery, and bell peppers. Cook until onions are clear, then add parsley, green onions and garlic. Add tomatoes to roux and simmer for 10 minutes. Brown chicken and sausage separately in skillet. Add enough water to fill roux pot about ⅔ full then add sausage and chicken. Season to taste. Continue to simmer gumbo for about 20 minutes. Add crab and shrimp and continue to simmer 10 minutes longer. Add file' and turn off pot and let remain on stove. Serve hot over rice. (Use 13" stock pot). Makes 18 servings. May be frozen.

Debra Horton Fields

Mrs. Cleo Fields, Wife of Representative (Louisiana)

> *Soup can be topped with a variety of garnishes such as crisp bacon bits, grated cheese, thin lemon slices, chopped parsley or green onions, or fresh diced tomatoes.*

CAROLINA CORN AND CRAB MEAT BISQUE

½ cup chopped onion
¾ cup chopped celery
4 tablespoons butter
2 tablespoons flour
¼ teaspoon curry powder
3 10 oz. frozen pkgs. of
    Cope's silver queen
    white double cut corn
    (thawed) OR 4 cups
    fresh corn
4 cups milk
1 cup heavy cream
    salt and pepper to taste
1 pound backfin or lump
    crab meat
    crumbled bacon

Saute onion and celery in butter. Add flour and curry powder and cook 2 minutes. Add thawed corn to onion/celery mixture and cook 5 minutes. Add milk, cream, salt and pepper and bring to a gentle boil. Stir in crab meat. Remove bisque from stove, cool, and chill in refrigerator overnight. Reheat in microwave. Serve hot, topped with crumbled bacon. Makes 10 servings. May be frozen.

Mrs. Alex McMillan, Wife of Representative (North Carolina)

IOWA CORN CHOWDER

¼ pound of bacon
1 large onion, chopped
1 cup celery, sliced
4 cups diced raw potatoes
1 cup water
2 1-pound cans corn
2 cups milk
1 14½ oz. can of evaporated
    milk
    salt, pepper, cayenne pep-
    per (optional)

Brown the bacon and remove from the pan. Pour off all but 2 tablespoons of bacon fat. Saute onion and celery about five minutes (do not burn). Add the potatoes and water and cook over medium heat about 10 minutes or until the potatoes are done. Stir in the corn. Add milk and the evaporated milk. Break the bacon into pieces and add to the chowder. Salt and pepper to taste. Add cayenne, as much or as little as you like. I have substituted low fat milk in this recipe and the flavor is still delicious. For a real taste treat, use fresh corn that has been cut from the cob. Makes 6 servings.

David Nagle, former Representative (Iowa)

PISTOU BASIL SOUP

4 shallots, finely chopped
3 tablespoons butter
3 cloves garlic, finely
   chopped
2 cans condensed tomato
   soup
2 cups water
1 can cut green beans
2 teaspoons dried sweet basil
1½ cups cooked spaghetti
   (broken)
½ cup Parmesan cheese

Saute shallots in 1 tablespoon butter until transparent. Add garlic. Saute two more minutes. Add the soup and water. Saute beans in two tablespoons butter and basil. Add beans and spaghetti to soup. Simmer five minutes. Pour into soup bowls. Sprinkle with cheese. Makes 1¾ quarts.

Connie Ewing

Mrs. Thomas Ewing, Wife of Representative (Illinois)

DEE'S WINTER SOUP

2 pounds ground beef
1 large onion, chopped
2 4 oz. cans green chilies
1 teaspoon salt
1 teaspoon pepper
4 16 oz. cans stewed to-
   matoes
1 pkg. ranch dressing mix
1 16 oz. can hominy
1 16 oz. can pinto beans
1 16 oz. can lima beans
1 16 oz. can kidney beans
1 pkg. taco seasoning
3 cups water

Brown ground beef and onions together in frying pan. Drain well. In a large colander, put the hominy, pinto beans, lima beans and kidney beans. Rinse and drain. When finished draining, combine all the ingredients together in a large soup pot and simmer for 30 minutes. I also rinse the green chilies, but you may prefer your soup a little hotter. To hurry the soup along, you can put the water, tomatoes and seasonings in the pot while the other ingredients are draining. This soup is also good served over taco chips with grated cheese as a topping. Makes 8 servings. May be frozen.

Kit Robinson

Mrs. J. Kenneth Robinson, Wife of former Representative (Virginia)

TEXAS TORTILLA SOUP

1 pound hamburger
1 large onion, chopped
1 can tomato chunks, with
   liquid
1 8 oz. can tomato sauce
1 8 oz. jar picante sauce
1 large can whole kernel
   corn, drained
1 large can ranch style
   beans, drained
3 to 4 drops Tabasco sauce
   tortilla corn chips
   sharp cheese, grated

Brown hamburger and chopped onion in Dutch oven. Add next six ingredients and heat thoroughly. Crumble corn chips in individual bowls. Ladle soup over chips and sprinkle with cheese. Makes 8 servings. May be frozen.

Charlotte Brooks

Mrs. Jack Brooks, Wife of Representative (Texas)

CHICKEN TACO SOUP

1 pound chicken, skinned,
   deboned and cut up
   small
2 16 oz. cans tomatoes,
   chopped (with liquid)
2 10¾ oz. cans chicken
   broth
1 4 oz. can green chilies
   (with liquid)
¼ teaspoon salt
4 corn tortillas, halved
½ cup chopped green onion
½ cup shredded Monterey
   Jack cheese
¼ cup chopped fresh cilantro
¼ cup green taco sauce

Combine chicken, tomatoes, broth, chilies, and salt in a large pot. Bring to a boil and simmer uncovered for 30 minutes. Lay tortilla half in each of 8 soup bowls. Top each with 1 cup soup, 1 tablespoon green onion, 1 tablespoon cheese, 1½ teaspoon cilantro and 1½ teaspoons of taco sauce. Makes 8 servings.

Lucille de la Garza

Mrs. Kika de la Garza, Wife of Representative (Texas)

POTAGE MONGOLE

1 can tomato soup
1 can green pea soup
1 can consomme
½ cup water
1 cup light cream
½ tablespoon curry powder
2 tablespoons sherry
chopped parsley (optional)

Combine first 5 ingredients. Mix curry powder, water and sherry. Add to other ingredients. Heat thoroughly, but do not boil. Garnish with chopped parsley. Makes 4 servings. May be frozen.

Jennette W Prouty

Mrs. Winston Prouty, Wife of former Senator (Vermont)

EASY SENEGALESE

2 cans condensed cream of
  chicken soup
2 cups of milk
2 heaping tablespoons plain
  yogurt
1 heaping teaspoon curry
  powder
1 to 2 sliced scallions, including some green tops

The day before serving, mix all ingredients in a blender or food processor for one minute. Refrigerate. When ready to serve, pour into chilled bouillon cups and garnish with chives. Makes 4 to 6 servings.

Marie Goss

Mrs. Porter Goss, Wife of Representative (Florida)

YOGURT CUCUMBER SOUP

1 medium cucumber, peeled and diced
¼ teaspoon salt or more as needed
2 cups plain yogurt
2 cups chicken broth
1 tablespoon olive oil
2 tablespoons (or more) finely chopped walnuts
1½ clove garlic, finely minced pepper
1 tablespoon chopped chives

Sprinkle cucumber with salt and let stand for 30 minutes. Beat yogurt and add chicken broth and oil slowly to give a smooth mixture. Rinse cucumber to remove excess salt and drain well on paper towel. Dice cucumber and add along with garlic and walnuts. Pepper to taste. Top with chopped chives. Chill. Makes 4 servings.

Betsy Mann

Mrs. David Mann, Wife of Representative (Ohio)

FRENCH ONION SOUP

6 medium onions, sliced
4 tablespoons butter
¼ teaspoon pepper
5 cups bouillon, or water and 6 bouillon cubes
½ cup sherry
1 teaspoon Worcestershire sauce
  salt (if necessary)
6 slices French bread
  grated Parmesan cheese

Cook onions in butter until golden, add pepper, bouillon, sherry, Worcestershire and salt (if necessary). Cover, simmer 20 to 30 minutes. Float slices of toast on top, sprinkle thickly with cheese. Bake in 400° oven about 10 minutes until cheese browns slightly. Makes 4 to 6 servings.

Virginia Lipscomb

Mrs. Glenard Lipscomb, Wife of former Representative (California)

HOPKINS COUNTY STEW

1 chicken or 4 chicken
  breasts
1 large onion, chopped
1 large can tomatoes,
  chopped and reserve
  liquid
4 potatoes, peeled and cubed
1 teaspoon sugar
  salt and pepper to taste
  chili powder to taste
1 can cream style corn
  paprika

Cover chicken with water in stew pot and boil until tender. Remove chicken from broth (cool, debone and cut in small pieces). While chicken is cooling, add onions, potatoes, tomatoes, sugar, salt, pepper and chili powder to broth and continue boiling until vegetables are tender. Add cooked chicken and cream style corn. Heat until boiling, but do not boil too long because the corn will burn on the bottom of the pan. You may need to add 2 tablespoons margarine, if the broth needs to be richer for your taste. Add paprika and extra chili powder if needed. Makes 4 servings. May be frozen.

Jim Chapman, Representative (Texas)

Instant soup stock will always be on hand if you save the pan juice from cooking meats. Pour liquid into ice cube trays and freeze. Place solid cubes in freezer bags or foil.

Steak, roast or poultry bones can be frozen until needed for soup stock.

WILD RICE SOUP

¼ cup butter or margarine
1 medium onion, chopped fine
1 teaspoon salt
1 teaspoon curry powder
½ teaspoon dry mustard
1 teaspoon dried chervil
½ teaspoon white pepper
½ pound mushrooms, sliced
½ cup celery, sliced thin
½ cup flour
6 cups chicken broth
2 cups wild rice, cooked
2 cups half and half
⅔ cup dry sherry
parsley or chives, chopped

In a large saucepan, melt butter over medium heat; add finely chopped onion and seasonings. Cook and stir about 5 minutes or until golden. Add mushrooms and thinly sliced celery; cook and stir two minutes. Mix in flour. Gradually add broth, stirring constantly for 5 to 8 minutes, until slightly thickened. Stir in rice and reduce heat to low. Stir in half and half and sherry. Bring to a simmer, stirring occasionally. Ladle hot soup into individual bowls; garnish with parsley. Makes 16 servings. May be frozen.

Mrs. Arne Carlson, Wife of Governor (Minnesota)

LENTIL BARLEY STEW

¼ cup butter
⅓ cup chopped onion
½ cup chopped celery
1 1 pound can of stewed tomatoes
2 cups water
½ cup lentils, well-rinsed
⅓ cup medium sized barley
½ teaspoon salt
dash pepper
¼ teaspoon crushed rosemary
⅓ cup shredded carrots

Melt butter in large heavy saucepan over moderate heat. Add onion and celery and cook until onion is lightly browned. Stir in tomatoes, water, lentils, barley, salt, pepper and rosemary. Bring to a boil, cover tightly and boil gently for 25 minutes, stirring occasionally. Add carrots and cook 5 minutes longer. Please note: I add a teaspoon of sugar to reduce the acidity of the tomatoes. Also, for a little zip, I add a few shakes of crushed red pepper. Makes 6 servings. May be frozen.

Mrs. Michael Castle, Wife of Representative (Delaware)

HERBED LENTIL VEGETABLE SOUP

1 cup lentils
3 cups water
18 ozs. tomato juice
1 wedged onion
1 tablespoon Worcestershire
    sauce
½ teaspoon salt
¼ teaspoon pepper
2 teaspoons beef bouillon
2 potatoes, cubed
10 ozs. green beans
1 cup grated cheese

Rinse lentils. Mix with water, tomato juice, onion, Worcestershire sauce, salt, pepper, and bouillon. Bring to a boil. Reduce heat. Add bouquet garni. Cover, simmer for 25 minutes. Add potatoes. Cover, cook for 20 minutes or until potatoes are tender. Add beans. Cover 5 to 10 minutes. Serve with grated cheese. Makes 4 to 6 servings.

Bouquet Garni:
    Place in cheesecloth:
¾ tablespoon parsley
¾ tablespoon thyme
2 cloves garlic

Debra Andrews

Mrs. Thomas Andrews, Wife of Representative (Maine)

If the soup or stew is too salty, add cut raw potatoes and discard them once they have cooked and absorbed the salt.

A leaf of lettuce dropped into the pot absorbs the grease from the top of the soup. Remove the lettuce and throw it away as soon as it has served its purpose.

EASY MINESTRONE

¼ cup butter
1 10 oz. pkg. frozen peas
1 cup chopped celery
1 cup chopped carrots
1 cup chopped onions
1 tablespoon chopped
   parsley
1 teaspoon basil
1 28 oz. can Italian tomatoes
7 packets chicken broth mix
7 cups water
1 cup shredded cabbage
1 small zucchini, sliced
2 19 oz. cans red kidney
   beans
½ cup spaghetti, broken in
   small pieces
   grated Parmesan cheese

In large pot, melt butter over medium heat. Cook peas and next 5 ingredients for 10 minutes. Stir in next 6 ingredients. Cook 20 minutes or until spaghetti is tender. Serve hot with a side dish of grated cheese. Makes 12 servings. May be frozen.

Mrs. Wilbur Mills, Wife of former Representative (Arkansas)

CHILLED CUCUMBER BISQUE

1 lb. cucumber
3 tablespoons butter
3 tablespoons flour
3 cups clam broth (strained)
1 cup whipping cream
   salt and pepper to taste

Garnish:
   sour cream and cucumber
   slices

Peel, quarter lengthwise, deseed then dice cucumbers. Sauté in butter until transluscent (do not brown). Blend in flour. Add clam broth—simmer slowly for 10 minutes. Put in blender—liquefy at high speed chill—add cream—season to taste. Serves 6.

Optional: garnish with dollop of sour cream and cucumber slices in each bowl.

Jack Buechner, former Representative (Missouri)

> *Add a pinch of herb, such as rosemary, tarragon, basil, thyme, or dill to canned soups while heating.*

PASTA FAGIOLI (BEAN AND PASTA SOUP)

3 tablespoons chopped yellow onion
¼ cup olive oil
3 tablespoons coarsely chopped celery
3 tablespoons coarsely chopped carrot
1 ham hock (the stronger it is, the more ham flavor you will have)
⅔ to 1 cup of canned Italian tomatoes and their juice
1 16 to 24 oz. can cannellini beans (depending on how thick you like your soup)
3 cups homemade beef broth or 1 cup canned broth plus 2 cups water
2 teaspoons freshly ground pepper
6 ozs. small macaroni
3 tablespoons freshly grated Parmesan

Saute onion over medium heat until translucent. Add celery and carrot and ham hock and saute 10 minutes. Add chopped tomatoes and their juices and cook for 20 minutes at medium low heat. Add drained beans and cook for 5 minutes, stirring thoroughly. Add broth and bring to moderate boil. Scoop up about ⅓ of beans and mash through a food mill. Add pepper and salt if necessary. Check density of soup, add water or more broth if you prefer a more liquid consistency. Add pasta and cook al dente. Let soup rest for a few minutes and just before serving, stir in Parmesan cheese. Makes 6 servings.

Kristy Gavin

Mrs. Stephen Gavin, Daughter of Representative Jon Kyl (Arizona)

Always start cooking bones and meat in cold, salted water.

To prevent curdling of the milk or cream in soup add the soup to the milk rather than vice versa. Or add a bit of flour to the milk and beat well before combining.

MONKEY BREAD

¾ oz. yeast or 1 pkg. dry
    yeast
1 to 1¼ cup milk
3 eggs
3 tablespoons sugar
1 teaspoon salt
3½ cups flour
6 oz. butter, room temper-
    ature
½ lb. melted butter
    two 9″ ring molds

In bowl, mix yeast with part of milk until dis-solved. Add 2 eggs, beat. Mix in dry ingredients. Add remaining milk a little at a time, mixing thoroughly. Cut in butter until blended. Knead dough, let rise 1 to 1½ hours until double in size. Knead again, let rise 40 minutes.

Roll dough onto floured board, shape into a log. Cut log into 28 pieces of equal size. Shape each piece of dough into ball, roll in melted butter. Use half of the pieces in each of buttered, floured molds. Place 7 balls in each mold, leaving space between. Place remaining balls on top, spacing evenly. Let dough rise in mold. Brush tops with remaining egg. Bake in preheated oven at 375° until golden brown, approximately 15 minutes.

With warmest holiday wishes,

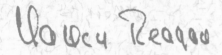

Mrs. Ronald Reagan, Wife of former President of the United States

BUTTERMILK BISCUITS

2 cups unsifted flour
2½ teaspoons baking powder
½ teaspoon salt
½ teaspoon baking soda
⅓ cup butter
¾ cup buttermilk
¼ cup melted butter for
    dipping

Combine all dry ingredients and sift into a mixing bowl. Add ⅓ cup butter and blend well. Stir in buttermilk and blend until dough holds together. Turn out on a floured board and flour the top of the dough lightly. Knead about 3 minutes and pat or roll out in a circle about ½ inch thick. Cut biscuits and dip them into melted butter, and arrange on a baking sheet or in a 9 × 9 inch buttered pan. Bake at 450° 12–15 minutes. Makes 1½ dozen. May be frozen.

Mrs. Mel Watt, Wife of Representative (North Carolina)

CLAUDE'S CAMPHOUSE BISCUITS

2 cups self rising flour
2 heaping and 1 level table-
    spoon Crisco
¾ cup buttermilk

Work Crisco into flour by hand. Add buttermilk slowly and continue to work by hand. Turn dough out onto lightly floured surface. Pat dough out by hand and fold in half. Pat dough out again and fold in half at least four times. Cut out biscuits and place in greased pan. Bake at 450° for 10 minutes or until lightly browned. Makes 10 biscuits. May be frozen.

Claude Harris, former Representative (Alabama)

IRISH SODA SCONES OR BREAD

2 cups unsifted all-purpose
    flour
1½ teaspoons baking powder
¾ teaspoon baking soda
1 teaspoon salt
4 tablespoons sugar
3 tablespoons shortening
1 cup buttermilk

Preheat oven to 375°. In medium bowl, combine flour, baking powder, baking soda, salt and sugar. Add shortening and cut into flour until shortening is in fine pieces. Make a well in center of flour mixture, pour in buttermilk, mix lightly. Turn out onto lightly floured board and knead gently a few times. Roll dough out to ½ inch thickness and cut in rounds with glass or cup. Bake until golden brown. Slice in half and butter, or add jam or jelly. Great for dinner or afternoon treat with a lovely pot of hot tea.

To make bread: Add ⅔ cup raisins to dough with buttermilk and shape dough into 5-inch round, if you wish to make loaf of bread instead. Bake at 375° for 35–40 minutes. Serve warm. "Cannot buy them for love or money." Makes 12 servings. May be frozen.

Mrs. Ed Royce, Wife of Representative (California)

EXIE'S ROLLS

1 cup potato water
1 cup scalded milk
1 cup melted shortening
    (Crisco)
1 pkg. yeast dissolved in ¼
    cup warm water
1 beaten egg
½ cup sugar
¼ teaspoon salt
    flour
    melted butter

Mix potato water, milk and shortening in large mixing bowl. Let cool. Add egg, sugar, salt and yeast. Mix well. Add two cups flour, beat well. Cover and keep in a warm place 1 hour. Add flour until consistency of rolls. Cover and let rise in warm place 1 hour. Roll out dough on floured board. Cut into rounds. Butter with melted butter. Fold over and put in greased roll pan. Brush top of rolls with melted butter. Cover and let rise 1 hour. Bake at 400° about 10 minutes. Makes 4 dozen. May be frozen.

Mike Heflin

Mrs. Howell Heflin, Wife of Senator (Alabama)

REFRIGERATOR ROLLS

Part 1:
1 cup sugar
1 cup Crisco
1 cup hot water
1 tablespoon salt

Part 2:
1 cup water
3 pkgs. of yeast
2 eggs

Put ingredients of part 1 in a large mixing bowl and melt in microwave for 3 minutes. Put ingredients of part 2 in a 2 cup measuring cup. Dissolve yeast and beat eggs. Add first ingredients when cooled. Add yeast mixture. Add 6 cups flour. Cover and refrigerate for 4 hours. Roll out amount needed and let rise. Bake at 400° for 10–15 minutes. (Dough keeps well in refrigerator for 2 weeks). Makes 4 dozen.

Mrs. Chet Edwards, Wife of Representative (Texas)

Adding water to bread dough makes crusty breads.

DILLY CASSEROLE BREAD

1 pkg. active dry yeast
¼ cup warm water
1 cup creamed cottage cheese (heated to lukewarm)
2 tablespoons sugar
1 tablespoon minced onion
1 tablespoon butter
2 teaspoons dill seed
1 teaspoon salt
¼ teaspoon soda
1 unbeaten egg
2¼ to 2½ cups flour

Soften yeast in water. Combine in mixing bowl the cottage cheese, sugar, onion, butter, dill seed, salt, soda, egg and softened yeast. Add flour to form a stiff dough—cover and let rise until light and double in size, 50 to 60 minutes, then stir down dough, turn into well greased round 1½ or 2 quart casserole. Let rise again. Bake at 350° for 40 to 50 minutes. Makes 12 servings. May be frozen.

Penny Ichord

Mrs. Richard Ichord, Wife of former Representative (Missouri)

ASHLEY'S STATE FAIR ROLLS

1 pkg. yeast
½ cup boiling water
¾ teaspoon salt
2 eggs
¼ cup lukewarm water
¼ cup plus 2 tablespoons lard
¼ cup plus 2 tablespoons sugar
3½ cups flour

Dissolve yeast in luke warm water. Mix water (boiling), shortening, sugar and salt. Beat eggs well and add to water mixture. When water mixture is cool, add yeast mixture. Add 1½ cups of the flour. Beat well with mixer about 3 minutes. Add the remaining flour and mix in. Knead your dough on a floured board for about 5 minutes. Place dough in a well greased bowl. Cover tightly. Store in refrigerator overnight, if desired, and let rise for 1½ to 2 hours. Bake at 400° for 10 minutes. Makes 18 servings. May be frozen.

Alice Baesler

Mrs. Scotty Baesler, Wife of Representative (Kentucky)

MONKEY BREAD RING

Rich Dough:

1	pkg. dry yeast
½	cup warm water
6	tablespoons sugar
½	cup milk
3	teaspoons salt
3½	to 4 cups all purpose flour or bread flour
1	egg
½	cup butter

Regular Dough:

1	pkg. yeast
1	cup warm water
1	tablespoon sugar
1	teaspoon salt
3	to 3½ cups flour
¼	cup butter
	no egg

Garlic:

1	large garlic minced or pressed
1	teaspoon dried parsley leaves
¼	teaspoon salt
⅛	teaspoon freshly ground pepper

Dissolve yeast in water. Add sugar. Stir to dissolve. Let stand for 5 minutes or until yeast bubbles. Sift flour and salt together. In saucepan, combine the milk and half the butter until very warm (130°F). At low speed, gradually beat the milk mixture into the flour, mix until satiny. Beat 2 minutes at medium speed. Beat in the egg. Stir in another cup of flour and beat 2 minutes longer. Stir in enough flour to make thick dough. Turn out on lightly floured surface. Cover and let rest 15 minutes. Knead about 5 minutes until smooth and satiny. Place into clean bowl that has been greased; turn dough over, cover and let rise until doubled. (For garlic: in a small bowl or saucepan, melt butter, garlic, parsley, salt and pepper). Turn dough out onto floured surface or counter. Cut into walnut sized pieces. Dip into butter or garlic butter mixture and place into buttered 10 inch, 1½ quart ring mold to make an even layer. Let rise about 1 hour or until doubled. Bake at 375° for 25 to 30 minutes. Makes a 10 inch ring. Makes 3 to 4 dozen rolls. May be frozen after baking.

Ms. Rachel Worby, Wife of Governor Gaston Caperton (West Virginia)

When bread is baking, a small dish of water in the oven will help to keep the crust from getting hard.

HUSH PUPPIES

1 cup self-rising cornmeal
½ cup self-rising flour
1 tablespoon sugar
1 egg
1 medium onion, finely
    chopped
½ green bell pepper or 1 jala-
    peno pepper, chopped
1 cup milk
  vegetable oil

Stir all ingredients, except oil, together. Drop mixture by tablespoons into hot vegetable oil, about 370°F, and fry until golden brown on all sides. Drain on paper towels.

Mrs. Trent Lott, Wife of Senator (Mississippi)

JENNIE SKURDALSVOLD'S RYE BREAD

2 cups boiling water
3 tablespoons shortening
3 tablespoons molasses
1 cup brown sugar
1 teaspoon salt
1 yeast cake (or packet of
    yeast moistened in ¼
    cup water)
2 cups rye flour
4 cups white flour

Combine water, shortening, molasses, sugar and salt. When mixture has cooled to lukewarm, add yeast, rye flour and 2 cups of the white flour. Mix and let rest about 10 minutes. Add the rest of flour and knead for short time. Let rise 1½ hours, or until doubled. Knead. Divide into two or three portions. Cover and let rise until double. Bake in moderate oven (375°) 35 to 45 minutes. You may use two 9½″ × 5″ × 3″ pans or simply form into rounded shapes on a cookie sheet. Makes 2 loaves. May be frozen.

Mrs. Martin Sabo, Wife of Representative (Minnesota)

CUCOLI (ITALIAN EASTER BREAD)

5 eggs
1 cup sugar
1 cup milk
¼ pound butter, melted
3 teaspoons baking powder
5 to 6 cups flour
  lemon or vanilla extract for
    flavoring (optional)
6 raw, colored eggs
1 egg, beaten for wash
  nonpareils

In a large bowl, combine sugar, baking powder and flour. Make a well in the center and add eggs with melted butter. Add the milk and flavoring and work mixture into a dough. Roll dough into a log. Cut into 6 equal portions. Using one portion at a time, remove ¼ of the dough and set it aside. Roll the larger portion into a rope about 20 inches long and form it into a horseshoe shape with the two ends facing you. Twist a loop at the top, leaving a space large enough to fit an egg, and continue twisting loosely until the end. Lay one egg in the loop formed by the dough. (Or you can take all the dough and form it into a ring). Roll out the reserved dough into a 12 inch rope. Lay it over the egg and twist it the same way. Repeat with remaining dough and eggs. Brush dough with beaten egg and sprinkle with nonpareils. Place on parchment-lined baking sheets. Bake in a 350° oven 25 to 30 minutes or until dough is golden brown. Makes 6 breads.

Mrs. Mario Cuomo, Wife of Governor (New York)

QUICK CORN LIGHT BREAD

2 cups self-rising cornmeal
  with hot rise (I use Martha White)
1 cup sugar
¾ cup flour
1 teaspoon salt
2 cups buttermilk
1 tablespoon oil or shortening

Pour oil in loaf pan and put in oven. Mix dry ingredients. Add buttermilk and oil that is hot from oven. Pour mixture in the well greased loaf pan. Bake at 350° for about 35–45 minutes, until done, especially check the center of loaf. Cool on wire rack. This is good with barbeque or ribs. Makes 15 servings. May be frozen.

Mrs. John Tanner, Wife of Representative (Tennessee)

Brush rolls with oil for tender crusts, with milk or one beaten egg diluted with 1 tablespoon milk for crisp crusts.

Rolls become crusty if placed one inch apart when baking.

CRUSTY WHITE HERB BREAD

3 cups lukewarm water
2½ tablespoons sugar
2 pkgs. yeast
2 teaspoons seasoned salt
7 to 8 cups flour
1 teaspoon dried thyme
1 teaspoon dried basil
1 teaspoon dried marjoram
1 teaspoon grated lemon rind
½ cup soft butter
egg wash for top

Grease two 9″ × 5″ × 3″ loaf pans. Combine ½ cup lukewarm water, 1 teaspoon sugar, and yeast. Dissolve seasoned salt in remaining water. Add rest of sugar and 3 cups flour. Add yeast mix, and beat until well mixed. Crumble herbs and add to mixture alone with lemon rind and soft butter. Add about 4 cups more flour and continue to mix. Let rest about 10 minutes before kneading. Lightly flour pastry board, knead about 10 minutes. Cover and let rise until double. Punch down. Knead again lightly. Divide in half and place shaped loaves in greased pans. Cover and let rise again until double. Paint with egg wash. Place in preheated 350° oven for about 50 minutes, or until golden brown. Let cool on rack. Makes 2 loaves.

Mrs. Richard Bryan, Wife of Senator (Nevada)

JALAPENO CORN BREAD

1 cup sifted flour
¼ cup sugar
4 teaspoons baking powder
1 teaspoon salt
¼ teaspoon garlic powder
1 cup yellow corn meal
2 eggs
1 cup milk
¼ cup soft shortening
1 cup finely chopped onion
1 can (8 oz.) cream style
    corn
2 tablespoons chopped jala-
    peno pepper

Sift together flour, sugar, baking powder, salt and garlic powder; stir in corn meal. Add eggs, milk, and shortening. Beat until smooth. Add onion, corn and pepper; mix well. Pour into greased 9″ × 9″ × 2″ pan. Bake at 425° for 35 to 40 minutes. Makes 10 to 12 servings. May be frozen.

Mrs. Olin Teague, Wife of former Representative (Texas)

MEXICAN CORNBREAD

2 eggs (beaten)
1 cup cream style corn
3 teaspoons baking powder
1 cup sour cream
1 cup cornmeal
1½ teaspoons salt
¼ cup jalapeno peppers (chopped)
⅔ cup oil
1 cup grated cheese

Mix together all ingredients, except cheese and peppers. Pour half of batter into greased pan; sprinkle ½ cheese and peppers over batter, pour rest of batter next and sprinkle top with remaining peppers and cheese. Bake at 350° for 1 hour. Makes one 9" × 13" loaf.

"Sug" Hancock

Mrs. Mel Hancock, Wife of Representative (Missouri)

WHITE MOUNTAIN CORNBREAD

1 cup flour
4 tablespoons sugar
1 cup cornmeal
2 teaspoons baking powder
1 teaspoon salt
½ teaspoon baking soda
1 egg
⅓ cup milk
4 tablespoons melted butter
1 cup sour cream

Sift dry ingredients. Set aside. Slightly beat egg; add milk, butter and sour cream. Mix thoroughly. Add dry ingredients to egg, milk, butter and sour cream mixture. Stir until mixed. Bake at 400° for 20 minutes, or until golden in a 8" × 8" sprayed pan. (I used melted Promise margarine and light sour cream to reduce the fat in this recipe). A flavorful, *moist* cornbread that is a favorite with chili and barbecue. Makes 9 servings. May be frozen.

Mary Jo Smith

Mrs. Robert Smith, Wife of Senator (New Hampshire)

Placing aluminum foil under the napkin in your bread basket helps keep rolls warm.

SAWMILL CORNBREAD

1 cup self-rising cornmeal
½ teaspoon salt
1 egg
½ cup buttermilk
1 tablespoon bacon grease
1 can cream-style corn
½ cup grated sharp cheddar
    cheese
small onion chopped and
    chili peppers (optional)

Sift together the dry ingredients. Add egg, milk, bacon grease, corn and cheese. Mix well. Pour batter into well-greased iron skillet. Bake at 425° for 30 minutes. Makes 8 servings. May be frozen.

Becky Browder

Mrs. Glen Browder, Wife of Representative (Alabama)

JALAPENO CORNBREAD

1 cup yellow cornmeal
2 eggs
½ cup bacon drippings
1 cup cream style corn
1 pound sausage
2 to 3 jalapeno peppers,
    chopped fine
1 cup milk
½ teaspoon baking soda
¾ teaspoon salt
1 large onion, chopped
1 pound yellow cheese,
    grated

Cook and drain sausage. Mix cornmeal, salt and soda. Add 2 eggs (beaten), milk, corn, bacon drippings, onion and peppers. Add sausage and cheese. Pour into large 2″ deep casserole dish (greased). Bake at 400° until brown—approximately 15 to 20 minutes. Makes 10 servings. May be frozen.

Suzie Brewster

Mrs. Bill Brewster, Wife of Representative (Oklahoma)

ALMOND BREAKFAST BREAD

1 cup butter
¾ cup sugar
1 egg, separated
½ cup almond paste
1 teaspoon vanilla
2 cups sifted flour
¼ cup sliced almonds

Preheat oven to 350°F. In a large bowl, cream butter and sugar until fluffy. Beat in egg yolk. Add almond paste and vanilla, and beat until smooth. At low speed, stir in flour just until well combined. Press into ungreased 8″ × 8″ pan. Beat egg white until frothy, brush over top, sprinkle with almonds, and bake 30 minutes or until golden brown. Cool completely. Wonderful! Makes 8 to 10 servings. May be frozen.

Lou B. Bevill

Mrs. Tom Bevill, Wife of Representative (Alabama)

APRICOT BREAD

¾ cup boiling water
1 cup dried apricots, chopped
3 cups unsifted flour
1 tablespoon baking powder
½ teaspoon salt
⅓ cup margarine
1 cup sugar
2 eggs
½ cup light corn syrup
1 cup chopped nuts

Pour water over apricots; let stand 15 minutes. Mix flour, baking powder and salt. Blend margarine, sugar, eggs and corn syrup. Stir in apricots with water, and add nuts. Gradually add dry ingredients. Grease and lightly flour 2 small loaf pans. Bake at 350° for 1 hour and 15 minutes. Check at 1 hour because ovens vary. Cool in pan 10 min. Remove from pans and cool on rack. Makes 2 loaves. May be frozen.

Dorothy W. Hungate

Mrs. William Hungate, Wife of former Representative (Missouri)

> *If the television is in use, it makes a nice warm spot for dough to rise.*

BANANA NUT BREAD

2 cups plain cake flour
½ teaspoon salt
½ teaspoon soda
½ cup butter
1½ cups sugar
2 eggs, well beaten
1 teaspoon vanilla
4 tablespoons buttermilk
½ cup chopped pecans
1 cup banana pulp (about 2 bananas)

Sift together flour, salt and soda. Cream butter and sugar. Add eggs and vanilla. Mix well. Add pecans and flour mixture alternately with milk and bananas. Pour into loaf pan. Bake at 350° for 1 hour.

Nancy Fountain Black

Mrs. William Black, Jr., Daughter of former Representative L. H. Fountain (North Carolina)

MOM DIMP'S* BEST BANANA BREAD

½ cup margarine
1 cup sugar
2 eggs, beaten
1 cup ripe bananas, mashed
1 cup chopped nuts
1 teaspoon lemon juice
2 cups sifted flour
1½ teaspoons baking powder
½ teaspoon soda
¼ teaspoon salt
1½ tablespoons milk

Cream margarine and sugar. Add eggs, bananas, nuts and lemon juice. Sift dry ingredients together. Add sifted ingredients and milk. Blend well. Pour into greased loaf pan. Bake at 350° for 1 hour. May be frozen. *Rod Chandler's mother, Edna, was nicknamed "Dimp" as a young child because of her dimples. She was born in Starkey, Oregon in 1906.

Rod Chandler

Rod Chandler, former Representative (Washington)

SUGARLESS BANANA BREAD

2 eggs
2 cups flour
1 cup raisins
1 cup nuts
½ cup honey
3 bananas, mashed
1 teaspoon baking soda
¾ cup oil (Crisco, Wesson or
    your preference)

Mix all ingredients together thoroughly, stirring until all lumps are gone. Pour into slightly greased loaf pan and bake at 350° approximately 40-45 minutes, checking the last 10 min. to see if it is done. Makes 1 loaf. May be frozen.

Mary Clement

Mrs. Bob Clement, Wife of Representative (Tennessee)

BANANA BREAD

1 cup flour
1 teaspoon baking soda
½ teaspoon salt
½ cup oil (scant)
1 cup sugar
2 eggs
2 bananas, mashed
1 teaspoon vanilla

Beat eggs, add sugar and oil. Add soda and salt to flour, mix egg and flour mixtures. Add vanilla, then the mashed bananas. Bake at 350° for one hour. Enjoy. May be frozen.

Mrs. Jamie L. Whitten

Mrs. Jamie L. Whitten, Wife of Representative (Mississippi)

If a dull-finish aluminum loaf pan is used it will brown the sides of the bread better.

BANANA BREAD

1 cup sugar
½ cup soft shortening or margarine
2 eggs
3 bananas (ripe or black)
2 cups flour
¼ cup milk
1 teaspoon baking soda
1 cup nuts (optional)

Mix flour and baking soda. Cream together sugar and shortening, add eggs 1 at a time. Add bananas (mashed with fork) to the milk and mix alternately to the flour mixture. When well blended, pour into greased bread pan. Bake at 350° for 35-45 min. Check with toothpick. "This is an old family recipe developed by my grandmother—Florina Marie Porter." Makes 10 servings. May be frozen.

Mrs. Ed Royce, Wife of Representative (California)

BANANA BREAD

1 cup flour
¾ cup whole wheat flour
1 cup sugar
1 teaspoon baking soda
1 teaspoon salt
3 bananas, mashed
¼ cup shortening
2 tablespoons orange juice
1 egg

Blend all ingredients and beat 3 minutes. Pour batter into a greased 9″ × 5″ pan and bake at 350° for 50 minutes. Makes 10 servings. May be frozen.

Mrs. David Hobson, Wife of Representative (Ohio)

BANANA NUT BREAD

3 bananas (1 cup)
1 cup sugar, brown or white
½ cup shortening
2 eggs, beaten
2 cups sifted flour
1 teaspoon baking soda
½ cup nuts, chopped

Preheat oven to 350°F. Mash bananas and add sugar, shortening and eggs. Mix well. Add other ingredients. Pour the batter into a loaf pan that has been greased and dusted with flour. Bake in 350° oven for about 1 hour and ten minutes. Cool before slicing. Enjoy!

Connie Morella

Connie Morella, Representative (Maryland)

HAWAIIAN BANANA NUT BREAD

3 cups all purpose flour
2 cups sugar
1 teaspoon baking soda
1 teaspoon salt
1 teaspoon cinnamon
1 cup chopped nuts
2 teaspoons vanilla
3 eggs beaten
1½ cups vegetable oil
2 cups of mashed RIPE bananas
1 8 oz. can of crushed pineapple, drained

Combine all dry ingredients, stir in nuts and set aside. Combine remaining ingredients. Add to dry ingredients, stirring just until moistened. Spoon into 2 greased 9″ × 5″ × 3″ loaf pans. Bake at 350° for 1 hour and 5 minutes—or until done. Cool 10 minutes before removing from pans. Yields two loaves. Makes 18 to 24 servings. May be frozen.

Ted Strickland

Ted Strickland, Representative (Ohio)

Refrigerate or freeze flour and it will last longer.

WHOLE WHEAT BANANA BREAD

½ cup (¼ lb.) butter or margarine
1 cup sugar
2 eggs, lightly beaten
1 cup mashed ripe banana
   (about 3)
1 cup all purpose flour, unsifted
1 cup whole wheat flour, unsifted
½ teaspoon salt
1 teaspoon baking soda
⅓ cup hot water
½ cup chopped walnuts

Melt butter and blend in sugar. Mix in beaten eggs and mashed banana, blending until smooth. In a bowl, stir together all purpose flour, whole wheat flour, salt and soda until thoroughly blended. Add dry ingredients alternately with hot water. Stir in chopped nuts. Spoon batter into greased 9" × 5" loaf pan. Bake at 325° oven for about 1 hour and 10 minutes, until bread begins to pull away from sides of pan and a wooden skewer inserted in center comes out clean. Let cool in pan for 10 minutes; then turn out onto rack to cool completely. Makes 1 loaf. Makes 6 to 8 servings. May be frozen.

Ms. Bob Filner, Wife of Representative (California)

CRANBERRY ORANGE QUICK BREAD

3 medium oranges
2 egg whites, beaten
2 tablespoon oil
1 cup flour
1 cup whole wheat flour
½ cup sugar
1½ teaspoon baking powder
½ teaspoon baking soda
1 cup cranberries, chopped
½ cup walnuts

Grate and measure 1 teaspoon orange peel. Squeeze and measure ¾ cup juice from oranges. Combine juice, orange peel with egg whites and oil. Stir together dry ingredients. Add the orange mixture. Fold in berries and nuts. Pour into greased 9" × 5" pan. Bake at 350° for 50–60 minutes. May be frozen.

Mrs. Laurie Kirby, Wife of Representative Earl Pomeroy (North Dakota)

LEMON BREAD

1 cup sugar
6 tablespoon melted butter
1 teaspoon baking powder
½ cup milk
2 eggs
1½ cups flour
1 teaspoon salt
rind of 1 lemon
½ cup chopped walnuts or pecans

Add butter to sugar and mix. Add slightly beaten eggs to butter mixture. Mix flour, baking powder and salt together. Alternately add flour, then milk to the butter mixture. Add lemon rind and nuts. Bake at 350° for one hour.

Glaze: Mix the juice of 1 lemon with ½ cup sugar. Spoon over bread while hot. Cool in pan. Makes 12 servings. May be frozen.

Jean Thompson

Mrs. Richard Thompson, Daughter of former Representative John Terry (New York)

LEMON BREAD

1 cup sugar
⅓ cup melted butter
1 tablespoon lemon extract
2 eggs
1½ cups plain flour
1 teaspoon salt
1 teaspoon baking powder
½ cup milk
½ cup powdered sugar
⅓ cup lemon juice
1 grated rind of 1 lemon (optional)
1 cup chopped pecans

Preheat oven to 325°. Grease and flour 1 large loaf pan. Cream together the sugar, melted butter and lemon extract. Add eggs, one at a time. Sift together the flour, salt and baking powder. Add sifted ingredients alternately with the milk. Fold in the grated lemon rind and pecans if desired. Put into the prepared loaf pan. Bake for 60 minutes. For glaze, combine the powdered sugar and lemon juice. Drizzle over the bread while still warm. This recipe may be doubled successfully. It is especially good if chilled before serving. Makes 1 loaf. May be frozen.

Lillian Darden

Mrs. George Darden, Wife of Representative (Georgia)

MANGO BREAD

1 stick butter or margarine
¾ cup sugar
2 eggs
1 tablespoon lemon juice
2 cups flour
¼ teaspoon cinnamon
⅛ teaspoon ginger
⅛ teaspoon nutmeg
1 teaspoon baking soda
½ teaspoon salt
1 chopped mango (about 1 cup)
½ cup chopped nuts

Cream butter and sugar. Add lemon juice. Add eggs, beating well. Sift all dry ingredients and add to the above mixture. Fold in mango and nuts. Bake in a loaf pan at 325° for 1 hour. Makes 20 servings. May be frozen.

Jeane Chappell

Mrs. Bill Chappell, Wife of former Representative (Florida)

HONEY OATMEAL BREAD

2½ cups boiling water
1¼ cups oatmeal
2½ tablespoons butter
2 pkgs. yeast dissolved in 1¼ cups warm water
1 tablespoon salt
¾ cup honey
7½ to 8 cups flour

Combine boiling water, oatmeal and butter. Let stand 30 minutes. Add salt and honey. Soak yeast 5 minutes and add oatmeal. Add flour and knead until dough is stiff and shiny (10 to 15 minutes). Put into greased bowl and let rise 1½ hours. Punch down and let rise another hour. Form into 3 loaves and let rise ½ hour. Bake at 350° approximately 1 hour. Recipe doubles well. Makes 3 loaves. May be frozen.

Lori McInnis

Mrs. Scott McInnis, Wife of Representative (Colorado)

Dough won't stick to your hands if it is kneaded inside a large plastic bag.

PUMPKIN BREAD

2 teaspoons vanilla
2 cups all-purpose flour
2 teaspoons baking powder
½ teaspoon baking soda
1 teaspoon salt
½ teaspoon ground nutmeg
¼ cup Wesson oil
¼ cup brown sugar
1 teaspoon ground cinnamon
2 eggs, well beaten
½ cup milk
1 cup sugar
1 cup canned pumpkin
1 cup chopped walnuts
¼ cup melted butter or margarine

Into a bowl, sift the flour, baking powder, soda, salt and spices. In another large bowl, combine eggs, milk, sugars, pumpkin, butter and oil. Add the sifted dry ingredients and mix until well blended. Fold in chopped nuts. Turn into a greased loaf pan, 9″ × 5″ × 3″. Bake in a moderate oven (350°) for about 55 minutes, or until a small fork inserted into the center comes out clean. Makes 6 servings. May be frozen.

Roscoe Dellums

Mrs. Ronald Dellums, Wife of Representative (California)

STRAWBERRY BREAD

3 cups all-purpose flour
1 tablespoon cinnamon
1 teaspoon baking soda
1 teaspoon salt
1¼ cups vegetable oil
3 eggs
2 cups sugar
2 10-oz. pkgs. frozen strawberries, thawed and drained
1 cup chopped pecans

Combine flour, cinnamon, baking soda and salt. Mix the vegetable oil, eggs and sugar well and gradually stir into the flour mixture. Stir in the strawberries and pecans. Pour into two greased and floured loaf pans 8½″ × 4½″ × 3″. Bake at 350° for 1 hour. Cool in pans 10 minutes. Remove and continue cooling on racks. Makes 16 servings. May be frozen.

Alice M. Lancaster

Mrs. Martin Lancaster, Wife of Representative (North Carolina)

ZUCCHINI-DATE BREAD

3 eggs
1 cup oil
2 cups sugar
2 cups grated zucchini
   squash
2 tablespoons vanilla
2 cups flour
¼ teaspoon baking powder
2 teaspoons baking soda
1 teaspoon salt
1 cup chopped dates
¾ cup chopped pecans

Mix eggs, oil, sugar, zucchini and vanilla. Add dry ingredients. Fold in dates and nuts. Bake at 350° in 2 greased and floured loaf pans for 45 minutes or until done. Makes 10 servings. May be frozen.

Joanne Kemp

Mrs. Jack F. Kemp, Wife of former Representative (New York) and former Secretary of Housing and Urban Development

BLUEBERRY MUFFINS

1½ cups sifted flour
½ cup sugar
2 teaspoons baking powder
½ teaspoon salt
1 egg
½ cup milk
¼ cup oil
1 cup fresh or frozen blueberries

Sift dry ingredients into bowl; then moisten with combined milk, egg and oil. Stir enough to thoroughly blend. Fold in blueberries. Bake in well-greased muffin tins or paper cup liners. Bake at 400° for 20–25 minutes. Makes 12 servings. May be frozen.

Jean Hastert

Mrs. Dennis Hastert, Wife of Representative (Illinois)

Let baked bread cool on a wire rack so the bottom won't be soggy.

HEALTHY MUFFINS WITH BLUEBERRIES

1½ cups flour (1 cup white +
    ½ cup whole wheat)
2 teaspoon baking powder
½ teaspoon salt
1 egg white and ½ shell
    filled with Egg Beaters
    (egg substitute)
½ cup skim milk
4 tablespoons Sweet One (no
    other sugar substitute
    holds up)
3 tablespoons margarine
1 cup frozen blueberries—do
    not thaw

Measure and set aside—flour, baking powder and salt. Blend sugars and margarine in bowl until course meal appearance. Add egg and mix lightly. Add flour mixture and milk alternately until blended. Do not overmix. Batter will be lumpy. Fold in gently 1 cup frozen blueberries. (Do not thaw). Fill muffin cups ⅔ full—bake at 325° for 20–25 minutes or until toothpick test is clean. Makes 6 to 8 servings. May be frozen.

Rachel Gillen Puetz

Mrs. Rachel Puetz, Daughter of former Representative Courtland Gillen (Indiana)

BANANA-BRAN MUFFINS

1 cup all-purpose flour
⅓ cup firmly packed brown
    sugar
1 tablespoon baking powder
½ teaspoon salt
2¼ cups bran cereal (All-Bran
    preferred)
1 cup milk
1 egg
½ cup vegetable oil
2 small well-ripened bananas
½ cup chopped dried fruit
    (your choice)
½ cup chopped walnuts

Mix flour, sugar, baking powder and salt in large mixing bowl. Set aside. Mix cereal and milk in separate bowl, and let stand 5 minutes until cereal softens. Add egg and oil to cereal mixture. Stir well. Mash 2 well-ripened bananas in food processor or blender until smooth. Add mashed bananas to cereal mixture. Blend well. Add cereal mixture to flour mixture stirring only until combined. Fold in dried fruit and nuts. Pour batter into lightly greased muffin pan evenly distributing batter. Bake at 400° for 20 minutes or until golden brown. Store in tightly sealed plastic baggies to maintain moisture. Keep in refrigerator to prevent mold. Makes 12 servings. May be frozen.

Sally J. Roemer

Mrs. Tim Roemer, Wife of Representative (Indiana)

BANANA MUFFINS

1 cup sugar
1 cup margarine
1 cup mashed bananas (approximately 2)
4½ tablespoons buttermilk
2 eggs, slightly beaten
1½ cups sifted plain flour
1 teaspoon baking soda
1 teaspoon cinnamon
1 teaspoon nutmeg
1 teaspoon vanilla
½ teaspoon salt

Cream sugar and margarine, add bananas, buttermilk and eggs. Mix dry ingredients, and fold into sugar/egg mixture. Add vanilla. Pour into greased muffin pans. Bake at 350° for 20 minutes. Makes 12 servings. May be frozen.

Barbara Valentine

Mrs. Tim Valentine, Wife of Representative (North Carolina)

JUDY'S ORANGE MUFFINS

1 cup sugar
½ cup (1 stick) unsalted butter
2 eggs
1 teaspoon baking soda
1 cup buttermilk
2 cups sifted all-purpose flour
½ teaspoon salt
1 cup raisins
zest and juice of one orange
½ cup sugar

Cream the sugar and butter until smooth with an electric mixer. Add the eggs and beat until fluffy. Add the baking soda to the buttermilk. Sift the flour and salt together, and add to the sugar-butter mixture alternately with the buttermilk. Stir until well mixed. In a food processor, grind the raisins and orange zest, add to the batter and combine. Spoon the batter into the muffin tins and bake at 400° until golden brown and firm to the touch, about 12 minutes. Remove the tins to a baking rack and set close together. Brush the tops of the muffins with orange juice and sprinkle with ½ cup sugar while still warm. Makes 30 servings. May be frozen.

Lydia de La Viña de Foley

Mrs. John R. Foley III, Daughter-in-law of former Representative John R. Foley (Maryland)

GRANOLA MUFFINS

1½ cups flour
1½ cups granola-style cereal
½ cup sugar
1 teaspoon baking soda
½ teaspoon salt
½ cup orange juice
2 eggs
½ cup margarine, melted

Combine flour, cereal, sugar and baking soda. In a separate bowl, beat orange juice, eggs and margarine. Add liquid ingredients to dry ingredients. Stir just enough to moisten. Fill 12 paper lined muffin cups ⅔ full. Bake at 375° for 15 to 20 minutes. Muffins will be a golden brown when done. Makes 1 dozen. May be frozen.

Barbara G. Johnson

Mrs. Tim Johnson, Wife of Representative (South Dakota)

SIX WEEK MUFFINS

1 box (15 ozs., approx. 6 cups) Raisin Bran cereal
2¼ cups sugar
5 cups flour
5 teaspoons soda
2 teaspoons salt
4 eggs slightly beaten
1 quart buttermilk

Combine first 5 ingredients in a large bowl. Mix eggs and buttermilk, then mix into dry mixture. Bake at 400° for 15 to 20 minutes in muffin cups. Store covered in refrigerator. Dough stores in refrigerator up to 6 weeks. Makes approximately 4½ dozen. May be frozen.

Pamela C. Herger

Mrs. Wally Herger, Wife of Representative (California)

To thaw, frozen bread loaves, place in clean brown paper and put in 325° oven for 5–6 minutes to thaw completely. For thawing rolls allow several more minutes.

MICHIGAN BRAN MUFFINS

1 cup oil
4 cups buttermilk
4 eggs
3 cups sugar
5 cups flour
5 teaspoons baking soda
2 teaspoons salt
7 cups (15 oz. box) Raisin
    Bran cereal

Mix together in a very large bowl, oil, buttermilk and eggs. Add remaining ingredients. Bake at 400° in paper cups or greased muffin tins 15–20 minutes. Batter will keep up to 6 weeks in refrigerator. Makes 4 dozen. May be frozen.

Gayle Kildee

Mrs. Dale Kildee, Wife of Representative (Michigan)

BRAN MUFFINS

1 cup shortening
2½ cups sugar
4 eggs
2½ cups buttermilk
6 cups Bran Buds
1½ teaspoons salt
2 cups raisins
1 cup chopped pecans
2 cups boiling water
5 cups flour
5 teaspoons baking soda

Cream shortening and sugar. Add eggs and beat well. Stir in buttermilk and Bran Buds. Add raisins and nuts. Stir in boiling water. Add all dry ingredients. Bake about 20 minutes in 400° oven in greased muffin tins. Batter can be kept in refrigerator in a covered container for several weeks. Add a little hot water to soften batter. Makes 2 dozen.

Connie Hansen

Mrs. George Hansen, Wife of former Representative (Idaho)

OAT BRAN MUFFINS

3 cups flour
2 cups bran cereal flakes
2 cups oat bran
1 cup brown sugar
½ teaspoon salt
1 tablespoon baking soda
2½ cups skim milk
2 egg substitutes
½ cup melted margarine (cholesterol-free)

Grease two 12 muffin tins. Combine first 6 ingredients in bowl. Add milk, eggs and margarine. Stir just until blended. May add walnuts, raisins or dates. Bake in a 400° oven for 15–20 minutes or until golden brown. Makes 24 muffins. Makes 20 servings. May be frozen.

Tommy Thompson, Governor (Wisconsin)

BRAN MUFFINS

1 cup boiling water
1 cup All Bran cereal
2 sticks margarine
1½ cups sugar
2 eggs, well beaten
2 cups buttermilk
2 cups All Bran cereal
1 teaspoon salt
2½ teaspoons baking soda
2½ cups all-purpose flour
½ pound dates, chopped
1 cup nuts, chopped. I use pecans

Combine one cup of boiling water and 1 cup of All Bran cereal. Set aside. Cream margarine and sugar, add eggs, buttermilk, 2 cups All Bran, salt soda and flour. Combine with bran and hot water mixture. Add dates and nuts. Bake 375° for 20 to 25 minutes in small muffin tins. Note: Batter may be stored in tightly covered container in refrigerator up to 6 weeks. Makes 50 servings. May be frozen.

Harold Volkmer, Representative (Missouri)

GOV. & MRS. BAYH'S FAVORITE CARROT MUFFINS

2 cups sugar
1¼ cups oil
4 eggs
3 cups flour
2 teaspoons baking powder
1 teaspoon baking soda
½ teaspoon salt
1 teaspoon cinnamon
½ teaspoon nutmeg
2¼ cups grated carrots
1 cup walnuts, coarsely chopped
1 cup raisins

Preheat oven to 350°. Mix oil, sugar and eggs in mixer for about 2 minutes at medium speed. In another bowl, sift dry ingredients and add gradually to sugar mixture. Add carrots, walnuts and raisins. Blend dough until no flour is seen. Fill muffin cups (either paper-lined or greased) ⅔ full. Bake 35–40 minutes or until a toothpick inserted in center comes out clean. Serve either warm or at room temperature. Makes 20 servings. May be frozen.

Evan Bayh, Governor (Indiana)

CRANBERRY MUFFINS

2 cups flour
2¼ teaspoons baking powder
¼ teaspoon baking soda
1 egg, slightly beaten
½ cup sugar
1 teaspoon salt (scant)
1 cup chopped cranberries
¼ cup melted butter
1 teaspoon honey

Combine dry sifted ingredients, set aside. Combine egg, buttermilk, honey and butter. Mix well. Make well in dry ingredients and pour in liquid ones. Stir until just moistened. Fold in cranberries which have been dredged in a little of the flour. Fill well greased muffin tins ⅔ full. Bake at 425° for 22 to 25 minutes until toothpick comes out clean. Let stand 5 minutes and remove from tins. Makes 18 servings. May be frozen.

Mrs. Thomas Kleppe, Wife of former Representative (North Dakota)

POPOVER SURPRISE

1 cup all-purpose flour, sifted
¼ teaspoon salt
1 cup milk
2 eggs

Grease popover pan or custard cups and place in a 425° oven to preheat while making the batter. Combine all ingredients and beat until smooth. Get pan out of the oven, and quickly pour batter into the hot cups, filling them half full. Immediately bake at 425° for 40 minutes. Puncture with a cooking fork to let out steam, and bake 5 more minutes. You may add walnuts, chocolate chips or whatever you desire to the batter, or fill the inside with vanilla, chocolate, etc. pudding, and ice the top with any frosting. Makes 8 servings.

Tyler Lott, Daughter of Senator Trent Lott (Mississippi)

GRANDMA'S BROWN SUGAR ROLLS

1¾ cups flour
⅓ cup shortening
2½ teaspoons baking powder
¾ teaspoon salt
¾ cup milk (approximately)
   butter
   brown sugar to sprinkle

Blend dry ingredients and shortening until mixture resembles fine crumbs. Stir in just enough milk so that dough leaves sides of bowl and rounds into ball. Turn dough onto lightly floured surface and knead gently ten times. Roll above or other biscuit dough out on lightly floured surface to ¼ to ½ inch. Spread with butter or margarine and sprinkle with brown sugar. Roll up and cut into 1 inch slices. Place sliced rolls, cut side down, on lightly greased baking sheet or dish and bake at 350° for approximately 30 minutes or until lightly brown. Do not overcook. Grandma's rolls were always served hot and with lots of love. I hope that you, too, enjoy serving our family favorite the same way. Makes 1 dozen.

Barbara Roberts, Governor (Oregon)

HONEY TWISTS

⅓ cup brown sugar
¼ cup butter
2 teaspoons honey
⅓ cup chopped nuts (pecans or walnuts)
2 8 oz. cans crescent dinner rolls
2 tablespoons butter, melted
¼ cup brown sugar
1 teaspoon cinnamon

Preheat oven to 400°. In small saucepan, combine first three ingredients; bring to a boil. Spread in ungreased 9″ × 13″ pan. Sprinkle with nuts; set aside. Separate one can crescent dough into four rectangles. Lay rectangles end to end to form one long rectangle. Firmly press perforations to seal. Brush rectangle with melted butter. Combine brown sugar and cinnamon; sprinkle over dough. Separate second can of dough into four rectangles. Place end to end over first dough rectangle; seal edges and perforations. Cut filled rectangle crosswise into twenty strips. Twist each strip two times. Place twists in prepared pan. Bake 15 to 20 minutes or until golden brown. Invert immediately to remove from pan. Makes 10 to 12 servings. May be frozen.

Mrs. John Doolittle, Wife of Representative (California)

CINNAMON PUFFS

¼ cup sugar
1 tablespoon cinnamon
¼ cup melted margarine
¼ cup chopped pecans
2 cans Pillsbury triangle rolls
1 bag large marshmallows

Glaze:
1 cup powdered sugar
1 teaspoon vanilla
6 teaspoons milk

Roll marshmallows in butter, sugar and cinnamon. Wrap triangle dough around marshmallow and seal. Roll triangle in sugar cinnamon mixture and dip in butter and place in large muffin tins. Bake at 350° for 10 to 15 minutes. Glaze by dribbling over rolls hot from the oven. Makes 20 servings. May be frozen.

Mrs. Ed Bethune, Wife of former Representative (Arkansas)

STICKY BUN PULL-APARTS

2 loaves frozen bread dough
    thawed
½ cup margarine
1 cup brown sugar
1 cup nuts
1 cup raisins
1 or 2 chopped apples
    (peeled)
1 large pkg. vanilla pudding
    (not instant)
2 tablespoons milk
    cinnamon to taste

Break one loaf into small pieces around bottom of 13″ × 9″ × 2″ buttered pan. Melt butter and add all other ingredients. Cream together. Pour over bread in bottom of pan. Break rest of bread in second loaf into small pieces. Place on top. Let rise for 2½-3 hours in 140° oven. Bake in 350° oven for 30 minutes. Turn upside down on rack to cool. Makes 24 servings. May be frozen.

William Baker, Representative (California)

WISCONSIN BLUEBERRY BUCKLE

2 cups sifted flour
2 teaspoons baking powder
½ teaspoon salt
¼ cup soft butter
1 cup sugar
1 egg
½ cup milk
2 cups fresh or frozen blue-
    berries

Sift together flour, baking powder and salt. Cream butter and sugar until light and fluffy. Add the egg and milk and beat well. Add the flour, baking powder and salt and stir until blended. Add blueberries. Spread mixture in 9″ × 13″ pan.

For topping: Cream together butter and sugar. Combine flour and cinnamon and add to creamed mixture. Stir until crumbly. Sprinkle over blueberry buckle and bake 35-45 minutes at 350°. Makes 24 servings.

Topping:
½ cup brown sugar
⅓ cup flour
¼ cup soft butter
½ teaspoon cinnamon

Tommy Thompson, Governor (Wisconsin)

BLUEBERRY BUCKLE

¾ cup sugar
¼ cup butter or margarine
1 egg
½ cup milk
2 cups flour
2 teaspoons baking powder
¼ teaspoon salt
2 cups well-drained blue-
    berries

Make batter by mixing together thoroughly sugar, butter and egg. Stir in milk. Sift together and add flour, baking powder, salt. Blend in blueberries. Spread batter into well-greased and floured 13" × 9" × 2" pan. Mix together topping ingredients with fork. Crumble over batter. Bake at 375° for 35 to 40 minutes. Makes 24 servings. May be frozen.

Topping:
⅔ cup sugar
⅓ cup sifted flour
½ teaspoon cinnamon
⅓ cup softened butter or mar-
    garine

Claire Schweiker

Mrs. Richard Schweiker, Wife of former Senator (Pennsylvania)

DAVID'S JOHNNY CAKE

2 cups flour
2 teaspoons baking powder
5 to 6 tablespoons sugar
1¾ tablespoons oil
⅔ cup water
½ teaspoon salt

Mix together and knead. Put into a greased 8" × 8" dish and place in preheated oven after you prick the top with a fork. Bake at 450° for 15 to 20 minutes. Makes 8 to 10 servings.

Faith H Battle

Mrs. James Battle, Daughter-in-law of former Representative Laurie C. Battle (Alabama)

Oil on your hands makes bread easier to knead.

SOUR CREAM COFFEE CAKE

½ pound butter or margarine
2 cups sugar
1 pint sour cream
2 teaspoons baking soda
4 eggs
2 teaspoons vanilla
2 cups regular flour
2 teaspoons baking powder

Topping:
½ cup sugar
2 teaspoons cinnamon
½ to 1 cup walnuts

Grease and flour 13″ × 10″ × 2″ pan. Preheat oven to 350°. Mix together butter and sugar, add sour cream and baking soda, then add eggs, vanilla, flour and baking powder. Mix all ingredients with electric beater until well blended. Pour mixture into pan using half of the mixture. Place half of the topping on batter and swirl. Pour remaining batter in pan. Swirl topping on top. Bake at 350° for 45-50 minutes. This is my husband's favorite cake. Makes 16 servings. May be frozen.

Mrs. Thomas Ewing, Wife of Representative (Illinois)

WHIT'S OVERNIGHT COFFEE CAKE

1 bag Rich's frozen rolls (for cloverleaf rolls)
1 small box Jello vanilla pudding (not instant)
½ cup brown sugar
¾ cup chopped nuts
1 stick oleo

Sprinkle ¼ cup nuts in bottom of bundt pan or angelfood cake tin which does not come apart. Mix sugar, pudding mix, and remaining nuts. Put layer of rolls in tin, then sprinkle with half of brown sugar mixture. Add another layer of rolls and finish with sugar mixture on top. Pour melted oleo on top. Cover with towel and leave at room temperature over night to rise. Bake at 350° for 30 minutes. Invert on plate. Makes 12 servings. May be frozen.

Mrs. Laurie C. Battle, Wife of former Representative (Alabama)

SOUR CREAM COFFEE CAKE

½ cup butter (1 stick)
1 cup sugar
2 eggs slightly beaten
1 teaspoon baking soda
1 cup sour cream
1½ cups flour
1½ teaspoons baking powder
2 teaspoons vanilla
¼ cup sugar
½ teaspoon cinnamon
½ cup chopped nuts

Cream butter and 1 cup sugar. Add 2 eggs slightly beaten. Add 1 teaspoon soda mixed with 1 cup sour cream. Sift flour and baking powder. Add to mixture. Add vanilla. Pour into greased bundt pan. Sprinkle with mixture of ¼ cup sugar, ½ teaspoon cinnamon and ½ cup chopped nuts. Bake at 350° for 35–45 min. Open door and allow cake to cool in oven. Remove from pan when cool. Makes 12 servings.

Mrs. Don Sundquist, Wife of Representative (Tennessee)

GRANDMA'S COFFEE CAKE

Mixture:
1 stick butter
1 cup sour cream
1½ cups sifted all-purpose
    flour
1 cup sugar
1 teaspoon baking soda
1½ teaspoon baking powder
2 eggs
1½ teaspoon vanilla extract

Cream butter, sour cream and sugar. Add baking soda. Add eggs one at a time, beating well. Sift flour and baking powder. Beat into other mixture. Add vanilla. Put ½ mixture in a bundt pan. Put in part of filling. Add rest of mixture and add the rest of filling on top all the way around bundt pan and cut through with a knife. Bake 40 minutes at 350°. Makes 1 bundt cake.

Filling:
½ cup brown sugar
1½ tablespoon cinnamon

Lucinda Bennett, Daughter of former Representative Charles Bennett (Florida)

NEW ENGLAND BLUEBERRY COFFEE CAKE

1½ cups all-purpose flour
½ cup sugar
1 tablespoon baking powder
1 teaspoon cinnamon
½ teaspoon salt
1½ cups fresh blueberries
1 egg
½ cup milk
¼ cup butter or margarine,
    melted

Topping:
¼ cup butter or margarine,
    melted
¾ cup packed brown sugar
1 tablespoon all-purpose
    flour
½ cup chopped walnuts

In a large mixing bowl, combine flour, sugar, baking powder, cinnamon and salt. Gently fold in blueberries. In a small bowl, whisk together the egg, milk and butter. Add to the flour mixture and stir carefully. Spread into a greased 8″ × 8″ baking pan. Combine all topping ingredients and sprinkle over batter. Bake at 425° for 20–25 minutes or until top is light golden brown. Serve warm or at room temperature. Makes 12 servings.

Peggy Soderberg

Mrs. William Soderberg, Daughter of former Representative Robert Grant (Indiana)

> *Add ½ teaspoon of sugar to the yeast when stirring it into the water to dissolve. If it foams and bubbles in ten minutes you know the yeast is alive and active.*

CRANBERRY COFFEE CAKE

¼ pound margarine
1 cup sugar
2 eggs
1 teaspoon baking powder
1 teaspoon baking soda
2 cups all-purpose flour
½ teaspoon salt
½ pint sour cream
1 teaspoon almond extract
8 ozs. whole-berry cranberry
   sauce
⅓ cup chopped nuts (op-
   tional)
¾ cup powdered sugar
1 tablespoon warm water
½ teaspoon almond extract

Cream margarine, sugar, and eggs. Add baking powder, baking soda, flour, and salt. Add sour cream, 1 teaspoon almond extract, and cranberry sauce. Grease and flour a 2 quart ring mold or two loaf pans. Pour in batter. Sprinkle ⅓ cup chopped nuts on top if desired. Bake at 350° for 40 to 45 minutes. Remove cake from pan 5 minutes after taking out of oven. Mix powdered sugar, water and ½ teaspoon almond extract. Spoon over cooled cake. This cake "keeps" very well. Makes 12 servings. May be frozen.

Mrs. Daniel Mica, Wife of former Representative (Florida)

INDIAN FRY BREAD

2 cups flour
1 teaspoon salt
2 teaspoons baking powder
½ cup dry milk
1 tablespoon sugar
1 cup warm water

Mix ingredients together. Pat out into 8″ circles, ½″ thick. Cut into wedges and slit each wedge in the center. Fry in oil which is just below the smoking point, working each piece quickly so that each piece is browned.

Pat Williams, Representative (Montana)

FRONTIER PANCAKES

2 cups buttermilk
2 cups flour
2 eggs
¼ cup sugar
1 teaspoon salt
1 teaspoon baking powder
1 teaspoon baking soda

Mix buttermilk, flour, eggs, sugar, salt and baking powder in bowl in this order. Mix batter well and add baking soda. Bake on very lightly greased grill at moderately hot temperature. ¼ cup buttermilk may be added if thinner pancakes are desired. Makes approximately 10 to 12 medium pancakes.

Mrs. George Hansen, Wife of former Representative (Idaho)

OATMEAL PANCAKES

1½ cups rolled oats (dry)—
quick cooking style
3 tablespoons flour
1 egg
1½ cups milk (skimmed)
dash of salt
1 teaspoon baking powder

Mix dry ingredients, add egg and half the skimmed milk. Stir together well. Add half the remaining milk and mix well. Let batter stand while preparing skillet or griddle. (Best prepared on iron skillet or griddle, using either liquid corn oil or shortening). When griddle is ready, stir in remaining milk, batter will not be smooth. Spoon batter onto griddle and spread evenly (to make pancake 4–5 inches, use 2 to 3 spoonfuls of batter). Fry over medium heat. Will be golden brown to brown when done. Top side will appear to be drying when ready to turn. Makes 2 to 3 servings. Serve immediately. Best taste is with cane syrup or molasses and butter or margarine.

Mick Staton, former Representative (West Virginia)

> *Small amounts of leftover corn may be added to pancake batter for variety.*

JUDITH'S PANCAKES

1 quart buttermilk
4 tablespoons melted butter
   or margarine
2 teaspoons baking soda
4 teaspoons baking powder
1 teaspoon salt
4 eggs
5 tablespoons brown sugar
2 cups flour

Beat eggs. Add all other ingredients and pour small amount of batter on lightly greased griddle or frying pan. Turn when lightly browned. Makes 4 servings.

Joanne Kemp

Mrs. Jack F. Kemp, Wife of former Representative (New York) and former Secretary of Housing and Urban Development

OLD FASHIONED BUCKWHEAT PANCAKES

1 pkg. dry yeast
½ cup warm water
2 cups cold water
2 cups buckwheat flour
1 cup all purpose flour
¼ cup oleo or sausage drippings
1 tablespoon sorghum
1 teaspoon baking soda dissolved in ½ cup hot
   water

Dissolve yeast in warm water, add cold water. Add flours to yeast and water and beat until smooth. Cover, refrigerate overnight. In morning, stir in oleo, sorghum and soda water. Let stand for 30 minutes. Bake as for pancakes. Delicious with pure maple syrup and fresh sausage patties. Makes approximately 36 4″ pancakes. Makes 12 servings. May be frozen.

Neal Smith

Neal Smith, Representative (Iowa)

Dough can rise with no problem even in a cold kitchen if the bowl is placed on a heating pad set on medium.

"ROLL-UP'S"

2 eggs
1¼ cups milk
1 cup flour
1 teaspoon sugar
½ teaspoon salt
¼ teaspoon baking powder
2 tablespoons melted butter

Blend first 6 ingredients in blender, then add the 2 tablespoons melted butter. Use omelette skillet or large crepe pan on medium heat. When pan is warmed, add a little butter, melt, then 1 to 2 tablespoons batter for each "roll-up". Swirl around pan, cooking until little bubbles begin forming on crepe. Turn and cook briefly for light golden brown color. Serve immediately generously spread with: best jelly, sour cream, confectioners sugar or dash of fresh lemon. Then roll up and devour. Recipe may be doubled. Our children request these constantly.

Mrs. Don Bonker, Wife of former Representative (Washington)

RAISED WAFFLES

1 pkg. dry yeast
½ cup warm water
2 cups lukewarm milk
1 stick melted butter
1 teaspoon salt
1 teaspoon sugar
2 cups flour
2 eggs
pinch of baking soda

Add yeast to warm water, dissolve and let sit for a few minutes. Add next 5 ingredients. Mix together the night before and the next morning add 2 eggs that are room temperature and a pinch of soda. Bake in waffle iron until crisp. Cool on rack completely and then freeze for later use. Then heat in oven on rack. Makes 8 servings. May be frozen.

Mrs. Jim Bunning, Wife of Representative (Kentucky)

LOW CHOLESTEROL WAFFLES

1¾ cups flour
2 teaspoons baking powder
3 teaspoons sugar
½ teaspoon salt
⅓ cup vegetable oil
1½ cups milk
6 egg whites, beaten stiff
½ teaspoon grated lemon rind
½ cup finely chopped pecans

Measure dry ingredients into mixing bowl. Blend. In two-cup measure or separate mixing bowl, mix oil and milk. Add liquid to dry ingredients. Stir until all ingredients are moistened. Beat egg whites with electric mixer until stiff but not dry. Fold into batter along with grated lemon rind and chopped pecans. Pour batter onto preheated grid on waffle iron and bake. Makes 6 to 8 servings. May be frozen.

Lou B. Bevill

Mrs. Tom Bevill, Wife of Representative (Alabama)

ANTIPASTO SANDWICH

1 large round loaf of bread
¼ cup wine vinegar
¼ cup olive oil
1 teaspoon oregano
1 small can pimentos, drained
1 large tomato, sliced
2 hard cooked eggs, sliced
1 small onion, sliced thin
4 pieces of lettuce, shredded
½ pound bologna, sliced
½ pound hard salami, sliced
½ pound provolone cheese, sliced
anchovies, to taste

Cut loaf of bread crosswise into fourths. Before filling each layer, sprinkle the bread with wine vinegar, olive oil, and oregano. Place bologna and canned pimento on bottom layer. Top with second slice of bread. Layer with lettuce, tomatoes, eggs, and anchovies. Top with third piece of bread. Layer with salami, cheese, and onion. Add remaining bread slice atop. Skewer sandwich to hold together. Cut in 4 wedges. Makes 4 servings.

Jon Dougher

Jon Dougher, Son-in-law of Representative Gerald Solomon (New York)

KENTUCKY HOT BROWN

Sauce:
2 tablespoons butter
¼ cup flour
2 cups milk
¼ cup grated Parmesan
¼ cheese
½ cup grated sharp cheddar
¼ cheese
teaspoon Worcestershire
sauce
¼ teaspoon salt

Sandwiches:
8 slices bread, trimmed and
toasted
1 pound sliced turkey breast
8 slices tomato
8 slices bacon, partially
cooked or ¼ pound
baked country ham,
thinly sliced
4 ozs. grated Parmesan
cheese
sprigs of parsley

Sauce: Melt butter in sauce pan. Blend in flour. Add milk, cheeses and seasonings, stirring constantly until smooth and thickened. Set aside.

Sandwiches: Cut toast into triangles. Arrange in baking dishes. Place turkey on the toast. Cover with hot cheese sauce. Top with tomato and bacon or ham. Sprinkle with Parmesan cheese. Bake at 400° until bubbly. Garnish with parsley. Makes 8 servings.

Brereton Jones, Governor (Kentucky)

Kneading the dough for a half minute after mixing improves the texture of baking power biscuits.

MIA'S HOT CHICKEN SANDWICH

16 slices firm white bread, buttered, crusts removed
2½ cups chicken, cooked
1 can or ½ pound mushrooms, cooked
3 eggs, hard boiled, sliced
3 tablespoons onions, minced, precooked
1 cup mayonnaise
   salt, pepper to taste
3 ozs. green stuffed or black olives

Topping:
1 can cream of chicken or mushroom soup
1 cup sour cream or substitute
   paprika
   parsley

Layer 8 slices bread on bottom of greased casserole. Mix above (7) ingredients and spread over bread. This mixture can be done the night before. Add second layer of bread slices on top. Spread topping over bread. Sprinkle paprika over top. Bake at 325° for 30 minutes. Sprinkle with parsley. Makes 8 servings.

Mrs. Charles Vanik, Wife of former Representative (Ohio)

> Do not use a wooden cutting board when handling uncooked chicken. The wood retains bacteria even after washing thoroughly.

HAM AND CHEESE SANDWICHES

1 Pillsbury crescent rolls
  Dijon prepared mustard
  poppy seeds
2 boiled ham slices
2 Swiss cheese slices
1 egg (optional)

Separate dough into 4 oblong pieces instead of the 8 triangles. Lightly spread each with mustard on one side. Heavily sprinkle with poppy seed—amount really depends on personal preference. Place a slice of ham and a slice of cheese on two pieces and cover with the other two. Gently press the edges together to seal. Place on an unbuttered cookie sheet. Brush tops with beaten egg if desired. Bake in 375° oven for 11–13 minutes until brown. Cut into serving pieces. One recipe will serve 2 as simple sandwiches, 3 or 4 in combination with soup or salad depending how you cut them. Makes 2 to 4 servings.

Donald Brotzman, former Representative (Colorado)

PEPPERONI BREAD

1 Pillsbury French bread
  (dairy case)
¼ pound sliced pepperoni
8 oz. grated mozzarella
  cheese
  Parmesan cheese

Unroll bread on cookie sheet. Sprinkle Parmesan cheese to cover bread. Place pepperoni slices on top of Parmesan cheese. Cover with mozzarella. Roll from long end. Bake at 350° for 25–30 minutes. Slice and serve. Makes 1 loaf.

Mrs. John Boehner, Wife of Representative (Ohio)

> *Hard cheeses can be frozen. Wrap airtight in small pkges.*
> *or grate and store in convenient serving amounts in freezer.*

VEGETABLE SANDWICH SPREAD

2 firm tomatoes
1 small onion
1 cup celery
1 bell pepper
1 cucumber
1 teaspoon salt
1 pint mayonnaise
1 envelope unflavored gelatin
¼ cup cold water
¼ cup boiling water

Chop all vegetables to fine texture and drain well on paper towels. Soften gelatin in cold water, then add boiling water and allow to cool to lukewarm. Fold mayonnaise and salt into gelatin, then add vegetables and mix thoroughly. Use as a spread for crackers or bread. May also be used to stuff tomatoes.

Faye Flippo

Mrs. Ronnie Flippo, Wife of former Representative (Alabama)

Old Amish Proverb: Eat it up, wear it out, make it do, or do without!

SPINACH QUICHE

1 10 oz. pkg. frozen
   chopped spinach
3 eggs
1 cup milk
½ teaspoon salt
   dash nutmeg
¼ teaspoon pepper
1 teaspoon instant minced
   onion
1 teaspoon instant minced
   garlic
½ teaspoon basil
1½ cups grated swiss cheese
   sauteed mushrooms, op-
   tional
2 strips fried bacon, optional
1 prepared pie crust,
   Pillsbury brand

Cook and drain spinach and set aside. Beat eggs, milk and spices. Stir in cheese, spinach and optional ingredients if desired. Pour into 9 inch baking pan lined with the pie crust. Crimp the edges and bake at 350° for 1 hour. Makes 4 to 6 servings.

Jane Sutermeister

Mrs. Richard Sutermeister, Daughter of former Representative Tom Kleppe (North Dakota)

SPINACH-CHEESE NO CRUST QUICHE

6 eggs
6 tablespoons flour
1 stick butter (or margarine), melted
½ pound sharp cheddar
2 pounds cottage cheese
2 pkgs. frozen chopped spinach
½ pound sliced fresh mushrooms

Beat eggs slightly gradually adding flour. Add melted butter and grated cheese. Next add cottage cheese and thawed and *well* drained spinach. Pour into 2 pie tins (9 inch), greased, or 9" by 13" casserole. Bake at 350° for 1 hour or until set. Makes 12 servings. May be frozen.

Dorothy W. Hungate

Mrs. William Hungate, Wife of former Representative (Missouri)

COTTAGE CHEESE SPINACH QUICHE

2 unbaked pie shells
4 tablespoons chopped onion
½ teaspoon nutmeg
½ teaspoon pepper
2 10-oz. pkgs. chopped spinach, thawed and drained
1 large carton (32 oz. low fat) cottage cheese
½ cup or more chopped ham
6 eggs mixed thoroughly with 1 teaspoon dry mustard
3 tablespoons parmesan cheese

Bake pastry shells for 8 minutes. Then combine all other ingredients and top with cheese. Bake at 350° about 50 minutes or until set. Makes 2 pies. May be frozen.

Mrs Fred Schwengel

Mrs. Fred Schwengel, Wife of former Representative (Iowa)

ZUCCHINI-CASHEW QUICHE

1 can (8 rolls) crescent-style
    refrigerator rolls
3/4 cup cashews
3 medium zucchini
3 tablespoons margarine
1/4 teaspoon garlic salt
1/4 teaspoon salt
1/8 teaspoon pepper
1/4 teaspoon dill weed
2 eggs
1 cup milk
4 ozs. Monterey Jack cheese

Preheat oven to 325°. Place dough in a 9 inch pie plate with points of triangles together in bottom. Seal seams to make a smooth pie shell. Sprinkle bottom of pie crust with cashews. Trim ends from zucchini and slice. Melt margarine in large skillet and saute zucchini slices until crisp-tender. Stir in garlic salt, salt, pepper, and dill weed. Spoon zucchini over cashews in pie crust. Combine eggs and milk well, pour over zucchini mixture. Sprinkle top with shredded cheese. Bake 45 minutes. Makes 6 servings.

Jean Grotberg

Mrs. John Grotberg, Wife of former Representative (Illinois)

BRIE QUICHE

1 9 inch pie crust
4 eggs, separated
1 pound brie cheese, broken
    into small pieces
1/8 teaspoon salt
1 1/2 cups light cream

Preheat oven to 375°. Line a 9 inch quiche pan with pastry. Bake 10 minutes. Cool and set aside. Beat egg yolks and cream, thoroughly blend in cheese and salt. Beat egg whites until stiff but not dry. Stir in 3 tablespoons of the egg whites and blend to lighten the mixture. Fold in the remaining whites. Pour into the cooled crust and bake at 375° for 30 minutes or until custard is set. Allow to cool slightly before cutting. Makes 6 servings.

Debbie Dingell

Mrs. John Dingell, Wife of Representative (Michigan)

GOVERNOR'S MANSION QUICHE LORRAINE

4 eggs
2 cups cream
³/₄ teaspoon salt
¹/₄ teaspoon sugar
¹/₈ teaspoon cayenne pepper
1 cup Swiss cheese, grated
6 slices bacon
¹/₃ cup onion, chopped

Combine eggs, cream, salt, sugar and cayenne pepper. Fry bacon crispy. Layer bacon, grated cheese and onion in bottom of pie shell. Pour in remaining egg mixture. Bake at 425° for 1 hour or until table knife comes out clean.

Pie Crust:
1³/₄ cups Wondra flour
1 teaspoon salt
³/₄ cup Crisco
ice water

Mix flour and salt. Cut in Crisco. Mix in enough ice water to make dough.

Bruce King, Governor (New Mexico)

CHRISTMAS BREAKFAST

7 slices white bread (regular, not thin sliced)
8 ozs. shredded cheddar cheese
6 eggs
3 cups milk
¹/₂ teaspoon salt
¹/₄ teaspoon pepper
1 teaspoon dry mustard
3 strips bacon, cut in half

You make it the day before, and it bakes while you open your gifts Christmas morning. Trim crusts from bread. Crumble bread. Mix bread and cheese and spread in bottom of greased 7¹/₂ inch × 12 inch flat baking dish. Beat eggs and milk together and stir in the salt, pepper, and mustard. Pour this over bread and cheese. Lay bacon on top. Refrigerate overnight. The next morning, bake, uncovered, at 350° for 50 to 55 minutes. Remove from oven just after guests sit down. Otherwise, it may tend to sink—tastes just as great, but doesn't look as pretty. Makes 6 servings.

Mrs. Jim Chapman, Wife of Representative (Texas)

WINE AND CHEESE OMELET CASSEROLE

1 large loaf french bread,
   torn up
6 tablespoons oleo, melted
¾ cup Swiss cheese,
   shredded
½ pound Monterey Jack
   cheese, shredded
12 slices hard salami or ham,
   chopped
16 eggs
3¼ cups milk
½ cup dry white wine
4 large green onions,
   chopped
1 tablespoon grey poupon
   mustard
¼ teaspoon ground pepper
⅛ teaspoon red pepper
2 cups sour cream (large carton and small carton)
   parmesan cheese

Butter two 9″ × 13″ baking dishes, spread bread on bottom, drizzle with oleo. Layer Swiss, Monterey Jack, and salami or ham. Beat together eggs, milk, wine, green onions, mustard, pepper, and red pepper until foamy. Pour over the cheese. Cover dish with foil and refrigerate overnight. Remove from refrigerator 30 minutes before baking. Bake casseroles at 325° for 45 minutes covered. Spread sour cream and parmesan cheese. Bake uncovered ten minutes. Great for brunch! Makes 24 servings.

Johnette Hand McCrery

Mrs. Jim McCrery, Wife of Representative (Louisiana)

Store cheese in a tightly covered container with sugar cubes to prevent mold.

MARTHA'S EGG CASSEROLE

10 eggs, lightly beaten
½ cup flour
1 teaspoon baking powder
½ teaspoon salt
½ cup melted butter
1 pound grated cheddar
   cheese
1 pint cottage cheese
1 8 oz. can chopped green
   chilies, drained

Stir together all ingredients and bake 5 minutes at 400°, then 40 minutes at 350°. Serve when top is golden brown. This can be prepared the night before and kept refrigerated until you put it in the oven for a morning breakfast or brunch. Also great for Christmas morning. Makes 12 servings.

Suzie Brewster

Mrs. Bill Brewster, Wife of Representative (Oklahoma)

BREAKFAST CASSEROLE

8 slices of bacon
½ cup crushed corn flakes
5 eggs
2½ cups frozen hash browns
1½ cups shredded Swiss
   cheese
⅓ cup milk
½ cup cottage cheese
1 sliced green onion
1 teaspoon salt
⅛ teaspoon pepper
4 drops of Tabasco

Cook 8 slices of bacon, crumble and set aside, reserving 1 tablespoon drippings. Mix both crumbled bacon and drippings with crushed corn flakes. Set aside. Mix together eggs, beaten until foamy, frozen hash browns, shredded Swiss cheese, milk, cottage cheese, sliced green onion, salt, pepper and Tabasco. Pour mixture into pie plate. Sprinkle with bacon and crumb mixture. Cover and refrigerate overnight. Uncover and bake at 325° for 50 minutes (or until firm in the center). Makes 6 servings. May be frozen.

Lynne Linder

Mrs. John Linder, Wife of Representative (Georgia)

Egg whites have more volume if they are at room temperature when beating for soufflés.

BRUNCH CASSEROLE

16 slices white bread (sour dough), crust removed
8 slices cheese
5 slices bacon, cut up (or ham)
¼ cup green pepper, chopped
2 teaspoons Worcestershire sauce
¼ pound butter or margarine
6 eggs
½ teaspoon salt
1 teaspoon dry mustard
dash pepper
3 cups milk

Place 8 slices bread in 9″ × 13″ greased baking dish. Place on each slice the bacon or ham and cheese. Sprinkle green pepper over all. Place 8 slices of bread over this. Mix eggs and beat into rest of ingredients, except butter. Pour over bread and refrigerate overnight. Melt butter and drizzle over top. Bake at 350° for 1 hour. Makes 8 servings. May be frozen.

Mrs. John Rhodes, Wife of former Representative (Arizona)

BREAKFAST SAUSAGE AND EGG CASSEROLE

10 slices bread, white or whole wheat
margarine
2 to 3 cups grated cheddar cheese
4 eggs
3 cups milk
1 pound ground sausage
salt/pepper
parsley
paprika
tomato (optional)

Remove crusts of bread, spread 1 side of bread with margarine. Cut bread into strips. Place strips margarine side down in Pam-coated casserole dish. Layer the cheese and sausage on top of bread. Combine milk, eggs and spices by beating together. Pour over layered casserole. Allow to sit overnight or up to 2 days. Bake at 350–375° for 45 minutes. Cool ten minutes and serve with fruit as a compliment. Option: slice tomato, arrange on top of casserole just before cooking. Makes 6 servings.

Mrs. Stan Parris, Wife of former Representative (Virginia)

BREAKFAST CASSEROLE

1½ to 2 pounds sausage, browned and drained
3 to 4 slices bread, cubed
1 cup or more cheddar cheese, grated
4 beaten eggs
¼ teaspoon dry mustard
1 teaspoon salt
2 cups milk

Butter a 2½ or 3 quart casserole. Put in layer of cubed bread. Layer sausage then cheddar cheese. Mix the remaining ingredients and pour over the top. Refrigerate overnight. Bake 1 hour at 325°. May be frozen and reheated.

Mrs. Hal Daub, Wife of former Representative (Nebraska)

JOAN'S ELEGANT EGGS

1 pound hot bulk sausage
1 pound regular bulk sausage
1 pkg. seasoned croutons for stuffing
4 eggs
2½ cups milk
1 can cream of mushroom soup
1 4 oz. can sliced mushrooms
¾ teaspoon dried mustard
1 cup grated cheddar cheese

Brown the two kinds of sausage, drain thoroughly and set aside. Lightly grease a large casserole dish. Pour croutons into dish with crumbled sausage on top. Beat together the eggs, milk, mushroom soup, mushrooms, and dried mustard. Pour this on top of the croutons and sausage and refrigerate overnight. Allow dish to reach room temperature before baking in 325° oven for 50 to 55 minutes uncovered. Sprinkle with cheese and return to oven until melted. This can be spiced up with passed picante sauce or fresh salsa. Makes 8 to 10 servings. May be frozen.

Mrs. John Bryant, Wife of Representative (Texas)

DODE'S SAUSAGE STRATA

6 slices enriched bread
1 pound bulk turkey sausage
1 teaspoon prepared mustard
1 cup (¼ pound) shredded
    Swiss or cheddar cheese
3 eggs, beaten slightly
1¼ cups milk
¾ cup light cream
½ teaspoon salt
    dash pepper and nutmeg
1 teaspoon Worcestershire
    sauce
    parsley

Trim crusts from bread. Fit bread in bottom of 6 individual casseroles, greased, or in a 10″ × 6″ × 1½dp dish. Brown sausage. Drain. Stir in mustard. Spoon sausage evenly over bread. Sprinkle with cheese. Combine remaining ingredients and pour over cheese. Bake in moderate oven (350°) for 25 to 30 minutes or until puffed and set. Trim with fluffs of parsley. Serve immediately. Makes 6 servings.

Mrs. Clarence Brown, Wife of former Representative (Ohio)

GREEN CORN TAMALE CASSEROLE

1 16 oz. can cream-style corn
1 4 oz. can chopped green
    chilies
½ cup grated cheddar cheese
⅔ cup yellow cornmeal
¾ cup milk
2 eggs
2 tablespoons vegetable oil

In a 2 quart glass, measure combine corn, green chilies, cheese, cornmeal, milk, eggs and oil. Pour into a 1½ to 2 quart casserole. Bake at 350° for one hour or until center is set. Microwave preparation: Cook on high, uncovered, for 20 to 22 minutes or until set. Makes 6 servings. May be frozen.

Mrs. Thomas Camarda, Daughter of former Representative James Mann (South Carolina)

ENCHILADAS RANCHERAS

¼ pound cheddar cheese,
   finely grated
1 pound Monterey Jack
   cheese, finely grated
2 green onions, finely
   chopped
⅓ cup butter, softened
   oil
12 corn tortillas
   Ranchera sauce
1 cup jack cheese, grated

Garnish:
   sour cream
   guacamole
   chopped green onion
   sliced olives
   cilantro sprigs

Ranchera Sauce:
¼ cup oil
½ cup chopped onion
2 stalks celery, chopped
1 green pepper, chopped
¼ cup flour
½ teaspoon dried marjoram
½ teaspoon salt
¾ teaspoon pepper
1½ teaspoons garlic powder
½ teaspoon dried oregano
2 cups water
3 teaspoons chicken stock
   base
2 cups finely chopped fresh
   tomatoes (peeled)

Mix grated cheeses and onions with the softened butter until well blended. Divide mixture into four (4) equal portions. Then form each portion into 3 sticks the length of one tortilla. Makes 12 sticks in all. Heat ¼ inch oil in heavy skillet. Soften tortillas (use tongs) one at a time for a few seconds on each side. Drain on paper towels. Place a cheese stick on each tortilla and roll up. Place seam side down in 9″ × 13″ baking pan. Cover with Ranchera sauce, and top with the 1 cup grated jack cheese. Bake at 450° 15 to 20 minutes until nicely browned. Makes 6 servings.

Method for sauce: Heat oil in heavy skillet. Cook onion, celery and green pepper until soft and onions are transparent. Combine flour and seasonings in bowl. Slowly add water, mix until smooth. Pour flour mixture into vegetables. Add chicken base and tomatoes. Cook over medium heat, stirring, until mixture boils and thickens. Reduce heat. Simmer one hour.

Nini Horn

Mrs. Steve Horn, Wife of Representative (California)

EGGS A LA BILL

2 eggs
2 tablespoons milk
  salt to taste
  pepper to taste
2 tablespoons orange juice
1 tablespoon butter or
  margarine

In a medium bowl, add all of the ingredients and mix well. Heat a skillet, melt the butter and pour in the eggs. With a fork, scramble the eggs until well cooked. When eggs are done, serve with two pieces of toast and some sausages or bacon. Makes 1 serving.

Bill Weld

Bill Weld, Governor (Massachusetts)

FANCY EGG SCRAMBLE

1 cup diced Canadian bacon
  (4 oz.)
¼ cup chopped scallions
3 tablespoons butter
12 beaten eggs
¼ pound mushrooms, sliced
2 tablespoons butter
2 tablespoons flour
2 cups warm milk
1 cup cheddar cheese
  salt and pepper
4 tablespoons butter
2 cups soft bread crumbs
⅛ teaspoon paprika

Saute first 3 ingredients until scallions are limp. Add eggs and scramble until just set. (Will be underdone). Make up sauce by blending 2 tablespoons of butter and flour. Add milk, cheese, salt and pepper and stir until thickened and bubbly. Fold sauce into eggs and add mushrooms. Put into 13″ × 9″ baking dish. Sprinkle crumbs and drizzle butter and paprika on top. May be refrigerated or frozen at this point. Bake at 350° for 30 minutes. Makes 8 servings.

Deborah Knapp Bonilla

Mrs. Henry Bonilla, Wife of Representative (Texas)

> *While cooking hard boiled eggs stir the water and it will help keep the yolks centered.*

HELENE'S CHEESE SOUFFLE

White Sauce:
- ¼ cup butter
- ¼ cup flour
- 1 cup milk

- 1 teaspoon salt
- ¼ teaspoon dry mustard
- ¼ teaspoon paprika
- ½ pound sharp american cheese, grated
- 5 eggs, separated

In double boiler, melt butter; gradually stir in flour; add milk slowly until thick. Add salt, dry mustard and paprika. Add cheese and keep warm. Beat egg yolks hard and add to sauce. Fold in stiffly beaten egg whites. Pour into buttered 3 quart casserole. Bake in 300° oven for 1 hour. Serve immediately. Makes 4 servings.

Annie Rhodes

Mrs. Jay Rhodes, Wife of former Representative (Arizona)

FINNISH PANCAKES

- 4 tablespoons butter
- 4 eggs
- 1 cup milk
- ½ cup flour
- 1 teaspoon salt
- 2 tablespoons sugar

Melt butter in a ten inch shallow square pan (in the oven while it is preheating). With a hand mixer, beat remaining ingredients well. Pour into pan (with melted butter). Bake at 400° for 25 to 30 minutes. Serve immediately with maple syrup and sliced strawberries, if desired. Makes 2 to 4 servings.

Debra Andrews

Mrs. Thomas Andrews, Wife of Representative (Maine)

Before grating cheese add a little oil on the grater and it will be easier to wash.

GARLIC CHEESE GRITS

1 cup quick grits
1 Kraft garlic cheese roll
2 sticks butter or margarine
2 eggs
½ cup milk

Cook grits in 4 cups boiling salted water. Cook until very dry. Melt cheese roll and butter and stir into cooked grits. Beat 2 eggs with milk and stir into grits. Put into casserole and bake at 350° for 45 minutes. Makes 8 servings.

Emilie C. Shaw

Mrs. E. Clay Shaw, Wife of Representative (Florida)

LOT'S CHEESE FONDUE

½ pound Swiss cheese
½ pound Gruyere cheese
3 tablespoons flour
  pinch salt
2 cups dry white wine
1 garlic clove
1 oz. Kirsch cut into cubes
  French bread

Microwave directions: Rub ceramic fondue dish with garlic clove—discard. Shred cheese and mix with flour and salt. Heat wine in two quart ceramic dish 2 minutes on high (10). Gradually stir in ½ cheese until smooth; cook medium (8) 2 to 3 minutes. Stir once. Add remaining cheese, stir until smooth. Cook medium (8) 2 to 3 minutes or until cheese is smooth. Add Kirsch. Put on fondue burner. Serve with bread cubes for dipping. Delicious! Makes 4 servings.

Nancy Beall

Mrs. J. Glenn Beall Jr., Wife of former Senator (Maryland)

A warm knife makes cheese easier to slice.

CHUTNEY CHEESE SPREAD

2 3 oz. pkgs. cream cheese,
  softened
4 ozs. sharp natural cheddar
  cheese, shredded (1
  cup)
4 teaspoons dry sherry
1/2 teaspoon curry powder
1/4 teaspoon salt
1/2 cup finely chopped
  chutney
1 tablespoon finely snipped
  chives or green onion
  tops

Blend thoroughly cheese, sherry and seasonings. Spread on flat serving platter, shaping a layer 1/2 inch thick. Chill until firm. To serve; spread chutney over top; sprinkle with chives; surround with crackers of choice.

Susan Dougher

Mrs. Jon Dougher, Daughter of Representative Gerald Solomon (New York)

STORE DAIRY PRODUCTS RIGHT! In refrigerator, store eggs in their own carton. To freeze, eggs must be removed from their shell first. For whole eggs, stir in 2 tablespoon sugar or 1 teaspoon salt for each pint of lightly beaten eggs. Pack in freezer containers, leaving half an inch of headspace. Label and date. Refrigerate cheese in its original wrapping, if possible; or cover cut surface tightly with plastic wrap or foil. To freeze cheese, wrap in moisture/vapor-proof wrap or store in the original wrap with a foil overlap. Do not freeze in amounts larger than 1 pound.

NOTES

NOTES

NOTES

Claudia Taylor (Lady Bird) Johnson
1963–1969

With memories and fond best wishes to my friends of the Congressional Club,

Lady Bird Johnson

Claudia Taylor (Lady Bird) Johnson

Lady Bird Johnson brought twenty-seven years of national government experience with her when she became First Lady. Her easy Southern charm and Texas hospitality soon made its mark on the White House.

Her true impact was found, however, in two divergent yet important causes— the beautification of America and the war on poverty. Beginning with the formation of the First Lady's Committee for a More Beautiful Capital, the first program was soon taken nationwide, increasing the public's awareness of the need to clean up litter and remove eyesores from the highways of America. In support of her husband's vision for "The Great Society," Mrs. Johnson became one of the primary advocates of the Head Start project for preschool children.

Navy-Marine Memorial in Lady Bird Johnson Park, Columbia Island, 1993

SALADS, SALAD DRESSINGS
AND
RELISHES

SWEET AND SOUR SLAW

3 pounds cabbage, grated
1 onion, chopped
1 green pepper, chopped
1 carrot, grated
1 cup sugar
¾ cup oil
¾ cup vinegar
1½ teaspoons salt
1 teaspoon celery seed
1 teaspoon dry mustard

Combine cabbage, onion and green pepper. Pour sugar over vegetables.

In saucepan, combine oil, vinegar, salt, celery seed and mustard; heat to boiling. Pour over slaw and stir. Refrigerate overnight.

Bill Clinton, President of the United States

STRAWBERRY SALAD

1 pint fresh strawberries,
  sliced
1 pound fresh spinach leaves
1 head Boston lettuce
½ cup pecan halves
  (browned in butter)

One day ahead, prepare the following:
⅓ cup raspberry wine vinegar
1 teaspoon salt
½ cup sugar
½ teaspoon dry mustard
1½ tablespoons minced fresh
  onion
¾ cup vegetable or olive oil
1½ teaspoons poppy seeds (optional)

Blend the first 5 ingredients in blender for 1 minute. While blender is still going, add oil slowly. Pour in poppy seeds. Put over other salad ingredients just before serving.

Lynn C. Hefley

Mrs. Joel Hefley, Wife of Representative (Colorado)

GINGER PEAR SALAD

Salad:
2 ripe pears peeled, cored
  and sliced
1 cup seedless grapes
1 head Boston lettuce, torn
  into bite-size pieces

Dressing:
6 tablespoons oil
2 tablespoons lime juice
1 teaspoon sugar
¼ cup crystallized ginger,
  chopped
  salt and pepper, to taste

In a bowl, put pears, grapes and lettuce. Mix ingredients of dressing. Add dressing to fruit and toss. Note: canned pears may be used. Makes 4 to 6 servings.

Pam Napier

Mrs. John Napier, Wife of former Representative (South Carolina)

CALIFORNIA AVOCADO SALAD

5 6 inch corn tortillas
4 oranges
4 grapefruit
1 tablespoon sugar
1 tablespoon raspberry
     vinegar
1 whole, soft, California av-
     ocado

Slice corn tortillas into thin strips. Bake the tortilla strips in a preheated oven set at 225°F for 10–15 minutes. Set aside. Grate the oranges to obtain 3 teaspoons rind. Peel oranges and grapefruit and seed. Section oranges and grapefruit. In large bowl, mix sugar, vinegar, orange and grapefruit sections. Add tortilla strips and orange rind. Toss. Top with avocado slices and chill for 15 minutes. Makes 6 servings.

Mrs. Norman Mineta, Wife of Representative (California)

MANDARIN ORANGE SALAD

Sauce:
½ cup vegetable oil
¼ cup tarragon wine vinegar
¼ cup sugar
½ teaspoon salt
¼ teaspoon pepper
½ teaspoon hot sauce

Mix together in large salad bowl:
1 head leaf lettuce
1 cup chopped celery
6 green onions, chopped
3 tablespoons fresh parsley
2 11 oz. cans mandarin or-
     anges, drained
½ cup slivered almonds,
     toasted

Shake and chill sauce. Pour over salad immediately before serving. Makes 6 to 8 servings.

Mrs. Kathleen Waters, Daughter of former Representative John R. Foley (Maryland)

GRAN'S APPLE ONION SALAD

1 medium head of lettuce
1 medium onion
2 medium MacIntosh apples
¼ cup salad oil
3 tablespoons lemon juice
1 tablespoon sugar
1 teaspoon of salt
½ teaspoon garlic powder
½ teaspoon dry mustard

15 minutes before serving: In salad bowl, break lettuce into large pieces, cut onion into paper thin slices, core apples, slice into thin rings. Cut rings of both the onions and apples in half, add to lettuce. In large (2 cup) measuring cup, add: salad oil, lemon juice, salt, sugar, garlic and mustard. Combine with lettuce and toss together. Makes 6 servings.

Donna Murtha, Daughter of Representative John P. Murtha (Pennsylvania)

FRUIT CASSEROLE

1½ cans sliced peaches
1½ cans pear halves
2½ cans sliced pineapple
     tidbits
     raisins
1 jar red cherries
     red grapes
1 jar Motts apple sauce

Drain fruit well overnight. Mix in apple sauce. Sprinkle cinnamon on top. Bake at 350° for 45 minutes. Makes 12 servings.

Mrs. William Soderberg, Daughter of former Representative Robert A. Grant (Indiana)

Do not use an aluminum sauce pan to make a white sauce. It tends to absorb the grayish color from the pan.

PINEAPPLE BAKE

¾ cup butter or margarine
¾ cup sugar
¾ cup brown sugar
2 eggs
1 20 oz. can pineapple
   chunks and juice
½ cup half & half (or milk)
   pinch of salt
4 cups cubed French bread

Cream butter and sugar. Add eggs and beat, add pineapple, half & half, salt, and bread cubes. Mix well. Bake 1 hour in 350° oven. Wonderful side dish with ham or pork. Makes 8 to 10 servings.

Doris Sangmeister

Mrs. George Sangmeister, Wife of Representative (Illinois)

PINEAPPLE SALAD

1 large can (20 ozs.) chunk
   pineapple (reserve juice)
1 egg
2 tablespoons flour
½ cup sugar
½ pound cream cheese, cut
   in cubes
1 dozen large marshmallows
1 cup sharp cheese, grated

Put pineapple juice in top of double boiler. Beat in egg, sugar, and flour. Cook until thickened. Layer the pineapple, cream cheese, marshmallows and pour cooked mixture over it. Top with grated cheese. Cook 10 minutes in a 450° oven until bubbly. Serve hot. Makes 8 servings.

Luella Rowland

Mrs. J. Roy Rowland, Wife of Representative (Georgia)

BAHAMIAN ORANGE AND ONION SALAD

3 sweet oranges
2 medium onions, (yellow or white) thinly sliced
2 teaspoons marjoram
  juice of 1 lime
3 tablespoons vegetable or olive oil
  salt and pepper to taste

Squeeze juice from 1 orange. Set aside. Peel the other oranges, removing all the white, and slice. Mix oranges, onions, and marjoram. Combine orange juice, lime juice, oil, salt, and pepper. Pour over salad. May be served on a bed of lettuce on salad plates. Makes 6 servings.

Susan Goldwater Keenan, Member of The Congressional Club

ESCALLOPED PINEAPPLE

4 cups soft bread crumbs
1 cup milk
3 beaten eggs
2 cups sugar
¾ cup butter or oleo
1 can (no. 2) chunk pineapple, drained, but saved

Soften bread with the milk. Juice from the pineapple may be used, adding milk to make a cup. Combine remaining ingredients. Bake in deep casserole for 30 to 40 minutes in 350°. Makes 8 servings.

Carol Ann Myers, Daughter of Representative John T. Myers (Indiana)

FROZEN CHERRY SALAD

1   8 oz. pkg. cream cheese,
      softened
1   8 oz. carton sour cream
¼   cup sugar
¼   teaspoon salt
2   cups miniature marsh-
      mallows
½   cup chopped nuts (pecans
      or walnuts)
1   16 oz. can pitted bing cher-
      ries, drained
1   8 oz. can crushed pineap-
      ple, drained
1   11 oz. mandarin oranges,
      drained

Beat cream cheese until smooth, add sour cream, sugar and salt. Mix well. Fold in marshmallows and nuts. Add fruit. Spoon mixture into an 8½″ × 4½″ × 3″ container and freeze at least six hours or until firm. (I freeze it overnight). Let stand five minutes at room temperature before serving. Makes 12 servings. May be frozen.

Mrs. Jamie L. Whitten, Wife of Representative (Mississippi)

PATRIOTIC SALAD

2   pkgs. raspberry Jell-O
3   cups hot water
1   pkg. unflavored gelatin
½   cup cold water
1   cup cream
½   cup sugar
1   pkg. (8 oz.) cream cheese
½   cup chopped nuts
1   teaspoon vanilla
1   #3 can blueberries, un-
      drained

Dissolve one package, raspberry gelatin in 2 cups hot water. Chill until set. Soften unflavored gelatin in cold water. Heat cream, sugar, and cream cheese, and add to softened gelatin mixture. Stir until all ingredients are dissolved. Cool. Add nuts and vanilla, pour over gelatin mix. Chill until set. Dissolve remaining raspberry gelatin in 1 cup hot water. Add blueberries. Pour over cream layer. Chill until set. Use a 9″ × 13″ glass dish. Makes 12 to 15 servings.

Bill Barrett, Representative (Nebraska)

BUTTERMILK SALAD

1 15¼ oz. can crushed
    pineapple
1 6 oz. pkg. orange flavored
    gelatin (may substitute
    any flavor)
2 cups buttermilk
1 12 oz. carton Cool Whip
½ cup pecans, chopped

Heat pineapple and add gelatin. Stir until dissolved. Let cool and add buttermilk, Cool Whip, and nuts. Mix well and pour into salad mold and chill. May use 13″ × 8″ × 2″ inch pan. Makes 6 to 8 servings. May be frozen.

Mrs. Terry Everett, Wife of Representative (Alabama)

WILMA'S FROZEN CHERRY SALAD LOAF

16 oz. can dark sweet pitted
    cherries
 8 oz. can crushed pineapple
11 oz. can mandarin oranges
 8 oz. pkg. cream cheese
 1 cup dairy sour cream
¼ cup sugar
¼ teaspoon salt
 2 cups miniature
    marshmallows
½ cup chopped pecans

Drain fruits; reserve a few cherries and orange segments for garnish. Let cream cheese stand at room temperature to soften. Beat until fluffy and blend in sour cream, sugar, and salt. Fold in fruits, marshmallows and pecans. Pour into 8½″ × 4½″ loaf pan and freeze overnight. Unmold and slice, and serve on lettuce leaves. Makes 12 servings. May be frozen.

Mrs. Jim Chapman, Wife of Representative (Texas)

If you wet the dish on which the gelatin is to be unmolded, it can be moved around until centered.

JEN'S AWESOME JELLO SALAD

2 pkg. strawberry Jell-O (3 oz.)
2 cups boiling water
1 pkg. frozen strawberries or 1 pint fresh, chopped
2½ cups crushed pineapple (drained)
3 mashed bananas
1 pint sour cream (or light variety)

Combine Jell-O and boiling water to dissolve. Add berries, pineapple and bananas. Pour half of Jell-O mixture in glass casserole (10″ × 10″ works well). Refrigerate. When jelled, spread with sour cream. Pour remaining liquid Jell-O mixture over the sour cream. Chill thoroughly. Cut into squares to serve. A very special "side dish". A Christmas dinner "must" for our family. Makes 8 servings.

Mary Jo Smith

Mrs. Robert C. Smith, Wife of Senator (New Hampshire)

MAMMY'S PEACHES AND CREAM SALAD

Cream Layer:
3 oz. pkg. lemon Jell-O
1 cup boiling water
1 cup orange juice
1 pkg. (2⅛ oz.) whipped topping mix
3 ozs. cream cheese
¼ cup chopped pecans

Peach Layer:
3 oz. pkgs. lemon Jell-O
1 cup boiling water
1 lb. 5 oz. can peach pie filling

Cream layer: Dissolve package of Jell-O in cup of boiling water. Add orange juice. Refrigerate until slightly thickened. Prepare topping mix according to directions. Blend in cream cheese. Add pecans. Fold into gelatin mixture. Pour into 9″ × 9″ × 2″ pan. Chill until firm.

Peach layer: Dissolve package of Jell-O in boiling water. Stir in peach pie filling. Pour over top of cream layer. Chill until firm. Cut into 9 or 12 portions. Serve on crisp greens. Makes 9 or 12 servings.

Claire Schweiker

Mrs. Richard S. Schweiker, Wife of former Senator (Pennsylvania)

FRUIT SALAD

1 large can pineapple chunks
1 can mandarin oranges
1 small pkg. tapioca pudding mix (not instant)
1 small pkg. lemon pudding mix (not instant)
1 small pkg. lemon, strawberry or orange Jell-O
1 cup miniature marshmallows
9 ozs. Cool Whip
bananas, as desired
strawberries, as desired

Drain pineapple and oranges, reserving liquid. Add water to fruit juice to make 1⅔ cups liquid. In large saucepan cook together until very thick, the liquid, puddings and Jell-O. Let this cool completely. When cool, add Cool Whip, marshmallows, pineapple, oranges, bananas and strawberries. Mix well. Makes 12 servings.

Sharon S Vander Schel

Mrs. Kevin VanderSchel, Daughter of Representative Neal Smith (Iowa)

LIME MOLD SALAD

2 pkgs. lime Jell-O
1 cup boiling water
1 20 oz. can crushed pineapple
½ cup finely chopped maraschino cherries (red, green and black)
½ cup chopped black walnuts
1 pint dairy sour cream

Dissolve Jell-O in hot water. Cool and add fruit and nuts. Fold in sour cream last. Put in mold and chill several hours before serving. Makes 8 servings.

Marilyn Burnside Weaver

Mrs. George Arthur Weaver, Daughter of former Representative M. G. Burnside (West Virginia)

SOUTHERN STRAWBERRY SALAD

2 cups crushed pretzels (not too fine)
¾ cup melted margarine
3 tablespoons sugar
1 8 oz. pkg. cream cheese softened
1 cup sugar
1 9 oz. Cool Whip
2 3 oz. pkgs. strawberry Jell-O
2 cups boiling water
2 10 oz. pkgs. frozen strawberries

First layer: Mix pretzels, margarine and 3 tablespoons sugar. Spread in 10″ × 13″ pan. Bake 8 to 10 minutes at 400°. (Don't get too brown!)

Second layer: Blend cream cheese and 1 cup sugar. Then fold in the Cool Whip. Spread on cooled crust.

Third layer: Dissolve Jell-O in boiling water. Stir in frozen strawberries. Refrigerate until partially congealed (consistency of blended cake mix). Pour over second layer. Refrigerate. Don't make more than one day ahead because pretzels will get soggy. Serve on bed of lettuce, if you like. Makes 12 servings.

Mary Morgan Reeves

Mrs. Eric Reeves, Daughter of former Senator Robert B. Morgan (North Carolina)

LEMON APPLE MOLD

2 pkg. lemon Jell-O
½ cup apples, sliced
½ cup walnuts, chopped
1 pkg. 3 oz. cream cheese
⅓ can Eagle brand milk
lemon juice to taste
vanilla to taste

Make lemon Jell-O according to package directions and place in 8″ × 8″ pan and allow to partially set. Place apple slices and walnuts on the Jell-O and top with another layer of Jell-O. Allow to set. Cream the cream cheese, Eagle brand milk together and season with lemon juice and vanilla. Spread this mixture over the top. You may add more apples and nuts if you desire. This is easily doubled for a larger pan.

Louise R. Brotzman

Mrs. Donald Brotzman, Wife of former Representative (Colorado)

BLUEBERRY SALAD

2 pkgs. black berry Jell-O
1 cup hot water
1 large can crushed pine-
   apple
1 can blueberries
1 8 oz. cream cheese (room
   temperature)
1 8 oz. sour cream
⅓ cup sugar
1 cup chopped pecans

Dissolve Jell-O, then add pineapple and blueberries (juice and all). Pour into 9″ × 13″ dish and let gel until firm. Mix cream cheese, sour cream and sugar with mixer. Pour on top of very firm Jell-O mixture, then sprinkle with chopped pecans. Makes 20 servings. May be frozen.

Barbara Harris

Mrs. Claude Harris, Wife of former Representative (Alabama)

LEMON CREME SALAD

1 3 oz. pkg. lemon gelatin
1½ cups boiling water
1 7 oz. jar marshmallow
   creme
1 cup heavy cream, whipped

Dissolve gelatin in water; cool. Gradually add gelatin to marshmallow creme, mix until well blended. Chill until thickened, whip until light and fluffy. Fold in whipped cream. Pour into 1 quart dessert dish. Chill until firm. Garnish with lemon slices and mint, if desired. Makes 4 to 6 servings.

Nancy Lightfoot

Mrs. Jim Lightfoot, Wife of Representative (Iowa)

> *If hollandaise curdles, gradually beat one well-beaten egg yolk into the mixture.*

ST. NICKS SALAD

2 3 oz. pkgs. red raspberry
     gelatin
2 cups hot water (boiling)
2 pkgs. frozen red raspber-
     ries (partially defrosted)
1 cup whipping cream
12 large marshmallows (or
     equiv. marshmallow
     cream)
2 3 oz. pkgs. cream cheese

Dissolve gelatin in boiling water, add raspberries and juice. Pour into 8″ Jell-O mold and chill. Combine marshmallows and cream cheese, add whipped cream and beat together. Spread over Jell-O mixture and chill thoroughly. Makes 10 servings.

Mikey Bilbray

Mrs. Jim Bilbray, Wife of Representative (Nevada)

CHEESE-PEAR SALAD

2 oz. blue cheese
1 tablespoon chopped
     toasted almonds
6 large pear halves, chilled
6 crisp lettuce leaves
2 tablespoon Italian dressing
6 tablespoon sour cream
     Paprika

Cream the cheese in a small bowl with a wooden spoon until smooth. Stir in the almonds. Fill each center of the pear halves with the cheese-almond mixture. Toss the lettuce leaves with dressing, coating them lightly. Arrange leaves on individual salad plates. Arrange the pears on the lettuce and top each pear with 1 tablespoon sour cream. Then sprinkle with paprika. Serves 6.

The Congressional Club

THREE-LAYER CHRISTMAS SALAD

Green Layer:

1	3 oz. pkg. lime gelatin
1	cup boiling water
1	cup cold water
½	cup frozen melon balls, thawed and drained
1	3 oz. pkg. cream cheese
½	cup chopped nuts

White Layer:

1	8 oz. can crushed pineapple
1	envelope unflavored gelatin
¼	cup granulated sugar
1½	cups canned or dairy eggnog

Red Layer:

1	3 oz. pkg. raspberry gelatin
1	cup boiling water
1	10 oz. pkg. frozen raspberries, thawed

Green Layer: Dissolve gelatin in boiling water. Add cold water. Pour into 6 cup mold. Chill until slightly thickened. Meanwhile, pat dry melon balls and chop coarsely. Fold into cream cheese. Spread nuts on waxed paper and drop teaspoonfuls of cream cheese mixture onto nuts. Roll and shape into balls. Chill in refrigerator while gelatin congeals. Carefully place balls in gelatin, positioning evenly in mold. Let chill until very thick, but not completely set.

White Layer: Drain pineapple, reserving syrup. Soften gelatin in syrup and heat until dissolved. Add sugar, stirring to dissolve. Combine with eggnog and drained pineapple and chill until slightly thickened. Pour over lime gelatin in mold and chill until thickened but not fully set.

Red Layer: Dissolve gelatin in boiling water. Stir in raspberries. Chill until slightly thickened. Pour over white layer in mold. Chill until completely set. To serve, unmold onto plate. Garnish with frozen melon balls, if desired. Makes 10 to 12 servings.

Mrs. Chalmers Wylie, Wife of former Representative (Ohio)

Perk up soggy lettuce by adding lemon juice to a bowl of cold water and soak for an hour in the refrigerator.

CONGEALED SALAD OR DESSERT

2 small boxes of orange
    gelatin
2 cups boiling water
1 10 oz. can crushed pineap-
    ple in juice
1 10 oz. can mandarin or-
    anges, drained and
    crushed
1 pint vanilla ice cream
1 cup sour cream
1 cup pecans

Dissolve gelatin in boiling water, cool slightly. Add crushed pineapple, drained mandarin oranges crushed, ice cream, sour cream, and pecans. Mix well and pour into casserole dish and refrigerate until firm. Sprinkle with additional pecans. Could be served as a dessert, just add whipped cream.

Mrs. Larkin Smith, Wife of former Representative (Mississippi)

MANDARIN ORANGE SALAD

1 12 oz. can apricot nectar
2 small pkgs. orange Jell-O
1 small can frozen orange
    juice (6 oz.)
1 small can mandarin or-
    anges (11 oz.), drained
1 8 oz. can crushed pine-
    apple

Heat apricot nectar to boiling and pour over Jell-O. Add orange juice. Stir until dissolved. Add oranges and pineapple. Refrigerate until set. This salad is a beautiful orange color and goes well with many menus. Makes 12 servings.

Mrs. Laurie C. Battle, Wife of former Representative (Alabama)

GRETTA'S KEY LIME MOLD SALAD

2 pkgs. lime Jell-O
1 cup boiling water
1 20 oz. can crushed pine-
    apple
½ cup finely chopped mara-
    schino cherries (green,
    red and black)
½ cup chopped black
    walnuts
1 pint dairy sour cream

Dissolve Jell-O in hot water. Cool and add fruit and nuts. Fold in sour cream last. Put in mold or bowl and chill thoroughly. May be topped with whipped cream and nuts. Makes 8 servings.

Cynthia Mitchell-Gingles

Mrs. Cynthia Mitchell-Gingles, Daughter of former Representative Donald J. Mitchell (New York)

EASY TOMATO ASPIC

1 envelope unflavored gelatin
2 cups tomato juice
½ teaspoon salt
    few drops bottled hot pep-
    per sauce
1 tablespoon grated onion
1 tablespoon lemon juice
1 tablespoon sugar

Soften gelatin in ½ cup cold tomato juice. Combine remaining 1½ cups tomato juice with salt, pepper sauce and onion. Bring to boiling point, add lemon juice and sugar. Add to gelatin. Stir until gelatin dissolves. Pour into individual molds. Chill.

Nancy Fountain Black

Mrs. William Black, Jr., Daughter of former Representative L. H. Fountain (North Carolina)

ANNIVERSARY HORSERADISH SALAD

1 box of lemon Jell-O (3 oz.)
1 box of lime Jell-O (3 oz.)
2 cups of boiling water
1 cup of real mayonnaise
1 can (#2) crushed pineapple, undrained
1 cup cottage cheese (large curd)
3 tablespoons cream style horseradish
2 tablespoons chopped pimento

Mix the 2 boxes of Jell-O together with the boiling water and dissolve. Add all the other ingredients and mix thoroughly. Pour in a large casserole and refrigerate. Serves 12. This is a wonderful dish with baked ham. Makes 12 servings.

Mrs. Glenn English, Wife of Representative (Oklahoma)

SEVEN-UP SALAD

2 3 oz. pkgs. lemon Jell-O
2 cups boiling water
2 cups cold 7-Up
1 20 oz. can crushed pineapple
2 large bananas
2 cups miniature marshmallows

Topping:
2 tablespoons butter
2 tablespoons flour
1/2 cup sugar
  pineapple juice and water to make 1 cup
1 egg
2 cups Cool Whip

Dissolve Jell-O in boiling water. Add 2 cups cold 7-Up and chill until slightly set. Drain juice from crushed pineapple and set aside for topping. Add crushed pineapple, diced bananas and marshmallows. Mix in well and chill until set.

Topping: Melt butter in medium sauce pan. Add flour and sugar, stirring constantly. Gradually add pineapple juice. Stir until thickened. Remove pan from heat. In separate bowl, beat egg slightly. Remove 1/2 cup of thickened custard and add to egg. Mix well. Return egg and custard mixture to custard in sauce pan and stir well. Allow mixture to cool slightly. Add Cool Whip and mix well. Pour over set Jell-O. Refrigerate for 1/2 hour before serving. Makes 12 servings.

Mrs. Wayne Allard, Wife of Representative (Colorado)

AVOCADO MOUSSE

1 tablespoon gelatin,
    dissolved in:
2 tablespoons cold water
1 pkg. lime Jell-O
2 cups hot water
1 cup mashed ripe avocado
½ cup of mayonnaise
½ cup cream, whipped

Dissolve gelatin mixture and Jell-O in the hot water. When partially congealed, stir in remaining ingredients. Pour into a mold greased with mayonnaise and set in refrigerator. Unmold on crisp dark green salad greens.

Garnish with clusters of strawberries, fresh pineapple sticks, orange sections, clusters of white grapes, bing cherries and mint.

Combine mayonnaise with pecans and grated orange peel for the center of mold/or as a side bowl. Present as a beautiful "party hat", tuck plastic ribbon on platter, wonderful for Easter dinner. Makes 8 servings.

Mrs. Harold S. Sawyer, Wife of former Representative (Michigan)

PORTOFINO MOLD

1¼ cups boiling water
1 6 oz. pkg. raspberry Jell-O
1 20 oz. can of crushed pineapple, undrained
1 16 oz. can of whole cranberry sauce
¾ cup port wine
1 cup chopped pecans

Add water to Jell-O in large mixing bowl. Stir in entire contents of pineapple and cranberries, mix well. Add port and pecans. Pour into 9″ × 12″ oblong dish. Chill until set.

Optional topping: Beat 1 cup sour cream into 8 oz. softened cream cheese until smooth. Frost set Jell-O. Chill an additional hour. Makes 8 servings.

Mrs. Tim Johnson, Wife of Representative (South Dakota)

BLUEBERRY SALAD

2 3 oz. pkgs. of raspberry
    Jell-O
3 cups hot water
1 envelope unflavored gelatin
½ cup cold water
1 cup sugar
1 cup half and half (cream)
1 teaspoon vanilla
1 8 oz. pkg. cream cheese
½ cup walnuts
1 #303 can blueberries

First layer: Dissolve 1 package raspberry Jell-O in 2 cups hot water and pour into 8″ × 12″ shallow dish.

Second layer: Soften 1 envelope, unflavored gelatin in ½ cup cold water. Heat 1 cup sugar and 1 cup half & half. Heat without boiling, then stir in the softened gelatin. Add vanilla and cream cheese. Cool to room temperature and add ½ cup nuts (crushed).

Third layer: Dissolve 1 package gelatin in 1 cup boiling water. Stir until dissolved, then add blueberries, including juice. Allow each layer to set well before adding another. Makes 12 servings.

Keely Burns, Daughter of Senator Conrad Burns (Montana)

ORIENTAL SLAW

Slaw:
1 head cabbage (½ green,
    ½ red)
2 bunches green onions
1 pkg. slivered almonds
    (toasted)
1 pkg. Ramen noodles, with
    chicken flavor packet

Dressing:
½ cup oil
¼ cup cider vinegar
2 teaspoons sugar
1 packet seasoning (from
    Ramen noodles)

Coarsely chop cabbage, green onions. Crumble dry noodles. Mix all ingredients for dressing, stirring constantly. Pour over cabbage mixture, stirring as you pour. Top with toasted slivered almonds. Makes 10 to 12 servings.

Mrs. Harold Runnels, Wife of former Representative (New Mexico)

ORIENTAL CABBAGE SALAD

1 large green cabbage
   noodles from 2 pkgs. of
   Ramen soup mix
1⅛ cups corn oil
12 tablespoons apple cider
   vinegar
2 teaspoons salt
   coarse pepper, to taste
⅓ to ½ cup sugar
6 scallions
¼ cup slivered almonds
¼ cup sesame seeds
   scant amount of cooking
   oil

Chop cabbage into small pieces, about ¼" square. Discard all tough pieces. Break up Ramen noodles into small pieces. Make marinade with oil, vinegar, salt, pepper, sugar. Marinate Ramen noodles only for 1 hour. Add scallions to cabbage. Saute almonds and sesame seeds in scant amount of oil until lightly brown. Set aside. Add marinade to cabbage and scallions. Add almonds and sesame seeds just before serving. Can be made 1 day ahead. Makes 8 servings.

Janet F Waxman

Mrs. Henry A. Waxman, Wife of Representative (California)

PINEAPPLE COLESLAW

Dressing:
¾ cup mayonnaise
2 tablespoons sugar
¾ cup sour cream
   juice of ½ lemon
4 slices pineapple, diced
½ head green cabbage,
   shredded
2 carrots, grated
½ cup coarsely chopped pecans (optional)

The Congressional Club

Combine ingredients for dressing. Combine the pineapple, cabbage and carrots in a bowl. Toss thoroughly with dressing. Cover and chill for 2 hours before serving. To serve, pile the pineapple coleslaw in a bowl and sprinkle with chopped pecans. Serves 4.

CRUNCHY CABBAGE SALAD

1 pkg. cabbage slaw or ½ head of chopped cabbage
1 bunch of diced green onions
8 tablespoons of toasted slivered almonds
2 tablespoons of toasted sesame seeds
1 pkg. Top Ramen oriental noodles

Dressing:
½ cup Bertinelli light olive oil
3 tablespoons rice vinegar
2 tablespoons sugar
½ teaspoon salt
½ teaspoon pepper
seasoning packet from Top Ramen noodles

Mix cabbage and green onions. Just before serving, add the almonds, sesame seeds and noodles. Combine dressing ingredients, shake well and pour over salad, then toss. Makes 6 servings.

Mrs. Elton Gallegly, Wife of Representative (California)

FAVORITE SLAW

1 medium cabbage
½ medium onion (to yield 1 tablespoon grated onion)
½ cup Hellmann's mayonnaise
1 tablespoon sugar
1 teaspoon salt
1 teaspoon celery seed
1 tablespoon lemon juice (freshly squeezed)
1½ teaspoons Dijon mustard

Using fine slicing disc of Cuisinart or a very sharp knife, slice cabbage *very* thin. Remove any large white parts of cabbage that get through the slicer. Soak sliced cabbage and the half onion in ice water for a couple of hours. Drain. Grate onion to yield 1 tablespoon and combine with remaining ingredients to make dressing; pour over cabbage. Stir until well mixed. Refrigerate before serving. Makes 6 to 8 servings.

Mrs. Alex McMillan, Wife of Representative (North Carolina)

SAUERKRAUT SALAD

1 large pkg. fresh sauerkraut
    (well drained)
1 cup thinly sliced white
    onion
1 cup thinly sliced celery
1 cup thinly sliced red and
    green pepper
2 cups shredded raw carrot
    (very thinly shredded)
1 cup white vinegar
2 cups white granulated
    sugar
1 tablespoon vegetable oil

Toss together the sauerkraut, onion, celery, pepper and carrot. Boil the vinegar, sugar and oil for 2 minutes, then chill. Pour chilled dressing over salad. Cover and let stand in refrigerator for 24 hours before serving. Keeps well for weeks! Makes 15 servings.

Mrs. David Bradley, Daughter of former Representative James Harvey (Michigan)

TOP RAMEN CABBAGE SALAD

1 medium head cabbage
2 pkgs. uncooked chicken
    Ramen noodles
1 cup sliced almonds
2 tablespoons sesame seeds
4 green onions
1 medium green pepper

Dressing:
6 tablespoons white vinegar
½ cup light virgin olive oil
2 tablespoons sugar
1 pkg. Ramen seasoning

Chop cabbage. Break up noodles slightly. Toast almonds and sesame seeds in small amount of butter or margarine. Chop green onions and green pepper. Mix all together, along with dressing. Marinate overnight in refrigerator. Makes 6 servings.

Mrs. Lionel Van Deerlin, Wife of former Representative (California)

NAPA CABBAGE SALAD

1 medium bunch Napa
   cabbage
1 bunch green onion
2 tablespoons of margarine
2 pkgs. Ramen oriental soup
   mix (only the noodles)
1 jar sesame seeds
1 pkg. slice almonds

Shred cabbage, slice green onions and add to cabbage. Set aside. In the 2 tablespoons of margarine, brown the Ramen noodles, the sesame seeds and the almonds. Set aside. In a small saucepan, combine vinegar, oil, soy sauce and sugar. Boil for 1 minute. Let cool. Place cabbage in a bowl. Top with noodle mixture. Shortly before serving, mix salad with dressing. Makes 8 to 10 servings.

Dressing:
1/4 cup vinegar
3/4 cup oil
2 tablespoons soy sauce
1/2 cup sugar

Corinne Michel

Mrs. Robert H. Michel, Wife of Representative (Illinois)

ARTICHOKE SALAD

1 pkg. Uncle Ben's chicken
   flavored rice
1 jar marinated artichoke
   hearts (reserve mar-
   inade)
1 can artichoke hearts
1/2 green pepper, chopped
2 green onions, chopped
8 green olives, sliced

Cook rice according to directions on box, slightly reducing water. Mix mayonnaise, marinade, and curry to make a dressing. Combine dressing with remaining ingredients and chill. Makes 4 servings.

Dressing:
1/2 cup mayonnaise
   marinade from artichokes
   dash curry

Jill Teague Cochran

Ms. Jill Cochran, Daughter of former Representative Olin E. Teague (Texas)

ARTICHOKE RICE SALAD

2 boxes Rice-A-Roni
4 green onions
1 bell pepper
4 jars marinated artichoke
    hearts
16 stuffed green olives
½ to 1 tablespoon curry
⅔ cup mayonnaise
    salt & pepper to taste

Cook Rice-A-Roni and cool. Chop ingredients together. Add oil from artichoke hearts to taste, add curry, mayonnaise, salt and pepper. Chill.

Nancy Schulze

Mrs. Richard T. Schulze, Wife of former Representative (Pennsylvania)

MARINATED GREEN BEAN SALAD

4 pound green beans,
    blanched
1 large red onion, coarsely
    chopped
½ pound feta cheese,
    crumbled
1 pint cherry tomatoes
1 cup walnut halves

Lemon vinaigrette:
3 tablespoons lemon juice
3 tablespoons wine vinegar
1 tablespoon Dijon mustard
    ground pepper to taste
    (ground fresh)
½ teaspoon sugar
½ teaspoon salt
1 cup oil

For Vinaigrette: Whisk together all items except oil. Add oil gradually until well blended. Add vinaigrette mixture to bean mixture. Makes 8 servings.

Mary A. Regula

Mrs. Ralph Regula, Wife of Representative (Ohio)

CONFETTI SALAD

1 teaspoon salt
½ teaspoon pepper
1 cup sugar
¾ cup white vinegar
½ cup oil
1 20 oz. French cut green
   beans (drain)
1 20 oz. Lasieuri *small* peas
   (drain)
1 20 oz. Shoe Peg *white*
   corn (drain)
½ cup chopped pimentos
1 cup chopped green pepper
1 cup chopped celery
1 cup chopped onions

Bring first 4 ingredients to a boil and then cool. Stir in oil. Mix all the rest and pour dressing over the salad fixins. Makes a large amount. Makes many servings

Shirley Volkmer

Mrs. Harold Volkmer, Wife of Representative (Missouri)

CAROLINA MARINATED VEGETABLES

1 can French cut green
   beans
1 can small early green peas
1 small onion, diced
1 green pepper, diced
1 medium sized can red pimento, diced
¼ cup corn oil
1 cup sugar
1 tablespoon water
½ teaspoon salt
½ cup vinegar
   dash of paprika

Combine first 5 ingredients: beans, peas, onion, green pepper and pimento. Heat the oil, sugar, water, salt, vinegar and paprika. Pour over vegetable mixture. Toss and refrigerate overnight. Very colorful! Makes 12 servings.

Katie O. Morgan

Mrs. Robert Morgan, Wife of former Senator (North Carolina)

MONA'S BEET SALAD

1 pkg. lemon Jell-O
1 cup boiling water
3/4 cup beet juice
1 tablespoon vinegar
1 tablespoon horseradish
1 cup diced celery
1 cup diced beets
2 tablespoons minced onion
    (optional)

Dissolve Jell-O in boiling water. Add all other ingredients. Pour into dish and put in refrigerator.

Mrs John Sparkman

Mrs. John Sparkman, Wife of former Senator (Alabama)

OUR BEST-LOVED CHURCH SUPPER SALAD

1 bunch broccoli
1/2 cup chopped onion
    (optional)
8 bacon strips; fried, drained,
    crumbled
    OR
1/2 cup nuts (sunflower seeds,
    walnuts, etc.)
3/4 cup mayonnaise
1/4 cup sugar
2 tablespoons vinegar
1/2 cup raisins

Cut broccoli in bite size pieces (I use stalk, too, peeled and then cut up). Mix with bacon and onion (or nuts), set aside. Mix mayonnaise, sugar and vinegar. Pour over broccoli mix. Toss gently. Stir in raisins. Toss again. Chill. This is such a hit at pot luck gatherings. Our most-requested recipe. Makes 6 servings.

Bob Smith

Robert C. Smith, Senator (New Hampshire)

BROCCOLI BACON MARINATED SALAD

½ cup rice wine vinegar
½ cup sugar (or 2 packages
    Equal)
1 cup mayonnaise
¼ cup olive oil
1 head broccoli, cut into
    bite-size pieces
1 pound bacon, cooked crisp
    and crumbled
1 small red onion, chopped
1 small red pepper, chopped
1 small yellow pepper,
    chopped

Mix together the first 4 ingredients and set aside. In a large bowl, mix together the broccoli, bacon, onion and peppers. Pour the liquid ingredients over the vegetables and let marinate overnight. Makes 8 to 10 servings.

Mrs. John Doolittle, Wife of Representative (California)

BROCCOLI SALAD

1 bunch broccoli, raw, use
    only flowerettes
3 hard-boiled eggs, chopped
1 small jar olives, chopped
    or sliced
4 small spring onions, sliced
½ cup mayonnaise
    juice from 1 lemon
½ teaspoon salt, if desired

Mix and serve well chilled. Will keep for several days if stored in sealed container in refrigerator.

Mrs. L. H. Fountain, Wife of former Representative (North Carolina)

DOT'S BROCCOLI SALAD

2 or 3 heads of broccoli
    (flowerettes)
1 cup chopped pecans
1 cup raisins
1 purple onion
1 cup grated cheese
    (medium)
    fried bacon, crumbled
1 cup mayonnaise
½ cup sugar
½ cup vinegar

Mix mayonnaise, sugar and vinegar. Combine all other ingredients except bacon. Refrigerate overnight. Sprinkle bacon over salad before serving. Makes 6 to 8 servings.

Margaret Morgan

Margaret Morgan, Daughter of former Senator Robert B. Morgan (North Carolina)

EASY BROCCOLI SALAD

1 large bunch broccoli (use
    just flowerettes)
1 small box cherry tomatoes,
    halved
    fresh mushrooms, sliced
1 can water chestnuts,
    drained and sliced
1 can ripe olives, sliced
1 purple onion, sliced
    Wish Bone Italian dressing

Pour the dressing over the vegetables and stir. Marinate up to 24 hours and drain before serving. Makes 6 to 8 servings.

Linda J. Mickelson

Mrs. George Mickelson, Wife of former Governor (South Dakota)

CHRISTMAS SALAD

1¼ pounds Brussel sprouts
1 teaspoon prepared mustard
1 teaspoon Worcestershire
1 teaspoon sugar
1 teaspoon salt
½ teaspoon dry basil
¼ teaspoon thyme leaves
¼ teaspoon pepper
¼ cup red wine vinegar
1 cup salad oil
2 cups cherry tomatoes
½ cup thinly sliced green onions

First cook Brussel sprouts. Trim off stem ends of Brussel sprouts, rinse thoroughly, then slice each in half lengthwise. In 3 quart pan, bring a large quantity of lightly salted water to boiling. Add Brussel sprouts and when water returns to boiling, reduce heat and simmer, uncovered, for 7 minutes, or until just tender crisp. Turn into colander and drain thoroughly. Meanwhile prepare dressing: Combine mustard, Worcestershire, seasonings, vinegar and oil and shake or stir to blend well. Transfer warm Brussel sprouts to bowl and pour over dressing, mixing to coat evenly. Cover and chill overnight. Just before serving, add cherry tomatoes and green onions. Stir gently to coat vegetables with dressing. Using slotted spoon, transfer salad to serving bowl. Makes 8 servings.

Mrs. Fran Symms, Member of The Congressional Club

CARROT SALAD

2 pounds (or more) carrots, sliced
½ cup vinegar
¼ cup salad oil
½ cup sugar
½ teaspoon Worcestershire sauce
1 small green pepper, chopped
1 medium purple onion, chopped
⅔ can tomato soup
¾ teaspoon prepared mustard
salt and pepper to taste

Slice carrots. Cook until tender, not soft. (This is the trick to this recipe). Mix remaining ingredients and pour over carrots. Stir to blend. Refrigerate. Makes 6 to 8 servings.

Mrs. Richard Thompson, Daughter of former Representative John H. Terry (New York)

EMMA'S VEGETABLE SALAD

1   8 oz. pkg. cream cheese
1   can undiluted tomato soup
2   packets gelatin
3/4 cup water
1¼ cups minced celery
1   yellow onion, minced
½   large green pepper,
       minced
1   cucumber, minced
¼   cup (or less) lemon juice
       (wine vinegar may be
       used)
½   cup chopped walnuts
1   cup (or less) mayonnaise

Melt the cream cheese in the soup in a double boiler. While still hot, add the gelatin softened in the water. When cool, add the vegetables, lemon juice or vinegar (to taste) the nuts and the mayonnaise (½ cup will be enough). Pour into a large mold at least 8 hours before serving. Excellent with ham or sliced turkey. Makes 12 to 14 servings.

Sara L. Matthews

Mrs. Donald Matthews, Wife of former Representative (Florida)

ANNA SZUCHY'S SPISSKA BELA HUNGARIAN CUCUMBER SALAD

5   medium size cucumbers
1   small onion
⅓   cup white vinegar
     paprika
     salt

Peel and thinly slice cucumbers and onion. Onion should be sliced as thin as possible. Place cucumbers and onion in a bowl and add the vinegar. Sprinkle freely with salt. Mix. Let sit at room temperature at least ½ hour, mixing occasionally. Drain off vinegar. Sprinkle paprika on top and serve. (Choose your cucumbers so they are not too seedy). My grandmother served these cucumbers with every meal. Makes 8 to 10 servings.

Christine Titus Daddario

Mrs. Richard Daddario, Daughter-in-law of former Representative Emilio Q. Daddario (Connecticut)

SWEET AND SOUR CUCUMBER SALAD

¼ cup cider vinegar
1 teaspoon sugar
½ teaspoon salt
¼ teaspoon white pepper
2 English cucumbers, sliced
1 red onion, sliced

In a medium bowl, whisk vinegar, sugar, salt, and pepper. Stir in cucumber slices and onion to coat with dressing. Cover and chill 2 hours. You may stir in ½ cup sour cream and 1 tablespoon dried dill into dressing for a sour cream cucumber salad variation. Makes 6 servings.

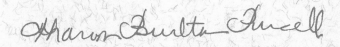

Mrs. Blaine Smith Purcell, Daughter-in-law of former Representative Graham Purcell (Texas)

PEA SALAD

1 cup mayonnaise
1 pkg. ranch dressing mix
2 10 oz. pkgs. frozen petite peas
1 cup diced celery
1½ cups cauliflower pieces

Combine mayonnaise and dry ranch dressing mix and set aside. Thaw frozen peas. Add celery and cauliflower pieces. Add mayonnaise mixture and combine. Makes 8 servings.

Mrs. Charles E. Grassley, Wife of Senator (Iowa)

> *To remove the core from a head of lettuce, hit the core end once against the counter sharply. The core will loosen and pull out easily.*

ENGLISH PEA SALAD

1 can (16 oz.) English peas
½ cup diced sweet pickles
¼ cup chopped pecans
1 cup cubed cheddar cheese
½ cup diced celery
½ cup diced onion
2 hard-cooked eggs, diced
1 teaspoon salt
1 tablespoon chopped pimento
1 tablespoon mayonnaise
lettuce leaves

Chill and drain the peas. Combine all ingredients and toss just enough to mix lightly. Serve on lettuce leaves. Makes 6 to 8 servings.

Freddie Teague

Mrs. Olin Teague, Wife of former Representative (Texas)

MARTHA'S MARVELOUS MORSELS

6 tablespoons mayonnaise
juice of 1 lemon
1 small onion, finely minced
salt and pepper to taste
2 cups of frozen peas (do not thaw)
1 cup of swiss or cheddar cheese strips
4 cups of lettuce, torn into bite size
8 slices crisp crumbled bacon

24 hours before serving, combine mayonnaise, lemon juice, onion, frozen peas and cheese strips in a bowl. Stir well and add salt and pepper. Cover and refrigerate. Before serving, add lettuce, bacon and toss. Makes 4 servings.

Annie Rhodes

Mrs. Jay Rhodes, Wife of former Representative (Arizona)

POTATO SALAD

5 pounds of potatoes
8 hard boiled eggs
½ bunch green onions
1½ cups of mayonnaise
1 tablespoon mustard
½ cup milk

Boil potatoes and eggs and let cool. Peel and grate potatoes, chop the eggs. Sauce: Mix mayonnaise, mustard and milk together to desired thickness and pour over potatoes and eggs. Add green onions and mix all together. Salt and pepper to taste. The secret to this recipe is grating the potatoes, which makes the salad very smooth, not chunky. Makes 15 servings.

Mrs. Dirk Kempthorne, Wife of Senator (Idaho)

POTATO SALAD

3 baking potatoes or 6 red
skinned potatoes
2 hard boiled eggs, use white
only, chopped
¼ cup celery, diced
¼ cup diced sweet red onion

Quarter baking potatoes (or halve red skinned potatoes). Boil until slightly resistant to fork. Cool and cube to size desired. Add chopped white only of hard boiled eggs, the celery and onion. Pour dressing over potatoes and stir gently. Improves when covered and refrigerated. Makes 4 servings.

Dressing:
½ cup mayonnaise with olive
oil to thin
¼ cup sour cream
white pepper
capers

Hamilton Fish, Jr., Representative (New York)

HERBED POTATO SALAD (Low Fat)

4 medium potatoes
⅓ cup sliced green onions
⅓ cup Chablis or other dry
   white wine
2 tablespoons white wine
   vinegar
1 teaspoon oil
1 teaspoon Dijon mustard
¼ teaspoon salt
¼ teaspoon freshly ground
   pepper
2 tablespoons chopped fresh
   parsley

Wash potatoes, pat dry, and slice ¼-inch thick slices. Arrange potato slices, overlapping in rows in a 10-inch pie plate. Sprinkle with green onions, wine, and vinegar. Cover with plastic wrap and microwave at high 10–12 minutes or until tender. Let stand, covered, 5 minutes. Uncover potato slices, drain and reserve liquid. Combine reserved liquid, oil and next 3 ingredients; stir with a small wire whisk until well blended. Pour mixture over potato slices, sprinkle with parsley and serve. Makes 4 servings.

Mrs. Fred Schwengel

Mrs. Fred Schwengel, Wife of former Representative (Iowa)

STUFFED TOMATO SALAD

6 firm tomatoes
1 can anchovy fillets
¼ cup chopped capers
1 clove garlic, minced
1 tablespoon olive oil
2 hard cooked eggs,
   chopped
¼ teaspoon black pepper
1 teaspoon lemon juice

Buy large, even-sized tomatoes. Cut a ½-inch piece from the stem end. Scoop out the pulp and chop it. Chop the undrained anchovies, mix with the chopped tomatoes, capers, garlic, olive oil, eggs, pepper and lemon juice. Stuff the tomatoes. Serve as an appetizer or salad. Makes 6 servings.

Rita Hanley

Mrs. James Hanley, Wife of former Representative (New York)

BETTY'S MARINATED TOMATOES AND ONIONS

2 pounds firm tomatoes, cored and sliced
2 medium onions (I prefer red onions)
2 tablespoons chopped fresh herbs (dill, chives, oregano, parsley, thyme, etc.)
½ cup salad oil
½ cup vinegar
¼ cup white wine
¼ cup granulated sugar
½ teaspoon salt
fresh ground pepper, to taste
fresh parsley for garnish

Put the tomatoes in a large bowl. Place onions on top. Sprinkle herbs on top. In a small bowl, blend the oil, vinegar, wine, sugar, salt, and pepper with a wire whisk until all the sugar is dissolved. Pour over the tomatoes and onions. Cover with plastic wrap and refrigerate for several hours. Serve chilled, garnished with parsley. Makes 6 servings.

Mrs. Carlos Moorhead, Wife of Representative (California)

BASIL VINAIGRETTE TOMATOES

tomatoes
balsamic vinegar
extra virgin olive oil
fresh basil leaves
salt
pepper

As close to serving as possible—plunge tomatoes into boiling water for 15 to 30 seconds. Run cold water over tomatoes, then skin and slice. Cover the bottom of a shallow serving dish with a layer of tomato slices (ceramic quiche or pie plate is perfect). Sprinkle with salt, freshly ground pepper and generous portions of balsamic vinegar and freshly cut or chopped basil leaves. Drizzle with olive oil. Additional layers of tomatoes should be seasoned the same way. Save leftover tomatoes and vinaigrette in separate containers. They can be served together again or the vinaigrette can be used as a salad dressing. Use Roma tomatoes in the winter for a little taste of summer.

Laurie Michel, Daughter of Representative Bob Michel (Illinois)

CAESAR SALAD WITH HOMEMADE CROUTONS

Caesar Salad:

10 cups romaine lettuce
 2 eggs
 1 lemon
 8 fillets of anchovies
 ¾ cup Parmesan cheese
   croutons (recipe below)
 2 garlic cloves
 ¾ cup olive oil
 1 teaspoon poupon mustard
 ¼ teaspoon Worcestershire
   sauce

Hold fork convex side against bottom of salad bowl with one hand, with other hand rub 1½ garlic cloves vigorously against prongs of fork. Rub inside of bowl with remaining garlic, then finish crushing it on prongs. Add anchovies and crush with fork. Add lemon juice, Worcestershire sauce and 2 eggs and mix well. Add olive oil, and mix well again. Add lettuce to bowl. Toss thoroughly, but gently. Sprinkle with Parmesan. Add croutons and toss again, briefly.

Homemade Croutons:

 1 loaf long, thin sandwich
   bread (refrigerate for a
   day)
 2 cups Wesson oil
 1 whole garlic head

Croutons: Cut bread in cubes and spread on 2 large cookie sheets. Chop peeled garlic into blender. Add oil slowly and process on blend. Pour evenly over bread cubes. Bake in slow over at 250-275° for 1 to 1½ hours or until golden brown. Sprinkle with parmesan cheese. Cool. Store in refrigerator in cans or jars. Will keep for at least a month! Makes 4 servings.

Carol Andrus

Mrs. Cecil Andrus, Wife of Governor (Idaho)

A small amount of baking soda added to gravy will eliminate excess grease.

SEMI-CAESAR SALAD

1 head romaine lettuce, broken
2 heads Bibb lettuce, broken
1 egg white
1 teaspoon garlic salt
3 tablespoons sour cream
½ teaspoon pepper
3 tablespoons oil
1 teaspoon rice vinegar
½ cup croutons
½ cup freshly grated Parmesan cheese

Place the lettuces in a large bowl. In a separate bowl, combine egg, garlic salt, sour cream, pepper, oil and vinegar. Mix. Before serving, toss lettuce, croutons and cheese with dressing. Makes 8 to 10 servings.

Mrs. Hank Brown, Wife of Senator (Colorado)

EASY CAESAR

1 head romaine lettuce
6 slices bacon
2 garlic cloves
½ cup grated Parmesan cheese
¼ cup plus 2 tablespoons of olive oil
¼ cup plus 2 tablespoons of vegetable oil
¼ cup lemon juice
1 tablespoon of Worcestershire sauce
2 ozs. of blue cheese, crumbled
1 cup Pepperidge Farm Caesar croutons

Clean romaine, refrigerate. Cook bacon, cool, crumble, set aside. Combine in blender or food processor the remaining ingredients. Toss with romaine, blue cheese, bacon, croutons and serve. Makes 4 servings.

Mrs. Robert Walker, Wife of Representative (Pennsylvania)

CAESAR SALAD (NO EGG—NO ANCHOVY)

3 heads romaine lettuce
2 tablespoons fresh lemon
  juice
1 tablespoon tarragon
  vinegar
2 cloves garlic, crushed
1/3 cup olive oil
1/4 cup blue cheese, crumbled
2 tablespoons Parmesan
  cheese
croutons (as you like)

Clean, wash, drain and dry romaine lettuce, then tear into small pieces. Mix together in separate bowl and let stand 2 hours before serving, remaining ingredients, except croutons. Toss romaine and dressing, add croutons, serve.

Priscilla Mack

Mrs. Connie Mack, Wife of Senator (Florida)

WATSON "NO EGG" CAESAR SALAD

1 large head romaine lettuce
  (about 1–1¼ pounds)
5 cups spinach (about 7 oz.)
4 slices of dried bread
1 large garlic clove, minced
  2 oz. tin of anchovies,
  chopped
2/3 cup olive oil
1/3 cup lemon juice (fresh or
  reconstituted)
2/3 cup Parmesan cheese
1/2 teaspoon Italian seasoning
  mix
1 to 3 dashes of white, red
  and black pepper
other spices/herbs to
  taste—suggestions
  include, oregano, basil,
  tarragon, Chinese five
  spices, and ginger

Tear lettuce and spinach into bite size pieces, and place in a large salad bowl. Dry bread in microwave oven on medium high for approximately 2 minutes. Turn bread over and microwave for another minute or until bread is dried out. Break bread into bite size pieces, and place bread cubes on top of lettuce. In a separate bowl, mix garlic, anchovies, olive oil, lemon juice, Parmesan cheese, Italian seasoning mix, peppers, and desired spices, and pepper. Add dressing to lettuce and bread cubes and toss ingredients until romaine and spinach are well coated. Serves 2, as a meal, or 8 with dinner. Makes 2 to 8 servings.

Diane Watson

Mrs. John Watson, Daughter of former Representative Glenard P. Lipscomb (California)

BACON AND BLUE CHEESE CAESAR SALAD

1 large head of romaine let-
    tuce, torn into bite size
    pieces
6 bacon slices, cooked,
    crumbled
½ cup crumbled blue cheese
    Easy Caesar Dressing
    (recipe follows)
1 cup Garlic Croutons
    (recipe follows)

Easy Caesar Dressing:
½ cup freshly grated
    Parmesan cheese
¼ cup plus 2 tablespoons
    olive oil
¼ cup plus 2 tablespoons
    vegetable oil
¼ cup fresh lemon juice
2 garlic cloves
1 teaspoon Worcestershire
    sauce

Garlic Croutons:
2 tablespoons butter
¼ cup olive oil
2 large garlic cloves, pressed
4 sourdough French bread
    slices, cut into cubes
    salt and pepper

Place first three ingredients in large bowl. Add enough dressing to season to taste and toss well. Garnish salad with croutons and serve.

Dressing: Combine all ingredients in a blender or food processor, blend until smooth. Season to taste with salt and pepper (can be prepared 2 days ahead. Cover and refrigerate).

Croutons: Preheat oven to 350°. Melt butter with olive oil and garlic in small saucepan. Place bread crumbs on a baking sheet. Pour butter mixture over top and toss well. Bake until bread cubes are golden brown and crisp (about 20 minutes). Season with salt and pepper, cool completely. Can be prepared in advance, store in refrigerator in airtight container. Makes 4 servings.

Elizabeth Rhodes Reich

Mrs. Frank Reich, Daughter of former Representative John J. Rhodes (Arizona)

> *To prevent soggy salads, place an inverted saucer in the bottom of the salad bowl. The excess dressing will drain under the saucer and keep the greens crisp.*

DEDY'S SUGAR MOUNTAIN PICNIC SALAD

1 head lettuce
1 15 oz. can french style
   green beans (well
   drained)
¼ cup chopped green onion
1 large tomato, diced
1½ cups grated sharp cheddar
   cheese
6 ozs. crushed Frito corn
   chips
1 bottle Catalina dressing
   (Kraft)

Toss first five ingredients. Add Catalina dressing and mix well. At last moment, sprinkle with Fritos and mix lightly. (Salad does not need salt because Fritos are salted). Makes 12 to 16 servings.

Annie Laurine Rankin Sanders

Mrs. John Sanders, Daughter of former Representative John E. Rankin (Mississippi)

SEVEN LAYER SALAD

1 head iceberg lettuce
½ cup celery, diced
1 red onion, diced
1 medium green pepper,
   diced
1 pkg. frozen peas
1 cup mayonnaise
1 tablespoon sugar
1 8 oz. pkg. cheddar cheese,
   shredded
1 pkg. blue cheese,
   crumbled

Clean, drain and dry the iceberg lettuce and break into bite size pieces. Layer ingredients as listed and refrigerate overnight, toss and serve.

Priscilla Mack

Mrs. Connie Mack, Wife of Senator (Florida)

> *Place individual salad plates in freezer about an hour before using.*

SPINNING BOWL SALAD

1 head lettuce, shredded
8 to 10 leaves romaine let-
    tuce, cut in four pieces
3 hard boiled eggs, chopped
4 ozs. blue cheese
1 cup seasoned croutons

Dressing can be made by mixing one 8 oz. bottle Wish Bone Italian and 1 cup Miracle Whip. Combine first 5 ingredients in a large serving bowl. Add dressing, toss and serve. Makes 8 to 10 servings.

Tish Traficant

Mrs. James Traficant, Wife of Representative (Ohio)

TEXAS SALAD

1 head shredded lettuce
1 onion, chopped
1 green pepper, chopped
1 can red kidney beans
    (drained and rinsed)
2 or 3 tomatoes, diced
1 small bag Fritos
½ cup grated cheddar cheese

Toss ingredients together. Marinate in Kraft Catalina dressing about 1 hour. Then add a small bag of crushed Fritos and ½ cup grated cheddar cheese. Makes 8 servings.

Dorothy F. Mathews

Mrs. Patrick Mathews, Daughter of former Representative Claude Albert Fuller (Arkansas)

Rubbing waxed paper over the inside and outside of a wooden salad bowl will prevent it from becoming sticky.

ENDIVE SALAD

1 head curly endive, broken into bite sized pieces
4 slices bacon, fried, reserve drippings
3 tablespoons mayonnaise
1 to 2 tablespoons vinegar

Stir mayonnaise into ⅔ of the bacon drippings. Add vinegar and more drippings if needed. Toss (warmed) over endive. Top with crumbled bacon. Makes 6 to 8 servings.

Ruth Fawell

Mrs. Harris Fawell, Wife of Representative (Illinois)

CITRUS AND GREENS

½ cup apricot nectar
3 tablespoons lemon juice
1 tablespoon unsweetened orange juice
1 teaspoon cornstarch
⅛ teaspoon ground ginger
  dash of ground nutmeg
1 teaspoon grated lemon rind
1½ cups torn iceberg lettuce
1½ cups torn green leaf lettuce
2 medium-size oranges, peeled and sectioned
2 medium grapefruit, peeled and sectioned

Combine first 6 ingredients in a glass bowl, stir well. Microwave at HIGH 2 minutes or until slightly thickened, stirring after 1 minute. Cool slightly, stir in lemon rind. Combine lettuce, oranges and grapefruit and toss with dressing. Makes 6 servings.

Mrs. Fred Schwengel

Mrs. Fred Schwengel, Wife of former Representative (Iowa)

Do not use metal bowls when mixing salads. Use wooden, glass or china.

CHINESE SLAW

1 head Chinese lettuce, chopped
4 green onions, sliced
1 tablespoon toasted sesame seeds
½ cup toasted slivered almonds
1 pkg. Ramen noodles (oriental section)
2 tablespoon sugar
1 teaspoon salt
¼ teaspoon pepper
½ cup oil
3 tablespoons vinegar
1 pkg. seasoning from noodles

Mix together chopped lettuce and green onions, add toasted sesame seed, almonds, and package noodles. Mix next 6 ingredients and shake well and then add to mixture. Toss all ingredients and serve. Makes 8 servings.

Mrs. Jim Bunning, Wife of Representative (Kentucky)

STUFFED CELERY RINGS

1 medium bunch celery
tangy cheese spread (or creamed cheddar, roquefort or pineapple cheese spreads may be used)
lettuce or watercress
French dressing

Cut top from celery, wash and dry each stalk. Fill smallest stalk with cheese, then the next smallest stalk and press firmly into the first one. Continue filling and pressing stalks together until all the celery is formed into a bunch. Tie with string and chill. Slice crosswise into ½-inch slices and serve on lettuce or watercress with French dressing. Serves 8.

The Congressional Club

Grease molds for congealed salads with mayonnaise.

GREEK SALAD

1 green cabbage
  kosher salt (coarse salt)
2 yellow onions
2 green peppers
1 large cucumber
1 to 2 large vine ripened
  tomatoes
¾ cup corn oil
¼ cup white vinegar
  pepper to taste
1 6 oz. jar Matje's herring
  handful Greek Mislines
  olives
  sugar to taste

Slice cabbage, as for coleslaw. Discard tough pieces. Generously salt cabbage. Set aside for 1 hour. Meanwhile, slice onions and add enough vinegar to soak them. Soak for 15 minutes. Dice green peppers. Slice cucumber. Cut tomato into bite size pieces. Squeeze the cabbage well. Combine the cabbage, drained onions, green pepper, tomato and cucumber. Make marinade of corn oil, vinegar, sugar and pepper. I don't measure, but use approximately ¾ cup oil to ¼ cup vinegar. Suit your own taste. Add enough sugar so that the marinade is not sour, yet not sweet. Test the taste of the marinade on the cabbage salad itself in order to get the salty taste as well. Add the olives. Can be made 1 day ahead. Makes 8 servings.

Janet F Waxman

Mrs. Henry A. Waxman, Wife of Representative (California)

ROMAN SALAD WITH NOODLES

½ lb. fettucine verde (green
  noodles)
1 lb. cooked ham, cut in
  finger-sized strips
2 cups fresh mushrooms,
  thickly sliced or quar-
  tered
½ cup pitted ripe olives
3 medium tomatoes, peeled
  and sliced
1 cup mayonnaise
  boiling water to thin mayonnaise
½ teaspoon Dijon-style
  mustard
For dressing:
2 tablespoons red wine
  vinegar
  salt and pepper to taste
6 tablespoons olive oil
¼ cup chili sauce or ketchup
1 tablespoon chopped parsley
1 teaspoon mixed herbs (oregano, thyme)

The Congressional Club

Cook the noodles in plenty of boiling salted water for 8 to 10 minutes or until just tender. Drain, rinse with cold water until shiny and drain again.

To make the dressing: Mix the vinegar with the salt and pepper, then whisk in the oil, chili sauce or ketchup, parlsey and mixed herbs. Put the ham in a bowl with the noodles, mushrooms and olives. Pour the dressing over the mixture and toss carefully. Pile the salad in a serving dish and arrange the tomato slices around the edge. Thin the mayonnaise with a little boiling water until it pours fairly easily; beat in mustard to taste and serve separately with the salad. Serves 4.

MARJORIE'S GREEK SALAD

2 dozen cherry tomatoes
2 cucumbers
1 green pepper
1 red pepper
1 large vidalia onion (or another kind)
1/4 pound feta cheese
   black olives
   fresh basil (or dried)

Dressing:
2 to 3 cloves of garlic
1/2 teaspoon salt
   fresh ground pepper
3 tablespoons balsamic vinegar
3 tablespoons good olive oil

Chop tomatoes, cucumbers, peppers and onion in small chunks. Mix all together in large salad bowl. Sprinkle feta cheese, sliced black olives and fresh basil over the salad. Dress with salad dressing ingredients, mixed together. Mix leftovers with wild or brown rice for lunch the next day. Makes 12 servings.

Sally Smith

Mrs. Peter Smith, Wife of former Representative (Vermont)

UKRAINIAN BEET SALAD

2 lbs. cooked beets, peeled
1 1/2 tablespoons freshly grated horseradish
2 tablespoon sugar
1/4 cup white vinegar
1/2 teaspoon caraway seeds (or to taste)

Grate the beets coarsely and mix them with the remaining ingredients. Cover and chill for at least 2 hours before serving. Serves 4.

The Congressional Club

PHOEBE'S LIMBERLOST INN SALAD & DRESSING

mixed greens
1 large red apple
1 large green pear
1 tablespoon extra fine granulated sugar
1 pkg. crumbled feta cheese

Dressing:
¼ cup Dijon mustard
½ cup raspberry vinegar
½ cup honey
1 cup olive oil

Use assorted fresh young mixed greens for six servings. Use any combination of baby lettuces, seasonal chicories, cilantro, dill, chevril, French sorrel, etc.

Wash and dry greens, crisp in refrigerator. Slice apple and pear in ¼ in slices, leaving peel on. Sprinkle apple and pear slices with sugar and broil in oven until golden brown. Set on a rack to cool. Combine lettuces with the slices of apple and pear and mix in feta cheese. Serve salad with raspberry honey vinaigrette dressing.

Method for dressing: Mix mustard, raspberry vinegar and honey in blender. Then slowly add 1 cup olive oil until thick. Pass dressing to serve over salad.

Gail McCandless

Mrs. Al McCandless, Wife of Representative (California)

CURRIED AVOCADO ROMAINE SALAD

Dressing:
1/3 cup safflower oil
1/3 cup melted bacon fat
1/4 cup red wine vinegar with
    garlic
2 tablespoons dry white
    wine
2 teaspoons soy sauce
1/4 teaspoon pepper
3/4 teaspoon salt
1/2 teaspoon curry powder
1 teaspoon dry mustard
1 teaspoon sugar

The Salad:
1/2 cup cashew nuts, toasted
3 tablespoons sesame seeds
4 to 6 slices of bacon, fried
    very crisp, crumble or in-
    stead sliver slices of ham
    or any smoked meat,
    chill the meat

Tear into bite sized pieces:
1 large head of romaine let-
    tuce OR
2 bunches of spinach or a
    combination of the two.

In large salad bowl, place:
1 or 2 ripe avocados, peeled
    and sliced thick
1/2 tart apple, chopped
1 14 oz. can of artichoke
    hearts, drained and cut
    in halves.
    sweet onion rings or
    chopped green onions
    (optional)

Make dressing early in the day by combining all ingredients in jar with lid. Shake well and chill. Arrange greens. Cover and chill. To serve salad: melt dressing by warming slightly to melt the bacon fat. Set to one side at room temperature. Pour over chilled lettuce, spinach or both, just enough dressing to moisten. Do not sog salad ingredients, so add dressing slowly toss and taste for piquancy then add cashews and sesame. Serve! Makes 8 servings.

Mldred Curtis

Mrs. Carl T. Curtis, Wife of former Senator (Nebraska)

STRAWBERRY GREEN SALAD

1 head Boston lettuce, washed and torn into pieces
1 bag fresh spinach, washed and torn into pieces
1 pint fresh strawberries, washed, hulled and sliced
4 slices bacon, cooked and crumbled
small pkg. fresh mushrooms, washed and sliced
½ head each broccoli and cauliflower, washed and chopped
2½ oz. pkg. slivered almonds, toasted

Dressing:
½ cup sugar
2 tablespoons sesame seeds
1 tablespoon poppy seeds
1 teaspoon minced onion
¼ teaspoon Worcestershire sauce
¼ teaspoon paprika
½ cup oil
¼ cup cider vinegar

Arrange salad ingredients in glass bowl. Make dressing in blender. Blend for short time only as it will become too thick. Drizzle dressing over salad and toss gently. Makes 10 servings.

Martha Mills Dixon

Mrs. David Jack Dixon, Daughter of former Representative Wilbur D. Mills (Arkansas)

WIEGERS SALAD

Salad:
    romaine lettuce
    iceberg lettuce
1/3 to 1/2 medium thinly sliced
        red onion
1 cup grated Parmesan
        cheese
1 14 oz. can artichoke hearts
    OR
1 can hearts of palm

Salad Dressing:
1   cup Crisco oil
1/4 cup white vinegar
1   teaspoon salt
1/2 teaspoon white pepper
1/2 teaspoon celery salt
1/4 teaspoon cayenne pepper
1/4 teaspoon dry mustard
    dash Tabasco
1   heaping teaspoon minced
        garlic

Salad: combine lettuce, red onion, Parmesan cheese, hearts of palm OR artichoke hearts together in salad bowl. Refrigerate until ready to serve.

Dressing: Mix ingredients for salad dressing in a container with a lid. Shake until mixed together. Refrigerate until ready to serve. Pour over salad and gently mix. Makes 6 servings.

Gina M. Sinovic

Ms. Gina Sinovic, Daughter of Representative Jerry F. Costello (Illinois)

Lettuce and celery keep longer if you store them in paper bags instead of plastic.

SPINACH SALAD

1 pound fresh spinach, torn
1 medium onion, chopped
½ head lettuce, torn
2 cans (11 oz.) mandarin
  oranges, drained

Dressing:
1½ cups sugar
1 teaspoon dry mustard
1 cup white vinegar
1 teaspoon salt
2 eggs, beaten frothy

Combine dressing ingredients, bring to a boil and boil for 1 minute. Cool and toss with greens when ready to serve. Refrigerate the remaining dressing. Makes 10 servings.

Carolyn Hobson

Mrs. David Hobson, Wife of Representative (Ohio)

SPINACH AND HEARTS OF PALM SALAD

3 tablespoons red wine
  vinegar
2 teaspoons Dijon mustard
1 teaspoon sugar
⅓ cup olive oil
1 pound fresh spinach, stems
  trimmed
1 14 oz. can hearts of palm,
  drained, sliced
1½ teaspoons grated lemon
  peel

Whisk first 3 ingredients in small bowl. Gradually whisk in oil. Season to taste with salt and pepper. Dressing can be prepared 1 day ahead. Cover and let stand at room temperature. Combine spinach, hearts of palm and lemon peel in bowl. Add enough dressing to season to taste and toss gently. Divide among plates and serve. Makes 8 servings.

Diane Nagle

Mrs. David Nagle, Wife of former Representative (Iowa)

SILVERGLADE SPINACH SALAD

6 cups spinach, rinsed/dried, stemmed & torn into pieces

6 ozs. Swiss cheese, cut into julienne strips

6 ozs. cheddar cheese, cut into julienne strips

2 cups seedless grapes, halved

Dressing:

½ cup vegetable oil

¼ cup cider vinegar

2 teaspoons Dijon mustard

2 teaspoons packed light brown sugar

4 slices bacon, fried crisp, drained and crumbled

2 tablespoons sliced green onions

To prepare dressing, whisk together oil, vinegar, mustard and brown sugar. Stir in bacon pieces and onion. Refrigerate. In large bowl combine spinach, cheese and grapes. Toss with dressing. Makes 6 servings.

Chris M. Rhodes

Mrs. Thomas H. Rhodes, Daughter-in-law of former Representative John J. Rhodes (Arizona)

SPINACH SALAD

¾ lb. spinach with stems removed

3 scallions, finely sliced

1 cup mushrooms, sliced

½ cup vinaigrette dressing made with lemon juice instead of vinegar (see recipe on page 84)

Clean and dry spinach. Make vinaigrette dressing and add scallions and mushrooms. Toss spinach with dressing just before serving. Serves 6.

The Congressional Club

SPINACH SALAD, POPPY SEED DRESSING

1 pound fresh spinach
11 oz. can mandarin orange
    segments, drained
1 large Granny Smith apple,
    cut in chunks
½ cup slivered almonds,
    toasted
1 cup golden raisins
    Poppy Seed dressing

Poppy Seed Dressing:
2 tablespoons onion,
    coarsely chopped
¾ cup honey
1 teaspoon dry mustard
1 teaspoon salt
3 tablespoons lemon juice
2 tablespoons vinegar
1 cup salad oil
1½ tablespoons poppy seeds

Wash spinach thoroughly, dry and remove stems, tear into pieces. Toss with orange segments, apple, almonds and raisins. Use just enough dressing to coat well.

Dressing: Put first 6 ingredients in blender, blend until onion is well chopped. Turn to low speed and gradually add oil. When thoroughly homogenized (but no longer) add poppy seeds and blend just until mixed. Refrigerate. Makes about 2 cups. Store in refrigerator up to 10 days. Makes 8 servings.

Charlotte Brooks

Mrs. Jack Brooks, Wife of Representative (Texas)

Thin gravy can be thickened by adding a mixture of flour or cornstarch and water, which has been mixed to a smooth paste, added gradually, stirring constantly, while bringing to a boil.

SPINACH SALAD

2 pkg. (20 oz.) fresh spinach
1 cup coarsely broken
    pecans
12 oz. cottage cheese, drained
    as much as possible
1 cup dairy sour cream
1/4 cup sugar
3 tablespoons seasoned rice
    vinegar
1 1/2 teaspoons dry mustard
4 teaspoons horseradish
1/2 teaspoon salt
1/2 teaspoon pepper

Wash spinach. Refrigerate spinach until crisp, then tear into bite size pieces. Combine spinach, pecans and cottage cheese. Mix lightly but thoroughly. Combine sour cream, sugar, vinegar, mustard, horseradish and salt and pepper. Mix well. Combine sour cream and spinach mixtures. Mix lightly, but thoroughly. Makes 12 servings.

Mrs. Hank Brown, Wife of Senator (Colorado)

SPINACH SALAD WITH POPPY SEED DRESSING

Salad:
2 grapefruit
1/2 pound fresh spinach
1 pint strawberries

Poppy Seed Dressing:
1 8 oz. bottle vinegar and oil
    dressing
1/2 cup sugar
1/2 teaspoon dry mustard
1 1/2 teaspoon grated grapefruit
    peel
1/4 cup grapefruit juice
2 tablespoons poppy seeds

Salad: Combine grapefruit sections, spinach torn in bite size pieces and strawberries in a bowl. Toss gently. Serve immediately with Poppy Seed dressing. Makes 6 servings.

Dressing: Combine all ingredients in electric blender. Cover and blend well. Refrigerate several hours before serving. Makes 1 1/2 cups.

Mrs. Tazewell Shepard, Daughter of former Senator John Sparkman (Alabama)

WARM SPINACH AND BASIL SALAD

6 pounds fresh spinach
  leaves
20 cups fresh basil leaves
4 cups best quality olive oil
24 cloves fresh garlic, finely
  chopped
4 cups pignoli nuts (pine
  nuts)
2 pounds prosciutto ham,
  diced
  salt and fresh ground
  pepper to taste
6 cups freshly grated
  Parmesan cheese

Toss the cleaned spinach and basil together in a large bowl. Heat the olive oil in a medium sized skillet over medium heat. Add the garlic and pignoli and saute until the nuts begin to brown slightly. Stir in the prosciutto and cook approximately 3 minutes more. Season to taste. Toss the spinach and basil with the warm dressing and sprinkle with the fresh Parmesan. Serve immediately and pass the peppermill. Makes 50 servings.

The Congressional Club

BROWN RICE SALAD

1 12 oz. box brown rice
1 10 oz. pkg. frozen peas
1 10 oz. pkg. frozen whole
  kernel corn
1 red bell pepper
1 green bell pepper
1½ cups dark raisins
1 jar sunflower seeds
   (7.5 oz.)
1 cup broken pecans
6 stalks celery
2 bunches green onions
  dash of salt

Cook rice according to package directions. Thaw and drain peas and corn. Thinly slice cored red and green peppers. Plump raisins in hot water; drain. Dice celery. Thinly slice onions. Thoroughly mix dressing ingredients; set aside. In large bowl, toss and gently mix all salad ingredients. Slowly fold dressing over the salad. Refrigerate 12–24 hours before serving, stirring mixture occasionally. Makes 16 servings.

Dressing:
¾ cup salad oil
¾ cup white vinegar
6 tablespoons brown sugar
5 teaspoons curry powder

Mrs. Ike Skelton, Wife of Representative (Missouri)

CORN AND RICE SALAD

1 16 oz. can whole kernel
    corn, drained
2 cups cooked rice
¼ cup chopped sweet red or
    green pepper (or both)
¼ cup sliced green onion
¼ cup chopped ripe olives
3 tablespoons olive or
    cooking oil
3 tablespoons white wine
    vinegar
2 tablespoons soy sauce
2 tablespoons snipped pars-
    ley or 1 tablespoon dry
    parsley flakes
½ teaspoon Dijon mustard
¼ teaspoon garlic powder
8 cherry tomatoes, sliced
    (1½ cups)
1 tablespoon finely shredded
    Parmesan cheese

In a medium bowl combine corn, rice, pepper, onion and olives. In a screw-top jar, combine oil, vinegar, soy sauce, parsley, mustard and garlic powder. Shake to mix, pour over corn mixture. Cover and chill several hours, or overnight. To serve, stir in tomatoes. Top with Parmesan cheese. Note: If using olive oil in dressing, let salad stand at room temperature for 20 minutes before serving. This is a great summer picnic salad! Can be made ahead. Makes 8 servings.

Jackie Lloyd

Mrs. Jim Lloyd, Wife of former Representative (California)

If you will brown the flour well before adding to the liquid when making gravy, you will avoid pale or lumpy gravy.

CORN, RICE AND BEAN SALAD

2 cups converted rice
3 teaspoons salt
2 cans (16 ozs. each) pink
    beans, rinsed and
    drained
1 can (12 oz.) vacuum-
    packed corn niblets
    OR
3 cups cooked fresh corn
    kernels
1 bunch scallions, chopped
    (about ¾ cup)
⅔ cup oil
¼ cup fresh lime juice
2 tablespoons cider vinegar
2 tablespoons (packed)
    brown sugar
4 pickled jalapeno peppers,
    stemmed, seeded and
    quartered
2 teaspoons chili powder
1 teaspoon cumin

Cook rice using 5 cups water and 1 teaspoon of the salt. In large bowl, combine the rice, beans, corn and scallions. Toss lightly to mix. In food processor, combine the oil, lime juice, vinegar, brown sugar, peppers, chili powder, cumin and remaining 2 teaspoons salt. Process until peppers are finely minced. Pour most of dressing over salad and toss to coat. Let stand at room temperature tossing occasionally for up to 4 hours, or cover and refrigerate for up to 2 days. Serve at room temperature. Makes 16 servings.

Joanne Kemp

Mrs. Jack F. Kemp, Wife of former Representative (New York) and former Secretary of Housing and Urban Development

RICE SALAD

1½ cups long grain rice
1 cucumber, peeled and
    sliced
    salt
1 large carrot, diced
1 cup diced green beans
1 cup shelled fresh peas or 1
    (4-oz.) package frozen
    peas, thawed
1 red bell pepper, cored,
    seeded and diced
2 medium tomatoes, peeled,
    seeded and cut in strips
½ cup vinaigrette dressing

Cook the rice in boiling salted water for 12 to 15 minutes. Drain, rinse with hot water and spread out to dry. Sprinkle the cucumber with salt, cover and let stand 30 minutes to draw out the juices, then rinse and dry on paper towels. Cook the carrots, beans and peas in boiling salted water for 6 to 8 minutes or until just tender, then drain, rinse in cold water and drain again. Blanch the pepper for 2 minutes in boiling salted water, drain, rinse and drain again. Add all the vegetables and tomatoes to rice and toss with vinaigrette dressing. Serves 6.

The Congressional Club

WILD RICE SALAD

6 oz. box wild rice
6 slices bacon, browned and crumbled
3 tablespoons bacon drippings
1 tablespoon flour
1 to 2 tablespoons sugar
½ teaspoon salt
¼ cup water
½ cup vinegar
1 head lettuce, torn in bite size pieces
1 cup sliced cucumber
1 cup sliced carrot

Cook rice as directed. In separate pan, put bacon drippings, flour, sugar and salt. Add water and vinegar. Cook over low heat until sauce is smooth. Mix vegetables and rice. Pour sauce over and toss. Sprinkle with crumbled bacon. Makes 4 to 6 servings.

Tim P. Johnson, Representative (South Dakota)

EASY RICE SALAD

2 cups cooked rice
2 cups golden raisins
1 tablespoon orange rind
½ cup orange juice
½ bottle ready-made Caesar salad dressing
2 tart apples (cored and chopped)
1 cup slivered almonds
⅛ teaspoon white pepper

Combine raisins with orange rind, orange juice and salad dressing. Add apples, slivered almonds, and white pepper. Toss mixture with rice. Chill for several hours. Makes 8 to 10 servings.

Mrs. John Watson, Daughter of former Representative Glenard P. Lipscomb (California)

TABBOULEH

1 cup bulgur wheat
water
1 cup finely chopped parsley
1 cup finely chopped green
onions
½ cup finely chopped fresh
mint
3 medium tomatoes, peeled,
seeded and chopped
⅓ cup freshly squeezed
lemon juice
⅓ cup olive oil
salt and pepper to taste

Soak the bulgur in water for 10 minutes to plump the grains. Drain well and add all the other ingredients, tossing well. Season and decorate with minced cucumber and mint. Makes 10 servings (as part of a buffet).

Mrs. Michael Oxley, Wife of Representative (Ohio)

TABBOULEH SALAD

1 cup uncooked bulgur
1 cup olive oil
½ cup lemon juice
1 cup scallions, finely
chopped, including
green tops
1 cup celery, chopped
3 tomatoes, finely chopped
3 green peppers, seeded and
finely chopped
2 large cucumbers, peeled
and finely chopped
2 teaspoon salt
black pepper to taste

Use a large glass jar, 2 quarts, with a screw top or a deep large glass bowl that can be easily covered. Place the bulgur in the bottom of the container. In a small bowl, mix the oil and lemon juice and pour over the bulgur. Add the vegetables in layers, in the order listed above. Sprinkle the last layer (cucumbers) with salt and pepper. Cover and refrigerate for at least 24 hours, or until the bulgur has expanded and is light in color. Just before serving, shake the jar well, or toss the salad to blend the ingredients completely. Makes 8 servings.

Mrs. Glenard Lipscomb, Wife of former Representative (California)

PRESTO (ARTICHOKE) PASTA SALAD

4 ozs. salad macaroni
1 jar (6 ozs.) marinated artichoke hearts
½ pound whole small mush-
 rooms
2 medium tomatoes, seeded
 and cut into bite size
 pieces or equivalent
 cherry tomatoes
1 cup medium size pitted
 ripe olives
 salt and pepper

Cook macaroni according to package instructions in a large kettle of salted, boiling water until al dente. Drain. Rinse with cold water and drain again. Turn into a large bowl. Combine artichokes with their liquid, mushrooms, tomatoes and olives. Add this mixture to the pasta and toss gently. Cover and refrigerate for 4 hours at least or until the next day. Before serving, add salt and pepper to taste. Makes 4 to 6 servings.

Joyce Brown

Mrs. Clarence Brown, Wife of former Representative (Ohio)

VERMICELLI SALAD

2 green peppers
2 medium cucumbers
4 medium tomatoes
1 large red onion
16 oz. box vermicelli
16 oz. Kraft Zesty Italian salad
 dressing
 McCormick's Salad
 Supreme

Chop all vegetables and combine in a very large bowl. Cook vermicelli according to box directions. Drain well and rinse with cold water. Combine vermicelli with chopped vegetables. Pour in Zesty Italian dressing and Salad Supreme. Mix well. Best if refrigerated overnight. You may also add shrimp or pepperoni, if desired. Makes 15 servings.

Laura Bateman Hehner

Mrs. Dee Bateman-Hehner, Daughter of Representative Herb Bateman (Virginia)

PASTA WITH SPINACH PESTO AND TUNA

10 oz. spinach, thawed and
    drained
1 cup fresh parsley, chopped
½ cup walnuts, chopped
⅔ cup fresh Romano cheese,
    grated
2 cloves garlic
3 tablespoons fresh basil,
    minced
1 teaspoon salt
¼ teaspoon fennel seeds,
    crushed
1 cup olive oil
½ pound rotelli (corkscrew
    pasta)
1 can (14 ozs.) tuna, drained
2 small green peppers, diced
¼ cup pimento, diced

Combine first 8 ingredients in food processor. With processor on, slowly add olive oil. Blend until smooth and well mixed. Cook rotelli in boiling, salted water, until al dente. Drain and mix with sauce, tuna, green peppers and pimento. Serve at room temperature. Makes 12 servings.

Caryll Kyl

Mrs. Jon Kyl, Wife of Representative (Arizona)

GREEN BEANS NICOISE

4 cups fresh green beans
1 small onion
2 tablespoons olive oil
2 tablespoons wine vinegar
½ teaspoon salt
    fresh ground pepper to
    taste
1 can flaked tuna packed in
    water
2 tablespoons grated
    Parmesan

Snap ends off beans, steam until tender but not soft. Toss with onion, oil, vinegar, salt and pepper. Chill. Toss again before serving. Divide between 2 plates, garnish each serving with half the tuna and half the Parmesan. Serve with an interesting bread. Makes 2 large servings.

Gayle Kildee

Mrs. Dale Kildee, Wife of Representative (Michigan)

ORIENTAL LUNCHEON SALAD

1 cup frozen peas
1 6½ oz. can tuna, drained
1 cup sliced celery
½ cup mayonnaise
1 tablespoon lemon juice
1½ teaspoons soy sauce
  dash garlic powder
1 cup chow mein noodles

Cook peas according to package directions. Drain and cool. In a salad bowl, combine tuna, celery, mayonnaise, lemon juice, soy sauce and garlic powder. Chill. Just before serving, add peas and chow mein noodles and toss gently. Makes 4 servings.

Mrs. Hamer Budge, Wife of former Representative (Idaho)

COOL TUNA SALAD

¾ cup Miracle Whip salad
  dressing or Kraft real
  mayonnaise
½ cup sour cream
¼ cup chopped, peeled
  cucumber
2 tablespoons finely chopped
  onion
2 hard-cooked eggs,
  separated
1 teaspoon dill weed
½ quart torn assorted greens
2 6½ oz. cans Starkist tuna,
  drained, flaked
  tomato wedges

Mix salad dressing, sour cream, cucumbers, onions, chopped egg whites and dill weed. Chill. For each serving, top greens with tuna and dressing. Garnish with sieved egg yolks and tomatoes. Makes 4 servings.

Mrs. Olin Teague, Wife of former Representative (Texas)

TUNA SALAD

1 pkg. frozen peas
1 can tuna
½ cup chopped celery
1 tablespoon soy sauce
½ cup chopped green onions
1 cup or less mayonnaise
1 small can Chinese noodles

Mix all the ingredients except noodles in a large bowl. Refrigerate. Just before serving, add the chinese noodles and mix. Makes very easy, but delicious lunch dish. Makes 4 servings.

Mrs. Edward Zorinsky-White, Wife of former Senator Ed Zorinsky (Nebraska)

SHRIMP AND PASTA SALAD

12 large cooked and deveined shrimp cut into small pieces
½ cup chopped celery
½ cup chopped red bell pepper
¼ cup minced onion
½ medium sized mango, sliced into small pieces
a little ground pepper to taste
enough mayonnaise to moisten

Salad Dressing:
1 packet Good Seasons Italian dressing
¼ cup wine vinegar
2 tablespoons water
⅔ cup V8 juice

Mix all ingredients together and serve chilled on a bed of lettuce. Serve with about ½ pound of cooked and chilled capellini pasta, tossed with a little oil and Locatelli Romano cheese and a no fat salad dressing.

Dressing: Mix vinegar and water, add packet of Good Seasons, mix until dissolved. Add V8 juice and again mix. Refrigerate until ready to use. Makes about 4 servings.

Mrs. William Hughes, Wife of Representative (New Jersey)

SHRIMP SALAD

2 pounds cooked, peeled and
    deveined medium
    shrimp
3 to 4 ribs celery, finely
    diced
3 cups mayonnaise
1 cup sour cream
1 cup chili sauce
2½ tablespoons grated onion
    dash of cayenne pepper

Mix together shrimp and celery, set aside. In separate bowl, mix the remaining ingredients to make dressing. Pour dressing over shrimp and toss well. Chill for at least three hours. Serve on lettuce bed garnished with tomatoes, hard-boiled egg slices and lemon wedges. Makes 6 servings.

Mrs. Craig James, Wife of former Representative (Florida)

WASHINGTON SALAD

4 cups grated carrots
4 cups grated sharp cheddar
    cheese
4 cups chopped celery
4 cups fresh tiny shrimp
1 cup chopped green onion
2 cups mayonnaise
1 3 oz. can chow mein
    noodles
    lettuce leaves
    chopped parsley for
    garnish

Toss together carrots, cheese, celery, shrimp, green onions, and mayonnaise and refrigerate overnight. Sprinkle chow mein noodles over salad just before serving. Serve on a bed of lettuce and garnish with parsley. Makes 10 servings.

Mrs. Rod Chandler, Wife of former Representative (Washington)

ANNIE WADE'S CRAB SALAD

1 pound crab meat (lump)
3 oz. vinegar (white)
4 oz. salad oil (Wesson)
¼ cup onion
4 oz. ice water
salt and pepper to taste

Put crabmeat in container. Pour other ingredients over and let sit in refrigerator 6 hours or overnight.

Ivo Sparkman

Mrs. John Sparkman, Wife of former Senator (Alabama)

CRAB LOUIS

1 egg yolk
2 teaspoons prepared imported mustard
½ teaspoons Worcestershire sauce
2 teaspoons red wine vinegar
salt and freshly ground pepper
½ cup vegetable or corn oil
1 tablespoons chili sauce
¼ cup finely chopped scallions
4 large stuffed green olives, chopped (about ¼ cup)
1 pound lump crab, picked over to remove all trace of shell and cartilage
lettuce leaves
2 hard-cooked eggs, sliced (optional)

Put yolk in a mixing bowl and add the mustard, Worcestershire sauce, and vinegar. Beat with a wire whisk. Add the oil gradually, beating rapidly with the whisk. When thickened and smooth, add chili sauce, scallions and olives, blend. Put the crab in a mixing bowl and add half the sauce. Blend gently so as not to break up the crab lumps more than necessary. Pile equal portions of the crab on a bed of lettuce leaves. Spoon the remaining sauce over. Garnish the crab filling, if desired, with egg slices. Makes 4 servings.

Rita Hanley

Mrs. James Hanley, Wife of former Representative (New York)

SALMON PASTA SALAD

12 oz. box pasta (I use
  twist trio)
6 to 8 oz. (leftover) baked or
  broiled salmon (frozen
  or canned salmon may
  be used)
1 tablespoon Italian herbs
2 tablespoons olive oil
½ cup no fat ranch dressing
2 tablespoons wine vinegar
½ cup chopped celery
⅓ cup low salt dill pickles,
  chopped
½ cup frozen peas

Cook pasta according to directions, drain. Add all ingredients, toss lightly and enjoy. Makes 6 to 8 servings.

Mrs. Tom Lewis, Wife of Representative (Florida)

SALMON SALAD

1 can red Sockeye salmon,
  15 oz.
¼ cup mayonnaise
¼ cup finely chopped onion
2 tablespoons sweet relish
2 tablespoons prepared horseradish

In bowl, separate salmon with fork, remove bones. Add remaining ingredients and mix until evenly combined. Use at once or refrigerate before serving. Recipe easily doubled. Serve on bed of greens with saltine crackers for light meal or as an appetizer. Makes 2 to 3 servings.

Mrs. Gerald Solomon, Wife of Representative (New York)

SEA LEG SALAD

1 pound sea legs
½ cup diced celery
1 cucumber
  garlic salt
  Tabasco sauce
2 tablespoons mayonnaise
½ teaspoon dill weed
4 lemon slices

In a medium sized mixing bowl, combine sea legs and celery. Add cucumber (remove seeds by scraping out the seeds after slitting cucumber). Add other ingredients. Use Tobasco sauce to suit taste. Serve in a fine salad dish. Sprinkle lightly with paprika. Garnish with lemon wedges. Makes 6 servings.

Mary H. Bateman

Mrs. Herbert Bateman, Daughter-in-law of Representative Herb Bateman (Virginia)

CHICKEN SALAD

4 cups chopped chicken
2 cups chopped celery
1 cup sliced water chestnuts
1 cup sliced almonds, lightly
  toasted
2 cups mayonnaise
1½ teaspoon curry powder
1 tablespoon soy sauce

I do not use quite two cups of celery or a full cup of water chestnuts, but this is the original recipe. I think you have to fix according to your taste. Mix ingredients and chill.

Mrs. Jamie L. Whitten

Mrs. Jamie L. Whitten, Wife of Representative (Mississippi)

HOT CHICKEN SALAD

4 large chicken breasts
2 cups chopped celery
³/₄ cup chopped roasted
     almonds
2 tablespoons grated onions
     (white)
1 cup sauted fresh
     mushrooms
³/₄ teaspoon salt
³/₄ teaspoon Accent
2 tablespoons lemon juice
1½ cups mayonnaise
¼ pound grated sharp
     cheddar cheese
   bread crumbs, buttered (to
     cover top of casserole)

Cook chicken in covered pan on top of stove until tender. Bone and cut into small pieces or chunks. Add all other ingredients, except bread crumbs, mix together lightly and place in 13″ × 9″ × 2″ casserole. Refrigerate overnight. Cover with buttered bread crumbs and bake in 350° oven for 30 minutes. Makes 8 to 10 servings. May be frozen.

Mrs. Lyle H. Boren, Wife of former Representative (Oklahoma)

ORIENTAL CHICKEN SALAD

4 to 6 cups cooked chicken,
     cubed
1 large can sliced water
     chestnuts
1 cup seedless grapes, cut in
     half
1 cup chopped celery
1 cup sliced almonds, toasted
1 cup mayonnaise
2 teaspoons soy sauce
1 teaspoon lemon juice
1 teaspoon curry powder
     (optional)
   lettuce

Combine chicken, water chestnuts, grapes, celery and almonds. Into the mayonnaise, mix the soy sauce, lemon juice and curry powder (optional). Fold mayonnaise mixture into the chicken mixture. More soy sauce may be added if necessary. Serve on lettuce. Makes 6 to 8 servings.

Mrs. Ernest F. Hollings, Wife of Senator (South Carolina)

CRUNCHY CHICKEN SALAD

2 cups cubed cooked
   chicken
1 cup cooked rice (cooled)
1 cup frozen uncooked
   green peas
½ cup diced water chestnuts
¼ cup sliced celery
¼ cup chopped bell pepper
¼ cup chopped onion
¼ cup chopped parsley
1 cup whole kernel corn
2 tablespoons chopped
   pimiento
½ cup Green Goddess bottled
   dressing
¼ cup sour cream

Combine all ingredients. Cover, chill until serving time. Makes 6 to 8 servings.

Lucille de la Garza

Mrs. Kika de la Garza, Wife of Representative (Texas)

If fresh vegetables are wilted or blemished, pick off the brown edges, sprinkle with cool water, wrap in paper towels and refrigerate for an hour or so.

CHICKEN SALAD CASSEROLE

2 cups cut up chicken
2 cups diced celery
½ cup almonds
½ teaspoon salt
2 teaspoons onion
1 cup mayonnaise
2 teaspoons lemon juice
½ cup grated cheese

Put in casserole. Sprinkle with 1 cup crushed potato chips. Bake 30 minutes at 450°. Makes 4 to 6 servings.

Frieda G. James

Mrs. Benjamin James, Wife of former Representative (Pennsylvania)

SHREDDED CHICKEN SALAD

2 boneless chicken breast
  halves (½ pound)
  skinned
4 large romaine lettuce
  leaves
2 cups shredded iceberg
  lettuce
1 cup thinly sliced cucumber
½ cup shredded zucchini
1 tablespoon olive oil
1 clove garlic, minced
¼ teaspoon dried whole
  oregano
¼ cup red wine vinegar
3 tablespoons water
⅛ teaspoon pepper
1 tablespoon grated parmesan cheese

Trim excess fat from chicken. Rinse chicken with cold water, pat dry. Place in a 1 quart glass baking dish. Cover with heavy-duty plastic wrap and vent, microwave at high for 4 to 6 minutes or until chicken is tender, turning chicken and rotating dish a half-turn after 2 minutes. Cool to room temperature. Shred chicken into bite size pieces, set aside. Arrange romaine leaves on a serving platter. Top with shredded lettuce, cucumber slices, zucchini and reserved chicken. Place oil in a 1 cup glass measure. Microwave, uncovered, at high for 30 seconds to 1 minute. Stir in garlic and oregano. Microwave at high for 30 seconds. Stir in vinegar, water and pepper. Pour mixture over salad. Sprinkle with cheese. (123 calories per serving). Makes 4 servings.

Franki Jean Roberts

Mrs. Pat Roberts, Wife of Representative (Kansas)

CHICKEN SALAD

3 whole chicken breasts
¼ cup slivered almonds
2 tablespoons sesame seeds
1 head medium size romaine
   lettuce
1 bunch green onions
1 3 oz. can chow mein
   noodles
2 tablespoons sugar
2 teaspoons salt
¼ teaspoon coarsely ground
   black pepper
¼ cup salad oil
¼ cup vinegar

Cook chicken in boiling water about 25 minutes, drain and cool. Skin and bone chicken. Cut into strips. Lightly toast almonds and sesame seeds. Tear lettuce into bite size pieces. Combine chicken, lettuce, onions, noodles, almonds, and sesame seeds in large bowl, set aside. Combine sugar, salt, pepper, oil and vinegar; mix well. Pour over chicken mixture. Toss lightly. Serve immediately. Depending on the size of the head of lettuce, the dressing may need to be increased. Makes 8 servings.

Ike Skelton, Representative (Missouri)

CHICKEN AND PASTA SALAD WITH CURRY AND CHUTNEY

1 pkg. of linguine
1 bottle of spicy peanut
   sauce
3 cups cooked chicken, cut
   into bite sized pieces
   mayonnaise (enough to
   make a creamy consis-
   tency)
1 jar chutney
   curry
   spring onions, chopped
1 can water chestnuts

Cook linguine and chill. Mix with peanut sauce. Mix chicken with enough mayonnaise to make a creamy consistency. Add chutney, spring onions and water chestnuts. Sprinkle curry to taste. Mix with linguine and serve. Makes 6 servings.

Mrs. Robert Beach, Daughter of former Senator James T. Broyhill (North Carolina)

CHICKEN AND PASTA SALAD

8 oz. Rotini pasta
1 cup Miracle Whip Light salad dressing
2 tablespoons soy sauce
1 teaspoon ground ginger
2 cups chopped cooked chicken
3 cups pea pods
1 cup chopped red pepper
¼ cup sliced green onions

Cook pasta as directed on package. In mixing bowl, combine Miracle Whip Light, soy sauce and ginger. Then add the cooked pasta, cooked chicken (you may use canned), pea pods (uncooked), chopped red pepper and green onion. Mix lightly and refrigerate for at least 1 hour before serving. A nice summer lunch for the patio! Serve with fresh fruit. Makes 4 to 6 servings.

Joyce Murtha

Mrs. John P. Murtha, Wife of Representative (Pennsylvania)

CHICKEN SALAD

¼ cup black or green olives, sliced
1 pkg. Rice-A-Roni, cooked as per package directions
6 green onions, sliced
½ cup green pepper, chopped
1 6½ oz. jar marinated artichoke hearts, drained (keep marinade)
1 cup chopped celery
2 cups cooked chopped chicken
⅓ cup mayonnaise
¼ teaspoon curry powder
¼ teaspoon dry mustard marinade from artichoke hearts

Combine olives, Rice-A-Roni, onions, green pepper, artichoke hearts (sliced), celery, chicken. Make dressing combining mayonnaise, curry powder, mustard, marinade. Toss dressing with other ingredients. Chill. Makes 8 servings.

Fran Symms

Mrs. Fran Symms, Member of The Congressional Club

DUCK AND SPINACH SALAD

Dressing:
1 egg yolk
3 hard-cooked eggs
1 clove garlic, chopped
2 teaspoons Dijon mustard
3 tablespoons sugar
3 to 4 tablespoons red wine
    vinegar
    salt and pepper
½ cup olive oil
½ cup cream

Salad:
2 cups shredded cooked
    duck
2 pounds fresh spinach,
    washed, dried and torn
    into pieces
1 red pepper, cut into slivers
1 bunch of scallions, minced,
    including some of the
    green
    crisped duck skin
    (optional)

Prepare the dressing: In a food processor or blender, blend egg yolk, hard-cooked eggs and garlic. Add mustard, sugar, vinegar, salt and pepper and blend again. With the machine running, slowly pour in oil and then the cream. To serve, combine the duck, spinach, red pepper and scallions in a large bowl and toss with the dressing. Garnish with the crisped duck skin. Makes 6 to 8 servings.

Mrs. George Hochbrueckner, Wife of Representative (New York)

THREE BEAN SALAD

1 cup cooked green beans,
    halved
1 cup cooked kidney beans
1 cup cooked wax beans
½ cup finely sliced celery
2 scallions, finely sliced
2 tablespoons chopped
    sweet pickle

For dressing:
¼ cup oil
2 tablespoons cider vinegar
    salt and pepper to taste
1 teaspoon dill

The Congressional Club

Drain the three different kinds of beans thoroughly and combine in a bowl with the celery, scallions and pickle. In another bowl, beat the ingredients for the dressing together until smooth and pour over the bean mixture. Turn the mixture with two wooden spoons until salad and dressing are thoroughly combined and taste for seasoning. Chill. Serves 4 to 6.

TACO SALAD

2 pounds ground round
1 head lettuce, broken
1 large can red kidney beans
1 can water chestnuts, sliced
6 radishes, sliced
1 block Muenster cheese, cubed
1 can black ripe olives, sliced
1 bell pepper, chopped
1 bunch green onions or 1 onion, sliced
2 avocados, in chunks
1 8 oz. bottle Golden Caesar salad dressing
6 ozs. cashews
Doritos and cheddar cheese

Cook beef and cool (season lightly with salt, pepper and garlic powder). Drain beans. Mix all ingredients down to avocados. Pour 1 bottle of Golden Caesar salad dressing. Add avocados, cashews, bag of Doritos and some grated cheddar cheese. Serve with warm tortillas. Makes 6 to 8 servings.

Mrs. Sam Johnson, Wife of Representative (Texas)

MACARONI AND VEAL SALAD

2 cups cooked elbow macaroni
1 cup chopped celery
6 sweet pickles, chopped
1½ cups diced cooked veal
mayonnaise to moisten
lettuce leaves for serving

Mix the macaroni, celery, pickles and veal in a bowl. Add enough mayonnaise to moisten thoroughly and mix. Serve on lettuce leaves. Serves 5.

The Congressional Club

TEX-MEX CHEF'S SALAD

1 onion
1 head lettuce
4 tomatoes
4 ozs. cheddar cheese, grated
8 ozs. Thousand Island or
   French dressing
1 medium bag tortilla chips
   (plain or taco), crushed
1 large avocado, sliced
   (reserve a few whole for
   garnish)
1 pound ground beef
1 can kidney beans (15 ozs.),
   drained
1/4 teaspoon salt

Chop onion, lettuce, and tomatoes (reserve a few tomato slices for garnish). Toss with the grated cheese and dressing. Add the crushed tortilla chips and the sliced avocado (reserve a few slices for garnish). Brown the ground beef, add the drained kidney beans and salt, and simmer for 10 minutes. Add into the cold salad. Garnish with tortilla chips, avocado, and tomato slices. Makes 6 servings.

Mrs. Anthony Beilenson, Wife of Representative (California)

CLAIRE'S FLAMING STEAK SALAD

1 large head of iceberg
   lettuce
4 carrots
4 stalks of celery
1/2 pound mild cheddar
   cheese, cubed
1 cup salad olives
1/2 cup Caesar or Italian
   dressing
2 pounds cubed sirloin steak
   butter and oil, enough to
   saute steak (about 1
   tablespoon)
1 to 2 cups fresh mushrooms
1/4 cup Dijon style mustard
1/4 cup horseradish sauce
   hot brandy (optional)

Make salad on large serving platter. Store in refrigerator. Just before serving, put over top of salad, the cheese, salad olives and dressing. Saute cubed sirloin in butter and oil until browned. Add mushrooms (whole if small, halved if larger), saute. Add mustard and horseradish sauce. Brown. If you are going to serve steak over salad, arrange on top and bring to table. Pour hot brandy over top and light if you want it fancy, or to keep it warm longer, serve salad on its separate platter, and put beef/mushroom mixture in chaffing dish, flame at table. Makes 8 servings.

Mrs. W. G. (Bill) Hefner, Wife of Representative (North Carolina)

BALSAMIC VINEGAR DRESSING

¼ cup Balsamic vinegar
1 clove garlic
¼ teaspoon salt
¼ teaspoon pepper
¼ teaspoon dry mustard
1½ teaspoon sugar
½ cup olive oil

Shake all ingredients together. Makes 4 servings.

Mrs. Charles Vanik, Wife of former Representative (Ohio)

THE PAYNES' BLUE CHEESE DRESSING

¾ cup sour cream
½ teaspoon dry mustard
½ teaspoon black pepper
½ teaspoon salt
¼ teaspoon garlic powder
1 teaspoon Worcestershire
    sauce
1½ cups mayonnaise
4 ozs. blue cheese

Mix all ingredients together in a food processor for 3–4 minutes. Bottle and seal the unused portion and refrigerate.

Mrs. Steve Neal, Wife of Representative (North Carolina)

1 tablespoon lemon juice or vinegar in 1 cup milk equals 1 cup buttermilk or sour milk.

SENSATIONAL SALAD DRESSING

½ pound finely ground
    Romano cheese
1 pint salad oil
  juice of 2 lemons
  juice of 3 cloves of garlic

Shake all ingredients in a quart jar. Dressing will keep indefinitely in refrigerator. Especially good tossed with lettuce, water cress, and parsley leaves. Salt and pepper greens as desired before adding dressing. Makes 6 to 8 servings.

Catherine Holloway

Mrs. Clyde Holloway, Wife of former Representative (Louisiana)

LEONARD'S RUSSIAN DRESSING

⅔ cup salad oil
½ cup catsup
¼ cup sugar
3 tablespoons lemon juice
2 tablespoons Worcestershire
    sauce
2 tablespoons vinegar
2 tablespoons water
1 + tablespoons grated or
    minced onion
½ teaspoon salt
½ teaspoon paprika

Mix all ingredients in pint jar with lid. Shake well. Chill. Shake again before serving. Optional: Crumble blue cheese over salad, or add to dressing. Makes 14 oz.

Nancy Schulze

Mrs. Richard T. Schulze, Wife of former Representative (Pennsylvania)

Add zip to store bought french dressing by putting a clove of garlic in the bottle.

TOMATO DRESSING

1 cup sugar
1 tablespoon salt
1 teaspoon pepper
¾ cup vinegar
1 cup salad oil
1 can tomato soup
2 to 3 cloves garlic, whole

In a large jar, combine all ingredients and shake well. Refrigerate. Before serving remove garlic cloves. Makes 4 cups.

Melanie Broyhill

Mrs. Edgar Broyhill, Daughter-in-law of former Senator James T. Broyhill (North Carolina)

FRENCH DRESSING

1 cup canola oil
¼ cup red wine vinegar
2 tablespoons lemon juice
   (Realemon lemon juice)
½ cup catsup
1 teaspoon salt
2 tablespoons onion juice
   red pepper to taste
   garlic to taste
4 pkgs. of Equal

Mix in order given. Shake well before using. Good for any vegetable or fresh fruit salad. Makes 1 pint.

Mike Heflin

Mrs. Howell Heflin, Wife of Senator (Alabama)

> *Put salad dressing in the bottom of the bowl, layer ingredients and toss just before serving.*

MAMA'S FAVORITE SALAD DRESSING

½ cup olive oil
2 tablespoon vinegar
1 teaspoon Dijon mustard
½ teaspoon salt
2 cloves garlic
   pinch basil
   pinch oregano
   pinch sugar

Mix all ingredients together in blender until smooth. Store in refrigerator. Best on a salad of tender leaf lettuce, with halved tiny tomatoes, and sprinkled with Grape Nuts. Makes 12 servings.

Fran DeWine

Mrs. Michael DeWine, Wife of former Representative (Ohio)

THOUSAND ISLAND DRESSING

2 cups mayonnaise
1 cup catsup
1 tablespoon Worcestershire
   sauce
1 tablespoon vinegar
¼ cup sugar
1 teaspoon granulated garlic
½ cup sweet pickle relish
½ cup chopped Spanish
   olives

Combine all ingredients using a wire whip to mix well. Refrigerate. Makes 1 quart.

Lynn Staton

Mrs. Mick Staton, Wife of former Representative (West Virginia)

Put salad greens or cole slaw in a metal bowl and place in the freezer for a few minutes to crisp quickly.

HONEY DRESSING

⅔ cup sugar
1 teaspoon dry mustard
1 teaspoon paprika
¼ teaspoon salt
1 teaspoon celery seed
⅓ cup honey
5 tablespoons vinegar
1 tablespoon lemon juice
1 tablespoon grated onion
1 cup salad oil

Mix dry ingredients; add honey, lemon juice, vinegar and onion. Mix well. Slowly pour oil into mixture, beating constantly. Blender may be used. Do not refrigerate! This will keep indefinitely. Dressing is good over fruit salad. Makes about 2 cups.

Mrs. Mick Staton, Wife of former Representative (West Virginia)

HANDY DANDY DIET DRESSING

1 6 oz. can tomato juice
1 tablespoon Dijon mustard
1 tablespoon lemon juice
2 teaspoons capers
2 cooked and chopped egg
   whites
3 garlic powder and black
   pepper to taste
   teaspoons chopped pimento (optional)

Mix well and chill. Makes 20 servings.

Beth Breaux, Daughter of Senator John Breaux (Louisiana)

JOHNNY'S NAVY DRESSING

Equal parts of each ingredient:
    apple vinegar
    white sugar
    crisco oil
    ketchup

Mix ingredients, shake well and serve over your salad. To use this recipe for slaw, delete the ketchup. Makes 4 to 6 servings.

Jerry F. Costello, Representative (Illinois)

HOUSE VINAIGRETTE

2 cups vinegar
2 cups salad oil
2 teaspoons garlic powder
2 teaspoons pepper
2 teaspoons salt
2 tablespoons sugar

Mix all the ingredients in a jar. Shake well before serving. Makes 50 servings.

Judy Hum, The Congressional Club Chef

> *Lumpless gravy can be your triumph if you add a pinch of salt to the flour before mixing it with water.*

PARMESAN DRESSING

¼ cup salad oil
2 garlic buds, minced
½ teaspoon salt
¼ teaspoon pepper, preferably fresh
1 tablespoon lemon juice
   pinch dry mustard
2 tablespoons Parmesan cheese, rounded

Put dressing in bottom of salad bowl. Break approximately 2 quarts greens on top of dressing. Just before serving, mix until each piece of green is coated. Delicious dressing for garlic lovers!

Jean M. Cole

Mrs. Thomas Cole, Daughter-in-law of former Representative Sterling Cole (New York)

OLD FASHIONED SALAD DRESSING

2 cups oil
1 cup cider vinegar
1 cup sugar
1 tablespoon garlic powder
1 tablespoons ground mustard
1 teaspoon salt
½ teaspoon black pepper

Put all ingredients in a jar and shake well. Shake again before putting on salad. This is good on a mixture of red and green leaf lettuce. Orange sections also make a nice addition.

Glenda Miller

Mrs. Dan Miller, Wife of Representative (Florida)

A different way of browning flour is to put it in a custard cup placed beside meat in the oven. Once the meat is done, the flour will be nice and brown.

VERMONT APPLESAUCE

25 Vermont McIntosh apples
4 cups water
  nutmeg
  cinnamon

Wash and quarter 25 Vermont McIntosh apples (no need to peel or core). Fill a large pot with 4 cups of water and fill pot to the top with apple quarters. Boil water and then simmer apples on low until they can be stirred and are crumbly. This may take 20 to 30 minutes. Stir from time to time to prevent the bottom from burning. Put apples through a food mill and grind vigorously. Best eaten when hot with nutmeg and cinnamon to taste. Adding sugar is not recommended.

Howard Dean, Governor (Vermont)

ESCALLOPED APPLES

4 cups apples, peeled and
    sliced (I prefer Jonathan,
    McIntosh or Winesap)
½ cup brown sugar
1 cup raisins
½ cup soft bread crumbs
    (about 4 slices)
¼ teaspoon cinnamon
¼ teaspoon nutmeg
⅛ teaspoon cloves
¼ teaspoon salt
1 tablespoon butter
¼ cup water
2 tablespoons lemon juice

Layer apples, brown sugar, raisins and bread crumbs in a 1–1½ quart casserole dish. Mix seasonings together and sprinkle over each set of layers, then dot with butter. After all layers have been assembled, mix water and lemon juice and pour over apples. Bake at 350° for 45 minutes. Makes 8 to 10 servings.

Doug Applegate, Representative (Ohio)

RAW CRANBERRY RELISH À LA NORVÉGIENNE

1 quart (1 pound) raw cranberries, fresh or frozen
1²⁄₃ to 2 cups sugar (more if
   you wish)
   grated rind of one orange

By Mixer: Wash cranberries and place in large bowl with sugar and orange rind. At low speed, take an electric hand mixer and run the mixer for 15 minutes. Let rest ½ hour and beat again. Continue until the sugar has dissolved completely.

By Hand: Stir with a wooden spoon for 5 minutes or more and give a vigorous turn for a few minutes whenever you feel like it, until it dissolves. It may take a day or two if you are lazy at the stirring. Store the relish in a jar (preferably a screw-top jar) where the relish will keep for weeks. This is an old Norwegian recipe. Norwegians use dwarf cranberries which we call lingonberries. This recipe is an adaptation of the original Norwegian dwarf cranberry recipe. Makes 12 servings.

Anne Neal Petri

Mrs. Thomas Petri, Wife of Representative (Wisconsin)

ALMOND CRANBERRY SAUCE

⅓ cup whole blanched al-
   monds
2 cups sugar
1 cup water
1 pound raw cranberries
½ cup apricot jam
¼ cup lemon juice

Spread almonds in shallow pan and place in 350° oven to warm for 5 minutes. Split almonds into halves with paring knife. Combine sugar and water in saucepan. Bring to a boil without stirring. Cook the syrup for 5 minutes over medium heat. Meanwhile wash cranberries. Add to syrup and cook for 3 to 5 minutes or until they burst. Remove from heat. Stir in jam and lemon juice. Chill sauce. Then add almonds. Makes 1 quart. May be frozen.

Florence Long

Mrs. Edward V. Long, Wife of former Senator (Missouri)

CRANBERRY CHUTNEY

2½ cups sugar
1 cup cider vinegar
1 cup chopped onions
1 cup currants or raisins, or
  ½ cup of each
1 teaspoon allspice
3 tablespoons finely grated
  fresh ginger
2 12-oz. pkgs. cranberries
½ cup water

In a medium saucepan, combine sugar, vinegar, onions, currants, allspice and ginger. Cook, uncovered, on medium-high until sugar dissolves. Add cranberries and cook on medium for 10 minutes or until all of them have popped. Stir and remove from heat. Pour into 1-cup jars, seal with paraffin or freeze. To serve, spoon over block of cream cheese and accompany with crackers. Makes 2 quarts. May be frozen.

Mrs. Hamer Budge, Wife of former Representative (Idaho)

CRANBERRY CHUTNEY

4 cups fresh cranberries
1 cup seedless white raisins
1⅔ cups granulated sugar
1 tablespoon cinnamon
½ teaspoon ginger
1½ teaspoons cloves
1 cup water
1 medium onion, chopped
1 medium apple, pared and
  chopped
½ cup sliced celery

Combine the cranberries, raisins, sugar, cinnamon, ginger, cloves and water in a large sauce pan. Cook approximately 15 minutes until the berries pop and the mixture thickens. Stir in the onion, apple and celery. Simmer approximately 15 minutes longer or until the mixture thickens. Cool. Refrigerate. Makes 6 to 8 servings.

Mrs. James Harvey, Wife of former Representative (Michigan)

Lemons at room temperature make the best juice.

CURRIED FRUIT

⅓ cup butter
2 teaspoon curry powder
¾ cup brown sugar
1 #2 can of each of the
    following:
    pineapple chunks
    sliced peaches
    halved apricots, sliced
    sliced pears
    cherries (red, maraschino,
      10½ oz. jar)

Drain fruit in colander at least ½ hour (cherries must be drained separately). Melt butter and stir in brown sugar and curry powder. Combine fruits and curry mixture in 3 quart casserole. Bake at 350° for 1 hour. Serve hot. Makes 8 servings. May be frozen.

Betsy Mann

Mrs. David Mann, Wife of Representative (Ohio)

HOT FRUIT COMPOTE

1 heaping cup dried, pitted,
    cut up prunes
1½ cups pineapple chunks,
    not drained
2 cups apricots, (or
    peaches), cut up
1 can cherry pie filling
1½ cups water
½ cup sherry

Stir all ingredients together and put into a casserole uncovered. Bake at 350° for 1 hour. Makes many servings.

Marguerite Nye

Mrs. Gerald P. Nye, Wife of former Senator (North Dakota)

---

*Ripen green fruits by placing in a perforated plastic bag
The holes allow air movement, yet retain the odorless gas
which fruits produce to promote ripening.*

SMOKE SEASONING

1 cup table salt
4 tablespoons black pepper
4 tablespoons white pepper
4 tablespoons sugar
2 teaspoons onion powder
2 teaspoons garlic powder
1 teaspoon sage
4 tablespoons paprika
1½ teaspoons rosemary
1½ teaspoons marjoram
1 teaspoon ground cloves

For use on smoked poultry, beef and wild game in outdoor smoker. Combine ingredients in quart jar punching holes in lid to make shaker. Thoroughly coat poultry, meat or wild game with above mixture. Cook according to smoker directions. Example: smoked turkey—coat with mixture, add 1 pan of water, 1 small bag of charcoal, several chunks of hickory. Cook 7-10 hours until all charcoal is burned. Cool, remove from smoker. Makes 1 quart.

Stan Parris, former Representative (Virginia)

GRANDMOTHER'S BARBECUE SAUCE

2 14 oz. bottles ketchup
1 12 oz. bottle chili sauce
½ cup prepared mustard
1 tablespoon dry mustard
1½ cups firmly packed brown
   sugar
2 tablespoons pepper
1½ cups red wine vinegar
1 cup lemon juice
½ cup Heinz 57 sauce
1 teaspoon Tabasco sauce
½ cup soy sauce
1 tablespoon Worcestershire
   sauce
3 tablespoons vegetable oil
1 12 oz. can beer

Blend all ingredients. Pour into glass jars, cover and refrigerate. Makes 1 gallon. May be frozen.

Mrs. Mark White, Daughter of former Representative Richard H. Ichord (Missouri)

COLMAN MUSTARD SAUCE

¾ cup Colman (use only Colman) dry mustard
   vinegar
2 eggs
1 cup sugar

Put mustard in a measuring cup. Add vinegar until it fills the cup. Stir mustard while pouring in vinegar. Let stand overnight. Beat eggs. Add sugar and mustard-vinegar mixture. Cook all together until thick.

Florence Long

Mrs. Edward V. Long, Wife of former Senator (Missouri)

MARINARA SAUCE

2 cloves garlic, minced
1 tablespoon olive oil
1 can Italian plum tomatoes
   (28 oz.)
¾ teaspoon marjoram
½ teaspoon salt
⅛ teaspoon pepper
2 tablespoons parsley
1 can tomato paste
   basil to taste
½ pound cooked spaghetti

Sautè garlic in olive oil, add remaining ingredients and simmer uncovered until the sauce is reduced to 2 cups. Makes 2 to 3 servings. May be frozen.

Sandi Knollenberg

Mrs. Joe Knollenberg, Wife of Representative (Michigan)

CHEESY WINE SAUCE STICK

½ cup soft style margarine
1 cup nonfat dry milk powder
½ cup non-dairy coffee creamer
½ cup all purpose flour
2½ cups shredded cheddar, Swiss, mozzarella or other favorite hard cheese (can also mix cheeses)
1 tablespoon dried parsley flakes
1 tablespoon dried chives or onion flakes
½ teaspoon onion salt or garlic salt
½ teaspoon dry mustard
3 to 4 tablespoons dry white wine

In a medium bowl, combine all ingredients except wine, mix well. Add wine and mix until mixture holds its shape. On a piece of plastic warp, shape cheese mixture into a stick. Use a table knife to score stick into quarters. Wrap in plastic wrap. Store in refrigerator.

To make thin sauce: Measure 1 cup water in a 4 cup glass measuring cup. Crumble in ¼ sauce stick. Microwave at full power (high) 3–4 minutes or until thickened and bubbly, stirring several times. Makes 1½ cups.

To make thick sauce: Follow directions for thin sauce above, except stir 1 tablespoon flour into water along with ¼ stick of sauce mix.

Makes a delicious rich tasting sauce to serve on vegetables or fish. Spices, cheeses and wine can be varied to suit individual taste. I like to add chili pepper, a dash of Tabasco, or cayenne pepper to give the sauce a slightly hotter taste. Makes 6 cups sauce. May be refrigerated for 3–5 weeks.

Martha Regula, Daughter of Representative Ralph Regula (Ohio)

ISLAND CHICKEN MARINADE

1 cup salad oil
⅓ cup lemon juice
3 tablespoons soy sauce
1 clove garlic, minced
1 teaspoon oregano
½ teaspoon salt
¼ teaspoon pepper
1 frying chicken, cut up

Combine all ingredients except chicken. Pour over cut up chicken and marinate for an hour or longer if desired. May be oven broiled, baked, or charcoal broiled. Makes 4 servings.

Daniel A. Mica, former Representative (Florida)

EASY CINNAMON JELLY

2½ cups sugar
1½ cups water
¼ pound cinnamon candy
½ a bottle of pectin

Combine the sugar, water and heat slowly in a saucepan. When dissolved, add the candy and bring to a rapid boil. Stir in the pectin when the candy is dissolved. Boil very hard for one half minute. Pour into properly scalded jars. Makes 2 jars.

Mrs. Robert McClory, Wife of former Representative (Illinois)

JOANNE'S GRAPE JAM

2 quart grapes, preferably
  Concord
2 quart sugar
4 tablespoons water

Cook slowly 25 minutes. Put through sieve (to remove skins and seeds). Heat again and put hot jam into sterilized jars. Simple! And good! May be frozen.

Mrs. Thomas Cole, Daughter-in-law of former Representative Sterling Cole (New York)

NANCY'S MAPLE BUTTER

1 cup soft unsalted butter
⅔ cup real maple syrup
1 teaspoon grated lemon
  peel
½ teaspoon nutmeg

Whip butter. Add next three ingredients. Store in container. It goes fast! Serve on toast or english muffins.

Mrs. Thomas Cole, Daughter-in-law of former Representative Sterling Cole (New York)

DILLED ONIONS

1 large Spanish onion, sliced in thin rings
½ cup sugar
2 teaspoons salt
1 teaspoon vinegar
¼ cup water

Slice onions in rings and separate each one. Place in large neck jar or bowl that can be covered. Make brine of sugar, salt, vinegar and water. Bring brine to a rolling boil for 2 or 3 minutes. Cool and pour over onion rings. Cover and let stand overnight or longer in refrigerator. Stir or shake them every once in a while.

Carol Ann Myers, Daughter of Representative John T. Myers (Indiana)

MOMMA'S PICKLES

1 quart dill pickles with garlic
2 cups sugar
1 tablespoon vinegar
¾ teaspoon mustard seed
¾ teaspoon celery seed
2 to 3 thin slices purple onion

Pour off pickle juice keeping some of the juice aside—approximately ¼ cup. Slice pickles, mix in bowl: pickle slices, sugar, vinegar, mustard seeds, celery seeds, and 2 to 3 thin slices of onion. Put back in pickle jar, pouring the remaining pickle juice over top. Close lid tightly and turn jar upside down for 1 day (24 hrs.). Then turn right side up for 1 day before eating. Makes 1 jar.

Lucinda Bennett, Daughter of former Representative Charles E. Bennett (Florida)

In pickling, do not use iodized table salt, it may darken pickles.

BREAD & BUTTER PICKLES

3 quarts sliced cucumbers
4 small onions, sliced
1 green pepper, cut up
½ cup coarse salt
  ice cubes

Vinegar Mix:
6 cups white vinegar
5 cups sugar
2 tablespoons mustard seed
1 teaspoon celery seed
1 tablespoon tumeric

Mix cucumber, onion, and pepper slices together in a large bowl. Pour salt over mixture. Cover with ice cubes, let stand 3 hours. Boil vinegar mix, set aside, keep hot. Drain cucumber mixture, do not wash off. Pack loosely in hot, sterile jars. Pour hot vinegar mix into jars. Wipe jars, seal at once with boiled lids.

Gayle Kildee

Mrs. Dale Kildee, Wife of Representative (Michigan)

KOSHER DILL PICKLES

4 qts. cucumbers
  iced water
4 cups vinegar
1 cup uniodized salt
3 qts. water
8 heads dill
4 garlic cloves

Wash cucumbers. Let stand overnight in ice water in refrigerator. Drain and pack whole or sliced cucumbers in 4 sterile quart jars. On stove, heat vinegar, salt and water to boiling. To each quart jar, add 2 heads of dill and 1 garlic clove. Pour the boiling brine over the cucumbers and seal jars tightly. Makes 4 quarts.

The Congressional Club

> *Run fork prongs down unpared cucumbers and you will have fluted edges.*

TOMATILLO SAUCE

⅓ cup oil
1 medium onion, chopped
1 7 oz. can green chilies, chopped
2 13 oz. cans tomatillos, drained
1 cup regular strength chicken broth
3 tablespoons lime juice
2 teaspoons sugar
2 teaspoons dry oregano
2 teaspoons dry cilantro (coriander) or 1 teaspoon chopped fresh cilantro
1 teaspoon ground cumin
1 teaspoon cayenne pepper or several dashes of bottled hot sauce (Tabasco)
1 teaspoon ground white pepper
salt to taste

Heat oil in 4 quart sauce pan over medium heat. Add onions and cook until soft (about 5–10 minutes). Stir in chopped green chilies, tomatillos, broth, lime juice, sugar and spices. Bring to a boil, then reduce heat and simmer uncovered, stirring occasionally, for 25 minutes. Blend sauce in electric blender until smooth. Serve with chicken enchiladas by placing a few spoonfuls on plate and placing enchiladas on top. Garnish with sliced tomatillo and fresh cilantro if desired. Sauce for chicken enchiladas. Makes 12 servings. May be frozen.

Mrs. Stephen Gavin, Daughter of Representative Jon Kyl (Arizona)

TEXAS HOT SALSA

2 to 3 jalapeno or serrano chilies
1 small onion, peeled and quartered
1 14½ oz. can Italian plum tomatoes including
4 juices
½ to 5 sprigs fresh cilantro teaspoon salt

Remove stems and cut chilies in half. Place chilies and onions in food processor or blender and mince. Add rest of ingredients and process to a puree. Serve with tostados as an appetizer, or can be used to spice up eggs or any Mexican food dish.

Mrs. Henry Bonilla, Wife of Representative (Texas)

NOTES

Elizabeth Bloomer Ford
1974–1977

With best wishes
Betty Ford

Elizabeth Bloomer Ford

Firestone Hall, The Betty Ford Center

Betty Ford brought a fresh, open manner to the White House. Her sense of humor and down-to-earth approach to life helped to make the role of First Lady more accessible.

Whether discussing her childrens' lives or her own, Mrs. Ford believed in telling people the truth. Her willingness to share the details of her breast cancer with the American public helped many women to find the courage to seek testing for themselves. This forthright policy has carried over into her new life in California, with the establishment of the Betty Ford Center in Rancho Mirage.

VEGETABLES, RICE, BEANS
AND
PASTA

LIMA BEAN AND MUSHROOM CASSEROLE

4 cups baby lima beans
1 cup canned mushrooms
3 tablespoons butter
1 cup milk
3 tablespoons flour
¼ cup grated cheese
1 teaspoon chili powder
¼ teaspoon pepper
½ teaspoon salt (or to taste)

Cook baby lima beans in salted water until tender. Drain thoroughly. Put butter in saucepan and melt. Add mushrooms and sear for 5 minutes. Add flour and milk to make thick sauce. Add grated cheese and let melt. Season with salt, chili powder and pepper. Add lima beans and serve very hot.

Mrs. Lyndon B. Johnson

Mrs. Lyndon B. Johnson, Wife of former President of the United States
Reprinted from the 1970 Congressional Club Cookbook, Eighth Edition

SUNDAY ARTICHOKES

½ cup butter or margarine
2 cups fresh mushrooms, sliced
1 teaspoon salt
½ teaspoon crushed oregano
¼ teaspoon garlic powder
1 teaspoon crushed sweet basil
1 tablespoon fine dry bread crumbs
2 tablespoons fresh lemon juice
2 8 oz. pkgs. frozen artichoke hearts, thawed (or 2 cans artichoke hearts)
½ cup Parmesan cheese

Melt butter in a large, heavy skillet. Saute mushrooms until golden. Sprinkle with salt, basil, oregano and garlic powder during cooking. Stir in bread crumbs and lemon juice, mixing well. Arrange artichoke hearts in a lightly buttered shallow glass baking pan. Spoon mushroom mixture over artichokes. Sprinkle cheese over all. Bake at 350° for 25–30 minutes until juices bubble and cheese is browned. Makes 8 servings.

Ralph Regula, Representative (Ohio)

Artichokes and red vegetables will not discolor if vinegar is added to the cooking water.

ASPARAGUS ALMOND CASSEROLE

1 can cut asparagus
1 can cream of mushroom
   soup
2 eggs, hard-boiled and
   chopped
2 tablespoons slivered almonds
½ cup grated cheddar cheese
   dash red pepper
   dash paprika

Drain asparagus. In bowl, add asparagus, soup, eggs and almonds. Season with red pepper and paprika. Mix well. Place in buttered casserole dish. Spread cheese over top. Bake 30 minutes at 350°. Makes 4 servings.

Tolise Norwood

Mrs. David Norwood, Daughter of former Representative E.C. "Took" Gathings (Arkansas)

ASPARAGUS CASSEROLE

2 cans asparagus, or equivalent fresh asparagus,
   cooked slightly
4 hard boiled eggs, sliced
1 can water chestnuts, sliced
1 can mushrooms, or fresh
3 tablespoons butter
3 tablespoons flour
1½ cups milk
6 ozs. American cheese

Cheese Sauce: Melt butter. Add flour and cook 2 minutes. Remove from heat and whisk in milk all at once. Add cheese and continue stirring to thicken.

Layer one half of asparagus, eggs, chestnuts, mushrooms and cheese sauce in that order. Repeat layering. Top with buttered bread crumbs. Bake in 350° oven until bubbly, about 30 minutes. May be frozen.

Florence Long

Mrs. Edward V. Long, Wife of former Senator (Missouri)

> *Asparagus—Stalks should be tender and firm, tips should be close and compact. Choose the stalks with very little white—they are more tender. Use asparagus soon—it toughens rapidly.*

SCALLOPED ASPARAGUS

⅓ cup butter
¼ cup flour
1 teaspoon salt
pepper
2 cans green asparagus
1 small jar chopped pimento
4 hard-boiled eggs, sliced
½ cup grated American
cheese
⅓ cup dry bread crumbs
milk

Melt 4 tablespoons butter. Add flour, salt and pepper. Drain liquid from asparagus and add enough milk to make 2 cups (may use skim milk). Cook until thickened, then add pimentos. Cover bottom of an 8 inch greased casserole with 1 can of asparagus. Layer sliced eggs, sauce and cheese. Repeat with remaining ingredients and top with bread crumbs. Melt remaining butter and pour over top. Bake at 425° for 20 minutes. Double recipe for a 10 × 15 casserole. This is a good luncheon dish with a salad and rolls. Makes 6-8 servings.

Mrs. Sam Johnson, Wife of Representative (Texas)

ASPARAGUS

2 bunches of asparagus
½ cup soy sauce
¼ cup sesame seed oil

Clean and cut asparagus into 1½ inch pieces. Boil in salted water for 1 minute. Drain and let cool in refrigerator. Toss together with soy sauce and sesame seed oil. You can also substitute broccoli or green beans for the asparagus. Makes 4 servings.

Mrs. Lloyd Meeds, Wife of former Representative (Washington)

FASOLAKIA (GREEK STYLE GREEN BEANS)

2 pounds green beans
2 medium onions, finely chopped
3 tablespoons olive oil
6 plum tomatoes, sliced
3 to 4 garlic cloves, crushed
2 15 oz. cans tomato sauce
salt, pepper, oregano, basil to taste

Clean the beans and cut off the tips. Cut into 4-5 inch lengths. In skillet, saute onions in olive oil until transparent. Add tomatoes and garlic. Simmer until tomatoes are soft. Put beans into heavy saucepan and add enough water just to cover beans. Add tomato sauce. Add onions and tomatoes and spices. Cook tightly covered over low heat until tender. Serve warm or cold. Makes 4 to 6 servings.

Lori Deutsch

Mrs. Peter Deutsch, Wife of Representative (Florida)

TASTY GREEN BEAN CASSEROLE

2 15 oz. cans green beans, cut or french style
1 8 oz. can sliced water chestnuts
½ cup sliced almonds
1 can cream of mushroom soup
1 small can French fried onions

Combine first four ingredients, mixing well. Put in greased 1 quart casserole. Sprinkle top with French fried onions. Bake in preheated 350° oven approximately 30 minutes. Makes 5 servings.

John R. Foley

John R. Foley, Former Representative (Maryland)

Leftover vegetables can be frozen. When you have a sufficient amount, thaw, blend and freeze in ice cube trays. They're good for adding additional flavor to soups, etc.

GREEN BEAN CASSEROLE

Casserole:

1 15 oz. can drained green
   beans
1 15 oz. can drained shoe
   peg corn
1 12 oz. can cream of celery
   soup
½ cup finely chopped onion
½ cup finely chopped bell
   pepper
½ cup finely chopped celery
½ cup grated cheddar cheese
2 cups light sour cream

Topping:

½ cup grated cheddar cheese
⅓ box Ritz crackers, crumbed
¼ cup slivered almonds
½ stick butter

Combine casserole ingredients and place in 9 ×
14 inch pyrex casserole dish. Top with: grated
cheddar cheese, Ritz crackers, slivered almonds
and melted butter or margarine. Bake at 350° for
45 minutes. Makes 12 servings. May be frozen.

Corinne S. Morris

Mrs. Thomas Morris, Wife of former Representative (New Mexico)

BEAN BUNDLES

2 16 oz. cans whole green
   beans, drained
12 to 16 slices bacon, cut in
   half
1 8 oz. bottle commercial
   French dressing
4 to 5 whole pimentos, cut
   into strips

Arrange green beans in bundles of 8, wrapping
a half slice of bacon around each bunch. Place
beans in a 13 × 9 × 2 inch baking dish. Pour
dressing over beans. Cover and chill for 3 hours.
Bake uncovered at 350° for 40 minutes, turning
beans after the first 20 minutes of cooking. Remove beans from dish with slotted spoon. Garnish bean bunches with strips of pimento before
serving. Makes 8 servings.

Luella Rowland

Mrs. J. Roy Rowland, Wife of Representative (Georgia)

GREEN BEAN CASSEROLE

3 cans string beans (French style)
garlic salt
1 small carton sour cream
1 can mushroom soup
8 ozs. Velveeta cheese
24 crackers crushed (butter flavored)

Drain green beans and place in bottom of 6 × 12 inch baking dish. Sprinkle garlic salt. Mix soup and sour cream and pour over beans. Slice cheese and place on top. Cover with cracker crumbs. Bake at 375°, covered, for 30 minutes, then uncovered 15 to 30 minutes (until no longer runny). Makes 9 servings.

Mrs. Jim McCrery, Wife of Representative (Louisiana)

BAKED BEANS

3 slices bacon
1 large onion, chopped
1 clove garlic, minced
1 pound ground beef
1 large can pork & beans
¼ cup molasses
½ cup *hot* ketchup
½ teaspoon dry mustard
1 teaspoon salt
1 tablespoon Worcestershire sauce

Brown bacon, onion, garlic and ground beef together. Combine with remaining ingredients. Bake at 325° for 40 minutes. Makes 4 servings. May be frozen.

Richard Bryan, Senator (Nevada)

SWEET AND SOUR BEANS

1 one pound can baked
   beans
6 tablespoons pineapple
   tidbits
5 tablespoons chopped red
   or green pepper
3 tablespoons brown sugar
3 tablespoons wine or balsamic vinegar
1 garlic clove, minced
1 teaspoon soy sauce

Combine all to taste. Bake at 350° for 1 hour.
Makes 4 servings.

Mrs. Emilio Daddario, Wife of former Representative (Connecticut)

LUSCIOUS LENTIL STEW

4 cups water
¾ cup dried lentils (rinsed and strained)
1 cup chopped onion
3 carrots-sliced
2 celery stalks, sliced
¾ teaspoon salt or salt substitute
½ teaspoon black pepper
1½ teaspoons lemon juice
¼ cup chopped fresh parsley
¼ teaspoon garlic powder
¼ teaspoon red pepper (optional)
½ cup sliced hot or mild chili peppers (optional)
¼ teaspoon dried leaf thyme
1 6 oz can tomato paste

This is a great, easy dish, low in calories and good for you too! In a 4 quart microwave-safe dish, combine water, lentils, onion, carrots, celery, salt, pepper, lemon juice, parsley, garlic powder, peppers and thyme. Cover tightly. Microwave on 70% power (medium-high) 40 minutes, stirring several times during cooking. Stir in tomato paste. Re-cover, microwave on 70% power 5 to 10 minutes more or until mixture is as thick as desired, stirring several times during cooking. 76 calories per serving—.2 grams fat. Makes 8 (¾ cup) servings. May be frozen.

Martha Regula, Daughter of Representative Ralph Regula (Ohio)

ED'S BAKED BEANS AND SAUSAGE

1 pound sausage
1 onion, chopped
2 bell peppers, chopped
2 16 oz. cans pork and beans
½ cup light brown sugar
¼ cup molasses
1 teaspoons dry mustard
2 teaspoons Worcestershire sauce
½ cup catsup
black pepper to taste

Brown meat and break into bite sized pieces, remove from skillet. Brown onion and bell pepper in meat drippings. Drain meat, onion and pepper well. Stir together pork and beans, brown sugar, molasses, mustard, Worcestershire, catsup and black pepper. Mix in meat, onions and bell pepper. Pour into lightly greased casserole. Bake at 325° for about 1 hour or until slightly thickened and meat is done. Makes 8 servings.

Ed Bethune, former Representative (Arkansas)

WHITE BEAN AND EGGPLANT GRATIN

¾ cup navy beans, dried
1 teaspoon dried sage or
    2 teaspoons fresh,
    chopped
2 bay leaves
2 cloves garlic, whole
7 tablespoons olive oil
    salt and pepper
½ teaspoon dried thyme or
    1½ teaspoons fresh,
    chopped
2 large yellow onions, sliced
    ¼ inch thick
½ bunch green onions,
    chopped
4 cloves garlic, finely
    chopped
1 12 oz. can Italian plum to-
    matoes with juice
1 large eggplant, cut into
    ¾" cubes
½ jar (6 oz.) picante salsa,
    hot
1 cup bread crumbs
¼ cup olive oil

Soak beans. Add to 4 cups water. Boil with half the sage, 2 cloves garlic and 1 tablespoon olive oil. Simmer 30 minutes, add ½ teaspoon salt and cook until tender, approximately 45 minutes. Drain. In skillet, heat oil (6 tablespoons) with the sage, thyme, onions, chopped garlic and salt. Cover and cook until onions are soft. Seed and chop tomatoes, strain juice. Add eggplant to onion mixture. Cook 10 minutes, add tomatoes with juice. Cook until eggplant is tender. Transfer to bowl and add beans. Add black pepper and salt. Preheat oven to 350°. Oil gratin dish. Add mixture. Liquid should come halfway up the sides of the dish. Mix crumbs with oil and spread on top. Bake about 30 minutes. May be frozen.

Bennett Johnston, Senator (Louisiana)

SAVORY WHITE BEAN AND HAM CASSEROLE

1 cup small white beans, washed, soaked in water to cover overnight, then simmered for 1 hour
1 medium yellow onion, chopped
3 garlic cloves, chopped
1 28 oz. can ready-cut, peeled tomatoes, with their juice
1 14 oz. can beef broth
1 cup cooked ham, diced
1 heaping tablespoon country dijon mustard
ground pepper to taste
1 box chopped spinach, thawed and water squeezed out
1½ heaping teaspoons dried summer savory

Drain cooked beans and set aside in a large bowl. Saute chopped onion and garlic in a little olive oil until they are soft. Add to beans, along with remaining ingredients. Stir until thoroughly combined. Place in a greased casserole, cover and bake in a preheated, 350° oven for 1 hour. Makes 4 servings. May be frozen.

Mrs. Ed Zschau, Wife of former Representative (California)

CALICO BAKED BEAN CASSEROLE

1 large can (#2½ or larger)
    pork & beans and juice
1 15½ oz. can red kidney
    beans and juice
1 15½ oz. can butter beans,
    drained
1 15½ oz. can baby limas,
    drained
1 teaspoon dry mustard
1 teaspoon garlic salt
½ cup vinegar
1 cup brown sugar
1 pound bacon, cut up

Mix all ingredients together in large casserole dish. Bake at 325° for 3 hours, uncovered. Makes 12 servings. May be frozen.

Charlotte Bruce

Mrs. Terry Bruce, Wife of former Representative (Illinois)

GEORGIA STYLE RED BEANS AND RICE

1 cup chopped onion
½ cup chopped bell pepper
½ cup thinly sliced celery
3 cloves garlic
3 tablespoons butter
2 16 oz. cans red kidney
    beans
    salt to taste
    pepper to taste
    thyme to taste
2 bay leaves
1 link sausage, sliced
    ham, cut in chunks
    cooked rice

Brown onion, pepper, celery, and garlic in butter. Add beans, seasonings, and meat. Simmer for 1 hour. Serve over hot rice. Makes 4 servings. May be frozen.

Kystek K. White

Mrs. Mark White, Daughter of former Representative Richard H. Ichord (Missouri)

BROCCOLI BUSH WOULD LOVE

2 boxes frozen chopped
    broccoli
1 can cream of mushroom
    soup
1 cup sharp cheddar cheese,
    grated
2 tablespoons minced onion
2 eggs, well beaten
1 cup mayonnaise
    salt and pepper, to taste
½ cup butter, melted
    Ritz crackers

Cook broccoli for about 5 minutes and drain. Mix eggs, soup, cheese, mayonnaise, onion and broccoli. Add salt and pepper to taste. Put into greased casserole dish and crumble Ritz crackers over top and dot with butter. Bake at 350° until bubbly and lightly browned, approximately 25-30 minutes.

Mrs. Larkin Smith, Wife of former Representative (Mississippi)

BROCCOLI CASSEROLE

1½ cups rice, cooked
1 can mushroom soup
1 box frozen cooked
    chopped broccoli
8 ozs. Monterey Jack cheese
    with jalapeno, grated
1 medium onion, chopped
    and braised

Mix rice, soup, broccoli, cheese and onion in large bowl. Pour into a casserole dish and bake at 350° for ½ hour. Makes 6 servings.

Carol Ann Myers, Daughter of Representative John T. Myers (Indiana)

Brussels sprouts should be washed, trimmed, and cut with an "X" in the stem end to insure uniform, faster cooking.

BROCCOLI CASSEROLE

2 pkgs. frozen chopped broccoli, cooked and drained
⅔ stick melted butter
⅔ cup crushed Ritz crackers
1 tube Nippy cheese

Add cheese to hot broccoli and mix until melted. Mix butter with crackers. Put ½ broccoli in greased casserole and top with ½ cracker mixture. Repeat with remaining broccoli and crackers. Bake at 325° for 25–30 minutes.

Mrs. Hal Daub, Wife of former Representative (Nebraska)

BROCCOLI CASSEROLE

2 10 oz. pkgs. frozen broccoli pieces (cook
   slightly)
¾ stick butter or oleo
1 pound Velveeta cheese
1 stack Ritz crackers
   pepper to taste

Combine all ingredients. Stir until melted. Pour into oblong pyrex casserole dish. Crumble crackers on top. Bake at 350° for 20–25 minutes until crackers are browned. Makes 10 servings. May be frozen.

Kirk Fordice, Governor (Mississippi)

> *Add a stalk of celery while cooking broccoli, cabbage and sauerkraut to prevent strong odors.*

FLAMMIFERO (MATCHSTICKS)

3 or 4 large broccoli stems
2 small tomatoes, peeled,
    seeded and chopped
1 clove garlic, mashed
¼ teaspoon coarse salt
2 teaspoons lemon juice
1 teaspoon wine vinegar
¼ cup olive oil
3 tablespoons Parmesan
black pepper to taste

Peel broccoli stems and cut into thin julienne strips, about 2 inches long. Put in dish, add tomatoes and set aside. Mash the garlic with the salt until a paste is formed. Beat in the lemon juice, vinegar and oil. Pour the dressing over the broccoli. Add the cheese and black pepper. Toss well. Chill at least 1 hour. Makes 4 servings.

Katharine S. McHugh

Mrs. John McHugh, Wife of Representative (New York)

GARLIC BEETS

5 medium size beets (about 1
    pound)
1 teaspoon fresh grated
    ginger
3 cloves garlic
¼ cup extra virgin olive oil
salt

Peel fresh beets (you may want to use gloves to avoid staining your hands) and cut into slices or cubes. Put beets in covered casserole together with the garlic cloves. Pour the olive oil over the beets and add grated fresh ginger and salt. Stir. Bake at 350° for about 1 hour. Stir occasionally. Beets should not be too soft. You can be pleasantly surprised when you taste these delicious beets, even if prepared without the ginger. They can be prepared in advance and served at room temperature. Goat cheese is a nice complement. Makes 8 to 10 servings.

Christine Titus Daddario

Mrs. Richard Daddario, Daughter-in-law of former Representative Emilio Q. Daddario (Connecticut)

SAUCE FOR BRUSSELS SPROUTS

⅓ cup butter or margarine
2 teaspoons prepared
   mustard
1 teaspoon Worcestershire
   sauce
1 tablespoon chili sauce or
   catsup
   salt and pepper to taste

Cook small sprouts, uncovered, in a large amount of boiling salted water for about 15 minutes, or until just tender. This special sauce makes an excellent flavor addition. Sauce: Melt butter in small saucepan. Add remainder of ingredients and stir until smooth. Pour over fresh-cooked, drained brussels sprouts, or pass in bowl. Sufficient for 2 pounds of vegetables.

Mrs. Dirk Kempthorne, Wife of Senator (Idaho)

GLORIFIED CABBAGE

1 medium head cabbage,
   chopped
½ cup water
6 tablespoons butter or margarine
½ cup onion, chopped
1 10¾ oz. can cream of
   mushroom soup
½ pound Velveeta cheese
   OR
   8 oz. Cheez Whiz spread
⅔ cup unseasoned bread
   crumbs
1 teaspoon salt
½ teaspoon cayenne pepper

In 4 quart dish, put cabbage in water. Cover with lid or plastic wrap. Microwave on high 25-30 minutes until very tender. Stir once during cooking. Drain and set aside. In 4 quart corning dish, put margarine and onion. Microwave on high 4 minutes. Add soup and cheese. Microwave on high 4 minutes or until cheese is melted. Add bread crumbs and cabbage, salt and pepper. Mix well. Put in 4 quart dish. Sprinkle with more bread crumbs. Microwave on 70% power 15 minutes, covered. Makes 6 to 8 servings.

Mrs. Gayle Tauzin, Member of The Congressional Club

CABBAGE CASSEROLE

1 stick oleo margarine, melted
5 cups shredded cabbage
1 can cream of celery soup
1 can milk
2 cups crushed corn flakes
1 can sliced water chestnuts
1 cup grated cheddar cheese

Mix margarine, cabbage, soup, milk and water chestnuts. Line a 9 × 13 greased ovenproof pan with 1 cup corn flakes, cover with the cabbage mixture. Top with the remainder of the corn flakes, then the shredded cheese. Bake at 350° for 35–40 minutes. Excellent with ham. Makes 6 to 8 servings.

Mrs. Donald Matthews, Wife of former Representative (Florida)

CARROT—GREEN BEAN CASSEROLE

1 tablespoon chopped onion
3 tablespoons cooking oil
2 tablespoons flour
½ teaspoon salt
⅛ teaspoon pepper
1½ cups milk
2 eggs, beaten
½ cup grated cheese
1¾ cups frozen green beans, cooked and drained
1¾ cups of sliced carrots, cooked and drained
bread crumbs
3 tablespoons melted butter

Cook onion slightly in oil. Add flour, salt and pepper. Blend well. Add milk gradually and cook until slightly thickened. Add eggs and cook slowly 1 minute, stirring constantly. Add cheese and vegetables. Pour into greased baking dish. Cover with buttered bread crumbs. Bake at 350° for 30 minutes. Makes 8 servings.

Mrs. Roy Taylor, Wife of former Representative (North Carolina)

When cooking cabbage, place a small tin cup or can half full of vinegar on the stove near the cabbage. It will absorb all odor from it.

MARINATED CARROTS

2 pounds carrots, sliced and
   cooked
1 cup sugar
1 can tomato soup
½ cup vinegar
½ cup Wesson oil
1 small jar cocktail onions
1 green pepper, chopped
1 tablespoon dry mustard
   (optional)

Bring all ingredients (except carrots) to a boil, pour over carrots. Refrigerate overnight. Serve cold or reheat and serve warm. Makes 12 servings.

Llebra Horton Fields

Mrs. Cleo Fields, Wife of Representative (Louisiana)

CARROT SOUFFLE

1 cup milk
2 cups cooked, mashed
   carrots
2 tablespoons butter or
   margarine
1 teaspoon salt
2 eggs, beaten
8 saltine crackers, crushed
1 teaspoon chopped onion

Combine all ingredients, pour into greased baking dish and bake at 350° for 35 minutes or until center is set. Makes 6 servings.

Carolyn Wolf

Mrs. Frank Wolf, Wife of Representative (Virginia)

Removing the tops of carrots before storing, prevents them from becoming limp and dry.

CAROLINE'S CARROT COINS

2 pounds carrots, sliced
1 small green pepper, chopped
1 medium onion, chopped
1 can tomato soup
½ cup salad oil
1 cup sugar
¾ cup vinegar
1 teaspoon prepared mustard
1 teaspoon Worcestershire sauce
salt and pepper to taste

Boil carrots in salted water until slightly tender. Drain and cool. Once carrots are cool, mix with onions and green peppers, set aside. Combine remaining ingredients and beat until well blended. Pour carrot mixture together with sauce and stir. Store in refrigerator. Can be served cold or warm. Makes 6 to 8 servings.

Nancy Fleetwood Miller

Mrs. James Miller, Daughter-in-law of former Senator Jack R. Miller (Iowa)

SWEET AND SOUR CARROTS

2 to 3 pounds of carrots
1 can tomato soup
1 cup vegetable oil
1 cup dark brown sugar
¾ cup vinegar
1 teaspoon salt
½ teaspoon pepper
1 green pepper, sliced thin
1 red onion, sliced thin

Parboil carrots. Slice. Marinate all ingredients together for 24 hours. Drain and serve.

Jacqueline Klein

Mrs. Herbert Klein, Wife of Representative (New Jersey)

BAKED CARROTS WITH APPLES

10 medium carrots
4 to 6 large Golden Delicious
   apples
⅓ cup firmly packed brown
   sugar
3 tablespoons butter
   salt and pepper to taste

Preheat oven to 350°. Butter a 9 × 13 inch baking dish. Wash and peel carrots and cut into strips. Peel, core, and slice apples into eighths. Steam apples and carrots together until tender but slightly crisp. Make a sauce by combining brown sugar and butter in a saucepan and stirring until sugar has dissolved. Transfer apples and carrots to prepared baking dish, cover with sauce, and toss gently. Sprinkle with salt and pepper, cover and bake 35 minutes. Makes 10 servings.

Mrs. Rod Chandler, Wife of former Representative (Washington)

CARROT CASSEROLE

2 cups sliced carrots
¼ cup margarine
½ cup milk
2 eggs
2 cups grated Velveeta
   cheese
   salt and pepper to taste
20 Ritz crackers
⅓ cup margarine
½ cup chopped pecans

Cook carrots until tender. Drain and mash carrots with pastry blender. Melt ¼ cup margarine and add to carrots. Beat eggs and add to carrots. Add milk, cheese, salt and pepper to taste. Pour carrot mixture into 9 × 9 casserole dish and bake at 350° for 20 minutes. Crush crackers and stir into ⅓ cup melted margarine, and chopped pecans. Sprinkle on top of carrot mixture and bake for 15 minutes more. Makes 6 servings. May be frozen.

Mrs. Thomas Barlow, Wife of Representative (Kentucky)

A teaspoon of sugar for every 3 cups of water used in cooking peas, carrots, cabbage, turnips, or onions will improve flavor.

DOROTHY'S CORN

2 cans white Shoepeg corn
   (drained)
1 8 oz. pkg. cream cheese
1 stick real butter
4 to 5 dashes garlic powder
1 large chopped green chili

Soften cream cheese and butter. Add chili, corn and garlic powder. Bake at 300° until bubbly, about 30 minutes. Makes 10 to 12 servings.

Mrs. Harold Runnels, Wife of former Representative (New Mexico)

CORN SOUFFLE

2 pkgs. Jiffy cornbread mix
4 eggs
1 can whole kernel corn
1 stick melted butter
16 oz. sour cream
1 can creamed corn

Beat eggs and then fold in other ingredients. Pour into a 9 × 13 pan. Bake at 350° for 45 minutes to 1 hour. Makes 10 to 12 servings.

Mrs. Jim Lightfoot, Wife of Representative (Iowa)

> *A dampened paper towel or terry cloth brushed downward on a cob of corn will remove every strand of corn silk.*

MARTIE'S CORN PUDDING

2 cups grated corn or 1 #2
    size can golden cream
    style corn
3 tablespoons flour
2 tablespoons melted butter
2 tablespoons sugar
3 eggs, separated
1 cup half & half
    salt to taste

Mix all ingredients except egg whites. Beat egg whites to stiffly beaten peaks. Fold egg whites into mixture. Pour into well greased casserole. Bake at 350° for 45 minutes. Makes 6 to 8 servings.

Mrs. W. G. (Bill) Hefner, Wife of Representative (North Carolina)

CHILI AND CORN CASSEROLE

2 cans yellow corn, drained
2 cans white corn, drained
½ stick or 4 tablespoons of
    butter, melted
1 8 oz. block cream cheese
1 large can chopped green
    chilies
2 cups grated cheddar
    cheese

Drain corn, melt butter. Soften cream cheese and mix with melted butter. Add corn and chilies to mixture. Add grated cheese and bake in a greased casserole at 350° until hot and bubbly, about 45 minutes.

This dish can be used as a wonderful dip as well as a side dish just by adding a chopped onion and a cup of picante sauce—serve hot with large Fritos.

Mrs. Graham Purcell, Wife of former Representative (Texas)

An easy way to remove the kernels of sweet corn from the cob is to use a shoe horn. It's built just right for shearing those kernels in a jiffy.

SCALLOPED CORN

1 can cream style corn
1 can whole kernel corn, undrained
2 eggs
½ cup chopped onion
1 teaspoon salt
¼ teaspoon pepper
1 cup sour cream
1 small box corn muffin mix

Mix both cans of corn. Add slightly beaten eggs, onion, salt, pepper and sour cream and mix. Add muffin mix and mix thoroughly. Put in greased 2 quart casserole and bake at 350° for 1 hour and 15 minutes, until puffed and brown. Makes 8 servings.

Barbara Ann Grassley

Mrs. Charles E. Grassley, Wife of Senator (Iowa)

DOROTHY'S CORN PUDDING

5 or 6 ears fresh corn (if un- available use 1 pound can cream-style corn)
4 eggs
3 tablespoons sugar
salt and freshly ground pepper
1 cup light cream
1 tablespoon melted butter

Slit center of corn kernels with sharp knife. Scrape cobs clean into bowl. Measure 2 cups. Beat eggs until thick. Add corn. Combine sugar, flour and salt and pepper to taste. Slowly stir in cream. Combine with corn mixture and blend well. Pour into 1½ quart casserole. Sprinkle with melted butter. Bake at 325° for 1¼ hours or until a knife in it comes out clean. Cool. Makes 6 servings. May be frozen.

Freddie Teague

Mrs. Olin Teague, Wife of former Representative (Texas)

CORN PUDDING

1 16½ oz. can of cream style
    corn
2 tablespoons flour
1½ teaspoons salt
2 tablespoons melted butter
1 cup milk
3 eggs, well beaten
1 tablespoon sugar (optional)

Mix ingredients in order given. Pour into well buttered casserole. Set casserole in pan containing enough water to come halfway up on casserole. Bake at 350° for 1 hour. Serve hot. Makes 6 servings. May be frozen.

Frances Hagan

Mrs. G. Elliott Hagan, Wife of former Representative (Georgia)

CORN PUDDING CASSEROLE

1 stick butter
1 can whole kernel corn
1 can creamed corn
1 cup sour cream
1 pkg. Jiffy cornbread mix
    (8½ oz.)
1 egg

Melt butter in 9 × 13 pan. Mix together creamed corn and whole kernel corn, undrained. Add cornbread mix, sour cream and hand beaten egg. Pour hot butter into this mixture. Stir all ingredients together and pour into hot pan. Bake at 350° for 1 hour. Makes 10 servings.

Lori B. Costello

Mrs. Jerry Costello, Daughter-in-law of Representative Jerry F. Costello (Illinois)

KENTUCKY CORN PUDDING

4 eggs
2 tablespoons flour
3 tablespoons sugar
1 teaspoon salt
1¾ cups milk
2 cups corn (fresh or frozen)
½ stick butter

Put corn, eggs, flour, salt and sugar in blender. Turn on and off twice at low speed. Add milk and stir until blended. Butter baking dish (cut up rest of butter in dish). Pour mixture in center of dish. Bake at 325°. Stir twice during the first 15 minutes to distribute butter. Continue baking for 30 minutes or until top is lightly browned. Makes 4 servings.

Alice Baesler

Mrs. Scotty Baesler, Wife of Representative (Kentucky)

MISS LOTTIE'S CORN PUDDING

1 cup milk
3 eggs
2 tablespoons butter, melted
½ teaspoon salt
3 tablespoons sugar
3 cups white Shoepeg corn
2 tablespoons butter

Preheat oven to 350°. Mix milk, eggs, butter, salt and sugar in a large mixing bowl. Add corn and blend well. Pour corn mixture into a lightly buttered 10 inch baking dish. Dot with butter. Bake, uncovered, for 30 minutes or until set. Makes 4 to 6 servings. May be frozen.

Melanie Broyhill

Mrs. Edgar Broyhill, Daughter-in-law of former Senator James T. Broyhill (North Carolina)

CHARLOTTE'S GRATED CORN PUDDING

2¼ cups milk
1 stick butter, melted
8 ears corn, grated, or 3-4 cups corn (Silver Queen if possible)
4 eggs, well beaten
2 tablespoons sugar
2 teaspoons salt
½ teaspoon white pepper
3 drops Tabasco

Scald milk, remove from heat, add rest of ingredients, mix well. Recipe may be prepared several hours ahead of time to this point. Stir well and pour into a 2 quart greased baking dish. Place baking dish in a pan half filled with warm water, and bake at 325° for approximately 1 hour and 15 minutes. Pudding is done when knife comes out clean from center of dish.

Mrs. Butler Derrick, Wife of Representative (South Carolina)

CORN SOUFFLE

1 8 oz. can whole corn, drained
1 8 oz. can creamed corn
1 8½ oz. box corn bread mix
2 eggs, beaten
1 cup light sour cream (milk can be substituted)
½ cup butter or margarine grated Swiss cheese for top (optional)

Combine eggs, cornbread mix, corn, sour cream and butter. Spread into 11 × 7 × 1¾ inch pyrex pan. Bake at 350° for 35 minutes. Put grated cheese on top for last 10 minutes if desired. Makes 6 servings.

Mrs. William Baker, Wife of Representative (California)

When boiling corn, add sugar to the water instead of salt. Salt will toughen the corn.

IVO'S CORN PUDDING

3 eggs
3 cups fresh corn kernels
2 teaspoons minced onion
3 tablespoons flour
1 teaspoon salt
2 tablespoons sugar
　 cayenne
　 freshly grated nutmeg
4 tablespoons (½ stick)
　 melted butter, cooled
1½ cups half & half

Preheat oven to 350°. Beat eggs in large mixing bowl until frothy, then stir in corn and onion. In small bowl, mix flour, salt, sugar, cayenne and nutmeg and add to corn mixture. Add butter and half & half and stir well. Pour into greased 1½ quart baking dish. Place in roasting pan filled 1 quart up the sides with boiling water. Bake 15 minutes, stir gently to distribute corn evenly. Bake 30 minutes more or until top is golden and a knife inserted into center emerges clean. Makes 6 servings.

Julia Ann Shepard

Mrs. Tazewell Shepard, Daughter of former Senator John Sparkman (Alabama)

CORN PUDDING

16 ozs. frozen corn
3 eggs
1 cup milk
1 cup heavy cream
1 tablespoon sugar
1 teaspoon salt
¼ cup prepared bread
　 crumbs
2 teaspoons melted butter

Microwave corn about 7 minutes or until hot, then mash slightly with potato masher. In a large mixing bowl, beat eggs until fluffy; add milk, cream, sugar and salt and mix. Stir in bread crumbs, butter and corn. Pour mixture into 1½ quart greased casserole. Place casserole into cake pan of water and bake in preheated 350° for 50 minutes. Makes 8 servings.

Anne Burhans

Mrs. Nicholas P. Burhans, Daughter of former Representative John C. Mackie (Michigan)

BAKED EGGPLANT PARMESAN

1 large eggplant
1¼ teaspoons salt
1 cup olive oil
1 clove garlic
¾ cup chopped mozzarella
   cheese
2 cups tomato sauce
¾ cup grated Parmesan
   cheese

Stem and peel eggplant and cut it into ¼ inch slices. Sprinkle with salt. Heat oil in a large skillet. Add garlic, cook for 1 minute and remove. Pat eggplant dry on absorbent paper and fry, a few slices at a time, until golden on both sides. Drain on absorbent paper. Arrange one layer of eggplant in a deep casserole dish. Sprinkle with some of the mozzarella, tomato sauce and Parmesan. Repeat this procedure until all eggplant is used, ending with a layer of tomato sauce and a sprinkling of Parmesan cheese. Bake in a preheated 400° oven uncovered for 20 minutes. Makes 4 to 6 servings. May be frozen.

Mrs. James J. Howard, Wife of former Representative (New Jersey)

JOHN'S CHEESE STUFFED EGGPLANT

1 eggplant
4 tablespoons lemon juice
2 cups water
½ teaspoon salt
1 8 oz. can tomato sauce
½ crushed oregano leaves
1 tablespoon butter
½ cup chopped onion
1 cup cubed ham
⅓ cup coarsely grated carrot
½ cup chopped celery
2 cups shredded cheddar
   cheese

Cut medium size eggplant in half lengthwise. Scoop out center, leaving one half inch around edge. Bring 2 tablespoons lemon juice, water, and salt to boiling point. Place eggplant shells in boiling water, cover and parboil 5 minutes, set aside. Chop eggplant pulp and combine with tomato sauce, 2 tablespoons lemon juice and crushed oregano leaves, heat to boiling. Separately, melt butter, add chopped onion and saute until tender. Remove from heat, stir in cubed ham, carrot, chopped celery and shredded cheddar cheese. In 1½ quart baking dish, spoon in ⅔ tomato mixture, then arrange the eggplant shells on top. Fill shells with ham and cheese mixture, pour remaining ⅓ of tomato sauce over the stuffed eggplants. Bake at 375° for 20–30 minutes or until hot. Makes 4 to 6 servings. May be frozen.

Mrs. Evan Howell, Wife of former Representative (Illinois)

EGGPLANT BALDUCCI

1 large eggplant
2 cups grated mozzarella
   cheese
2 cups spaghetti sauce
1 teaspoon oil

Peel eggplant, removing stem end. Cut into ½ inch slices. Grease 9 × 12 inch shallow baking pan. Alternate layers of eggplant, sauce and cheese. Bake at 350° for 1 hour or until eggplant is tender. Makes 4 servings. May be frozen.

Virginia Mann Camarda

Mrs. Thomas Camarda, Daughter of former Representative James R. Mann (South Carolina)

BIRENGENAS (CHAMORRO EGGPLANT)

4 fresh local eggplants
1 cup coconut cream
   juice of 2 lemons
½ cup finely chopped onions
   chili peppers to taste
½ teaspoon salt
½ teaspoon aji-no-moto

Grill fresh whole eggplant over open fire until skin blisters. (Or stick eggplant on a fork and cook one at a time over burner of stove until skin blisters.) Hold under cold water, then peel against and soak in enough water to cover. Drain and mix with remaining ingredients. Serve warm or cold. (Remember to chop up the chili peppers very fine or you might set someone's mouth on fire.) Makes 4 servings. May be frozen.

Lorenzo I. De Leon Guerrero, Governor (Commonwealth of the Northern Mariana Islands)

EGGPLANT ITALIANO

1 medium eggplant
2 cans 8 oz. each, tomato
    sauce
1 to 2 teaspoons oregano
½ cup shredded sharp cheese
    (optional)
1 pkg. 6 oz. mozzarella
    cheese, sliced

Pare eggplant. Slice ⅛ inch thick. Spread 2 table-spoons tomato sauce in bottom of 2 quart casserole. Layer ½ of eggplant, 1 can tomato sauce, ½ of oregano and ½ of sharp cheese. Repeat layers. Cover. Microwave on high 14–16 minutes, rotating dish ¼ turn after 8 minutes. Add mozzarella cheese. Microwave on high 1–2 minutes, until cheese has melted. Makes 4 to 6 servings.

Mrs. Gayle Tauzin, Member of The Congressional Club

SPINACH FRITTATA

2 10 oz. pkgs. frozen,
    chopped spinach
3 cups cottage cheese
1 cup plain breadcrumbs
½ cup grated romano (any
    cheese can be used
    except mozzarella)
5 eggs
    paprika

Preheat oven to 350°. Parboil and drain spinach thoroughly. Blend with cottage cheese, ¾ cup breadcrumbs and romano cheese. In a separate bowl, beat 3 eggs well and blend in spinach mixture. Lightly oil bottom of 9″ × 9″ baking dish and sprinkle in remaining breadcrumbs. Place pan in oven until breadcrumbs are golden brown, 3 to 5 minutes. Spread spinach mixture evenly in baking dish. Beat remaining eggs and pour evenly over spinach. Sprinkle with paprika. Bake for 45 minutes. Cool for about 10 minutes before cutting. Makes 9 servings.

Mrs. Mario Cuomo, Wife of Governor (New York)

CREAMED SPINACH

1 10 oz. pkg. frozen,
    chopped spinach
1/8 teaspoon ground nutmeg
2 tablespoons chopped
    onion
4 slices chopped bacon
1 tablespoon flour

Cook spinach as directed on package. Add nutmeg. Meanwhile, cook chopped bacon with onion until brown. Add flour to bacon mixture until dissolved. Combine spinach and bacon mixture. Serve warm. Makes 4 servings.

John Boehner, Representative (Ohio)

BAKED SPINACH IN SHERRY

3 pkgs. chopped spinach
1/4 cup sherry wine (or to
    taste)
3 hard boiled eggs, sliced
1/4 teaspoon nutmeg
3 tablespoons chopped
    onions
1 can mushroom soup
1/2 cup grated sharp cheese
1/2 cup soft bread crumbs
    paprika

Cook spinach according to directions. Drain. Saute onion in butter until golden brown. Blend into mushroom soup. Stir in wine. Mix with spinach, eggs, nutmeg and season. Turn into greased casserole. Sprinkle with bread crumbs, cheese and paprika. Place in oven at 350° until brown and bubbly. Makes 6 to 8 servings.

Mrs. David Mann, Wife of Representative (Ohio)

HOT SPINACH CASSEROLE

2 pkgs. frozen, chopped
   spinach
4 tablespoons butter
2 to 3 tablespoons chopped
   onion
2 tablespoons flour
1/2 cup evaporated milk
3/4 teaspoon celery salt
3/4 teaspoon garlic
1 teaspoon Worcestershire
   sauce
   dash cayenne pepper
   black pepper
1 6 oz. roll jalapeno cheese
   bite-size bread crumbs

Cook 2 packages spinach, drain well, save 1/2 cup cooking liquid. Melt butter. Saute chopped onion in the butter. Add flour and mix well. Add evaporated milk and the spinach liquid. Season with: black pepper, celery salt, garlic, Worcestershire sauce and dash cayenne. Cup up the jalapeno cheese, melt in the sauce. Add the drained spinach. Put the mixture into a casserole dish. Top with bite-size bread crumbs sauteed in butter. Cook at 350° until bubbly (or about 30 minutes).

Mrs. Charles S. Robb, Wife of Senator (Virginia)

ARTICHOKE AND SPINACH CASSEROLE

1 large can artichoke hearts
2 pkgs. frozen spinach
1/2 cup chopped onion
1/2 stick butter or margarine
1 pint sour cream
1/2 cup cheddar cheese, grated

Cook spinach and saute onion in butter or margarine. Mix all ingredients, place in casserole and bake at 350° for 30 minutes.

Mrs. Robert Beach, Daughter of former Senator James T. Broyhill (North Carolina)

CRESPELLE (CREPES)

2 tablespoons butter
2 cups sifted flour
2 whole eggs plus 1 egg yolk
2 cups cold milk
  pinch of salt

Melt butter in saucepan and let stand until cool. Place flour in bowl and make a well in the flour. Place eggs and egg yolk in well and stir carefully, absorbing some flour from the edges. Start adding the milk, stirring continuously with wooden spoon until all flour is incorporated. Add cooled butter and salt, mix well and place the bowl in a cool place for a 1 hour rest. For each crespelle, use ⅛ cup or 2 tablespoons batter, using a 8½ inch crepe pan. Brush pan with oil before cooking each one. Pan is ready when drops of water bounce and dance. Stack as they are finished placing a paper towel between each two. These keep in the refrigerator separated by squares of waxed paper and wrapped in plastic for 2 days. Frozen in batches of six and wrapped air tight for up to 6 months. Then by placing in covered dish for 10 minutes at 300°. Makes 24. May be frozen.

Norma Lagomarsino

Mrs. Robert Lagomarsino, Wife of former Representative (California)

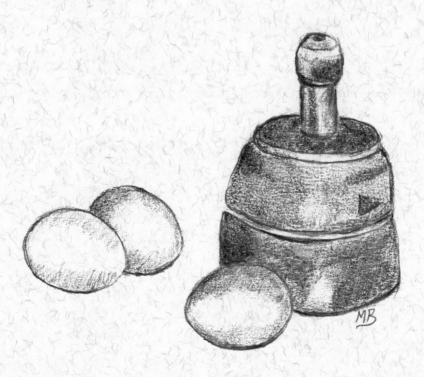

CRESPELLE (CREPES) ALLA FIORENTINA

Make 8 Crespelle rolls
[see recipe].
frozen fresh or canned
    spinach
1 pound ricotta cheese
3 whole eggs
5 tablespoons freshly grated
    Parmesan cheese
salt, pepper and nutmeg to
    taste

White Sauce (Bechamel):
2½ tablespoons butter
2½ tablespoons flour
2 cups warm milk
salt to taste

Tomato Sauce:
1 cup tomato sauce
1 tablespoon olive oil
salt and pepper to taste
3 or 4 basil leaves

Filling: Drain spinach, remove large stems, squeeze very dry, then chop fine. Place spinach, ricotta, eggs and Parmesan cheese in bowl with salt, pepper and ½ teaspoon nutmeg. Mix well with wooden spoon.

White Sauce: Melt butter in saucepan and stir in flour. Stir over medium heat for 3 minutes. Slowly add warm milk, stirring constantly. Adjust heat so that the mixture bubbles and cook for 4 minutes longer. Stirring constantly, add salt, and pepper. Let sauce cool.

Tomato Sauce: Heat tomato sauce, olive oil, salt and pepper to taste. Add basil leaves each torn in 2 or 3 pieces. Let stand until cold.

To Assemble Dish: Butter 2 13½ × 8¾ inch baking dishes. Preheat oven to 375°. Place 2 heaping tablespoons of filling on one end of each crespella roll, place in baking dish one next to the other. Lightly drizzle white sauce, then tomato sauce over each crespelle. Place dishes in preheated oven to bake for about 20 minutes. Remove from oven, allow to cool for 2 minutes, then serve. Makes 8 servings.

Norma Lagomarsino

Mrs. Robert Lagomarsino, Wife of former Representative (California)

SPINACH BAKE

½ cup butter
½ quart small curd cottage cheese
4 eggs
5 tablespoons flour
½ pound grated cheddar cheese
1 garlic clove, minced
  salt and pepper
2 tablespoons Danish fried onions
2 10 oz. pkgs. frozen chopped spinach (thawed and drained)
2 tablespoons butter
½ cup bread crumbs

Cut butter into coarse pieces. Add cottage cheese, eggs, flour, cheese, garlic, salt and pepper, and onions and mix well. Stir in spinach and pour into well greased casserole. In frying pan, melt the remaining butter, add bread crumbs and brown. Top spinach with bread crumb mixture. Bake at 350° for 1 hour. Makes 6 servings. May be frozen.

Sharon Archer

Mrs. Bill Archer, Wife of Representative (Texas)

DATE AND SWEET POTATO COMBO

5 medium sweet potatoes, cooked and drained
3 eggs
½ cup light cream
2 teaspoons sherry
¼ cup melted butter
½ teaspoon cinnamon
¾ teaspoon salt
¾ cup pitted dates
10 pecan halves

Mash sweet potatoes and set aside. Combine the next 6 ingredients in blender and blend at high speed. Add the dates, a few at a time, until well blended. Add sweet potatoes gradually, blending well. Put mixture in a greased 1 quart casserole. Garnish with pecan halves. Bake at 350° for 30 minutes. Makes 6 servings.

Lucy Foley

Mrs. John R. Foley, Wife of former Representative (Maryland)

YAM PRALINE CRUNCH

1 28 oz. can yams, drained
    and mashed
¼ teaspoon salt
¼ cup butter or margarine
2 eggs, slightly beaten
1 teaspoon vanilla
½ teaspoon cinnamon
½ cup sugar

Topping:
3 tablespoons margarine
3 tablespoons flour
¾ cup dark brown sugar
¾ to 1 cup pecans, chopped

Topping: Mix all ingredients in separate bowl until margarine is mixed in thoroughly. Sprinkle over yams. Makes 6 servings.

In 8 × 8 inch casserole dish, put mashed yams, salt, butter, eggs, vanilla, cinnamon and sugar. Mix well. Sprinkle with topping. Microwave on high 8 minutes.

Mrs. Gayle Tauzin, Member of The Congressional Club

PECAN SWEET POTATOES

6 yams
    salted boiling water
½ cup light brown sugar
⅓ cup chopped pecans
1 cup orange juice
1 tablespoon grated orange
    rind
⅓ cup sherry
2 tablespoons butter

Cook yams in boiling salted water until tender. Peel and cut in half lengthwise. Place in casserole one layer thick, sprinkle with brown sugar, pecans, pour over orange juice, grated rind and sherry, dot with butter. Cover and bake at 350° for about 45 minutes or until all the juice has cooked into the yams. (Mini-marshmallows and a sprinkling of nutmeg may be added on top, if desired.) Makes 6 servings.

Mrs. Howard Cannon, Wife of former Senator (Nevada)

EDNA'S SWEET POTATO PUDDING

3 medium size sweet pota-
  toes, grated
½ stick margarine
½ cup sugar
1½ cups milk
1 egg
1 tablespoon flour
½ teaspoon vanilla
½ teaspoon cinnamon
¼ teaspoon nutmeg

Melt margarine in 8″ × 8″ casserole dish. In a small bowl, mix sugar, spices, flour, vanilla and milk. Stir in egg. Put sweet potatoes in casserole and pour mixture over. Bake at 350° for 1 hour and 15 minutes. Makes 8 servings. May be frozen.

Cynthia L.B. Rice

Mrs. Christopher Rice, Daughter of former Representative Laurie C. Battle (Alabama)

SWEET POTATO CRUNCH

3 cups canned sweet pota-
  toes, mashed in own
  juice
¼ cup milk
¼ cup margarine, melted
¾ cup sugar
1 teaspoon vanilla
2 eggs, beaten
1 cup coconut (optional)

Crunch Topping:
1 cup brown sugar
¼ cup margarine, melted
½ cup flour
1 cup chopped pecans

Combine all ingredients and mix well. Pour into well greased baking dish. Prepare topping.

Topping: Mix together brown sugar and butter, gradually add flour. Mix well. Stir in pecans. Sprinkle over potato mixture. Bake at 350° for 30 minutes, until bubbly. Makes 4 to 6 servings. May be frozen.

Barbara Everett

Mrs. Terry Everett, Wife of Representative (Alabama)

SWEET POTATO CASSEROLE

3 cups sweet potatoes
½ cup sugar
½ cup butter
2 eggs, beaten
1 teaspoon vanilla
⅓ cup milk

Topping:
⅓ cup melted butter
1 cup brown sugar (light or
   dark)
½ cup flour
1 cup chopped pecans

Boil potatoes until tender, then peel and mash. Mix in sugar, butter, eggs, vanilla and milk. Put in 13 × 9 baking dish.

Topping: Melt butter and mix in remaining ingredients. Sprinkle on top of potato mixture. Bake at 350° for 25 minutes. Makes 10 to 12 servings.

Jim McCrery, Representative (Louisiana)

BAKED SQUASH

7 yellow squash
1 onion, diced
½ cup cream
¼ cup crushed saltines
2 tablespoons butter or
   margarine
½ cup bread crumbs,
   buttered

Slice, boil, drain and mash squash. Saute onion in butter. Add cream and crushed crackers, then squash. Put mixture in greased casserole. Cover with bread crumbs. Bake at 400° for ½ hour. Makes 6 servings.

Mrs. Thomas J. Bliley, Jr., Wife of Representative (Virginia)

SQUASH CASSEROLE

1½ to 2 pounds yellow squash, sliced thin (or zucchini, patty pan, etc.) 3 or 4 medium

4 or 5 strips of bacon, fried, drained and crumbled

1 medium onion, chopped (½ to ¾ cup)

1 cup carrots, shredded

1 can condensed cream of chicken soup, undiluted (10½ oz. size)

1 cup sour cream

1 2 oz. jar of pimentos, drained

1 8 oz. box or bag Pepperidge Farm Blue Label stuffing mix

1 cup grated cheddar cheese

1 stick margarine

salt and pepper to taste

Cook squash in just enough water to cover until tender, and drain. Saute the onion in a small amount of the bacon drippings. Crumble bacon and combine with the onion, squash, carrots, soup, sour cream, pimentos, ½ the stuffing mix and ½ the cheese. Season to taste. Melt margarine and combine with remaining stuffing mix. Line 9 × 13 inch pan or glass dish with the stuffing/margarine mixture (reserving small amount). Add squash mixture. Sprinkle reserved stuffing mixture around the outer edges on the top. Sprinkle remaining cheese in center of top meeting stuffing mixture. Bake at 350° for 30 minutes. Makes 8 servings.

Mrs. Sam Gibbons, Wife of Representative (Florida)

JO'S SQUASH CASSEROLE

3 or 4 summer squash, cooked (but not too done)

½ bag Pepperidge Farm herb stuffing

1 to 2 cups broth from chicken

1 egg

1 small carrot, grated

Mix all ingredients. Mixture should not be too loose. Pour into greased casserole and bake at 350° for 30 to 40 minutes. Sprinkle with grated cheese after oven is turned off. Let stand in oven until cheese melts. Makes 4 to 6 servings.

Mrs. John P. Murtha, Wife of Representative (Pennsylvania)

SQUASH CASSEROLE

1 12 oz. pkg. frozen squash
½ teaspoon salt
1 egg, slightly beaten
3 tablespoons orange mar-
   malade
½ teaspoon lemon juice
¼ cup chopped blanched almonds
1 tablespoon butter
¼ cup bread crumbs

Cook squash. Season with salt. Stir in eggs, marmalade, lemon juice and almonds. Place in 1 quart casserole. Melt butter and add crumbs and sprinkle on top. Bake at 350° for 20 minutes. Makes 4 servings.

Margaret Grant

Mrs. Robert A. Grant, Wife of former Representative (Indiana)

SQUASH CASSEROLE

2 to 3 cups cooked yellow
   squash
1 medium onion
½ stick margarine
5 saltine crackers, crushed
2 eggs, slightly beaten
1 teaspoon sugar
3 dashes red pepper
½ cup mayonnaise
   salt and pepper to taste
1 cup medium cheese,
   coarsely grated
   saltine crackers, crumbled
   on top

Boil squash and onion in lightly salted water until tender. Drain well and mash. Add margarine, crushed crackers, eggs, sugar, red pepper, mayonnaise, salt, pepper, and cheese. Mix well. Place in buttered casserole, sprinkle crumbled crackers on top. Bake at 350° for 30–45 minutes, until crackers begin to brown. Makes 8 to 10 servings.

Dorothy Runnels

Mrs. Harold Runnels, Wife of former Representative (New Mexico)

CORN AND ZUCCHINI SAUTE

4 ears fresh corn
1 medium zucchini
3 slices bacon, diced
½ cup minced onion
1 can tomatoes, broken up
   (1 pound)
2 teaspoons sugar
1 teaspoon salt
¾ teaspoon ground cumin
   seed
⅛ teaspoon black pepper
1 tablespoon cornstarch
1 tablespoon cold water

Cut kernels from cobs to make about 2 cups. Set aside. Cut zucchini into ½ inch thick slices and set aside. Saute bacon until crisp in large skillet. Add onion and saute for 3 minutes. Add reserved corn and zucchini, tomatoes, sugar, salt, cumin, and black pepper. Bring to boiling point, reduce heat, cover and simmer 6–8 minutes or until vegetables are tender. Mix cornstarch with water, blend into hot vegetable mixture. Cook stirring gently until mix thickens slightly. Makes 6 servings.

Valery J. Moorhead

Mrs. Carlos Moorhead, Wife of Representative (California)

MOM'S BAKED STUFFED ZUCCHINI

6 small zucchini
2 eggs, well beaten
⅓ cup seasoned dry bread
   crumbs
⅓ cup grated Parmesan
   cheese (*NOT* out of a
   carton)
¼ cup olive oil
1 small yellow onion, minced
4 sprigs of parsley, minced
   (1–2 tablespoons dried
   parsley)
2 sprigs thyme, minced (¼
   teaspoon dried thyme)
  salt, pepper and garlic salt
   to taste
  butter

Parboil zucchini in salted water until tender but not falling apart (about 10 minutes). Cool and carefully cut each zucchini in half lengthwise. Scoop out center of zucchini, being careful not to tear outside shell. Arrange shells in a greased baking pan and sprinkle them with a little salt. Mash zucchini pulp and add other ingredients, garlic salt and pepper to taste, and mix well. Fill shells with mixture. Dot with thin slivers of butter and bake in preheated 350° oven for 25 to 30 minutes. Makes 6 servings.

Jo Zschau

Mrs. Ed Zschau, Wife of former Representative (California)

CARMELIZED ONIONS

12 small onions
4 tablespoons butter
½ teaspoon salt
2 tablespoons brown sugar

Remove skin and prick centers of onions. Place in 1 inch boiling water. Cook them, covered, until almost tender. Dry on cloth. Melt butter. Add salt and brown sugar. Cook this syrup for 1 minute then add onions. Move them to coat, very gently. This glaze and method may be used for carrots, pearl onions or sliced onions. Excellent with meats.

Mrs. Frank H. Miller, Daughter of former Senator Edward V. Long (Missouri)

APPLE-ONION CASSEROLE

6 medium onions, peeled and cut crosswise into ⅛ inch slices
4 medium apples, peeled, cored and slice
8 slices of bacon
½ cup soft bread crumbs
½ teaspoon salt
¾ cup beef bouillon

Saute bacon, reserving fat. Remove bacon from pan and mince. Toss ½ cup bread crumbs in 2 tablespoons bacon fat. Grease a casserole dish. Arrange onions, apples and bacon in alternate layers. Mix salt with beef bouillon and pour over mixture. Place breadcrumbs on top. Bake 30 minutes covered at 375°. Uncover and bake 15 minutes longer. Makes 6 servings.

Mrs. Paul Gillmor, Wife of Representative (Ohio)

No more tears when peeling onions if you place them in the freezer for 4 or 5 minutes first.

VEGETABLE CASSEROLE

4 to 5 tomatoes, sliced
3 zucchini, sliced
1 spanish onion, sliced
4 medium potatoes, sliced
3 green peppers, sliced
½ cup raw rice
　salt, pepper
　oregano
　tarragon
½ cup melted butter
2 cups light cream
2 cups grated cheddar
　cheese
2 cups bread crumbs

In a buttered 9″ × 13″ glass dish, layer vegetables, sprinkling each layer with seasoning and melted butter. Sprinkle rice. Make as many layers as you wish, always ending with tomato. Pour ½ cup water over the vegetables. Cover tightly with foil. Bake at 350° for 1½ hours. Remove foil, pour on cream, bake 20 minutes more. Sprinkle with cheese and crumbs. Bake 10 minutes more until cheese is melted. Cooked meat may be added. Makes 8 to 10 servings.

Gayle Kildee

Mrs. Dale Kildee, Wife of Representative (Michigan)

CONGRESSIONAL CLUB STIRFRY

4 pounds carrots, julienned
　thin
3 red peppers, julienned thin
8 pounds medium asparagus,
　tips only
¼ pound butter
　salt and pepper to taste

Melt butter and saute carrots over medium heat for 3 minutes. Add asparagus tips, saute for an additional 4 minutes. Add red peppers and heat through. Salt and pepper to taste. Serve immediately. Makes 50 servings.

The Congressional Club

VEGETABLE CURRY WITH STEAMED BARLEY

4 cups cooked pearl barley
2 tablespoons vegetable oil
2 medium (8 ozs. each) onions
1 clove garlic, minced
1 to 2 tablespoons curry powder
1 medium green pepper, diced
½ cup sliced celery
2 carrots, sliced
1 medium zucchini, sliced
1 cup chopped broccoli
1 15½ oz. can garbanzo beans, drained
2 cups chicken broth
2 tablespoons cornstarch dissolved in 3 tablespoons water

To Cook Barley: Place 1⅓ cups pearl barley, 4 cups water and 1 teaspoon salt (optional) in large saucepan. Bring to boil. Cover and cook on low heat for 1 hour, or until tender and liquid is absorbed.

For Vegetable Curry: Heat oil in large saucepan over medium heat. Add onions, garlic and curry powder. Saute 3–4 minutes. Add remaining ingredients, except cornstarch. Cover and simmer 10–15 minutes or until vegetables are tender. Stir in cornstarch mixture, cook until thickened. Spoon hot barley around edge of a deep platter. Pour curried vegetables into center. This is a great entree for the nutrition conscious cook, whose family may not be quite so motivated! It's hearty, tasty, and if you like curry, it's rather exotic, and SO good for you! Makes 6 servings. May be frozen.

Mrs. Jim Lloyd, Wife of former Representative (California)

SPICY PEPPER CASSEROLE

6   medium bell peppers (3 red, 3 green)
1½ cups thinly sliced onions
2   tablespoons olive oil
2   tablespoons butter
3   medium garlic cloves, crushed
1   teaspoon salt
1   teaspoon cumin
1   teaspoon coriander
½   teaspoon dry mustard
¼   teaspoon black pepper
¼   teaspoon red pepper
2   tablespoons flour
½   pound sharp cheddar cheese, thinly sliced
    paprika

Custard:
4   large eggs
1½ cups sour cream

Beat together custard ingredients, eggs and sour cream, and set aside. Slice the peppers into thin strips. Heat butter and olive oil together in large, heavy skillet. Saute onions and garlic with salt and spices. When onions become translucent, add peppers. Saute over low heat for approximately 10 minutes. Sprinkle in flour. Mix well and saute until there is no extra liquid. Butter a deep casserole dish. Spread in ½ saute and top with half of the sliced cheese. Repeat these layers. Pour custard over and sprinkle with paprika. Bake for 40–45 minutes; uncover for last 15 minutes. Makes 6 servings.

James Miller, Son of former Senator Jack R. Miller (Iowa)

BROILED TOMATOES

4   ripe tomatoes
2   tablespoons olive oil
2   cloves garlic, crushed
½   cup fine bread crumbs
½   teaspoon dried basil
2   teaspoons Romano cheese

Slice 4 tomatoes in half (cross-grain) and place on oven sheet. In a mini-processor, mix bread crumbs, garlic and olive oil. Sprinkle on tomato halves. Garnish with basil and cheese. Broil until browned, then bake at 375° for 15 minutes. Do not overcook! Makes 8 servings.

Mrs. Nicholas P. Burhans, Daughter of former Representative John C. Mackie (Michigan)

MUSHROOM CASSEROLE

1 pound fresh mushrooms
8 slices white bread
½ cup chopped onion, cel-
  ery, green pepper
½ cup mayonnaise
  salt and pepper
2 beaten eggs
1½ cups whole milk
1 can mushroom soup
  grated cheese

Brown mushrooms in butter. Butter 3 slices bread, cut in squares and cut edges off. Place in bottom of casserole. Combine celery, mushrooms, onions, green pepper, mayonnaise, salt and pepper. Place on top of bread in casserole. Add 3 more slices of bread cut in squares and buttered on top of this. Combine eggs and milk and pour over mixture in casserole. Refrigerate at least 1 hour. Remove from refrigerator and let stand. Add soup. Add 2 slices buttered, cut bread. Put cheese on top. Bake at 300° for 1 hour. Makes 8 servings.

Barbara Valentine

Mrs. Tim Valentine, Wife of Representative (North Carolina)

STUFFED MUSHROOMS

1 pound large mushrooms
3 tablespoons grated Parmesan cheese
1 clove garlic, chopped
1 small onion, chopped
1 cup Italian bread crumbs
1 tablespoon chopped
  parsley
2 tablespoons melted mar-
  garine
6 tablespoon olive oil
  salt and pepper to taste

Clean and remove stems from mushrooms. Mix thoroughly, bread crumbs, cheese, parsley, margarine, garlic, onion, salt and pepper. Fill mushroom caps. Pour 2 tablespoons of oil in bottom of baking pan. Place mushrooms in pan, stuffed side up. Pour balance of oil equally over all mushrooms. Bake at 350° approximately 20 minutes in medium oven. When tops are brown, remove. Serve hot. Makes 4 to 6 servings.

Lori Deutsch

Mrs. Peter Deutsch, Wife of Representative (Florida)

Always store mushrooms in a paper bag; plastic causes a moisture to build up. Also be aware that mushrooms are their freshest if the gills are not open.

CREAMED PARSNIPS

1 pound parsnips
2 tablespoons flour
½ cup milk
¼ teaspoon salt
⅛ teaspoon pepper
1 teaspoon grated lemon
   peel
¼ cup chopped parsley

Peel parsnips, cut into thin slices, cook parsnips in boiling water until tender about ten minutes. Drain parsnips, reserve ½ cup of cooking liquid from parsnips. Stir together flour and milk in saucepan over medium heat until well blended. Add reserved parsnip liquid, salt, pepper and lemon peel. Stir constantly until thick and smooth. Add parsnips to sauce. Sprinkle with chopped parsley. Serve. Makes 6 servings.

Mildred Curtis

Mrs. Carl T. Curtis, Wife of former Senator (Nebraska)

BARLEY CASSEROLE

1 cup minced onion
⅔ cup butter or margarine
2 cup uncooked pearl barley
6 cups beef consomme
   (heated)
1 pound mushrooms, sliced
   (or two 8 oz. cans)
2 teaspoons salt
½ teaspoon pepper
   garlic salt

In a large heavy skillet saute onions in ⅓ cup butter until soft (not brown). Add barley, stir until it begins to brown. Very slowly add hot consumme. Cook over low heat 1 hour until almost tender. Stir occasionally and add more hot water to liquid if necessary. Saute mushrooms in rest of butter, salt, pepper and garlic salt, add this to barley and cook until tender. Can fix ahead and reheat. I think you cook the barley covered for 1 hour, might read recipes on side of barley package as to how to cook in general. Makes 12 servings. May be frozen.

Jane Sullivan

Mrs. Mike Sullivan, Wife of Governor (Wyoming)

WILD RICE AND SAUSAGE

1 pound bulk pork sausage
½ cup celery, chopped
1 tablespoon dried green
    pepper flakes
1 can cream of mushroom
    soup
1½ cups water
1 cup wild rice
4 ozs. diced pimento,
    drained
2½ ozs. sliced mushrooms,
    drained
1 cup shredded cheddar
    cheese (4 ozs.)
1 tablespoon instant minced
    onion
2 teaspoons dried leaf marjo-
    ram, crushed
1 teaspoon dried leaf thyme

Brown sausage in dutch oven, stirring to crumble. Add celery and pepper flakes, saute until celery is tender. Drain off pan drippings. Stir in soup, water, wild rice, pimento, mushrooms, cheese, onion, marjoram and thyme. Pour into a lightly greased 12 × 8 × 2 baking dish. Cover with foil. Bake at 350° for 1½ hours, until rice is tender. Makes 8 servings.

Sharon S Vander Schel

Mrs. Kevin Vander Schel, Daughter of Representative Neal Smith (Iowa)

PHOEBE'S WILD RICE

½ pound of bacon, cut into
    very small bits
3 medium onions, chopped
2 small green peppers,
    chopped
½ pound sliced mushrooms
¼ cup melted butter
1 quart canned tomatoes, cut
    into small pieces
1 teaspoon salt
1 cup wild rice

Fry bacon bits until crisp. Saute onions, green peppers and mushrooms in drippings of bacon. Mix together the onions, green peppers, mushrooms, canned tomatoes (with the canned liquid), rice, butter and salt. Place in casserole, cover and bake at 325° for 2 hours. Makes 8 servings.

Gail McCandless

Mrs. Al McCandless, Wife of Representative (California)

RICE DRESSING

1 pkg. Uncle Ben's long grain
   and wild rice
3 large onions, chopped fine
4 large stalks of celery,
   chopped fine
1 green pepper, chopped
   fine
   ground heart, liver and
   gizzard
1/2 cup butter, or low fat substitute
1 tablespoon salt
1 tablespoon poultry
   seasoning
2 eggs
2 cup chopped nuts (preferably pecans)
1/2 cup parsley, chopped
   oysters and mushrooms to
   taste, if desired

Cook rice according to directions on package. While rice is cooking, saute onions, celery, pepper, liver, gizzard and heart together in butter until thoroughly cooked. Add seasonings and mix. Beat eggs until frothy. Remove sauteed onion mixture from heat. Add rice and fold in beaten eggs, mixing thoroughly. Add chopped nuts and parsley. Add oysters and mushrooms if desired. Stuff cooked turkey and bake at 350° for 30 minutes more or bake in a buttered shallow casserole for 25 minutes. Flavor improves if frozen several days then baked. Makes 6 to 8 servings.

Maria S. Sawyer

Mrs. Harold S. Sawyer, Wife of former Representative (Michigan)

WILD RICE CASSEROLE

1 cup uncooked wild rice
1/4 to 1/2 cup chopped onion
3 stalks chopped celery
1 teaspoon seasoned salt or
   Mrs. Dash
1/2 cup white wine
2 tablespoons butter
1 quart chicken broth (your
   own or low salted
   brand)
   pepper to taste

Mix all ingredients well. Bake in a casserole, covered, at 350° for 1 1/2 to 2 hours. Check during last hour. You can prepare this a day ahead. This fact and that it is not necessary to precook the rice makes it a convenient one at holiday times. Suitable for freezing.

Abigail McCarthy

Mrs. Eugene McCarthy, Wife of former Senator (Minnesota)

NUTTED WILD RICE

3 cups golden raisins
1½ cups dry sherry
10 cups Uncle Ben's wild rice blend
4 cups Uncle Ben's rice
22 cups fresh chicken stock (or canned broth)
½ pound unsalted butter
2½ cups slivered almonds, toasted
1 cup parsley (1 bunch), chopped

Heat the raisins and sherry in a small saucepan to boil, reduce heat and simmer 5 minutes. Set aside. Divide the rice evenly between 2 hotel pans. Boil the chicken stock and pour 11 cups into each pan of rice. Cover with foil and cook 25 minutes at 350°. Add ¼ pound of butter to each pan, stir rice, recover and cook an additional 25–30 minutes. Uncover rice, stir in raisin mixture. Add almonds and parsley before serving. Makes 50 servings.

The Congressional Club

MARY JANE'S RICE AND GREEN CHILIES CASSEROLE

3 cups of cooked rice (minute or converted)
1 cup of sour cream
1 4 oz. can chopped green chilies, drained
12 ozs. Monterey Jack cheese, sliced
2 ozs. grated cheddar cheese

Mix sour cream and chilies together. Put 1 cup of the rice in a greased casserole. Cover with ½ the sour cream mixture and a layer of the Monterey Jack slices. Repeat layers and end with rice. Bake uncovered at 325° for 30 minutes. Cover with grated cheddar cheese and return to oven until cheese is melted. Makes 6 servings.

Glenn English, Representative (Oklahoma)

Brown rice has more food value, roughage and taste than white. It takes longer to cook, but is worth the effort.

JONNIE'S CHICKEN RICE CASSEROLE

1 can mushroom soup
1 can chicken broth
1 can cream of celery soup
 OR
1 can cream of chicken soup
1 pkg. French onion soup
   (optional)
2 cups rice, long grain
1 chicken, skinned and cut
   up, or 2 chicken breasts,
   boned and skinned

Mix soups and broth together. Spray baking dish with Pam. Spread rice in bottom of dish. Place chicken pieces on top of rice. If chicken breasts, cut in half. Pour soup mixture over chicken and rice. Bake at 350° for 1 hour. If using wild rice, bake for 2 hours. Makes 5 to 6 servings.

Bea Smith

Mrs. Neal Smith, Wife of Representative (Iowa)

GREAT GRAINS AND GRAPES

½ cup brown rice
½ cup chopped carrots
½ cup chopped onions
½ cup sliced fresh mush-
   rooms
2 tablespoons vegetable oil
½ cup wild rice
1 teaspoon fresh thyme
1 teaspoon fresh rosemary
2 cups chicken broth
2 cups seedless grapes,
   halved
¼ cup pistachio nuts, toasted
2 tablespoons minced green
   onions
2 tablespoons minced parsley
   salt and pepper to taste

In 1½ quart saucepan, saute brown rice, carrots, onion and mushrooms in oil until rice is golden. Rinse and drain wild rice. Add wild rice, herbs and broth to brown rice mixture. Bring to boil, reduce heat, cover and simmer 45 to 55 minutes or until wild rice is tender and all liquid is absorbed. Gently stir in grapes, nuts, green onion, parsley, salt and pepper. Let stand, covered, 5 minutes. Makes 6 to 8 servings. May be frozen.

Betty Rhodes

Mrs. John J. Rhodes, Wife of former Representative (Arizona)

RICE CASSEROLE

1 cup uncooked rice
1 can beef bouillon soup
1 cup water
½ stick butter

Mix the above ingredients. Cook at 325° for 1 hour. Makes 4 servings. May be frozen.

Beth Valentine

Beth Valentine, Daughter of Representative Tim Valentine (North Carolina)

MUSHROOM RICE

3 cups hot, cooked white
   rice
1 4 oz. can mushrooms,
   sliced and drained
1 cup cooked green peas
2 tablespoons butter, melted
2 tablespoons diced pimento
¼ teaspoon onion powder
   salt and pepper to taste

Combine rice, mushrooms, peas, butter, pimento, onion powder, salt and pepper. Heat until vegetables are hot, about 3 or 4 minutes. Toss lightly. Makes 6 servings.

Nancy Fountain Black

Mrs. William Black, Jr., Daughter of former Representative L. H. Fountain (North Carolina)

For a special rice, add a little white wine or sherry to uncooked rice and butter in pan. Add liquid and cook as usual.

In choosing a casserole dish, remember that wild rice almost triples in bulk while cooking.

CHICKEN FRIED RICE

3 eggs
2 teaspoons salt
½ teaspoon cooking sherry
5 tablespoons cooking oil
2 tablespoons minced onion
4 cups cooked rice
1 teaspoon Kitchen Bouquet
1 cup shredded cabbage
1 cup chicken, cooked,
   boned and diced
   soy sauce

Beat eggs with salt and sherry. Pour oil in hot skillet over medium/high heat. Stir in minced onion and egg mixture. Scramble and break into small pieces until quite dry. Add rice, Kitchen Bouquet and cabbage. Stir until ingredients are well blended and thoroughly heated. Add chicken. You may also use pork, ham, shrimp, or beef. Do not use soy sauce until ready to serve, then only as desired. Makes 10 servings. May be frozen.

Mrs. Ronnie Flippo, Wife of former Representative (Alabama)

TERRY'S FRIED RICE

2 tablespoons peanut oil
⅓ cup thinly sliced green
   onions
½ teaspoon fresh ginger,
   chopped
½ teaspoon minced garlic
2 eggs
¼ teaspoon salt
¼ teaspoon sugar
⅓ pound diced ham or
   chicken (or both)
⅓ cup peas (frozen)
2 tablespoons soy sauce
2 cups cold cooked rice
½ teaspoon sesame oil

Heat peanut oil in electric skillet at 325°. Add onions, ginger and minced garlic. Stir fry for 1 minute. Add eggs, cook until hard. Break into bits. Add salt, sugar, meat, peas and soy sauce. Stir fry 2 minutes. Add rice. Heat 1 minute or until rice is warm. Add sesame oil. Stir in. Serve. Makes 4 servings.

Terry Bruce, former Representative (Illinois)

RICE CASSEROLE

¼ pound butter
1 medium onion, chopped fine
1 cup long grained rice
1 small can mushrooms, including juice
½ teaspoon oregano
1½ cans consomme
1 can water

Melt butter in frying pan. Add onion, rice, mushrooms (including juice) and oregano. Cook over low heat for 20 minutes, stirring constantly. Place rice mixture in a casserole and add consomme and water. Bake at 400° for 1 hour. Makes 6 servings.

Jean Thompson

Mrs. Richard Thompson, Daughter of former Representative John H. Terry (New York)

LAYERED RICE MONTEREY

2 cups cooked rice
7 ozs. canned chopped green chilies
3 cups shredded Monterey Jack cheese
3 medium zucchini, sliced
1 large tomato, sliced
2 cups sour cream
1 teaspoon oregano
1 teaspoon salt
2 tablespoons chopped green pepper
2 tablespoons chopped green onion
1 tablespoon chopped parsley

Place rice in buttered casserole. Layer it with chilies, 2 cups of the cheese, zucchini and tomato. Combine the sour cream with the oregano, salt, green pepper, onion and parsley. Pour over the zucchini and tomato layer and top with remaining cheese. Bake at 350° for 30 minutes. Makes 8 servings. May be frozen.

Sharon Archer

Mrs. Bill Archer, Wife of Representative (Texas)

Leftover rice freezes well. To reheat, steam, covered in a colander until thoroughly heated. Fluff with a fork.

FRENCH RICE

1 10½ oz. can onion soup, undiluted
½ cup butter or margarine, melted
1 4½ oz. can sliced mushrooms
1 8 oz. can sliced water chestnuts
1 cup uncooked regular rice

Combine soup and butter, stir well. Drain mushrooms and water chestnuts, reserving liquid. Add enough water to reserved liquid to equal 1⅓ cups. Add mushrooms, water chestnuts, liquid and rice to soup mixture, stir well. Pour into a lightly greased or Pam sprayed 10 × 6 × 2 baking dish. Cover and bake at 350° for 1 hour. Makes 6 servings.

Mrs. Sam Gibbons, Wife of Representative (Florida)

BASQUE RICE

4 chorizos cut in half lengthwise, then sliced into small pieces
4 chicken breasts, boned, diced in small chunks
3 to 4 cloves garlic or more, minced
½ cup chopped onions
1 large jar pimentos, chopped
1½ cups Uncle Ben's rice
4½ cups water
2 small cans tomato sauce
salt to taste (maybe ½ teaspoon at first)
pepper—sprinkle generously, it should be spicy
chopped parsley

Brown the chorizos, chicken, garlic, and onions together until pretty well done. Add the pimentos with all their juice. Add the rice to the frying pan and fry it a while. Add water and tomato sauce and cook about 10 minutes on the stove. Add the salt, pepper and parsley and pour into casserole. Bake covered at 325° for 45 minutes to 1 hour. Add more parsley to decorate. Note: Some Basque families add peas, carrots, and celery to make it more like a paella. For decorative look, add sliced boiled eggs all around the top with pimentos in a pinwheel design. Serve with green salad and sour dough bread, red wine.

Mrs. Larry LaRocco, Wife of Representative (Idaho)

CONNIE'S CANNELLONI

Crepe:
- 3 eggs
- ¾ cup sifted flour
- 1 cup milk
- 3 tablespoons melted butter
- ½ teaspoon salt

Beef Filling:
- ⅔ cup chopped onion
- ½ cup butter
- 1½ to 2 pounds or 4 cups left over meat
- 1 can Spanish style tomato sauce
- 3 tablespoons chopped fresh parsley
- 1 teaspoon salt
  sliced Monterey Jack and/ or mozzarella cheese
  Parmesan or Romano cheese

Sauce:
- ⅓ cup butter
- 6 tablespoons flour
- 3 cups milk
- 1½ teaspoons salt
- ⅛ teaspoon white pepper
  dash nutmeg (optional)

Crepe: Beat all ingredients until smooth. Heat a 7 to 8″ crepe pan and brush well with oil. For each crepe add 3 tablespoons butter. Tilt pan quickly to spread batter. Brown and turn. Brown other side.

Filling: Saute onion in butter. Add meat, brown. Add all but cheese. Simmer 20 minutes. Spoon mixture on crepes, add pieces of cheese and roll. Place seam side down in single layer in part of sauce. Pour remaining sauce. Sprinkle with parmesan and or romano cheese and bake at 350° for 20 minutes.

Sauce: Melt butter and blend in flour. Stir in milk, salt, white pepper and dash nutmeg if desired. Cook to thick. Makes 6 servings. May be frozen.

Shirley H. Wilson

Mrs. Bob Wilson, Wife of former Representative (California)

Add a lump of butter or a few teaspoons of cooking oil to the water. Rice, noodles or spaghetti will not boil over or stick together.

SPINACH NOODLE CASSEROLE

1 12 oz. pkg. wide egg
   noodles
1 32 oz. jar spaghetti sauce
3 eggs, lightly beaten
1 24 oz. carton cottage
   cheese
1 pkg. frozen spinach
   (10 oz.)
2 cups shredded mozzarella
   cheese
1 onion, chopped

Cook noodles as directed and drain. Mix with all but 1 cup spaghetti sauce. Mix eggs, cottage cheese, thawed spinach (press water out of spinach), mozzarella cheese and onion. Place ½ noodles in Pam sprayed 3 quart casserole. Cover with egg, cheese, spinach mixture, cover with remaining noodles and pour 1 cup spaghetti sauce over top. Cover and back at 350° for 30-35 minutes. This is quick and easy and tastes like spinach lasagna, but much easier! Makes 8 servings. May be frozen.

Mrs. William Wampler, Wife of former Representative (Virginia)

MOM'S PASTA FAZOOL

1 onion, chopped
2 cloves garlic, minced
½ celery stalk, chopped fine
   olive oil
3 8 oz. cans Hunt's tomato
   sauce
3 cans Cannelini beans or
   butter beans or combination of both
½ pound elbows, bows, or
   ditalini pasta

Saute onion, garlic and celery in about 1 tablespoon olive oil until clear and soft. Add tomato sauce and 1 can of water to it and simmer. (Also add salt and pepper to taste and a little sugar). Then add the beans (undrained) and simmer for about ½ hour. Meanwhile, cook pasta al dente according to directions on box. When done, strain and add to tomato mixture, serve, adding Parmesan cheese and hot pepper flakes. BONA APPETITO!! Makes 4 to 6 servings. May be frozen.

Mrs. Henry Nowak, Wife of former Representative (New York)

One pound of dry pasta will yield about 2.2 pounds of cooked pasta.

TWO CHEESE PASTA

½ teaspoon minced garlic
¼ cup olive oil
½ cup fresh basil, finely cut
2 large tomatoes
½ pound cheddar cheese
½ pound fontina cheese
1 box small pasta shells

Combine garlic, olive oil, basil, and diced tomatoes in saucepan and cook over low heat, stirring occasionally. Cut all cheese into small cubes. Cook and drain pasta shells. In large pasta dish, combine all ingredients and stir thoroughly to melt cheese. Place in 325° oven for 15 minutes, stirring every couple of minutes. Serve hot. Makes 6 servings.

Robyn Porter, Daughter of Representative John Edward Porter (Illinois)

PIZZA

For Dough:
1 pkg. yeast
1 teaspoon sugar
1 cup warm (not hot) water
2 tablespoons olive oil
2½ cups flour

For Standard Topping:
1 jar pizza sauce
6 oz. shredded mozzarella
   cheese
2 tablespoons grated cheese
   pinch oregano
   pinch basil

Dissolve yeast and sugar in water. Let stand 10 minutes. Add yeast mixture to large bowl and add olive oil and flour. Mix with a spoon until blended, then knead with your hands. You may have to add some additional flour if the dough is too sticky to handle. Shape into ball, cover bowl and let stand 1 hour. Meanwhile, spray a cookie sheet with non-stick cooking spray. After dough has risen, spread onto sheet until it meets the sides. Let stand until dough has risen again—maybe 20 or 30 minutes. Top with sauce, cheeses and seasonings. Bake in 425° oven for 20 to 25 minutes. For variations, top with shredded chicken, sun dried tomatoes, and ricotta cheese. Makes 1 pie, 8 servings.

Mrs. David Levy, Wife of Representative (New York)

One pound of fresh pasta will yeild about 1.6 to 1.8 pounds of cooked pasta, depending on the amount of moisture in making the fresh pasta.

TOFU CANNELLONI

16 manicotti shells
28 ozs. firm tofu
2 eggs, slightly beaten
1 teaspoon nutmeg
1 teaspoon basil
1 teaspoon salt
½ teaspoon pepper
½ cup Parmesan cheese
1 cup grated cheddar cheese
1 cup grated mozzarella
   cheese
32 ozs. Italian tomato sauce

Cook and drain manicotti shells. Mix tofu (mashed) with eggs, spices and cheeses (reserve Parmesan for top). Fill shells with mixture. Lay shells in oiled casserole dish and cover with sauce. Sprinkle with parmesan cheese. Bake at 350° for 30 minutes. Makes 8 servings.

Gail McCandless

Mrs. Al McCandless, Wife of Representative (California)

PASTA WITH PEPPERS

8 oz. pkg. mostaccioli
   salt
1 large red pepper
1 large yellow pepper
1 large green pepper
1 large onion
3 tablespoons olive oil
1 tablespoon sugar
1 tablespoon balsamic
   vinegar
¾ teaspoon dried basil leaves
½ teaspoon cracked black
   pepper

Cook mostaccioli as label directs, using ½ teaspoon salt in water. Drain. Return pasta to saucepan. Meanwhile, cut peppers and onion into ½ inch wide strips. In 12 inch skillet, over medium heat, in hot oil, cook peppers, onion and 1½ teaspoons salt until browned and tender, about 15 minutes. Stir in sugar, vinegar, basil, and cracked black pepper, heat through. Toss pepper mixture with pasta. Delicious! Makes 4 to 6 servings.

Joyce Murtha

Mrs. John P. Murtha, Wife of Representative (Pennsylvania)

One pound of cooked pasta will serve four people as a main dish.

FAMILY PASTA SAUCE

3 tablespoons olive oil
3 to 4 tablespoons garlic, chopped
2 slices bacon, finely chopped
1 medium onion, chopped
¼ cup + 2 tablespoons chopped fresh basil (or ¼ cup dried)
3 tablespoons oregano
3 tablespoons fresh parsley, chopped
1 can tomato paste
1 tablespoon anchovy paste
3 cans stewed tomatoes (15 oz.)
1 cup red wine (any kind will do)
1 tablespoon sugar
1 large can mushrooms with liquid

Heat olive oil, add garlic, bacon, and onion. Saute for a few minutes. Add basil, oregano, parsley and tomato paste. Stir in anchovy paste. Saute 5 more minutes. Add tomatoes and wine and cook for 20 minutes. Add sugar and more wine if needed. Add mushrooms. May be served with your favorite pasta. Penne, angle hair, etc. This is wonderful served with fresh cooked shrimp. Put pasta in large round flat bowl, add sauce, and top with shrimp. Makes 10 to 12 servings. May be frozen.

Loretta Symms

Mrs. Steve Symms, Wife of former Senator (Idaho)

The water should be boiling furiously before adding 1½ tablespoons salt and 1 tablespoon oil. After adding pasta, maintain a steady boil, uncovered, stirring occasionally with wooden spoon or fork.

PUTTANESCA

½ cup olive oil
1 large onion, chopped
8 large cloves garlic, pressed
2 tablespoons tomato paste
2 cans Italian plum tomatoes, peeled (28 oz. cans) cut up and liquid
2 cans anchovies packed in oil (2 oz. cans), chopped
¾ cup pitted and coarsely chopped oil cured black olives
5 tablespoons drained large capers
1 teaspoon dried basil
1 teaspoon dried oregano
½ teaspoon crushed red peppers
½ teaspoon freshly ground black pepper
1 pound rigatoni pasta
Parmesan cheese for grating

Heat oil in heavy saucepan. Add the onion and garlic. Cook until soft (about 10 minutes). Add tomatoes, stir and add tomato paste. Stir and cook for about 5 minutes. Add anchovies with their oil, the olives, capers, basil, oregano and the red and black peppers. Simmer for 30 minutes, stirring occasionally. In a separate pot, cook pasta according to the directions on package until just tender (about 10–12 minutes). Do not over cook! Drain pasta. Mix into puttanesca sauce. Grate Parmesan cheese on top. Makes 6 servings. May be frozen.

Mrs. Bennett Johnston, Wife of Senator (Louisiana)

> *Use a fry basket in the pot when cooking pasta. The pasta can be lifted out all at once and rinsed in the same basket.*

TORTELLINI IN BALSAMIC DRESSING

2 pounds premium frozen
    tortellini (fresh if
    available)
¼ cup balsamic vinegar
½ cup extra virgin olive oil
2 to 3 cloves of garlic,
    chopped fine
    oregano (to taste)
1 bunch broccoli
2 to 3 medium onions
½ to 1 cup Parmesan cheese
1 red bell pepper
    parsley (optional)

Cook tortellini as directed in boiling water. Prepare balsamic vinaigrette as follows: Combine vinegar, olive oil, garlic, and oregano. Whip vinegar and oil with wire whisk until smooth. Add 1–2 cloves of garlic and oregano to taste. Shake vigorously before use. Cook broccoli florets in steamer until just tender. Saute onions and remaining garlic. Stir broccoli into onions. Set aside. Drain tortellini. Toss in balsamic vinaigrette. Add broccoli mixture, Parmesan cheese, sliced strips of red pepper and mix well. Garnish with parsley. Let this dish cool awhile. It is much better warm than hot. Perfect for buffet dish for fund raisers and campaign gatherings. For a spicier taste, add more balsamic vinaigrette, garlic or Parmesan cheese. Makes 6 to 8 servings.

Mrs. Maurice Hinchey, Wife of Representative (New York)

PASTA WITH GREEN SAUCE

¼ cup sun dried tomatoes
⅓ cup pine nuts
4 tablespoons olive oil
2 cloves garlic, pressed fine
1 red bell pepper, julienned
2 to 3 cups raw spinach
⅓ cup basil, chopped
2 cups chicken stock or
    broth
9 to 12 oz. bow tie pasta
    (large)
½ cup grated Parmesan
    cheese

Soak sun dried tomatoes in boiling water to cover for 10 minutes. Drain and chop. Set aside. Saute pine nuts in 1 tablespoon olive oil. Set aside. Heat remaining olive oil in a large skillet. Saute garlic and red peppers for 1 to 2 minutes. Add spinach, basil and chopped sun dried tomatoes. Saute until spinach begins to wilt. Add broth, lower heat and cook gently for 5 minutes. Spinach should remain vivid green. Cook pasta in boiling water, drain. Toss pasta, spinach sauce, pine nuts, Parmesan cheese and serve immediately. Makes 4 servings.

Beth Schermer, Wife of Representative Sam Coppersmith (Arizona)

PASTA WITH SPINACH AND TOMATO

1 pound fresh spinach
1 large can Italian plum
  tomatoes
2 tablespoons olive oil
2½ teaspoons chopped garlic
  salt
  pepper
  grated Parmesan
1 pound favorite pasta,
  cooked

Trim spinach, rinse in several changes of cold water. Drain well in a salad spinner. Chop spinach. Drain and chop tomatoes. Add oil to saute pan. Add garlic and cook until colored a pale gold. Add spinach, salt and a few grindings of pepper. Cook, stirring frequently, for a minute or two. Add tomatoes, lower heat and simmer for about 10 minutes. Toss with cooked pasta. Top with grated Parmesan. Makes 2 to 3 servings.

Mary Sasser

Mrs. Jim Sasser, Wife of Senator (Tennessee)

TALLIROONI

2 tablespoons Crisco or oil
2 pounds ground chuck
2 onions, chopped
3 pods garlic, chopped
2 green peppers, chopped
1 tablespoon salt
2 cans tomato soup
½ pound grated, or sliced
  cheese
1 pkg. (12 oz.) medium egg
  noodles
1 can ripe olives
1 can yellow whole kernel
  corn

Brown until meat is done—onions, garlic, peppers, and salt. Then add tomato soup and cheese. Cook noodles, drain and combine with meat mixture. Add olives and corn last and let stand before serving to absorb flavorings. Makes 10 to 12 servings. May be frozen.

"Sug" Hancock

Mrs. Mel Hancock, Wife of Representative (Missouri)

PASTA WITH TOMATOES, SHITAKE MUSHROOMS AND PROSCIUTTO

2 cup chopped onion
2 garlic cloves, minced
1/4 teaspoon dried hot pepper flakes
1 teaspoon dried basil, crumbled
1 teaspoon dried oregano, crumbled
2 tablespoons olive oil
1 pound fresh shitake mushroom caps, sliced
1/2 stick butter
3 tablespoons flour
2 cups milk
2 28 oz. cans Italian tomatoes, drained and chopped
1/4 pound sliced prosciutto, cut into strips
1/4 pound Italian fontina, grated (about 1 cup)
1/4 pound Gorgonzola, crumbled (about 1 cup)
1 1/2 cup freshly grated Parmesan
2/3 cup minced fresh parsley
1 pound large bow-tie shaped pasta or penne

Saute the onion, garlic, red pepper flakes, basil and oregano in the oil over moderately low heat, stirring until the onion is softened. Add mushrooms, cook over moderate heat, stirring for 10 to 15 minutes. Transfer to a large bowl. Melt 3 tablespoons butter over moderately low heat, whisk in the flour, and cook the roux, stirring for 3 minutes. Add the milk in a stream, whisking and simmer the mixture for 2 minutes, stirring constantly. Pour the sauce over the mushroom mixture and add the tomatoes, the prosciutto, the fontina, Gorgonzola, 1 1/4 cup of the Parmesan and the parsley. Cook the pasta for 5 minutes in boiling water (the pasta will not be tender) and drain well. Add the pasta, salt and pepper to taste to the mushroom mixture. Combine well and transfer to a buttered 3 to 4 quart casserole. Sprinkle pasta with remaining 1/4 cup Parmesan, dot with remaining 1 tablespoon butter (cut into bits) and bake for 25 to 30 minutes in a 450° oven. Makes 6 to 8 servings. May be frozen.

Mary Sasser

Mrs. Jim Sasser, Wife of Senator (Tennessee)

Adding vegetable oil to pasta cooking water before you add the pasta will cut down on sticking.

BILLIE'S NOODLES AU TIM

8 oz. thin egg noodles
2 cups cottage cheese
1¼ cups sour cream
¼ cup melted butter
¼ cup minced onion
1 mashed clove of garlic
1 teaspoon Worcestershire
    sauce
1 can green chilies, mashed
1 to 2 dashes Tabasco sauce
3 heaping tablespoons
    freshly chopped parsley
salt and pepper to taste
paprika sprinkled on top
    for color

Slightly undercook noodles (al dente). Combine remaining ingredients and mix with drained noodles. Turn into greased casserole (12″ × 8″ × 2″) or large round dish. Sprinkle with paprika, cover with foil and bake at 350° for 45 minutes. Makes 8 to 10 servings.

Janet Bryant

Mrs. John W. Bryant, Wife of Representative (Texas)

CHICKEN WITH VEGETABLES AND PASTA

¼ cup olive oil
1½ pound boneless chicken
    breast
2 medium onions, chopped
2 garlic cloves, chopped
1 teaspoon fennel seeds
2 carrots, peeled and sliced
    in ¼ inch pieces
½ cup sliced sun dried toma-
    toes (blanche for 2
    minutes)
12 ozs. angel hair pasta
2 cups grated Parmesan

Heat oil in heavy skillet over medium-high heat. Add chicken and saute until cooked through. Using slotted spoon, transfer chicken to large bowl. Keep warm. Add onion, garlic and fennel seeds to skillet and saute until onion is tender. Add carrots and sun dried tomatoes. Cook until carrots are tender. Cook pasta, drain, add 1 cup of cheese to pasta. Add remaining ingredients including the second cup of cheese. Toss well and serve. Makes 6 servings.

Barbara B. Johnson

Mrs. Tim Johnson, Wife of Representative (South Dakota)

LINGUINE IN CLAM SAUCE

3 cloves garlic, minced
1/2 cup melted butter or margarine
4 4 oz. cans sliced mushrooms, drained
2 6 1/2 oz. cans minced clams, drained
1/2 cup chopped parsley
1/2 teaspoon pepper
8 ozs. linguine or spaghetti, cooked and drained
grated Parmesan cheese

Saute garlic in butter in large skillet over low heat for 1 minute. Add mushrooms and cook 5 minutes. Stir in clams, parsley, salt and pepper. Heat thoroughly. Combine linguine and mushroom mixture, toss well and heat until hot. Top with Parmesan cheese. Makes 4 to 6 servings.

Mrs. Douglas (Pete) Peterson, Wife of Representative (Florida)

BAKED ZITI

6 cups (16 ozs.) cut ziti, uncooked
3 1/2 cups (32 oz. jar) spaghetti sauce
2 cups (16 ozs.) ricotta cheese
2 cups (8 ozs.) shredded mozzarella cheese
1/4 cup chopped fresh parsley
1 egg, slightly beaten
1 teaspoon oregano
1/2 teaspoon garlic powder
1/4 teaspoon pepper
1 tablespoon grated Parmesan cheese

Cook cut ziti according to package directions for 10 minutes, drain. In large bowl, combine cooked ziti, 1 1/2 cups spaghetti sauce, ricotta cheese, mozzarella cheese, parsley, egg, oregano, garlic powder and pepper. In 3 quart casserole, pour 1/2 cup spaghetti sauce, spread ziti mixture evenly over sauce. Top with remaining 1 1/2 cups spaghetti sauce, sprinkle with Parmesan cheese. Bake at 375°, covered for 30–35 minutes or until hot and bubbly. Makes 8 servings. May be frozen.

Mrs. Richard Shoup, Wife of former Representative (Montana)

ORZO WITH SAUTEED ONIONS

2 quarts water
1 teaspoon salt
1 cup orzo (tiny greek pasta beads, available in gourmet stores)
3 tablespoons unsalted butter
2 medium onions, chopped

In a large pot, bring salted water to a boil. Add orzo and cook for 12 minutes, or until just tender. Drain. In a skillet, melt butter and saute onions over medium heat for about 4 minutes. Add the orzo to the onions. Stir well and serve immediately. Makes 4 servings.

Mrs. Michael Oxley, Wife of Representative (Ohio)

BAKED ZITI

1 pound sweet Italian sausage, skinned
2 onions, minced
3 cans mushrooms
6 cups drained canned tomatoes
½ cup minced peppers
½ teaspoon dried sage leaves
1 teaspoon dried basil
1 teaspoon salt
¼ teaspoon black pepper
1 cup water
1 pound ziti pasta
½ pound mozzarella cheese, diced
1 cup grated Parmesan cheese

Combine sausage, onions and mushrooms in a large heavy saucepan and cook over medium heat, stirring constantly to break up sausage. Continue cooking until all the fat has cooked out of the sausage. Pour off excess fat. Add the remaining ingredients except the pasta, mozzarella and the parmesan. Simmer, uncovered, over very low heat for 2 hours, stirring occasionally to prevent sticking. Parboil ziti and drain. Put in a deep casserole dish, cover with hot sauce, add the mozzarella cheese and mix well. Sprinkle Parmesan over the top, cover and bake in a preheated 350° oven for 15 minutes. Remove cover and continue baking for 10 minutes. Makes 6 to 8 servings. May be frozen.

Mrs. James J. Howard, Wife of former Representative (New Jersey)

PASTA AND PEPPER MEDLEY

2 tablespoons olive oil
1 clove garlic, sliced
1 small onion, quartered and sliced
½ green pepper
½ red pepper
½ yellow pepper
1 medium tomato, diced
2 tablespoons capers
½ cup mushrooms, sliced
2 tablespoons ripe olives, sliced
2 tablespoons green olives, sliced
salt to taste

Brown garlic in olive oil. Then remove garlic. Saute onion, then add peppers and all other ingredients. Continue to stir until they have reached your desired texture, whether crisp or well done. Serve over prepared linguine pasta. Just as good served chilled the next day. Makes 6 servings.

Ronnie Flippo

Ronnie Flippo, former Representative (Alabama)

LINGUINE WITH MARINARA SAUCE

1 pound cooked linguine
3 tablespoons olive oil
6 garlic cloves
1 small onion, chopped
½ cup chopped green pepper
1 cup chopped fresh mushrooms
2 8 oz. cans crushed tomatoes in puree
2 tablespoons basil
2 tablespoons oregano
¼ cup parsley flakes

Cook linguine according to directions on package. Heat olive oil in skillet and add the next 4 ingredients. Saute 5 minutes. Add the remaining ingredients and simmer 35–40 minutes. Serve over linguine. Makes 4 servings. May be frozen.

Tish Traficant

Mrs. James Traficant, Wife of Representative (Ohio)

LINGUINE AND PROSCIUTTO WITH CREAMY, LOW-CHOLESTEROL PARMIGIANO-REGGIANO SAUCE

4 tablespoons extra-virgin olive oil
¼ cup red onion, finely chopped
1 teaspoon salt
1½ cups evaporated skimmed milk
1 teaspoon grated lemon rind
3 ozs. Prosciutto de Parma, thinly sliced
10 fresh basil leaves
¼ cup chopped fresh parsley
4 fresh mint leaves
1 pound linguine
¾ cup freshly grated Parmigiano-Reggiano
freshly ground pepper

Heat olive oil in a large saute pan set over medium heat. Add onion and season with salt. Saute 5 minutes, until soft. Add evaporated milk and the grated lemon rind. Heat 1 minute. Remove from heat. Cut prosciutto into thin strips. Finely chop basil, parsley and mint together. Combine with prosciutto and set aside. Cook linguine in a large quantity of very well-salted, rapidly boiling water. Just before the pasta is done, set the saute pan with the sauce back over medium-high heat to warm it briefly. Drain pasta when "al dente". Add it to the pan with the sauce, along with the herbs and prosciutto. Toss well over medium heat. Then, while tossing, add the Parmigiano-Reggiano, tossing until a light sauce is formed. Season generously with pepper. Serve immediately into warm pasta bowls. Note: Parmigiano-Reggiano is used to thicken and flavor this sauce based on evaporated skim milk. This produces a rich tasting dish *low* in cholesterol, with only 25% of its calories derived from fat. Makes 6 servings.

Mrs. Paul Laxalt, Wife of former Senator (Nevada)

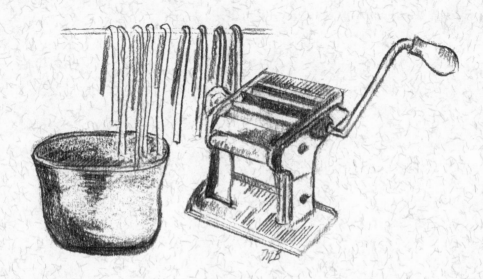

AUNT MART'S CHICKEN FETTUCINE

¼ cup butter
¼ cup flour
1 cup milk
1 cup chicken broth
1 large chicken, boned and cubed
1 4 oz. jar pimentos
½ cup chopped onions
⅓ cup lemon juice
½ teaspoon cayenne pepper
1 teaspoon salt
9 oz. fettucine, cooked and drained
2 cups sour cream
1 pkg. frozen chopped spinach, cooked and drained
1 6 oz. jar sliced mushrooms
1 can sliced water chestnuts
½ cup chopped celery
2 teaspoons seasoned salt
1 teaspoon paprika
1 teaspoon pepper
1½ cups grated Monterey Jack cheese

Melt butter and stir in flour. Add milk and broth, stirring continually until it begins to thicken. Add remaining ingredients except for cheese. Pour into buttered casserole dish. Top with grated cheese and bake at 300° for 25–30 minutes. Makes 10 to 12 servings.

Janet Bryant

Mrs. John W. Bryant, Wife of Representative (Texas)

Run cooked spaghetti under HOT water to prevent stickiness.

CHEDDAR CHEESE FETTUCINE

8 ozs. fettucine
⅓ cup onion, chopped
1 clove garlic, minced
1 tablespoon margarine
1 tablespoon all-purpose
  flour
½ teaspoon instant chicken
  bouillon granules
¼ teaspoon pepper
1 cup milk
1½ cups shredded cheddar
  cheese
1 tablespoon parsley
  fresh ground pepper

Cook fettucine according to directions on package. Drain and keep warm. For cheese sauce, in a saucepan, cook onion and garlic in margarine until tender. Stir in flour, bouillon granules and the ¼ teaspoon pepper. Add milk all at once. Cook and stir until thickened and bubbly. Cook and stir for 1 more minute. Stir in cheese. Cook and stir until cheese melts. Stir in parsley. If cheese sauce is too thick, stir in 1 to 2 tablespoons additional milk. Serve cheese sauce over hot pasta. Sprinkle with freshly ground pepper. Makes 4 servings.

Jill DeWine Darling

Mrs. William Darling, Daughter of former Representative Mike DeWine (Ohio)

FETTUCINI MILANI

1 pound Italian sausage
  (sweet or hot)
½ cup olive oil
1 cup onion
2 cloves minced garlic
½ cup butter
3 cups mushrooms, sliced in
  half
1 cup fresh parsley
1 teaspoon basil
½ teaspoon oregano
¼ teaspoon rosemary
1 pound fettucine, cooked

Brown sausage in olive oil, set aside. Saute the onion and garlic in butter, add mushrooms and brown lightly. Add sausage and spices, warm thoroughly. Serve over the fettucini. Makes 8 servings.

Sally J Patterson

Mrs. Jerry Patterson, Wife of former Representative (California)

"QUICK" SHRIMP FETTUCINI

12 oz. fresh fettucini (spinach or egg noodles or combined)
Frozen or fresh shrimp (as many as desired)
2 tablespoons garlic spread or garlic butter
1 medium onion, chopped very fine
½ cup whipping cream
¼ cup butter
grated Parmesan cheese

Cook fettucini according to directions. While this is cooking, place shrimp in a skillet and simmer with garlic butter or spread with finely chopped onion. Saute until onion is tender. Set aside and keep warm. Mix cooked fettucini with whipping cream, butter and a little garlic butter. When ready to serve, put fettucini on plate and top with shrimp mixture and Parmesan cheese. Garnish with parsley. Makes 6 servings.

Mary Clement

Mrs. Bob Clement, Wife of Representative (Tennessee)

FETTUCINI CON PORI

4 to 6 leeks (white part only, sliced crosswise)
½ cup olive oil
4 tablespoons butter
½ cup sun-dried tomatoes, reconstituted and slivered
½ pound slivered prosciutto
½ cup grated assiago or Parmesan cheese
½ cup toasted pignolis
½ cup chopped cilantro
1 pound fettucini

Saute leeks in olive oil and butter. Then add sun-dried tomatoes. Cook the pasta and just before pasta is finished, add the slivered prosciutto (do not add too soon). Sprinkle with cheese, pignolis and cilantro. Toss in large bowl. Mangia! Makes 4 to 6 servings. May be frozen.

Susan Dougher

Mrs. Jon Dougher, Daughter of Representative Gerald Solomon (New York)

SPINACH LASAGNA

1 medium onion, chopped
4 tablespoons olive oil
1 pound chopped spinach
   (fresh or frozen)
1 cup pesto (store bought
   varieties are fine)
4 cups ricotta cheese
1 cup grated Parmesan
   salt and pepper to taste
2 cups favorite tomato sauce
1 pound mozzarella cheese
   (sliced or grated)
24 lasagna noodles (fresh or
   dried)

Saute chopped onion in 2 tablespoons olive oil until soft. Add chopped spinach to onions and saute briefly. (If using frozen spinach, defrost and drain spinach first). Transfer mixture to a large bowl. Add the pesto, ricotta and ½ cup Parmesan cheese to mixture. Blend well. Add salt and pepper to taste. If using dried noodles, boil noodles about 2 minutes until slightly softened. Fresh noodles are ready to use without boiling. Oil the bottom of a 9″ × 13″ pan. Place a layer of noodles into the bottom of the pan. Spread ⅓ of the filling on the noodles. Spread ½ cup tomato sauce over spinach mixture. Place ⅓ mozzarella over that. Place another layer of noodles on top. Repeat layers of spinach filling, tomato sauce and mozzarella. More noodles. Repeat layers. One final layer of noodles. Drizzle with 2 tablespoons olive oil. Spread remaining tomato sauce on top. Sprinkle with remaining Parmesan. Cover with foil and bake at 350° for 40 minutes. Makes 6–8 servings. May be frozen.

Sally J. Roemer

Mrs. Tim Roemer, Wife of Representative (Indiana)

CHICKEN TETTRAZINI

4 single skinned boned
   chicken breasts
1 can cream of mushroom
   soup
8 ozs. spaghetti noodles
   Parmesan cheese
   milk
1 small green pepper
   salt and pepper

Boil chicken breast until tender, remove and cut into bite size pieces. Cook spaghetti in broth from chicken, add more water if necessary. Saute green pepper. Mix chicken, green pepper, soup and 1 soup can of milk together. Sprinkle in Parmesan cheese and mix again. Put in casserole dish and top with more Parmesan. Bake at 375° for 40 minutes or until very hot. Makes 4 servings. May be frozen.

Sheila Wellstone

Mrs. Paul Wellstone, Wife of Senator (Minnesota)

RATATOUILLE LASAGNA

2 tablespoons olive oil
2 small eggplants, diced
1 each red and yellow pep-
    per, seeded and diced
2 coarse zucchini, coarsely
    chopped
1/8 teaspoon cayenne pepper
3 cups strained tomatoes
1 tablespoon olive oil
1/2 cup fresh basil leaves,
    chopped or 2 table-
    spoons dried basil
salt and pepper
10 black olives, halved
12 oz. pkg. lasagna noodles,
    cooked according to
    pkg. directions
1 1/2 cups low-fat ricotta cheese
1 1/2 cups shredded mozzarella
    cheese
1/2 cup Parmesan cheese

To make ratatouille, heat 2 tablespoons of oil in a large nonstick saucepan over medium heat. When hot, add eggplant, peppers, zucchini and cayenne pepper and cook for 5 minutes. Reduce heat to low, cover and cook for 20 minutes. Uncover, increase heat to medium and cook until most of the liquid has evaporated.

To make sauce, combine strained tomatoes, remaining oil, basil, salt, pepper and olives in saucepan. Slowly bring to a boil.

To assemble: place a ladleful of sauce in 9″ × 13″ baking dish. Cover with a layer of cooked noodles, then the ricotta and drizzle with a ladleful of sauce. Add another layer of noodles, the ratatouille and more sauce. Finish with a final layer of noodles, the remaining sauce, and top with mozzarella and Parmesan cheese. Bake at 350° for 20 minutes. Makes 6 to 8 servings. May be frozen.

Mrs. Harris Livingstain, Daughter of former Representative Don Fuqua (Florida)

CHICKEN TETRAZZINI

1 4 1/2 pound chicken
1 pound dry spaghetti
2 cans cream of mushroom
    soup, heat and thin with
    chicken broth
1 small jar pimento

Cook chicken, debone and skin, save broth. Cook spaghetti. Add cut up chicken, mushroom soup with broth, spaghetti and chopped pimento. Put into baking dish, cover with fine bread crumbs and cheese. Bake until cheese is melted and ingredients hot and bubbly. Bake at 350° for about 15 minutes.

Mrs. L. H. Fountain, Wife of former Representative (North Carolina)

VEGETARIAN MICROWAVE LASAGNA

6 uncooked lasagna noodles
15 oz. jar of spaghetti sauce
1 medium green or red pepper, diced
2 ozs. of fresh spinach, diced
15 ozs. low fat cottage cheese
8 ozs. part-skim milk mozzarella cheese
15 oz. can of beans, drained (choices include, vegetarian, baked, kidney or pinto)
1 carrot, diced (optional)
1 small onion, diced (optional)
2 tablespoons of Parmesan cheese

Use a microwave rectangular dish (7½″ × 11″). Spread a thin layer of spaghetti sauce in bottom of dish and cover spaghetti sauce with 3 uncooked lasagna noodles. In a separate bowl, mix the diced pepper, diced spinach, cottage cheese, mozzarella cheese, drained beans, and other optional items (carrot and onion) if desired. Spread ½ of the cottage cheese mixture on top of the 3 uncooked lasagna noodles and cover with a layer of spaghetti sauce. Add the 3 remaining uncooked lasagna noodles and another layer of the cottage cheese mixture. Cover the lasagna noodles with the remaining spaghetti sauce. Sprinkle with the Parmesan cheese. Cover dish and microwave on high for 11 minutes; rotate dish 90° and microwave on high for another 11 minutes. Allow lasagna to cool for 30–60 minutes or overnight in refrigerator. Delicious hot or cold. Makes 6 servings.

John Watson, Son-in-law of former Representative Glenard P. Lipscomb (California)

KIP'S LOBSTER PASTA

½ cup chopped onion
2 tablespoons olive oil
1 can Italian plum tomatoes
salt and pepper to taste
2 teaspoons tarragon
1 cup heavy cream
½ pound lobster meat (cook a 3-pound lobster)
1 pound spaghetti

Saute onion in oil until soft. Add tomatoes, salt, pepper and tarragon, simmer for 20 minutes. Stir in cream and simmer for 15 minutes. Cook the lobster for 8 minutes in boiling water. Chop lobster meat into small pieces. Add lobster to pot and cook for 3 more minutes. Pour the sauce over the cooked pasta and serve. Makes 2 servings. May be frozen.

Mrs. Steve Neal, Wife of Representative (North Carolina)

POLLO TETRAZZINI (CREAMED CHICKEN WITH NOODLES)

4 pound stewing chicken
1 teaspoon salt
½ teaspoon white pepper
½ teaspoon dried rosemary
water
½ pound fettucine (or other egg noodles)
¼ cup butter
1 onion, minced
1 pepper, minced
1 can mushrooms, drained
½ cup heavy cream
1½ cups grated Parmesan cheese
¼ cup minced parsley

Place chicken in a deep pot. Add salt, pepper, rosemary and enough water to cover. Bring to a gentle boil and simmer for 2½ hours. Drain the broth into a large saucepan. Add enough water to make 2 quarts. Bring to a rolling boil and add the noodles. Cook until tender and drain. Meanwhile, bone and skin the chicken and cut the chicken meat into bite size pieces. Melt the butter in a large skillet. Add onion and pepper and saute for 5 minutes, stirring constantly. Add mushrooms and cook for 5 minutes longer. Add cream, chicken meat, noodles, 1 cup of cheese and parsley. Mix and heat through. Serve with remaining cheese. Makes 4 to 6 servings. May be frozen.

Mrs. James J. Howard, Wife of former Representative (New Jersey)

CHICKEN TETRAZZINI CASSEROLE

4 cups cooked chicken
2 cans cream of mushroom soup
2 bay leaves
½ cup chopped pimento
½ cup chopped green pepper
1 large onion, chopped
1 tablespoon Worcestershire
¾ pound grated mild cheddar cheese
1 cup chicken stock
10 oz. Ronco thin spaghetti

Boil chicken and remove from bones and chop. Strain stock (reserve 1 cup for sauce).

Sauce: To mushroom soup, add stock, bay leaves, pimento, green pepper, onion, Worcestershire and cheese (reserving some cheese for topping). Simmer until well blended. Cook spaghetti in remaining stock, adding water if necessary. Mix cooked spaghetti, sauce and chicken and place in large casserole (4 quart). Sprinkle top with grated cheese. Bake at 350° 1 hour in large casserole. ½ hour if using 2 small casseroles (2 quart). Makes 12 servings. May be frozen.

Mrs. Brock Adams, Wife of former Senator (Washington)

CHICKEN TETRAZZINI

4½ to 5 pound stewing
    chicken
  3 cups hot water (or enough
    to cover liberally)
    salt to taste or health
  1 teaspoon onion salt
  ½ pound cooked spaghettini
    (very thin)

Sauce:
6   tablespoons butter or mar-
      garine
½   to 2 pounds fresh mush-
      rooms or 1 large can
1   tablespoon lemon juice
2   tablespoons flour
      paprika
½   teaspoon pepper
⅛   teaspoon nutmeg
1   cup heavy cream (for not
      as rich, use tablecream)
⅔   cup grated Parmesan
      cheese (for thickening,
      may need more)
½   cup buttered, seasoned
      crumbs
½   cup dry sherry or good
      white wine (optional)
2   cups finely shredded pro-
      cessed yellow cheese

Simmer chicken covered with water and onion salt until tender, about 1 to 1½ hours. Be careful not to overcook and dry out. Add water if needed. Remove chicken from the broth and cool. Cut meat off bone in good size hunks. Set aside 2½ cups of broth. Saute sliced mushrooms in 3 table-spoons butter or margarine (don't let fat smoke) and with a slotted spoon, set aside. Add remaining 3 tablespoons butter or margarine. Slowly stir in lemon juice, flour, paprika, pepper and nutmeg, stirring over very low heat to make a thick paste. Very slowly stir in reserved cups of broth. At this point, add the sherry if using it. Stir sauce until it thickens. Remove from heat and add heavy cream. Blend mushrooms and chicken (and shred-ded processed cheese, if desired) into spaghettini in baking dish. Gently pour sauce over all, making sure it is fully blended into the chicken, etc. Alter-nate layers of bread crumbs and Parmesan cheese on top until about ¼ inch thick. Bake at 325°, for 45 minutes or longer if not yet bubbly. Good served at a buffet with ham, herb rice, tossed salad, vegetable gelatin salad or aspic. Makes 8 servings. May be frozen.

Bethine Church

Mrs. Frank Church, Wife of former Senator (Idaho)

CHICKEN SPAGHETTI

1 large fryer chicken
  onion
  celery
  bay leaf
  salt
  pepper

Sauce:
1/4 cup oil
3 tablespoons flour
2 large onions, chopped
1 bell pepper
  crushed garlic
2 cups celery, chopped
1 can tomato paste
1 large and 1 small can
  tomatoes
1 jar sliced mushrooms with
  juice
1 jar prepared spaghetti
  sauce
1/2 stick butter
3 bay leaves
  red pepper
  black pepper
  Tabasco
  salt
  Lea & Perrins
1 tablespoon sugar
  small bunch chopped
    parsley
1/2 bunch green onions

Chicken: Boil large fryer with onion, celery, bay leaf, salt and pepper for 30 minutes. Or boil a hen 1 1/2 hours. Reserve chicken stock. Remove from bones.

Sauce: Mix oil and flour—make into a brown roux. Add chopped onions, cook with chopped bell pepper. Then add crushed garlic and chopped celery. Cook, then add can tomato paste, then small and large can of tomatoes, sliced mushrooms with juice, prepared spaghetti sauce and 1/2 stick butter. Season with 3 bay leaves, red pepper, black pepper, Tabasco, salt, Lea & Perrins, and sugar. Add chicken stock (about 4 cups) and simmer 1 hour. Add cut chicken. Cook 1/2 hour. Add more stock if necessary. Stir often during cooking time. Serve over spaghetti with Parmesan cheese.

Dan Miller, Representative (Florida)

WINKIE'S CLAM SPAGHETTI

½ cup olive oil
1 dried red chili pepper,
    finely chopped
1 large onion, chopped
3 large garlic cloves, minced
½ cup fresh basil leaves,
    chopped OR 1 table-
    spoon dried
1 tablespoon oregano
    salt and pepper to taste
3 4½ oz. cans chopped
    clams (drained with liq-
    uid reserved)
1 pound dried spaghetti
1 cup chopped fresh parsley
½ cup grated Romano or
    Parmesan cheese

Put olive oil in large cast iron skillet and heat. Cook slowly, 30 minutes until onion is very soft. Add to pan, basil, oregano, salt, pepper and liquid from the clams. Continue to simmer until liquid is reduced. Keep warm. Bring kettle of water to a boil, add pasta, cook until al dente. As pasta is cooking, add the clams, parsley and ¼ cup cheese to the sauce. Keep warm. Drain pasta. Stir into sauce and toss. Sprinkle with ¼ cup cheese. Serve from skillet. Makes 6 servings.

Mrs. Jay Rhodes, Wife of former Representative (Arizona)

'HOT' SPAGHETTI

1 large round steak
1 large onion
1 can tomato sauce
½ can water
¼ teaspoon cloves, chili pow-
    der, garlic salt
    salt and pepper to taste

Cut steak in strips, chop onions and brown together in a large fry pan. Add tomato sauce, water and spices. Simmer on low for 3 hours. Thicken with flour when ready to serve. Serve over spaghetti. Makes 6 servings.

Mrs. Pat Williams, Wife of Representative (Montana)

LUCENTE SAUCE (SPAGHETTI SAUCE)

For Sauce:

2 large country ribs
1 large onion, diced
4 cloves garlic, chopped
4 tablespoon olive oil blend
3 6 oz. cans tomato paste
1 #2½ size can Italian pack tomatoes
1 #2½ size can of water
½ cup grated Parmesan
8 or 9 basil leaves
8 sausage links
salt to taste

For Meatballs:

1 pound ground beef
1 cup Italian bread crumbs
¾ cup grated Parmesan
½ to 1 cup of water
1 unbeaten egg
3 cloves chopped garlic
3 tablespoons fresh parsley
salt and pepper

First brown meat, then add onion and garlic. Add all remaining ingredients for sauce. Add meatballs gently. Stir often and simmer for 1½ hours. Keep covered.

For meatballs: Mix all ingredients in a big bowl. Consistency should be easy to work with and similar to a meatloaf. Shape into small balls and place into sauce. Makes 12 servings. May be frozen.

Susan Nunner

Mrs. Jeffrey Nunner, Daughter of Representative David L. Hobson (Ohio)

BETTY'S SPAGHETTI SAUCE

½ cup onion, sliced
2 tablespoons olive or salad oil
1 pound ground beef
2 cloves garlic, minced
2 1 pound cans tomatoes (4 cups), blend in blender
2 8 oz. cans seasoned tomato sauce (2 cups)
1 cup water
1 3 oz. can broiled sliced mushrooms (⅔ cup)
¼ cup chopped parsley
1½ teaspoons oregano
1 teaspoon salt
¼ teaspoon thyme
1 bay leaf
long spaghetti, cooked
grated Parmesan (optional)

Cook onion in hot oil until golden. Add meat and garlic; brown lightly. Add remaining ingredients simmer uncovered 2-2½ hours (or until thick). Remove bay leaf. Serve over cooked spaghetti. Top with grated Parmesan. Makes 6 servings. May be frozen.

Jill DeWine Darling

Mrs. William Darling, Daughter of former Representative Mike DeWine (Ohio)

GRANDMOTHER LILLIAN'S BAKED SPAGHETTI

2 pounds ground beef
4 whole medium sized onions
1½ pounds spaghetti
8 cans (8 oz. each) tomato puree
8 tablespoons olive oil
4 buds garlic
12 bay leaves
Parmesan cheese

Brown ground beef and onion in skillet. Boil spaghetti in 2 quarts of water. Combine cooked ground beef mixture and cooked spaghetti in large casserole dish. Add tomato puree, olive oil, garlic and bay leaves. Stir together thoroughly. Sprinkle ¼-½ cup of Parmesan cheese on top. Bake at 350°, uncovered for 1-1½ hours, until top is browned and mixture is cooked thoroughly. Makes 12 servings. May be frozen.

Charlotte Bruce

Mrs. Terry Bruce, Wife of former Representative (Illinois)

VENISON SPAGHETTI SAUCE

3 cloves garlic
1 large bell pepper
1 large onion
½ pound fresh mushrooms
2 pounds ground venison
1 jar Prego tomato sauce
  (plain)
1 can tomato sauce
1 tablespoon dry Italian seasoning
1 tablespoon sugar
  salt to taste
  pepper to taste

Saute garlic, pepper, onion and mushrooms. Add venison and brown. Add remaining ingredients and simmer 2 to 3 hours. Makes 4 servings. May be frozen.

Carroll Campbell, Governor (South Carolina)

PESTO SAUCE FOR PASTA

1 cup washed basil leaves,
  firmly packed
⅓ cup pine (pignoli) nuts
⅓ cup grated Parmesan
  cheese
4 large cloves of garlic
½ cup good olive oil
½ cup chicken broth (skim
  off fat)

Add all ingredients into blender and blend to creamy consistency. Serve at room temperature on your favorite pasta. Pesto sauce may be frozen in ice cube trays, then stored in freezer bags for use as needed.

Mrs. Gerald Solomon, Wife of Representative (New York)

SPAGHETTI BAKE

1½ pounds lean ground beef
1 cup chopped onion
1 clove garlic, minced
1 15 oz. can tomatoes, cut up with juice
1 15 oz. can tomato sauce
1 4 oz. can mushroom pieces, drained
2 teaspoons sugar
1 teaspoon salt
½ teaspoon dried basil
½ teaspoon oregano
8 ozs. spaghetti, broken in half, cooked and drained
1 8 oz. pkg. shredded mozzarella cheese
⅓ cup Parmesan cheese

Brown beef, onion and garlic until beef is browned. Drain off fat. Stir in tomatoes, tomato sauce, mushroom pieces and seasonings. Bring to a boil and then simmer 20–25 minutes. Remove from heat and stir in spaghetti. Place ½ of mixture in 9″ × 13″ pan, sprinkle with mozzarella cheese, top with remaining spaghetti mixture, then sprinkle with Parmesan cheese. Bake at 375° for about 30 minutes. Makes 6 servings. May be frozen.

George E. Sangmeister, Representative (Illinois)

POMMES DAUPHINOISE

5 pounds potatoes, peeled and sliced
2 teaspoons garlic, minced
salt and pepper to taste
1 quart heavy cream
2 cups Swiss cheese, shredded

Mix garlic and salt and pepper with potatoes; layer in baking dish. Cover with heavy cream. Cover baking dish with foil and bake at 375° for 1 hour. Remove foil, sprinkle with shredded cheese and bake an additional 15 minutes, or until cheese is melted and browned. Makes 8 servings.

Mrs. Arne Carlson, Wife of Governor (Minnesota)

CONNIE'S PASTA CARBONARA

1 pound bacon, cooked
1 pound pkg. spaghetti, linguini or angel hair
2 eggs
1 medium onion, chopped
1 stick butter, melted
2 teaspoons prepared minced garlic
½ cup white wine or additional ½ stick butter, melted
½ cup grated Parmesan cheese
dash of pepper and oregano

Crumble bacon and set aside. Cook spaghetti in boiling water as directed. Beat eggs very well and set aside. Use a pan large enough to hold all ingredients and keep it over heat during the entire preparation. Brown onions in the melted butter, adding garlic. When onion is browned, stir in the wine or additional melted butter so as to maintain a liquid. Stir in eggs vigorously so they are absorbed rather than cooked. Add drained spaghetti, bacon, cheese, pepper and oregano, stirring quickly and thoroughly until cheese is melted. Serve immediately. Makes 6 servings.

Mrs. John R. Foley, Wife of former Representative (Maryland)

PALMETTO PASTA

1 pound fresh linguine or fettucine
½ cup chopped bell pepper
½ cup chopped red peppers or chopped pimento, drained
6 ozs. fresh mushrooms, sliced
½ cup fresh grated Parmesan cheese
4 ozs. fresh butter
1 pkg. Old Monk Instant Alfredo Sauce
1 pint half and half cream
2 ozs. ham (Smithfield or prosciutto) chopped or bacon, crumbled

In a large pot, cook linguine or fettucine according to package directions. Drain and set aside. In a large skillet, saute peppers and mushrooms in butter. Add package of Alfredo sauce. Stir in half and half until creamy on low heat. Toss ham or bacon with Parmesan cheese and broccoli if desired. Add to sauce mixture. To serve, place pasta on a heated platter or chaffing dish, pour sauce over top. Serve immediately. Optional: 4 ozs. fresh broccoli, broken into florets. Cook in a small amount of boiling water until crisp/tender. Makes 4 servings.

Carroll Campbell, Governor (South Carolina)

POTATO WEDGES

4 potatoes (3½ oz. each) A
    combination of brown &
    sweet potatoes is deli-
    cious
2 egg whites, unbeaten
    salt-free seasoning to taste

Preheat oven to 425°. Cut potatoes into wedges. Dip wedges into unbeaten egg whites and place on a non-stick pan sprayed with vegetable spray. Season with salt-free seasoning and bake for 25 minutes or until golden brown. Makes 4 servings.

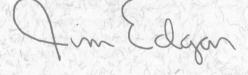

Jim Edgar, Governor (Illinois)

POTATO CASSEROLE

2 pound bag frozen hash
    brown potatoes
1 can cream of chicken soup
8 ozs. sour cream
8 ozs. french onion dip
2 cups grated sharp cheese
1 stick margarine, melted
1 cup potato chips, crushed

Thaw hash browns enough to combine with soup, sour cream, onion dip and cheese. Stir well. Pour into buttered 9″ × 13″ casserole. Drizzle melted butter over top and sprinkle with crushed potato chips. Bake at 400° for 1 hour. Good for buffet dish. Holds heat well and is good at room temperature. Makes 12 servings. May be frozen.

Mrs. Jack Brooks, Wife of Representative (Texas)

A thin slice cut from each end of the potato will speed up baking time.

KROPPKAKOR (SWEDISH POTATO DUMPLINGS)

5 cups mashed potatoes
½ teaspoon salt
3 eggs, slightly beaten
1 cup sifted flour
¾ pound salt pork

Cream Gravy:
4 tablespoons butter
2 tablespoons flour
2 cups milk
½ teaspoon salt

Peel, cook and mash enough potatoes to make 5 cups. Add salt, slightly beaten eggs and flour. Cut salt pork into small pieces and fry until lightly browned. Shape potato mixture into 2-inch balls (add more flour if hard to handle), flatten the ball and place 1 teaspoon of the salt pork in the center. Reshape into balls. Add 1 tablespoon salt to 3 quarts boiling water. Carefully add the potato balls and cook slowly for 15 minutes. Remove from water with a slotted spoon and serve with cream gravy. Dumplings may be cut in half and fried the next day.

Cream Gravy: Melt butter in pan, add flour and salt, stirring carefully until mixture bubbles. Add milk gradually, cooking and stirring until mixture thickens. Reduce heat to very low and simmer a few minutes. Makes 8 servings.

Mrs. Don Sundquist, Wife of Representative (Tennessee)

POTATO CASSEROLE

2 pound pkg. hash browns
   (thawed)
½ cup grated onion
½ cup melted margarine
8 oz. sour cream
1 can cream of chicken soup
1 cup grated cheddar cheese
1 cup crushed corn flakes
¼ cup melted margarine

Mix first 6 ingredients. Place in a 9″ × 12″ pan. Top with crushed corn flakes and melted margarine (mixed together). Bake at 350° for 45 minutes. Makes 12 servings.

Mrs. Jim Slattery, Wife of Representative (Kansas)

BOUREKAS (GREEK POTATO PASTRIES)

1 box Pepperidge Farm puff
    pastry sheets
2 large baking potatoes
1 medium onion, finely
    chopped
3 tablespoons margarine
3 tablespoons flour
1 egg yolk
    sesame seeds

Thaw frozen pastry sheets for approximately 20 minutes before gently unfolding. Cut into 18 squares. For easier handling, flour board. Peel skin off potatoes and boil for 20–25 minutes until soft. Drain potatoes and mash until smooth. Fry onions in 1 tablespoon of margarine until golden brown. Add to potatoes and mix. Put teaspoon of potato mixture into center of each square. Fold over to make triangle. Seal edges of overlapped dough by pressing together with a fork all around so filling will not run out while baking. Put a little egg yolk on top of each boureka. Sprinkle on sesame seeds. Put bourekas on baking sheet. Bake at 325° for approximately 30 minutes until golden brown.

Lori Deutsch

Mrs. Peter Deutsch, Wife of Representative (Florida)

CRAB-TOPPED POTATOES

2 baking potatoes
1 small onion, chopped
¼ cup shredded crab
¼ cup pecans
2 tablespoons thinly sliced
    green onions
2 tablespoons thinly sliced
    celery
1 teaspoon lemon juice
¼ cup plain nonfat yogurt

Microwave potatoes on high power for 12 minutes, or cook potatoes in oven at 350° until soft. Remove from oven and keep warm. Combine remaining ingredients except yogurt, in a glass container. Cover, microwave on high power until vegetables are tender. Split potatoes and remove the pulp. Mix all ingredients, including the yogurt and pulp. Mix and stuff potato shells. Cook at 350° for 10 minutes. Makes 2 servings. May be frozen.

Danealia Mineta

Mrs. Norman Mineta, Wife of Representative (California)

Potatoes will bake in a hurry if they are boiled in salted water for about ten minutes before popping into a very hot oven.

SHREDDED POTATO CASSEROLE

1 32 oz. pkg. frozen shredded potatoes
½ cup melted butter
1 can cream of chicken
   soup, undiluted
12 ozs. grated American
   cheese
1 8 oz. carton sour cream
1 teaspoon salt
½ small onion, chopped
2 cups crushed corn flakes
½ cup melted butter

Place thawed potatoes in a 9″ × 13″ baking dish. Mix together next 6 ingredients and pour over potatoes. Top with crushed corn flakes and drizzle melted butter over all. Bake uncovered at 350° for 45 minutes. Makes 12 servings. May be frozen.

Betty Thornton

Mrs. Ray Thornton, Wife of Representative (Arkansas)

SISTER DOLLY'S BESTEST POTATOES

1 pound small red potatoes
¼ cup dry white wine
1 cup firmly packed part of
   leek (up to light green)
3 tablespoons unsalted butter
¼ cup heavy cream
¼ cup sour cream
2 to 4 small garlic cloves,
   minced
nutmeg to taste

Thinly slice leek, wash and pat dry. In boiling water, (salted) simmer potatoes covered for 10–15 minutes until tender. Drain. Transfer to bowl. In skillet cook leek in butter over low heat, stirring until soft. Add wine and cream. Simmer stirring for 5 minutes. Mash potatoes with fork coarsely still leaving lumpy. Add leek mixture to potatoes and add sour cream, garlic, nutmeg, salt and pepper to taste. Mix well and enjoy. Makes 4 to 6 servings.

Amey Upton

Mrs. Fred Upton, Wife of Representative (Michigan)

For fluffier mashed potatoes add a pinch of baking soda as well as milk and butter.

AUNT JANET'S GOURMET POTATOES

6 Maine potatoes
2 cups shredded cheddar
  cheese
¼ cup butter
1½ cups sour cream with
  chives (room temper-
  ature)
¼ teaspoon pepper
1 teaspoon salt
2 tablespoons butter

Cook potatoes in skins and cool. Peel and shred coarsely. In saucepan over low heat combine cheese and ¼ cup butter, stirring until almost melted. Remove from heat and blend in sour cream, salt and pepper. Fold in potatoes and turn into 2 quart greased casserole. Dot with butter. Bake at 350° for 25 minutes or until slightly brown. Makes 6 to 8 servings.

Judy Clinger

Mrs. William Clinger, Wife of Representative (Pennsylvania)

GARLIC MASHED POTATOES (LOW FAT)

8 or 10 potatoes, peeled
2 leeks, chopped
¼ cup sun dried tomatoes
1 whole garlic bulb
  pinch cumin
1 tablespoon lemon juice
1½ tablespoons olive oil
  pinch salt

Cook potatoes until done, drain and add all other ingredients—whip together until smooth (small amount of skim milk may be used if needed for smoother consistency). Bake garlic until soft and peel. Add to cooked potatoes. Delicious! Makes 10 servings. May be frozen.

Marian Lewis

Mrs. Tom Lewis, Wife of Representative (Florida)

HANK'S FAVORITE POTATOES AND BUTTERMILK

6 to 8 potatoes (cut in quarters or eighths)
½ pound salt pork, cut up in tiny pieces
1 whole onion, sliced
buttermilk

In small frying pan, slowly saute salt pork and onions until clear and lightly brown (pork should be well done—dark brown). Set aside, and keep warm. Meanwhile boil potatoes, when soft drain and mash. Add salt pork and onions and mix thoroughly with spoon. Add buttermilk in desired amounts as eaten. (This is an old Polish dish— usually served as Friday supper!!) Makes 4 to 6 servings.

Mrs. Henry J. Nowak, Wife of former Representative (New York)

MOM'S MASHED POTATOES SUPREME

8 to 10 potatoes, cooked and mashed
salt to taste
1 stick butter, softened
8 oz. pkg. cream cheese
8 oz. container sour cream

Blend butter, cream cheese and sour cream in blender. Add to mashed potatoes. Mix well in baking dish and refrigerate overnight. Remove and bake at 350° for 30 minutes. (Good for company because you can do the night before.) Makes 8 servings.

Mrs. Carroll Hubbard, Wife of former Representative (Kentucky)

> *A few drops of lemon juice in the water will whiten boiled potatoes.*

HOMINY CASSEROLE

2 regular cans hominy
   (drained)
1 small can pimento
½ stick butter, melted
8 oz. sour cream
1 pkg. cheddar cheese (6 to
   8 oz.)

Mix 2 cans of hominy (drained) with all ingredients except cheddar cheese. Place in casserole dish and top with cheddar cheese. Bake at 350° for 20–30 minutes. This makes an excellent side dish. Makes 6 to 8 servings.

Mary Clement

Mrs. Bob Clement, Wife of Representative (Tennessee)

POTATO CASSEROLE AU GRATIN

6 medium potatoes (about 2
   pounds)
¼ cup butter or margarine
¼ cup all-purpose flour
1 cup chicken broth
⅓ cup light cream
¼ teaspoon salt and pepper
½ cup finely chopped celery
½ cup finely chopped onion
¼ cup chopped pimento,
   drained
1 cup grated cheddar cheese
½ cup melted butter or margarine
1 teaspoon salt
1 cup dairy sour cream
½ cup corn flake crumbs

Boil potatoes with jackets or until almost tender, about 15 minutes. Drain and let cool. Melt butter in saucepan, stir in flour. Slowly add chicken broth and cook, stirring constantly until thickened and bubbly. Stir in cream, salt and pepper. Remove from heat, cover and let cool. Peel and grate potatoes. Combine with celery, onion, pimento, cheese, melted butter and salt. Stir sour cream into cooled cream sauce, then fold sauce into grated potato mixture. Turn into 9″ × 13″ shallow baking dish. Sprinkle with corn flake crumbs. May be refrigerated at this point, if desired. Bake at 325° for 1 hour. Makes 10 to 12 servings. May be frozen.

Marjorie A. Wylie

Mrs. Chalmers Wylie, Wife of former Representative (Ohio)

NOTES

Rosalynn Smith Carter
1977–1981

Best Wishes ———

Rosalynn Carter

Rosalynn Smith Carter

Community, the elderly and mental health were the principal concerns of First Lady Rosalynn Carter. In addition, she continued to focus national attention on the performing arts, inviting classical artists from around the world as well as recognizing traditional American culture.

Hardworking and serious, Mrs. Carter brought her business acumen and drive to the White House. She attended Cabinet meetings and other high-level briefings and also served as the President's personal emissary to Latin American countries. She was also responsible for a lasting legacy to future First Ladies by helping push through legislation to provide funding and staff support for the essential activities of the position.

Her concern and energy remain unabated as she travels the world today helping to build homes for the disadvantaged as part of Habitat for Humanity.

New Roof and Porch

SEAFOOD

FISH CHOWDER

2 pounds haddock
2 ounces salt pork, diced
2 onions, sliced
4 large potatoes, diced
1 cup chopped celery
1 bay leaf, crumbled
1 quart milk
2 tablespoons butter
1 teaspoon salt
Freshly ground pepper

Simmer haddock in 2 cups water for 15 minutes. Drain. Reserve broth. Remove bones from fish. Saute diced pork until crisp, remove and set aside. Saute onions in pork fat until golden brown. Add fish, potatoes, celery, bay leaf, salt and pepper. Pour in fish broth plus enough boiling water to make 3 cups of liquid. Simmer for 30 minutes. Add milk and butter and simmer for 5 minutes. Serve chowder sprinkled with diced pork. Serves 6.

Jacqueline Kennedy

Mrs. John F. Kennedy, Wife of former President of the United States
Reprinted from the 1961 Congressional Club Cookbook. Sixth edition.

PRESIDENT CARTER'S FRIED FISH RECIPE

Filet fish, cut in strips about size of French fries.
Marinate several hours in A-1 or Heinz 57 sauce with touch of Tabasco.
Shake in bag with Bisquick or pancake mix.
Deep fry in peanut oil (or substitute).
Eat hot or cold.

Rosalynn Carter

Mrs. Jimmy Carter, Wife of former President of the United States

SAVORY LO-CAL FISH DISH

1 pound firm-flesh fish fillets (I use Orange Roughy) or steaks, about ½ inch thick

1 tablespoon fresh lime juice

1 medium onion, sliced

1 medium green pepper, cut in ¾ inch chunks

1 clove garlic, minced

2 tablespoons vegetable oil

1 16 oz. can tomatoes, drained and chopped up

⅛ teaspoon crushed red pepper or a few dashes Tabasco sauce

Sprinkle fish with lime juice, set aside. In large skillet, saute onion, green pepper, and garlic in oil until tender-crisp. Add tomatoes and red pepper. Boil until most of liquid is evaporated, about 3–5 minutes. Place fish over sauce, cover and simmer 5–7 minutes or until fish is completely cooked. (Thicker fish requires longer). Remove fish, simmer sauce to thicken, if necessary. Spoon sauce over fish. Serve with plain rice or Spanish rice. Fish will continue to cook while it waits for you to complete the sauce. Makes 4 servings.

Valery J. Moorhead

Mrs. Carlos Moorhead, Wife of Representative (California)

Whole fish are more perishable so they are usually fresher than fillets.

BAKED FILLET OF SOLE

2 pkgs. fillet of sole (or 1½–
   2 pounds fresh)
½ cup chopped parsley
2 tablespoons butter
2 tablespoons lemon juice
1 tablespoon flour
1½ cups heavy cream
1 tablespoon dry sherry
1 tablespoon Parmesan
   cheese
1 tablespoon bread crumbs
½ pound sliced fresh mushrooms
   garlic salt
   salt and white pepper
   paprika
   chopped parsley for
   topping

Cook mushrooms in butter, lemon juice and parsley for 10 minutes. Stir in flour and cream and simmer 10 minutes. Add sherry, salts, and pepper to taste. Pour over fish in a flat baking dish. Sprinkle with Parmesan cheese and bread crumbs, paprika, and parsley. Bake at 350° for 30 minutes or until done. Makes 3 to 4 servings.

Mrs. Cecil Andrus, Wife of Governor (Idaho)

TUNA BROCCOLI CASSEROLE

2 10 oz. pkgs. frozen broccoli spears
1 12 oz. can tuna
1 can cream of mushroom
   soup
¼ cup cooking sherry
8 slices cheddar cheese
   paprika

Cook broccoli according to package directions. Do not overcook. Drain and arrange in buttered 8″ × 11″ × 1½″ baking dish. Cover with a layer of tuna. Dilute soup with sherry and pour over tuna. Top with cheese slices. Sprinkle with paprika and bake at 325° for 20 to 25 minutes. Makes 6 servings. May be frozen.

Mrs. Richard Simpson, Wife of former Representative (Pennsylvania)

ROCKY MOUNTAIN TROUT WITH CRABMEAT MAYONNAISE

3 whole trout, 10 ozs. each, cleaned, boned, heads and tails removed
1 egg
2 tablespoons lemon juice
½ teaspoon salt
¼ teaspoon dijon mustard
1 cup oil: ½ olive, ½ vegetable
1 cup crabmeat
lemon slices
fresh cilantro

Grill trout under broiler, turning halfway. Put in blender the egg and lemon juice, salt, dijon mustard and 2 tablespoons of the oil. Blend on low speed 5 to 6 seconds. Add remaining oil slowly. After oil is added, blend at high speed 4 to 5 seconds. Transfer contents to mixing bowl. Fold in crabmeat. Take trout from broiler and arrange on serving plate. Place hearty dollop of crabmeat mayonnaise on top of fish. Garnish with lemon slices and fresh cilantro. Makes 6 servings.

Jean Grotberg

Mrs. John Grotberg, Wife of former Representative (Illinois)

POACHED HALIBUT

1 slice halibut per person
1 medium white onion
1 bay leaf
1 stalk celery
1 carrot

Halibut topping:
fresh chopped tomato
chopped celery
chopped red and green peppers
chopped green onion

Cover fish with water. Add onion, bay leaf, celery and carrot. Poach for 15–20 minutes or until fish flakes and is done. Remove fish to a warm plate. Cover with tomato, celery, peppers and green onion.

Mrs Mark Hatfield

Mrs. Mark Hatfield, Wife of Senator (Oregon)

FISH NORMANDY

4 fish fillets (haddock, sole, firm fleshed white fish)
salt
pepper
lemon juice
1 egg, beaten
flour
3 tablespoons butter
2 tart apples, peeled, cored, sliced into thin rings
2 sweet onions, peeled and thinly sliced
fresh bread crumbs (heels and crust from French bread. Make crumbs in blender)

Dry fish fillets with paper towel. Sprinkle lightly with salt and pepper. Dip fillets in flour, beaten egg and then in bread crumbs. Gently fry in butter until golden brown on each side. Cover fish with layer of thinly sliced onions. Top onions with layer of apple rings. Squeeze small amount of lemon juice over apples. Baste with butter from frying pan. Cover pan, reduce heat to very low and cook just until onions and apples are wilted (about 5 minutes). Baste with butter from pan several times during cooking. Allow 2 pieces per person.

Mrs. Richard Bryan, Wife of Senator (Nevada)

BAKED FISH

1 pound fish fillets (perch, haddock)
2 tablespoons butter
1 can cream of shrimp soup
¼ cup shredded Parmesan
ground pepper
paprika
lemon wedges

Arrange fish fillets in buttered pie plate (or shallow baking dish). Dash with pepper, dot with butter. Spread soup over fillets and sprinkle with cheese and paprika. Bake at 400° for 25 minutes. Serve with lemon. Makes 4 servings.

Mrs. John McHugh, Wife of Representative (New York)

BAKED FILLETS OF OCEAN PERCH

⅓ to ½ pound per person, ocean perch fillets (or other fish)
1 lemon
small bunch parsley, stems removed
4 to 6 mushroom caps per person
plum tomatoes (optional)
nutmeg, sugar, cracker crumbs
paprika, salt, pepper
butter or margarine

Grease a baking dish. Place fillets in a single layer, skin side down. Squeeze ½ of a lemon over the fish. Place mushroom caps around the fish. Season with salt, pepper and paprika as desired. Add parsley leaves. Dot generously with small, thin slices of butter. If using the tomatoes, slice in half lengthwise. Dust with nutmeg, sugar, salt, pepper, cracker crumbs and a dot of butter. Place atop fish. Cook at 350° in a covered baking dish for 30 minutes. Increase time slightly if over a pound of fish is used. Lift tomatoes off carefully when serving so they do not spill. Serve with wedges of lemon.

Mary H. O'Neal, Daughter of former Representative Emmet O'Neal (Kentucky)

FISH NEOPOLITAN

3 tablespoons vermouth
1 onion, chopped
¼ green pepper, chopped
2 tablespoons chopped parsley
3 medium tomatoes, cut in pieces
½ cup tomato juice
½ teaspoon basil
⅛ teaspoon pepper
1 pound of fish fillets (sea bass, snapper or perch)

Heat vermouth in large frying pan and cook onions 2 to 3 minutes. Add rest of ingredients except fish. Simmer until tomatoes and peppers are soft, or about 10 minutes. Add fish and simmer until fish flakes. Great low cal meal! Makes 4 servings.

Beth Breaux, Daughter of Senator John Breaux (Louisiana)

JURICH FAMILY POLENTA AND BRODIT (CHOWDER)

Polenta:

1 cup yellow corn meal
2 cup water
1 tablespoon butter or olive oil
salt to taste

Bodit (Sauce-Chowder):

1 tablespoon olive oil
¼ cup onions, cut fine
¼ cup green peppers, diced
1 garlic clove, diced
1 tablespoon chopped parsley
½ pound cooked cod, white fish or tuna, chopped
8 Roma tomatoes, peeled and diced

Mix cornmeal in ½ cup of the 2 cups of water, stir with wooden spoon. Add remaining water, butter and salt. Cook on top of stove until done, 10–20 minutes, lower heat. When firm, turn onto a plate, upside down. Cool. Sauce: Brown onions, pepper and garlic in oil until clear, but not brown. Add tomatoes and fish, cook for 15 minutes. Spread chowder (Brodit) on Polenta. Serve like pie, in wedges. Makes 6 to 8 servings.

Olga Esch

Mrs. Marvin Esch, Wife of former Representative (Michigan)

LIME-BROILED SNAPPER

1½ pounds snapper fillets
2 tablespoons melted butter
4 tablespoons lime or lemon juice
salt, pepper and paprika to taste
2 tablespoons finely minced fresh dill or parsley

Spray a non-stick pan with cooking spray. Arrange fish in a single layer. Combine butter and lime juice and spread over fish. Add salt and pepper. Broil 4 inches from heat source without turning, until fish flakes easily. Spoon any juices that form over the fish. Sprinkle fish with paprika and minced parsley or dill, if desired. Before serving, garnished with lime wedges. Makes 6 servings.

Carol Myers

Mrs. John T. Myers, Wife of Representative (Indiana)

CHEESY BROILED FLOUNDER

2 pounds flounder fillet or
   other similar fish
2 tablespoons fresh lemon
   juice
½ cup Parmesan cheese,
   grated (preferably fresh)
¼ cup butter, softened
3 tablespoons mayonnaise
3 green onions, chopped
¼ teaspoon salt
   dash of hot pepper sauce
   lemon twists
   fresh parsley, chopped

Place fillets in a single layer on the greased rack of a broiler pan. Brush fish with lemon juice. Combine the next 6 ingredients in a bowl, set aside. Broil fillets 4–6 minutes until firm. Remove from oven and spread with cheese mixture. Broil an additional 30 seconds or until cheese is lightly browned and bubbly. Garnish with lemon twists and parsley. Makes 6 servings.

Emilie C. Shaw

Mrs. E. Clay Shaw, Wife of Representative (Florida)

BETTY'S SALMON CROQUETTES

1 15½ oz. can salmon,
   drained and mashed
½ pkg. saltines, crumbled
1 egg, beaten
   green onions, chopped
½ teaspoon Cavender's seasoning
   vegetable oil for frying

Combine salmon, saltines, egg, green onions and Cavender's seasoning. Form into golf-ball sized croquettes. Roll in flour. Brown in ½ inch hot vegetable oil, serve with southern-style vegetables. Makes 6 to 8 servings.

Betty Thornton

Mrs. Ray Thornton, Wife of Representative (Arkansas)

> *Poaching fish in the pan you serve in keeps the fillets from breaking.*

ESCABECHE

1 whole fish (a dolphin or red snapper about 1½ feet long will do nicely for a pretty buffet)
1 large onion, sliced thin
5 cloves garlic, chopped fine
1 one-inch piece fresh ginger root, sliced thin
2 cups green papaya, peeled and sliced or cubed
⅓ cup vinegar
2 cups water
2 tablespoons soy sauce
2 fresh tomatoes, sliced
3 green onions, chopped

Clean and wash fish, leaving head and tail on. Sprinkle fish inside and outside with salt and let stand 10 minutes. Fry fish until done, or bake it if your frying pan is not big enough. Keep fish warm. Fry onions, garlic and ginger in small amount of oil until onion is soft. Add papaya, and ¼ cup water, cooking until half done, about 10 minutes. Add vinegar, water and soy sauce to vegetables, heat to boiling, and thicken if you like with cornstarch mixed with cold water. Continue cooking until papaya is tender but not mushy. Place fish on large platter and cover with thin tomato slices. Pour vegetables and vinegar mixture over all, spooning some inside the fish. Let stand a while before serving so flavors can mingle. Just before serving, garnish with chopped green onions or very thin small raw onion and pepper rings. Nice if you can keep fish warm in chafing pan. Escabeche can also be prepared with smaller fish or frozen fish fillets layering fried fish with cooked vegetables in a casserole, pouring hot broth over all. When serving, make sure each plate gets both fish and vegetables. Sweet green peppers, sliced, or ½ pound pepper leaves are wonderful substitutes for the green papaya. Makes buffet serving. May be frozen.

Lorenzo I. De Leon Guerrero, Governor (Commonwealth of the Northern Mariana Islands)

Truly fresh fish smell fresh like the ocean and are not slimy.

BOUILLABAISSE OR FISH STEW

4 tablespoons olive oil
1 large onion, chopped
2 leeks, with 1 inch of
    green, chopped
4 cloves garlic, chopped
½ teaspoon saffron
1 bay leaf and sprig of thyme
¼ teaspoon red pepper flakes
4 tomatoes peeled, seeded
    and quartered
3 pounds white fish, either
    in big chunks, or cut
    into 1½ inch pieces, or
    fillets rolled and held
    with toothpicks (remove
    before serving)
1 piece of orange rind
1 celery stalk, chopped
2 fennels, quartered
2 zucchini, cut into big
    chunks
8 cups water
2 cups dry white wine

In a large pot, heat the olive oil and saute the onions until tender. Add garlic at last minute. Add tomatoes. Cook 5 more minutes. Add wine and raise heat. Boil 2-3 minutes. Add potatoes, leeks, bay leaf, spices, zucchini, celery and fennel. Saute 5-10 minutes. Add water, bring to a boil. Lower heat and simmer 30-45 minutes. Add fish gently and simmer about 8 minutes. If in chunks, add another 10 minutes. Remove bay leaf, thyme and orange rind. Serve with toasted slices of French bread with minced garlic, parsley, grated Swiss cheese, saffron and mayonnaise. Makes 6 to 8 servings.

Adeline P. Rhodes

Mrs. Scott Rhodes, Daughter-in-law of former Representative John J. Rhodes (Arizona)

EDITH'S SALMON TARRAGON

1 to 2 pound fillet of salmon
2 teaspoons lemon juice
2 tablespoons dried tarragon
    leaves
½ cup dry white wine
    pepper to taste
2 tablespoons butter

Grease baking pan with butter. Place cleaned fillet of salmon into baking dish. Mix together lemon juice, tarragon, white wine and pepper until well combined. Pour sauce over fish and bake in preheated 450° oven for 10 minutes or until fish is cooked through. Makes 4 servings.

Gisela Lager Blatnik

Mrs. John Blatnik, Wife of former Representative (Minnesota)

SALMON LOAF

1   15 oz. can salmon (retain
    liquid, remove skin,
    bones and flake)
¾ cup cracker crumbs
¼ cup milk
2   tablespoons melted butter
2   tablespoons lemon juice
2   tablespoons grated onion
2   egg yolks
2   egg whites, beaten sepa-
    rately

Mix ingredients together. Fold in beaten egg
whites. Bake at 350° for ½ hour in oiled loaf
pan. Serve with creamed peas and new potatoes.
Makes 4 servings.

Virginia Lipscomb

Mrs. Glenard Lipscomb, Wife of former Representative (California)

BROILED SALMON WITH DILL

2   tablespoons olive oil
¼ teaspoon freshly ground
    pepper
½ teaspoon salt
4   6 to 8 oz. center cut skin-
    less salmon fillets (¾ to
    1 inch thick)
2   tablespoons dry white
    wine
2   tablespoons minced fresh
    dill

Preheat the broiler. In a nonreactive baking dish
large enough to hold the salmon in a single layer,
combine the oil, salt and pepper. Add the salmon
fillets and turn to coat thoroughly. Broil the
salmon in the baking dish about 2 inches from
the heat for 6 minutes, or until almost cooked
through. Sprinkle the wine on top and broil, without turning, for about 2 minutes, or until the
salmon is just opaque at the center. Transfer the
fillets to plates and spoon a little of the pan juices
on top. Garnish with the dill and serve. Makes
4 servings.

Rebecca Rogers

Mrs. Paul G. Rogers, Wife of former Representative (Florida)

FILLET OF SALMON

1 to 1½ pounds salmon fillet (Nova Scotia, North Atlantic, or Scottish are all wonderful)
1 lemon
1 small bunch parsley, stems removed
1 tablespoon butter
salt and pepper to taste
large teaspoon capers, drained (may be added to the fish before cooking, if desired)

Put the salmon fillet, skin side down, on a piece of aluminum foil large enough to envelope it. Squeeze half a lemon over it. Salt and pepper it to taste. Sprinkle parsley over it. Dot with small slices of butter. Wrap in the aluminum foil, folding so no steam can escape. Cook at 350° for 35 minutes in a hot oven on a baking sheet. Serve with lemon wedges. Parsley potatoes are a nice accompaniment. Makes 2 servings.

Mary H. O'Neal, Daughter of former Representative Emmet O'Neal (Kentucky)

BROILED SALMON STEAKS

juice of 1 lime
2 teaspoons soy sauce
2 center-cut salmon steaks, 1¼ inches thick
kosher salt to taste

Preheat the broiler. In a bowl, combine lime juice and soy sauce. Put the salmon steaks on a baking sheet and baste with the lime-soy mixture and lightly sprinkle with salt. Broil 4 inches from the flame for about 5 minutes. Turn the salmon, brush with lime-soy mixture, sprinkle with salt and cook 5 minutes more, or until fish is done. Serve at once. Makes 2 servings.

Mrs. Michael Oxley, Wife of Representative (Ohio)

BAKED SALMON WITH SOUR CREAM STUFFING

4 to 6 pounds dressed
   salmon (fresh or frozen)
1½ tablespoon salt
2 tablespoon melted fat or
   oil

Stuffing:
¾ cup chopped celery
½ cup chopped onion
¼ cup fat (melted)
1 teaspoon salt
½ cup sour cream
¼ cup lemon, peeled and
   diced
1 tablespoon lemon rind,
   grated
1 teaspoon paprika
1 quart dry bread crumbs

Cook celery and onion in fat until tender. Combine all stuffing ingredients and mix thoroughly. Thaw frozen salmon. Clean, wash and dry fish, sprinkle inside and out with salt. Stuff fish loosely. Close opening with small skewers or toothpicks. Place fish in well greased baking pan, brush with fat. Bake at 350° for approximately 1 hour or until fish flakes easily when tested with a fork. Baste occasionally. Makes 6 to 8 servings.

Patricia Kempthorne

Mrs. Dirk Kempthorne, Wife of Senator (Idaho)

BAKED FISH FILLETS CANE RIVER QUISINE

¾ cup Wishbone creamy on-
   ion salad dressing
4 tablespoons mayonnaise
   juice of 1 lemon
   salt and pepper
8 fish fillets
   bread crumbs, Parmesan
   cheese, chopped parsley

Make a sauce of creamy onion salad dressing, mayonnaise, lemon juice, salt and pepper. Dip fish in sauce, roll in bread crumbs, parsley and cheese mixed together. Place on foil covered cookie sheet and bake at 425° for 25 to 30 minutes.

Glenda Miller

Mrs. Dan Miller, Wife of Representative (Florida)

STEAMED BLUE CRABS THE "TRULY MARYLAND" WAY

½ cup seafood seasoning
½ cup salt
3 cups white vinegar
3 cups beer (or water)
3 dozen live (and lively)
    Maryland Blue hard crabs

Mix seasonings, vinegar and beer (or water) well. Put ½ of crabs in very large pot with rack and TIGHT fitting lid. Pour ½ of seasoning mixture over top. Add rest of crabs and remaining liquid. Steam, covered, until crabs turn bright red in color, about 20 to 30 minutes. Serve hot or cold. Makes about 9 to 12 servings, depending upon size of crabs. If two pots are used, layer crabs and measure seasoning mixture accordingly. Note: Serve crabs immediately if to be eaten hot. To serve cold, bring to room temperature and refrigerate until ready to use. Under NO circumstances should live and steamed crabs ever be stored in such a manner that they could come into contact with each other.

William Donald Schaefer, Governor (Maryland)

CRAB IMPERIAL

1 pound of crabmeat
1 egg, slightly beaten
½ teaspoon salt
⅛ teaspoon pepper
½ teaspoon celery salt
½ teaspoon Worcestershire
1 tablespoon vinegar
2 teaspoons prepared
    mustard
½ cup mayonnaise
½ stick oleo or butter

Mix and put in shallow casserole. Dot with butter. Bake at 350° for 15 to 20 minutes. Makes 4 servings.

Mrs. Herbert Bateman, Wife of Representative (Virginia)

AL ALFORD'S DEVILED CRAB

1 pound crab
2 hard-boiled eggs
4 tablespoons butter
3 tablespoons flour
1 teaspoon dry mustard
1 teaspoon salt
¼ teaspoon pepper
2 tablespoons lemon juice
   toasted bread crumbs
   paprika

Melt butter. Add flour, mustard, salt and pepper. Add milk and heat with constant stirring until it just begins to thicken. Meanwhile, put crabmeat in mixing bowl. Add minced boiled eggs and lemon juice. Mix sauce with crab mixture. Put in greased casserole. Top with bread crumbs, sprinkle with paprika. Heat in 350° oven to bubbly stage and brown crumbs. Serve at once. Makes 8 servings.

Ivo Sparkman

Mrs. John Sparkman, Wife of former Senator (Alabama)

BAKED CRABMEAT

1 pound crabmeat
2 cups fresh bread pieces (3
   slices)
1 cup mayonnaise
4 hard boiled eggs, forked
½ cup milk
1 teaspoon Worcestershire
   sauce
1 teaspoon onion juice
   dash Tabasco

Mix all ingredients together before putting into greased casserole. Heat thoroughly at 375° for 20 minutes. Serve at once. Makes 4 servings.

Mary Virginia Bliley

Mrs. Thomas J. Bliley, Jr., Wife of Representative (Virginia)

SIMPLE CRAB CAKES

2 cups crabmeat (lump preferred), picked over
¼ teaspoon salt
⅛ teaspoon pepper
   dash Worcestershire sauce
1 egg, slightly beaten
   flour
   sweet butter for cooking

Gently mix crabmeat with salt, pepper, Worcestershire sauce and egg. Shape into small cakes.
Chill for several hours. When ready to cook,
dredge crab cakes in flour. Either saute in a frying
pan in enough sweet butter to prevent sticking
(3-4 minutes per side) or until browned, or fry
in deep hot fat 2-3 minutes. Makes 4 servings.

Judy Clinger

Mrs. William Clinger, Wife of Representative (Pennsylvania)

CRAB IMPERIAL

1 pound lump crabmeat
   (picked carefully for
   shells)
½ cup green bell pepper,
   minced
¼ cup onion, minced
¾ cup mayonnaise
3 tablespoons butter, melted
½ cup fresh bread crumbs

Combine the crabmeat, peppers and onion.
Gently fold in the mayonnaise. Mold the mixture
into a clean crab shell or other heat-proof serving
dish, and cover with melted butter and bread
crumbs. Bake at 350° for 12 minutes, or until
crumbs are golden brown. Serve immediately.
Makes 4 to 6 servings.

Tim Valentine

Tim Valentine, Representative (North Carolina)

> *When pan frying fish, cook it last, when the rest of the dinner
> is almost ready and serve it immediately.*

CRABMEAT DELIGHT

1 pound crabmeat
1 egg, well beaten
½ cup mayonnaise
2 tablespoons melted margarine
2 tablespoons evaporated milk
1 teaspoon salt
¼ teaspoon pepper
½ cup sour cream
½ cup grated cheddar cheese

Combine all ingredients except cheese, mix well and pour in greased 9″ × 13″ casserole dish, sprinkle with cheese. Bake at 350° for 25–30 minutes. Makes 4 to 6 servings.

Larkin I. Smith, former Representative (Mississippi)

CRABMEAT AU GRATIN

1 pint whipping cream
4 tablespoons flour
4 tablespoons lemon juice
4 tablespoons wine
1 cup grated cheese (sharp cheddar)
1 pound can crabmeat
salt to taste
bread crumbs

Mix cream and flour. Let thicken under low heat. Add remaining ingredients. Put in small casseroles. Sprinkle bread crumbs on top. Bake at 350° about 20 minutes. Makes 4 servings.

J. Roy Rowland, Representative (Georgia)

CHESAPEAKE BAY CRAB IMPERIAL

2 pounds Maryland back fin crabmeat
2 tablespoons lemon juice
2 tablespoons chopped pimento
1 tablespoon Worcestershire sauce
½ cup lite mayonnaise
½ teaspoon salt
½ stick margarine or butter, melted
paprika

Remove cartilage from crabmeat and put crabmeat in large mixing bowl. In separate bowl, mix lite mayonnaise, lemon juice, pimento, Worcestershire sauce and salt until blended. Add mayonnaise blend to crabmeat and mix gently. Spoon crabmeat mixture lightly into 8 individual aluminum shells. Brush top of each shell with melted butter or margarine and sprinkle lightly with paprika. Bake in 400° oven for about 15 minutes or until golden brown. Makes 6 to 8 servings.

Tony Morella, Husband of Representative Connie Morella (Maryland)

CRAB IMPERIAL DELUXE

1 pound lump crabmeat
½ teaspoon salt
dash of pepper
1 cup mayonnaise (not salad dressing)
1 egg
¼ teaspoon Worcestershire sauce
dash of paprika

Place crab in bowl. Sprinkle with salt and pepper. In another bowl, beat egg and blend in mayonnaise and Worcestershire. Add just enough egg mixture to crabmeat to moisten, not bind. Lightly spoon crab mixture into 4 or 6 oiled baking shells. Heap high, don't pack down. Spread a thin coating of remaining dressing entirely over each. Place on cookie sheet. Bake at 375° for 30 minutes. Sprinkle with paprika. Makes 4 to 6 servings.

Mrs. Richard S. Schweiker, Wife of former Senator (Pennsylvania)

OREGON CRAB CASSEROLE

½ pound mushrooms
4 tablespoons butter
2 green onions, chopped
3 tablespoons flour
1½ cups half and half
½ pound crabmeat
1 teaspoon Worcestershire
   sauce
⅓ cup white wine
1 cup cooked rice
   salt and pepper to taste
1¼ cup grated Monterey Jack
   cheese

Slice mushrooms and saute in butter. Add green onions. Blend in flour, add half and half and crab. Fold in the remaining ingredients, except cheese. Place in casserole and top with cheese. Bake at 350° until cheese is melted and bubbly. Makes 6 to 8 servings.

Mrs. Jeff Minckler, Daughter of former Senator Ernest Lundeen (Minnesota)

CRABMEAT SUPREME

8 slices white bread, cubed
2 cups fresh claw crabmeat
1 yellow onion, chopped
½ cup mayonnaise
1 cup celery, chopped
½ cup green pepper,
   chopped
4 eggs, beaten
1 cup canned mushroom
   soup
3 cups milk
1 cup cheddar cheese,
   shredded
   dash paprika

Cook celery in water for 10 minutes. Put 4 slices (cubed) pieces of bread in bottom of 9½″ × 13″ pan. Mix crabmeat, onion, mayonnaise, green pepper and celery together. Spread over bread. Put 4 slices (cubed) pieces of bread on top of crabmeat mixture. Mix egg and milk, pour over all. Cover and place in refrigerator for 1 hour or more. Bake at 325° for 15 minutes. Spoon soup over top. Sprinkle paprika and cheese on top. Bake 1 hour. Serve. Makes 4 servings. May be frozen.

Mrs. Connie Mack, Wife of Senator (Florida)

CRAWFISH MAQUE CHOUX

butter to cover bottom of
  pot
2 large onions, chopped
1 clove garlic, diced or
  pressed
1 bell pepper, chopped
5 ears fresh corn, cut
1 can Rotel tomatoes
2 pounds crawfish or shrimp
  tails or crabmeat
parsley and onion tops,
  chopped

Place onions, garlic, bell pepper in medium size heavy pot with butter. Saute. Add fresh corn with corn milk from corn and season to taste. Stir well. Cover and let simmer stirring occasionally. Add Rotel, a little bit of water, cover and simmer 1 hour on low heat. Add seafood and cook another 15–20 minutes. Can also add parsley and green onions. You may substitute 2 cans whole kernel corn with 1/3 cup evaporated milk. Makes 6 to 8 servings.

Catherine Hollaway

Mrs. Clyde Holloway, Wife of former Representative (Louisiana)

LOBSTER IN CREAM SAUCE

2 cups fresh lobster meat
4 tablespoons melted butter
2 tablespoons flour
1 cup cream
2 egg yolks, slightly beaten
1/4 teaspoon salt
1 teaspoon lemon juice
  paprika

Heat lobster, previously boiled and diced, in 3 tablespoons melted butter. In another pan, stir flour well into remaining butter, cook for a minute without browning, stirring until sauce thickens and is smooth. When sauce reaches a boil, remove from heat and add beaten egg yolks, stir over low heat until mixture thickens. Add lobster and seasoning. Dry sherry may be added to flavor, if desired. Serve with toasted crackers or thin dry toast. Makes 4 servings.

Dorothy S. Cannon

Mrs. Howard W. Cannon, Wife of former Senator (Nevada)

> *To store fish, wrap in waxed paper, plastic wrap or foil and refrigerate in coldest section of the refrigerator. Use the same day if possible.*

TOM ANDREWS' "WICKED GOOD" MAINE LOBSTER CHILI

1 pound dried black beans
4 whole lobsters, boiled and chopped medium size
3 green jalapeno peppers, coarsely chopped
4 dried red chili peppers, finely chopped
4 cups fish broth
4 tablespoons olive oil
4 medium size shallots, finely chopped
2 medium size garlic cloves, finely chopped
1 large (28 oz.) can crushed tomatoes
1 tablespoon dried leaf oregano
1/2 tablespoon dried leaf basil
1 teaspoon dried leaf thyme
1 bay leaf
1/4 cup unsalted butter, melted
1 tablespoon sweet paprika
1/3 cup finely chopped fresh chives
1/3 cup finely chopped cilantro
salt, pepper, chili powder to taste

In a large saucepan, cover beans with cold water. Bring to a boil over high heat, boil briskly 5 minutes, then remove from heat and let soak 1 hour. Drain and rinse under cold running water. Set beans aside. In a blender or food processor fitted with the metal blade, put dried chilies with 1/2 fish broth. Puree and set aside. In a saucepan, heat oil over medium heat. Add fresh chilies, shallots, garlic, and saute until shallots are transparent, 2 to 3 minutes. Add drained beans, remaining fish broth, pureed red chilies, tomatoes, oregano, basil, thyme, bay leaf, salt and pepper. Bring to a boil, reduce heat and simmer, covered, until beans are tender, 1 1/2 to 2 hours, adding a little water if necessary to keep beans barely covered. Saute cooked chopped lobster in butter with paprika, adding chives, cilantro, chili powder, salt and pepper. Add lobster to beans 1/2 hour before serving. Makes 6 to 8 servings.

Tom Andrews, Representative (Maine)

> *Thaw frozen fish in milk. The milk draws out the frozen taste and provides a fresh-caught flavor.*

SCALLOPED OYSTERS

1 pint oysters (remove all
    shells)
2 cups medium coarse
    saltines (48)
½ cup melted butter
¾ cup light cream
½ teaspoon salt
½ teaspoon Worcestershire
    sauce

Butter a shallow baking dish. Drain oysters, reserve ¼ cup liquid. Melt butter, combine with crackers. Spread ⅓ crackers in shallow dish. Cover with ½ oysters (sprinkle with pepper). Repeat with a second layer. Combine cream, reserved oyster liquid, salt and Worcestershire sauce, pour over oysters, top with cracker crumbs. Bake at 350° for 40 minutes or until nicely browned. Makes 4 servings.

Nancy Beall

Mrs. J. Glenn Beall, Jr., Wife of former Senator (Maryland)

EDGEFIELD'S OLD FASHIONED SCALLOPED OYSTERS

2 cups fine cracker crumbs
½ cup butter, melted
1½ pints small shucked
    oysters, or 18 large
    oysters
¾ teaspoon salt
    freshly ground black pepper to taste
2 tablespoon chopped parsley (optional)
½ teaspoon Worcestershire
    sauce
6 tablespoons cream

Preheat oven to 350°. Mix the cracker crumbs and water. Place half the crumb mixture on the bottom of a greased 1 quart casserole. Add half the oysters, reserving the liquor, and sprinkle with half the salt, pepper and parsley. Add the remaining oysters and sprinkle with the remaining salt, pepper and parsley. Mix ⅓ cup oyster liquid with the Worcestershire sauce and milk and pour over the oysters. Top with the remaining crumb mixture. Bake uncovered, until puffy and brown, about 45 minutes. Makes 4 servings.

Beverly Derrick

Mrs. Butler Derrick, Wife of Representative (South Carolina)

CHEF MICHAEL FUNDABURK'S OYSTERS BIENVILLE

2 dozen fresh or canned oysters
1 pound shrimp, chopped finely
1 bunch green onions, chopped finely
½ cup chopped parsley
1 pint half and half
1 tablespoon sherry
3 tablespoons flour
salt and pepper to taste

Saute shrimp in ½ stick butter for 10 minutes. In another skillet, saute onions and parsley in 1 stick butter. Blend in flour and add half and half. Add sherry and shrimp. Place oysters in lightly greased individual shells or in large casserole. Cover with 1 tablespoon sauce per oyster. Bake at 350° for 10 minutes or until edges of oysters curl. Can use sauce on broiled fish. Makes 4 to 5 servings.

Mrs. John Sanders, Daughter of former Representative John E. Rankin (Mississippi)

OYSTER PIE

1 pint of oysters
1 cup cracker crumbs
½ cup melted butter or margarine
¼ cup half and half
1 teaspoon Worcestershire sauce
seasoned salt to taste
¼ teaspoon pepper
bread for topping

Drain oysters and reserve liquid, toss cracker crumbs with melted butter, reserving 2 tablespoons of butter for the topping. Mix together in a bowl, the oyster liquid, Worcestershire sauce, half & half, seasoned salt and pepper. Place ⅓ of cracker crumbs in bottom of a 2 quart casserole dish, top with ½ oysters and part of the liquid. Continue to alternate crumbs, oysters and liquid finishing with bread topping and remaining butter that was set aside. Heat oven to 350° and bake for 30 minutes. Makes 4 servings.

Carroll Campbell, Governor (South Carolina)

SHRIMP WITH RICE

½ cup butter
1 large onion, finely chopped
1 cup sliced mushrooms
1 green pepper, finely
    chopped
1¼ cups raw rice
¼ teaspoon nutmeg
1 teaspoon salt
½ teaspoon freshly ground
    pepper
1 cup dry white wine
3 cups hot chicken stock or
    water
2 tablespoons chopped
    parsley
¼ teaspoon thyme
½ bay leaf
2 pounds raw shrimp,
    shelled and deveined

In a large skillet or wok, heat the butter, add the onion, mushrooms, green pepper, rice, nutmeg, salt and pepper and cook, stirring until the rice is golden brown. Add the wine and simmer 5 minutes. Add the stock, parsley, thyme and bay leaf, cover and cook 10 minutes, stirring occasionally. Add the shrimp and simmer 5 to 10 minutes, depending on the size of the shrimp. Remove the bay leaf and serve immediately. Makes 4 to 6 servings.

Jo Ann Emerson

Mrs. Bill Emerson, Wife of Representative (Missouri)

FRIED SCALLOPS

1 cup dry bread crumbs
½ teaspoon celery salt
1 teaspoon salt
1 lb. scallops
1 egg, beaten and diluted
    with 2 tbsp. water
    fat for frying
    tarter sauce to serve with

Combine crumbs, celery salt and salt. Dip scallops into crumbs, then into egg mixture and back into crumbs. Sauté or fry in hot deep fat (365 degrees) for 4 to 5 minutes. Serve with tartar sauce. Serve 4.

The Congressional Club

CHAMORRO SHRIMP PATTIES

1 pound shrimp, cleaned, deveined, chopped (or frozen shrimp)
1 10 oz. pkg. frozen mixed
   vegetables
1 7 oz. can corn
1 medium onion, chopped
½ cup chopped green pepper
½ cup chopped celery
2 cloves garlic, crushed
2 eggs
½ cup canned milk
½ cup flour
1 teaspoon baking powder
   salt and pepper to taste
   oil for frying

Mix all ingredients in a bowl (except oil). Heat oil to 350°. Drop from spoon into oil. Fry until golden. Drain on paper towels. Makes 10 servings.

Christine K. Knuth

Mrs. Charles Knuth, Daughter of former Representative David S. King (Utah)

GRILLED SHRIMP SANIBEL

4 to 5 jumbo shrimp per person, peeled and de-
   veined
1 cup olive oil
   juice of 2 lemons
1 large clove garlic, pressed
   chopped parsley

Mix all ingredients except the shrimp in a bowl. Whisk. Pour over the shrimp and marinate for at least 2 hours. Thread shrimp on skewers. Grill over hot coals 2 to 3 minutes a side.

Mariel Goss

Mrs. Porter Goss, Wife of Representative (Florida)

SHRIMP AND ARTICHOKE-HEART CASSEROLE

6½ tablespoons butter (divided)
4½ tablespoons flour
¾ cup each milk and heavy cream
½ teaspoon salt, or to taste
fresh ground pepper to taste
1 20 oz. can artichoke hearts, drained
OR
1 10 oz. pkg. frozen, cooked
1 pound shrimp, cooked and cleaned
4 oz. mushrooms, sliced (1¼ cups)
¼ cup dry sherry
1 tablespoon Worcestershire sauce
¼ cup grated Parmesan cheese
paprika

In medium saucepan, melt 4½ tablespoon butter. With whisk, stir in flour until blended. Gradually beat in milk and cream, cook and stir until thickened and smooth. Season with salt and pepper, set aside. In greased shallow baking dish, arrange artichoke hearts, then shrimp. In small skillet saute mushrooms in remaining 2 tablespoons butter for 6 minutes. Spoon over artichoke hearts and shrimp. Add sherry and Worcestershire to cream sauce, pour over mushrooms. Sprinkle with Parmesan cheese and paprika. Bake in preheated 375° for 20 minutes or until bubbly. Makes 4 servings.

Mary A. Regula

Mrs. Ralph Regula, Wife of Representative (Ohio)

The best way not to overcook fish is to calculate 10 minutes per inch of thickness for whatever cooking method you are using.

BROILED GARLIC SHRIMP

40 large shrimp, shelled and
    deveined
1 cup lemon juice
1 cup olive oil
6 cloves crushed garlic
2 teaspoons chopped parsley
1 teaspoon red pepper

Wash shrimp in cold water, dry and put in large bowl. Mix remaining ingredients, pour over shrimp and cover bowl. Refrigerate overnight, stirring several times. Remove shrimp from marinade and broil 3 inches from the source of heat. Broil about 5 minutes on each side. Heat marinade, pour desired amount over the shrimp or serve on the side. Makes 4 servings.

Mrs. Craig James, Wife of former Representative (Florida)

SHRIMP AND ARTICHOKES LA BRETAGNE

2 pounds shrimp
1 teaspoon seafood seasoning
2 14 oz. cans artichoke
    hearts, halved
1 6 oz. can pitted black
    olives
3/4 cup olive oil
2 tablespoons tarragon
    vinegar
2 cloves garlic, crushed
1 1/2 teaspoons salt
1 1/2 teaspoons dry mustard
1 teaspoon sugar
1/2 teaspoon black pepper,
    freshly ground
    leaf or Bibb lettuce
    watercress

Cook shrimp in boiling water with seafood seasoning until done (about 5 minutes). Cool and clean shrimp. Combine shrimp, artichokes and olives. Combine oil, vinegar and seasonings. Pour over shrimp mixture. Marinate in refrigerate for several hours or overnight. Serve as a first course on a bed of lettuce topped with a sprig of watercress. May serve as hors d'oeuvres with toothpicks in a large iced compote. Serves 12 as first course or 16 for hors d'oeuvres.

Mrs. Susan Goldwater Keenan, Member of The Congressional Club

SCAMPI

30 large fresh shrimp
½ cup butter
1 cup fresh bread crumbs
2 large garlic cloves
2 tablespoons chopped
   parsley

Heat oven to 350°. Place butter in a 9″ × 13″ shallow baking dish and place in oven to melt. Squeeze garlic into melted butter and stir. Arrange shrimp in a baking dish and cover with bread crumbs. Bake 4 minutes. Turn shrimp and bake for 4 minutes more, or until done. Garnish with chopped parsley. Makes 6 servings.

Lowell P. Weicker, Jr., Governor (Connecticut)

TRENT'S SHRIMP CREOLE

⅓ cup shortening or cooking
   oil
¼ cup flour
1 pound raw shrimp, peeled
   and deveined
1 garlic clove, minced
½ cup minced onion
2 tablespoons minced parsley
½ cup chopped green pepper
1 cup water
1 8 oz. can tomato sauce
2 bay leaves
¼ teaspoon cayenne pepper
½ teaspoon Accent

Melt shortening in heavy skillet over high heat. Add flour and stir until light brown. Lower heat, add shrimp and cook about 3 minutes or until pink. Add garlic, onion, parsley, and green pepper. Cook 2 minutes longer, gradually add water and the remaining ingredients. Bring to boil and then simmer covered 20 to 30 minutes. Serve very hot over fluffy rice. Makes 4 servings.

Mrs. Trent Lott, Wife of Senator (Mississippi)

JIFFY SHRIMP CASSEROLE

1½ cups rice
3 cups water
1 cup diced green pepper
1 cup diced celery
2 tablespoons butter or margarine
2 10 oz. cans cream of mushroom soup
2 teaspoons curry
dash of pepper
1 10 oz. pkg. frozen shrimp

Boil rice in water for 10 minutes. Set aside. In large skillet, cook green pepper and celery in butter until crisp. Add mushroom soup, curry and frozen shrimp. Mix in the rice and bring to boil. Simmer slowly until rice is crisp. Do *not* overcook. Makes 6 servings. May be frozen.

Lionel Van Deerlin, Former Representative (California)

BAKED STUFFED SHRIMP

12 jumbo shrimp (5″ long)
½ pound scallops

Filling:
4 tablespoons butter
¼ teaspoon paprika
2 tablespoons crushed potato chips
¼ cup cracker meal
3 tablespoons grated Parmesan cheese
1 to 2 tablespoons cooking sherry (add just before removing from oven)
lemon wedges

Cut shrimp in back to remove black vein then put toothpicks in to keep shrimp open. Melt 4 tablespoons of butter in small saucepan. Add ¼ teaspoon of paprika and cook over very slow heat for 10 minutes to take raw taste out of paprika. Combine potato chips, cracker meal and grated Parmesan cheese and scallops. Stuff shrimp with scallop filling. Place in shallow baking pan. Bake with a little water in bottom of pan. Just before taking shrimp from oven, sprinkle shrimp with cooking sherry and bake a short time more. Bake at 350° for 20 to 25 minutes.

Mrs. Patrick Mathews, Daughter of former Representative Claude Fuller (Arkansas)

SHRIMP IN SCALLOP SHELLS

1 pound shrimp, cooked in court bouillon (save bouillon)

Herbed Butter:
1 cup butter, softened
2 tablespoons lemon juice
  salt
6 shallots, small and green tops
¼ teaspoon thyme
  fresh parsley sprigs
1 cup bread crumbs, fresh
¼ teaspoon Tabasco
6 tablespoons court bouillon, strained
2 garlic cloves, chopped
  chives, 4 sprigs, chopped

Cook shrimp and save bouillon. Chop shallots, garlic, parsley, chives, thyme. Add to butter. Add other ingredients and fold in bread crumbs last. Smear butter mixture about ¼″ thick over scallop shells and press the shrimp down into butter. Bake at 400° for 10 minutes and broil to brown if you like. Makes 4 servings.

Mrs. Andy Ireland, Wife of former Representative (Florida)

SHRIMP CURRY LOLLY

1 tablespoon butter
1 medium onion, chopped
2 cans frozen shrimp soup
1 pound cleaned and shelled shrimp, cooked
1 cup sour cream
1 tablespoon (about) curry powder (to taste)

Saute onion in butter. Add shrimp soup. Cook over medium heat, stirring until smooth. Add shrimp and blend, (cooking) add sour cream. Blend over low heat. Season with curry powder. Serve very hot over white rice with chutney, shredded coconut and chopped peanuts on the side. Makes 4 servings. May be frozen.

Mrs. Evan Howell, Wife of former Representative (Illinois)

CURRIED SHRIMP WITH SAFFRON RICE

pkg. of rice of choice
¼ teaspoon ground whole saffron
1¼ pound shelled and de-veined large shrimp
¼ teaspoon grated fresh lemon peel
½ teaspoon ground ginger
½ teaspoon ground cardamon
3 large garlic cloves, minced
1 bay leaf
2 teaspoons curry powder
4 tablespoons golden raisins
2 tablespoons fresh lime juice
2 apples cored and cut into small pieces
1½ cup thinly sliced onions
2 tablespoons margarine

Garnish:
½ cup julienne cut green bell peppers
½ cup diced red bell peppers
½ cup diced tomatoes
¼ cup cucumber slices
¼ cup diced onion

Prepare rice as direct on package, adding the saffron. Heat margarine in large, non-stick skillet over medium high heat until bubbly and hot. Add sliced onions and saute until golden. Stir in remaining ingredients *except* shrimp and garnish. Reduce heat and let simmer until apples are soft, around 5 minutes. Increase heat to high and add shrimp. Cook, stirring, until shrimp turn pink. To serve: Stir rice and spoon it on 1 side of warm serving platter. Arrange shrimp mixture next to rice and decorate with garnish. Makes 4 servings.

Jean Grotberg

Mrs. John E. Grotberg, Wife of former Representative (Illinois)

> *The odor from baking or broiling salmon may be eliminated by squeezing lemon juice on both sides of each salmon steak or on the cut surface of the salmon and letting it stand in the refrigerator for one hour or longer before cooking.*

GRILLED SHRIMP

2 pounds shelled shrimp
1¼ cups Italian dressing
½ teaspoon pepper

Place shrimp in shallow dish. Pour dressing over shrimp and sprinkle with black pepper. Cover and refrigerate 2 to 3 hours. Put shrimp on skewers (don't place shrimp too close together or they won't cook evenly). Broil on grill over medium flame for 3 to 4 minutes. Cook only until shrimp begin to curl. Be careful not to overcook or shrimp will be dry and tasteless. Makes 4 to 6 servings.

John L. Napier, Former Representative (South Carolina)

SHRIMP SCAMPI

1 stick butter
1 large onion, diced
4 cloves garlic
½ teaspoon garlic salt
½ teaspoon salt
½ teaspoon pepper
1 teaspoon Cavender's All Purpose Greek seasoning
1 teaspoon parsley
1 teaspoon Worcestershire sauce
1 tablespoon fresh lemon juice
1½ pounds large peeled and deveined raw shrimp

Saute onion in butter, then add remaining ingredients. Simmer for approximately 7 minutes or until shrimp are done. Best when served over long grain brown rice. Makes 4 servings.

Elton Gallegly, Representative (California)

SHRIMP CREOLE OR JAMBALAYA

1 pound or more shrimp, raw and peeled
4 cups cooked rice
2 tablespoons tomato paste
1 teaspoon sugar
4 cloves garlic, crushed
2 cups stock or bouillon
½ cup celery
½ cup bell pepper
¾ stick butter
¼ teaspoon cornstarch
1 cup green onions
1 cup onions
½ cup parsley
Parmesan cheese

Seasoning Mix:
¾ teaspoon white pepper
1 teaspoon salt-pepper seasoned salt
⅜ teaspoon ground black pepper
1½ teaspoons thyme
¾ teaspoon basil
1 bay leaf

Melt butter, add onion, celery, pepper and garlic. Cook in heavy pot until onions are wilted. Add seasoning mix and tomato paste, cook stirring constantly 14 minutes. Add 1¼ cup stock and sugar and heat over medium heat 40 minutes, stirring occasionally. Skim off all that floats to top. Add additional stock to get right consistency. Refrigerate overnight. 20 minutes before serving, reheat and add raw shrimp. Add cornstarch dissolved in water if too thin. Add parsley and green onions 5–10 minutes before ready to serve. Serve on top of rice for creole or mix with *appropriate* amount of rice for Jambalaya. Serve with Parmesan cheese.

Dan Miller, Representative (Florida)

Always serve fresh lemon wedges with shellfish.

SHRIMP STEW OVER RICE

2 10½ oz. cans of celery
    soup, undiluted
1 medium size green pepper,
    diced
1 medium onion, chopped
1 tablespoon Worcestershire
    sauce
1 tablespoon hot sauce
1 bay leaf
⅛ teaspoon pepper
1 16 oz. pkg. peeled frozen
    small shrimp
   cooked rice

Combine first 7 ingredients in a dutch oven; stir well. Bring to a boil over medium heat, reduce heat, and simmer uncovered, 20 minutes. Add shrimp and cook 5 to 7 minutes, stirring occasionally. Remove bay leaf. Serve over buttered rice. Makes 8 servings.

Carse Myers

Mrs. John T. Myers, Wife of Representative (Indiana)

FISH IN RAMEKINS

1 cup leftover fish
8 mussels or clams
½ cup bread crumbs
⅔ cup milk
1 teaspoon chopped parsley
1 garlic clove
1 onion, chopped
   salt and pepper to taste
3 tablespoons fat
½ cup buttered bread crumbs

Chop fish and mussels or clams. Add crumbs (soaked in 2 tablespoons of milk), parsley, garlic, onion, salt and pepper. Cook in fat for several minutes. Stir in remaining milk and fill small ramekins or scallop shells. Cover with buttered crumbs and bake in a 350 degree oven for about 15 minutes. Serves 5.

The Congressional Club

SHRIMP/CRAB CASSEROLE

2 pounds cooked and peeled shrimp
1 can crabmeat (or you may use crabmeat substitute—pollock)
½ pound dried mushrooms which have been soaked in Chablis wine for 1 hour
1 can artichoke hearts
2 cans cream of mushroom soup
1 bunch shallot onions, sliced
grated Gruyere or Parmesan cheese

Put the shrimp, crab and artichoke hearts in saucepan. Add shallots and mushrooms and saute in butter until they are light brown. Add the grated cheese, the 2 cans of soup and cook briefly. Put in a greased casserole, sprinkle with a little cheese and a few dabs of butter. Broil in the oven for 1 minute. Makes 4 to 6 servings.

Mrs. Robert McClory, Wife of former Representative (Illinois)

SEAFOOD DREAM

1½ pounds of king crab
½ pound shrimp, cooked and cleaned
½ green pepper, chopped
½ cup fresh parsley
2 cups cooked rice
1½ cups of Hellmann's mayonnaise
1 10 oz. pkg. frozen peas, thawed, but not cooked

Combine all ingredients and turn into 1½ quart casserole. Bake 1 hour at 350°. Makes 4 to 6 servings.

Mrs. John T. Myers, Wife of Representative (Indiana)

SEAFOOD LASAGNA

3 tablespoons olive oil
1 yellow onion, chopped
4 minced cloves of garlic
5 cups canned plum
    tomatoes
½ cup white wine
1 tablespoon dry basil
2 teaspoons fennel seeds
1 to 1½ pound mozzarella
    salt and pepper
1 cup milk
2 tablespoons pernod
    (liquor)
2 pounds shelled shrimp
3 cups ricotta cheese
8 ozs. cream cheese
2 eggs
1 small pkg. cooked, drained
    spinach
1 pound lumped crabmeat
8 lasagna noodles. cooked

Sauce: Heat olive oil, add onion and garlic. Saute 5 minutes. Add tomatoes (not all of juice), white wine, basil, fennel and salt and pepper. Simmer 45 minutes. Add milk, pernod, shrimp and simmer 5 minutes. Remove from heat.

Filling: Mix ricotta, cream cheese and eggs. Beat with wooden spoon. Add spinach and crab meat.

Layer starting with the sauce, noodles, filling, mozzarella, repeat and end with the mozzarella. Cook 350° for 50 minutes. Makes 8 to 10 servings. May be frozen.

Mrs. Joe Knollenberg, Wife of Representative (Michigan)

SEAFOOD NEWBURG

1 lb. (3 cups) clean cooked
    crabmeat
1 lb. (3 cups) lobster tail
    meat
1 cup clean cooked shrimp
⅓ cup butter
3 teaspoons flour
½ teaspoon salt
½ teaspoon paprika
    dash cayenne
1½ cups cream (flavored with
    chicken bouillon)
3 large egg yolks, beaten
2 tablespoons sherry
    toast points (sliced toast
    cut into quarters)

Remove any shell or cartilage from the shellfish, being careful not to break the meat into small pieces. Melt the butter and blend in the flour and seasonings (salt, paprika, cayenne). Add cream and cook until thick and smooth, stirring constantly. Beat hot mixture into the beaten egg yolks, a little at a time. Remove from heat and slowly stir in the sherry. Serve immediately on toast points. Serves 10.

The Congressional Club

JAMBALAYA

½ cup olive oil
1 pound sausage, smoked
2 cloves garlic, minced
½ cup onion, chopped
½ cup celery, chopped
1 cup green pepper, chopped
2 tomatoes, chopped
1 can tomato paste (6 oz.)
1 can stewed tomatoes, (14 oz.)
1 teaspoon thyme, basil, salt pepper to taste
4 tablespoons lemon juice
2 pounds shrimp, peeled
3 cups rice, cooked
  hot sauce to taste

Brown sausage in oil and set aside. Saute garlic, onion, celery, green pepper. Add tomatoes, seasonings, tomato paste and simmer for 20 minutes. Add rice and sausage. Cover and heat a few minutes. Add shrimp (uncooked) to pot and cook until shrimp turn pink. Add hot sauce to taste. Makes 8 servings. May be frozen.

Nancy H. Ireland

Mrs. Andy Ireland, Wife of former Representative (Florida)

SCAMPI

2 dozen scampi or jumbo shrimp
⅔ cup cognac
24 thin slices of prosciutto or very lean bacon
24 fresh sage leaves or 1 tsp. ground dried sage
  salt and freshly ground black pepper to taste
  lemon wedges for garnish

Split shrimp shells up the back with a small, sharp knife or kitchen shears. Devein and shell, if desired. Marinate in cognac for one hour at room temperature. Pre-heat broiler. Drain and wrap each shrimp in a thin slice of prosciutto. Thread on skewers alternately with a leaf of sage (or sprinkle shrimp with ground sage if fresh is not available). Sprinkle with salt and pepper. Broil about 5 inches from heat for 5 to 7 minutes on each side or until ham fat is sizzling hot. Garnish with lemon wedges and serve immediately. Serves 2 to 4.

The Congressional Club

Nancy Davis Reagan
1981–1989

To the Congressional Club - thank you for making me always feel so welcome.
Best Wishes Nancy Reagan

Nancy Davis Reagan

The glittering, star-studded years of the Reagan White House were skillfully overseen by Mrs. Reagan. As First Lady she added a sense of style and panache to that role.

She is perhaps best remembered for her "Just Say No" to drugs campaign which continues to focus attention on the prevention of drug and alcohol abuse among America's youth. Her 1982 book "To Love A Child" was about another subject close to her heart, the Foster Grandparents Program. This marvelous program was an effective way to address the fears of those who see the disintegration of the traditional family. Nancy Reagan continues her support of these projects from her home in California.

Just Say No

POULTRY

BAJA CALIFORNIA CHICKEN

8 boned chicken breasts
seasoning salt and pepper,
to taste
2 cloves garlic, crushed
4 tablespoons olive oil
4 tablespoons tarragon
vinegar
2/3 cup dry sherry

Sprinkle chicken with seasoning salt and pepper. Crush garlic into oil and vinegar in a skillet. Saute chicken pieces until golden brown, turning frequently. Remove, place in a baking dish. Pour sherry over pieces and place in 350° oven for 10 minutes. Makes 8 servings.

Nancy Reagan

Mrs. Ronald Reagan, Wife of former President of the United States.
Reprinted from the 1982 Congressional Club Cookbook, Tenth Edition

BARBEQUED CHICKEN

Marinade
1 3-lb. fryer, quartered
1 large garlic clove, crushed
1 teaspoon salt
1/2 teaspoon freshly ground
     pepper
1 tablespoon oil
3 tablespoon lemon juice

Put ingredients in a heavy ziplock bag. Shake to coat well. Refrigerate for 24 hours if possible, turning the bag several times. When coals are ready, place chicken on the grill, skin side up, basting with the marinade. Cook until well browned before turning. (If baking in oven, bake at 400°, skin side down first.) About 20 minutes before chicken is done, begin using your favorite bottled barbeque sauce or the homemade version which follows.

Barbeque Sauce
1/4 cup cider vinegar
2 1/4 cups water
3/4 cup sugar
1 stick butter or margarine
1/3 cup yellow mustard
2 onions, coarsely chopped
1/2 teaspoon each, salt and
     pepper

Bring to a boil, cook on low 20 minutes or until onion is tender.

Then add:
1/2 cup worcestershire
2 1/2 cups catsup
6-8 tablespoons lemon juice
     cayenne pepper to taste

Simmer slowly for 45 minutes. Taste for seasoning. This sauce freezes well. Serves 4.

Barbara Bush

Mrs. George Bush, Wife of former President of the United States

> *Getting the catsup out of the bottle isn't so tough. Insert a drinking straw, push it to the bottom of the bottle, and then remove. Enough air will be admitted to start an even flow.*

SAN ANTONIO CHICKEN WITH PICANTE BLACK BEAN SAUCE

6 chicken breast halves, boned and skinned
2 teaspoons ground cumin
1 teaspoon garlic salt
1 tablespoon vegetable oil
1 cup rinsed and drained canned black beans
1 10 oz. can whole kernel corn, drained
2/3 cup picante sauce
1/2 cup diced red bell pepper
2 tablespoons chopped cilantro

Sprinkle both sides of chicken with 1 teaspoon of the cumin and the garlic salt. Heat oil in 12-inch skillet over medium-high heat. Add chicken, cook 3 minutes. In medium bowl, combine beans, corn, picante sauce, red pepper and remaining 1 teaspoon cumin. Turn chicken and spoon bean mixture evenly over chicken. Reduce heat to medium and cook uncovered 6 to 7 minutes or until chicken is cooked through. Push bean mixture off chicken into skillet and transfer the chicken to serving platter and keep warm. Cook bean mixture over high heat 2 to 3 minutes or until thickened, stirring frequently. Spoon over chicken and sprinkle with chopped cilantro. I recommend serving this with long grain brown rice. Makes 6 servings.

Janice Gallegly

Mrs. Elton Gallegly, Wife of Representative (California)

6 half chicken breasts equal 2 2/3 cups diced cooked chicken.

CHICKEN TORTILLA

12 corn tortillas, cut into 4 tri-
    angles each
4 cups coarsely chopped
    cooked chicken
1 can condensed cream of
    chicken soup
1 can condensed cream of
    mushroom soup
1 7 oz. can green chili salsa
    or ½ cup picante salsa
1 4 oz. can diced green
    chilies
1 cup sour cream
1 tablespoon grated onion
1½ cups grated cheddar
    cheese

Lightly grease sides and bottom of 3 quart casserole dish. Arrange alternate layers of tortillas with
chicken, and mixture of undiluted soups, salsa,
sour cream, onion and green chilies. Cover and
cook 30 minutes at 350°. Remove cover and sprinkle cheese on top and cook for 5 minutes more,
or until cheese is melted. Cheese can also be used
in between layers, leaving about ¼ cup for the
top. Makes 8 to 10 servings.

Kristy Gavin

Mrs. Stephen Gavin, Daughter of Representative Jon Kyl (Arizona)

CHICKEN FAJITA CASSEROLE

6 to 8 chicken breasts
1 pkg. frozen flour tortillas
2 large bell peppers
2 large onions
    fajita seasoning (liquid)
1 can chicken soup
½ cup sour cream
2 cups grated cheddar
    cheese
    jalapeno peppers, sliced
    salt, pepper, garlic salt to
    taste

Cook chicken until tender, season with salt, pepper and garlic salt to taste. Debone and cut into
strips. Saute onions and green peppers. In large
casserole, layer small amount sauce (chicken
soup, sour cream), tortillas, chicken (which has
been mixed with fajita seasoning to taste), peppers and onions, repeat layers. Top with grated
cheese and peppers. Bake at 350° until cheese
melts and bubbles (uncovered) about 30 minutes.
Garnish with guacamole, salsa and sour cream
when served. Makes 8 servings. May be frozen.

Lana Bethune

Mrs. Ed Bethune, Wife of former Representative (Arkansas)

CREAMED CHICKEN ENCHILADA CASSEROLE

2 cups cooked chicken, diced
½ medium onion, diced
1 tablespoon of margarine or butter
1 12 oz. can of evaporated milk
1 can of cream of chicken soup
1 can of cream of mushroom soup
4 oz. can of chopped green chilies
2 cups of grated cheddar cheese
1 bag of original flavor tortilla chips

Saute diced onion in butter or margarine. Put this in a mixing bowl and add milk, soups, chilies and chopped chicken. Mix. Spray casserole with Pam and pour about ⅓ of the mixture in casserole. Add 1 cup of grated cheese over this and ½ of the bag of broken chips (not too fine). Add remainder of chicken mixture and the rest of the grated cheese. Bake at 350° for 30 minutes, uncovered. Use the remainder of chips with picante sauce or guacamole salad. Makes 8 servings. May be frozen.

Mrs. Glenn English, Wife of Representative (Oklahoma)

WILSON'S BARBECUE CHICKEN

4 to 6 skinless chicken breasts
2 tablespoons Paul Newman Italian salad dressing
2 tablespoons Dijon mustard Lawry's seasoned salt pepper to taste

First baste chicken on all sides with mustard, then baste with salad dressing, seasoned salt and pepper. Place chicken on grill and sear until meat turns from pink to white on both sides. Baste once again with same ingredients and continue grilling until meat is done. Enjoy! Makes 4 to 6 servings.

Mrs. Pete Wilson, Wife of Governor (California)

LAYERED MEXICAN CASSEROLE

1 can cream of mushroom
   soup
1 can cream of chicken soup
½ cup milk
1 large onion, chopped
2 small cans green chilies,
   chopped
1 pkg. corn tortillas (flour
   may be used)
1 pound cheese, grated
2 cups cooked, cubed
   chicken (optional)

Mix soups and milk in saucepan and heat slightly, until smooth. In a 1¾ quart casserole dish with deep sides, place one tortilla. Cover tortilla with a thin layer of soup mixture, chilies, onions and cheese. Top this with another tortilla, and repeat layers until casserole is filled, ending with cheese. The chicken may be added to the layers, but we like it better without the chicken. Bake at 350° for 30 minutes until bubbly. The size and shape of the casserole dish is important so that the layers stay in place and don't slide around while cooking. Makes 4 servings. May be frozen.

Betty Chapman

Mrs. Jim Chapman, Wife of Representative (Texas)

GARLIC CHICKEN BREASTS

½ to ¾ pound of butter,
   melted
4 cloves of garlic, crushed
3 cups unseasoned croutons
1 cup Parmesan, grated
¼ cup parsley, chopped
¼ cup basil, chopped
2 teaspoons salt
1 teaspoon pepper
8 chicken breasts

Place chicken breasts flat in a large, buttered baking dish. Combine the remaining ingredients and pour over chicken breasts. Bake at 350° for 1 hour. Makes 8 servings.

Sharon Thomas

Mrs. William Thomas, Wife of Representative (California)

SHANNON'S FAVORITE CHICKEN FAJITAS

8 flour tortillas, warmed

Filling:
 8 ozs. nonfat yogurt
 2 tablespoons lime juice
 1 clove garlic, finely
     chopped
 1 teaspoon ground cumin
 ¼ teaspoon salt
 ¼ teaspoon pepper
 4 skinless, boned chicken
     breast halves

Tomato Salsa:
 3 medium ripe tomatoes,
     chopped
 2 green onions, finely sliced
 1 tablespoon balsamic
     vinegar
 1 teaspoon olive oil
 ½ teaspoon salt
 ¼ teaspoon pepper
 ¼ cup chopped fresh
     coriander

Start by mixing filling 2 hours ahead of time. Substituting nonfat yogurt for oil as a marinade not only lowers fat but produces a delicious, moist piece of chicken.

Prepare filling: Combine yogurt through pepper in shallow dish. Add chicken, turn to coat. Refrigerate 2 hours.

Prepare tomato salsa: Mix together ingredients. Set aside.

Preheat broiler. Remove chicken from marinade. Line broiler pan with aluminum foil. Arrange breasts, smooth side down, on broiler rack. Broil with bottom of pan 6 inches from heat for 4 minutes. Turn over. Spoon any remaining marinade over chicken. Broil until lightly browned and cooked through, about 4 minutes longer. Slice chicken diagonally into strips. Place strips on warm tortillas, dividing equally. Top with salsa. Wrap up tortillas. (452 calories, 4 g fat, 972 mg sodium). Serve immediately. Makes 4 servings.

Mrs. Daniel Donovan, Daughter of Representative Al Swift (Washington)

CHICKEN OLE

1 skinned and boned chicken
     breast per person
picante sauce
Monterey Jack cheese

Place chicken in baking dish and cover with picante sauce. Bake at 350° until tender. Top with Monterey Jack cheese and melt.

Mrs. Paul Wellstone, Wife of Senator (Minnesota)

POLENTA WITH CHICKEN

8 deboned and skinned chicken breasts (cut to bite size)
  olive oil
1 medium sized onion, chopped
1 medium sized whole garlic, chopped
1 cup finely grated carrots
2 medium size cans of peeled tomatoes
1 can tomato sauce
8-10 sliced mushrooms
1 cup corn meal
1 tablespoon powdered chicken
1 stick butter
1 cup grated Parmesan
1/2 pound havarti or soft white cheese
1/2 cup grated Parmesan

In large roasting pan, brown chicken breasts in olive oil. Add onions, garlic, then add grated carrots. Add tomatoes, tomato sauce and mushrooms. Place roaster in 300° oven for 2 hours. Cook corn meal in 3 cups cold water, stirring constantly over medium heat until thick. Add powdered chicken, butter and Parmesan cheese. Set aside, keeping warm. Spread corn meal mush onto large platter or dish, cover with thinly sliced soft white cheese, cover with chicken stew. Spread grated Parmesan on top. Serve immediately or keep warm in oven. Makes 8 servings. May be frozen.

Robert Lagomarsino, former Representative (California)

GRILLED CHICKEN

4 skinless, boned chicken breasts
  bottled Italian dressing (we use no fat dressing)

Marinate chicken breasts in no-fat Italian dressing overnight. Grill on your barbeque. These are great for a main course. They are also excellent served sliced and chilled with a salad. These are easy and have low fat. Makes 4 servings.

Jim Slattery, Representative (Kansas)

CHICKEN WITH A SPANISH FLAIR

1 dozen tortillas
2 large fryers, stewed and
   boned in large chunks or
   8 whole chicken breasts
1 can green chilies (large)
   roasted and peeled
1 onion, chopped fine
2 cans cream of chicken
   soup
½ can water or chicken broth
2 8 oz. pkgs. sliced swiss,
   american or cheddar
   cheese, whichever you
   prefer
paprika

In baking dish, put layer of tortillas down first, cut in strips about width of large noodles, then put layer of chicken, green chili, chopped onion, and cheese. Pour chicken soup which has been mixed with ½ can water or chicken broth and heated. Repeat layers, ending with cheese on top. Sift paprika on top. Bake at 300° for 40 to 45 minutes. Makes 8 to 10 servings. May be frozen.

Alta Leath

Alta Leath, Member of The Congressional Club

MUSTARD CHICKEN

4 boned and skinned chicken
   breast halves
4 tablespoons spicy brown
   mustard
4 tablespoons Italian bread
   crumbs
4 tablespoons melted butter
2 teaspoons lemon juice
4 tablespoons white wine
paprika

Spread each breast half with mustard and cover with crumbs. Pour butter, juice and wine over chicken. Sprinkle with paprika. Cover tightly. Bake at 350° for 45 minutes. Makes 4 servings.

Martha Mills Dixon

Mrs. Jack Dixon, Daughter of former Representative Wilbur D. Mills (Arkansas)

TURKEY SOPA

½ stick butter or margarine
1 medium onion, chopped
1 can diced chilies
1 jar Old El Paso taco sauce
3 cups cooked turkey or
   chicken
1 dozen corn tortillas, cut in
   1 inch strips
1 can cream of mushroom
   soup
1 can cream of chicken soup
1 can consomme
1 pound jack cheese,
   shredded
1 pound cheddar cheese,
   shredded

Melt butter. Add onions. Cook until tender. Add green chilies, taco sauce, soup and turkey or chicken. Place layer of tortillas on bottom of 2″ deep casserole. Place alternate layers of soup mixture, tortillas and cheese. Repeat for 3 layers, making sure top layer is cheese. Bake at 350° for 30 minutes to 1 hour, until thoroughly heated and cheese is melted. Makes 8 to 10 servings.

Fife Symington, Governor (Arizona)

BAKED MUSTARD CHICKEN

4 chicken breast halves,
   skinned
¼ cup Italian (bold) spicy
   brown mustard
½ cup Italian-flavored breadcrumbs (can be optional)
¼ cup butter or margarine,
   melted
2 tablespoons lemon juice
2 tablespoons water or white
   wine
   paprika

Brush chicken with mustard and dredge in breadcrumbs (also good without the bread crumbs). Place in a 13″ × 9″ × 2″ inch baking dish. Combine butter, lemon juice, and water. Drizzle 1 tablespoon over each piece of chicken and pour the remainder in the baking dish. Cover and bake at 350° for 45 minutes. Remove cover. Sprinkle with paprika and bake an additional 15 minutes. Makes 4 servings. May be frozen.

Mrs. Ted Strickland, Wife of Representative (Ohio)

TAMALE PIE

1½ cup onion, chopped
1½ cup green pepper, chopped
 whole fryer, steamed and boned
 3 cans tomato sauce
 3 tablespoons butter (if butter is used)
24 oz. creamed corn
 2 cloves minced garlic
 2 to 3 teaspoons sugar
 3 tablespoons chili powder, salt and pepper
 olives
 3 cups shredded cheese (jack or cheddar)
2¼ cups corn meal, yellow
 3 teaspoons salt
 6 cups water or chicken broth

Cook onion, pepper in little fat until soft. Add garlic, tomato sauce, creamed corn, sugar, salt and pepper and chili and chicken. Then cheese and olives. Simmer 10 minutes. Pour into greased dish. Stir corn meal, salt and chicken broth together. Keep stirring constantly until thick. Add butter and spread over meat. Baked at 375° for 20–30 minutes or until cheese is bubbly. Makes 6 servings. May be frozen.

Barbara Vucanovich, Representative (Nevada)

GRILLED MARINATED CHICKEN

 4 chicken breast halves, boned and skinned
 4 tablespoons vegetable oil
 4 tablespoons white wine
 2 tablespoons lemon juice
 ½ teaspoon dry mustard
 ½ teaspoon dried whole rosemary
 ½ teaspoon parsley flakes
 ¼ teaspoon garlic powder

Mix well all ingredients except chicken. Pour marinade over chicken, cover and refrigerate at least 2 hours. Remove chicken from marinade, but save marinade. Grill chicken ½ hour (or until done), turning chicken and basting with reserved marinade every 10 minutes. Makes 4 servings.

Mrs. Wilbur D. Mills, Wife of former Representative (Arkansas)

GOVERNOR'S MANSION CHICKEN ENCHILADA CASSEROLE

1 small can chopped green chili
1 large can Ashley enchilada sauce
1 can cream of chicken soup
1 small can Pet milk
2 cups chicken broth
1½ dozen corn tortillas
2 cups grated longhorn cheese
2 tablespoons chopped onion
1 stewing chicken, boned and chopped

Saute onions and chili in butter. Combine all liquids and add onion and chili. Break tortillas into pieces, place in casserole in layers with chicken and cheese, ending with cheese. Pour liquid over all and refrigerate overnight, or several hours. Bake at 350° for 1 hour.

Bruce King, Governor (New Mexico)

After stewing a chicken for diced meat for casseroles, etc., let cool in broth before cutting into chunks. It will have twice the flavor.

BAR-B-QUE TURKEY

1 10-12 pound turkey, split

Sauce:
3 sliced onions
1 pint vinegar
1 tablespoon mustard
3 tablespoons ketchup
3 tablespoons Worcestershire
1/3 tablespoon garlic powder
2 tablespoons salt
1 tablespoon black pepper
1 stick margarine
1 tablespoon crushed red
    pepper
1/3 tablespoon hot sauce

Combine all ingredients, except turkey, to make sauce. Cook sauce 20-25 minutes. Brown turkey halves on grill 30-45 minutes each side. Place half turkey in broiler pan, pour sauce over, cover with aluminum foil and cook on grill (or can cook in oven) for 1-1½ hours, or until tender.

Pat Roberts, Representative (Kansas)

AUNT BOO'S TURKEY MEATLOAF

1½ to 2 pounds ground turkey
1½ tablespoons sesame oil
3 cloves garlic, crushed
2 tablespoons soy sauce
1 tablespoon Worcestershire
    sauce
2 tablespoons sherry
2 tablespoons honey
1 small onion, diced
1/4 cup oatmeal
1/4 cup breadcrumbs
1/2 cup chicken broth
1/2 cup water

Mix all ingredients, except chicken broth and water, thoroughly, then form into customary meatloaf shape. Place in pan (optional: surround with pieces of onion, celery, and carrots). Cover with foil, and bake at 375° for scheduled 1 hour, however, after 45 minutes, pour the chicken broth and water over the meatloaf and resume baking for the final 15 minutes or until done. Makes 4 to 6 servings. May be frozen.

Sam Coppersmith, Representative (Arizona)

TURKEY A LA KING

2 cups thinly sliced celery
½ cup chopped green pepper
1 8 oz. can chopped mush-
    rooms, drained
¾ cup butter or margarine
2 teaspoons salt
¼ teaspoon pepper
2 quarts milk
¼ pound cheddar cheese,
    chopped
1 pkg. frozen mixed vege-
    tables
2½ cups diced turkey

Saute first 3 ingredients in butter for 5 minutes, blend in flour and seasonings. Gradually add milk, stirring until thickened and add remaining ingredients. I simmer in crock pot a couple of hours. Serve over biscuits or toast. Makes 20 servings.

Jim Bilbray, Representative (Nevada)

"GOODBYE TURKEY" CASSEROLE

5 tablespoons sifted flour
1 teaspoon salt
¼ teaspoon onion salt
¼ cup butter, melted
2½ cups milk or light cream
1⅓ cups minute rice
1½ cups turkey or chicken
    broth
½ cup grated American
    cheese
1½ cups cooked asparagus
2 cups sliced turkey
2 tablespoons toasted, sliv-
    ered almonds

Stir flour, half of salt, onion salt into butter. Stir in milk. Cook over hot water, stirring occasionally until thickened. Pour minute rice into 2 quart shallow baking dish. Combine broth, remaining salt, pour over rice. Sprinkle half of cheese over rice. Top with asparagus, then turkey. Pour on sauce. Sprinkle with remaining cheese. Bake at 375° about 20 minutes. Top with almonds. Makes 6 servings. May be frozen.

Joyce Hubbard, Member of The Congressional Club

KOGAN TURKEY CHILI

1 large onion, diced
2 cloves garlic
3 tablespoons oil
1 pound ground turkey
½ green pepper, chopped
½ red pepper, chopped
1½ teaspoons salt
½ teaspoon cumin
3 tablespoons oil
1 8 oz. can tomato sauce
1 20 oz. can canned to-matoes
1 teaspoon crushed chili
2 bay leaves
1 16 oz. can red beans (op-tional)

Saute onion and garlic until soft. Add and saute turkey and peppers until soft. Then add rest of ingredients. Cook over low heat for 1 hour. This chili may be served over pasta or rice or else served plain in a bowl. Makes 4 servings. May be frozen.

Mrs. Dan Glickman, Wife of Representative (Kansas)

CHICKEN-N-JAM

½ cup Russian salad dressing
⅔ cup apricot jam
½ pkg. dehydrated onion soup mix
4 halves of chicken breast

Heat salad dressing, jam and soup mix together in saucepan while stirring until jam melts. Arrange pieces of chicken in baking dish and cover, bake at 350° for 30 minutes. Remove foil and bake another 25 minutes. Makes 4 servings.

Tyler Lott, Daughter of Senator Trent Lott (Mississippi)

ROAST DUCK WITH ORANGE SAUCE

1   4 to 5 pound duck, Wisconsin C & D brand
1   orange (sliced into quarters)
    salt, pepper and poultry seasoning
½   cup sugar
1   tablespoon wine vinegar
    juice of 2 oranges
1   bay leaf
½   teaspoon thyme leaves
    salt and pepper to taste
½   cup Grand Marnier
    grated rind of 1 orange

Preheat oven to 425°. Wash duck in cold water and remove excess fat. Season the inside cavity and the outside of duck with salt, pepper, and poultry seasoning. Place orange quarters inside duck and place in a shallow roasting pan. Cook in hot oven for 30 minutes, then remove duck from oven and prick breast with heavy tine kitchen fork to drain grease. Turn oven down to 300° and return duck to oven for 1 hour or 1 hour and 15 minutes until tender.

Orange Sauce: In a heavy saucepan, combine sugar and wine vinegar. Cook the mixture over a medium flame until sugar melts and begins to carmelize. Add the juice of 2 oranges, Grand Marnier and grated orange rind. Stir well and cook for 5 minutes. Add ½ cup orange peel cut into julienne strip, cooked in a little water for 5 minutes and drained. Correct the seasonings and pour over the duckling on a serving platter. Makes 4 servings.

Tommy G. Thompson, Governor (Wisconsin)

It is easy to skin and bone chicken if slightly frozen.

WILD DUCK

wild ducks
salt
pepper
onions
carrots
celery
prunes
oranges
apples
Red Wine (Port)

Gravy:
1 can beef gravy
1 jar red currant jelly

Clean ducks. Soak in salt water overnight, or a few hours. Dry ducks, salt and pepper inside and out. Stuff with: onion, carrot, celery or prune, orange, apple, or any combination. Place in covered roaster with room between ducks. Put roaster in pre-heated 450° oven, roast 1 hour. Then quickly pour red wine over ducks, ½ cup per duck. Cover pan, turn oven off—leave ducks covered in oven for 1 hour more. Remove stuffing. Heat together gravy and jelly. Serve with ducks and wild rice. Ducks can be quartered and cooked in the same manner. Makes 1 duck per person. May be frozen.

Mrs. Harold S. Sawyer, Wife of former Representative (Michigan)

CHICKEN AMARETTO

1 broiler-fryer chicken, cut in parts
1 teaspoon salt
¼ teaspoon pepper
½ cup orange juice
⅓ cup steak sauce
½ cup honey
2 tablespoons almond flavored liquer

In large shallow baking pan place chicken in single layer, skin side up. Sprinkle salt and pepper on chicken. In bowl, mix together orange juice, steak sauce, honey and liquer. Pour ¾ of mixture on chicken. Bake, uncovered, in 350° oven for 1 hour. Pour on remaining sauce and bake about 15 minutes longer or until fork can be inserted in chicken with ease. I have sometimes added walnuts to the sauce for a special taste. Makes 4 servings.

Tony Morella, Husband of Representative Connie Morella (Maryland)

BASQUE CHICKEN

4 skinless, boneless chicken
    breast halves
1 32 oz. can peeled toma-
    toes, chopped
2 green peppers, cut into
    thin strips
1 medium onion, finely
    chopped
2 tablespoons olive oil
1 teaspoon oregano, dried
1 teaspoon basil, dried
1/2 teaspoon salt
1/4 teaspoon pepper
1/8 teaspoon cayenne pepper
1 large clove garlic, finely
    chopped

Cut cleaned chicken breasts into strips. Brown chicken in olive oil until light brown and cooked throughout, approximately 15 minutes. Remove chicken from pan and place on warm plate. Add onions to pan and saute until translucent, add garlic and cook for 1 minute. Add green peppers and saute until soft. Add tomatoes, oregano, basil, salt, pepper and cayenne pepper. Mix well. Add cooked chicken to this mixture and simmer covered for 45 minutes. Serve over rice. Makes 4 servings.

Stephanie Blatnik, Daughter of former Representative John Blatnik (Minnesota)

KATHY'S CHICKEN AND PEPPERS

1 green pepper
1 yellow pepper
1 red pepper
1 red onion, thinly sliced
3 oranges, peeled and sec-
    tioned
1/2 cup corn meal
1/4 cup flour
1/4 teaspoon cayenne pepper
1/4 teaspoon ground fennel
4 boneless skinless chicken
    breasts
1 1/4 teaspoon olive oil

Slice peppers thinly, toss with onion and oranges and set aside. Pound chicken with back of knife until are flat. Coat well with cornmeal, flour and spices mixture and saute in olive oil about 2 minutes on each side. Put chicken on plate and salad on top and serve. Makes 4 servings.

Mrs. Martin Sabo, Wife of Representative (Minnesota)

BURROS BAKED IMPERIAL CHICKEN WITH CUMBERLAND SAUCE

Chicken:

½ cup grated Parmesan
2 cups seasoned bread crumbs
3 tablespoons sesame seeds
2 2½ to 3 pound broilers or fryers—I use chicken breasts
½ cup melted margarine or butter

Sauce:

1 cup red current jelly
1 6 oz. can frozen orange juice
4 tablespoons dry sherry
1 teaspoon dry mustard
⅛ teaspoon ground ginger
¼ teaspoon hot pepper sauce

Mix first 3 ingredients. Melt margarine, cut up chicken into serving pieces. Dip chicken pieces into margarine then into crumb mixture. Freeze or refrigerate up to 2 days. When ready to serve, bring chicken to room temperature, place in shallow pan and dot with margarine, bake at 350° for 1 hour. Combine and simmer sauce ingredients until smooth. Spoon sauce over chicken when serving. Makes 6 to 8 servings. May be frozen.

Mrs. Norm Dicks, Wife of Representative (Washington)

RUSSIAN CHICKEN

6 to 10 boneless chicken breast halves
1 pkg. Lipton onion soup
8 ozs. Russian dressing
8 ozs. apricot jam or preserves

Mix together and pour over chicken. Bake 1 hour or until tender. Makes 9 to 10 servings.

Mrs. William H. Ayres, Wife of former Representative (Ohio)

LAURIE ANNE'S APRICOT CHICKEN

12 chicken breasts, skinned
    and boned
1 12 oz. can apricot nectar
1 teaspoon ground allspice
½ teaspoon salt
¼ teaspoon ground ginger
¼ teaspoon pepper
¾ cup apricot preserves
½ cup chopped pecans,
    roasted

Place chicken breasts in 13″ × 9″ × 2″ dish. Combine nectar, allspice, salt, ginger, pepper. Stir well and pour over chicken. Cover. Chill 8 hours. Remove chicken. Let stand at room temperature for 30 minutes. Cover and bake at 350° for 30 minutes. Uncover and drain liquid. Heat preserves until warm. Brush over chicken. Bake, uncovered 25 minutes, basting occasionally. Sprinkle with pecans. Garnish. Makes 12 servings.

Faith H Battle

Mrs. James Battle, Daughter-in-law of former Representative Laurie C. Battle (Alabama)

CHICKEN LEG PILAF

6 to 8 chicken legs
1 large onion, chopped
¼ cup butter or margarine
⅔ cup long grain white rice
1⅓ cups beef bouillon
    (one can)
⅓ cup seedless raisins
1 cup almond flakes or slices
4 tablespoons chopped
    parsley

Wash and pat dry chicken legs. In a large saucepan or dutch oven, cook onion in butter until tender. Add rice, cook 3 minutes, stirring. Add beef bouillon, raisins, and chicken pieces. Bring to a boil, reduce heat, cover and simmer about 1 hour or until chicken is tender. Remove chicken to platter, keep warm (e.g., in oven). Stir almonds and parsley into rice, fluff with a fork. Serve chicken with rice on the side. Makes 4 to 6 servings. May be frozen.

Frances B. Hagan

Frances B. Hagan, Daughter of former Representation G. Elliott Hagan (Georgia)

CHICKEN AND SWEET POTATO BAKE

3 medium sweet potatoes,
    peeled and cut into
    small chunks
3 whole chicken breasts,
    skinned and split
1 small onion, diced
1 celery stalk, diced
½ cup apple juice
2 teaspoons chicken bouillon
    powder
2 9 oz. pkgs. frozen cut
    green beans, thawed

Put all ingredients in a 3 quart casserole, toss well. Cover and bake, stirring occasionally, at 375° for 1 hour, or until chicken is tender. This is a very low fat entree with LOTS of nutritional content. (Sweet potatoes are one of the most nutritional vegetables there is.) Makes 6 servings. May be frozen.

Mrs. Jim Lloyd, Wife of former Representative (California)

CHICKEN A LA PECHE

2 3 to 4 pound fryers, cut in
    quarters
2 teaspoons salt
¼ cup butter, melted

Glaze:
1 29 oz. can cling peach
    slices, with syrup
2 tablespoons honey
1 tablespoon instant onion
1 teaspoon curry
1 teaspoon powdered ginger

Dry chicken quarters. Sprinkle with salt, brush with butter. Bake skin side down at 425° about 45 minutes. Meanwhile, prepare glaze. Drain can of cling peach slices, saving syrup. Set aside 1 cup peaches for garnish. Combine remaining peaches, syrup, honey, onion, curry and ginger. Simmer 5 minutes until thick. Use a wire whip to break up peaches in syrup. When chicken is done, turn skin side up and spoon heavily with glaze. Bake another 15 minutes. Garnish with reserved 1 cup peach slices and heat slightly. Serve immediately with hot rice. Makes 6 to 8 servings.

Mrs. Anthony Beilenson, Wife of Representative (California)

APRICOT STUFFED CHICKEN BREASTS

6 boneless chicken breasts
⅔ cup chopped dried apricots
3 tablespoons fine chopped onion
2 tablespoons slivered almonds
1 tablespoon chopped parsley

Sauce:
1 cup sour cream
⅔ cup apricot preserves
¼ cup Dijon mustard

Combine all. Spread chicken breast flat, skin side down. Place 1 to 2 tablespoon mixture in center of each breast. Fold tightly and secure with food pick if necessary. Place skin side up on foil lined sheet pan. Bake uncovered 30 to 40 minutes at 375°. Brown 2 to 3 minutes under broiler, to golden.

Sauce: Heat to warm. Do not boil. Top each chicken breast with 1 tablespoon sauce. Serve with rice and the extra sauce. Makes 6 servings. May be frozen.

Mrs. Bob Wilson, Wife of former Representative (California)

CHICKEN KELAGUIN—CHAMORRO

1 chicken, halved
1 grated mature coconut
½ onion (or 1 small), diced
salt to taste
juice of 2 or 3 fresh lemons
Aji-no-moto to taste
hot pepper to taste (optional)

Barbeque or broil chicken until only half done. Cool it so it will be easier to debone chicken. Chop meat into small pieces. Mix chicken with all other ingredients in a bowl. Allow to marinate at least 1 hour. For variety substitute 1 pound shrimp or 1 pound fresh raw white fish such as jack or parrot fish. Makes 6 servings. May be frozen.

Lorenzo I. DeLeon Guerrero, Governor (Commonwealth of the Northern Mariana Islands)

HEALTHY CURRY FRIED CHICKEN

4 chicken breasts or 8 drumsticks
½ cup plain yogurt
¼ cup lime juice
1 tablespoon curry powder
1 teaspoon garlic powder

Line a glass or aluminum baking pan with foil or cooking spray. Remove skin and fat from chicken. Combine yogurt, lime juice, curry powder, and garlic and coat chicken. Bake at 425°, uncovered for 30 minutes. Makes 4 servings. May be frozen.

Elizabeth Albert

Mrs. David Albert, Daughter-in-law of former Representative Carl Albert (Oklahoma)

CHICKEN CURRY

6 chicken breasts
2 cloves garlic
2 bay leaves
4 whole peppercorns
1 teaspoon salt
1 carrot, sliced
1 onion, diced
½ cup chopped celery
1 apple, peeled, cored and
   chopped
3 tablespoons butter or oleo,
   melted
2 teaspoons curry powder
½ teaspoon chili powder
3 tablespoons flour
¼ teaspoon ground mace
¼ teaspoon ground allspice
¼ teaspoon ground nutmeg
¼ teaspoon ground cinnamon
¼ teaspoon ground cloves

Place first 5 ingredients in a dutch oven, add water to cover. Bring to a boil over medium heat, cover, reduce heat, simmer 45 minutes. Drain, but reserve broth. Skin and bone chicken, cut into bite size pieces. Set aside. Saute carrot, onion, celery, and apple in butter in large skillet for 15 minutes. Add curry and chili powder, cook 5 minutes, stirring occasionally. Add ½ cup reserved chicken broth. Stir. Place mixture in blender, process until smooth. Add flour, process until smooth (well-blended). Return mixture to dutch oven, cook until thickened. Gradually add 2 cups reserved chicken broth, stirring constantly. Cook 5 minutes. Stir in mace and next 4 ingredients. Gently stir in chicken. Serve over rice. Optional, may serve with the following condiments: flaked coconut, peanuts, chopped bell pepper, chopped green onions, chutney, and/or raisins. Makes 6 servings.

Mrs. Ike Skelton, Wife of Representative (Missouri)

CHICKEN CURRY

2 medium size onions,
   chopped
2 cloves garlic, chopped
2 tablespoons vegetable oil
1 teaspoon cinnamon
¼ teaspoon ground cloves
1 tablespoon curry
1 teaspoon salt
1 teaspoon tumeric
1 teaspoon ground ginger
1 teaspoon ground cumin
2 tablespoons ground coriander
3 to 4 pounds chicken
   pieces
1 can tomato juice
1 cup chicken broth
1 to 2 tablespoons corn-
   starch dissolved in ¼
   cup cold water

In a large pot, saute onions and garlic in oil. Add spices. Add chicken and saute until it is well coated with spices and golden in color. Add liquids, cover and simmer over low heat 1-2 hours until chicken is tender. Thicken sauce with cornstarch and serve over rice. Makes 4 servings.

Jane Sutermeister

Mrs. Richard Sutermeister, Daughter of former Representative Tom Kleppe (North Dakota)

LIME CHICKEN

2 1 lb., boneless, skinless
   chicken breasts
3 limes
   fresh ground pepper
   white wine
   olive oil
   Tabasco

Preheat oven to 375. Rinse chicken breasts and put in shallow baking dish. Drizzle with olive il. Add juice of 2 limes and white wine (about ¼ cup). Sprinkle the tops of the chicken breasts with fresh ground pepper to taste, 2 tsp. of Tabasco sauce and a couple of pinches of ground ginger. Thinly slice 1 whole lime. Cover chicken breasts with the lime slices. Cover baking dish and bake for 35-40 minutes. Baste once or twice during the last 15 minutes of cooking. Use cooking juices on rice or steamed vegetables. Serves two.

David Norcross

David Norcross, Son-in-Law of Representative Bob Michel (Illinois)

GOURMET CURRY CHICKEN

8 chicken breasts
1 can cream of chicken soup
1 can cream of celery soup
1 cup sour cream
1 small can sliced mush-
   rooms
1 tablespoon parsley flakes
1 teaspoon curry powder
1 tablespoon lemon juice
½ teaspoon salt
½ teaspoon paprika
½ cup Parmesan cheese
¼ cup slivered almonds

Cook chicken breasts until tender, remove skin and bones, and place chicken in baking dish. Mix together chicken soup, celery soup, sour cream, mushrooms, parsley, curry powder, lemon juice, salt and paprika. Pour this mixture over chicken. Sprinkle cheese and almonds over the top. Bake at 350° for 30 minutes. May microwave, cover dish and cook on high 10 minutes. Makes 8 servings. May be frozen.

John Marsh, Former Representative (Virginia)

RITZ CHICKEN

chicken breasts
Ritz cracker crumbs
oil or egg whites, slightly
   beaten

May use boned or unboned, skinned chicken breasts. Dip in vegetable oil or slightly beaten egg whites or Egg Beaters. Then coat with cracker crumbs. Place on cookie sheet. Bake 1 hour at 350°.

Mrs. Edward V. Long, Wife of former Senator (Missouri)

> *Maximum freezer storage for poultry and game birds is 6-8 months.*

MOM'S CHICKEN POT PIE

1 stewing chicken cut into
    pieces (an oven roaster
    may be substituted)
4 quarts water and chicken
    bouillon to taste
  seasonings: onion, celery,
    salt and pepper

Dough:

2 cups flour
⅔ cup shortening
4 tablespoons cold water
  salt to taste

Bring chicken, water and seasonings to a boil and simmer until tender. Add water to keep covered as needed. When chicken is done, fork tender, remove from the water and keep warm and covered. Reserve broth adding enough water to make at least 3 quarts. Season to taste before adding the rolled dough. Mix flour and salt in a mixing bowl, cut in shortening until shortening and flour are well mixed, add water a little at a time until all the flour is moistened. Press into a ball. On a floured board, rollout dough until very thin, cut into 2″ by 3″ strips. Sprinkle lightly with flour. Bring seasoned reserve broth to a good rolling boil. Drop the pieces of rolled dough into the boiling broth making sure that there is enough broth to cover the dough. Stir gently to make sure that the dough is not sticking, reduce the heat and cover for about 10 minutes, remove cover and cook until dough is done, about 10 more minutes. Time depends on the amount of dough and the desired tenderness of dough. Makes 6 servings.

William J. Hughes, Representative (New Jersey)

A different way of browning flour is to put it in a custard cup placed beside meat in the oven. Once the meat is done, the flour will be nice and brown.

CHICKEN POT PIE

2 to 3 pound hen
½ stick butter
1 chopped onion
1 cup celery
1 can English peas and
    carrots
1 cup chicken broth
1 teaspoon flour
biscuit mix for 10 biscuits

Boil hen until tender. Remove meat from bone and cut into small pieces. Melt butter in ovenware pan. Add onion and celery. Cook very slowly for 15 minutes. Add can of peas and carrots, blend broth and flour. Add broth mixture, chicken, salt and pepper to taste. Top with biscuits and bake at 425° until brown. If desired, add ½ cup chopped bell pepper or can of mushrooms as onion and celery cooks.

Zell Miller, Governor (Georgia)

HOMESTYLE CHICKEN POT PIE

2 cans (10¾ oz. each) cream
    of broccoli soup
1 cup milk
¼ teaspoon dried thyme
    leaves, crushed
¼ teaspoon pepper
4 cups cooked cut-up vegeta-
    bles (broccoli, cauli-
    flower, carrots and
    potatoes)
2 cups cooked, cubed
    chicken
1 10 oz. can refrigerated
    flaky biscuits

In a 3 quart baking dish, combine soup, milk, thyme and pepper. Stir in vegetables and chicken. Bake at 400° for 15 minutes or until mixture begins to bubble. Meanwhile, cut each biscuit into quarters. Remove from oven and stir. Arrange biscuits over top of mixture and bake another 15 minutes or until biscuits are golden brown. Makes 5 servings.

(You can use frozen vegetables, cooked and drained and 1 cup cubed, cooked and peeled potato).

Allison Lightfoot, Daughter of Representative Jim Lightfoot (Iowa)

RUTH'S CHICKEN PIE

6 tablespoons butter
6 tablespoons flour
½ teaspoon salt
¼ teaspoon pepper
1¾ cups chicken broth
⅔ cup half and half cream
2 cups cooked chicken, cubed
¼ cup diced pimento

Mix first 5 ingredients in a saucepan and bring to a boil over medium heat. Remove from heat and add cream, chicken and pimento. Use any pie pastry recipe and line a 9 inch casserole dish with pastry. Pour chicken mixture on top and cover with remaining pastry. Bake for 35 minutes at 425°. Makes 6 servings.

Annie Ben Kornegay

Mrs. Horace R. Kornegay, Wife of former Representative (North Carolina)

TIB'S CHICKEN PIE

1 4 pound stewing hen, cut in pieces
4 sprigs of parsley
1 stalk of celery, cut in large hunks
1 bay leaf
1 onion stuck with 2 cloves
2 or 3 carrots, cut into thin rounds
1 cup fresh or frozen peas
12 small white onions
2 tablespoons butter
2 tablespoons flour
½ cup cream
salt and pepper to taste
pastry

In a kettle, put the hen and next 4 ingredients. Add just enough water to cover hen. Bring to a boil and simmer until hen is tender. Let stand in the stock until cool enough to handle. Remove hen and strain stock. Reserve. Discard skin and bones of chicken and cut meat into pieces. Cook separately in a little boiling water, 2 or 3 carrots cut into thin rounds and 12 small white onions. When almost done, add 1 cup peas. Drain when cooked. In a saucepan, melt 2 tablespoons butter. Stir in 2 tablespoons flour until smooth and cook over low heat until it bubbles. Pour in 2 cups of reserved chicken stock and ½ cup cream. Add salt and pepper to taste. Continue cooking sauce until smooth and thick. Combine chicken, vegetables and sauce in a deep glass pie dish. Roll out pastry (cheddar cheese best) about ¼ inch thick on a lightly floured board and prick pastry well with fork. Cover the top of the dish with pastry. Bake pie in a preheated oven at 425° for 10 minutes. Reduce heat to 350° and bake for 25 to 30 minutes longer. May be frozen.

Annie Laurie Rankin Sanders

Mrs. John Sanders, Daughter of former Representative John E. Rankin (Mississippi)

CHICKEN BREASTS PIQUANT

2 cups seasoned bread crumbs (Italian style)
½ cup grated Parmesan cheese
½ cup minced fresh parsley
1 3 oz. can french fried onions, crushed
½ cup butter or margarine (1 stick)
2 large cloves of garlic, minced
1 teaspoon Worcestershire sauce
1 teaspoon dry mustard
8 halves of chicken breasts, boned, skinned

Combine bread crumbs, cheese, parsley and onions in a shallow dish. Saute garlic in butter or margarine for 1 minute. Add Worcestershire sauce and mustard. Dip chicken breasts in butter mixture and then in bread crumb mixture, coating well. Arrange coated breasts in a foil lined baking dish in a single layer. Pour any remaining butter mixture over them. Bake now or prepare and refrigerate earlier in the day. Bake, uncovered, at 350° for 50 to 60 minutes. Makes 4 to 6 servings.

Freda Solomon

Mrs. Gerald B. Solomon, Wife of Representative (New York)

CHICKEN 'N' RICE

2 pounds chicken parts
1 can chicken broth
⅔ cup raw regular rice
½ cup chopped green pepper
½ cup peas
2 tablespoons salad oil
2 medium cloves garlic, minced
½ cup chopped canned tomatoes
½ cup chopped onion
2 tablespoons Goya Sofrito seasoning

In skillet, brown chicken in oil, pour off fat. Add Sofrito seasoning, onion, garlic and cook for 2 minutes. Add broth and cover, simmer 15 minutes. Add remaining ingredients, simmer 30 minutes or until done. Stir often. Makes 4 servings.

Elena Skelton

Mrs. Ike Skelton IV, Daughter-in-law of Representative Ike Skelton (Missouri)

MOROCCAN LEMON CHICKEN

1½ teaspoons vegetable oil
1½ cups onions, ¼″ × 1½″
    julienne strips
½ teaspoon garlic, minced
    fine
¼ teaspoon ginger, ground
¼ teaspoon tumeric
¼ teaspoon salt
    dash black pepper
¾ teaspoon oregano
¼ cup lemon juice
¾ cup chicken broth
1 tablespoon cornstarch
2 tablespoons cold water
1½ teaspoons minced parsley
¾ teaspoon minced cilantro
2 teaspoons margarine
6 boneless chicken breasts

Prepare sauce by sauteing onions and garlic in oil until tender. Add seasonings, lemon juice and chicken broth. Cover and simmer for 15 to 20 minutes. Combine cornstarch and cold water and add to the hot mixture. Stir well and simmer for 5 minutes. Add parsley, cilantro and margarine, stirring well to combine. Keep sauce hot. Place chicken breasts on a baking sheet and place in a 400° oven for 15 to 20 minutes to brown lightly. Place browned chicken breasts in a baking dish. Pour 1½ cups sauce evenly over chicken. Cover and bake in a 350° oven for 30 to 45 minutes or until chicken is thoroughly cooked. Makes 6 to 8 servings.

Mrs. Kathleen Waters, Daughter of former Representative John R. Foley (Maryland)

MANUEL'S FAVORITE CHICKEN

1 frying chicken, cut up with
    skin removed
2 lemons
½ cup olive oil or corn oil
½ teaspoon salt
½ teaspoon pepper
4 potatoes, quartered
    lengthwise

In bowl, mix lemon, oil, salt, pepper and oregano. Dip pieces of chicken and potatoes in mixture and place in baking pan. Add 1 cup of water and remaining lemon-oil mixture. Cover with foil and bake at 400° for 1 hour. Serve with vegetable or salad. Makes 4 servings.

Mrs. Michael Bilirakis, Wife of Representative (Florida)

CHICKEN KIEV

4 chicken breasts, skinned
   and boned
½ pound butter
2 tablespoons green onions
½ teaspoon garlic salt
¼ teaspoon pepper
¼ cup flour
2 eggs, beaten
½ cup seasoned bread
   crumbs

Pound chicken breasts ¼ inch thick. Form 8 balls from butter and roll them lightly in mixture of green onions, salt and pepper. Place the butter balls in the middle of the breasts, roll up, and secure with toothpicks. Dust breasts with flour, then dip in beaten egg and roll in bread crumbs. Bake at 350° for 30 minutes. Makes 4 servings.

Marge Shoup

Mrs. Richard Shoup, Wife of former Representative (Montana)

LAZY CHICKEN

4 chicken breasts with skin
   & 4 legs OR 6 breasts
1 medium onion, quartered
3 to 4 medium potatoes, cut
   into large chunks
6 or 7 carrots, cut into large
   chunks
3 to 4 cloves chopped garlic
   (optional)
1 to 1½ teaspoons salt
   freshly ground pepper to
   taste
1 teaspoon dry thyme
1 cup white wine
1 to 2 cups chicken broth, as
   needed
3 tablespoons butter
   chopped parsley for
   garnish

Preheat oven to 500°. Place oven rack in upper third of oven. Lay chicken in large baking pan. Add onion (pulling quarters apart), potatoes, and carrots. Pieces should be propped up onto each other. Pour wine and 1 cup of chicken broth over mixture. Sprinkle garlic, thyme, salt and pepper. Dot with butter. Reduce heat to 350° and bake in upper third of oven for 50 minutes to 1 hour. Chicken and vegetables will brown. Turn chicken and baste as needed to brown. Add more broth if evaporating. Please note: I like to use more thyme—it's so good. Also, this dish is very good leftover. Makes 3 to 4 servings.

Mike Castle

Mrs. Michael Castle, Wife of Representative (Delaware)

CHICKEN WITH MUSTARD SAUCE

⅓ cup whole mustard seeds
¼ cup chopped fresh basil, or
   2 tablespoons dried
6 tablespoons Dijon mustard
2 large whole chicken
   breasts, skinned, boned
   and split
2 tablespoons olive oil
½ cup chicken broth
½ cup white wine
1 garlic clove, minced

Combine mustard seeds, basil and 4 tablespoons mustard. Pound chicken breasts to ¼ inch thickness. Spread mustard seed mixture on larger half of each breast. Starting at the end with the mixture, roll up each breast and secure with toothpicks. In a skillet, brown chicken in hot oil on all sides. Pour fat from pan. Add broth, wine, garlic and remaining 2 tablespoons mustard. Cover and simmer 10 minutes or until tender. Remove chicken and keep warm. Heat liquid to boiling and cook about 2 minutes or until sauce thickens. Discard garlic. Spoon some sauce on each of four plates. Remove toothpicks from chicken breasts and cut each into ½ inch thick slices. Place on top of sauce. Makes 4 servings.

Laura Livingstain

Mrs. Harris Livingstain, Daughter of former Representative Don Fuqua (Florida)

BUTTERMILK CHICKEN

5 pounds cut-up chicken,
   washed and dried
1 cup buttermilk
1½ teaspoons salt
¼ teaspoon pepper
2 cloves garlic
2 tablespoons corn oil
1 cup chopped onion
2 tablespoons curry powder
   chopped almonds (optional)

Mix buttermilk, salt, pepper, garlic and corn oil. Marinate chicken in buttermilk mixture for 2 hours. Drain and save liquid. Brown chicken lightly in hot oil. Add onion, saute slowly 10 minutes. Add curry powder. Add the almonds and reserved liquid. Cover, cook at 350° for 1 hour or until done. Suggestion: Serve the meal with rice to give an Indonesian flavor. May be frozen.

Betty Bumpers

Mrs. Dale Bumpers, Wife of Senator (Arkansas)

ALEXA'S CHICKEN NUGGETS

2 full chicken breasts
melted margarine or butter
1 cup unseasoned bread
   crumbs
¼ cup Parmesan cheese
½ teaspoon salt
1 teaspoon thyme
1 teaspoon basil
1 teaspoon parsley flakes

Bone and skin chicken. Cut into 1″ × ½″ pieces. Dip into melted butter (margarine) then into crumb mix. Bake on cookie sheet in a single layer for 10 minutes at 400°.

Allison Lightfoot

Allison Lightfoot, Daughter of Representative Jim Lightfoot (Iowa)

CAROLYN'S COQ AU VIN

2 tablespoons butter
¼ pound diced bacon
3½ pounds chicken, cut into
   pieces
1 tablespoon diced onion
2 cloves diced garlic
2 tablespoons flour
2 cups red wine
1 tablespoon brandy
1 tablespoon minced parsley
¼ teaspoon thyme
1 bay leaf
   salt and pepper to taste
1 teaspoon tomato paste
1 teaspoon beef bovril
1 pint of pearl onions, boiled
   for 10 minutes and
   peeled
½ pound of mushrooms,
   sliced

Melt butter in a heavy skillet. Brown the bacon in the butter. Remove the bacon and brown the chicken in the pan drippings. Remove the chicken and cook the diced onion and garlic until softened. Stir the flour into the mixture and stir until all lumps are gone. Add the wine and brandy. Add the browned bacon and chicken. Add the parsley, thyme, bay leaf, salt, pepper, tomato paste and bovril. Simmer for 30 minutes. Add the boiled pearl onions and mushrooms and cook for 10 more minutes. Makes 4 servings. May be frozen.

Lardie M. Neal

Mrs. Steve Neal, Wife of Representative (North Carolina)

CHICKEN BREASTS WITH WINE

6 to 8 whole chicken
    breasts, flattened and
    thinly sliced
  flour
  salt and pepper
  garlic powder
2 to 4 tablespoons margarine
    or butter and 2 table-
    spoons oil
6 to 8 scallions
1 pound mushrooms
1 cup chicken bouillon soup
3/4 cup white wine

Dredge chicken breasts in flour, salt, pepper and garlic powder. Heat 1 tablespoon margarine and 1 tablespoon oil in frying pan, sauteing breasts quickly and adding more margarine and oil as necessary. Remove breasts as they are browned to shallow casserole in single layer; add scallions and mushrooms to pan drippings and fry to lightly brown. Add bouillon and wine and bring to boil, deglazing pan. Pour over breasts and bake at 350° for about 15 minutes. Garnish with green stems of scallions. Serve over rice or make ahead party dish. Bake at time of serving. Makes 6 servings. May be frozen.

Mrs. Henry J. Nowak, Wife of former Representative (New York)

BARBARA'S CHICKEN CASSEROLE

4 chicken breasts
1 cup sour cream
1 can golden mushroom
    soup
  small can of mushrooms

Put chicken in casserole dish. Mix ingredients and pour over chicken. Cook at 350° for 1¼ hours. Makes 4 servings. May be frozen.

Beth Valentine, Daughter of Representative Tim Valentine, (North Carolina)

> *When freezing game birds, wrap in plastic wrap followed by heavy foil then freezer paper. Remember to date the package.*

CHICKEN FILLETS WITH THREE-COLOR PEPPER SAUCE

6 tablespoons light olive oil, divided
1 medium onion, sliced
1 medium green pepper, cut into thin strips
1 medium red pepper, cut into thin strips
1 medium yellow pepper, cut into thin strips
1 clove garlic, minced
1 cup low sodium chicken broth
¼ cup chopped cilantro
½ teaspoon ground cumin
¼ teaspoon pepper
¼ cup lemon juice
flour
1 pound chicken breast fillets

In large skillet, heat 4 tablespoons olive oil over medium heat. Add onion, peppers and garlic, stirring occasionally, cook 10 minutes. Stir in chicken broth, cilantro, cumin and pepper. Cook 10 minutes longer or until peppers are soft. Add lemon juice. Place mixture in food processor or blender, cover. Process until almost smooth. Remove and keep warm. Lightly coat chicken with flour. In large skillet, heat remaining 2 tablespoons olive oil over medium heat. Add chicken. Cook, turning once, 8 to 10 minutes or until golden brown. Serve with pepper sauce. Makes 4 servings. May be frozen.

Thomas M. Camarda, Son-in-law of former Representative James R. Mann (South Carolina)

EASY CHICKEN AND RICE

½ cup butter or margarine
1 medium size onion, chopped
1 medium size bell pepper, chopped
1 cup uncooked rice
2 cans chicken broth
1 pound raw chicken pieces

Saute onion and bell pepper in butter. Stir in rice and brown the rice with the onion and pepper. Add broth and pour into a 1 quart casserole dish. Add chicken pieces and cook uncovered for 30 to 40 minutes at 350°. Makes 4 servings.

Mrs. Gene Green, Wife of Representative (Texas)

LOUISE'S CHICKEN CASSEROLE

2 cups cooked chicken
⅓ cup chopped onions
  enough margarine for
    sautéing
1 cup chopped celery
½ cup mayonnaise
1 can cream of chicken soup
1 can cream of mushroom
    soup
1 small jar diced pimentos,
    drained
1 cup cooked rice
½ teaspoon salt
  almonds (optional)
½ tablespoon Worcestershire
  bread crumbs or potato
    chips

Saute onions and celery in margarine. Mix with other ingredients. Pour into buttered dish and top with bread crumbs or potato chips. Bake at 350° for 30 to 40 minutes. Makes 6 to 8 servings. May be frozen.

Barbara Harris

Mrs. Claude Harris, Wife of former Representative (Alabama)

YOGURT CHICKEN

4 tablespoons margarine
4 chicken breast halves,
    boneless and skinless
3 tablespoons flour
½ cup chicken bouillon
¾ cup low-fat yogurt
¼ cup white wine
1 teaspoon dry mustard
1 teaspoon salt
½ teaspoon pepper
½ cup sliced mushrooms

Preheat oven at 350°. Melt 2 tablespoons margarine in a shallow pan. Place chicken breasts in pan and bake, uncovered, 30 minutes. Meanwhile, melt remaining margarine in a saucepan, add flour and cook briefly, stirring. Add bouillon, stirring until mixture is thick and smooth. Add yogurt, wine, mustard, salt and pepper, stirring until blended. Remove pan from oven and turn chicken breasts. Cover with mushrooms and sauce. Bake 30 minutes, uncovered. Serve with couscous or rice. Makes 4 servings.

Nancy Hamilton

Mrs. Lee Hamilton, Wife of Representative (Indiana)

CHICKEN À LA SMITH

4 large chicken breasts, cooked, cut in large chunks
2 pounds fresh broccoli (or in season, asparagus)
2 cans cream of chicken soup (10¾ oz., undiluted)
½ cup mayonnaise
2 tablespoons lemon juice
½ teaspoon curry powder

Cook chicken (save broth for cooking rice to accompany this dish). Cook broccoli or asparagus in bite-size pieces until crunchy-tender. Place chicken and broccoli (or asparagus) in shallow baking dish in alternate layers. Mix soup, mayonnaise, lemon juice and curry powder. (Use more curry if you wish, to taste). Pour mixture over chicken, broccoli layers. Bake at 350° until bubbly. Serve over rice. This is our family's favorite chicken dish and it has been for 25 years. Makes 4 servings.

Mary Jo Smith

Mrs. Robert C. Smith, Wife of Senator (New Hampshire)

MABEL'S BAKED CHICKEN BREASTS

8 chicken breast halves, skinned and boned
8 slices Swiss cheese, 4 × 4 inches
1 can cream of chicken soup (thin a bit with milk)
¼ cup dry white wine
1 cup herb seasoned stuffing mix, crushed
¼ cup butter or margarine, melted

Arrange chicken in greased 9″ × 13″ casserole. Top with cheese slices. Combine soup with wine, stirring well. Pour on chicken and cheese. Sprinkle with stuffing mix. Drizzle butter over crumbs. Bake at 350° for 45–55 minutes. Makes 8 servings.

Cynthia L. B. Rice

Mrs. Christopher Rice, Daughter of former Representative Laurie C. Battle (Alabama)

CHICKEN, HAM AND CHEESE BAKE

3 large chicken breasts,
   skinned, boned, halved
   and flattened
6 slices cooked ham
6 slices Swiss cheese
1 cup flour
1 egg, beaten with 2 tablespoons milk
1 cup bread crumbs
8 tablespoons sweet butter
2 cups Mornay sauce
   paprika

Mornay Sauce:
4 tablespoons butter
4 tablespoons flour
½ teaspoon salt
¼ teaspoon white pepper
2 cups milk
¼ cup Gruyere cheese
¼ cup Parmesan cheese
2 tablespoons butter

Arrange ham and cheese on one chicken breast half. Form into a roll and skewer if necessary. Dredge in flour, then egg mixture, then bread crumbs. Melt butter and brown chicken. Arrange in an oven proof dish, cover and bake at 350° for 25 minutes. Pour sauce over when done baking and dust lightly with paprika. Makes 6 servings.

Mornay Sauce: Melt butter, add flour and cook a few minutes. Add milk gradually, stirring constantly, until thick and smooth. You now have Bechamel Sauce. To make Mornay, add ¼ cup (1 oz.) each Gruyere and Parmesan (grated) and 2 tablespoons additional butter to 2 cups hot Bechamel and stir until cheese melts.

Mrs. Barbara Burlison, Member of The Congressional Club

BAKED CHICKEN BREASTS

10 half chicken breasts, boned
2 cups sour cream
1 tablespoon Worcestershire
   sauce
2 teaspoons salt
1 tablespoon lemon juice
½ teaspoon pepper
3 teaspoons celery salt
1½ cups (or more) dry bread
   crumbs
¾ cup butter
   parlsey

Mix Worcestershire, lemon juice, salt, pepper and celery salt with the sour cream in large bowl. Add chicken breasts to sour cream mix. Stir well. Put in the refrigerator overnight. The next day, roll up each breast and then roll breast in bread crumbs. Place on greased shallow baking pan. Return to refrigerator for at least 1 hour. Melt butter, baste breast with ½ of the butter. Bake breast at 325° for 40 minutes. Then baste breasts with the remainder of butter. Return to oven and bake another 30 minutes. Garnish with parsley. Makes 10 servings. May be frozen.

Mrs. Gerald P. Nye, Wife of former Senator (North Dakota)

BESS'S HOT CHICKEN SALAD

2 cups diced cooked chicken
1 cup celery
1 cup cooked rice
¾ cup mayonnaise
1 can sliced water chestnuts, drained
1 can cream of chicken soup, undiluted
1 teaspoon chopped onion
1 teaspoon salt
2 hard boiled eggs (optional)
½ stick oleo, melted
1 cup crushed Corn Chex or Corn Flakes
½ cup slivered almonds

Mix first 9 ingredients together and put in greased casserole. Bake at 350° for 15 minutes and remove from oven. Sprinkle Corn Chex and almonds over casserole and pour melted oleo on top. Return to oven and bake for 30 minutes longer. Makes 6 servings.

Janis N. Battle

Mrs. Laurie Battle, Wife of former Representative (Alabama)

CHICKEN CRESCENT ALMONDINE

3 cups cooked, cubed chicken
1 can cream of chicken soup
1 8 oz. can sliced water chestnuts, drained
1 4 oz. can sliced mushrooms, drained
⅔ cup mayonnaise
½ cup chopped celery
¼ cup chopped onion
½ cup sour cream
1 8 oz. can crescent rolls
½ stick margarine
⅔ cup cheddar cheese, grated
½ cup slivered almonds

Mix first eight ingredients and heat until bubbly (in microwave or saucepan). Pour mixture into ungreased 8″ × 12″ pan. Unroll 1 8 oz. can crescent roll dough into long rectangle. Place dough over hot chicken mixture. Spread shredded cheese over dough. Melt margarine and combine with slivered almonds. Pour over all. Bake at 375° for 25 minutes until golden brown. (You might bake without cheese and almonds until crust forms, then add cheese and almonds and finish baking). Makes 8 servings.

Marian N. Adair

Mrs. E. Ross Adair, Wife of former Representative (Indiana)

CHICKEN DELIGHT

1 chicken bouillon cube
2 chicken breasts with skin
   (4 halves)
1 10¾ oz. can cream of
   chicken soup
1 15 oz. can Lesueur early
   peas with mushrooms
   and pearl onions
1 stick margarine
1 cup buttermilk
1 cup Bisquick

Boil chicken in water with dissolved bouillon cube until well done. Save broth. Chop chicken and spread in bottom of 9″ × 13″ inch Pyrex dish. Mix chicken broth (2 cups) with cream of chicken soup and heat. Combine soup mixture with Lesueur vegetables and pour over chicken. Melt margarine and mix with buttermilk and Bisquick until smooth and pour over chicken combination. Bake at 425° for approximately 40 minutes. Makes 8 servings. May be frozen.

Louise Broyhill

Mrs. James Broyhill, Wife of former Senator (North Carolina)

CHICKEN BREASTS PIQUANT

3 chicken breasts, split and
   skinned
¾ cup rose wine
½ cup soy sauce
¼ cup vegetable oil
2 tablespoons mushroom
   liquid
1 clove garlic, minced
1 teaspoon ginger
½ teaspoon oregano
1 tablespoon brown sugar
1 4 oz. can mushrooms,
   drained, liquid reserved

Arrange chicken breasts in baking dish. Combine all other ingredients except mushrooms and pour over chicken. Cover and bake at 375° for 1½ hours. Add mushrooms last 15 minutes of baking time. If not browned, place under broiler for a few minutes. Makes 6 servings. May be frozen.

Blaine S. Purcell

Blaine S. Purcell, Son of former Representative Graham Purcell (Texas)

CHICKEN BREASTS IN SOUR CREAM SAUCE

4 skinless chicken breast
  halves, bone in or
  boneless
10 to 20 fresh mushrooms,
  sliced
1 can creamy chicken mushroom soup
1 cup sour cream
½ can white wine
  paprika

Place single layer of chicken breasts in casserole. Cover with mushrooms. Mix soup, sour cream and wine. Pour over chicken. Sprinkle with paprika. Bake uncovered at 350° for 1½ hours. Serve over noodles or rice. Makes 4 servings.

Audrey L. Hagen

Mrs. Harold Hagen, Wife of former Representative (Minnesota)

CHICKEN CONTINENTAL

9 pieces of chicken, skinned
¼ cup margarine
1¾ cups water
1 can cream of mushroom
  soup
2½ tablespoons chopped
  onion
2 tablespoons parsley flakes
2 tablespoons celery seed
2 cups minute rice

Brown chicken pieces in margarine. Remove chicken. To margarine and drippings, add water, soup, chopped onion, parsley flakes and celery seed. Bring to a boil and remove from heat. Pour rice in a 9″ × 13″ casserole dish. Pour half of liquid mixture over rice, place chicken pieces on top of rice, and pour remainder of liquid mixture over top of chicken and rice. Cover and bake at 400″ for 40 minutes. Makes 9 servings. May be frozen.

Shirley Barlow

Mrs. Thomas Barlow, Wife of Representative (Kentucky)

> *Pale gravy may be browned by adding a bit of instant coffee straight from the jar, no bitter taste either.*

SHITAKE CHICKEN CASSEROLE

¼ pound margarine or butter
1 cup finely chopped onion
2 cups sliced shitake mush-
　　rooms
1 cup wild rice
3 cups chicken broth
⅛ teaspoon pepper
2 or 3 cups cooked, diced
　　chicken breasts

Melt margarine or butter in skillet. Add onion and cook until soft. Add mushrooms and cook until dark. Place all ingredients except chicken in greased casserole, cover and bake at 325° for 30 minutes. Add chicken and bake another 30 to 45 minutes until rice is tender and liquid absorbed. Makes 6 servings.

Marguerite R. Cederberg

Mrs. Elford Cederberg, Wife of former Representative (Michigan)

CHICKEN ASPARAGUS CASSEROLE

2 14½ oz. cans asparagus
　　spears
6 chicken breasts, cooked
　　and cut in bite size
　　pieces
1 medium onion, chopped
1 4 oz. can sliced mush-
　　rooms, drained
½ cup margarine
2 10¾ oz. cans cream of
　　mushroom soup
¾ cup evaporated milk
1 8 oz. pkg. cheddar cheese,
　　shredded
¼ teaspoon hot sauce
1 teaspoon Accent
2 tablespoons soy sauce
½ teaspoon pepper
2 tablespoons chopped pi-
　　mento
½ cup chopped almonds

Place asparagus in a greased 13″ × 9″ inch pan, cover with chicken. Saute onion and mushrooms in margarine. Add remaining ingredients except almonds. Simmer until cheese melts. Pour sauce over chicken. Sprinkle with almonds. Bake at 350° 35–45 minutes or until bubbly. Serve over hot cooked rice. Makes 6 servings.

Martha H. Gibbons

Mrs. Sam Gibbons, Wife of Representative (Florida)

CHICKEN CASSEROLE

2 cups cooked chicken
2 cups cooked rice
1 cup mayonnaise
2 tablespoons chopped onion
1 teaspoon garlic salt
½ teaspoon white pepper
1 cup chopped celery
1 can cream of chicken soup
1 can water chestnuts, drained and sliced
1 pkg. of dry herb stuffing

Mix all ingredients together and top with the package of dry herb stuffing. Bake at 350° for 30 to 40 minutes. Makes 6 to 8 servings. May be frozen.

Marilyn Burnside Weaver

Mrs. George Weaver, Daughter of former Representative M. G. Burnside (West Virginia)

CREAMY BAKED CHICKEN BREASTS

4 whole chicken breasts, split, skinned and boned
8 (4 × 4 inch) slices Swiss cheese, or grated similar amount
1 10¾ oz. can cream of chicken soup, undiluted
¼ cup dry white wine
1 cup herb-seasoned stuffing mix, crushed
¼ cup butter or margarine, melted

Arrange chicken in a lightly greased (or better yet, Pam sprayed) 13″ × 9″ × 2″ inch baking dish. Top with cheese slices. Combine soup and wine, stirring well. Spoon sauce evenly over chicken, and sprinkle with stuffing mix. Drizzle butter over crumbs. Bake at 350° for 45 to 55 minutes. Makes 6 servings.

Martha H. Gibbons

Mrs. Sam Gibbons, Wife of Representative (Florida)

POPPY SEED CHICKEN

6 chicken breasts
1 4 oz. can mushrooms, drained
1 can cream of chicken soup
1 small carton sour cream
1 cup white wine
½ stick butter
1 cup crumbled Ritz crackers
2 tablespoons poppy seed

Cook chicken and remove bone. Cut into small pieces and put in 2 quart casserole dish. Pour drained mushrooms over chicken. Mix cream of chicken soup with sour cream and white wine, spread over chicken. Melt butter with crackers and poppy seed, sprinkle over soup mixture. Cover and bake at 350° for 30 minutes, or until bubbly. Makes 6 servings. May be frozen.

Luella Rowland

Mrs. J. Roy Rowland, Wife of Representative (Georgia)

ALMOND CHICKEN

6 to 8 boneless, skinless chicken breasts
2 cans chicken with rice soup
1 can cream of mushroom soup
¼ cup melted butter or margarine
½ cup sherry or white wine
1 small pkg. shaved almonds
1 pkg. Uncle Ben's long grain & wild rice (unprepared) with seasoning packet

Place all ingredients in a large, greased baking pan. Be sure wild rice is completely covered with liquid. Cover with foil and bake at 275° for 30 minutes. Remove foil and bake another 2 hours. This recipe can be cut in half. Only bake total of 1½ hours if cut in half. Makes 10 to 12 servings. May be frozen.

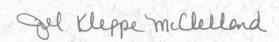

Mrs. Scott McClelland, Daughter of former Representative Thomas Kleppe (North Dakota)

> *CAUTION: Never freeze poultry with the stuffing inside. Stuffing may be frozen separately.*

HERBED CHICKEN IN CASSEROLE

3 large chicken breasts
  salt and pepper
¼ cup butter or margarine
1 can condensed cream of
  chicken soup
¾ cup white cooking wine
1 5 oz. can water chestnuts,
  drained and sliced
1 3 oz. can broiled sliced
  mushrooms, drained
2 tablespoons chopped green
  pepper
¼ teaspoon crushed thyme

Lightly season chicken with salt and pepper, brown slowly in skillet. Arrange browned chicken, skin side up, in baking dish. For the sauce, add soup to drippings in skillet, slowly add wine, stirring until smooth. Add remaining ingredients, heat to boiling. Pour sauce over chicken. Cover with foil and bake at 350° for 25 minutes. Uncover, continue baking 25 to 35 minutes. Serve with hot fluffy rice. Makes 6 servings. May be frozen.

Jennette W Prouty

Mrs. Winston Prouty, Wife of former Senator (Vermont)

SMOTHERED CHICKEN

½ cup all-purpose flour
  salt and pepper to taste
2½ to 3 pound fryer, cut up
1 tablespoon sage
1 tablespoon poultry sea-
  soning
1 cup olive/vegetable oil
1 sliced, medium onion
1 can cream of mushroom
  soup
1½ cups water

Combine flour, seasonings, salt and pepper. Coat chicken with flour mixture. Heat oil in large heavy skillet and brown chicken. Remove chicken. Brown remaining flour mixture in oil until golden brown, stirring constantly. Slowly stir in water and soup. Return chicken to skillet, add onion. Cook and cover over low heat until done (about 25–30 minutes). Makes 4 servings.

Roscoe Dellums

Mrs. Ronald Dellums, Wife of Representative (California)

PAPER BAG BARBECUED CHICKEN

3 tablespoons catsup
2 tablespoons vinegar
1 tablespoon lemon juice
4 tablespoons water
2 tablespoons butter
2 tablespoons Worcestershire
   sauce
3 tablespoons brown sugar
1 teaspoon salt
1 teaspoon dry mustard
1 teaspoon chili powder
1 teaspoon paprika
1 frying chicken, cut up

Combine ingredients for sauce and simmer for 5 minutes. Grease interior of a large paper bag. Salt and pepper a frying chicken. Dip each piece of chicken into the sauce and put it inside the greased bag. Pour remaining sauce over the chicken in the bag. Tie end of bag with string and place in shallow pan. Bake for 2 hours at 350°. Makes 4 servings.

Dorothy F. Mathews

Mrs. Patrick Mathews, Daughter of former Representative Claude Fuller (Arkansas)

CASHEW CHICKEN

¼ cup soy sauce
1 cup unsalted raw cashews
⅛ cup cooking sherry
½ cup chicken stock
¼ cup Hoisin sauce
2 tablespoons peanut oil
2 tablespoons cornstarch
3 chicken breasts, diced
3 celery stalks, chopped
1 can sliced water chestnuts
2 cups snow peas
1 cup bean sprouts

Mix first 4 ingredients to form marinade. Pour over chicken and let stand 30 minutes. Pour 2 tablespoons peanut oil into wok or large frying pan and stir-fry chicken until meat turns white, about 5 minutes. Pour in celery and stir until tender-crisp. Add water chestnuts, bean sprouts and snow peas. Cook 3 minutes. Add cashews and chicken stock. Simmer 3 minutes. Serve over rice or Chinese noodles. Makes 6 servings.

Lenora Moeller

Mrs. Walter Moeller, Wife of former Representative (Ohio)

MEGHAN'S FAVORITE STIR-FRY WITH PEANUT SAUCE

Sauce:
- 5 tablespoons peanut butter
- 2 tablespoons soy sauce
- 4 tablespoons water (+/− use water to thin sauce)
- 2 tablespoons brown sugar
- 2 tablespoons oriental sesame oil
- $\frac{1}{2}$ teaspoon crushed red pepper flakes (omit when serving children)

Ingredients for Wok:
- 1 tablespoon peanut oil
- 1 pound skinless boned chicken breast, cut into 3" × $\frac{1}{2}$" strips
- 1 clove garlic, finely chopped
- 1 teaspoon fresh ginger, finely chopped
- 4 green onions, cut into 1 inch pieces
- 1 medium size red pepper, cored, seeded and cut into $\frac{1}{4}$ inch wide strips

Combine peanut butter, soy, water, brown sugar, sesame oil and red pepper flakes in container of electric blender or food processor. Whirl to mix. Heat peanut oil in large wok or nonstick skillet over high heat until hot. Add chicken and stir-fry until browned, 4 minutes. Add garlic, ginger, green onion and red pepper. Reduce heat to medium high and stir-fry 3 minutes. Add peanut butter mixture to wok. Cook 1 minute, stirring. Serve over rice. Makes 4 servings.

Mrs. Daniel Donovan, Daughter of Representative Al Swift (Washington)

STORE IT RIGHT! In the refrigerator, remove giblets and wrap and store them separately. Store poultry loosely wrapped in the coldest part of the refrigerator. To freeze, wrap in a moisture/vapor-proof wrap. Label and date it.

BOB'S PORK OR CHICKEN SATAY WITH PEANUT SAUCE

1 pound boneless, skinless chicken breast or lean pork cut into strips

10 inch long wooden skewers

Satay marinade:

½ cup soy sauce

¼ cup firmly packed brown sugar

2 tablespoons lemon juice

¼ cup vegetable oil

1 teaspoon ground ginger

½ teaspoon garlic powder

Peanut Sauce:

½ cup crushed dry roasted peanuts

1 cup peanut butter

½ cup light soy sauce

dash of Tabasco and garlic powder

2 tablespoons brown sugar

1 tablespoon lemon juice

½ cup yellow onion rings

Marinade: Combine all ingredients in shallow bowl. Mix well. Add chicken or pork evenly and marinate several hours or over night in refrigerator. After marinating, thread chicken strips onto skewers. Grill on barbeque or broil in the oven. Serve with peanut sauce and grilled veggies such as onions, mushrooms, zucchini and cherry tomatoes.

Peanut Sauce: Saute onions. Add peanut butter and other ingredients, cook until smooth. Serve on or along side grilled chicken or pork.

Soak wooden skewers in water to prevent burning.

Bob Livingston, Representative (Louisiana)

Tart or sweet and sour fruit is best garnish or accompaniment for game.

CHINESE CHICKEN

2 half chicken breasts, boned
   and cut in strips
2 tablespoons soy sauce
1 tablespoon sherry wine
1 tablespoon corn starch
2 tablespoons water

Sauce:
2 tablespoons oyster sauce
2 tablespoons water
1 tablespoon sugar

Marinate first 5 ingredients for 3–4 hours or overnight. Heat 2 tablespoons olive oil in pan. Cook chicken 2–3 minutes. Mix sauce and add to chicken. Cook 1 minute. Add any remaining marinade, cover, cook 6 minutes over medium heat. Makes 2 servings. May be frozen.

Mrs. Charles Vanik, Wife of former Representative (Ohio)

SPICED ALMOND CHICKEN

2 chicken breasts, skinned,
   boned and diced
1/2 teaspoon salt
1 clove garlic, mashed
1/2 cup sauterne
2 tablespoons peanut oil
1 teaspoon hot chili powder
1 cup whole blanched almonds
1 tablespoon soy sauce
1/2 teaspoon sugar
1/4 teaspoon pepper
1 cup diced carrots
1 cup diced green pepper

Marinate chicken in garlic, salt and wine for 4 hours before cooking. Place oil in frying pan. Add chili powder and chicken. Stir continuously for about 5 minutes. Add almonds, carrots, soy sauce and sugar. Add 1/2 cup water, stir, cover and cook at high heat for 5 minutes. Reduce heat, add green pepper. Stir for 2 minutes. Remove and serve. Makes 6 to 8 servings.

Mrs. Lloyd Meeds, Wife of former Representative (Washington)

CHICKEN DELIGHT

6 single, boned and skinned chicken breasts
1 small can mandarin oranges
flour, salt, pepper, garlic powder
1/2 cup lemon juice
2 tablespoons honey
2 tablespoons soy sauce
1/2 teaspoon ginger
2 tablespoons oil
2 tablespoons olive oil

Mix flour, salt, pepper and garlic powder in a small bag and coat chicken, brown in hot oils. Mix juice from oranges and all other ingredients together. Pour over chicken and simmer 1 hour or until chicken is very tender. Add oranges last 5 minutes of cooking. Makes 6 servings.

Mrs. Paul Wellstone, Wife of Senator (Minnesota)

CHINESE CHICKEN CASSEROLE

3 cups cooked chicken, cut in large chunks
2 teaspoons lemon juice
1 tablespoon soy sauce
1/4 cup chopped green onions
1 cup chopped celery
1 5 oz. can water chestnuts, drained and sliced
1/2 pound fresh bean sprouts (or 1 pound can)
1/2 teaspoon salt
1 cup mayonnaise
1/2 cup chow mein noodles (topping)
slivered almonds (topping, optional)

Sprinkle chicken with lemon juice and soy sauce. Cover and chill 2 hours or longer. Add green onions, celery, water chestnuts, washed and drained bean sprouts, salt (pepper), and mayonnaise. Mix lightly but thoroughly. Turn into greased 1 1/2 quart casserole. Sprinkle noodles (and slivered almonds) on top. Bake at 350° for 25 to 30 minutes. Makes 6 servings.

Mrs. Hamer Budge, Wife of former Representative (Idaho)

SWEET AND SOUR CHICKEN

4 chicken breasts, skinless
1 medium bottle of Catalina dressing
1 medium jar of peach preserves
½ packet French onion soup mix

Place chicken breasts on bottom of dish. Mix other ingredients and pour over chicken. Cook in covered dish for 45 minutes at 350°. Makes 4 servings.

Johnette Hant McCrery

Mrs. Jim McCrery, Wife of Representative (Louisiana)

LEMON CHICKEN

3 pounds boneless chicken breasts
1 tablespoon sherry
1 tablespoon soy sauce
2 eggs
¼ cup cornstarch
½ teaspoon baking powder
2 cups vegetable oil
⅓ cup sugar
1 tablespoon cornstarch
1 cup chicken broth
1 tablespoon lemon juice
2 tablespoons vegetable oil
1 lemon, thinly sliced

Combine chicken with sherry and soy sauce. Marinate for 15 minutes. Beat eggs, cornstarch, and baking powder to form a smooth batter. Heat oil to 350°. Coat chicken with batter and fry until brown. Remove from pan and cut into 1½ inch wide pieces and arrange on a serving dish. Put in warm oven. Combine sugar, 1 tablespoon cornstarch, broth and lemon juice. Heat remaining oil. Stir-fry the lemon slices for 30 seconds. Slowly stir in cornstarch mixture. Cook, stirring constantly until sauce is clear. Pour over chicken and serve immediately. Makes 6 servings.

Elizabeth Rhodes Reich

Mrs. Frank Reich, Daughter of former Representative John J. Rhodes (Arizona)

> *You can clean darkened aluminum pans easily by boiling in them two teaspoons of cream of tartar mixed in a quart of water. Ten minutes will do it.*

CRUNCHY CHICKEN CASSEROLE

3 cups chopped, cooked
   chicken
½ cup slivered almonds
1 can sliced water chestnuts
1 can undiluted cream of
   mushroom soup
1 small jar red pimentos
¼ teaspoon salt
⅛ teaspoon paprika
1 tablespoon chopped
   parsley
1 can french fried onion
   rings
½ cup shredded cheddar
   cheese

Combine all ingredients except cheese and onion rings. Pour into greased 1½ quart casserole. Sprinkle cheese and onion rings over top. Bake in preheated 350° for 30 minutes.

Mrs. John S. Cross, Daughter of former Representative Claude Fuller (Arkansas)

ITALIAN CHICKEN BREASTS

3 whole boned and skinned
   chicken breasts, cut in
   half
⅓ cup all-purpose flour
½ teaspoon salt
⅛ teaspoon white pepper
⅛ teaspoon ground nutmeg
⅛ teaspoon marjoram leaves
1 egg, beaten with 1 tablespoon water
⅓ cup fine dry bread crumbs
¼ cup freshly grated Parmesan cheese
¼ cup butter or margarine
2 tablespoons olive oil

Place chicken breasts, one at a time, between pieces of wax paper or plastic warp and pound with flat side of a mallet until about ¼ inch thick. Mix flour, salt, pepper, nutmeg and marjoram in a shallow dish. Have egg mixture ready in a second shallow dish. Mix crumbs and cheese in a third. Coat chicken breasts lightly with flour mixture, then with egg, and finally with crumb mixture. In a wide frying pan over medium-high heat, place butter and oil. When butter is melted, add chicken breasts, without crowding and cook, turning once until golden brown on each side. Serve with lemon wedges. Makes 6 servings.

Mrs. Guy Vander Jagt, Wife of former Representative (Michigan)

CHICKEN SCARPARIELLO A LA DOLCE VITA

6 chicken breasts, split in 2,
    skinned and boned
  chicken thighs and legs,
    skinned and boned
  chicken broth
  olive oil
  flour
2 to 4 cloves garlic, minced
    fine
  red wine vinegar
1 tablespoon butter
  dry sauterne wine
  fresh parsley, minced fine
  salt
  pepper

Cut skinned and boned chicken into 3-inch pieces. Salt and pepper chicken pieces and flour lightly. In a large skillet, heat a small amount of olive oil. Saute chicken until golden brown. Remove excess oil. Add 2–4 cloves garlic, minced fine. Cook until garlic is brown. Add 1 tablespoon red wine vinegar for every 7 pieces of chicken. Add enough chicken broth to cover chicken halfway. Cover and cook until done (about 15 minutes). The liquid should be cooked down when chicken is done. Then, add 1 tablespoon butter, salt and pepper to taste, minced fresh parsley and dry sauterne wine (½ oz. per 7 pieces of chicken). Figure approximately 7 pieces per serving.

Mrs. Richard Bryan, Wife of Senator (Nevada)

CHICKEN CACCIATORE

1 2½ pound fryer, cut up
½ cup flour
2 teaspoons salt
¼ teaspoon pepper
¼ cup oil
2 onions, chopped
1 16 oz. can chopped
    tomatoes
1 8 oz. can tomato sauce
2 cloves garlic, minced
1 teaspoon oregano
1 teaspoon celery seed

Dredge chicken in flour, salt and pepper and brown in oil. Remove chicken from oil and cook onions until soft. Add rest of ingredients and return chicken to pan. Simmer for 40 minutes, turning chicken occasionally. Serve over hot egg noodles. Makes 4 servings. May be frozen.

Mrs. Barbara Burlison, Member of The Congressional Club

CHICKEN STRATA

8 slices bread, buttered
2 cups cooked, diced
  chicken
1/2 cup chopped onion
1/2 cup chopped celery
1/2 cup chopped green pepper
3/4 teaspoon salt, dash of
  pepper
1/4 cup mayonnaise
2 eggs, beaten
1 1/2 cups milk
1 can mushroom soup
1/2 cup shredded cheese

Butter bread and cut in cubes. Place half in 9″ × 13″ greased baking dish. Combine chicken, onion, peppers, celery, seasonings and mayonnaise. Spoon mixture over the bread cubes. Top with rest of bread cubes. Mix together milk, eggs and soup, pour this over the top of casserole. Top with cheese. Chill in refrigerator at least 1 hour or overnight. Bake for 50 minutes at 325°. Makes 10 to 12 servings. May be frozen.

Mrs. Frank Wolf, Wife of Representative (Virginia)

PESTO CHICKEN

Pesto:
1 cup fresh basil leaves
1/2 cup olive oil
1 tablespoon pine nuts
1/3 cup grated Parmesan
  cheese
1/2 teaspoon salt

Chicken:
2 whole chicken breasts,
  boned and skinned
6 to 8 slices prosciutto
5 to 6 tablespoons pesto
2/3 cup ricotta cheese
1/3 cup pine nuts
3 tablespoons olive oil
2 tablespoons butter
  salt and pepper
1 1/2 cups white wine

Combine all pesto ingredients in a blender or food processor. Process and set aside. Lay chicken breasts flat and pound. Place prosciutto slices on top. In small bowl, combine pesto, ricotta and pine nuts. Spread on prosciutto. Roll up chicken breasts and secure with toothpicks. Place in baking dish, seam side down. Rub chicken with olive oil and dot with butter. Sprinkle with salt and pepper. Pour wine over chicken and bake at 375° for 25 minutes. Makes 4 servings. May be frozen.

Mrs. Bill Archer, Wife of Representative (Texas)

GREEN PEPPERCORN STUFFED CHICKEN

50 chicken breasts, boned and
    skinned
4 pounds filo dough
3/4 stick butter, melted

For stuffing:
5 pounds frozen spinach,
    thawed and drained
1/2 pound Swiss cheese,
    shredded
1 1/2 pounds ricotta cheese
2 tablespoons oil
2 large onions, chopped
1 dozen eggs, hard boiled
    and finely chopped
4 large cloves garlic, minced
4 1/2 tablespoons green pepper-
    corns, crushed in
    blender or processor
4 teaspoons salt

For sauce:
12 tablespoons butter or mar-
    garine
12 tablespoons all-purpose
    flour
12 tablespoons dry Madeira
    wine
6 cups chicken broth
4 tablespoons tomato paste
2 cups sour cream
2 cups chopped chives or
    green onion tops
    salt and white pepper to
    taste

Pound chicken breasts to 1/4 inch thick. Season with salt and pepper, set aside. Saute garlic and onions in oil until tender, remove from heat. Add the remaining stuffing ingredients, mix thoroughly until the peppercorns are evenly distributed. May be refrigerated overnight. Spread 1/3 cup of stuffing over each breast. Roll up jelly roll fashion. Cut filo dough into 3 1/2 inch strips, keep filo under a damp cloth to avoid drying out. While using 2 strips of filo, place 1 chicken at the end of the strips and roll. Place on a rimmed baking sheet with the seam side down. Brush tops with butter. Repeat. May be refrigerated overnight or frozen for up to 2 weeks. In a medium saucepan, melt butter. Add flour and cook, stirring until mixture is golden. Remove from heat and whisk in Madiera and chicken broth. Return to heat and cook until mixture boils and thickens. In a small bowl mix together tomato paste and sour cream. Add a little of the hot sauce to the bowl, mix and pour into saucepan. Stir in chives and green onions, salt and pepper to taste. Sauce will thicken as it cools, while reheating add Madiera or cream to thin. Bake chicken (room temperature) at 400° for 25–30 minutes. To serve, drizzle sauce over top. Pass the remaining. Makes 50 servings. May be frozen.

The Congressional Club

CORNBREAD DRESSING

2 loaves bread
1 large pan cornbread
2 dozen eggs
1 cup cooked rice
1 cup minced onions
2 cups chopped celery
2 tablespoons poultry seasoning
5 quarts rich stock
1 pound oleo
   salt and pepper to taste
   sage to taste

Combine all of above and spread in 2-3 quart casserole dishes. Amount of ingredients may vary in either direction. Heat at 350° until slightly brown on top, approximately 25 minutes. Makes 16 servings. May be frozen.

Janice H DeMeritte

Mrs. Fred DeMeritte, Daughter of former Associate Justice of the Supreme Court Hugo L. Black

TURKEY STUFFING

4 pounds pork sausage (bulk
   or remove sausage from
   casing)
4 medium onions
4 medium white potatoes
1 bunch of celery
2 pkgs of carrots
4 medium yams
2 pounds of mushrooms
4 medium Cortland apples
   (peeled and diced)
1 dozen eggs
1½ pounds chestnuts

Stuffing for 20 pound turkey, measurements are approximate. Clean and dice all vegetables and remove sausage from casing or use bulk sausage. Pan fry sausage and add diced vegetables. Pepper to taste, no salt. Add diced apples. Let mixture cool. After it has cooled, blend in beaten eggs and fold into vegetables. Stuff turkey and roast as directed.

Matilda Cuomo

Mrs. Mario Cuomo, Wife of Governor (New York)

SAGE SAUSAGE DRESSING

1 stick butter
1 cup chopped onions
½ cup chopped celery
6 cups cubed bread
1 pound sage sausage (room
  temperature)
1 cup chopped walnuts
¼ cup chopped parsley
2 eggs, beaten
1 teaspoon salt
½ teaspoon thyme
½ teaspoon ground pepper

Melt butter in medium skillet over medium-high heat. Add onions and celery. Saute until softened. Add to bread cubes in large bowl. Stir in rest of ingredients and blend well. Stuff into poultry of choice and bake per its instructions.

William Thomas, Representative (California)

> *If the food is too sharp, a teaspoon of sugar will soften the taste.*

ORANGE STUFFING

2 cups finely diced celery
¼ cup butter, melted
3 cups toasted bread cubes
  (about 5 slices cut in ½-
  inch cubes)
1 teaspoon grated orange
  peel
⅔ cup diced orange sections
  (2 medium oranges)
½ teaspoon salt
½ teaspoon poultry seasoning
1 beaten egg

Cook celery in butter till tender but not brown. Add remaining ingredients and dash pepper; toss lightly. Makes enough stuffing for a 5-pound duckling.

The Congressional Club

OYSTER STUFFING

1 bay leaf
½ cup chopped celery
½ cup chopped onion
¼ cup butter
6 cups dry bread cubes
1 tablespoon snipped parsley
2 beaten eggs
1 pint raw oysters, chopped
1 teaspoon poultry seasoning
1 teaspoon salt
  dash of pepper
  milk

Cook bay leaf, celery and onion in butter until tender. Discard bay leaf. Add bread cubes and parsley to butter mixture; mix thoroughly. Add eggs, oysters, poultry seasoning, and salt and pepper. Add milk to oyster liquor to make ¼ to ½ cup; add enough liquid to stuffing to moisten. Makes enough stuffing for a 10-pound turkey.

The Congressional Club

NOTES

NOTES

Barbara Pierce Bush
1989–1993

With admiration and best wishes to my
friends and fellow member of the Congressional Club
Barbara Bush

Barbara Pierce Bush

Gracious, warm and witty are all very apt descriptions of Barbara Bush. Known for her ability to put people at ease, she brought a sense of home, family and tradition to the White House.

Early in her tenure, Mrs. Bush announced that she would not be involved with controversial issues, but rather would focus on family and volunteer work. By choosing this route, she was able successfully to project her image as an involved, concerned humanitarian.

Long an advocate of universal literacy, Mrs. Bush continues to be devoted to this cause and is honorary chairman of the Barbara Bush Foundation for Family Literacy. Her belief in volunteerism is also exemplified by her work with such causes as the homeless, AIDS, the elderly and school volunteer programs.

Foundation for Family Literacy

MEATS

BEEF COOKED WITH PEEL OF MANDARIN ORANGE

1⅓ pounds beef tenderloin
    slices, ⅛ inch thick
½ cup Chinese rice wine
½ ounce soy sauce
6 ounces corn oil
12 ounces chicken broth
4 dried aniseed buds
4 scallions, chopped
½ ounce fresh ginger, minced
    peel of 3 mandarin
    oranges, thinly sliced
4 shakes powdered cloves
¼ pound sugar
¼ cup vinegar
5 dried hot red peppers
1 tablespoon salt
½ tablespoon spice powder

Coat beef with rice wine and soy sauce. Cook in hot oil in a heavy frying pan until all water evaporates from beef. Add chicken broth, aniseed buds, ½ of the scallions, ½ of the ginger, orange peel, powdered cloves, sugar, vinegar and red peppers. Cover and simmer ½ hour. Just before serving add salt, spice powder, and remaining scallions and ginger. Red peppers may be removed. Serve hot or cold. May be frozen. Makes 4 to 6 servings.

Barbara Bush

Mrs. George Bush, Wife of former President of the United States
Reprinted from the 1976 Congressional Club Cookbook, Ninth Edition

BARBEQUED BRISKET

4 to 5 pound boneless beef
    brisket
  onion salt to taste
  garlic salt to taste
  celery salt to taste
3 ozs. liquid smoke
2 teaspoons Worcestershire
    sauce
1 cup brown sugar
½ cup lemon juice
1 cup bottled barbeque
    sauce

Trim brisket of 75% fat. Sprinkle with onion, garlic, and celery salt to taste. Pour on the 3 ozs. of liquid smoke. Wrap in foil and marinate overnight in refrigerate fat side up. Next day, open foil and add 2 teaspoons Worcestershire sauce. Wrap completely and put in shallow pan. Bake 4–5 hours at 275°. Remove from oven. Open a corner of foil and pour out all liquid and fat into saucepan. Cool brisket and slice across the grain in thin slices. May be wrapped and frozen or stored overnight. Skim fat off liquid and simmer to reduce amount of liquid. In shallow pan, spread meat with brown sugar, lemon juice and barbeque sauce combined. Bake 1 hour at 350°. Baste with hot liquid. Pour all drippings into liquid and serve with meat. Makes 8 servings. May be frozen.

Barbara L. Battle

Mrs. L. Hunt Battle, Daughter-in-law of former Representative Laurie C. Battle (Alabama)

And remember the first rule of carving . . . *"Cut across the grain"* If you cut with the grain, long meat fibers give a stringy texture to the slice. Steaks are the exception.

JIMMY OWEN, JR. BAR-B-QUE BRISKET

10 pounds charcoal
5 or 6 hickory blocks
1 large untrimmed beef brisket (do not trim fat)
Lea & Perrins sauce
Tony Chachere's seasoning
or its equivalent
salt and black pepper
heavy aluminum foil

Bar-B-Que Sauce:
1¼ cup of catsup
½ cup of Lea & Perrins sauce
2 heaping tablespoons
brown sugar
4 tablespoons meat drippings
1 teaspoon Tabasco sauce
juice of 2 lemons
½ cup of water

Put charcoal on one end of a closed top Bar-B-Que pit or smoker so the brisket will not be directly over the flame. A water pan baffle will have the same effect. Light it now. Put 5 or 6 hickory blocks in water to soak. Pour a liberal amount of Lea & Perrins sauce on brisket and season well with Tony's seasoning, salt and black pepper on all sides. When the charcoal fire is real hot, put the hickory blocks on the coals and place the brisket fat side up on the opposite side of the grill from the fire. Close the top and let cook for 4 to 5 hours at approximately 400°. Remove brisket and wrap tightly in heavy aluminum foil, seal well. Place in oven fat side up 220° and leave for 12 to 14 hours. Save drippings. When ready to serve, cut with a sharp knife or an electric knife. The brisket will be so tender that a dull knife will tend to tear it. If you want to reheat it, cover tightly and put in the oven at 220° again for about an hour. This gets better with age. Simmer bar-b-que sauce ingredients in covered saucepan for 1 hour. Stir occasionally, serve this on the side.

Leslie Owen Hayes

Mrs. Jimmy Hayes, Wife of Representative (Louisiana)

> *When broiling or barbecuing meat, slash the fat to prevent curling.*

BEER BRISKET

3 or 4 pound beef brisket
salt
pepper
1 onion, sliced
¼ cup chili sauce
2 tablespoons brown sugar
1 clove of garlic, minced or
    garlic powder
1 12 oz. can beer
½ cup water
2 tablespoons flour

Trim excess fat from brisket (important), season with salt and pepper and place in 9″ × 13″ baking dish, cover with onion slices. In bowl, combine chili sauce, brown sugar, garlic and beer, pour over meat. Cover tightly with foil. Bake at 350° for 3½ hours. Uncover and bake 30 minutes more, basting occasionally. Remove meat to platter. Skim off excess fat from drippings, measure liquid and add water to make 1 cup. Blend flour and ½ cup water, combine with drippings in saucepan. Cook, stirring constantly, over medium heat until thickened and bubbly. Cut meat across grain, pass beer gravy. Makes 8 to 10 servings. May be frozen.

Martha Jane Shriver

Mrs. Garner Shriver, Wife of former Representative (Kansas)

JIM'S IOWA FAIR PRIZE BRISKET

3 or 4 pound beef brisket

Marinade:
¼ cup lemon juice
½ cup soy sauce
3 tablespoons liquid smoke
¼ cup red wine

Barbecue Sauce:
¼ teaspoon pepper
1½ teaspoon salt
½ cup catsup
¼ cup vinegar
½ cup chopped onion or 2 ta-
    blespoons onion flakes
1 tablespoon Worcestershire
    powder or liquid
1½ teaspoon liquid smoke

Rub brisket with salt, pepper, Worcestershire and paprika. Place brisket in the marinade in a plastic bag for 24 to 48 hours. Grill brisket, basting with barbecue sauce, for 4 hours or 1 hour per pound. Slice thin, crosswise and serve. Makes 10 to 12 servings. May be frozen.

Jim Lightfoot

Jim Lightfoot, Representative (Iowa)

CHINESE FLANK STEAK

1 good sized flank steak, sliced thin
1 bunch green onions (or more) into 2 inch slices
4 cloves garlic, crushed
½ cup oil

Fry flank steak quickly in hot oil using an up and out frying technique, takes only a short time. Remove from pan and stir fry green onions and garlic in remaining oil for a minute. Return flank steak to pan. Add a shot of sherry, some light soy sauce, and lots and lots of freshly ground pepper. Serve on rice or be adventurous and try frying a section of molded noodles in small amount of hot oil with flat skillet. It makes a crispy bed for your flank steak.

Mrs. Bob Livingston, Wife of Representative (Louisiana)

STUFFED FLANK STEAK

1 flank steak
   sliced sharp cheddar cheese
1 can whole green chilies
   liquid oil
   Lawry's seasoning salt
   garlic powder
   salt
   pepper

Cut a pocket in the flank steak (lengthwise). Do not pierce sides, If sides are pierced, close with toothpicks prior to stuffing. Open and spread flat the chilies. Layer chilies and cheese (amount will depend on size of pocket) and slide into pocket. Close opening with wooden skewer or tooth-picks. Brush steak on both sides with oil. Generously sprinkle seasoning salt, garlic, pepper and salt on both sides. Put steak in plastic bag and let flavors blend for several hours. Broil or BBQ 6 minutes per side for rare. Let the cooked steak stand a few minutes so the melted cheese inside can thicken to ease in the slicing. Slice on the diagonal and serve.

Thomas H. Rhodes, Son of former Representative John J. Rhodes (Arizona)

HANK'S FLANK STEAK

juice of 1 lemon
½ cup soy sauce
¼ cup seasoned rice vinegar
1 tablespoon vegetable oil
2 tablespoons Worcestershire
1 large clove garlic, sliced
½ teaspoon pepper
dash Tabasco
chopped green onion
chives
fresh ginger
2 pound flank steak

Mix all ingredients in the pan in which the meat will be marinated. Marinate flank steak for 2-12 hours, turning occasionally. Broil over hot coals for 5 minutes on each side. Slice on the diagonal across the grain of the meat. Makes 4 servings.

Nan Brown

Mrs. Hank Brown, Wife of Senator (Colorado)

CHUCK WAGON PEPPER STEAK

1 3 pound top round steak, 2 inches thick
2 teaspoons unseasoned meat tenderizer
2 tablespoons minced onion
2 teaspoons thyme
1 teaspoon marjoram
1 bay leaf, crushed
1 cup wine vinegar
½ cup oil
3 tablespoons lemon juice
coarsely ground black pepper to taste

Sprinkle steak evenly on both sides with meat tenderizer. Combine onion, thyme, marjoram, bay leaf, vinegar, oil and lemon juice in small bowl, mix well. Pierce steak with fork. Place in shallow baking dish. Pour marinade over steak. Marinate for 1 to 3 hours, turning steak every half hour. Remove steak from marinade, drain. Sprinkle both sides generously with pepper, pound pepper into steak. Grill 6 inches above hot coals for 20 minutes per side. Slice ¼ inch thick. Makes 4 servings.

Joan Allard

Mrs. Wayne Allard, Wife of Representative (Colorado)

PEPPER STEAK

2 pounds round steak
1 clove garlic, crushed
½ teaspoon salt
1/16 teaspoon pepper
¼ teaspoon ginger
¼ teaspoon sugar
½ cup water
¼ cup soy sauce
2 green peppers, sliced
1 can drained bean sprouts
1 medium onion, sliced
4 medium tomatoes, quartered
1 tablespoon cornstarch

Cut beef into strips and brown on all sides. Add garlic, salt, pepper, ginger and sugar. Cover and cook on low heat for 20 minutes. Move meat to side, add soy sauce, green pepper, bean sprouts and onion. Cook covered, 5 minutes. Move food away from center of skillet. Add tomatoes and cook 5 minutes longer. Make a paste of cornstarch and water, add to hot mixture. Stir gently and cook until thickened. Makes 10 servings. May be frozen.

Mrs. Conrad Burns, Wife of Senator (Montana)

LOUISIANA GRILLADES AND GRITS

2½ pounds round steak
salt, pepper or Tony Chachere's creole seasoning
½ cup flour
3 tablespoons vegetable oil
3 tablespoons vermouth
2 large onions, coarsely chopped
1 large green bell pepper, coarsely chopped
½ cup coarsely chopped celery
3 cloves garlic, minced
2 cups of water
grits

Pound the steak and cut into 2″ × 3″ pieces and season with salt and pepper or creole seasoning. Dredge meat in flour and shake off the excess. In a heavy skillet, heat oil and brown meat. Remove meat from skillet and set aside. Pour off remaining fat in skillet and add vermouth. Add onions, green bell pepper, celery and garlic. Cook for about 5 minutes, stirring frequently, or until the vegetables are tender. Stir in water and bring to a boil. Return meat to pan and reduce heat to low, cover the skillet, and simmer for about 1 hour or until meat is tender and gravy has been reduced to a thick sauce. Adjust seasonings. Cook grits according to package directions. Mound grits on warm plates and ladle grillades and gravy over grits. Makes 6 servings.

Mrs. John Breaux, Wife of Senator (Louisiana)

VEGETARIAN CHILI

¾ cup chopped onions
2 cloves garlic, minced
2 tablespoons (or less) olive oil
2 tablespoons chili powder
¼ teaspoon basil
¼ teaspoon oregano
¼ teaspoon cumin
2 cups finely chopped zucchini
1 cup finely chopped carrots
1 28 oz. can tomatoes and 1 small (14½ oz.) can tomatoes, drained and chopped
1 15 oz. can kidney beans, undrained
2 15 oz. cans kidney beans, drained and rinsed
chopped onions, tomatoes, lettuce, green pepper to garnish (optional)

In a large pot, saute onion and garlic in oil until soft. Mix in chili powder, basil, oregano and cumin. Stir in zucchini and carrots, cook 1 minute. Stir in chopped tomatoes and beans and bring to a boil. Then simmer for 30–45 minutes. Serve in bowls and top with garnishes, if desired. Makes 8 servings. May be frozen.

Dan Glickman, Representative (Kansas)

CORNISH PASTIES

Pastry:
- 3 cups flour
- 1 teaspoon baking powder
- ½ teaspoon salt
- 1 cup shortening
- ½ cup cold water

Filling:
- 4 large potatoes
- 2 large onions
- ½ cup chopped parsley
  salt and pepper
- 2 tablespoons butter
- 1 pound round steak

Sift flour, baking powder and salt together. Cut in shortening. Add water, mixing well. Divide dough into 6 pieces. Roll out each section so that it is thin, round and the size of a pie pan. Put a ⅙th of the potato and onion mixture in the center of the dough, keeping it within an inch of the edge. Add ⅙th of the meat. Season with salt and pepper and dot with butter. Fold top half of pastie over the filling crimping edges together and slitting the top of each. Place two pasties in each pie pan. Bake at 400° for 30 minutes. Reduce heat to 350° and bake 30 minutes more. Makes 6 servings. May be frozen.

Carol Williams

Mrs. Pat Williams, Wife of Representative (Montana)

For a juicier hamburger add cold water to the beef before grilling (½ cup to 1 pound of meat).

SPICY CHILI

2 pounds ground beef
¾ cup chopped green pepper
1 cup chopped onion
¾ cup chopped celery
2 cloves minced garlic
2 19 oz. cans kidney beans,
   drained
2 8 oz. cans tomato sauce
1 6 oz. can tomato paste
1 cup water
2 16 oz. cans tomatoes
1 4 oz. can peeled and
   chopped green chilies
1 tablespoon plus 1 teaspoon
   chili powder
2 teaspoons ground cumin
½ teaspoon dried whole basil
2 teaspoons oregano
1 bay leaf
2 teaspoons sugar substitute
¼ teaspoon pepper
¼ teaspoon hot sauce
¼ teaspoon paprika
   shredded cheddar cheese
   corn chips

Combine first 5 ingredients in large pot. Cook over medium heat on top of stove until meat is brown. Drain. Add remaining ingredients except cheese and chips. Reduce heat. Cover and simmer 1 hour, stirring often. Serve with cheese and chips. Makes 6 servings. May be frozen.

Martha Mills Dixon

Mrs. David Jack Dixon, Daughter of former Representative Wilbur D. Mills (Arkansas)

CRACKERJACK GEORGIA CHILI

5 large vadalia onions, chopped
5 pounds top round beef
2 pounds pork tenderloin
6 ozs. chili powder OR 3 ozs. Hot Texas
3 tablespoons salt
1 tablespoon pepper
½ teaspoon ground red pepper
2 28 oz. cans whole tomatoes
1 medium can tomato paste
1 teaspoon Tabasco
2 tablespoons minced garlic
2 tablespoons brown sugar
6 tablespoons white vinegar
⅓ cup canola oil

Chop onions and set aside. Remove fat and gristle from beef. Cut half of the beef into chunks of about ½ inch. Coarse grind the other half. Set aside. Cut the pork tenderloin into chunks of about ½ inch. Set aside. Mix the chili powder and other dry ingredients in a bowl. Set aside. Mix the whole tomatoes with the tomato paste, cutting the whole tomatoes so that the juice mixes with the paste. Stir in the garlic and Tabasco, set aside. Mix the brown sugar with the vinegar. Set aside. Into an 8 quart pot, pour vegetable oil. On medium-high heat, bring to smoking point. Add onions and stir continuously for about 12–15 minutes. Do not brown the onions. Add all of the meat, stir frequently for another 15 minutes or until the onions and meat are at a good simmer in their own juices. Add the chili powder with the other dry ingredients and stir frequently for another 10 minutes. Add the tomatoes with tomato paste and all other ingredients. Reduce heat to maintain simmer for about 2 hours. Stir frequently to prevent scorching. Add a little boiling water if chili becomes too thick. If beans are desired, heat and serve separately or drain and add to chili about 20 minutes before serving. Serve chili plain or over rice or pasta. Makes 45 servings. May be frozen.

Colleen Nunn

Mrs. Sam Nunn, Wife of Senator (Georgia)

HEARTLAND CHILI

6 tablespoons butter, margarine or oil
6 medium onions, chopped
3 pounds ground beef
3 20 oz. cans whole tomatoes, broken up
1 6 oz. can tomato paste
1 cup beer
1 tablespoon salt
½ teaspoon Tabasco
4 tablespoons chili powder
2 cans (12 oz. each) whole kernel corn

Melt the butter in a large pan, add onions, cook very slowly until the onions are tender, not browned. Add the ground beef and cook over medium low heat until lightly browned, use a fork to break it up. Add the tomatoes, tomato paste, beer, salt, Tabasco and chili powder. Cover and simmer 45 minutes. Add corn and simmer another 15 minutes. Makes 8 servings. May be frozen.

Mrs. David Nagle, Wife of former Representative (Iowa)

DAVE'S LONG ISLAND CHILI

1½ pound ground turkey
1½ pound ground beef
2 large chopped onions
8 finely chopped garlic cloves
2 12 oz. cans beer
5 tablespoons chili powder
2 tablespoons chili sauce
3 chopped jalapeno peppers
1 tablespoons cumin
2 tablespoons sweet paprika
    pinch cayenne pepper
1 large can black beans
1 28 oz. can chopped tomato
3 tablespoons sugar

Brown meat in a large dutch oven sprayed with a non-stick cooking oil. Add onions and garlic until tender. Stir in all remaining ingredients and bring to a boil. Reduce heat and simmer, adding more water if too thick. Adjust seasoning after 45 minutes. Serve with shredded cheddar cheese, chopped red onion and avocado. Makes 6 servings. May be frozen.

David Levy, Representative (New York)

FIRST LOVE CHILI

1 tablespoon lard or Crisco
   vegetable shortening
1 large onion, finely chopped
2 medium cloves garlic,
   finely chopped
1 pound lean ground beef,
   coarse chili grind
1 teaspoon ground cumin
½ teaspoon dried basil
1 teaspoon salt
1 16 oz. can plum tomatoes
1 small bay leaf
3 cups water
1 small cinnamon stick
2 whole cloves
1 green bell pepper, corded,
   seeded and coarsely
   chopped
1 16 oz. can kidney beans

Melt the lard or shortening in a large heavy pot over medium-high heat. Add the onion and garlic and cook until the onion is translucent. Add the meat to the pot. Break up any lumps with a fork and cook stirring occasionally until the meat is evenly browned. Stir in the remaining ingredients up through the cloves. Bring to a boil and then lower the heat and simmer uncovered for 2½ hours. Stir occasionally. Stir in the green pepper and kidney beans and simmer, uncovered for ½ hour longer. Remove the cinnamon stick, bay leaf and if possible, the cloves. Taste and adjust seasoning. Makes 2 to 4 servings.

Mrs. James Florio, Wife of Governor (New Jersey)

CHILI MADE EASY

2 pounds ground beef
2 large onions, chopped
3 red or green peppers,
   chopped
1 celery stalk, chopped
1 15 oz. can pinto beans
1 15 oz. can kidney beans
3 8 oz. cans tomato sauce
3 16 oz. cans whole to-
   matoes
1 pkg. chili mix

Cook ground beef in large skillet. Drain fat. Saute separately the onions, pepper and celery. Add these and all other ingredients to skillet with ground beef. Simmer for 15–20 minutes, stirring occasionally. Serve over rice or noodles. Makes 6 servings.

Mrs. David Norwood, Daughter of former Representative E. C. "Took" Gathings (Arkansas)

CHILI MAC

4 to 6 oz. fettucine, dried
1 15 oz. can Stagg chicken
   chili with beans
1 scallion, diced
½ tomato, diced
   shredded cheddar cheese

Cook fettucine by method suggested on box. Meanwhile, open the can of chili, put it in a bowl and then in microwave, turn on the microwave (full power) for 3–4 minutes. Chop or dice the tomato and scallion (you can do this together). Drain the fettucine, put it on a plate, spoon chili on top and then sprinkle with tomato, scallion and shredded cheddar cheese. This makes two servings which you can eat at once or save for next night. If she's in the "house" and you are alone again. Makes 2 servings.

Hugh Friedman, Husband of Representative Lynn Schenk (California)

LOW-FAT CHILI

½ pound ground buffalo or
   lean sirloin
1 cup chopped onions
½ cup chopped green pep-
   pers (optional)
1 14½ oz. can beef broth
   (no fat)
1 8 oz. can low salt tomato
   sauce
1 6 oz. can low salt tomato
   paste
2 15½ oz. cans dark red kidney beans, undrained
2 teaspoons chili powder
½ teaspoon cumin
   brown sugar to taste (optional)

Cook beef or buffalo, onion and green peppers over medium heat until meat is well done and onion and peppers are soft. Strain all and run under hot water until meat loses oily feel when touched. Add remaining ingredients and bring to a boil. Reduce heat and simmer. Adjust seasonings to taste. (1½ cup servings = 4.5 g total fat, 1.5 g saturated fat). Makes 8 servings. May be frozen.

Jim Edgar, Governor (Illinois)

GREEN CHILI STEW

1 pound very lean beef, cubed
2 tablespoons olive oil
1 medium onion, chopped
2 to 3 cloves garlic, crushed
water (or part bouillon) to cover
2 to 3 cans Ortega whole green chilies, cut in several pieces
2 medium potatoes, red, unpeeled
chopped tomatoes (optional)

Toss beef in seasoned flour and brown in oil. Add onion and garlic, liquid and green chili. Simmer for 1 hour and add cubed potatoes. Simmer until potatoes are cooked, about 20 minutes. This is basic recipe, pork rather than beef may be used, more or less of any ingredient is acceptable. Makes 6 servings. May be frozen.

Jennette I. Prouty

Mrs. Winston Prouty, Wife of former Senator (Vermont)

When choosing meat for the grill, allow about 3/4 to 1 pound per serving for cuts with bone, or 1/3 to 1/2 pound per serving for boneless cuts.

TENNESSEE CHILI

2 teaspoons butter or margarine

3 pounds beef chuck, cut into ½" pieces

1 large onion

1 green pepper, chopped

1 garlic clove, crushed

4 to 6 tablespoons chili powder

2 bay leaves

2 teaspoons each oregano and sugar

1 teaspoon each cumin and salt

½ teaspoon freshly ground pepper

1 14½ or 16 oz. can stewed tomatoes

1 13¾ or 14½ oz. can beef broth

1 16 oz. can red kidney beans, drained and rinsed

1 8 oz. can tomato sauce

1 cup water

1 tablespoon cornmeal

In dutch oven, melt butter or margarine over high heat. Add beef and brown. Drain excess fat. Stir in onion, green pepper and garlic, saute until vegetables are softened, 3 minutes. Stir in next 7 ingredients, cook 2 minutes. Add remaining ingredients. Bring to a boil, reduce heat, cover and simmer 1 hour. Simmer uncovered 1-1½ hours more. Discard garlic and bay leaves. Makes 2 quarts, 660 calories per cup.

This favorite recipe of Governor McWherter's mother, Lucille, won Honorable Mention in the 1988 *Ladies: Home Journal* "Great Chili Cook-Off".

Ned McWherter, Governor (Tennessee)

BEEF A LA KARLSSON

1 pound lean ground beef
2 egg yolks
½ cup liquid from pickled
   beets
⅓ cup whipping cream
2 teaspoons salt
   pepper to taste
4 tablespoons finely chopped
   onion, sauteed in butter
2 to 4 tablespoons drained,
   finely chopped capers
½ cup drained, finely
   chopped pickled beets
   butter for frying

In a large bowl, mix well the ground beef, egg yolks, juice from pickled beets, whipping cream, salt and pepper. Gently stir in sauteed onions, capers and pickled beets. Shape into patties about 2 inches in diameter. Melt butter in large heavy skillet over moderate heat and fry patties 3-4 minutes on each side. They should be rosy inside. Makes 6 servings. May be frozen.

Elsie Barrett

Mrs. Bill Barrett, Wife of Representative (Nebraska)

CABBAGE PUDDING

1 head cabbage
1 pound ground beef
1 pound ground pork
¾ teaspoon salt
¼ teaspoon pepper
1 egg
⅓ cup mashed potatoes

Remove core and chop cabbage into large pieces. Cook cabbage in boiling water until it wilts. Drain. Combine beef, pork, salt, pepper, egg and mashed potatoes. Work mixture until well mixed. In a well greased 2 quart casserole dish, alternate layers of meat mixture and cabbage, the last layer being meat. Cover casserole and place in large baking pan with 1 inch of boiling water and bake at 400° for 1-1½ hours. Let stand 5 minutes, then turn out onto warm serving platter. Makes 6 servings.

Elsie Barrett

Mrs. Bill Barrett, Wife of Representative (Nebraska)

FLORIDA PORCUPINES

1 pound hamburger
1/3 cup uncooked rice
1 teaspoon salt
1/2 teaspoon pepper
   dash Tabasco
1 can tomato soup
1/2 cup water

Mix hamburger, rice, salt, pepper and Tabasco. Form small meatballs and put in 2 quart casserole. Cover with tomato soup and water. Bake covered for 1/2 hour at 350°. Uncover and continue baking for another 1/2 hour. Makes 4 servings. May be frozen.

Mrs. Don Fuqua, Wife of Former Representative (Florida)

CABBAGE CASSEROLE

1 small head cabbage
1 pound ground beef
1/2 cup chopped onion
1/2 cup uncooked rice
1 can tomato soup
1 1/2 cups of water
1/2 tablespoon salt
1/2 tablespoon pepper
1 small pkg. grated cheese

Chop cabbage into small pieces, spread in a 13" × 9" pan. Brown meat and onions, drain grease, stir in rice and heat both tomato soup and water, salt and pepper to boiling. Pour soup over cabbage and meat. Sprinkle cheese over top, cover with foil and bake at 350° for 1 hour. After 45 minutes, remove foil and bake an additional 15 minutes. Makes 6 to 8 servings. May be frozen.

Donna Murtha, Daughter of Representative John Murtha (Pennsylvania)

LOOSE CABBAGE ROLLS

2 pounds ground beef
1 head of cabbage
1 large onion
2 cloves garlic
2 ribs celery
1 large hand full raw rice
3 small cans Spicy V-8 juice (6 oz.)
1 10 or 12 oz. pkg. cheddar cheese, grated
salt, pepper and other seasoning (Tony's) to taste

In a Dutch oven, place the ground meat on a stove burner. Heat it until it is soft and pliable and break it up. Turn off the fire and add the chopped onions, celery, squeezed garlic, rice and all of the seasoning. Mix this thoroughly and place in a bowl. Chop the cabbage and put a layer about ½ to 1 inch thick in bottom of the Dutch oven. Salt and pepper it. Add ½ of the meat mixture and pour 1 can of the V-8 juice over it evenly. Add another layer of cabbage, salt and pepper. Add the other half of the meat mixture and a can of V-8 juice. Add the third and final layer of cabbage, salt and pepper and add the third can of V-8. All of the above can be done in 20 or 25 minutes. Can be refrigerated and cooked later or cooked immediately. Place the Dutch oven, covered, into preheated 350° oven. Cook for 1½ hours. Remove and cover the casserole with the grated cheese. Replace pot cover and let stand for 10 minutes and serve. Don't be bashful with the seasoning, it usually needs more at the table. Makes 8 servings.

Leslie Owen Hayes

Mrs. Jimmy Hayes, Wife of Representative (Louisiana)

A roast with the bone in will cook faster than a boneless roast—the bone carries the heat to the inside of the roast quicker.

ROSE'S MACARONI GOULASH

1½ pounds ground beef
1 medium onion, chopped
2 stalks celery, sliced
1 16 oz. can stewed toma-
   toes (Italian style)
1½ tomato cans of water
1 clove garlic
1 6 oz. can tomato paste
1 tablespoon Worcestershire
   sauce
1 teaspoon salt
½ teaspoon pepper
1 7 oz. pkg. uncooked elbow
   macaroni (2 cups)
1 cup bread crumbs
¼ cup margarine

Cook and stir ground beef, onion and celery in 4 quart ovenproof Dutch oven until beef is brown. Drain. Stir in remaining ingredients. Top with bread crumbs browned in butter or margarine. Throwing in a little garlic salt on the melted butter adds a little zest to the topping. Bake at 350° until liquid is absorbed and goulash is hot, about 40 minutes. Note: The above recipe is a reasonable facsimile of my mother's after-church Sunday dinner. I say reasonable because she could add or subtract a little here or there depending upon what she had left over in the refrigerator, such as peas, carrots, corn, etc.! Makes 6 servings. May be frozen.

Doris Sangmeister

Mrs. George Sangmeister, Wife of Representative (Illinois)

CHACHI'S BEEF AND RICE

1 pound ground beef
1 large onion, chopped
2½ cups water
1 cup long grain rice
3 beef bouillon cubes,
   crushed
1 teaspoon mustard
1 medium green pepper,
   chopped
1 medium tomato, chopped
1 cup Monterey Jack cheese

Brown ground beef and onion in a 10 inch skillet and drain fat. Stir in rice, water, crushed bouillon cubes and mustard. Bring to boil. Reduce heat, cover and simmer until liquid is absorbed. Stir in green pepper and tomato. Sprinkle cheese over top. Cover and remove from heat. Let stand 3 minutes to melt cheese. Makes 4 to 6 servings.

Annie Bea Kornegay

Mrs. Horace R. Kornegay, Wife of former Representative (North Carolina)

BAKED BEANS WITH GROUND BEEF

1 pound ground beef
1 cup catsup
1 2 pound can pork and
   beans
½ cup molasses
   dash garlic powder and salt
½ cup chopped onion
½ cup brown sugar
1 medium chopped green
   pepper
½ cup Heinz thick BBQ sauce
   with mushrooms

Brown ground beef and drain. Add remaining ingredients and cook in 350° oven tightly covered for 20 minutes. Then uncover and continue cooking for 10–15 minutes. Delicious! Makes 8 servings. May be frozen.

Trent Lott, Senator (Mississippi)

SYMPHONY CASSEROLE

4 cups uncooked noodles (or
   8 oz. pkg. noodles)
1 pound ground chuck
1 envelope Lawry's spaghetti
   sauce mix
2 8 oz. cans tomato sauce
1 8 oz. cream cheese
1 carton cottage cheese
1 large onion, chopped
½ medium green pepper,
   chopped
3 tablespoons melted
   margarine

Cook noodles. Brown meat in a little oil, when brown add tomato sauce and mix, remove from heat. Have cream cheese at room temperature and cream together with cottage cheese and add chopped onion and green pepper and blend. In large casserole, put layer of noodles, add all cheese mixture, put remaining noodles on top. Pour over it melted margarine and then all the meat sauce. Chill ½ day if possible. Bake at 350° for 30 minutes. Makes 8 servings. May be frozen.

Mrs. E. Ross Adair, Wife of former Representative (Indiana)

TENDERLOIN OF BEEF

1 Whole tenderloin
  Mix equal parts of salt, pepper and paprika

Trim fat from whole tenderloin. Rub with oil, then sprinkle mixture on entire tenderloin. Heat oven to 450°. Place tenderloin on broiler rack above ½″ of water. Cook at 450° for 18 minutes. Turn off oven. Do not open. Let set for 45 minutes.

Laura Y. Bateman

Mrs. Herbert Bateman, Wife of Representative (Virginia)

MARINATED TENDERLOIN OF BEEF

1 beef tenderloin, well trimmed (6 pounds)
2 cloves garlic, halved
1 cup port wine
5 tablespoons low-sodium soy sauce
1 teaspoon hot sauce (Tabasco)
1 tablespoon dried whole thyme
1 teaspoon pepper
  dash of salt
1 bay leaf
  vegetable cooking spray
  orange slices
  fresh parsley sprigs

Trim any fat from tenderloin. Spear meat in several places, and rub with garlic. Mince garlic. Combine garlic and next 7 ingredients in a large zip-top plastic bag. Add tenderloin. Marinate in refrigerator 8 hours turning bag occasionally. Remove tenderloin from bag, reserving marinade, discard bay leaf. Fold under small ends. Place meat on a rack coated with cooking spray, place rack in a shallow roasting pan. Brush reserved marinade over tenderloin. Insert meat thermometer into thickest portion of meat. Bake at 425° for 35 minutes or until thermometer registers 140° (rare) to 160° (medium), basting frequently with marinade. Place tenderloin on a large serving platter, cover loosely with foil and let stand 10 minutes before slicing. Garnish with orange slices and fresh parsley. Can also cook on the grill. Makes 10 servings.

Loretta Symms

Mrs. Steve Symms, Wife of former Senator (Idaho)

PRIME RIB AND MUSHROOM SAUCE

1 to 3 pound boned small end prime rib seasoned with minced garlic, salt and pepper and Cavender's Greek seasoning

Sauce:

1 large onion
1 stick butter
¾ pound fresh mushrooms (some sliced and some whole)
1 teaspoon salt
1 teaspoon lemon pepper
1 teaspoon Worcestershire sauce
1 teaspoon Cavender's Greek seasoning
1 pkg. Knorr dry mushroom soup
1½ cups water
3 jiggers brandy (optional)

Roast room temperature prime rib at 400° for 8 minutes per pound and then reduce temperature to 200° for 2 hours.

Sauce: Saute onion in butter. Add mushrooms and seasonings. Mix soup with water and simmer for 20 minutes. Just before serving, add brandy. Makes 6 servings.

Elton Gallegly, Representative (California)

Never cook a roast cold—let stand for at least an hour at room temperature. Brush with oil before and during roasting—the oil will seal in the juices.

GRILLED EYE OF ROUND

3 to 4 pound eye of round
    prepared mustard
    Jane's Crazy salt

Trim fat from eye of round. Coat with prepared mustard and sprinkle generously with salt. Let marinate for 1 to 2 hours. Cook over hot coals on grill for 45 minutes to 1 hour, preferably in covered kettle type grill. If using open grill, wrap roast in heavy foil.

Herbert H. Bateman, Representative (Virginia)

SKEWERED BEEF TENDERLOIN

1½ pounds beef tenderloin,
    cut into 1½ inch cubes
3 tablespoons olive oil
8 tablespoons (1 stick)
    melted butter
1 tablespoon chopped fresh
    thyme or ½ teaspoon
    dried
1 tablespoon Dijon mustard
⅛ teaspoon red pepper flakes
    salt and freshly ground
    pepper
6 tablespoons fresh lemon
    juice

Divide the beef between 2 long skewers. Combine the oil, 4 tablespoons of melted butter, thyme, mustard, and red pepper flakes and mix well. Brush over all sides of the beef cubes. Season to taste with salt and pepper. Grill for about 3 minutes per side, brushing with more of the oil mixture. Combine the remaining melted butter with the lemon juice. Heat quickly and pour over the skewered meat just before serving. Makes 4 to 6 servings.

Mrs. Frank Reich, Daughter of former Representative John J. Rhodes (Arizona)

A large roast can be carved more easily after it stands for about thirty minutes.

ROAST BARBECUE

3 pounds chuck roast
2 tablespoons shortening
2 tablespoons butter
1 large onion
½ cup chopped celery
2 tablespoons cider vinegar
2 tablespoons lemon juice
¾ cup water
2 cups catsup
2 tablespoons soy sauce
2 tablespoons brown sugar
1 tablespoon Dijon mustard
1 teaspoon salt
¼ teaspoon pepper
1½ tablespoons chili powder

Trim meat and brown in shortening and drain. Add butter, onions and celery. Saute until onions are soft. Add remaining ingredients. Bring to a boil, cover, reduce heat to low and simmer 3 hours until meat is tender. Use 2 forks to shred meat and continue cooking 2-3 hours. Serve over buns. Makes 10 servings.

Jan Sutermeister

Mrs. Richard Sutermeister, Daughter of former Representative Tom Kleppe (North Dakota)

POT ROAST

3½ to 4 pound boneless arm or chuck roast
1 envelope Lipton onion soup mix
1 can Campbell's cream of mushroom soup
6 to 8 medium potatoes, scrubbed
1 large pkg. fresh carrots, peeled
1 cup water

Spray heavy roaster with Pam. Place roast in pan and sprinkle dry soup mix over roast, evenly. Spoon soup from can over the dry soup mix. Pour 1 cup water around edge of pan. Cover and bake for 2½ hours at 300°. About 2 hours before serving, add potatoes and carrots. Spoon some of the gravy over vegetables to keep them moist. Cover pan again and return to oven for 2 more hours. This is delicious and is great left over. The slow cooking makes this meat very tender. Makes 6 to 8 servings.

Betty Ann Tanner

Mrs. John Tanner, Wife of Representative (Tennessee)

FAVORITE WINTER POT ROAST

5 pounds boneless pot roast
   (or a size appropriate for
   your meal)
flour (for dredging)
Johnny's Dock seasoning
   salt (or any beef seasoning salt)
olive oil (for browning the
   meat)
¼ cup shallots, finely
   chopped
1 bottle prepared horseradish
   (not sauce)
red wine (good quality)
water or beef broth
potatoes, halved
carrots, in chunks
boiling onions
pea pods, fresh or frozen
   or broccoli florets

Dust the roast all over with the flour and rub in seasoning salt on all sides. Brown the meat in hot oil in a heavy, oven-proof casserole. Reduce heat and lightly brown the shallots. Scoop up most of the shallots and distribute on top of the roast. Spread a thick layer of the prepared horseradish over the top surface of the potroast. Be generous, this is a tenderizer and trust me, it won't be hot. Add a mixture of wine and water or broth (at the ratio of 2-wine to 1-water) until it measures half way up on the roast. Cover and put in oven at 350° for 2½ to 4 hours, depending on the size of the roast. It will test done when the meat pulls off easily with a fork. About 45 minutes before serving, remove the roast to an ovenproof platter, cover and keep hot. Put cut vegetables (except pea pods) in the liquid left from the roast, cover and return to the oven. When done, arrange vegetables on the platter with the meat, sprinkle pea pods on the surface and place in the oven with the heat turned off while you make a gravy with the wonderful winy, beefy broth. Serve with a tossed green salad, French bread and a bottle of hearty red wine. Makes 6 to 8 servings.

Paula J Swift

Mrs. Al Swift, Wife of Representative (Washington)

> *STORE MEATS RIGHT! Meat keeps best in the refrigerator if it's loosely wrapped in plastic wrap or wax paper. To freeze it, wrap in moisture/vapor-proof wrapping, such as heavy plastic wrap. Always remember to label and date it.*

SWEDISH POT ROAST

4 pounds boneless roast or
   brisket
1 teaspoon nutmeg
1 teaspoon cinnamon
½ teaspoon ginger
2 teaspoon salt
⅛ teaspoon pepper
1 tablespoon oil
2 onions, sliced
1 clove garlic, diced
½ cup brown sugar
½ cup red wine
4 bay leaves
8 large or 16 small carrots
8 potatoes, halved

Combine spices, salt and pepper and rub into meat. Brown meat on all sides and add onion, garlic, brown sugar dissolved in wine and bay leaves. Roast at 350° in covered dutch oven 2½ hours. Add potatoes and carrots and roast an additional 45 minutes. Make brown gravy with drippings. Makes 8 servings.

Mrs. Barbara H. Burlison, Member of The Congressional Club

ROAST LEG OF LAMB

½ leg of lamb
2 cups white vinegar
12 garlic cloves
4 fresh lemons
   oregano, salt, pepper
    (enough to sprinkle over
    meat)
4 potatoes, quartered length-
    wise (optional)

Prepare lamb the night before. Cut off all visible fat and wash with vinegar. Rinse thoroughly and cut slits an inch deep in all parts of lamb and insert garlic cloves. Marinate overnight in lemon juice. Sprinkle with salt, pepper, and oregano after adding lemon juice. Cover and refrigerate. The next day, place in baking pan with rack and add 1 cup water to pan. Pour remaining marinade over lamb. Bake at 350° uncovered about 20 minutes per pound. Baste periodically. Optional: When lamb is half done, you may add potatoes. Add more water to pan if needed. Cover for remaining cooking period. Makes 6 servings.

Mrs. Michael Bilirakis, Wife of Representative (Florida)

CURRIED LAMB

2 cups lamb, cooked
1 onion, chopped
1 large apple, chopped
1 tomato, chopped
1 clove garlic, minced
4 tablespoons butter
1 tablespoon cornstarch
1 tablespoon curry or more
½ teaspoon ginger, ground
¼ teaspoon pepper
1 cup beef stock
¼ to ½ cup raisins
   juice of 1 lemon
   toasted almonds
   chutney
   cooked rice (4 servings)

Cook onion, apple, tomato and garlic in butter until soft. Add seasonings and cornstarch slowly (whisk in cornstarch). Add meat, raisins and lemon juice. Serve over cooked rice and garnish with toasted almonds and chutney. May easily be doubled and made ahead. Makes 4 servings.

Emilie C. Shaw

Mrs. E. Clay Shaw, Wife of Representative (Florida)

BARBECUED BUTTERFLY LAMB

1 leg of lamb, butterfly cut
1 cup dry red wine
½ cup olive oil
2 tablespoons parsley,
   snipped
2 tablespoons chives,
   chopped
½ teaspoon Worcestershire
¼ teaspoon pepper
⅛ teaspoon marjoram
⅛ teaspoon rosemary
⅛ teaspoon thyme
2 cloves garlic, crushed
1 teaspoon salt

Combine all ingredients to make marinade. Pour over lamb and marinate overnight in refrigerator. Barbecue on both sides, about 25 minutes per side on an *open* grill. Baste frequently with marinade. Makes 6 to 8 servings.

Nancy Fleetwood Miller

Mrs. James Miller, Daughter-in-law of former Senator Jack R. Miller (Iowa)

LAMB SHANKS SUPREME

3 lamb shanks
   small head of cabbage
   small eggplant
1 28 oz. can whole peeled
   tomatoes
1 cup uncooked white rice
1 teaspoon salt

Place lamb shanks in bottom of covered casserole. (Do not trim off skin, it enhances the flavor). Cover with sliced cabbage (¼-½″ thick), peeled and cubed eggplant, tomatoes (cut them in pieces) with juice. Sprinkle salt over mixture. Cover and bake 1 hour at 350° then reduce heat to 325° for last 2 hours. Last hour add 1 cup rice, stir into liquid around edges. This is a wonderfully delicious one dish meal served with salad. It is our favorite and is even better the second day. Makes 3 servings.

Ann Simpson

Mrs. Alan Simpson, Wife of Senator (Wyoming)

BARBECUED LAMB RIBLETS

3 pounds lamb riblets
   salt
   pepper
1 lemon
¾ cup catsup
¾ cup water
½ cup chopped onion
2 tablespoons brown sugar
3 tablespoons Worcestershire
   sauce
1 tablespoon vinegar
1½ teaspoons monosodium
   glutamate
¾ teaspoon salt
   dash bottled hot pepper
   sauce

Brown 3 to 4 pounds lamb riblets slowly in skillet. Drain off excess fat. Season with salt and pepper, top with 1 lemon, sliced. Combine catsup, water, chopped onion, brown sugar, Worcestershire sauce, vinegar, monosodium glutamate, salt and hot pepper sauce, pour over meat. Cover, simmer about 1½ hours or until done. Remove meat to serving dish. Skim off excess fat from sauce. Pass sauce with meat. Makes 6 to 8 servings. May be frozen.

Phyllis J. Burns

Mrs. Conrad Burns, Wife of Senator (Montana)

THE BEST SHISHKABOBS

Marinade:
1½ cups olive oil
¾ cup soy sauce
¼ cup Worcestershire sauce
2 tablespoons dry mustard
2½ teaspoons salt
1 tablespoon coarse black
  pepper
½ cup wine vinegar
1½ teaspoons dried parsley
  flakes
2 cloves garlic, crushed
½ cup fresh lemon juice
  zucchini
  green peppers
  large mushrooms (optional)

Whip marinade ingredients in blender until thick. Pour over meat and marinate two days. Marinade will keep in refrigerator for 1 week or can be frozen. Be sure and whip again before pouring over meat. Cut meat into approximately 1 inch cubes and alternate with pan broiled zucchini cubes, green pepper cubes and mushrooms on skewers. Makes 8 servings.

Alta Leath

Alta Leath, Member of The Congressional Club

MARINATED SHISH KEBAB

6 tablespoons soy sauce
6 tablespoons oil
6 teaspoons sugar
1 clove garlic, minced
1 pound flank steak, cut into
  cubes
  pineapple chunks
  whole mushrooms
  green peppers
  onions

Combine the soy sauce, oil, sugar and garlic. Add the meat and let marinate for 2 hours uncovered. Remove the meat and place on skewers, alternating with chunks of pineapple, whole mushrooms, green peppers and onions. Place on grill and baste vegetables with Italian dressing. Cook over medium hot coals. Makes 4 servings.

Lori Kerns

Mrs. Brian Kerns, Daughter of Representative John Myers (Indiana)

GRILLED BEEF STRIPS ON SKEWERS

1½ pound sirloin or top round
    steak (or boneless
    chicken breasts)
⅓ cup oil
½ cup brown sugar
2 teaspoons Worcestershire
    sauce
¼ cup soy sauce
¼ cup wine vinegar
2 cloves garlic, chopped

Cut steak into strips about ½" thick and 1" wide. Make marinade of oil, brown sugar, Worcestershire sauce, soy sauce, wine vinegar, and chopped garlic. Marinate meat in sauce 5-6 hours in refrigerator. Thread strips of steak loosely back and forth on long skewers. Grill about 5 minutes on each side, depending on desired doneness. Can also skewer on small onions, mushrooms, green peppers, small tomatoes, par-boiled potatoes, peaches and fresh pineapple.

Mike DeWine

Michael DeWine, former Representative (Ohio)

SWEET LAMB KEBABS

1 pound ground lamb
1 egg
¼ cup cracker crumbs
1 teaspoon salt
¼ teaspoon dry sage
⅛ teaspoon pepper
1 can (1 pound) sliced cling
    peaches, drained
8 marischino cherries
¼ cup melted butter or mar-
    garine
4 skewers

Combine lamb, egg, cracker crumbs, salt, sage and pepper, mix well. Shape mixture into 12 balls and arrange on 4 skewers. Place on grill and broil for approximately 10 minutes, turning once. Remove from grill and slip lamb balls off skewers and brush with half the butter. Return the lamb to the skewers, alternating with the sliced peaches and cherries. Return to grill, brush with butter and cook 3 or 4 minutes longer, turning once. Makes 4 servings.

Nancy Fleetwood Miller

Mrs. James Miller, Daughter-in-law of former Senator Jack R. Miller (Iowa)

GRILLED LAMB KABOBS

8 tablespoons olive oil
10 tablespoons soy sauce
1 teaspoon freshly ground
 pepper
1 large onion, grated fine
3 tablespoons freshly
 squeezed lemon juice
3 pounds lean lamb (from
 leg or shoulder of lamb),
 cut in large cubes
large fresh mushrooms
small parboiled onions
green pepper, cut in 1
 inch squares

Whisk together olive oil, soy sauce, pepper, onion and lemon juice to make marinade. Cut lamb in cubes and leave in marinade for 2 hours or longer, turning and rubbing the seasonings into the meat. Thread on skewers with mushroom, onion and green pepper. Broil in oven or grill over hot coals, brushing often with marinade, for about 15 minutes. Makes 6 servings.

Alex McMillan, Representative (North Carolina)

SUPER-MOIST MEAT LOAF

1½ pound hamburger
1 pkg. onion soup mix
1 cup Pepperidge Farm dressing mix
1 cup catsup
½ cup half and half
3 cup chopped celery
 eggs
 dash of garlic salt
 dash of celery salt
¼ pepper to taste
 cup chopped onion
 (optional)

Mix all ingredients well. Bake at 325° for 1 hour. Makes 8 servings. May be frozen.

Mrs. Conrad Burns, Wife of Senator (Montana)

LUCY'S LUSCIOUS MEATLOAF

1½ tablespoons butter or mar-
    garine
1 tablespoon olive oil
½ cup minced onion
1 large clove garlic, minced
1 large minced shallot
2 pkgs. frozen spinach
¼ pound ground sausage
3 pounds ground chuck
½ pound ground veal
1 tablespoon Dijon mustard
½ teaspoon salt
¼ teaspoon black pepper
½ teaspoon nutmeg
½ teaspoon mace
⅓ cup chopped parsley
    dash of Tabasco
½ green bell pepper,
    chopped
¾ cup bread crumbs
2 eggs, slightly beaten
1 tablespoon Madeira or
    Marsala wine
¼ tablespoon dried thyme
    leaves

Preheat oven to 375°. Saute onion, garlic and green pepper in olive oil and margarine/or/butter in a medium sized skillet until soft. Add the thawed spinach. Stir until all moisture has evaporated (2 minutes or so). Set aside to cool. Combine three meats in a large mixing bowl and add all spices, bread crumbs, eggs, and spinach/onion etc. Mix. Sprinkle with the wine and mix well. Place in the loaf pan. Be sure to fill bottom corners. Smooth the top and sprinkle with the thyme leaves. Bake about 1 hour until well browned (when done, juices will run clear when center is pierced with a fork). Invert on platter and allow to cool to room temperature. Then chill, to facilitate slicing. Use a sharp serrated knife. Note: I like this dish served as the mainstay of an evening supper, and the loaf tastes best when served cold; however, it can of course be served hot. Makes 10 servings.

Mrs. James H. Scheuer, Wife of former Representative (New York)

MOM'S APPLESAUCE MEATLOAF

1 pound lean ground beef
½ cup applesauce
½ cup ketchup
¾ cup bread crumbs

Mix ingredients together and put in loaf pan. Bake in preheated 350° oven for 45 to 60 minutes. Makes 4 to 6 servings. May be frozen.

John Miller, Former Representative (Washington)

MEAT-ZA-PIE

1 to 1½ pounds of ground
    beef
⅔ cup evaporated milk (5⅓
    oz. size can)
½ cup bread crumbs
    salt and pepper to taste.
1 small can mushrooms
1 6 oz. can tomato paste
    oregano
    Parmesan cheese

Press firmly into pie tin, on bottom and sides. Spread ⅓ cup tomato paste (6 oz. can). Cover with mushrooms, either fresh or canned. Sprinkle with oregano and parmesan cheese. Bake at 325° for 30 minutes. Makes 4 to 6 servings.

Frieda G. James

Mrs. Benjamin James, Wife of former Representative (Pennsylvania)

PORK ROAST WITH SAUERKRAUT

1 5 to 6 pound pork loin
    roast, bone in
¾ teaspoon salt
½ teaspoon coarse pepper
2 pounds sauerkraut, canned
    and drained or (prefera-
    bly) from delicatessen
1 large onion, coarsely
    chopped
3 to 4 cloves garlic, sliced
1 6 oz. can frozen apple
    juice, thawed
    heavy duty aluminum foil

Preheat oven to 500°. Rub the pork with salt and pepper, place on rack in roasting pan and brown in hot oven for 10 minutes. Drain any accumulating grease. Mix sauerkraut, onion in a separate saucepan and heat thoroughly. When pork has browned, remove from oven and pour sauerkraut, onion mixture over it. Sprinkle sliced garlic over the top. Dribble the thawed apple juice over the pork and sauerkraut mixture. Turn oven down to 200°. Cover tightly with foil. Seal the entire top of baking pan, so that it is totally covered and no steam can escape. Return to oven and let cook until serving time, at least 8 hours. Drain any grease out of the pan with a baster. Serve with mashed potatoes and green vegetable. Makes 6 to 8 servings.

Loretta Symms

Mrs. Steve Symms, Wife of former Senator (Idaho)

CROWN ROAST OF PORK AND MIXED FRUIT DRESSING

1 crown roast of pork

Mixed Fruit Dressing:
1 11 oz. pkg. mixed dried fruit
1/2 cup butter or margarine
1 medium onion, chopped
1 cup celery, chopped
6 cups bread cubes
1 1/2 teaspoons salt
1/4 teaspoon pepper
1 teaspoon thyme, crumbled
1/4 teaspoon ground allspice

Ask your butcher to cut and tie a pork roast crown the size you desire. Count on 1 to 2 ribs per person. Have the butcher remove the backbone, for easier carving. Wrap the rib ends with foil to prevent charring them. Place the roast, ribs end up, in a shallow baking pan. Bake at 325° 35 to 40 minutes per pound or until meat thermometer placed in center of meat registers 170°. If desired, fill center of crown roast with dressing before serving. To carve, slice between ribs. Spoon out dressing to serve alongside.

Mixed Fruit Dressing: Cover mixed fruit with water and bring to a boil. Reduce heat, cover and simmer 15 minutes or until tender. Drain and dice fruit. You should have about 2 cups. Cook onion and celery in butter until tender, about 10 minutes. Combine with seasonings, fruit and bread cubes, tossing to combine thoroughly. Turn into a greased shallow casserole and bake, uncovered at 325° for 30 minutes. If desired, serve inside the crown roast. Makes 6 to 8 servings. May be frozen.

Chalmers Wylie, former Representative (Ohio)

BAKED PORK CHOPS AND SAUERKRAUT

1 16 oz. can of sauerkraut
4 pork chops salted and peppered
2 tablespoons water

Wash sauerkraut in a sieve. Put in oblong casserole 10″ × 6″ × 1¾″. Place pork chops on top of kraut. Cover with aluminum foil. Bake at 350° for 1 hour. Uncover the last 15 minutes to brown. Makes 2 to 4 servings.

Mrs. Howell Heflin, Wife of Senator (Alabama)

SOUTHWESTERN PORK ROAST

3 pound boneless pork loin
   roast
1 teaspoon chili powder
½ teaspoon garlic salt
½ teaspoon salt
½ cup catsup
½ cup apple jelly
1 tablespoon vinegar

Combine ½ teaspoon chili powder, the garlic salt and salt. Rub into the roast. Bake uncovered at 325° for 2 hours until meat temperature reaches 170°. Combine the catsup, apple jelly, vinegar and remaining ½ teaspoon chili powder in pan. Simmer 5 minutes. Cover the roast with the glaze and continue baking for 10–15 minutes until done. Remove roast. Measure pan drippings, adding water to make 1 cup. Serve sauce with the roast. Makes 8 servings.

Jon Kyl, Representative (Arizona)

CURRY GLAZED PORK CHOPS

4 large pork chops
1 large onion
2 tablespoons flour
2 tablespoons brown sugar
1 tablespoon curry powder
1 teaspoon salt
1 teaspoon cinnamon
1 beef flavor bouillon cube
1 cup water
2 tablespoons catsup
1 jar strained apples and apricots (4 ozs.)

Place 4 pork chops in baking dish. Chop the onion and saute in butter. Blend in the flour, brown sugar, curry powder, salt and cinnamon. Bring to a boil. Add bouillon cube, water, catsup and apples/apricots. Stir together and then allow to simmer for 5 minutes. Spoon ½ of the mixture over the pork chops. Bake at 400° for 20 minutes. Spoon on the rest of the sauce. Bake at 400° for an additional 20 minutes. Makes 4 servings. May be frozen.

Mrs. Ted Strickland, Wife of Representative (Ohio)

> *To tenderize meats, marinate in vinegar and olive oil for at least 2 hours.*

APPLE CINNAMON PORK FILETS

2 pounds pork tenderloin
1 large apple
1 teaspoon sugar
¼ teaspoon cinnamon
¼ teaspoon garlic powder
1 teaspoon salt
¼ teaspoon pepper
¼ cup olive oil
½ cup dry red wine
1 cup stock

Slice tenderloin into 6 pieces. Peel, core, and finely chop apple. Combine apple, sugar and cinnamon, mix well. Make horizontal slash in center of each tenderloin without cutting through. Stuff with apple filling. Press meat together, secure with metal clamps or skewers if necessary. Combine garlic powder, salt and pepper. Rub tenderloins with mixture. Heat oil in deep skillet, brown tenderloins on all sides. Add wine and stock, bring to boil. Reduce heat, simmer 1 hour, turning meat at 15 minute intervals. Makes 4 servings.

Lori Kerns

Mrs. Brian Kerns, Daughter of Representative John Myers (Indiana)

PORK N' APPLES WITH STUFFING

12 pork chops
2 20 oz. cans pie-sliced apples, drained
½ cup brown sugar
6 cups herb-seasoned stuffing mix
½ cup chopped celery
¼ cup butter, melted
3 tablespoons instant minced onion
1 teaspoon salt
1 teaspoon ground sage
2 cups beef bouillon

Trim off excess fat. Brown chops in large skillet with 2 tablespoons oil or fat drippings. Sprinkle meat with salt and pepper. Brown well on both sides. Place in two 11¾" × 7½" baking dishes. Combine apples and brown sugar. Spoon over pork cops. Combine stuffing mix, celery, melted butter, onion, salt and sage. Toss with beef bouillon until moistened. Spread dressing over each pork piece. Cover tightly. Seal, label and freeze. Bake *frozen* casserole *covered* in 400° oven for approximately 1¼ hours or until pork is done. Bake *unfrozen* casserole in 375° oven for 1 hour. This recipe makes 2 casseroles of 6 servings each. Makes 12 servings. May be frozen.

Carol Andrus

Mrs. Cecil D. Andrus, Wife of Governor (Idaho)

GOURMET PORK CHOPS

6 loin pork chops, ½ inch thick
2 tablespoons all-purpose flour
1 teaspoon salt
   dash pepper
2 tablespoons shortening
1 10½ oz. can condensed cream of mushroom soup
¾ cup water
¼ teaspoon ginger
¼ teaspoon rosemary, crushed
1 3½ oz. can french-fried onions
½ cup sour cream

Coat chops with a mixture of flour, salt, and pepper. In skillet, brown on both sides in hot shortening. Place in 11″ × 7″ × 1½″ baking dish. Combine soup, water, ginger and rosemary, pour over chops. Sprinkle with half the onions. Cover and bake at 350° for 50 minutes, or until meat is tender. Uncover, sprinkle with remaining onions and continue baking 10 minutes. Remove meat to platter. Blend sour cream into soup mixture, heat. Pass with meat or serve over white rice. Makes 6 servings.

Marc Racicot, Governor (Montana)

GRILLED PORK CHOPS

¾ inch boneless pork chops (2 to 3 per person)
   Johnny's Dock seasoning salt (or a favorite seasoning salt)

Sprinkle pork chops on both sides with seasoning salt. Heat Bar-B-Q grill until very hot. Lay chops on hot grill. Brown each side until done. Serve immediately.

Mrs. Al Bellamy, Daughter of Representative Al Swift (Washington)

> *To season pork chops for cooking on a charcoal grill, sprinkle with lemon-pepper seasonings, meat tenderizer, soy sauce, a dash of ground cloves and a little butter.*

APRICOT PORK MEDALLIONS

1 pound pork tenderloin, cut into 1" slices
1 tablespoon butter + 1 teaspoon butter
½ cup apricot jam
2 sliced green onions
¼ teaspoon dried mustard
1 tablespoon cider vinegar

Flatten each piece of pork tenderloin slightly. Heat 1 tablespoon butter over medium-high heat in a skillet. Saute pork about 2 minutes each side. Remove from pan. To juices, add 1 teaspoon butter, apricot jam, sliced green onions, mustard and vinegar. Cover and simmer for 3–4 minutes. Add pork to heat through. Serve with buttered noodles and green salad as side dishes. Makes 4 servings.

Mrs. Chalmers Wylie, Wife of former Representative (Ohio)

MARINATED PORK CHOPS

¼ cup wine vinegar
¼ cup soy sauce
1 teaspoon salt
½ teaspoon black pepper
½ teaspoon Accent
½ cup water
¼ cup oil
12 1-inch thick pork chops

Mix together first 5 ingredients, add water and oil and mix. Cover pork chops with sauce and refrigerate over night, basting several times. Clean and prepare bar-be-que grill and cook pork until golden brown. Makes 12 servings. May be frozen.

Terry Everett, Representative (Alabama)

MARINATED PORK TENDERLOIN

3 pounds fresh pork strip
    tenderloin

Marinade:
¼ cup soy sauce
¼ cup bourbon
2 tablespoons brown sugar

Mustard Sauce:
⅓ cup sour cream
⅓ cup mayonnaise
1 tablespoon dry mustard
1 tablespoon finely chopped
    scallions
1½ teaspoons vinegar
    salt to taste

Marinate meat several hours at room temperature, turning occasionally. Remove from marinade and bake in slow oven at 325°, basting frequently with marinade for 1 hour or until tender. Carve the tenderloin on the diagonal in thin slices and serve it with mustard sauce.

Sauce: Mix together sour cream and mayonnaise. Stir in remaining ingredients. Makes 6 servings.

Mrs. Guy Vander Jagt, Wife of former Representative (Michigan)

STUFFED PORK CHOPS

6 center-cut pork chops,
    about 1½″ thick
2 cups cornbread, crumbled
1 cup light bread, crumbled
1 can chicken broth
1 teaspoon sage
½ teaspoon salt
2 eggs
    pepper to taste
½ cup diced celery
½ cup diced onion

Mix stuffing ingredients together and stuff in pork chops. Roll pork chops in flour and brown in skillet. Fasten with toothpicks. Bake in roasting pan, covered at 350° for 2 hours or until done. During the last ½ of cooking time, uncover roasting pan and thicken broth for gravy. Makes 4 to 6 servings.

Mrs. Dale Bumpers, Wife of Senator (Arkansas)

PORK TENDERLOIN WITH ORANGE MARMALADE

1½ tablespoons coarse mustard
1 clove garlic, minced
¼ teaspoon dried whole rosemary
¼ teaspoon pepper
1 pork tenderloin (1 pound)
¼ cup low-sugar orange marmalade, divided
vegetable cooking spray
½ cup water
¼ cup ready-to-serve, no-salt-added chicken broth

Combine first 4 ingredients and set aside. Trim fat from tenderloin. Slice tenderloin lengthwise, cutting almost to, but not through, outer edge. Spread mustard mixture in pocket, press gently to close. Tie tenderloin with heavy string at 2 inch intervals. Spread 2 tablespoons of orange marmalade over tenderloin. Place tenderloin on a rack that has been coated with cooking spray. Place rack in broiler pan, add water to pan. Bake at 325° for 40 to 50 minutes or until meat thermometer inserted into thickest portion registers 160°. Cook remaining 2 tablespoons orange marmalade and chicken broth 2 to 3 minutes until thickened. Slice tenderloin, spoon sauce over slices and serve. Makes 4 servings.

Pam Napier

Mrs. John Napier, Wife of former Representative (South Carolina)

PORK TENDERLOIN WITH PINEAPPLE

1½ pound pork tenderloin
4½ ozs. non-sweetened pineapple juice
¼ pineapple, cut into big chunks or 6 slices cut into large triangles
⅛ teaspoon each of the following powdered spices mixed together: cloves, nutmeg, pimento and cinnamon
1 tablespoon of margarine or butter
salt and pepper to taste

Broil the meat 15 minutes to remove extra fat. Place meat in an oven dish and pour on top, pineapple juice, salt, pepper and half of the spice mixture. Cook in preheated 450° oven for 20 minutes. In the meantime, peel pineapple and cut. Melt butter in a pan and saute the pineapple until golden. Add salt, pepper and the rest of the spices. Serve the pork tenderloin with the pineapples around it. Makes 4 servings. May be frozen.

Scott Rhodes

Scott Rhodes, Son of former Representative John J. Rhodes (Arizona)

SPIT-ROASTED CINNAMON PORK

1 center-cut pork loin, boned
    (3½ to 4 pounds)
2 tablespoons cinnamon
2 teaspoons salt
1 teaspoon freshly ground
    white pepper
2 teaspoons sugar
1 onion, finely grated (about
    ½ cup)
4 garlic cloves, minced
    (about 2 tablespoons)
1 to 3 tablespoons soy sauce

Prepare the pork by scoring the surface in 1 inch diamonds with a sharp knife, cuts should be ⅛ to ¼ inch deep. Combine all other ingredients except soy sauce. When well mixed, blend in 1 tablespoon soy sauce. If mixture is not spreadable, add another 1 to 2 tablespoons soy sauce. Rub mixture into loin as completely as possible, using your hands and penetrating the scored lines. Let pork stand at room temperature for 3 hours or refrigerate overnight. Bring to room temperature before grilling. Secure pork on the spit. Arrange coals at far end of grill, or set gas grill on indirect or low heat. Set drip pan under spit and insert when fire is ready. Roast for 1½ or 2 hours or until pork is slightly pink inside, basting with juices from drip pan, do not over-cook. Allow to rest 5 to 10 minutes before cutting into thin slices. Makes 6 servings.

Frank J. Reich, Son-in-law of former Representative John J. Rhodes (Arizona)

MARINATED PORK ROAST

½ cup soy sauce
½ cup dry sherry
2 cloves garlic, minced
1 tablespoon dry mustard
1 teaspoon ginger and thyme
1 4 to 5 pound boned, rolled
    and tied pork loin roast

Combine soy sauce, sherry, garlic, mustard, ginger and thyme. Place roast in large, clear plastic bag. (Set in deep bowl to steady roast). Pour in marinade and close bag tightly. Let stand 2 to 3 hours at room temperature or overnight in refrigerator. Roast, uncovered at 325° for 2½ to 3 hours or 175° on meat thermometer. Baste during last hour. Makes 10 to 12 servings. May be frozen.

Mrs. Tim Valentine, Wife of Representative (North Carolina)

COMPANY HAM

20 pound ham from butcher, deboned, rolled and tied

Peach Sauce:
1 10 oz. jar of peach chunks with juice
  dash of brandy extract
  dash of cloves
1 cup of honey
1 teaspoon dry mustard
  dash of cayenne pepper

Boil ham three hours in water.

Peach Sauce: Heat on stove and boil down to ¾ of the original liquid to thicken sauce. The sauce can be made ahead and heated just before serving. Serve on the side with Company Ham. Makes 10 to 15 servings.

Mrs. Dirk Kempthorne, Wife of Senator (Idaho)

HAM LOAF

2 pounds ground ham
2 pounds ground pork
2 cups soft bread crumbs
4 eggs, slightly beaten
1 cup milk
½ cup onion, finely chopped
  salt and pepper to taste

Sauce:
2 9 oz. cans crushed pine-apple
⅔ cup catsup
⅔ cup vinegar
¼ cup soy sauce
1 cup brown sugar
1 tablespoon ginger

Loaf: Combine ingredients and form into individual sized loaves. Place in shallow pan and brown in oven. Drain off grease and add sauce. Bake at 350° for about 1 hour. Baste occasionally with sauce.

Sauce: Mix all ingredients together. Makes 10 to 12 servings. May be frozen.

Mrs. Robert A. Grant, Wife of former Representative (Indiana)

SAUSAGE HOMEMADE

8 pounds freshly ground
   sausage meat
8 teaspoons salt
3 teaspoons pepper
6 teaspoons sage

Mix sausage and spices together. Divide into 1 pound portions and freeze in plastic freezer bags or make individual patties and freeze. May be frozen.

Neal Smith

Neal Smith, Representative (Iowa)

SWEET AND SOUR SPARERIBS

2 pounds lean spareribs, cut
   1 inch long and sliced
   separately
1 cup green pepper, cut in 1
   inch pieces
1 cup sauterne
¾ cup soy sauce
1 teaspoon cornstarch
½ cup water
1 cup vinegar
1 cup sugar

Marinate spareribs in soy sauce and sauterne overnight. Heat peanut oil in frying pan at high heat. Place drained ribs in frying pan and brown on both sides. Reserve marinade and stir a little into cornstarch. Mix until smooth, return to remaining marinade. Combine marinade with ½ cup water, 1 cup sugar and 1 cup vinegar and mix well. Add to ribs. Cover and simmer for ½ hour at low heat. Add green pepper. Simmer uncovered for about 5 minutes. Serve. Makes 4 servings. May be frozen.

Mary K Meeds

Mrs. Lloyd Meeds, Wife of former Representative (Washington)

> *To slice meat into thin strips, as for Chinese dishes—partially freeze and it will slice easily.*

OVEN BAR-B-QUE RIBS

4 pounds country style ribs
1 lemon
1 large sliced onion
1 cup catsup
⅓ cup Worcestershire sauce
1 teaspoon chili powder
1 teaspoon salt
2 dashes Tabasco sauce
2 cups water

Place ribs in a shallow roasting pan. On each piece, place a slice of unpeeled lemon and a thin slice of onion. Roast in a very hot oven (450°) for 30 minutes. To make sauce, combine catsup, Worcestershire sauce, chili powder, salt, Tabasco sauce and water, in a saucepan. Let this come to a boil and pour over ribs. Do not use all of the sauce. Continue baking in moderate oven (350°) until tender, about 1½ to 2 hours. Baste ribs with sauce every 15 minutes. Makes 6 to 8 servings.

John T. Myers

John T. Myers, Representative (Indiana)

VEAL SCALLOPINE

1 pound veal cutlets, sliced
    thin
flour
6 tablespoons butter
salt and pepper
4 cloves garlic, crushed
¾ cup white wine
2 tablespoons parsley,
    chopped
1 can mushrooms, sliced
1 large onion, cut thin in
    rings

Veal should be sliced thin. Pound it with a mallet to make it almost transparent. Dip veal into flour. Saute garlic in butter in large skillet, then add the veal slices. Saute for 3 to 4 minutes on each side. Sprinkle with salt and pepper and remove veal from the skillet, place in casserole and keep warm in oven. Next saute the onions and mushrooms in the butter and garlic, then add the wine and parsley. Simmer so it thickens and makes a light gravy. Pour over the veal. Great with pasta tossed with garlic and olive oil. Makes 4 servings. May be frozen.

Christine LaRocco

Mrs. Larry LaRocco, Wife of Representative (Idaho)

When broiling or barbecuing meat, slash the fat to prevent curling.

VEAL SCALLOPINE WITH CHEESE AND MADIERA SAUCE

2 pounds veal scallopine, sliced thin and lightly breaded
½ cup butter
3 tablespoons Madiera
1 tablespoon flour
½ cup milk
½ cup water
1 bouillon cube
¼ teaspoon nutmeg
½ pound Gruyere or Ementhaler cheese, grated
freshly ground black pepper

Heat 6 tablespoons of butter in a skillet over medium heat, add veal and cook until browned on both sides. (Do not over cook!) Remove veal to a plate. Add Madiera to the skillet and cook for a few seconds, scraping particles on the bottom. Set skillet aside.

To make sauce: Bring water and milk to a boil in a saucepan and dissolve the bouillon cube in the mixture. In another small saucepan, melt remaining 2 tablespoons butter, add flour and stir with a wire whisk until blended. Add Madiera and water-milk mixtures to this at once, stirring continuously until thickened, well blended, and smooth. Add nutmeg and season with pepper. Arrange veal in a single layer in a shallow baking dish. Pour sauce over veal and top with grated cheese. Dish can be refrigerated at this point for several hours. Before serving, heat oven to 425° and heat veal until cheese melts and turns brown, about 20 minutes. Makes 6 servings.

Lowell P. Weicker, Jr., Governor (Connecticut)

Store cooked meats and leftovers right! Always chill leftovers and cooked meats quickly. Keep covered in the refrigerator. Separate leftover poultry meat from the stuffing when refrigerating. To freeze package and freeze quickly. Meat stuffing should always be frozen separately.

VEAL SUPREME

1 cup flour
¼ teaspoon salt
1 pound veal scallopini
2 tablespoons butter
1 cup chicken broth
¼ cup dry vermouth
½ teaspoon Worcestershire
   sauce
½ teaspoon marjoram
¼ teaspoon garlic powder
1 bay leaf
1 can artichoke hearts, rinsed
   and quartered
6 lemon slices
1 small jar (2 ozs.) chopped
   pimentos
1 pound cooked noodles
½ teaspoon dillweed

Dredge veal in flour and salt, and brown veal in butter. Remove veal from skillet. Add broth, vermouth, Worcestershire sauce, marjoram, garlic, bay leaf and bring to a boil. Add veal, artichokes and lemon slices. Simmer 10–15 minutes or until liquid thickens. 5 minutes before serving, discard bay leaf and add pimentos. Serve over warm noodles and garnish with dillweed. Makes 4 servings.

Betty J. Applegate

Mrs. Doug Applegate, Wife of Representative (Ohio)

VEAL SCALOPPINE CASSEROLE

6 veal scaloppine, pounded
   thin
1 egg, beaten
   bread crumbs
   butter or margarine
1 can mushroom soup
1 small can chopped mush-
   rooms
½ cup white wine

Dip veal in egg and then in bread crumbs. Brown lightly in butter or margarine and place in buttered casserole. Add mushroom soup, chopped mushrooms and wine. Heat at 325° for 45 minutes. Serve with noodles or rice. Makes 6 servings. May be frozen.

Jean Terry

Mrs. John Terry, Wife of former Representative (New York)

PORK SCALLOPINI

1½ pounds pork tenderloin,
    sliced 1″ thick
½ cup flour
2 tablespoons butter
2 tablespoons oil
½ cup dry sherry
½ cup water
½ cup chopped onions
1 clove garlic, minced
1 teaspoon salt
¼ teaspoon pepper
¼ teaspoon each, thyme, rose-
    mary and oregano
1½ cups fresh mushrooms,
    sliced

Dredge meat in flour. Brown meat in butter and oil. Stir in sherry and water. Add onion, garlic and seasonings. Cover and cook at 225° for 30 minutes. May add water. Add mushrooms and cook covered 15 minutes. Makes 2 to 3 servings.

Linda J. Mickelson

Mrs. George Mickelson, Wife of former Governor (South Dakota)

AL'S VEAL MEDALLIONS

2 veal tenderloins (1 pound
    each)
    sesame oil
1 teaspoon powdered garlic
1 teaspoon powdered onion
½ cup butter
2 cups mushrooms
    juice of 1 lemon
¼ cup dry white wine

Cut veal filets into ¼″ slices. Brush slices on 1 side with sesame oil and then sprinkle lightly with garlic powder. Turn slices over and sprinkle other side lightly with onion powder using heavy iron skillet, melt butter. Over high heat, "sear" pieces of veal very quickly until lightly browned. Total time: 1 minute. Do not overcook! Remove veal from pan to warm platter. In skillet, saute mushrooms until tender, add juice of lemon and the wine, simmer for several minutes and then pour over veal. Serve immediately. Makes 4 servings.

Al McCandless

Al McCandless, Representative (California)

BEEF STEW

2 pounds boneless chuck or bottom round cut into 2 inch squares
2 tablespoons flour
1 tablespoon salt
½ teaspoon pepper
¼ pound or 1 stick of butter or oleo
1 medium onion, sliced
½ pound mushrooms, sliced or 1 can drained
1 cup water
1 cup dry red wine
1 10 oz. can tomatoes
few sprigs of parsley
2 stalks celery with leaves, cut diagonally into 1 inch pieces
2 carrots cut into 1 inch pieces
1 teaspoon thyme
1 bay leaf
2 tablespoons flour
3 tablespoons water

Coat meat with combined 2 tablespoons flour, salt and pepper. Melt butter in Dutch oven or large skillet. Add meat, brown lightly on all sides, add onions and mushrooms. Cook over low heat until onion is tender. Add water, wine, tomatoes, parsley, celery, carrot, bay leaf and thyme. Cover, simmer gently, stirring occasionally, 2 to 2½ hours, or until meat is tender. Blend the 2 tablespoons of flour and 3 tablespoons of water. Stir into mixture, simmer 5 minutes, add salt to taste. Serve in hot cooked rice ring. If you don't want rice ring, add a few potatoes, cut in quarters, about an hour before stew is finished. Makes 4 servings. May be frozen.

Marguerite Nye

Mrs. Gerald P. Nye, Wife of former Senator (North Dakota)

"WYOMING JOHN'S WESTERN BEEF STEW"

1½ to 2 pounds beef cubes
 4 large potatoes, peeled, cut
     in ⅓'s
 1 pound mushrooms, sliced
¾ cup minced onion
 1 tablespoon tarragon
 2 tablespoons Worcestershire
     sauce
   salt
   pepper
   water
 1 cup frozen peas
 5 large carrots, peeled, cut in
     ¼'s
 5 large celery stalks, cut in
     chunks
¼ cup A-1 Steak Sauce
½ cup dry white wine
½ teaspoon Tabasco sauce
 3 tablespoons flour

Brown beef cubes over high heat in skillet lightly oiled with olive oil. Transfer to 5 quart pot and add potatoes, mushrooms, ½ of the minced onions, tarragon, 1 tablespoon Worcestershire sauce. Lightly salt and pepper and add just enough water to cover these ingredients. Stir, cover and simmer for 2 hours. Stir occasionally while simmering. Add peas, carrots, celery, peeled white onions, A-1 Steak Sauce, 1 tablespoon Worcestershire sauce, dry white wine, Tabasco sauce. Add just enough water to cover these additional ingredients. Whisk in flour to thicken gravy. Cover and simmer for 1 hour, stirring occasionally while simmering. When ready to serve, stir in remaining minced onion, salt and pepper to taste. Makes 6 to 8 servings. May be frozen.

Cynthia Mitchell-Gingles

Mrs. Cynthia Mitchell-Gingles, Daughter of former Representative Donald J. Mitchell (New York)

To prevent splashing when frying meat, sprinkle a little salt into the pan before putting the fat in.

LAST-MINUTE BRUNSWICK STEW

1 24 oz. can Brunswick stew
1 small can barbecue beef
1 small can barbecue pork
1 can creamed corn
1½ tablespoons Worcestershire
    sauce
½ cup Johnny Harris (or
    other barbecue sauce)
⅓ cup catsup

Combine all ingredients in large saucepan or Dutch oven. Heat and stir until bubbly hot. Makes 10 servings. May be frozen.

Frances B. Hagan, Daughter of former Representative G. Elliott Hagan (Georgia)

IRISH STEW

4½ pounds lamb neck chunks
2 tablespoons butter
2½ cups water
2 teaspoons salt
¼ teaspoon pepper
¼ teaspoon thyme
3 medium potatoes
6 small white onions
1 pkg. frozen green peas
¼ pound fresh or canned
    sliced mushrooms
1 cup light cream or milk
¼ cup flour

Brown lamb in butter in large Dutch oven or kettle. Add water and seasonings, cover and simmer for 45 minutes. Peel potatoes, cut into medium-sized chunks. Skim excess fat from top of kettle. Add potatoes and onions. Simmer, covered, for 15 minutes. Add peas and mushrooms, simmer, covered, for 15 minutes longer or until lamb and vegetables are tender. Blend cream into flour, stirring until well mixed. Pour flour mixture into bubbling stew, boil for 1 minute, stirring constantly. Add more seasoning if desired. Makes 6 servings.

Mrs. Tom Harkin, Wife of Senator (Iowa)

ALL DAY GONE BEEF STEW

2 pounds beef chuck, cut in
   2-inch cubes
1 10-oz. can tomato soup,
   undiluted
1 cup water or red wine
¼ cup of flour
3 medium-size carrots, cut in
   1-inch slices
6 white boiling onions or 4
   medium-size yellow
   onions, quartered
4 medium-sized potatoes, cut
   to 1½-inch slices
12 whole large fresh mushrooms (optional)
2 beef bouillon cubes
1 tablespoon Italian herbs or
   mixed seasoning
1 teaspoon oregano, thyme,
   rosemary
   fresh pepper
1 bay leaf

Mix together soup, water or wine with flour until smooth. Combine remaining ingredients in covered roasting pan and bake at 275° for 4 to 5 hours. When ready to serve, adjust seasonings. Serve over noodles with crusty French bread. (I use Bergundy wine in this recipe). Makes 6 servings. May be frozen.

Mary Jo Van Deerlin

Mrs. Lionel Van Deerlin, Wife of former Representative (California)

STORE CURED MEATS RIGHT! Keep meat loosely covered in refrigerator. To freeze, wrap it tightly in moisture/vapor-proof wrapping, pressing out as much air as possible. When freezing smoked meat, wrap extra well so its odors won't permeate other foods. Cured meats don't keep their high quality for long when frozen, because the seasonings that are added in the curing process speed rancidity.

BEEF STROGANOFF

Grandma's Recipe

- 2 pounds filet of beef
- 4 tablespoons butter
- 1 cup chopped onion
- 1 clove garlic, finely chopped
- 3 tablespoons flour
- 2 teaspoons meat extract paste
- 1 tablespoon catsup
- ½ teaspoon salt
- ⅛ teaspoon pepper
- 1 can beef bouillon, undiluted
- ¼ cup dry white wine
- 1 tablespoon fresh snipped dill or 1 teaspoon, dried
- 1½ cups sour cream
- 1½ cups cooked wild rice
- 1½ cups cooked white rice or 3 cups cooked noodles

Trim fat from beef and cut filet crosswise into ½ inch thick slices. Cut each slice across grain into ½ inch wide strips (about 2 inches long). Slowly heat large heavy skillet. Melt 1 tablespoon butter, add beef strips, just enough to cover skillet bottom. Over high heat, sear quickly on all sides. Remove with tongs as meat finishes browning (it should be brown on outside and rare inside). In 3 tablespoons hot butter in same skillet, saute onion, garlic and mushrooms until onion is golden (about 5 minutes). Remove from heat, add flour, meat extract paste, catsup, salt and pepper. Stir until smooth. Gradually add bouillon, bring it to a boil, stirring. Reduce heat and simmer 5 minutes. Over low heat, add wine, the snipped fresh dill or dried dill and sour cream stirring until well combined. Add beef and simmer until sauce and beef are hot. Lightly toss wild and white rice. Surround stroganoff with rice. Snip dill or parsley on top.

Jim Guy Tucker, Governor (Arkansas)

BEEF STROGANOFF

4 tablespoons butter
1 pound sliced beef (top round)
5 tablespoons flour
½ cup chopped onion
1 clove fresh garlic, minced
1 tablespoon tomato paste
1 can beef bouillon
½ teaspoon salt
1 cup fresh mushrooms
1 cup sour cream
2 tablespoons sherry
2 cups cooked rice

Melt 2 tablespoons butter in pan. Dredge meat in 2 tablespoons flour and brown in butter. Add onion and garlic, remove and set aside. To the drippings, add 2 tablespoons butter, 3 tablespoons flour, tomato paste, beef bouillon and salt. Add the meat mixture and mushrooms and heat until it reaches boil. Add sour cream and sherry. Serve over prepared rice. Makes 4 servings.

Sydna Zeliff

Mrs. William H. (Bill) Zeliff, Wife of Representative (New Hampshire)

BUL GO GI (BARBECUE ORIENTAL)

2 pounds beef sirloin (or chicken pieces)
2 large green onions, sliced thin
1 clove of garlic, minced
1 tablespoon brown sugar
4 ozs. soy sauce
3 tablespoons salad oil (or sesame oil)
¼ teaspoon salt
¼ teaspoon pepper
½ teaspoon Accent (optional)

Mix all ingredients together, marinate for about 15 minutes. Barbecue over charcoal. If chicken is to be used, score pieces well to obtain better marination. You can also cook this dish in the electric skillet right on your table.

Cindy Daub

Mrs. Hal Daub, Wife of former Representative (Nebraska)

REUBEN CASSEROLE

3 medium potatoes, cooked
1 16 oz. can sauerkraut, drained
½ pound smoked sausage or kielbasa, thinly sliced
½ cup Thousand Island dressing
2 tablespoons chopped parsley
¾ 3 cup (3 ozs.) shredded Swiss cheese
½ green pepper, cut into strips (about ⅓ cup)

Pare and cube potatoes, set aside. Combine sauerkraut, potatoes (about 2 cups), sausage, dressing and parsley. Spoon into greased 10″ × 6″ × 1¾″ oven-proof glass baking dish. Bake at 350° for 25 to 30 minutes. Sprinkle cheese and green pepper strips over top. Bake 5 minutes more. Makes 5 servings.

Dolores Beilenson

Mrs. Anthony Beilenson, Wife of Representative (California)

LIVER SURPRISE

1 pound liver (calf or beef)
1 can applesauce
1 teaspoon cinnamon

Sear liver on both sides in hot pan or cast iron skillet. Place liver in a greased baking dish and pour applesauce over the top. Sprinkle with cinnamon and bake ½ hour at 350°. Simple, but tasty. Makes 2 to 4 servings.

Marion Giaimo

Mrs. Robert Giaimo, Wife of former Representative (Connecticut)

MONTANA BEEF CREPES

1⅓ cups milk
  2 tablespoon butter, melted
  2 eggs, beaten
 ½ cup flour
  1 teaspoon baking powder
 ½ teaspoon salt
  2 cups sour cream
1½ pound cooked roast or
    steak cut into strips
 ½ cup sliced ripe olives
 ½ cup sliced green onion
    tops
 ½ cup grated mozzarella
    cheese
 ⅓ cup milk

Make batter of milk, butter, eggs, flour, baking powder and salt. (You can also use your favorite pancake or crepe mix). Makes 10 (4-5 inch), as thin as possible, crepes, browning each side. Spread 1 side of each with sour cream, using about 1 cup of sour cream. Place strips of beef, olives and green onion on each crepe. Roll up and put into a 7″ × 11″ baking dish. Mix 1 cup sour cream and ⅓ cup milk. Pour over crepes. Sprinkle with cheese. Bake uncovered for 20 minutes at 350° or until heated through. Makes 10 servings. May be frozen.

Phyllis J. Burns

Mrs. Conrad Burns, Wife of Senator (Montana)

SWEET AND SOUR MEATBALLS

1 pound ground hamburger
¼ cup milk
1 teaspoon salt
1 egg
½ cup dry bread crumbs
2 tablespoons finely chopped onion
½ teaspoon Worcestershire sauce

Sauce:
½ cup packed brown sugar
1 tablespoon cornstarch
1 13½ oz. can pineapple chunks
1 tablespoon soy sauce
⅓ cup vinegar
1 coarsely chopped small green pepper

Meatballs: Mix ingredients and shape into 20 1½-inch balls. Cook over medium heat in small amount of cooking oil, turning occasionally, until brown, about 20 minutes. Or, bake in ungreased oblong baking dish, 13″ × 9″ × 2″, in 400° oven until lightly browned, 20 to 25 minutes.

Sauce: Mix brown sugar and cornstarch in skillet. Stir in pineapple chunks with juice, vinegar and soy sauce. Heat to boiling, stirring constantly, reduce heat. Add meatballs. Cover and simmer, stirring occasionally, for 10 minutes. Stir in green pepper, and continue simmering until crisp-tender, about 5 minutes. Makes 4 servings. May be frozen.

Helen Hunt

Mrs. Guy Hunt, Wife of Governor (Alabama)

> *To freeze meatballs, place them on a cookie sheet until frozen. Place in plastic bags and they will stay separated so that you may remove as many as you want.*

LOW-FAT BAR-B-QUE MEATBALLS

Meatballs:
1½ pounds ground turkey
1 small can of canned milk
1 cup oatmeal
¼ teaspoon pepper
¼ teaspoon garlic powder
1 egg
½ cup onion (dehydrated is fine)
1 teaspoon salt
1 teaspoon chili powder

Sauce:
1 cup catsup
1 small can tomato sauce
¾ cup brown sugar
1½ teaspoons liquid smoke

Mix all ingredients for the meatballs together well and form into 1½ inch balls. Place on flat baking dish. Cover with sauce and bake at 350° for 45 minutes to 1 hour. Makes 4 servings. May be frozen.

Mrs. Buck McKeon, Wife of Representative (California)

NOTES

NOTES

Hillary Rodham Clinton
1993–

To my good friends at the Congressional Club
With best wishes,

Hillary Rodham Clinton

Hillary Rodham Clinton

With Hillary Rodham Clinton dawns a new generation of First Ladies. She proves that there is room for a First Lady who can lead alongside a President.

As a career attorney, she reflects the revolution of women in today's society and sets a shining example for young women. Much of her life has been spent improving the lives of children—the future of our country.

Mrs. Clinton has fought for funds for the first neonatal hospital in Arkansas; she has improved education standards there, and she made the state a national leader in parenting programs for low-income mothers. Now charged with changing our nation's health care system, she is again working to help those who have been forgotten.

DESSERTS

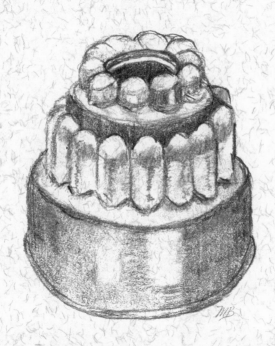

HILLARY CLINTON'S CHOCOLATE CHIP COOKIES

INGREDIENTS:

1½ cups unsifted all-purpose flour
1 teaspoon salt
1 teaspoon baking soda
1 cup solid vegetable shortening
1 cup firmly packed light brown sugar
½ cup granulated sugar
1 teaspoon vanilla
2 eggs
2 cups old-fashioned rolled oats
1 (12-ounce) package semi-sweet chocolate chips

METHOD:

Preheat oven to 350 degrees. Grease baking sheets. Combine flour, salt and baking soda. Beat together shortening, sugars and vanilla in a large bowl until creamy. Add eggs, beating until light and fluffy. Gradually beat in flour mixture and rolled oats. Stir in chocolate chips. Drop batter by well-rounded measuring teaspoonfuls onto greased baking sheets. Bake 8 to 10 minutes or until golden. Cool cookies on sheets on wire rack for 2 minutes. Remove to wire rack to cool completely. Makes 7½ dozen.

Hillary Rodham Clinton

Hillary Rodham Clinton, Wife of the President of the United States

FRESH PEACH FLAN

For pastry:

3¾ cup flour
1 cup butter
1 cup sugar
8 egg yolks
2 tsp. vanilla extract

For filling:

4 to 6 tablespoons kirsch or
   maraschino liqueur
¼ cup orange juice or juice
   from canned peaches
10 to 12 large macaroons,
   crushed
8 or 9 fresh peaches
1½ cups apricot jam glaze

To make the French flan pastry dough: Mix flour, butter, sugar, egg, yolks and vanilla extract. Chill 30 minutes. Roll out. Line 2 9-inch flan rings and bake in a 375 degree oven for 15 to 20 minutes or until the pastry is lightly browned.

To make filling: Spoon the kirsch or maraschino liqueur and orange or peach juice over the macaroons and let soak.

Scald, peel and halve fresh peaches. Spread the soaked macaroon crumbs in the cooled flan shells and arrange the peach halves on top. Brush the peaches and the pastry generously with hot apricot jam glaze. Makes 2 9-inch flans.

The Congressional Club

APRICOT AND BANANA MOUSSE

1 tablespoon unflavored
   gelatin
¼ cup cold milk
½ cup apricot juice, hot
2 ripe bananas, mashed
1 cup sweetened stewed
   apricots
2 cups heavy whipping
   cream
1 cup confectioners sugar

Soften gelatin in milk for 5 minutes, dissolve in hot apricot juice and cool. Add bananas and stewed apricots. Whip cream until thick enough to hold a soft peak and beat in sugar. Fold cream into fruit mixture and freeze until firm. Serves 8 to 10.

The Congressional Club

CHOCOLATE SOUR CREAM CAKE

2 cups sugar
1 cup Crisco
½ cup cocoa
2 eggs
1 8 oz. carton sour cream
2½ cups flour
2 teaspoons baking soda
1 teaspoon salt
1 cup boiling water
2 teaspoons vanilla

Cream together sugar, Crisco and cocoa. Add eggs. Add alternately; sour cream, flour, baking soda and salt. Add boiling water and vanilla. Bake 1 hour at 350°. Can be frozen.

Jim Guy Tucker, Governor (Arkansas)

GRANDMA DUNHAM'S CHOCOLATE CAKE

2 eggs
2 cups sugar
½ teaspoon salt
2 heaping tablespoons shortening (lard)
1 tablespoon vinegar
2 level teaspoons baking soda
1 cup sour milk (whole milk)
2½ cups flour
6 heaping teaspoons cocoa
1 cup boiling water

Beat eggs, sugar, salt, shortening together thoroughly. Put vinegar in a cup, stir into it the baking soda. Pour this effervescent mixture into the milk and add to the above mixture. Add the flour with 3 heaping teaspoons of cocoa sifted into each cup of flour. Add the one cup of boiling water last. The batter will be very thin. Pour into baking pan and bake for 35–40 minutes. Heat oven to 350°. Grease and flour a 9″ × 12″ baking dish. Makes 12 servings.

Mrs. Tony Hall, Wife of Representative (Ohio)

NANCY'S SOUR CREAM CHOCOLATE CAKE

Cake:

  3 blocks Hershey's semi-
      sweet chocolate
  ¼ cup butter
  1 cup boiling water
  2 cups firmly packed brown
      sugar
1½ teaspoons baking soda
  2 cups flour
  1 teaspoon salt
  1 teaspoon vanilla
  ½ cup sour cream
  2 eggs

Icing:

  ¼ cup cocoa
  ¼ cup sugar
  ¼ cup brown sugar
  ¼ cup melted butter
5¾ oz. can evaporated milk
  ¼ teaspoon salt
  1 teaspoon vanilla
    powdered sugar

Cake: Combine chocolate squares, butter and boiling water. Stir until chocolate is melted. In a large bowl, combine sugar, flour, baking soda and salt. Make a well and gradually add the chocolate mixture, then the eggs one at a time, beating with each addition. Add sour cream and vanilla and beat at medium speed with electric mixer for 1 minute. Bake at 350° for 35 to 40 minutes or until tests done. Use a 9″ × 13″ pan.

Icing: Bring first 6 ingredients to a boil. Boil for 5 minutes and add vanilla. Add powdered sugar to taste. Let cake cool *completely* before icing. Makes 8 to 10 servings.

Allison Lightfoot

Allison Lightfoot, Daughter of Representative Jim Ross Lightfoot (Iowa)

Dust a little flour or cornstarch on your cake before icing; this way the icing won't run off.

BILLIE'S RED VELVET CAKE AND FROSTING

Cake:
- ½ cup shortening
- 1½ cups sugar
- 2 eggs
- 2 ozs. red food coloring
- 2 tablespoons cocoa
- 1 teaspoon salt
- 2¼ cups cake flour
- 1 cup buttermilk
- 1 teaspoon vanilla
- 1 teaspoon baking soda
- 1 tablespoon vinegar

Frosting:
- 3 tablespoons flour
- 1 cup milk
- 1 cup sugar
- ½ pound butter
- 1 teaspoon vanilla

Cake: Cream shortening. Add sugar gradually, then eggs, one at a time. Make paste of food coloring and cocoa and add to mixture. Add salt and flour, buttermilk and vanilla, alternately. Mix, but do not overbeat. Add baking soda and vinegar (sprinkle baking soda over batter and pour vinegar over it) and mix thoroughly. Bake at 350° in 3 layer pans for 30 to 35 minutes.

Frosting: Cook flour and milk over medium heat until thick, stirring constantly. Cool. Combine sugar, butter and vanilla and add to flour and milk mixture. Beat with electric mixer on high until smooth and creamy. Frost cooled cake. Makes 8 to 10 servings.

Nancy Lightfoot

Mrs. Jim Lightfoot, Wife of Representative (Iowa)

Use cocoa rather than flour to dust pans for chocolate cake.

NO FAT MOCHA CAKE

Cake:
1 cup flour
⅓ cup + 1 tablespoon cocoa
1 teaspoon instant expresso
 or instant coffee
1 teaspoon baking powder
1 teaspoon baking soda
6 large egg whites (room
 temperature)
1 cup firmly packed brown
 sugar
1 teaspoon vanilla
1 cup coffee flavored non-fat
 yogurt

Topping:
1 tablespoon cocoa
1 teaspoon powdered sugar
½ teaspoon cinnamon

Preheat oven to 350°. Line bottom of pan with waxed paper. Spray pan and paper with Pam and dust with flour. Sift flour, cocoa, expresso, baking powder and baking soda into medium bowl. Beat egg whites, sugar, yogurt and vanilla in large bowl for about 1 minute, until well blended. Mix in dry ingredients and pour into pan. Bake until center tests done (about 35 minutes). Cool cake in pan on wire rack about 15 minutes, then turn out on plate and sprinkle with topping. Makes 8 servings. May be frozen.

Marian Lewis

Mrs. Tom Lewis, Wife of Representative (Florida)

SOLDATI/WHEELER DEATH BY CHOCOLATE

1 chocolate cake mix
2 large containers Cool Whip
4 Skor candy bars, chopped
4 boxes Jell-O instant chocolate mousse

Bake cake as normal. Make all 4 boxes of Jell-O mousse at once, according to package directions. In large crystal bowl, layer proportionally: crumbled cake, mousse, Cool Whip, chopped Skor bars. Continue until ingredients are gone. Garnish with chopped Skor bars. Refrigerate until ready to serve. Makes 10 to 12 servings.

Anne Rhodes

Mrs. Jay Rhodes, Wife of former Representative (Arizona)

GEORGE'S DECADENT CHOCOLATE CAKE

Cake:

1 cup boiling water
4 ozs. unsweetened choc-
   olate
8 tablespoons (1 stick) sweet
   butter
1 teaspoon vanilla extract
2 cups granulated sugar
2 eggs, separated
1 teaspoon baking soda
½ cup sour cream
2 cups less 2 tablespoons unbleached, all-purpose
   flour, sifted
1 teaspoon baking powder
   chocolate frosting (recipe
   follows)

Chocolate Frosting:

2 tablespoons sweet butter
¾ cup semisweet chocolate
   chips
6 tablespoons heavy cream
1¼ cups sifted confectioners
   sugar or as needed
1 teaspoon vanilla extract
   Frosting: Place all ingredients in a heavy saucepan
   over low heat and whisk
   until smooth. Cool
   slightly, add more sugar
   if necessary to achieve a
   spreading consistency.
   Spread on cake while
   frosting is still warm.

Cake: Preheat oven to 350°. Grease and flour a 10″ tube pan, knock out excess. Pour boiling water over chocolate and butter, let stand until melted. Stir in vanilla and sugar, then whisk in egg yolks, one at a time, blending well after each addition. Mix baking soda and sour cream and whisk into chocolate mixture. Sift flour and baking powder together and add to batter, mixing thoroughly. Beat egg whites until stiff, but not dry. Stir a quarter of the egg whites thoroughly into the batter. Scoop remaining egg whites on top of the batter and gently fold together. Pour batter into the prepared pan. Set on the middle rack of the oven and bake for 40 to 50 minutes, or until the edges have pulled away from the sides of the pan and a cake tester inserted into the center comes out clean. Cool in pan 10 minutes, unmold and cool completely before frosting.

Beverly Derrick

Mrs. Butler Derrick, Wife of Representative (South Carolina)

MONIE'S CHOCOLATE CAKE

Cake:
- 2 sticks margarine
- 1 cup Crisco
- 2¾ cups white sugar
- 1 cup milk
- 3 cups cake flour, sifted
- ½ cup cocoa
- 5 eggs
- 1 teaspoon vanilla
- ½ teaspoon baking powder
- 2 tablespoons milk

Icing:
- 1 stick butter
- 2 squares semi-sweet chocolate
- 1 egg
- 1 teaspoon lemon juice
- 1 teaspoon vanilla
- 1 box powdered sugar

Cake: Cream margarine, Crisco and sugar. Add 1 cup milk and mix. Sift together pre-sifted flour with cocoa 3 times. Add flour mixture and eggs to batter, alternating flour then eggs, beginning and ending with the flour mixture. Add vanilla. Combine baking powder and 2 tablespoons milk in separate container. Add to batter, mix well and pour into large tube pan. Bake at 325° for 1 hour and test for doneness.

Icing: Melt butter and chocolate together. Using a mixer, beat egg and add lemon juice and vanilla. Mix in chocolate/butter mixture with egg then fold in powdered sugar until desired consistency, (about 1 box). Cool, then ice cake. Makes 18 servings. May be frozen.

Shelly Hefner, Daughter of Representative W. G. (Bill) Hefner (North Carolina)

Place a paper doily on top of cake, dust with powdered sugar and lift off for intricate design.

ALABAMA PEANUT BUTTER WHITE CHOCOLATE COCONUT CAKE

Cake:
- 1 cup margarine
- 1¾ cups sugar
- 4 eggs
- 2½ cups self-rising flour
- 1 cup buttermilk
- ½ pound (4 squares) white chocolate, melted

Filling:
- ¼ cup margarine, melted
- ½ cup crunchy peanut butter
- ¼ cup milk
- 1 square white chocolate, melted
- 1 16 oz. box confectioners sugar

Icing:
- 1 16 oz. box confectioners sugar
- ⅓ cup Crisco shortening
- ½ teaspoon coconut flavoring dash of salt
- ½ cup milk
- 1 cup frozen coconut (optional)

Cake: Preheat oven to 325°. Grease and flour three 9″ cake pans. Cream butter and sugar. Add eggs and beat well after each addition. Stir in flour and buttermilk. Add melted chocolate. Beat for 2 minutes. Pour batter into pans and bake at 325° for 35 minutes or until toothpick inserted in center comes out clean.

Filling: Put all filling ingredients in bowl and stir until well-blended and spread between layers. You may need to add extra milk for spreading consistency.

Icing: In large bowl, beat all ingredients until very smooth adding more milk, if necessary, to make good spreading consistency.

Barbara Everett

Mrs. Terry Everett, Wife of Representative (Alabama)

To keep the top of a cake from browning too quickly, put a pan of warm water on the rack above.

CHOCOLATE ZUCCHINI CAKE

½ cup soft margarine
½ cup oil
1¾ cups sugar
2 eggs
1 teaspoon vanilla
½ cup sour milk
2½ cups unsifted flour
4 tablespoons cocoa
½ teaspoon baking powder
1 teaspoon baking soda
½ teaspoon cinnamon
½ teaspoon cloves
2 cups finely sliced or shredded zucchini
¼ cup chocolate chips

Cream margarine, oil and sugar. Add eggs, vanilla and sour milk, beat with mixer. Mix together dry ingredients and add to creamed mixture. Beat well with mixer. Stir in zucchini. Spoon batter into greased and floured 9" × 13" pan. Sprinkle top with chocolate chips. Bake at 325° for 40-45 minutes, or until toothpick comes out clean.

Linda L. Klink

Mrs. Ron Klink, Wife of Representative (Pennsylvania)

MIX-IN-THE-PAN CHOCOLATE CAKE

3 cups flour
2 cups sugar
6 tablespoons cocoa
2 teaspoons baking soda
1 teaspoon salt
⅔ cup oil
2 tablespoons vinegar
2 teaspoons vanilla
2 cups water

Measure dry ingredients (flour, sugar, cocoa, baking soda and salt) into 9" × 13" cake pan and stir together. Make 3 holes in ingredients. Put oil in one, vinegar in one and vanilla in one. Pour water over all and mix well with spoon. Bake at 350° for 30 minutes. Good served warm, even without icing. Makes 12 servings.

Fran DeWine

Mrs. Michael DeWine, Wife of former Representative (Ohio)

GOVERNOR CASEY'S CHOCOLATE CAKE

Cake:
 ¾ cup Hershey's cocoa
 1½ teaspoons baking soda
 1½ cups hot water
 2 cups sugar
 1 cup safflower oil
 2 cups flour
 1½ teaspoons baking powder
 2 eggs (substitute egg
    beaters)
 2 teaspoons vanilla

Icing:
 6 tablespoons softened marga-
    rine (Fleischmann's or
    Weight Watcher's)
 ½ cup Hershey's cocoa
 2⅔ cups 10X sugar
 ⅓ cup skim milk
 1 teaspoon vanilla

Cake: Combine all above ingredients. Spray a 13″ × 9″ × 2″ pan with Pam. Bake at 350° for 40–45 minutes.

Icing: Cream margarine in bowl. Add cocoa and 10X sugar alternately with milk. Blend in vanilla. Beat to spreading consistency.

Robert P. Casey, Governor (Pennsylvania)

TUNNEL OF FUDGE CAKE

 3 sticks butter
 1½ cups sugar
 6 eggs
 2 cups flour
 1 pkg. Betty Crocker's dry
    chocolate fudge frosting
    mix

Blend softened butter with mixer. Add sugar, ½ cup at a time. Add eggs, 2 at a time, blending well after each pair. By hand, stir in flour and dry frosting mix. Put in well-greased and floured bundt pan. Bake for 50–55 minutes at 350°. (Use high altitude conversions where needed.) Do not test with toothpick. Remove cake from pan after cooling 20 minutes. Will form a tunnel of fudge with brownie-type cake on the outside.

Mrs. Joel Hefley, Wife of Representative (Colorado)

WHITE CHOCOLATE CAKE

¼ pound white chocolate
1 cup butter
2 cups sugar
4 eggs
2½ cups cake flour
¼ teaspoon baking powder
1 cup buttermilk
1 cup chopped pecans
1 cup flaked coconut
1 teaspoon vanilla

Melt chocolate over hot water and cool slightly. Cream together butter and sugar until light. Add melted chocolate. Add eggs, one at a time, beating well after each addition. Stir dry ingredients together and add alternately with buttermilk, beating well as you go. Fold in vanilla, pecans and coconut. Pour into greased and floured 9″ pans. Bake at 350° for 45 minutes. May be frozen.

Cecile Cox Quillen

Mrs. James H. Quillen, Wife of Representative (Tennessee)

SYLVIE'S CHOCOLATE CAKE

1 cup butter
8 ozs. semi-sweet chocolate
2 tablespoons milk
6 eggs, separated
1 cup sugar
4 ozs. powdered blanched almonds
3 tablespoons cornstarch
½ teaspoon baking powder

Have the butter ready at room temperature. Melt the chocolate in the milk, about two minutes in the microwave. Separate egg yolks from whites. Add sugar to the yolks, pour the chocolate with the yolks. Mix and add vanilla extract. Combine cornstarch, powdered almonds and baking powder, add to the chocolate. Cream in the softened butter, cut into small pieces. Beat egg whites stiff and include gently. Butter and flour a round, 10½″ diameter pan. Preheat oven and bake at 350° for 40 minutes in the center rack. Makes 8 servings.

Adeline P. Rhodes

Mrs. Scott Rhodes, Daughter-in-law of former Representative John J. Rhodes (Arizona)

CHOCOLATE JIFFY CAKE

 2 cups white sugar
 3 cups flour
 2 teaspoons baking soda
10 tablespoons cocoa
 2 teaspoons salt
 1 cup salad oil
 3 cups sour milk OR but-
    termilk
 4 teaspoons vanilla
 2 teaspoons red food color-
    ing (optional)

Mix together sugar, flour, baking soda, cocoa and salt. Add dry ingredients together and to salad oil and buttermilk OR sour milk and vanilla. Beat together well with wire whip or spoon. Bake in 13″ × 9″ pan at 350° for 35 minutes. Check with toothpick. Cover with favorite frosting. (To sour sweet milk, add 1 tablespoon vinegar to 1 cup milk). Everyone has these ingredients on hand. This is delicious, moist cake!! No eggs!! Makes 15 large or 30 small servings. May be frozen.

Mrs. Ed Royce, Wife of Representative (California)

CEMA'S CHOCOLATE CAKE

Cake:
 3 cups flour
 2 cups sugar
½ cup cocoa
 1 teaspoon salt
 2 teaspoons baking soda
 2 teaspoons vanilla
 2 teaspoons vinegar
⅔ cup vegetable oil
 2 cups ice water

Mix all dry ingredients together. Add wet ingredients. Beat all together, then put in greased 13″ × 9″ baking pan. Sprinkle on top a 6 ounce package of chocolate chips. Bake at 350° for 40–50 minutes. Makes 10 to 12 servings.

Topping:
 6 oz. pkg. chocolate chips

Mrs. Paul Gillmor, Wife of Representative (Ohio)

CHOCOLATE STEAMED PUDDING CAKE

Cake:
- 1 tablespoon butter
- ½ cup sugar
- 1 egg
- 1 square unsweetened chocolate
- ½ cup milk
- 1 cup flour
- ½ teaspoon baking soda
- 1 teaspoon cream of tartar

Sauce:
- ⅔ cup butter
- 2 cups 10X (confectioners) sugar
- 2 teaspoons vanilla
- 4 eggs

Cake: Cream butter and sugar until fluffy. Add egg and melted chocolate. Add alternately to above: Milk and the mixture of flour, baking soda and cream of tartar. Place in a steam pan, cover with cloth and steam for 45 minutes.

Sauce: Cream butter and sugar until fluffy. Add vanilla and egg yolks and beat until lemon colored. Fold in egg whites that have been beaten until stiff and dry. Cook over double boiler until sauce is warm (about 15 minutes).

Serve: Serve cake with sauce poured over top. You can cook the cake early and then put all sauce ingredients together except for the stiff whites and finish while you clear the table and make coffee. Makes 6 servings.

Mrs. William (Bill) Zeliff, Wife of Representative (New Hampshire)

HIGH ALTITUDE CHOCOLATE CAKE

- 3 eggs
- 1 cup cooking oil
- ½ cup buttermilk
- 1 teaspoon vanilla
- 1¾ cups cocoa
- 1 teaspoon salt
- 1 teaspoon baking soda
- 1 teaspoon cinnamon
- 2 cups unsifted flour
- 1 cup boiling water

Beat together eggs, oil, buttermilk and vanilla until smooth. Sift together sugar, cocoa, salt, baking soda, cinnamon and flour. Add dry ingredients to egg mixture. Mix until smooth. Add boiling water all at once. Mix until smooth. (Batter will be extremely thin). Pour batter into greased, floured 8″ cake pans and bake at 350° for about 30 minutes until done.

Mrs. Scott McInnis, Wife of Representative (Colorado)

JL'S MILKY WAY CAKE

Cake:

6 Milky Way bars ($1^{11}/_{16}$ oz. only 5 if 2.10 oz.)
½ cup butter or oleo
2 cups sugar
1 cup butter or oleo
4 eggs
2½ cups flour
1 teaspoon salt
1½ cups buttermilk
½ teaspoon baking soda
1 teaspoon vanilla

Frosting:

2 cups sugar
1 13 oz. can evaporated milk
½ cup butter
1 6 oz. pkg. chocolate chips
1 cup marshmallow creme

Cake: Melt candy and ½ cup butter, stirring constantly. Combine sugar and butter and beat until creamy. Add eggs and beat until light and fluffy. Combine flour and salt. Dissolve baking soda in buttermilk. Add dry ingredients to creamy mixture and alternate with buttermilk mixture. Stir in vanilla and candy bar mixture. Pour into 3 greased and floured 9″ pans. Bake at 350° for 30 minutes. Cool and frost.

Frosting: Combine sugar, milk and butter in saucepan. Cook until "softball" stage. Remove and add chips and creme and stir until melted. Makes 20 servings. May be frozen, prior to frosting.

Alta Leath

Alta Leath, Member of The Congressional Club

Refrigerate cheesecake overnight for ease in cutting.

DOUBLE ICING CHOCOLATE CAKE

Cake:
- 1²/₃ cups sugar
- ½ cup shortening
- 1¾ cups flour
- 1½ teaspoons baking powder
- ½ teaspoon baking soda
- ½ teaspoon salt
- ½ cup cocoa
- 1½ cups milk
- 2 eggs
- 1 teaspoon vanilla

Chocolate Icing:
- 1 12 oz. pkg. milk chocolate chips
- ²/₃ of can sweetened condensed milk

Cream Icing:
- 1 cup & 2 tablespoons shortening (Crisco-solid)
- ¾ cup sugar
- ½ teaspoon salt
- 3 eggs
- 1 teaspoon vanilla

Cake: Cream sugar and shortening. Add flour, baking powder, baking soda, salt, cocoa and ¾ cup milk. Mix and add ¾ cup milk, eggs and vanilla. Grease and flour a 9″ × 13″ cake pan. Pour cake batter into prepared pan and bake at 350° for 25–30 minutes, until it tests done. Cool and remove from pan before icing.

Chocolate Icing: Melt milk chocolate chips in double boiler. Remove from heat and stir in sweetened condensed milk. Mix well. Ice cake on top and sides. Let cool.

Cream Icing: In small mixing bowl cream sugar and shortening. Add remaining ingredients. Beat until creamy and fluffy and sugar is dissolved. Ice only the top of the cake. Makes 16 servings. May be frozen.

Mrs. Thomas Barlow, Wife of Representative (Kentucky)

TEXAS CHOCOLATE SHEET CAKE

Cake:
 2 cups flour
 2 cups sugar
 1 teaspoon baking soda
 1 teaspoon cinnamon
 1 teaspoon vanilla
 1/2 cup buttermilk (1/2 cup
    milk and 1 1/2 teaspoon
    lemon juice)
 2 eggs, beaten well
 2 stick margarine
 2 tablespoons cocoa
 1 cup water

Icing:
 2/3 stick margarine
 4 teaspoon cocoa
 1 teaspoon vanilla
    powdered sugar
    Texas pecans

Cake: Combine first 7 ingredients in a bowl. Bring margarine, cocoa and water to a boil and stir into other ingredients. Do not beat, stir only until mixtures blend. This batter will be thin. Pour into a greased, floured pan (13" × 9"). Bake at 375° for 30–35 minutes.

Icing: Bring margarine, cocoa and vanilla to a boil. Add enough powdered sugar to make spreading consistency. Ice cake immediately after removing it from oven. Place Texas pecans on top. Makes 12 servings. May be frozen.

Deborah Knapp Bonilla

Mrs. Henry Bonilla, Wife of Representative (Texas)

WHITE FUDGE FROSTING

 3/4 cups white chocolate
 2 1/2 tablespoons flour
 1 cup milk
 1 cup butter, softened
 1 cup sugar
 1 1/2 teaspoons vanilla

Melt chocolate. Add flour. Blend in milk and cook over medium heat, stirring constantly until mixture is very thick. Cool completely. In a large bowl, cream butter, sugar and vanilla. Beat until light and fluffy, about 3 minutes. Gradually add completely cooled white chocolate mixture. Beat at high speed until mixture is the consistency of whipped cream.

Cecile Cox Quillen

Mrs. James H. Quillen, Wife of Representative (Tennessee)

GRANDMA'S ICEBOX CAKE

1 pound vanilla wafers
½ cup butter or margarine
½ cup sugar
2 eggs, separated
4 cups canned, crushed pine-
    apple
1 teaspoon vanilla
½ cup chopped nuts
    whipped cream or Cool
    Whip

Drain pineapple into bowl. Combine pineapple juice, butter, sugar and egg yolks. Cook in double boiler until thickened slightly. Cool and add pineapple. Fold in stiffly beaten egg whites. In a 10″ × 13″ cake pan, place a layer of vanilla wafers. Cover with ½ of mixture. Add another layer of wafers and the rest of the mixture and sprinkle with the nuts. Put final layer of wafers on top. Store in refrigerator overnight. Serve with whipped cream or Cool Whip. Makes 15 servings.

Mrs. Bob McEwen, Wife of former Representative (Ohio)

APPLE CAKE

2 cups flour
2 teaspoons baking soda
2 teaspoons vanilla
2 eggs
½ cup oil
2 cups white sugar
2 teaspoons cinnamon
¼ teaspoon salt
1 cup chopped walnuts
4 cups cooking apples,
    peeled and cubed

Place all ingredients in large bowl and mix with hands. Dough will be stiff. Bake at 350° in flat 9″ × 13″ pan for 45 minutes.

Frosting: Whip 3 tablespoons butter, 3 ozs. Philadelphia cream cheese, 1½ cups powdered sugar and ½ teaspoon vanilla. Frost while in the pan. Sprinkle grated walnuts on top. Makes 12 servings. May be frozen.

Mrs. Jeff Minckler, Daughter of former Senator Ernest Lundeen (Minnesota)

Brown sugar won't harden if an apple slice is placed in the container.

GREEN APPLE CAKE

Cake:
- 1 cup vegetable oil
- 2 cups sugar
- 3 eggs
- ½ cup milk
- 3 cups unsifted flour
- 2 cups sugar
- 1 teaspoon baking powder
- 1 teaspoon salt
- ½ teaspoon cumin
- 1 teaspoon vanilla
- 3 Granny Smith green apples, peeled and coarsely chopped
- ½ cup chopped dates or raisins
- 1 cup walnuts

Glaze:
- ½ cup soft butter
- 1 cup confectioners sugar
- 3 tablespoons brandy (or lemon juice, if prefer)
- ½ teaspoon nutmeg

Cake: Beat top 4 ingredients in mixer until creamy. Gradually add dry ingredients to above mixture and beat on low for 2 minutes. Add vanilla. Fold in apples, nuts and dates. Bake in a greased and floured 10″ tube pan at 350° in a preheated oven for 1 hour or until cake tester comes out clean. Cool on wire rack until completely cooled, then spread glaze over it. Sprinkle a few nuts over the glaze.

Glaze: Beat ingredients together in a small bowl until smooth and fluffy. Spread over cake. Makes 15 to 25 servings. May be frozen.

Jeane Chappell

Mrs. Bill Chappell, Wife of former Representative (Florida)

Sending cookies to children through the mail? Pack them in popcorn, it keeps the cookies from breaking and is good to eat too.

GRANNY LIDDLE'S APPLE SAUCE CAKES

½ cup shortening
1 cup sugar
2 cups flour
1 teaspoon salt
2 teaspoons baking soda
1 teaspoon cinnamon
1 teaspoon nutmeg
¼ teaspoon cloves
1½ cups unsweetened apple-
    sauce

Cream together sugar and shortening. Stir together flour, soda, salt, cinnamon, nutmeg and cloves. Add applesauce and dry ingredients to creamed mixture and stir just until mixed. Fill greased (or paper lined) cupcake pans half full. Bake at 350° for 15–20 minutes. (These can also be made in mini-muffin pans). Cool. Ice. Makes 12 servings. May be frozen.

Rebecca DeWine

Rebecca DeWine, Daughter of former Representative Michael DeWine (Ohio)

MERĆEDÈS' APPLE CAKE

1 egg
2 tablespoons oil
3 tablespoons milk
4 tablespoons sugar
5 tablespoons flour
1 big apple, peeled, quar-
    tered and thinly sliced
½ cup sugar
1 egg
½ teaspoon vanilla
½ cup sour cream
½ cup sliced almonds

Butter and flour a 9″ pie pan. Cream together the first 5 ingredients and pour into pan. Add sliced apples on top and bake 15 minutes at 350°. In the meantime, cream the sugar, egg, vanilla and sour cream. Remove pan and pour the mixture. Sprinkle the almonds and bake at 350° until golden brown, about ½ hour. Serve warm with favorite ice cream. Makes 6 servings.

Adeline P. Rhodes

Mrs. Scott Rhodes, Daughter-in-law of former Representative John J. Rhodes (Arizona)

IOWA APPLESAUCE CAKE

½ cup butter, margarine or
    shortening
¾ cup sugar
¾ cup packed brown sugar
1 egg
2 cups all-purpose flour
2 teaspoons baking powder
1 teaspoon baking soda
1 teaspoon ground cinnamon
½ teaspoon ground cloves
1½ cups applesauce
1 cup raisins
½ cup chopped walnuts or
    pecans

In a large mixing bowl, beat the butter, margarine or shortening for 30 seconds. Add the sugars and egg, beat until combined. Stir together the flour, baking powder, baking soda and spices. Add flour mixture alternately with applesauce to butter mixture. Stir in raisins and nuts. Pour batter into a greased 13″ × 9″ × 2″ baking pan, spreading evenly. Bake in a 350° oven for 30–35 minutes, or until a toothpick inserted near the center comes out clean. Cool in pan on wire rack.

Cream Cheese Frosting: Beat together two 3-ounce packages softened cream cheese, ½ cup softened butter (or margarine) and 2 teaspoons vanilla until light and fluffy. Gradually beat in 2 cups sifted powdered sugar. Add additional sifted powdered sugar to make a spreadable frosting. (A butter frosting could be used instead of the cream cheese.) Note: For a decorative finish, set a doily lightly on the frosted cake and sprinkle lightly with a mixture of cinnamon and nutmeg. Carefully remove the doily.

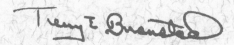

Terry Branstad, Governor (Iowa)

If your brown sugar is already brick-hard, put your cheese grater to work and grate the amount you need.

BANANA PINEAPPLE CAKE

3 cups sifted flour
1 teaspoon baking soda
1 teaspoon cinnamon
2 cups sugar
1 teaspoon salt
1½ cups liquid cooking oil
1 8 oz. can crushed pine-
    apple
1½ teaspoons vanilla
3 eggs
2 cups diced ripe bananas
1 cup chopped nuts, pecans
    or walnuts (optional)

Measure and sift dry ingredients. Add oil, crushed pineapple with its juices, vanilla, eggs and bananas. The mixture is stirred to blend, but is not beaten. It is then poured into a greased and floured 9″ tube pan and baked in preheated oven of 350° for 1 hour and 20 minutes. Let cool in pan. May be frozen.

Mrs. Steven Schiff, Wife of Representative (New Mexico)

BANANA PUDDING CAKE

1 pkg. yellow cake mix
1 pkg. banana cream or va-
    nilla pudding and pie
    filling
1 cup water
¼ cup oil
4 eggs
1 or 2 small ripe bananas
    (mashed)
½ cup chopped pecans or
    walnuts

Combine cake mix, pudding, water and oil; add eggs 1 at a time (mixing well after each). Fold in bananas and chopped nuts. Pour into tube pan and bake in 350° oven for 60-70 minutes or in 13″ × 9″ pan for 50-55 minutes.

Ned McWherter, Governor (Tennessee)

MARGARET CHASE SMITH'S BLUEBERRY CAKE

½ cup shortening
¾ cup sugar
2 eggs
2 cups sifted cake flour
4 teaspoons baking powder
½ teaspoon salt
1 teaspoon nutmeg
1 cup milk
2 cups fresh or frozen blueberries

In a large mixing bowl, cream shortening and sugar until creamy. Add eggs, beat until light and fluffy. Sift together flour, baking powder, salt and nutmeg; add alternately to creamed mixture with milk. Beat well after each addition. Fold in blueberries. Divide batter between two greased and floured 9″ round cake pans. Bake in a 350° oven for about 25 to 30 minutes or until no batter remains when tested with a wooden pick. Remove pans from oven to cooling racks; cool for 10 minutes. Remove cake from pan to cool completely. If desired, put together layers and frost top with a cream cheese icing. Makes one 2-layer cake.

Margaret Chase Smith, former Senator (Maine)

SUPREME LEMON CAKE

1 pkg. instant lemon pudding
1 box Duncan Hines Lemon
   Supreme cake mix
4 eggs
½ cup salad oil
¾ cup of water

Beat the above ingredients on medium speed for 10 minutes and pour into prepared bundt cake pan and bake at 350° for 50 minutes. Cool 10 minutes and ice in pan. Icing: 6 tablespoons lemon juice and 1½ cups of powdered sugar. Makes 15 servings. May be frozen.

Mrs. Dennis Hastert, Wife of Representative (Illinois)

FRESH CRANBERRY CAKE

Cake:
2¼ cups flour
1 cup sugar
¼ teaspoon salt
1 teaspoon soda
1 teaspoon baking power
1 cup whole fresh cranberries
1 cup chopped walnuts
1 cup chopped dates
3 eggs
¾ cup Wesson oil
1 cup buttermilk

Topping:
1 cup sugar
1 cup fresh orange juice

Mix together flour, sugar, salt, baking soda, baking powder; then add cranberries, walnuts and dates. Beat eggs well, add Wesson oil and buttermilk. Combine these ingredients with flour mixture and mix in large bowl. Pour into greased and floured tube cake baking pan. Bake 1 hour at 350°. Heat 1 cup sugar and 1 cup orange juice, pour over hot cake. Makes 40 servings. May be frozen.

Mrs. John Marsh, Wife of former Representative (Virginia)

LEMON CAKE

1 ready made angel food cake, tear into bite-sized pieces
2 3 oz. pkgs. lemon pudding mix.

Cook pudding according to directions, reducing water to 2 cups for each mix and adding an extra egg yolk for each mix. Cool. Toss the cake pieces and the lemon pudding very lightly and put into a tube pan. Chill. About an hour before serving turn out onto serving plate. Frost with lightly sweetened whipped cream. Keep refrigerated.

Mrs. William Darling, Daughter of former Representative Mike DeWine (Ohio)

OATMEAL CAKE WITH RASPBERRY ICING

Cake:

- 1 cup oatmeal (old fashioned Quaker Oats)
- ½ stick butter or shortening (¼ cup)
- 1 cup light brown sugar
- ½ cup sugar
- 2 eggs
- ¼ teaspoon salt
- 1 teaspoon baking soda
- 1 teaspoon cinnamon
- 1½ cups white flour

For icing:

- ¾ stick butter or margarine
- ½ teaspoon vanilla
- ¼ cup brown sugar
- ½ cup raspberry fruit spread
- ½ cup coconut
- 1 cup coarsely chopped pecans

Cake: Combine oatmeal with 1¼ cups boiling water, set aside, stir occasionally. Cream together butter or shortening, sugars and eggs. In separate bowl, sift flour with salt, baking soda and cinnamon. Combine with creamed ingredients and blend well. Add oats and bake at 350° in greased and floured 9″ × 13″ pan for 30 to 35 minutes or until toothpick pulls out clean.

Icing: Heat all ingredients until combined well, spread evenly on warm cake and broil top in oven until golden, about 5 minutes. Makes 12 servings. May be frozen.

Rosalie L. King

Mrs. David S. King, Wife of former Representative (Utah)

A slice of soft bread placed in the package of hardened brown sugar will soften it again in a couple of hours.

GRANDMA CASSERLY'S PINEAPPLE UPSIDE DOWN CAKE

½ cup butter
1 medium can pineapple
1 cup brown sugar
3 eggs, separated
1 cup granulated sugar
5 tablespoons fruit juice
1 cup sifted flour
1 teaspoon baking powder

Melt butter and brown sugar, add pineapple. In separate bowl, beat egg yolk, add sugar and juice. Add sifted flour and baking powder and fold in stiffly beaten egg whites. Bake at 350° for 45 minutes.

Mickey Bilbray

Mrs. Jim Bilbray, Wife of Representative (Nevada)

PRUNE CAKE

Cake:
- ½ cup soft shortening
- 1½ cups sugar
- 3 large eggs
- 1 cup buttermilk
- 1 cup nuts (optional)
- 2 cups sifted flour
- 1 teaspoon baking powder
- 1 teaspoon soda
- 1 teaspoon salt
- 1 cup cooked, chopped prunes

Icing:
- 1 cup sugar
- 1 teaspoon baking soda
- ½ cup buttermilk
- 1 stick margarine
- ½ teaspoon vanilla
- 1 tablespoon white Karo syrup

Cake: Cream shortening and sugar. Beat in eggs. Sift flour, baking powder, soda, salt and add to mixture alternately with buttermilk, beginning and ending with dry mixture of flour. Bake at 350° in either a 13″ × 9″ × 2″ cake pan or 2 round layer cake pans, for 35-45 minutes in oblong pan or 25-30 minutes in round pans.

Icing: Combine ingredients in saucepan and cook over low or medium heat for 25 minutes. Pour over hot cake. May be frozen.

Corinne S. Morris

Mrs. Thomas Morris, Wife of former Representative (New Mexico)

MARGARET SMITH'S CAKE

- 2 egg whites, beaten
- 1½ cups sugar
- ½ cup water
- 1¼ cups sifted cake flour
- ½ teaspoon salt
- ½ teaspoon cream of tartar
- ½ teaspoon vanilla

Cook sugar and water until it spins a thread. Beat egg whites until stiff, pour over syrup. Add flour, extracts and bake at 350° in angel food cake pan for about 45 minutes. Makes 12 servings.

Bea Smith

Mrs. Neal Smith, Wife of Representative (Iowa)

RHUBARB CAKE

Cake:
1½ cups frozen rhubarb
½ cup sugar
2 cups sifted all-purpose
    flour
½ cup Wesson oil
1 cup buttermilk
1 teaspoon cinnamon
1 teaspoon baking soda
1½ cups sugar
1 egg
1 teaspoon salt
1 teaspoon baking soda

Topping:
6 tablespoons margarine
⅔ cup brown sugar
1 cup chopped nuts
1 cup coconut
¼ cup milk
1 teaspoon vanilla

Cake: Combine rhubarb and the ½ cup sugar. Set aside. When thawed, stir and cut up any large pieces of rhubarb. In large bowl, combine all remaining ingredients and stir with a spoon until thoroughly blended. Add the rhubarb mixture and blend. Pour into well greased and floured pan. Bake at 350° for 40 to 45 minutes. Remove from oven when it tests done with a toothpick or cake tester. While still warm, spoon on the topping.

Topping: Combine margarine, coconut, brown sugar, milk, nuts and vanilla. Boil 3 minutes. Spoon over the warm cake. Makes 12 to 15 servings.

Martha Jane Shriver

Mrs. Garner E. Shriver, Wife of former Representative (Kansas)

Cream will whip faster and better if you: first chill the cream, bowl and beaters well. The freezer is really fast.

SOUR CREAM POUND CAKE

6 eggs, separated
2 sticks margarine or butter
3 cups sugar
1 teaspoon vanilla
¼ teaspoon baking soda
3 cups all-purpose flour
1 8 oz. container sour cream

Separate eggs, beat egg whites until stiff. Set aside. Cream margarine or butter, slowly adding sugar then add egg yolks one at a time. Add vanilla and baking soda. Alternately add sifted flour and sour cream. Gently fold in beaten egg whites. Pour into greased and floured tube pan. Bake at 350° for 1½ hours or until toothpick comes out clean when used for testing doneness. Cool at least 30 minutes before removing from pan. Makes 10 servings. May be frozen.

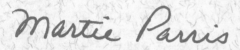

Mrs. Stan Parris, Wife of former Representative (Virginia)

STRAWBERRY CAKE

1 pkg. white cake mix
1 cup cooking oil
1 cup thawed frozen strawberries
1 cup chopped pecans
4 eggs
1 3 oz. box strawberry Jell-O
½ cup milk
   whipped cream or white
   frosting
   strawberries

Mix ingredients and beat with mixer at medium speed for 3-4 minutes. Pour into 3 greased and floured 8″ layer cake pans and bake at 350° for 25-30 minutes. Frost with whipped cream or any white frosting. Decorate with strawberries. Makes 8 to 10 servings.

Mrs. Maurice Burnside, Wife of former Representative (West Virginia)

SPECIAL BUTTER CAKE

1 pkg. yellow cake mix (pud-
    ding included style)
4 eggs
1 stick melted butter
8 oz. cream cheese, softened
1 teaspoon vanilla
1 pound powdered sugar
    pecans or fresh strawber-
    ries may be added as a
    garnish

Preheat oven to 350°. Mix 1 slightly beaten egg with dry cake mix and melted butter to moist dough consistency. Grease a 13″ × 9″ × 2″ pan. Press mixture evenly in pan. Soften cream cheese and beat in electric mixer with remaining eggs and vanilla until creamy. Beat in powdered sugar gradually, and beat until smooth; this takes several minutes. Pour over crust. Bake at 350° for 35 to 40 minutes. Watch carefully so base doesn't get too brown. The cheese mixture sinks into the center somewhat leaving a firmer crust around the edges. Cut in squares to serve. Pecans, powdered sugar, or fresh strawberries can be used as a garnish when serving. Makes 20 servings.

Helen Green

Mrs. Gene Green, Wife of Representative (Texas)

ONE-EGG CAKE

⅔ cup sugar
⅓ cup shortening
⅛ teaspoon salt
1 teaspoon vanilla flavoring
1 egg
1½ cups flour
½ cup milk
2 teaspoons baking powder

Cream shortening and sugar. Add unbeaten egg. Add flavoring. Beat thoroughly. Sift flour, measure and sift with salt and baking powder. Add alternately with milk to creamed shortening and sugar. Pour into well oiled loaf or 8″ × 8″ pan. Bake at 375° for 35 minutes. Makes 8 servings.

Lucille K. Carter

Mrs. Steven V. Carter, Wife of former Representative (Iowa)

CHARLIE'S LAMB CAKE

1 pkg. white deluxe cake
    mix
1 pkg. instant vanilla pud-
    ding mix
4 eggs
1 cup water
½ cup oil

Grease and flour upper and lower half of a lamb cake mold baking pan. Mix all ingredients together for 2 minutes. Pour batter into lower half of lamb mold pan, to just below the top rim. Place empty top half over the lower and bake in preheated 350° oven for 50 minutes. Test for doneness with toothpick through steam hole in top of mold. Remove from oven. Remove top half of pan. Replace lower half in oven. Cook at same temperature for another 5–10 minutes. Allow 5 minutes to cool. Place on cake platter. Trim bottom edges so that the lamb will stand upright. Frost with white frosting. Coat with coconut shreds and decorate eyes, nose and mouth with candied fruit. Makes 8 to 10 servings. May be frozen.

Charles A. Vanik, former Representative (Ohio)

LEMON GLAZE POUND CAKE

Cake:
1 box Duncan Hines lemon
    cake mix
½ cup sugar
¼ cup Crisco cooking oil
1 cup sour cream
1 cup apricot nectar
4 eggs, beat well

Glaze:
1½ cup confectioners sugar
¼ cup lemon juice

In a mixer blend together cake mix, sugar, oil, sour cream, apricot nectar and eggs (well beaten). Blend until smooth (approximately 2 minutes). Pour batter into 10″ tube pan or fluted pan (spray pan with Pam cooking spray). Bake at 350° for 30 minutes, reduce temperature to 325° and bake for 30 minutes more.

Glaze: Combine confectioners sugar and lemon juice (if too thin, add more confectioners sugar) pour immediately over warm (not hot) cake. Makes 8 to 10 servings. May be frozen.

Mrs. Larkin Smith, Wife of former Representative (Mississippi)

SOUR CREAM CAKE

Cake:
- 2 sticks margarine
- 2 cups sugar
- 2 eggs
- 2 cups cake flour
- 1 teaspoon baking powder
- 1 teaspoon vanilla
- 1 small carton sour cream

Topping mix:
- 1 teaspoon cinnamon
- 2 teaspoons sugar
- ½ cup chopped pecans

Cream margarine and sugar well. Add eggs one at a time and beat well. Add cake flour and baking powder. Mix well. Add vanilla and sour cream. Mix briefly. Fold in ½ of topping mix. Grease bundt pan. Pour rest of topping mix in bottom of pan and roll around to coat all sides. Pour in cake mixture and bake for 1 hour at 325°. Do not open the oven door while baking. Flop cake on plate as soon as it comes out of oven. Makes 10 servings. May be frozen.

Nancy Hamilton

Mrs. Lee Hamilton, Wife of Representative (Indiana)

GRANDMOTHER'S POUND CAKE

- 2 sticks butter at room temperature
- 1⅔ cups sugar, sifted 5 times before measuring
- 5 eggs at room temperature
- 2 cups flour, sifted 5 times before measuring
- 2 teaspoon flavoring (I use ½ teaspoon lemon, then 1½ teaspoon of either almond or vanilla)

The sifting is very important as is the room temperature. Set the butter and flour out the night before you bake. Cream the butter and sugar while sifting flour. Take 5 minutes or more to make sure it's light and fluffy. Add eggs one at a time, letting each one mix a minute before adding another. Add flavoring. Blend or fold in flour. Put in a tube pan that is only greased and floured on the bottom. (No butter on the sides because the cake has to hold onto something to rise well.) Bake at 325° for 1 hour and 15 minutes. Use the toothpick test. Cool on a rack for 10 minutes. Run a knife around between the cake and the pan and then invert and finish cooling on a rack. The reason for all the sifting and beating is that there is no leavening in the cake. Makes 25 servings. May be frozen.

Kit Robinson

Mrs. J. Kenneth Robinson, Wife of former Representative (Virginia)

CHOCOLATE POUND CAKE

2 sticks butter
1 cup Crisco
3 cups sugar
5 eggs
3 cups cake flour
½ teaspoon baking powder
½ cup Hersheys cocoa
1 cup milk
1 teaspoon vanilla

Cream butter and Crisco with sugar, then add eggs. Sift flour, baking powder and cocoa and add alternately with milk and vanilla. Bake at 325° in well greased and floured 10″ tube pan for 1 hour 30 minutes. Makes 8 to 10 servings. May be frozen.

Margaret Grant

Mrs. Robert A. Grant, Wife of former Representative (Indiana)

ALABAMA RUM CAKE

1 cup chopped pecans
1 18 oz. yellow cake mix
1 3.4 oz. instant vanilla
   pudding
4 eggs
½ cup cold water
½ cup Wesson oil
½ cup dark rum

Syrup:
¼ pound butter
¼ cup water
1 cup sugar
½ cup dark rum

Grease and flour 10″ bundt or tube pan. Sprinkle chopped pecans in bottom of pan. Mix all ingredients including rum. Bake 1 hour at 325°, check at 55 minutes. Do not overbake. Cool 10 minutes. Place on serving plate. Prick top and sides with toothpick. Brush and spoon rum syrup on cake.

Rum Syrup: In small saucepan, mix butter, water and sugar until mixture boils and sugar is melted. Remove from heat. Add rum. Brush over hot cake. Best made the day before serving.

Karen Callahan

Mrs. Sonny Callahan, Wife of Representative (Alabama)

SALLY'S QUICK RUM CAKE

Cake:
- 1 cup chopped pecans
- 1 pkg. yellow cake mix (Duncan Hines preferred)
- 1 pkg. French vanilla instant pudding
- ½ cup water
- ½ cup Wesson oil
- ½ cup dark rum
- 4 eggs

Glaze:
- 1 stick butter
- 1 cup sugar
- ¼ cup water
- 2 ozs. dark rum

Cake: Sprinkle chopped pecans on bottom of greased tube or bundt pan. Mix together cake mix, pudding, water, Wesson oil and rum with electric mixer. Beat in eggs one at a time. Pour batter into pan and bake for 1 hour at 325°. Let cake cool.

Glaze: Boil sugar, butter, water and rum together in saucepan. Pour over the cooled cake while still in pan. Let glaze soak into cake (overnight is best). Cake and glaze should be completely cooled before removing from pan. This cake is divine. Makes 10 servings. May be frozen.

Mrs. Tim Roemer, Wife of Representative (Indiana)

HEATH CAKE

- 2 cups sugar
- 2 cups flour
- 2 sticks margarine, divided
- ½ cup Crisco
- 8 tablespoons cocoa, divided
- 1 cup water
- ½ cup buttermilk
- 2 slightly beaten eggs
- 1 teaspoon baking soda
- 1 teaspoon cinnamon
- 2 teaspoons vanilla, divided
- 6 tablespoons milk
- 1 box powdered sugar
- 1 cup chopped pecans

Sift together: sugar and flour. Put in saucepan and bring to boil: 1 stick margarine, Crisco, 4 tablespoons cocoa and water. Remove when boiling and pour over flour and sugar. Mix well. Add: buttermilk, eggs, baking soda, cinnamon and 1 teaspoon vanilla. Mix well. Pour into greased cookie sheet. Bake at 400° for 20 minutes. Frosting: Start 5 minutes before cake is done. Put in saucepan: 1 stick margarine, 4 tablespoons cocoa and 6 tablespoons milk. Mix and bring to a boil. Remove from heat and add: powdered sugar, 1 teaspoon vanilla and pecans. Beat and spread on cake while hot.

Mrs. E. Benjamin Nelson, Wife of Governor (Nebraska)

BUTTERSCOTCH CAKE

1 box instant vanilla pudding
  and pie filling
4 eggs
½ cup oil
1 box yellow cake mix
8 oz. container of sour cream
8 ozs. (1 cup) butterscotch
  morsels
1 cup chopped pecans

Mix the first 5 items, then fold in butterscotch morsels and nuts. Cook in a greased bundt pan at 350° for 1 hour if tested done.

Evelyn Taylor

Mrs. Roy Taylor, Wife of former Representative (North Carolina)

DIANA'S TOFFEE ANGEL FOOD CAKE

Angel Food Cake:
10 egg whites at room temperature
¼ teaspoon cream of tartar
¼ teaspoon salt
1 teaspoon vanilla extract
1¼ cups sugar
1 cup cake flour, sifted

Frosting:
4 tablespoons unsweetened
  cocoa
1 cup confectioners sugar
6 Heath bars, chopped finely
1 pint heavy cream

Beat egg whites and cream of tartar until they form soft peaks. Then add salt and vanilla. Gradually add sugar, beating until whites are stiff but not dry. Slowly fold flour into egg whites using a rubber spatula. Spoon into an ungreased 10″ tube pan. Bake at 350° for 40 minutes. Cool completely before taking the cake out of the pan. Two hours prior to serving, prepare frosting. Mix cocoa and sugar together. Add chopped Heath bars. Whip the cream and fold it into mixture. Frost top and sides of cake completely. Note: To help you chop heath bars, put them in the freezer for 30 minutes to harden. Makes 10 to 12 servings.

Rhoda Glickman

Mrs. Dan Glickman, Wife of Representative (Kansas)

CARAMEL CAKE

Cake:
  1 box Duncan Hines butter recipe cake mix

Frosting:
2½ cups sugar
  1 stick margarine
  ½ pint whipping cream
  2 teaspoon vanilla

Cake: Mix cake according to package directions. You may use a sheet pan or 2 layers—8″ or 9″. Bake at 350°, instead of 375° as directed.

Frosting: This is a two step process, done simultaneously: 1. In a small heavy skillet, caramelize ½ cup sugar until a golden brown. Watch carefully, this will burn. Stir to help dissolve sugar and to promote browning. 2. In a large heavy pan (I use the pressure cooker pan), melt the margarine, whipping cream and 2 cups sugar. When this is bubbling, add the caramelized sugar from step 1. Using a candy thermometer, cook to the "soft ball" stage. Remove from heat and cool for 5 minutes. Pour in mixing bowl and beat until spreading consistency. If it gets too stiff, add a teaspoon of milk. Add 2 teaspoons vanilla and spread on cake. Makes 15 servings. May be frozen.

Mrs. John Tanner, Wife of Representative (Tennessee)

NANNY'S MOLASSES CAKE

  1 cup white sugar
  ½ cup molasses
  ½ cup shortening
  2 cups flour
  2 teaspoons cinnamon
  1 teaspoon ginger
  2 eggs, beaten
  1 cup hot water
  2 teaspoons baking soda
  1 cup raisins
    nuts (optional)

Mix white sugar, molasses, shortening, flour, cinnamon, ginger and eggs. Add 1 cup hot water in which 2 teaspoons baking soda have been dissolved. Beat all together, with raisins and nuts. Grease a 13″ × 9″ × 2″ pyrex. Bake at 325° for 25 minutes. Makes 24 servings. May be frozen.

Mrs. William Baker, Wife of Representative (California)

OLD FASHIONED GINGER BREAD

2½ cups flour
1½ teaspoons baking soda
½ teaspoon salt
1 teaspoon cinnamon
1 teaspoon ginger
½ teaspoon cloves
½ cup butter or other shortening
½ cup sugar
1 egg, well beaten
1 cup molasses or cane sugar
1 cup boiling water

Lemon Sauce:

½ cup sugar
1½ tablespoons cornstarch
1 cup boiling water
1 tablespoon butter
1 tablespoon lemon juice
pinch of salt
⅓ cup raisins
dash nutmeg (optional)

Sift and measure flour. Sift with baking soda, salt and spices. Cream shortening until light and fluffy. Add sugar gradually, beating after each addition. Add well beaten egg and molasses, beat until smooth. Add sifted dry ingredients. Mix thoroughly and add hot water, stir until smooth. Turn into well greased pan. Bake in preheated oven at 350° for 35 to 40 minutes. Makes 16 servings. May be frozen.

Lemon Sauce: Mix sugar and cornstarch. Add boiling water, cook 5 minutes. Add remaining ingredients in order given. May be served warm or cold with gingerbread.

Frances Hagan

Mrs. G. Elliott Hagan, Wife of former Representative (Georgia)

AGGIE'S SPICE CAKE

1½ cups seeded raisins
1 cup water
½ cup butter
¾ cup sugar
1 well beaten egg
1½ cups flour
1 teaspoon baking soda
nutmeg, cinnamon, cloves, salt
nuts (if desired)

Cook raisins in water for 20 minutes, save liquid. Cream butter, sugar and egg. Add dry ingredients alternating with raisins, water (and vanilla or bourbon, if desired). Bake at 350° for 20 minutes. Makes 8 servings.

Frosting: Powdered sugar creamed with butter. Add bourbon or brandy. Amounts vary depending on amount wanted. About 1 cup sugar per ¼ cup butter.

Mary Kennedy

Mrs. Anthony Kennedy, Wife of Associate Justice, U.S. Supreme Court

CARROT CAKE

Cake:
3 cups unbleached all-purpose flour

3 cups sugar

1 teaspoon salt

1 tablespoon baking soda

1 tablespoon ground cinnamon

1½ cups corn oil

4 large eggs, lightly beaten

1 tablespoon vanilla extract

1½ cups chopped walnuts

1½ cups shredded coconut

1⅓ cups pureed cooked carrots

¾ cup drained crushed pineapple

Cream Cheese Frosting:
8 ozs. cream cheese, at room temperature

6 tablespoons unsalted butter, at room temperature

3 cups confectioners sugar

1 teaspoon vanilla extract

juice of ½ lemon (optional)

Cake: Preheat oven to 350°. Grease two 9″ layer cake pans lined with wax paper. Sift dry ingredients into bowl. Add oil, egg and vanilla. Beat well. Fold in walnuts, coconut, carrots and pineapple. Pour batter into prepared pans. Set on middle rack of oven and bake for 30–35 minutes until edges have pulled away from pan and cake tester inserted in center comes out clean. Cool on cake rack for 3 hours. Fill cake and frost with cream cheese frosting. Makes 10 to 12 servings. May be frozen.

Cream Cheese Frosting: Cream together cream cheese and butter in a mixing bowl. Slowly sift in confectioners sugar and beat until fully incorporated. Stir in vanilla and lemon juice.

Jane Merrill Filner

Ms. Bob Filner, Wife of Representative (California)

Soupy whipped cream can be saved by adding an egg white, then chilling thoroughly. Rebeat for a fluffy surprise.

TWENTY-FOUR CARAT CARROT CAKE

Cake:
- 2 cups flour
- 2 teaspoons baking powder
- 2 teaspoons baking soda
- 2 teaspoons cinnamon
- 1 teaspoon salt
- 2 cups sugar
- 1½ cups vegetable oil
- 4 eggs
- 3 cups grated carrots
- ½ cup chopped nuts
- 1 cup raisins

Frosting:
- 8 ozs. cream cheese, softened
- ¼ cup softened butter
- 2 teaspoons vanilla
- 3 to 4 cups confectioners sugar

Stir together flour, baking powder, baking soda, cinnamon, salt and sugar; add oil and beat well. Add eggs, one at a time, beating after each addition. Stir in carrots, nuts, and raisins, blend thoroughly. Pour into a greased 13″ × 9″ baking pan, bake at 350° for 45–60 minutes. Serve plain sprinkled with confectioners sugar or frost with cream cheese frosting. Makes 10 to 12 servings.

Frosting: Beat together cream cheese, butter and vanilla until smooth. Add confectioners sugar until spreading consistency. Beat until smooth.

Karen S. Gillmor

Mrs. Paul Gillmor, Wife of Representative (Ohio)

A meringue pie may be covered with waxed paper or plastic wrap with no fear of sticking. If you'll first spray the paper with non-stick spray.

DIANE'S FABULOUS CARROT CAKE

Cake:
- 3 cups grated carrots
- 2 cups sugar
- 4 eggs
- 1½ cups oil
- 3 teaspoons cinnamon
- 1 teaspoon salt
- 2 teaspoons baking soda
- 2 teaspoons vanilla
- 2 cups flour

Icing:
- 1 stick margarine
- 1 pkg. cream cheese
- 1 box powdered sugar (don't need to use all)
- 2 teaspoons vanilla

Combine all ingredients in one bowl. (I just use a carrot peeler for carrots). Mix all ingredients thoroughly. Spray pan(s) with Pam. Bake at 350° for 30-45 minutes. When cake is cool, mix together icing ingredients and frost cake.

Suzie Dicks

Mrs. Norm Dicks, Wife of Representative (Washington)

Once your meringue is baked, cut it cleanly, using a knife coated with butter.

CARROT CAKE

Cake:
- 1½ cups oil
- 2 cups sugar
- 4 eggs
- 2 cups flour
- 2 teaspoons baking soda (scant)
- 1 teaspoon salt
- 3 teaspoons cinnamon
- 2 teaspoons vanilla
- 3 cups grated carrots

Icing:
- 1 stick of margarine
- 8 oz. pkg. of cream cheese
- 1 pkg. of confectioners sugar
- 2 teaspoons vanilla

Cake: Combine sugar and oil and add eggs, beat well. Sift flour, baking soda, salt and cinnamon together. Add to sugar mixture and beat well, add vanilla and grated carrots. Bake in three 8″ layer cake pans, which have been well greased. Bake at 325° for 45 minutes, when cool, ice with cream cheese icing. This cake is tasty enough for a party.

Icing: Soften margarine and cream cheese and beat together. Add confectioners sugar and vanilla. Beat well. Frost cake. Refrigerate until ready to serve. Makes 10 servings. May be frozen.

Marguerite Nye

Mrs. Gerald P. Nye, Wife of former Senator (North Dakota)

Cream whipped ahead of time will not separate if you add ¼ teaspoon unflavored gelatin per cup of cream.

CARROT CAKE

Cake:
- 2 cups flour
- 2 teaspoons baking powder
- 1½ teaspoons soda
- 2 teaspoons cinnamon
- 1 teaspoon salt
- 2 cups sugar
- 4 eggs
- 1½ cups Wesson oil
- 2 cups raw carrots, grated
- 1½ cups crushed pineapple, undrained
- ½ cup chopped pecans

Frosting:
- 1 box powdered sugar
- 1 stick (½ cup) oleo or butter, softened
- 1 8 oz. pkg. cream cheese
- 1 teaspoon vanilla
- 1 tablespoon milk

Cake: Sift dry ingredients. Mix oil, sugar and eggs and beat well. Add dry ingredients, mix. Add carrots, pineapple and nuts. Bake at 350° for 35 to 40 minutes.

Frosting: Mix all ingredients together.

Terry Branstad, Governor (Iowa)

A dampened and folded dish towel placed under the bowl in which you are whipping cream will keep the bowl from dancing all over the counter top.

CARROT CAKE

Cake:
- 2 cups flour
- 2 cups sugar
- 2 teaspoons cinnamon
- ½ teaspoon salt
- 1 teaspoon baking powder
- 2 teaspoons baking soda
- 3 cups grated carrots
- 1½ cups oil
- 4 eggs
- 1 teaspoon vanilla

Frosting:
- 1 8 oz. pkg. cream cheese
- ½ cup butter or margarine
- 1 box powdered sugar
- 1 teaspoon vanilla
- 1 cup chopped pecans

Cake: Mix all dry ingredients together. Add grated carrots. Add oil, eggs and vanilla and blend well. Bake in three 9″ pans at 350° for about 30 minutes or until done. Spread frosting between layers and on top and sides of cake. May be frozen.

Frosting: Mix cream cheese and butter. Add sugar, vanilla and pecans. Blend well. Add milk if necessary to spread.

Note: This is Senator Bumpers' favorite cake.

Betty Bumpers

Mrs. Dale Bumpers, Wife of Senator (Arkansas)

A few drops of lemon juice added to whipping cream helps it whip faster and better.

CARROT CAKE

Cake:
- 3 cups all-purpose flour
- 2 cups sugar
- 2 teaspoons baking powder
- 2 teaspoons baking soda
- 1 teaspoon cinnamon
- 1 teaspoon salt
- 3 cups grated carrots
- 1⅓ cups vegetable oil
- 4 eggs
- 2 teaspoons vanilla
- ¾ cup raisins
- ½ cup chopped walnuts

Icing:
- 1 8 oz. pkg. cream cheese
- 1 tablespoon butter
- 1 teaspoon vanilla
- dash salt
- 1½ cups confectioners' sugar

Combine flour, sugar, baking powder, baking soda, cinnamon and salt in mixing bowl. Add carrots, oil, eggs and vanilla. Mix with electric mixer at medium speed, beating 3 to 4 minutes. Stir in raisins and walnuts. Pour mixture into greased and floured 10″ tube pan. Bake at 350° for 1 hour or until cake tester comes out clean. Makes 16 servings. May be frozen.

Icing: Blend cream cheese, butter and vanilla in a small bowl with mixer or fork until mixture is smooth. Stir in salt. Gradually add confectioners' sugar, beating until mixture is fluffy. Drizzle icing over baked cake.

Nancy Hamilton

Mrs. Lee Hamilton, Wife of Representative (Indiana)

If you've over sweetened a dish, add salt.

CARROT PINEAPPLE CAKE

Cake:
- 2 cups flour
- 2 cups sugar
- 2 teaspoons cinnamon
- 1½ teaspoons baking soda
- ½ teaspoon salt
- 1½ cups cooking oil
- 4 eggs, beaten
- 2 cups grated raw carrots
- 1 15 oz. can crushed pineapple, drained
- 1 cup chopped nuts

Frosting:
- 1 8 oz. pkg. cream cheese, softened
- ½ box confectioners' sugar
- ½ cup butter (or margarine), softened
- ½ teaspoon vanilla
- milk

Cake: Sift together first 5 ingredients. Add oil, eggs, carrots, pineapple and nuts. Mix well. Pour into 9″ × 13″ pan and bake at 350° for 35 to 45 minutes. Cool before frosting. Makes 12 servings. May be frozen.

Frosting: Combine cheese, sugar, butter and vanilla in small bowl and blend thoroughly. Add small amount of milk, if necessary, to make frosting the proper consistency to spread on cake.

Mae J. Simpson

Mrs. Richard Simpson, Wife of former Representative (Pennsylvania)

JUDY'S PUMPKIN CAKE

- 1 box yellow cake mix (reserve 1 cup for
- ½ topping)
- 1 cup oil
- 30 egg
- 2 oz. can pumpkin pie mix
- ⅔ eggs
- ½ cup evaporated milk
- ¼ cup sugar
- 1 cup margarine
- cup chopped nuts

To dry cake mix, add oil and 1 egg. Mix together and pat in bottom of a 9″ × 13″ sheet cake pan. To pumpkin pie mix, add 2 eggs and evaporated milk. Mix well and pour over raw dough mixture. For topping, mix reserved cup of cake mix with sugar and margarine until crumbly. Sprinkle over pumpkin mix and add nuts over top. Bake at 350° for 1 hour 15 minutes. Makes 16 servings.

Kit Robinson

Mrs. J. Kenneth Robinson, Wife of former Representative (Virginia)

GLORIOUS CHEESE CAKE

½ cup graham cracker
    crumbs
3 8 oz. pkgs. cream cheese
1 cup sugar
5 eggs
¼ teaspoon salt
2 teaspoons vanilla
½ teaspoon almond extract
1 pint sour cream
    canned fruit filling or fresh
    strawberries

Grease spring-form pan (10″) and sprinkle with graham cracker crumbs. Blend together softened cream cheese and sugar. Add eggs and flavorings. Then add sour cream. Blend until smooth, use hand or electric mixer. Bake for 35 minutes at 375°. Open oven door (when baking time is over) and let cake cool gradually. Top with canned fruit filling or fresh strawberries. Makes 12 to 16 servings.

Connie Ewing

Mrs. Thomas Ewing, Wife of Representative (Illinois)

FRANK'S CHEESE CAKE

Crust:
1 pkg. graham crackers,
    rolled to crumbs
¼ cup sugar
6 tablespoons butter, melted

Filling:
3 8 oz. pkgs. cream cheese
1 cup sugar
3 eggs
1 teaspoon vanilla

Topping:
1½ cups sour cream
2 tablespoons sugar
1 teaspoon vanilla

Crust: Mix cracker crumbs and sugar. Stir in butter and mix with fork until well moistened. Press all but a few tablespoons of crumbs into bottom and sides of spring-form pan. The crumbs should come approximately half way up sides of pan. Bake at 375° for 8 minutes. Cool.

Filling: Beat cream cheese, eggs, sugar and vanilla until smooth and pour into the crust. Bake 40 minutes at 350°.

Topping: Mix ingredients together and spread on baked cheese cake. Sprinkle with reserved cracker crumbs and bake 5 minutes at 400°. Cool, then chill. May be frozen.

Frank H. Miller

Frank H. Miller, Son-in-law of former Senator Edward V. Long (Missouri)

CREAM CHEESE CAKE

Cake:
- 4 eggs
- 1 cups sugar
- 1 tablespoon lemon juice
- 4 8 oz. pkgs. cream cheese, softened
- 2 cups sour cream
- 1 teaspoon vanilla
- 4 tablespoons sugar

Graham Cracker Shell:
- 2 cups graham cracker crumbs
- 4 tablespoons confectioners sugar
- ½ cup melted butter

Cake: Preheat oven to 375°, a moderately hot oven. Beat eggs, sugar and lemon juice until light. Add the cheese and beat thoroughly. Pour filling into crust and bake for 20 minutes. Remove cake from oven; increase oven heat to 475°, a very hot oven. Top cake with sour cream mixed with vanilla and sugar. Sprinkle with remaining crumbs and bake 10 minutes longer. Cool and chill in refrigerator overnight before serving.

Graham Cracker Shell: Blend all ingredients together thoroughly. Spread and press mixture on buttered sides and bottom of spring-form (13″ × 9″ pyrex works just as well). Chill for several hours before filling. Reserve ¼ cup of mixture to sprinkle on top of cheesecake.

Mrs. William Thomas, Wife of Representative (California)

FROZEN MOCHA CHEESE CAKE

Crust:
- 1½ cup chocolate wafer crumbs
- ¼ cup granulated sugar
- ¼ cup margarine, melted

Cheese Cake:
- 1 8 oz. pkg. cream cheese
- 1 14 oz. Eagle brand milk
- ⅔ cup chocolate syrup
- 2 tablespoons instant coffee
- 1 teaspoon hot water
- 1 cup (½ pint) whipping cream, whipped

Crust: In small bowl, combine crumbs, sugar and margarine. In a buttered 9″ spring-form pan or 13″ × 9″ baking dish, pat crumbs on sides and bottom. Chill.

Cake: In large bowl, beat cheese until fluffy. Add milk and chocolate syrup. In a cup, dissolve the coffee in water, add to cheese mixture. Fold in whipped cream. Pour into pan. Cover and freeze. Garnish with chocolate crumbs. Keep in freezer. Makes 12 servings.

Mrs. James Harvey, Wife of former Representative (Michigan)

AMARETTO CHEESECAKE

1 cup graham crackers,
   crushed
3 tablespoons butter
4 8 oz. pkgs. cream cheese
   dash salt
1 teaspoon vanilla
4 eggs
1⅓ cups sugar
½ cup amaretto (or more)
2 cups sour cream
½ cup sliced almonds

Butter 10″ spring-form pan and coat with graham cracker crumbs. Beat together cream cheese, salt, vanilla, eggs, sugar and Amaretto. I use a food processor. Fold in the sour cream. Bake at 375° for 45 minutes or until set. I add sliced almonds to brown on top, the last 10 minutes. (If you don't like Amaretto, other flavorings will work.) Makes 12 servings.

Linda Slattery

Mrs. Jim Slattery, Wife of Representative (Kansas)

INCREDIBLE CHEESECAKE

Crust:
1¾ cups graham cracker
   crumbs
¼ cup chopped walnuts
¼ cup butter or margarine,
   melted
½ teaspoon cinnamon

Filling:
3 eggs
2 8 oz. pkgs. cream cheese
1 cup sugar
¼ teaspoon salt
¼ teaspoon vanilla
½ teaspoon almond extract
3 cups sour cream or plain
   yogurt

Crust: Mix together graham cracker crumbs, walnuts, butter and cinnamon. Press into the bottom and onto the sides of a 9″ spring-form pan.

Filling: Beat eggs and add cream cheese until mixed. Add sugar, salt and extracts. Beat until smooth. Fold in sour cream or yogurt. Pour into crust and bake at 375° for 40–50 minutes or until sides of top become golden brown. Cool for 24 hours before serving. Top with cherries, pineapple, blueberries or raspberries. Makes 10 servings. May be frozen.

Lacy Bergen Levy

Mrs. David Levy, Wife of Representative (New York)

HEALTHY CHEESECAKE

Crust:
- ½ cup graham cracker crumbs
- ½ cup Grape Nuts cereal
- 2 tablespoons vegetable oil

Filling:
- 2 cups non-fat cottage cheese
- 2 cups yogurt cheese, grated on rough grater
- 1 8-ounce package low fat cream cheese

(all cheeses at room temperature)
- 1¾ cups sugar
- 2 large eggs, plus 2 egg whites
- 1 tablespoon cornstarch
- 1 tablespoon vanilla
- 2 teaspoons grated lemon zest
- 1 teaspoon lemon juice

Topping:
- 2 cups lowfat sour cream
- ⅓ cup sugar
- 1 teaspoon vanilla

Glaze:
- ⅓ cup apricot preserves
- 2 tablespoons orange liqueur
- 4 kiwi fruit, peeled and sliced

Crust: Coat a 9″ or 10″ spring-form pan with non-stick spray. Mix crumbs with cereal and oil and press into bottom of pan.

Filling: Place cottage cheese in sieve and press with wooden spoon to drain off liquid. Put cottage cheese in food processor and process until smooth. Add yogurt cheese, cream cheese, sugar, eggs, egg whites, cornstarch, vanilla, zest and juice. Process until smooth. Spoon into crust. Bake at 350° for 40–45 minutes until set. Remove pan from oven and let stand 15 minutes.

Topping: Stir sour cream, sugar and vanilla. Spoon over cheesecake. Bake 5 minutes longer. Cool on rack. Refrigerate 12 hours to 3 days.

Glaze: Skin and slice kiwi. Place slices on top of cake. In small pan, melt apricot preserves. Remove from heat. Add orange liqueur. Spread over top of cake and kiwi. Makes 16 servings.

Richard S. Schweiker, former Senator (Pennsylvania)

CHEESECAKE

Crust:
- 2½ cups graham cracker crumbs
- 6 tablespoons sugar
- 1 stick butter
- 1 teaspoon cinnamon

Filling:
- 3 8 oz. pkgs. cream cheese (room temperature)
- 1½ cups sugar
- 4 jumbo eggs (room temperature and separated)
- 1 cup sour cream (room temperature)
- 1 teaspoon vanilla
  powdered sugar

Crust: Mix and press into springform pan and place in freezer or ice box.

Mix cream cheese and sugar then cream in a large mixing bowl. Add egg yolks one at a time and beat well. Fold in sour cream and vanilla. Beat egg whites in separate bowl and gradually fold into cream cheese mixture. Pour entire mixture into cold graham cracker crust. Cook for 1 hour or longer (until browned) at 300°. Let cheesecake cool completely and then put powdered sugar on top. After cooling, I usually put it in refrigerator, but it can be eaten warm.

Mrs. Charles S. Robb, Wife of Senator (Virginia)

TOFFEE COOKIES

- 24 graham crackers
- 1 cup butter
- 1 cup brown sugar
- 1 cup chopped nuts

Place graham crackers on buttered jelly roll pan to cover pan. Then boil butter and brown sugar two minutes. Than add nuts and spread over the crackers. Bake at 350° for 10 minutes. Cut warm. To get best flavor, boil the toffee mixture on the lowest heat possible to get it boiling. Stir occasionally. Makes 24 to 48 cookies.

Mrs. Dennis Hastert, Wife of Representative (Illinois)

MRS. BUTLER'S CARAMEL BROWNIES

1 cup butter
4 ozs. (squares) unsweetened
  chocolate
4 eggs
2 cups sugar
1 cup flour
1 teaspoon vanilla
1 teaspoon salt
½ cup nuts
1 14 oz. pkg. caramels
  scant ⅓ cup evaporated
  milk

Preheat oven to 350°. Grease one 9″ × 13″ baking pan. Melt together butter and chocolate. Beat eggs and sugar together in large mixing bowl. Add cooled chocolate mixture. Add flour, vanilla and salt. Stir in nuts. Pour ½ the mixture into the baking pan. Bake 15 minutes. Heat milk and caramels over low heat, stirring until caramels are melted. Spread caramel mixture on brownies. Top with remaining ½ batter. Bake another 30 minutes. Note: Since the addition of caramel makes these brownies stick slightly to the pan, run a knife around the edge of the pan soon after removing it from the oven. Makes 30 servings. May be frozen.

Mrs. George Darden, Wife of Representative (Georgia)

CHOCOLATE ECLAIR SQUARES

1 box graham crackers
2 small pkgs. instant vanilla
  pudding
4 tablespoons milk
9 ozs. Cool Whip
1 cup chocolate chips
4 tablespoons shortening
4 tablespoons corn syrup

Line the bottom of 13″ × 9″ pan with graham crackers. Combine pudding, milk and Cool Whip. Spread ½ mixture over graham crackers. Repeat graham crackers, rest of mixture, then graham crackers again. Melt chocolate chips and shortening. Add 4 tablespoons corn syrup. Pour on top of crackers and chill 24 hours. Makes 8 to 10 servings. May be frozen.

Mrs. Maurice Burnside, Wife of former Representative (West Virginia)

CHOCOLATE CARAMEL BARS

50 light caramels (14 oz. pkg.)
⅔ cup evaporated milk, divided
1 pkg. German chocolate cake mix
¾ cup butter or oleo melted
1 cup chopped nuts
1 cup chocolate chips

In saucepan, combine caramels and ⅓ cup evaporated milk. Cook (low heat) until caramels melt. Cool while cake bakes. Combine cake mix, butter and ⅓ cup evaporated milk and nuts until mixture holds together. Spread ½ of mixture in a 9″ × 13″ pan. Bake at 350° for 6 minutes. Test with toothpick for doneness. Sprinkle chocolate chips over crust. Spread caramel mixture over chocolate chips. Spread rest of cake mixture over all. Bake for 15–18 minutes. Makes 28 bars.

Glen Kleppe

Mrs. Thomas S. Kleppe, Wife of former Representative (North Dakota)

CHAMPION BROWNIES

1 cup butter
4 squares unsweetened choc-
    olate
4 eggs
1 cup of sugar
1 cup of flour

Melt butter and chocolate in saucepan over low heat. Beat eggs and sugar together. Add flour and slightly cooled chocolate and butter mixture. Mix well. Pour into greased 13″ × 9″ pan. Top with nuts if desired. Bake at 350° for 40 minutes. Makes 4 dozen. May be frozen.

Mary Hamilton O'Neal

Mary H. O'Neal, Daughter of former Representative Emmet O'Neal (Kentucky)

MINT BROWNIES

3 ozs. unsweetened choco-
    late melted and cool
¾ cup butter
3 eggs
1½ cup sugar
¾ cup flour
⅓ teaspoon baking powder
¼ teaspoon salt
¾ cup chopped nuts

Icing:
6 tablespoons butter
3 tablespoons heavy cream
3 cups confectionary sugar
3 teaspoons peppermint ex-
    tract
2 oz. unsweetened chocolate
2 tablespoons butter

Melt and cool chocolate and butter. Add slightly beaten eggs, sugar and mix. Add dry ingredients and mix. Fold in nuts. Bake in greased 9″ × 13″ or jelly roll pan at 350° for 15 minutes. Cool and ice.

For icing soften butter, add cream and gradually add sugar. Beat well adding peppermint extract. Melt 2 oz. unsweetened chocolate and 2 table-spoons butter. Drizzle over cold brownies. May be frozen.

Nancy Purcell

Mrs. Graham Purcell, Wife of former Representative (Texas)

CHOCOLATE MINT BROWNIES

Step 1:
½ cup margarine
2 squares unsweetened chocolate
1 cup sugar
2 eggs
½ cup flour
½ teaspoon salt
1 teaspoon vanilla
½ cup chopped nuts

Melt butter and chocolate and cool. Beat eggs, salt and sugar. Add chocolate. Add remaining ingredients. Bake at 325° for about 20-25 minutes. Cool.

Step 2:
2 tablespoons butter
1 cup confectioners sugar
1 teaspoon peppermint flavor
1 drop green food color

Mix all ingredients and spread on top of cooled brownies. Refrigerate until cold.

Step 3:
1 tablespoon butter
1 square unsweetened chocolate

Melt chocolate with butter and spread over cold brownies. Refrigerate. Cut into squares and serve.

Ann Richards, Governor (Texas)

PEANUT GOODIES

12 ozs. chocolate chips
12 ozs. butterscotch chips
 2 cups peanut butter
 1 cup margarine
½ pkg. (3½ oz. pkg.) vanilla
   pudding (not instant)
½ cup evaporated milk
 2 pounds powdered sugar
12 ozs. dry roasted peanuts

Melt together chocolate chips, butterscotch chips and peanut butter (may be done in microwave). Pour ½ of this mixture into a 15″ × 10″ × 1″ cookie sheet. Place cookie sheet in refrigerator or freezer until filling is done.

Filling: Beat together until smooth, margarine, pudding, milk and sugar. Spread this mixture over chocolate layer on cookie sheet. Add peanuts to remaining chocolate mixture and spread over bottom layers. Refrigerate until firm. Store in refrigerator. Makes 24 servings. May be frozen.

Sharon S Vander Schel

Mrs. Kevin Vander Schel, Daughter of Representative Neal Smith (Iowa)

APRICOT BARS

 1 cup unsulphered dried
   apricots
½ cup unsalted butter,
   softened
¼ cup granulated sugar
1⅓ cups unbleached all-purpose pre-sifted flour
½ teaspoon baking powder
¼ teaspoon salt
 1 cup light brown sugar,
   packed
 2 eggs, beaten
½ teaspoon vanilla extract
   confectioners sugar

In a saucepan, cover the apricots with water and boil slowly for 10 minutes. Drain, cool, chop and set aside. Preheat oven to 350°. Mix butter, granulated sugar and 1 cup flour with a pastry blender fork or your hands until crumbly. Firmly press mixture into a lightly greased 8″ square pan. Bake for 25 minutes, or until lightly golden, and remove from oven. Meanwhile, sift together the remaining ⅓ cup flour, baking powder and salt. In a separate bowl, beat the brown sugar into the eggs. Gradually stir in the flour mixture. Add the vanilla extract and apricots (will be gooey) and mix well to combine ingredients. Spread the apricot mixture over the pre-baked shortbread layer and bake for 25–30 minutes. Remove from oven, cool in the pan, then cut into 2″ bars and dust each one liberally with confectioners sugar. Makes 16 servings. May be frozen.

Ann Simpson

Mrs. Alan Simpson, Wife of Senator (Wyoming)

CHOCOLATE SARATOGAS

saltine crackers
1 cup unsalted butter
1 cup dark brown sugar
1 12 oz. pkg. semisweet
   chocolate morsels

Line a jelly roll pan (with sides) with foil. Cover foil with one layer of crackers, sides touching. Melt butter in saucepan. Add sugar. Bring to a boil and continue boiling 3 minutes. Remove from heat and pour evenly over crackers. Bake at 400° for 5 minutes. Immediately upon removing from oven, sprinkle on chocolate morsels. As chocolate melts, spread evenly with spatula. Cut into bars as chocolate starts to set. Chill. Edges may be trimmed easily with knife when cold. Break into bars. Makes 50 servings.

Mrs. Frank H. Miller, Daughter of former Senator, Edward V. Long (Missouri)

MOCK HEATH BARS

saltine crackers
2 sticks butter (not oleo)
½ cup brown sugar
12 oz. pkg. chocolate chips
½ cup Heath's Bits 'o Brickle

Cover bottom of 9″ × 13″ pan with foil extending over edges. Cover bottom with saltines, salt side up. Use broken saltine pieces to edges. Melt butter and add brown sugar cooking until sugar melts, stirring gently. Pour over crackers. Bake at 400° only 5 minutes. Remove from oven. Turn oven off. Sprinkle chocolate chips over the mixture. Put back in oven briefly to melt chocolate. Remove and spread chocolate. Sprinkle over chocolate Heath's Bits 'o Brickles. Cool. Cover with Saran Wrap and refrigerate until hard. Break into pieces and store in a tin.

Mrs. Roy Taylor, Wife of former Representative (North Carolina)

NEOPOLITAN COOKIES

1 pkg. or can (7 or 8 oz.) almond paste
1 cup (2 sicks) butter or margarine
1 cup sugar
4 large eggs, separated
1 teaspoon almond extract
2 cups unsifted all-purpose flour
  red and green food coloring
¼ cup seedless raspberry jam
¼ cup apricot preserves
1 pkg. (6 oz.) semisweet-chocolate pieces

Grease bottom and side of microwave-safe 13″ × 9″ × 2″ baking dish; line with waxed paper; grease. In large bowl, with electric mixer, beat almond paste, butter, sugar, egg yolks and almond extract until fluffy; stir in flour. In small bowl, beat egg whites until soft peaks form; stir into almond-paste mixture. Place 1⅓ cups of the batter in each of two small bowls. Add red food coloring to one and green food coloring to the other. Spread red batter in prepared dish. Microwave on MEDIUM 5 minutes, rotating dish after 2 minutes. Microwave on HIGH 2 minutes more. Holding edge of waxed paper, lift layer onto wire rack. Reline dish, and microwave, in turn, the green batter and white batter as above. Cool completely. Invert green layer; spread with raspberry jam. Add white layer; spread with apricot preserves. Top with red layer; cover; set heavy pan on top; refrigerate. Next day, in small glass bowl, microwave chocolate pieces on HIGH 3 minutes, stirring once; spread over red layer; trim edges. Let chocolate set slightly; cut crosswise into ½-inch strips; cut each into four pieces. Makes 8 dozen. May be frozen.

Catherine Hollaway

Mrs. Clyde Holloway, Wife of former Representative (Louisiana)

Candy & Frosting Chart

230 degrees–234 degrees	Thread
234 degrees–240 degrees	Soft Ball
244 degrees–248 degrees	Firm Ball
250 degrees–266 degrees	Hard Ball
270 degrees–290 degrees	Soft Crack
300 degrees–310 degrees	Hard Crack

LEMON BARS

Crust:
1 cup (2 sticks) lightly salted butter
2 cups sifted all-purpose flour
½ cup sifted confectioners sugar

Filling:
4 large eggs, room temperature
2 cups granulated sugar
grated zest of 2 large lemons
6 tablespoons lemon juice
1 tablespoon flour
pinch salt
½ teaspoon baking powder

Make crust: In a bowl, beat together butter, flour and confectioners sugar until fluffy. Scrape mixture into greased 9″ × 13″ pan and smooth into a thin layer on the bottom. Bake in preheated 325° oven for 15 minutes.

Make filling: In a bowl, beat eggs and sugar until light. Mix in lemon zest and juice. Add flour, salt, baking powder. Combine well.

Pour lemon mixture into warm or cool baked crust and return to oven for 35 minutes, or until filling is set. Cool slightly and cut into squares. Loosen crust from edges of pan.

Rebecca Rogers

Mrs. Paul Rogers, Wife of former Representative (Florida)

LEMON SQUARES

Crust:
2 cups flour
½ cup 10X sugar
1 cup butter or margarine

Filling:
4 eggs, beaten
2 cups sugar
¼ teaspoon salt
½ teaspoon baking powder
⅓ cup fresh lemon juice
2 teaspoons lemon rind

Crust: Preheat oven to 350°. Mix above ingredients, flour, sugar and butter with pastry blender until crumbly. Press into bottom of greased 9″ × 13″ pan, bake 20 minutes until golden.

Filling: Mix together beaten eggs, sugar, salt, baking powder, lemon juice and lemon rind. Pour into hot crust. Bake for another 20 minutes. Dust with 10X sugar while still warm. Cut into squares when cool.

Rita Hanley

Mrs. James Hanley, Wife of former Representative (New York)

AUNT DOLLY'S GOURMET GOOEY BROWNIES

5 oz. unsweetened chocolate
¼ cup butter
2 large eggs
2 cups sugar
1 teaspoon vanilla
1½ cups all-purpose flour
¼ cup water

Preheat oven to 425°. Melt chocolate and butter. Let cool. Beat eggs and gradually add sugar, then mix with chocolate and butter, *alternating*. Add water and flour. Line pan with *buttered foil*. Spoon in mixture. Bake at 425° for 20–25 minutes until gooey. Remove and cool. Makes 1 dozen.

Amey Upton

Mrs. Fred Upton, Wife of Representative (Michigan)

BABE RUTH BARS

1 cup light Karo syrup
1 cup sugar
1½ cups peanut butter
5 cups Rice Krispie cereal
6 oz. pkg. chocolate chips
6 oz. pkg. butterscotch chips

Bring syrup and sugar to a full boil. Remove immediately from heat. Mix in peanut butter. Add cereal. Press into 9" × 13" buttered pan. Melt chocolate and butterscotch chips over hot water. Spread over first layer as icing. Cool. Cut into bars. Makes 20 servings.

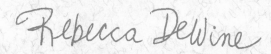

Rebecca DeWine, Daughter of former Representative, Michael DeWine (Ohio)

BABY RUTH BARS

1 cup light Karo syrup
1 cup white sugar
1½ cups peanut butter
4 cups Special K or Rice Krispies cereal
1 6 oz. pkg. chocolate chips
1 6 oz. pkg. butterscotch chips

Bring syrup and sugar to full boil. Remove immediately from heat. Mix in peanut butter and cereal. Press into buttered 9½" × 13" pan. Melt chocolate and butterscotch chips together. Spread as icing over first mixture. Cut into 1 inch bars to serve. Makes 117 one-inch bars.

Mary Morgan Reeves

Mrs. Eric Reeves, Daughter of former Senator, Robert B. Morgan (North Carolina)

ROCKY ROAD BARS

½ cup butter or margarine
¾ cup sugar
2 eggs
1 teaspoon vanilla
¾ cup flour
¼ teaspoon salt
½ cup chopped pecans
2 tablespoons cocoa powder, unsweetened
¼ teaspoon baking powder
2 cups tiny marshmallows
1 6 oz. pkg. (1 cup) semi-sweet chocolate pieces
1 cup peanut butter
1½ cups crisp rice cereal

Cream butter or margarine and sugar, beat in eggs and vanilla. Stir together flour, salt, chopped nuts, cocoa and baking powder. Stir into egg mixture. Spread in bottom of greased 13″ × 9″ × 2″ pan. Bake in 350° oven for 15 to 20 minutes or until bars test done. Sprinkle marshmallows evenly on top, bake 3 minutes more. Cool. In small saucepan, combine chocolate pieces and peanut butter. Stir over low heat until chocolate is melted. Stir in cereal. Spread mixture atop cooled bars. Chill, cut into bars. Refrigerate. Makes 3 to 4 dozen. May be frozen.

Doris Sangmeister

Mrs. George Sangmeister, Wife of Representative (Illinois)

MANTEO MARCUS BARS

1 pkg. yellow cake mix
1 egg
1 stick margarine, softened
1 cup pecans, chopped
8 ozs. cream cheese, softened
1 box confectioners sugar
2 eggs

Mix first 4 ingredients and pat in 9″ × 13″ pyrex baking dish. Mix last 3 ingredients with beater. Pour over crust. Bake at 350° for 40 minutes. Cool and slice. Makes 32 bars. May be frozen.

Alice M. Lancaster

Mrs. Martin Lancaster, Wife of Representative (North Carolina)

BROWN SUGAR COOKIES

¼ pound butter
2 eggs
2 cups brown sugar
1 cup self-rising flour
1 teaspoon vanilla
1½ cups pecans, chopped
    coarsely
¼ teaspoon salt
1 teaspoon baking powder
    (only if not using self-ris-
    ing flour)

Mix together ingredients and pour in 9″ × 12″ slightly greased pan. Bake 35 minutes at 350°. Let stand in pan before cutting. Makes 24 cookies.

Katie O. Morgan

Mrs. Robert Morgan, Wife of former Senator (North Carolina)

DATE BARS

2 sticks of margarine
1 cup granulated sugar
4 eggs
1 cup flour
1 pound pitted dates,
    chopped
1 pound chopped walnuts
    powdered sugar

Melt the margarine. Cool and pour into a mixing bowl. Add sugar gradually while beating with hand mixer. Add eggs one at a time, beating well. Fold in flour. Stir in walnuts and dates. (It's easiest to cut dates with kitchen shears or to buy chopped dates.) The mixture is thick. Put into a greased 12″ × 15″ pan. Bake in 350° oven for 40 minutes. Test with toothpick. Cut while warm. Sprinkle powdered sugar on top. Makes 20 or more bars. May be frozen.

Cece Zorinsky-White

Mrs. Edward Zorinsky-White, Wife of former Senator Ed Zorinsky (Nebraska)

CHOCOLATE PEANUT BUTTER BITES

¾ cup brown sugar
1 pound confectioners sugar
8 tablespoons (1 stick) sweet butter
2 cups peanut butter
1 cup unsalted peanuts
12 ozs. semi-sweet chocolate chips
1 tablespoon sweet butter

Mix first 5 ingredients together. Pat into an ungreased jelly-roll pan, about 15" × 10" × 1". Flatten top with a rolling pin. Melt chocolate chips and butter in the top part of a double boiler over simmering water. Spread chocolate on peanut butter mixture. Cut into bite-size squares. Chill for 15 to 20 minutes. Remove from pan. Serve chilled. Makes 50 bites. May be frozen.

John Robert Foley III

John R. Foley III, Son of former Representative John R. Foley (Maryland)

EXECUTIVE MANSION BISCOTTI

1 cup butter
2 cups sugar
6 eggs
¼ cup anise seed
2 teaspoons anise extract
¼ cup Galliano liqueur
5½ cups flour
1 tablespoon baking powder
2 cups slivered almonds, chopped
2 cups golden raisins
½ cup chopped citron

Beat butter in the bowl of an electric mixer until light and fluffy. Gradually beat in sugar and then beat in eggs, one at a time. Add anise seed, anise extract and Galliano, mix until well combined. Mix flour and baking powder together and slowly blend into butter mixture. Stir in almonds, golden raisins and citron. Cover and chill mixture for 2 hours. Form dough into 2-inch wide by ½-inch thick loaves directly on parchment lined baking sheets. Bake in a 375° for 20 minutes. Remove from oven and immediately cut on the diagonal, turn each piece cut-side up on baking sheet and bake for another 15 minutes or until lightly browned. Makes 9 dozen.

Mary Lowry

Mrs. Mike Lowry, Wife of Governor (Washington)

INDIANA MINT BROWNIES

Brownies:
- 1 cup all-purpose flour
- 1 cup sugar
- 1 16 oz. can chocolate-flavored syrup (1½ cups)
- 4 eggs
- ½ cup butter or margarine, softened

Mint Cream:
- 2 cups powdered sugar
- ½ cup softened butter or margarine
- 1 tablespoon water
- ½ teaspoon mint extract
- 3 drops green food coloring

Chocolate Topping:
- 1 cup semi-sweet mint-flavored chocolate pieces OR semi-sweet chocolate pieces
- 6 tablespoons butter or margarine

In a mixing bowl, beat together the flour, sugar, syrup, eggs and butter or margarine with an electric mixer on low speed until combined, then 1 minute on medium speed. Turn mixture into a greased 13″ × 9″ × 2″ baking pan. Bake in a 350° oven for 30 to 35 minutes or until top springs back when lightly touched (top may still appear wet). Let cook in pan on wire rack. Meanwhile, prepare Mint Cream and Chocolate Topping.

Mint Cream: In a small mixing bowl, beat together sifted powdered sugar, softened butter or margarine, water, mint extract and food coloring, if you like. Beat until smooth.

Chocolate Topping: In a heavy, small saucepan, combine semi-sweet mint-flavored chocolate pieces or semi-sweet chocolate pieces and butter or margarine. Cook over low heat until chocolate melts. Or, in a small microwave-safe bowl, micro-cook on 100% power (high) for 1 to 1½ minutes or until chocolate melts, stirring occasionally. Makes 50 small brownies.

Evan Bayh, Governor (Indiana)

Save margarine wrappers to grease baking pans.

ICE BOX COOKIES

1 cup butter
2 cups brown sugar
1 teaspoon vanilla
2 eggs
3½ cups flour
½ teaspoon baking soda
½ teaspoon salt
1½ teaspoons baking powder
1 cup chopped nuts

Cream butter and sugar. Add vanilla. Add one egg at a time. Sift flour, baking soda, salt and baking powder together. Add nuts and flour to the mixture. Mix well. Makes 3 rolls of dough and wrap in wax paper. Put in refrigerator for 24 hours. Slice thin and bake at 350° for 15 minutes. Makes 3 dozen. May be frozen.

Christine Fountain

Mrs. L. H. Fountain, Wife of former Representative (North Carolina)

ICE BOX COOKIES

1½ cups of margarine
6 oz. "2nd Nature" (egg substitute) or 3 well beaten eggs
1 cup of white sugar
1 cup of brown sugar
½ teaspoon of nutmeg
½ teaspoon of cinnamon
1 tablespoon of vanilla
½ teaspoon of cloves
1½ cups of raisins
1½ cups of nuts, chopped fine
3½ cups of flour
½ teaspoon of salt
1 teaspoon of baking soda

Cream margarine with sugars. Add beaten eggs or egg substitute. Sift spices, salt and baking soda with flour. Mix dry ingredients, raisins and nuts with creamed mixture, add vanilla last. Shape dough into two logs then wrap in plastic wrap. Place in refrigerator at least 6 hours to chill. When ready to bake, slice in ¼ inch circles. Place on greased cookie sheet. Bake in 350° oven for 10 to 12 minutes or until lightly browned. May be frozen.

Lawton Chiles

Lawton Chiles, Governor (Florida)

"CAN'T FAIL" CHRISTMAS COOKIES

1 cup shortening
²/₃ cup sugar
³/₄ teaspoon salt
2 teaspoons vanilla
    exactly ¹/₃ cup of eggs (1
      to 2, depending on size)
3 cups sifted, all-purpose
    flour

Combine shortening, sugar, salt, flavoring and eggs and beat until smooth and light. Stir in flour. Wrap in waxed paper and chill at least 2 hours. Remove ¼ of the dough at a time. Roll out ¼″ to ³/₈″ thick on slightly floured surface. Cut into desired shapes. Bake at 350° on baking sheet for 12 to 15 minutes. Do not allow to get brown. Remove from cookie sheet and cool thoroughly on cake racks.

Mrs. Dirk Kempthorne, Wife of Senator (Idaho)

SUGAR COOKIES

1 cup sugar
1 cup confectioners sugar
1 cup butter or margarine
2 eggs, beaten
1 cup oil
1 teaspoon vanilla
4 cups flour
1 teaspoon baking soda
1 teaspoon cream of tartar

Cream sugars and margarine or butter. Mix beaten eggs, oil and vanilla and add to sugars. Mix dry ingredients, flour, baking soda and cream of tartar, add to rest. Chill dough, roll in balls, roll in sugar, flatten slightly. Bake at 350° for 10 minutes until lightly browned. Makes 5 dozen. May be frozen.

Mrs. Jeff Minckler, Daughter of former Senator, Ernest Lundeen (Minnesota)

GRANDMA'S CHRISTMAS COOKIES

2 cups sugar
1 pound butter
4 eggs, beaten
3 teaspoons water
1 tablespoon vanilla
6½ to 7 cups flour
½ teaspoon baking soda
1 teaspoon baking powder
½ teaspoon salt
   various colored sugars
   multicolored sprinkles

Cream sugar with butter. Add beaten egg, water and vanilla. Combine dry ingredients and add to sugar mixture. Let stand overnight in refrigerator covered. Roll out thinly on floured pastry cloth. Cut with Christmas cookie cutters and decorate with various colored sugars, multicolored sprinkles, etc. Bake at 350° for 8–10 minutes or less. Watch carefully, baking time varies with thickness. Makes 10 dozen. May be frozen.

Jean Terry

Mrs. John Terry, Wife of former Representative (New York)

INCREDIBLY EASY SUGAR COOKIES

1 cup butter
1½ cups sugar
2 eggs
¼ teaspoon salt
1 teaspoon vanilla
1 teaspoon baking powder
1 teaspoon baking soda
3 cups flour

Cream butter and sugar. Add eggs, vanilla and sifted flour with salt, baking powder and baking soda. Drop by spoonfuls on a baking sheet. Flatten with a glass greased on the bottom with butter and dipped in sugar. Bake at 350° for 8–12 minutes (depending on size). When cool, you can frost with your favorite frosting. Makes 4 dozen.

Patricia McKeon

Mrs. "Buck" McKeon, Wife of Representative (California)

HOLLY COOKIES

1 stick margarine
40 large marshmallows
1½ teaspoons of green food
    coloring
4 cups Cornflakes
    red hots (candy)

Melt margarine and marshmallows in large pan. Add food coloring. Fold cornflakes into above mixture until all are covered. Quickly, drop by spoonsful on wax paper. Place 5 or 6 red hots on each "wreath". These may be used to add color to a plate of Christmas cookies. Makes 15 servings.

Lenora Moeller

Mrs. Walter Moeller, Wife of former Representative (Ohio)

BUTTER COOKIES

1 pound Imperial margarine
1½ cups sugar
1 egg
4 cups sifted flour (regular)
1 teaspoon vanilla extract
    whole pecans

Cream margarine and sugar. Add whole egg and mix well. Add vanilla. Add flour gradually. Drop by teaspoonful (heaping) on ungreased cookie sheet. Press with fork and add pecan to top of each. Bake at 375° for 15 minutes. Place on brown paper until cool. Store in tight cookie container or freeze. Makes about 85 cookies.

Quitha F. Cross

Mrs. John S. Cross, Daughter of former Representative Claude Albert Fuller (Arkansas)

> *When you are doing any sort of baking, you get better results if you remember to preheat your cookie sheet, muffin tins, or cake pans.*

SHORTBREAD

1 cup butter, unsalted
¾ cup powdered sugar
2 cups plus 3 tablespoons
   flour
1 tablespoon vanilla

Mix all ingredients together in Cuisinart until a ball is formed. Divide in half and spread each half in a 9″ removable bottom, round cake pan, lightly sprayed with Pam. Score with a knife into 16 triangles in each pan. Prick very well. Bake at 325° for 25 to 30 minutes until very lightly browned. Cut again over scored marks while warm. Let cool in pans. Makes 32 servings. May be frozen.

Mrs. Frank H. Miller, Daughter of former Senator Edward V. Long (Missouri)

NUTTY OATMEAL HEALTH COOKIES

1¼ cup butter
1 teaspoon olive oil
1¼ cup brown packed sugar
¼ cup white granulated sugar
1 egg
2 teaspoons vanilla
1¾ cups unbleached flour
1 teaspoon baking powder
2 teaspoons nutmeg
1 teaspoon cinnamon
¾ teaspoon salt
2½ cups oats
1¾ cups chopped nuts
1½ cups raisins

Preheat oven to 375°. Mix butter, olive oil, sugars to a smooth consistency. Add egg, vanilla, flour, baking powder, nutmeg, cinnamon, salt, oats, nuts and raisins. Mix well. Place rounded tablespoons of dough on ungreased cookie sheet. Bake at 375° for 10-12 minutes. Upon removal from oven, allow cookies to cool to enhance cunchiness. Delicious served with apple slices. Makes 5 dozen.

Mrs. Royal Kastens, Daughter of former Representative Gus Yatron (Pennsylvania)

GRAHAM CRACKER OBLONGS

40 or 50 graham crackers
½ cup butter
¼ cup sugar
1 tablespoon cinnamon
½ cup chopped nuts

Break crackers apart and lay on cookie sheet (40–50 pieces). Melt butter. Mix sugar and cinnamon. Sprinkle ½ of the butter over the crackers. Sprinkle ½ of the sugar mixture over the crackers. Sprinkle ½ of the nuts over the crackers. Repeat sprinkling remainder of butter, sugar and nuts. Bake at 350° for 12 minutes. Allow to cool a little. Remove from sheet. Makes 40 servings. May be frozen.

Audrey L. Hagen

Mrs. Harold Hagen, Wife of former Representative (Minnesota)

LEMON-RASPBERRY CHESS TASSIES

Dough:
1 3 oz. pkg. cream cheese, softened
½ cup butter, softened
1 cup sifted flour

Filling:
½ cup sugar
1 egg
2 tablespoons butter, softened
2 tablespoons whipping cream
½ teaspoon vanilla
juice and grated peel of ½ lemon
24 raspberries

To prepare dough: Mix together cream cheese and butter in small bowl or food processor. Add flour and blend thoroughly. Chill 5-15 minutes if hard to handle. Divide dough and roll into 24 small balls. Wrap balls in plastic wrap and chill again briefly, 5 minutes or so. Place each ball in tiny, ungreased fluted tart pan (1-1½" diameter cups) or miniature muffin tin and press dough with fingertips against bottom and sides. Place pans in refrigerator to chill while you prepare filling.

To prepare filling: Beat together sugar, egg, butter, cream, vanilla, lemon juice and peel. Spoon dough into pans about ¾ of the way up the sides. Bake at 325° until filling is set, 25–30 minutes. Remove tarts from pans before they cool completely and finish cooling on wire rack. Place 1 raspberry in depression in center of each tart and refrigerate until serving. Tassies will keep several days in refrigerator if tightly wrapped and up to 3 months in freezer. Makes 24 small tarts, 8 to 12 servings. May be frozen.

Colleen Nunn

Mrs. Sam Nunn, Wife of Senator (Georgia)

PECAN TASSIES

1 3 oz. pkg. cream cheese
½ cup butter
1 cup sifted plain flour
1 egg
¾ cup brown sugar
1 tablespoon soft butter
1 teaspoon vanilla
    dash salt
⅔ cup broken pecans

Cheese pastry: Let cream cheese and ½ cup butter soften at room temperature, blend. Stir in sifted flour. Chill about 1 hour. Shape into 2 dozen 1-inch balls. Place in ungreased 1¾" muffin cups. Press dough against bottom and sides of cups.

Pecan filling: Beat together egg, brown sugar, 1 tablespoon butter, vanilla and salt just until smooth. Divide half the pecans among the pastry cups, add egg mixture and top with remaining pecans. Bake at 325° for 25 minutes or until the filling is set. Cool, remove from pan. Makes 2 dozen.

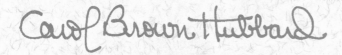

Mrs. Carroll Hubbard, Wife of former Representative (Kentucky)

GAGY'S PEANUT BUTTER COOKIES

1 stick of butter
½ cup brown sugar
½ cup white sugar
½ cup peanut butter plus 1
    level tablespoon
1 egg
½ teaspoon baking powder
½ teaspoon baking soda
½ teaspoon salt
    dash of vanilla
1½ cups flour

Combine all ingredients and stir until mixed well. Roll into walnut sized balls and place on cookie sheet. Press with a fork. If they seem too sticky to roll, add a little flour to dough. Bake at 350° until light brown, approximately 10–12 minutes. Makes 48 cookies.

Mrs. Eric Reeves, Daughter of former Senator, Robert B. Morgan (North Carolina)

GERMAN CHOCOLATE THUMBPRINT COOKIES

Topping:
- 1 cup sugar
- 1 cup evaporated milk
- ½ cup unsalted butter or margarine, softened
- 1 teaspoon vanilla
- 3 egg yolks, beaten
- 1½ cups flaked coconut
- 1½ cups chopped pecans

Cookies:
- 1 pkg. Pillsbury Plus German Chocolate cake mix
- ½ cup unsalted butter or margarine, softened

In heavy 2 quart saucepan, combine sugar, milk, ½ cup butter, vanilla and egg yolks, blend well. Cook over medium heat for 10 to 13 minutes or until thickened and bubbly, stirring frequently. Stir in coconut and pecans. Remove from heat. Cool to room temperature. Reserve 1¼ cups of topping mixture, set aside. In large bowl, combine cookie ingredients and remaining topping mixture, stir by hand until thoroughly moistened. Heat oven to 350°. Shape dough into 1-inch balls. Place 2 inches apart on ungreased cookie sheets. With thumb, make an indentation in center of each ball. Fill each indentation with rounded ½ teaspoon of reserved topping. Bake for 10 to 13 minutes or until set. Cool 5 minutes, remove from cookie sheets. Cool completely. Makes 5 dozen. May be frozen.

Helen Green

Mrs. Gene Green, Wife of Representative (Texas)

MEZZA LUNA COOKIES

- 1 cup sweet butter
- ½ pound cream cheese
- ¼ teaspoon salt
- 2 cups sifted flour
- 1 cup chopped nuts
- 1 cup currants
- ½ cup sugar
- 1 tablespoon cinnamon

Mix butter, cheese and salt. Mix in flour. Shape into 14 balls. Chill overnight. Roll each ball into 6 inch circle. Cut into quarters. Mix nuts, currants, sugar and cinnamon. Drop rounded teaspoonful onto each quarter. Pinch edges of dough together. Form into crescents. Place on ungreased cookie sheet. Bake at 350° for 12 minutes. Makes 7 dozen. May be frozen.

Berenice C. Daddario

Mrs. Emilio Daddario, Wife of former Representative (Connecticut)

SWEETHEART COOKIES

¾ cup margarine
½ cup sugar
1 yolk of egg
1½ cup flour
  tart jelly or jam
  powdered sugar

Cream ¾ cup margarine in a large mixing bowl, gradually add sugar and yolk of egg. Continue mixing in flour. Knead gently and chill for several hours. Roll into small balls and place on greased cookie sheet. With your thumb, make a small depression in the center of the ball. Spoon in your choice of jam or jelly into the hole and bake in a 350° oven until lightly brown. No more than 10–15 minutes. Roll in powdered sugar and enjoy! Makes 2 dozen.

Susan Nunner

Mrs. Jeffrey Nunner, Daughter of Representative David L. Hobson (Ohio)

RAISIN OATMEAL COOKIES

1 cup (2 sticks) margarine or
  butter, softened
1¼ cups firmly packed brown
  sugar
½ cup granulated sugar
2 eggs
2 tablespoons milk
2 tablespoons vanilla
1¾ cups all-purpose flour
1 teaspoon baking soda
½ teaspoon salt (optional)
2½ cups oats (quick or old
  fashioned, uncooked)
1 cup raisins
1 cup pecans

Preheat oven to 375°. Beat margarine and sugars until creamy. Add eggs, milk and vanilla, beat well. Add flour, baking soda and salt, mix well. Stir in oats, raisins and nuts, mix well. Drop by rounded measuring tablespoonfuls onto ungreased cookie sheet. Bake 9 to 10 minutes for a chewy cookie or 12–13 minutes for a crisp cookie. Cool cookies on wire rack. Makes 5 dozen.

Shirley Volkmer

Mrs. Harold Volkmer, Wife of Representative (Missouri)

OATMEAL COOKIES

¼ pound butter (do not use oleo)
1 cup oatmeal (Quick Quaker Oats)
2 tablespoons flour
1 cup sugar
½ teaspoon baking powder
¼ teaspoon salt
1 cup chopped pecans or walnuts
1 egg, beaten
1 teaspoon vanilla

Melt butter, add all dry ingredients, then add beaten egg and vanilla, put about ½ teaspoon on aluminum foil on cookie sheet. Bake for 8 minutes at 325°. Watch closely, they will burn. Let cookies cool well and peel off cookies. Place cookies about ½ inch apart. Makes 24 servings.

Mrs. Jamie L. Whitten, Wife of Representative (Mississippi)

OATMEAL COOKIES

1 cup raisins
½ cup water
½ teaspoon baking soda
1 cup shortening
1 cup brown sugar
1 cup white sugar
2 eggs
2 cups flour
2 cups oatmeal
1 teaspoon salt
1 teaspoon vanilla
½ teaspoon almond extract

Cook raisins in water until ¼ cup of water remains. Cream shortening, add sugar, then beaten eggs. Dissolve baking soda in raisin juice and add to creamed mixture. Add flour, oatmeal, salt and flavoring. Mix in raisins and drop by teaspoonful on greased sheet. Bake at 350° until brown, about 10 minutes. Makes 4 dozen.

Mrs. Christopher Rice, Daughter of former Representative, Laurie C. Battle (Alabama)

OATMEAL SCOTCH CHIPPERS

1¼ cups butter flavor vegetable shortening
1½ cups firmly packed brown sugar
1 cup granulated sugar
3 eggs
1¼ cups extra crunchy peanut butter
4½ cups old-fashioned oats (not quick or instant)
2 teaspoons baking soda
1 cup semi-sweet chocolate chips
1 cup butterscotch chips
1 cup chopped walnuts

Heat oven to 350°. Combine shortening, brown sugar and granulated sugar in large bowl. Beat at medium speed of electric mixer until well-blended. Beat in eggs. Add peanut butter. Beat until blended. Combine oats and baking soda. Stir with spoon into creamed mixture. Stir in chocolate chips, butterscotch chips and nuts until well blended. Drop rounded teaspoonsful of dough 2 inches apart on ungreased baking sheet. Bake at 350° for 10 to 11 minutes, or until lightly browned. Cool 2 minutes on baking sheet. Remove to cooling rack. Makes 6 dozen. May be frozen.

John J. Rhodes, former Representative (Arizona)

COCONUT GEMS

1 cup butter
1 cup sugar
1 cup brown sugar
2 eggs
2 cups flour
1 teaspoon baking soda
½ teaspoon salt
1 teaspoon vanilla
1 small can coconut
4 cups Corn Flakes

Cream butter and sugars. Add eggs and mix well. Add dry ingredients, vanilla, coconut and corn flakes. Drop by teaspoon onto cookie sheet. Bake at 350° for 10 minutes. Makes 2 to 3 dozen.

Mrs. Chet Edwards, Wife of Representative (Texas)

THE ULTIMATE CHOCOLATE COOKIE

1 cup margarine or butter
1 cup brown sugar
1 cup sugar
2 eggs
½ teaspoon vanilla
2 cups flour
1½ cups oatmeal, blended in blender to fine powder
1 teaspoon baking powder
1 teaspoon baking soda
12 ozs. chocolate chips
1 8 oz. Heath bar, broken into chips
1 cup chopped pecans

Cream margarine or butter and sugars. Add eggs and vanilla. Mix together flour, oatmeal, baking powder and baking soda and add to creamed mixture. Add chips, Heath chips and pecans. Drop by tablespoonful onto greased cookie sheet. Bake at 350° for 8 to 10 minutes. Makes 2½ dozen. May be frozen.

Marguerite R. Cederberg

Mrs. Elford Cederberg, Wife of former Representative (Michigan)

COCONUT MACAROONS

2 egg whites
⅛ teaspoon salt
⅛ teaspoon cream of tartar
1 teaspoon vanilla
¾ cup sugar
1 4 oz. can moist shredded coconut (1½ cups)

Beat egg whites, salt and cream of tartar together until soft peaks form. Beat in vanilla and sugar until peaks are stiff. Fold in coconut. Cover cookie sheet with waxed paper. Drop coconut mixture from a teaspoon onto prepared cookie sheet about 1 inch apart. Bake at 300° for 25 minutes. Cool slightly before removing from paper. Makes 2 dozen.

Mariel Goss

Mrs. Porter Goss, Wife of Representative (Florida)

REUNION COOKIES

2 cups shortening
2 cups white sugar
2 pounds brown sugar
12 eggs
2 teaspoons vanilla
3 pounds peanut butter
1 large box quick oatmeal
8 teaspoons baking soda
1 pound M&M's candies
12 oz. pkg. chocolate chips

A very large roaster or other large utensil is needed for mixing this batter. Cream the shortenings and sugars. Add eggs and vanilla. In a very large pan, combine the peanut butter and oatmeal. Add the baking soda, chips and candies to the first mixture, then combine with peanut butter and oatmeal mixture. Use hands to mix well. Drop onto cookie sheet about 2 inches apart. Bake at 350° for 10 minutes. Makes 20 dozen. May be frozen.

Connie Hansen

Mrs. George Hansen, Wife of former Representative (Idaho)

VIRGINIA'S CHOCOLATE CHIP COOKIES

½ cup Crisco
½ cup sugar
½ cup brown sugar
½ teaspoon vanilla
1 egg
1 cup plus 1 tablespoon flour (not sifted)
½ teaspoon baking soda
½ teaspoon salt
chocolate chips

In large bowl, combine Crisco, sugar, brown sugar and vanilla, beat until creamy. Beat in egg. Combine flour, baking soda and salt. Add to creamy mixture. Stir in chocolate chips. Drop tablespoon size on ungreased cookie sheet. Bake at 375° until done. May be frozen.

Cindy Stenholm

Mrs. Charles Stenholm, Wife of Representative (Texas)

MAUREEN'S COWBOY COOKIES

1 cup shortening
1 cup sugar
1 cup brown sugar
2 eggs
1½ teaspoons vanilla
1½ cups flour
1 teaspoon baking soda
1 teaspoon salt
3 cups quick-cooking
    oatmeal
1 cup chopped pecans
1 pkg. chocolate chips

Cream shortening and sugars until mixture is light. Add eggs and vanilla and beat well. Sift flour, baking soda and salt together and gradually add creamed mixture. Stir in oatmeal, pecans and chocolate chips. Blend well. Drop by teaspoonful on well greased cookie sheets. Bake at 350° for 10 minutes or until done. Makes 5 dozen.

Lucy Foley

Mrs. John R. Foley, Wife of former Representative (Maryland)

LUCY'S NO-BAKE PEANUT BUTTER COOKIES

½ cup Karo syrup
½ cup sugar
1 cup peanut butter
2 cups Special K cereal or
    other similar dry cereal

Bring syrup and sugar to a boil. Remove from heat, stir in peanut butter. Add cereal. Drop by spoonfuls on cookie sheet covered by wax paper. Makes 24 cookies.

Paul Gillmor

Paul Gillmor, Representative (Ohio)

Dip the spoon in hot water to measure shortening, butter, etc., the fat will slip out more easily.

MONSTER COOKIES

2 one pound boxes of light brown sugar
3½ cups white sugar
12 eggs
1 pound butter softened
8 teaspoons baking soda
3 pounds peanut butter
18 cups oatmeal
1 tablespoon honey
1 pound M&M's
2 12 oz. pkgs. chocolate chips

Mix all ingredients (works best in a commercial mixer), or divide all ingredients in half and mix in the electric mixer in two batches. Use ice cream scoop for large cookies, or use a tablespoon for smaller ones. Place on greased cookie sheets or non-greased for non-stick pans. Bake at 350° for 12 minutes. Great for college kids care packages. Makes 12 dozen. May be frozen.

Eulada P. Watt

Mrs. Mel Watt, Wife of Representative (North Carolina)

MONTANA WHOPPERS

⅔ cup margarine or butter
1¼ cups brown sugar
¾ cup white sugar
3 beaten eggs
1½ cups chunky peanut butter
6 cups old fashioned oatmeal
2 teaspoons baking soda
6 to 8 ozs. chocolate chips
¾ cup raisins or chopped nuts

Melt margarine or butter over low heat. Blend in sugars, peanut butter and beaten eggs. Mix until smooth. Add remaining ingredients and mix. Chill dough. Drop on greased baking sheet with ice cream scoop or large spoon, fairly well packed. Flatten slightly. Bake at 350° for 10–12 minutes or until golden brown. Watch while baking as they burn easily. Montana Whoppers are a great favorite with men. May be frozen.

Nancy Schulze

Mrs. Richard T. Schulze, Wife of former Representative (Pennsylvania)

SUNSHINE MUNCHIES

¾ cup honey
½ cup sugar
1 cup peanut butter
5 cups Corn Flakes (or other flake cereal)

Combine honey and sugar in a medium saucepan. Boil mixture on medium-high heat for 1 minute. Add and stir peanut butter and Corn Flakes together and stir. Drop by spoonfuls onto covered cookie sheets. Refrigerate until firm. Makes 36 cookies.

Faith H Battle

Mrs. James Battle, Daughter-in-law of former Representative Laurie C. Battle (Alabama)

WHITE CHOCOLATE AND MACADAMIA NUT COOKIES

2 sticks margarine, melted
1 cup brown sugar
1 cup white sugar
2 cups oatmeal
2 beaten eggs
2 cups flour
1 teaspoon almond extract
¼ teaspoon salt
1 teaspoon baking soda
1 teaspoon baking powder
1 cup macadamia nuts
1 cup white chocolate pieces

Mix all ingredients. Chill well. Spray cookie sheet with Pam. Bake at 325° for 10 minutes.

Betty Thornton

Mrs. Ray Thornton, Wife of Representative (Arkansas)

REESE'S COOKIES

1 cup shortening or ¾ cup
  butter
1 cup sugar
½ cup light brown sugar
1 teaspoon vanilla
2 eggs
2 cups all-purpose flour
1 teaspoon baking soda
1 cup Reese's peanut butter
  chips
1 cup Hershey's semi-sweet
  chips

Heat oven to 350°. Cream shortening, sugar, brown sugar and vanilla. Add eggs and beat well. Combine flour and baking soda and blend into other mixture. Stir in chips. Drop by teaspoonful on baking sheet. Bake at 350° for 10 to 12 minutes. Makes 5 dozen. May be frozen.

Margaret Grant

Mrs. Robert A. Grant, Wife of former Representative (Indiana)

MONSTER COOKIES

1 cup margarine
2¼ cups peanut butter
2 cups sugar
2¼ cups brown sugar
6 eggs
1½ teaspoons light corn syrup
1½ teaspoons vanilla
3 teaspoons baking soda
9 cups oatmeal
2 cups chocolate chips
2 cups M&M candy

Cream margarine, peanut butter and sugars until light and fluffy. Add eggs and beat well. Stir in corn syrup, vanilla and baking soda. Add oats, chocolate chips and M&M's and beat thoroughly. Drop by tablespoons on cookie sheet and bake at 350° for about 12 minutes. Makes 9 dozen. May be frozen.

Marge Shoup

Mrs. Richard Shoup, Wife of former Representative (Montana)

GRANDMA'S BROWN EDGE COOKIES

2 sticks butter
1 cup sugar
2 unbeaten egg whites
1½ cups flour
1 teaspoon vanilla
  cinnamon and sugar

Cream butter. Add sugar and mix well. Add egg whites gradually. Add flour and vanilla. Mix well. Drop by teaspoons on teflon baking sheet. Sprinkle cookies with a mixture of cinnamon and sugar as soon as cookies come from oven. Bake at 350° for 15 minutes or until edges turn brown. Makes 36 cookies. May be frozen.

Kathryn Sellers Howell

Mrs. Evan Howell, Wife of former Representative (Illinois)

MARK'S BOURBON BALLS

2½ cups crushed vanilla wafers
2 tablespoons cocoa
1 cup powdered sugar
1 cup finely chopped pecans
3 tablespoons light corn
  syrup
¼ cup bourbon
  powdered sugar

Mix dry ingredients. Then add nuts, corn syrup and bourbon. Using a teaspoon, make into balls and roll in additional powdered sugar. If mixture dries out while making balls, add a few drops of water to hold together. Place in tins that have been lined with plastic wrap. Seal tins with tape. Note: These are best when left sealed for 3 weeks. Makes 3 to 4 dozen. May be frozen.

Mark E. White

Mark White, Son-in-law of former Representative Richard H. Ichord (Missouri)

Before measuring honey or other syrup, oil the cup with cooking oil and rinse with hot water.

GINGER MOLASSES COOKIES

1 pound butter
¾ cup dark molasses
¼ cup water
½ tablespoon salt
3 cups brown sugar
3 large eggs
7 cups flour
1 tablespoon baking soda
1 tablespoon cinnamon
2 teaspoon cloves
2¼ teaspoons ginger

Cream butter, molasses, water and brown sugar. Add eggs. Sift together dry ingredients and add to creamed mixture. Mix well. Chill. Roll into balls and roll in regular sugar. Bake at 375° for about 10 minutes. Do not overbake, keep soft. Do not grease cookie sheets. Makes 6 to 7 dozen.

Mrs. Scott McInnis, Wife of Representative (Colorado)

CHINESE ALMOND COOKIES

1 cup butter
¾ cup sugar
2 cups sifted flour
½ teaspoon baking powder
½ cup ground almonds
36 whole almonds
1 teaspoon almond extract
extra sugar

Combine butter and sugar. Add flour, baking powder, ground almonds and almond extract. Refrigerate dough until solid. Form into balls walnut size. Roll in extra sugar then press almond into each cookie. Bake at 375° on ungreased cookie sheets for 15 to 20 minutes or until lightly browned. Cool on rack. Makes 3 dozen. May be frozen.

Mrs. William L. Hungate, Wife of former Representative (Missouri)

DATE-RICE CRISPIES FINGERS

½ stick oleo or butter
1 cup sugar
1 beaten egg
1 teaspoon vanilla
1 cup dates, cut fine
1 cup chopped nuts
2 cups Rice Crispies
powdered sugar

In double boiler, melt butter, then stir in sugar and beaten egg, vanilla and dates. Cook 10 minutes stirring constantly. Cool. When cool, add nuts and the Rice Crispies. Pinch off and roll in powdered sugar.

Evelyn Taylor

Mrs. Roy Taylor, Wife of former Representative (North Carolina)

APRICOT BOWLING BALLS

¾ cup Grape Nuts cereal
¾ cup finely crushed graham crackers
¾ cup finely snipped dried apricots
½ cup finely chopped pecans
¾ cup sifted powdered sugar
¼ cup light corn syrup
1 tablespoon orange juice or water

Combine cereal, crackers, apricots, nuts and ½ cup sugar. Stir in syrup and juice. With buttered hands, shape into ¾ inch balls. Roll in remaining powdered sugar. Makes 36 servings. May be frozen.

Marion Giaimo

Mrs. Robert Giaimo, Wife of former Representative (Connecticut)

Try substituting ground nuts in a one crust pie. Press pie shell just like you would with a graham cracker crust.

BOURBON BALLS

1 cup crushed vanilla wafers
1 cup chopped pecans
1 cup powdered sugar
2 tablespoons cocoa
¼ cup bourbon
2 teaspoons light corn syrup
½ cup powdered sugar for
   rolling

Combine all dry ingredients. Mix bourbon and corn syrup, mix with dry ingredients. Roll into 1-inch balls and roll balls in powdered sugar. Age 2–3 days in air tight containers. May be frozen.

John Paul Hammerschmidt, former Representative (Arkansas)

PEANUT BUTTER CHOCOLATE KISS COOKIES

1¾ cups flour
 2 tablespoons milk
 1 teaspoon baking soda
½ teaspoon salt
½ cup sugar
½ cup shortening
½ cup brown sugar, firmly
   packed
½ cup peanut butter
 1 teaspoon vanilla
 1 pkg. chocolate kisses

Mix all ingredients except chocolate kisses in one bowl. Roll into balls about the size of a quarter. Roll each ball in sugar. Flatten on the cookie sheet. Bake at 375° for 10–12 minutes. Place kisses on top each cookie when they are removed from oven. Makes 3 dozen. May be frozen.

Mrs. Doug Applegate, Wife of Representative (Ohio)

EUNICE'S PRALINES

2 cups white sugar
1 cup brown sugar
¾ cup water
  pinch salt
½ cup Karo
2 cups broken pecans
1 teaspoon vanilla
2 tablespoons butter

Combine first 5 ingredients and cook. Cook to soft ball stage (240°) and remove *immediately* from heat. Add next 3 ingredients. Beat until mixture starts to thicken. Quickly drop from teaspoon onto wax paper. Cool. Makes 32 cookies. May be frozen.

Cindy Stenholm

Mrs. Charles Stenholm, Wife of Representative (Texas)

CHOCOLATE MINT CREAMS

1¼ cups all-purpose flour
½ teaspoon baking soda
⅔ cup brown sugar, packed
6 tablespoons butter or margarine
1 tablespoon water
1 6 oz. pkg. semi-sweet chocolate chips (1 cup)
1 egg
½ to ¾ pound pastel cream mint kisses

Stir together flour and baking soda. In a medium saucepan, heat and stir brown sugar, butter or margarine and water until butter is melted. Add chocolate chips. Heat and stir until chocolate is melted. Pour into a large mixing bowl and let stand for 10–15 minutes or until cool. Beat egg into chocolate mixture. Stir in flour mixture until well mixed. (Dough will be soft). Cover and chill 1–2 hours or until the dough is easy to handle. Shape into 1 inch balls and place 2 inches apart on ungreased cookie sheet. Bake at 350° for 8 minutes. Quickly remove and place on top of each cookie a mint kiss and return to oven for 2 minutes more until cookies are done. Remove cookies from oven and swirl the melted mints with a knife to "frost" cookies. "Frosting" will become firm when cookie cools. Makes 48 cookies.

Sam Napier

Mrs. John Napier, Wife of former Representative (South Carolina)

JACK'S CINNAMON CANDY

2 cups sugar
2 cups Karo syrup
1 teaspoon oil of cinnamon
   red food coloring

Boil sugar and Karo to 300° on low heat. Use a candy thermometer. Stir occasionally. Add oil of cinnamon and red food coloring. Pour on buttered cookie sheet or foil. Crack when hard. May vary by using oil of peppermint and green food coloring or orange and orange or lemon and lemon, etc. Makes 12 servings.

Mrs. Wilbur D. Mills, Wife of former Representative (Arkansas)

MICROWAVE PEANUT BRITTLE

1 cup raw peanuts
½ cup white syrup
1 teaspoon vanilla
1 teaspoon baking soda
1 cup sugar
1 teaspoon butter
⅛ teaspoon salt

Put peanuts, sugar, syrup and salt in 2 quart microwave bowl. Microwave for 4 minutes. Take out and stir. Put back in microwave for 4 minutes. Take out and put in vanilla and butter and stir. Microwave for 2 minutes, take out and put in baking soda. Stir until good and bubbly. Pour on cookie sheet. When cool, break into pieces.

Mrs. Garner E. Shriver, Wife of former Representative (Kansas)

To melt chocolate, grease pan in which it is to be melted.

PEANUT BRITTLE (EASY)

1 cup sugar
1 cup light corn syrup
1½ cup peanuts (raw)
1 tablespoon butter
1 teaspoon salt
1 teaspoon baking soda

Bring syrup and sugar to hard boil and cook to hard ball stage. Add peanuts and cook until they begin to pop (about 10 minutes). Add butter, salt and baking soda (mixture will be foamy and bubbly), mix well and pour in large buttered pan. Cool, crack and enjoy!

"Sug" Hancock

Mrs. Mel Hancock, Wife of Representative (Missouri)

PEANUT BRITTLE

3 cups sugar
1 cup Karo (white)
½ cup water
13½ ozs. or more of salted cocktail peanuts
2 baking soda, set aside in
   bowl

In heavy 4 quart saucepan, stir together sugar, Karo, water (stirring) until sugar dissolves and mixture boils. Continue cooking without stirring to 280° (about 15 minutes). Stir in peanuts gradually, cook stirring until 300°. Remove from heat and dump in baking soda all at once. Blend quickly and gently pour brittle on 2 greased cookie sheets. Cool and break. Store in an airtight tin and the candy will stay fresh for several weeks. Make candy on a sunny day, humid days make sticky candy.

Nancy Purcell

Mrs. Graham Purcell, Wife of former Representative (Texas)

For a curdled custard, slowly blend a beaten egg into the hot liquid.

CARMELS

2 cups sugar
3 cups whipping cream
1⅓ cup white Karo syrup
1 tablespoon vanilla
dash salt

Combine sugar and Karo syrup in heavy saucepot. Add cream 1 cup at a time. Cook to 228° after first 2 cups have been added. After last cup is added, cook to 238° and remove from heat. Add vanilla and salt. Mix together and pour out into buttered dripper pan. Cool before cutting, wrap individually in waxed paper, twisting the ends.

John T. Doolittle, Representative (California)

OHIO BUCKEYES

3 one pound boxes confec-
tioners sugar
4 cups creamy peanut butter
1 pound margarine, room
temperature
1 6 oz. pkgs. semi-sweet
chocolate chips
1 6 oz. pkg. milk chocolate
chips
¼ bar parafin

Mix together peanut butter, softened margarine and add the confectioner's sugar. Make into balls about the size of walnuts and chill. Melt together chocolate and parafin over hot water. Use a toothpick and dip balls into chocolate halfway—to look like buckeyes. Set on waxed paper to cool and store in refrigerator. Makes 100. May be frozen.

Rebecca DeWine, Daughter of former Representative Michael DeWine (Ohio)

MDC'S FUDGE

2 cups semi-sweet chocolate chips
1 cube butter (¼ pound)
1 teaspoon vanilla
1 7 oz. jar of marshmallow creme
2¼ cups sugar
¾ cup plus 2 tablespoons of evaporated milk

Place chocolate chips, butter, vanilla and marshmallow creme in large mixing bowl. Place sugar and evaporated milk in a heavy saucepan over heat. Stir until the mixture starts to boil. Reduce heat to a low boil and try not to stir. Boil about 4 to 6 minutes. Pour over ingredients in mixing bowl. Stir for 3 to 5 minutes. Pour in 8″ × 8″ square buttered pan. Let cool and eat.

Mrs. Mike Crapo, Wife of Representative (Idaho)

CHRISTMAS CRUNCH

12 ozs. chocolate chips
¾ cup salted peanuts
¾ cup raisins
½ cup miniature marshmallows

Melt chocolate chips in top of double boiler over gently boiling water. Cool. Stir in peanuts, raisins and miniature marshmallows. Drop chocolate mixture 1 teaspoon at a time onto cookie sheet. Refrigerate overnight. Makes 24.

Mrs. Sam Nunn, Wife of Senator (Georgia)

ANNE'S ENGLISH TOFFEE

1⅓ cups sugar
1 cup butter
1 tablespoon dark Karo
    syrup
3 tablespoons water
8 plain Hershey bars
⅓ cup toasted, chopped almonds

Cook sugar, butter, water and Karo syrup to 298° (hard crack). Remove from heat and add half of almonds. Pour immediately on a greased cookie sheet and spread thin with a spatula. Then lay Hershey bars on top and spread. Sprinkle remaining almonds on top. Put in refrigerator to cool. Crack with knife. Makes 40 pieces.

Cynthia L.B. Rice

Mrs. Christopher Rice, Daughter of former Representative Laurie C. Battle (Alabama)

EMPANADAS—PASTRY

2 cups flour
¼ teaspoon salt
1¾ teaspoons cinnamon, divided
¾ cup granulated sugar
1 cup butter or margarine
2 egg yolks
2 tablespoons sherry
2½ tablespoons milk
    fruit jam
1 egg, slightly beaten

Sift flour with salt, ¼ teaspoon cinnamon, ¼ teaspoon sugar and cut in butter until the consistency of corn meal. Blend well egg yolk, sherry and milk. Add to flour mixture and mix until a dough. Refrigerate until chilled. Heat oven to 400°. Roll out half of dough ⅛" thick, cut into 2 inch rounds, spread with filling, fold over and seal by pressing with fork. Brush tops with beaten egg, sprinkle with ⅓ cup sugar mixed with 1½ teaspoons cinnamon. Bake to golden, remove to rack.

Filling: I use strawberry jam, or apricot jam, about 1 teaspoon per pastry. Makes 24 servings. May be frozen.

Alta Leath

Alta Leath, Member of Congressional Club

SUE SIMS' ALL PURPOSE PIE CRUST

3 cups flour, sifted
1 teaspoon salt
1 tablespoon sugar
1 cup Crisco (butter flavored)
1 tablespoon butter
8 tablespoons water

Mix flour, sugar and salt, cut in butter flavor Crisco and butter. Make a well and add water. Mix with a fork to form a ball. Roll out on floured wax paper. After pricking crusts, bake at 400-425° until brown. Makes four 10″ shells. May be frozen.

Cindy Stenholm

Mrs. Charles Stenholm, Wife of Representative (Texas)

PEACH CRUMBLE PIE

pastry for pie shell
17 to 18 medium, ripe, fresh peaches
1 cup brown sugar, divided
¼ teaspoon cinnamon, mixed with 3 tablespoons flour
1 cup flour
½ cup butter or substitute

Roll out pastry and line 9″ pie plate, flute edge. Peel, pit and halve peaches. Place peaches in lined pie plate, cut side up. Sprinkle on fruit: ¼ cup brown sugar and the 3 tablespoons of flour and cinnamon. Mix ¾ cup (remaining) brown sugar with the cup of flour. Cut butter into this until mixture is like crumbs. Sprinkle over fruit completely covering. Bake at 450° for 15 minutes or at 350° for 35 minutes or until peaches are tender. Makes 8 servings. May be frozen.

Jacqueline Klein

Mrs. Herbert Klein, Wife of Representative (New Jersey)

To cut a pie into five equal pieces, first cut a Y in the pie and then two large pieces can be cut in half.

CHEESEY PEACH PIE

¾ cup flour
1 teaspoon baking powder
½ teaspoon salt
  small pkg. French vanilla pudding
3 tablespoons soft margarine
1 egg
½ cup milk
15 to 20 oz. can sliced peaches
1 8 oz. cream cheese
½ cup sugar
3 tablespoons peach juice
  cinnamon, if wanted

Combine all of the above *except* peaches, cream cheese, sugar and juice. Beat 2 minutes at medium speed. Pour into 10″ cake pan (greased). Drain 15 to 20 oz. can sliced peaches, reserve juice. Place peaches over top batter. In small bowl combine: cream cheese, sugar and peach juice. Beat 2 minutes. Spoon over batter and peaches to within 1 inch rim of pan. Mix 1 tablespoon sugar and ½ teaspoon cinnamon. Sprinkle over batter. Bake at 350°. Cool before serving.

Mrs. Joyce Hubbard, Member of Congressional Club

KEY LIME PIE

1 can sweetened condensed milk
4 egg yolks
3 large limes, juiced
1 tablespoon grated lime peel
1 graham cracker crust

Beat milk until thick and fluffy, gradually add egg yolks beating at medium speed until thoroughly blended. Add lime juice and peel slowly. Beat until smooth and creamy. Add to pie shell and bake at 350° for 10 minutes. Top with whipped cream if desired. Makes 8 servings.

Mrs. Roy Muth, Daughter of former Senator J. Glenn Beall, Jr. (Maryland)

KEY LIME PIE

1 can sweetened condensed
   milk (15 oz.)
1/3 cup fresh lime juice
1 tablespoon grated lime rind
1/4 teaspoon salt
1 baked graham cracker
   crust

Combine condensed milk, lime juice, grated rind and salt. No need to cook! Pour into baked pie shell and chill at least 3 hours. Top with whipped cream if desired. Makes 6 servings.

Mrs. Jim Sasser, Wife of Senator (Tennessee)

LIME CHIFFON PIE

4 egg yolks
1 15 oz. can sweetened condensed milk
1/2 cup lime juice
1/4 teaspoon salt
6 egg whites
1/2 cup sugar
1 9″ baked pie shell

Beat four egg yolks until lemon colored, stir in milk, lime juice and salt blending well. Beat 6 egg whites until foamy, gradually add sugar and continue beating until meringue stands in peaks. Fold 1/4 cup of meringue into egg yolk mixture and pour into baked pie shell. Cover with remaining meringue. Bake in 400° oven for 8–10 minutes or until lightly browned. Makes 6 servings.

Mrs. William Proxmire, Wife of former Senator (Wisconsin)

The lower crust should be placed in the pan so that it covers the surface smoothly. And be sure no air lurks beneath the surface, for it will push the crust out of shape in baking.

LEMON PIE

1½ sticks margarine, melted
1½ cups plain flour
2½ cups chopped pecans
1 8 oz. cream cheese
2 8 oz. Cool Whip
1½ cups confectioners sugar
6 egg yolks
2 cans Eagle Brand sweet-
    ened condensed milk
1 cup lemon juice

First layer: Combine melted margarine, flour and 1 cup chopped pecans. Press over bottom of 9″ × 13″ glass dish. Bake at 375° for 15 minutes. Let cool. Second layer: Combine cream cheese, one 8 oz. Cool Whip and confectioners sugar and spread over first layer. Third layer: Beat egg yolks, Eagle Brand milk and lemon juice until thick. Spread over second layer, then sprinkle with ½ cup chopped pecans. Topping: Spread Cool Whip over third layer and sprinkle with 1 cup chopped pecans. Makes 20 servings. May be frozen.

Barbara Harris

Mrs. Claude Harris, Wife of former Representative (Alabama)

LEMON CHESS PIE

2 cups sugar
1 tablespoon flour
1 tablespoon corn meal
4 eggs, unbeaten
¼ cup melted butter
¼ cup milk
3 tablespoons grated lemon
    rind
¼ cup lemon juice
1 uncooked pie shell

Mix sugar, flour and corn meal in bowl. Beat eggs, butter, milk and lemon juice with rind until smooth and well blended. Pour into uncooked pie shell. Bake at 350° for 35 to 40 minutes. Makes 6 servings.

Nancy Fountain Black

Mrs. William Black, Jr., Daughter of former Representative L. H. Fountain (North Carolina)

LEMON MERINGUE PIE

1 9″ pie shell, baked
¾ cup flour
2½ cups sugar
2½ cups boiling water
4 teaspoons butter
6 egg yolks, slightly beaten
grated peel of 2 lemons
½ cup fresh lemon juice

Meringue:
6 egg whites
½ cup powdered sugar
pinch of cream of tartar

Preheat oven to 325°. In large saucepan, mix flour and sugar. Add boiling water, stirring constantly. Cook 2 minutes. Add butter, egg yolks, lemon peel and juice. Continue cooking and stirring until thick. Pour into shell. Top with meringue and bake.

Meringue: Beat egg whites, gradually add sugar and cream of tartar. Beat until stiff peaks form. Spread over pie and bake as directed above.

Karen Callahan

Mrs. Sonny Callahan, Wife of Representative (Alabama)

CHERRY-BANANA PIE

1 can pie cherries, drained
1 small can crushed pineapple
2 cups sugar
7 tablespoons cornstarch
salt
1 teaspoon vanilla
1 teaspoon red food coloring
1 cup chopped pecans
6 bananas, sliced
½ pint whipping cream

Drain fruit and add enough water to make 2 cups. Mix cornstarch, salt and sugar. Gradually add liquid. Add vanilla and color. Cook until thick, stirring often. Remove from heat. Add cherries and pineapple. Let cool. Fold in bananas and nuts. Pour into 2 baked pie shells. Top with whipped cream as served. Makes 14 servings.

Shirley Johnson

Mrs. Sam Johnson, Wife of Representative (Texas)

VIRGINIA APPLE CRUMB PIE

1 unbaked 9″ pie crust
5 to 6 apples, peeled, cored and thinly sliced
½ cup sugar
1½ tablespoons cornstarch
½ teaspoon cinnamon
¼ teaspoon nutmeg
⅛ teaspoon salt

For crumb topping:
¾ cup flour
½ cup sugar
⅓ cup butter

Mix sugar, cornstarch, cinnamon, nutmeg and salt together. Stir into apple slices to coat. Arrange apples in pie crust. To make topping: blend flour, sugar and butter, working into small crumbs with fingers or pastry blender. Sprinkle crumbs over apples. Bake at 425° for 10 minutes, then at 350° for 35 additional minutes. Makes 6 to 8 servings.

Frank R. Wolf, Representative (Virginia)

SCRUMPTIOUS APPLE PIE

Pie Crust:
4½ cups unsifted flour
¾ teaspoon salt
1½ cups plus 2 tablespoons shortening
¾ cup water

Pie Filling:
¾ cup sugar
4 teaspoons butter
8 Granny Smith apples
½ tablespoon cinnamon

Pie Crust: Lightly mix flour and salt, add shortening and cut in with pastry blender. Add water slowly until dough is sticky. Divide dough in half, roll out 2 pie crusts. Put in 9″ pie pan (deep dish pan).

Pie Filling: Sprinkle sugar and cinnamon on crust. Dot with butter. Peel and cut apples and fill pie shell to heaping. Make slits in top of crust, place over pie, seal edges. Bake on lower rack of oven at 425° for 1 hour. (Lower temperature after 15–20 minutes to 300° if crust browns too quickly). May be frozen.

Donna Murtha, Daughter of Representative John P. Murtha (Pennsylvania)

JUNEAN'S CHRISTMAS APPLE PIE

Filling:
- 8 cups of apples (½ Golden Delicious and ½ Granny Smith apples)
- ⅓ cup sugar
- ½ teaspoon cinnamon
- 2 tablespoons butter
- ¾ cup sugar
- 3 tablespoons flour (level)

Pie Crust:
- 2 cups flour
- 1 cup Crisco
- ⅛ teaspoon salt
- ½ cup milk

In a mixing bowl, combine the apples, ⅓ cup sugar, cinnamon and butter which has been cut into thin chunks. In a separate small bowl, mix ¾ cup of sugar and the 3 tablespoons of flour.

Prepare crust: Cut Crisco into the flour and salt. When it is pebble-like, not sticky, add milk and stir until you can make two balls with your hands. Roll out on a floured surface. Makes 2 crusts. Put bottom crust in pan.

Sprinkle about ⅓ of the sugar-flour mixture in the bottom of the crust so that it is covered. Add the apple mixture. Cover this with the remaining sugar-flour mixture. Put on top pie crust, seal edges and cut slits in the top. Brush the top with milk and sprinkle with sugar. This pie will be quite high! Bake 15 minutes at 425° and 45 minutes at 375° or until golden brown. This pie is also great if you reduce the apples about a cup and add ½ cup of whiskey soaked raisins and a handful of coarsely cut walnuts. This pie freezes well. Wrap lightly in several layers of aluminum foil and don't brush with milk or sprinkle with sugar until just before you bake it. Let set about 10 minutes before baking. Makes 8 servings. May be frozen.

Mrs. David Nagle, Wife of former Representative (Iowa)

> *Sending cookies to children through the mail? Pack them in popcorn, it keeps the cookies from breaking and is good to eat too.*

STRAWBERRY-RHUBARD PIE A.K.A. SHINNECOCK DELIGHT!

3 cups sliced rhubarb, cut in 1" pieces
1 cup sliced fresh strawberries
1½ cups sugar
3 tablespoons minute tapioca
½ teaspoon cinnamon
¼ teaspoon nutmeg
¼ teaspoon salt
1 9" unbaked pie shell

Topping:
⅔ cup flour
½ cup brown sugar
⅓ cup butter or margarine

Mix rhubarb and strawberries in bowl with sugar and tapioca. Let stand 20 minutes. Add seasonings, mix, and turn into the pie shell. Mix flour and sugar and cut butter or margarine into the mixture until crumbly. Sprinkle over pie and bake for 1 hour in 400° oven. Makes 8 servings. May be frozen.

Mrs. George Hochbrueckner, Wife of Representative (New York)

ELDERBERRY PIE

1 double pie crust (may use frozen which has been thawed)
4 cups elderberries, rinsed (these berries grow wild along railroad tracks and highways)
¾ cup sugar
3 tablespoons lemon juice
3 tablespoons cornstarch butter or margarine

Carefully mix the berries with the sugar, lemon juice and cornstarch. Pour it all into the defrosted or freshly made crust. Put dots of butter/margarine on top. Cover this with the second crust. Prick the top with a fork after crimping edges of crust. (It is vitally important that you prick the top)! Bake in a 450° oven for 10 minutes. Turn the oven down to 350° and bake for 30 minutes more, until the crust is a golden color. Marvelous served slightly warm with vanilla ice cream. Makes 8 servings. May be frozen.

Mrs. Robert McClory, Wife of former Representative (Illinois)

RHUBARB CUSTARD PIE

Custard:
- 3 eggs
- 2 cups sugar
- ¼ teaspoon salt
- 1 tablespoon butter
- 3 tablespoons milk
- ⅓ cup flour
- 4 cups rhubard, sliced

Oatmeal Crust:
- 1 cup flour
- 1 stick margarine
- 1 cup brown sugar
- 1 cup quick cooking oatmeal

Custard: Beat the eggs and milk. Mix flour, sugar and salt, then blend into the egg mixture. Stir in the rhubarb. Pour into 9″ pie shell (there are many fine ready-made crusts on the market). Top with the oatmeal crust. Bake 10 minutes at 425° and 25 minutes longer at 350°. Pie is done when you insert a thin knife and it comes out clean.

Oatmeal Crust: First, blend the flour, brown sugar and oats with 1 stick of margarine until crumbly. Use ¾ cup for each pie. This mixture stores for a long time in the refrigerator in a covered dish. Also a good topping for apple or cherry pie with a little cinnamon added. Makes 8 servings.

Bethine Church

Mrs. Frank Church, Wife of former Senator (Idaho)

RASPBERRY PIE

Crust:
- 1½ cups flour
- ½ cup lard
- 1 egg
- 2 tablespoons vinegar
- dash salt

Filling:
- 2 cups fresh or frozen red raspberries
- 3 tablespoons minute tapioca
- 1 generous cup sugar
- a pat butter

Crust: Cut flour and lard together with pastry blender. Mix egg, vinegar and salt. Lightly mix with fork until flour is moistened. Gather dough together and press into a ball. Divide dough in half and roll out to fit your pie pan. Place in pan, add filling and top with the top crust.

Filling: Mix together, pour into prepared pie crust. Cover with top crust. Make a couple of splits in the top crust. Bake at 400° for 35–40 minutes until brown. Makes 6 to 8 servings. May be frozen.

John Engler

John Engler, Governor (Michigan)

PENNY'S PEANUT BUTTER PIE

1 9" baked pie crust
1 8 oz. cream cheese
½ cup sugar
½ cup creamy peanut butter
1 teaspoon vanilla
1 cup whipped cream
   chopped peanuts

Bake pie crust. Beat sugar and cream cheese until smooth (medium). Add vanilla and peanut butter. Fold (remember fold only) in whipped cream. Pour into baked pie crust. Chill at least 3 hours. Sprinkle chopped peanuts on top. Makes 6 servings. May be frozen.

Penny Ichord

Mrs. Richard Ichord, Wife of former Representative (Missouri)

CHOCOLATE PEANUT ICE CREAM PIE

2 9" prepared chocolate
   crumb crust
½ gallon fudge ripple ice
   cream
1 10 oz. jar peanut butter
   (crunchy or creamy)

Soften ice cream in mixing bowl. Blend in peanut butter. Pour in pie shells, cover, freeze. Remove from freezer 15 minutes before serving. Cut, drizzle with fudge sauce if desired. May be frozen.

Laura G. Bateman

Mrs. Herbert Bateman, Wife of Representative (Virginia)

Mix a half gallon of vanilla ice cream with 4 cups mashed figs to make fresh fig ice cream.

KATHY'S FRENCH CHOCOLATE PIE

¾ cup sugar
1 stick butter, softened
1 square unsweetened chocolate
1 teaspoon vanilla
2 eggs
   chocolate crumb crust
   pecans

Cream together the sugar and butter. Melt 1 square of unsweetened chocolate in double boiler and let cool. Combine cooled chocolate with sugar/butter mixture and add 1 teaspoon vanilla. Add 2 eggs, mixing 5 minutes after each. Pour into chocolate crumb crust and add pecans on top. Chill. Makes 6 servings.

Mrs. Guy Vander Jagt, Wife of former Representative (Michigan)

CHOCOLATE BERRY PIE

1¼ cup graham cracker
   crumbs
⅓ cup butter or margarine,
   melted
3 tablespoons sugar
½ cup plus 2 tablespoon
   semi-sweet chocolate
   morsels, divided
1 8 oz. pkg. cream cheese,
   softened
¼ cup firmly packed brown
   sugar
½ teaspoon vanilla extract
1 cup whipping cream,
   whipped
1 pint fresh strawberries
1 teaspoon shortening

Combine first 3 ingredients, mixing well. Firmly press onto bottom and sides of a lightly greased 9″ pie plate. Bake at 325° for 10 minutes. Cool completely. Place ½ cup chocolate morsels in top of a double boiler, bring water to a boil, reduce heat to low, cook until chocolate melts, set aside to cool slightly. Beat softened cream at low speed of mixer until light and fluffy, add brown sugar and vanilla, mixing well. Fold whipped cream into cream cheese mixture, spoon into prepared crust. Chill at least 8 hours. Set aside 1 large strawberry, cut remaining straw-berries into thick slices. Arrange over filling, place whole strawberry in center. Combine remaining 2 tablespoons chocolate morsels and shortening in a small saucepan, cook over low heat until melted. Drizzle over berries. Makes 8 servings.

Mrs. Tennyson Guyer, Wife of former Representative (Ohio)

CHOCOLATE SILK PIE Á LA RICHMOND

1 stick butter
¼ cup sugar
2 eggs
1 teaspoon vanilla
3 squares semi-sweet chocolate
1 9" pie shell

Cream butter and sugar. Add melted chocolate and then vanilla. Add eggs one at a time and beat at high speed on the electric mixer for 5 minutes after adding each egg. Pour into baked pie shell which has cooled. Top with whipped cream and grated bitter chocolate. Refrigerate. Makes 6 servings.

Laura Bateman Hehner

Mrs. Dee Bateman Hehner, Daughter of Representative Herbert H. Bateman (Virginia)

CHOCOLATE CHIP NUT PIE

2 eggs
½ cup flour
½ cup sugar
½ cup brown sugar
1½ sticks softened Promise margarine
1 cup chopped English walnuts
6 oz. semi-sweet chips
1 unbaked pie crust

Beat 2 eggs for 3 minutes on high speed. Add next 3 ingredients, mix well. Add softened margarine, mix well. Add nuts and chips. Pour into unbaked pie crust. Bake at 350° for 50–60 minutes. Makes 8 to 10 servings.

Deborah Boehner

Mrs. John Boehner, Wife of Representative (Ohio)

> *A super-fast 'company' pie can be made by using a prepared crust. Add one box of instant pudding mix to prepared whipping topping. Mix well and fill crust. Reserve enough whipped topping to cover pie. Any flavor pudding mix can be used.*

KANSAS GERMAN-CHOCOLATE PIE

1 4 oz. pkg. German sweet
   chocolate
¼ cup butter or margarine
1 12 oz. can evaporated milk
   (1⅔ cups)
1½ cups sugar
3 tablespoons cornstarch
⅛ teaspoon salt
2 slightly beaten eggs
1 teaspoon vanilla
1 9″ unbaked pie shell
1⅓ cups coconut
½ cup chopped nuts

In a heavy, small saucepan, warm the chocolate and butter over low heat until chocolate melts, stirring occasionally. Remove from heat. Stir the evaporated milk into the melted chocolate mixture. In a medium mixing bowl, combine sugar, cornstarch and salt. Stir in the eggs and vanilla. Add the chocolate mixture to the egg mixture, stirring well. Pour into a prepared pie shell. Combine the coconut and nuts. Sprinkle over the filling in the shell. Bake in a 375° oven for 25 minutes. Cover with foil, continue baking for 25 to 30 minutes more or until puffed and browned. (Filling will be soft). Let cool, then chill for at least 4 hours or until serving time. Note: For a decorative touch, place semi-sweet chocolate pieces around the edge of the pie crust just after you remove it from the oven. Cut out pastry scraps in desired shapes and bake until golden. Place chocolate pieces on the baked pastry shapes while hot, then cool and place on pie before serving. Makes 8 servings. May be frozen.

Joan Finney, Governor (Kansas)

CHOCOLATE CHESS PIE

¼ pound butter or margarine
1 square chocolate
1 cup sugar
2 eggs, beaten
1 teaspoon vanilla
1 9″ unbaked pie shell
vanilla ice cream or
   whipped cream

Melt butter and chocolate. Add sugar, eggs and vanilla. Stir together thoroughly and pour into unbaked pie shell. Bake at 350° for 25 or 30 minutes. Top baked pie with ice cream or whipped cream. May be served warm or cold. Makes 6 to 8 servings. May be frozen.

Mrs. George Arthur Weaver, Daughter of former Representative M. G. Burnside (West Virginia)

MUD PIE

35 Oreos, crushed
⅓ cup melted butter
½ gallon vanilla ice cream
5 to 6 teaspoons Suisse Mocha coffee mix (optional)
1 can Hershey's hot fudge topping
1 4 oz. carton Cool Whip

First Layer: 35 Oreos crushed. Mix with ⅓ cup melted margarine. Freeze.

Second Layer: ½ gallon vanilla ice cream, softened a little. (Can mix Suisse Mocha coffee mix, 5-6 teaspoons). Layer on top of crumb mixture. Freeze.

Third Layer: 1 can Hershey's hot fudge topping. Warm a little and spread on ice cream. Freeze 15 minutes.

Fourth Layer: 1 4 oz. carton Cool Whip. Spread on top of chocolate. (Sprinkle almonds on top if desired). Makes 10 servings. May be frozen.

Marc Racicot, Governor (Montana)

RUM CHIFFON PIE

1 tablespoon unflavored gelatin
¼ cup cold water
3 eggs, separated
1½ cups milk
¾ cup sugar
⅛ teaspoon salt
3½ tablespoons rum
1 graham cracker pie shell
½ pint whipping cream
sweet chocolate, shredded

Soften gelatin in water 5 minutes. Beat egg yolks, add milk, sugar and salt and cook over low heat, stirring constantly. When mixture coats a spoon, stir in gelatin and cool until mixture begins to thicken. Beat egg whites until stiff and fold into custard with rum. Turn into pie shell, cover with whipped cream, sprinkle with chocolate. Chill. Makes 6 servings.

Mrs. John S. Cross, Daughter of former Representative Claude Albert Fuller (Arkansas)

SHERRY CREAM PIE

1½ cups crushed crisp chocolate cookies (may use Oreos with filling scraped from between)
¼ cup melted butter
¼ envelope unflavored gelatin
¼ cup cold milk
3 eggs, separated
½ cup sugar
1 cup milk
⅛ teaspoon salt
¼ teaspoon nutmeg
½ cup sherry wine
½ pint whipping cream

Crush cookies on waxed paper with rolling pin until very fine (or use food processor). Mix cookies with melted butter and pat mixture into 10″ greased pie plate to form pie shell. Put pie shell into refrigerator for 1 hour's chilling. From here you must work like a cyclone. Soften gelatin in cold milk. Put egg yolks in top of a double boiler, beat slightly, add sugar, 1 cup milk, stir well and cook 10 minutes or until mixture coats the spoon. Take off stove. Add gelatin mixture, salt and nutmeg to egg custard, stirring until gelatin is dissolved. Add wine very slowly, stirring constantly. (If added too fast, it might curdle). Custard filling goes to refrigerator to thicken. When thick, beat egg whites gently and fold in cream. By now pie shell will be firm. Take out of refrigerator and fill shell with chilled custard, sprinkling top with grated sweet chocolate or crushed cookies. Chill in refrigerator 8 hours before serving. Makes 6 to 8 servings. May be frozen.

Lou B. Bevill

Mrs. Tom Bevill, Wife of Representative (Alabama)

PECAN PIE

3 eggs
⅔ cup sugar
½ teaspoon salt
⅓ cup butter or oleo, melted
1 cup dark corn syrup
1 cup pecan halves, cut in two

Beat ingredients together with rotary beater, mixing pecans in last. Pour into pastry-lined 9″ pie pan. Bake at 375° for 40 to 50 minutes, until set and pastry is nicely browned. Serve cold or slightly warm. Makes 7 to 8 servings. May be frozen.

Laurie C. Battle

Laurie C. Battle, former Representative (Alabama)

PUMPKIN PIE

1 9″ pie shell
2½ cups cooked, mashed fresh
    or canned pumpkin
3 large eggs
1 cup sugar
¼ teaspoon salt
1 stick butter
1 teaspoon powdered cin-
    namon
1 teaspoon nutmeg
1 teaspoon allspice

If using fresh pumpkin, peel and cut into thin slices. Place pumpkin in a heavy saucepan with enough water to cover. Cook slowly over low heat until all water is absorbed. Mash pumpkin and set aside. Beat eggs and add ¾ cups sugar, salt and ½ stick of melted butter. Add spices to this mixture and blend. Add mashed pumpkin and mix. Pour into pie shell and spread mixture even with edge of pie shell. Sprinkle remaining ¼ cups sugar over top of pie and dribble remaining ½ stick of melted butter over sugar. Bake in preheated 350° oven for about 45 minutes. Makes 6 to 8 servings. May be frozen.

Ms. Rachael Worby, Wife of Governor Gaston Caperton (West Virginia)

CHEESE PIE

1 8 oz. pkg. softened cream
    cheese
½ cup sugar
2 cups thawed Cool Whip
1 unbaked 9″ graham cracker
    crust
1 cup canned cherry pie
    filling

Beat together the cream cheese and sugar until creamy. Blend in the Cool Whip. Pour into graham cracker crust. Top with the cherry pie filling. Chill at least 3 hours before serving. Makes 8 servings.

Mrs. Harold Hagen, Wife of former Representative (Minnesota)

PECAN PUDDING PIE

1 9″ uncooked pie shell
½ cup butter or margarine
⅓ cup firmly packed brown
    sugar
⅓ cup chopped pecans
⅓ cup coconut
1 6 oz. chocolate pie filling
    (cooked)
    Cool Whip

Bake pie shell until it begins to brown, remove and set aside. Melt sugar and butter in small saucepan, stirring. Add pecans and coconut, mix and pour into pie shell. Return pie to oven and bake until filling is bubbly. Remove from oven. When cool, spread with chocolate pie filling. Top with Cool Whip. Makes 5 to 6 servings.

Mary Jo Van Deerlin

Mrs. Lionel Van Deerlin, Wife of former Representative (California)

MEL'S FAVORITE PECAN PIE

¾ cup chopped pecans
3 tablespoons bourbon
¼ cup melted butter
1 cup sugar
3 eggs
¾ cup Mrs. Butterworth's
   syrup
1 teaspoon vanilla
¼ teaspoon salt
¾ cup chocolate chips
1 9″ prepared butter recipe
   pie crust

Soak pecans in the bourbon. Set aside. In a mixing bowl, beat melted butter, sugar and eggs until fluffy. Blend in syrup, vanilla and salt. Stir in chocolate chips until evenly distributed. Pour mixture into pie crust. Sprinkle bourbon-soaked pecans over top of filling. Bake in 375° oven for 45–55 minutes. Check at 45 minutes, it may brown quickly. Makes 8 servings. May be frozen.

Eulada P. Watt

Mrs. Mel Watt, Wife of Representative (North Carolina)

SOUTHERN BUTTERMILK PIE

2 cups sugar
1 stick butter, softened
3 eggs
1 teaspoon vanilla
½ cup buttermilk
   pinch of salt
1 tablespoon flour
   unbaked deep pie shell

Cream sugar and butter. Add eggs, vanilla, buttermilk, salt and flour. Mix thoroughly, pour into unbaked deep pie shell. Bake at 350° for 1 hour. Delicious and so easy. Makes 6 to 8 servings.

JoLane Edwards

Mrs. Jack Edwards, Wife of former Representative (Alabama)

> *Folding the top crust over the lower crust before crimping will keep the juices in the pie.*

AMAZING COCONUT PIE

2 cups milk
¾ cup sugar
½ cup biscuit mix
4 eggs
¼ cup butter or margarine
1½ teaspoons vanilla
1 cup angel flake coconut
1 9″ pie shell

Combine milk, sugar, biscuit mix, eggs, butter and vanilla in electric mixer. Blend on *low* speed 3 minutes. Pour into greased 9″ pie pan. Let stand about 5 minutes, then sprinkle with coconut. Bake at 350° for 40 minutes. Serve warm or cool. Makes 6 servings.

Mrs. James Hanley, Wife of former Representative (New York)

SARAH'S BROWN SUGAR PIE

1 cup brown sugar
½ cup white sugar
1 tablespoon flour
2 eggs
2 tablespoons milk
½ cup melted butter (1 stick)
1 teaspoon vanilla
1 unbaked pie shell

Mix all ingredients and pour into an unbaked pie shell. Bake at 375° for approximately 45 minutes. Makes 6 to 8 servings. May be frozen.

Mrs. Horace R. Kornegay, Wife of former Representative (North Carolina)

> *In making custard type pies, bake at a high temperature for about ten minutes to prevent a soggy crust. Then finish baking at a low temperature.*

CHOCOLATE DELIGHT

First Layer:
1½ cups plain flour
1½ sticks margarine
¾ cup chopped pecans
¼ cup sugar

First Layer: Mix all ingredients and press into 9″ × 13″ baking dish. Cook for 30 minutes at 300°. Cool.

Second Layer:
1 8 oz. cream cheese
1½ cups 10X sugar (powdered)
½ of 9 oz. carton Cool Whip

Second Layer: Cream the cheese and sugar. Fold in Cool Whip and spread over cooled crust, first layer.

Third Layer:
2 small pkgs. instant chocolate pudding
3 cups milk
¾ cup sugar

Third Layer: Mix all ingredients and pour over second layer. Place in refrigerator for at least 2 hours. When chilled, cover with remaining Cool Whip or whipped cream. Cut into squares and serve. Makes 16 servings.

'Peatsy' Hollings

Mrs. Ernest F. Hollings, Wife of Senator (South Carolina)

HOPSCOTCH

½ cup peanut butter
1 cup butterscotch morsels (1 6 oz. pkg.)
2 cup chow mein noodles (1 3 oz. can)
2 cups miniature marshmallows

Combine peanut butter and butterscotch morsels in the top of a double boiler and melt on low heat. Add and coat noodles and marshmallows. Drop by teaspoon onto waxed paper and chill. This is a favorite among children. Makes 30 servings. May be frozen.

Elizabeth Albert

Mrs. David Albert, Daughter-in-law of former Representative Carl Albert (Oklahoma)

KANSAS APPLE DUMPLINGS

1 pastry for 9″ two crust pie
6 baking apples (each about
    3 inches in diameter)
    pared and cored
3 tablespoons raisins
3 tablespoons chopped nuts
2 cups brown sugar, packed
1 cup water

Heat oven to 425°. Prepare pastry as directed except roll ⅔ of dough into 14 inch square, cut into 4 squares. Roll remaining dough into rectangle, 14″ × 7″, cut into 2 squares. Place apple on each square. Mix raisins and nuts, fill center of each apple. Moisten corners of squares, bring 2 opposite corners of pastry up over apple and press together. Fold in sides of remaining corners (as if wrapping a package). Bring corners up over apple and press together. Place dumplings in ungreased baking dish. Heat brown sugar and water to boiling, carefully pour around dumplings. Spoon syrup over dumplings 2 or 3 times during baking. Bake at 425° for 40 minutes or until crust is golden and apples are tender. Serve warm or cool, if desired, top with sweetened whipped cream. Makes 6 servings. May be frozen.

Joan Finney, Governor (Kansas)

APRICOT MOUSSE

1 cup Sunsweet dried
    apricots
⅔ cup water
⅓ cup granulated sugar
1½ tablespoons orange juice
½ teaspoon brandy extract
1½ cups whipping cream

Combine apricots, water and sugar in small saucepan. Bring to boil, reduce heat and simmer uncovered 12 minutes. Puree in food processor or blender. Stir in orange juice and brandy extract. Cool. Beat cream until stiff and fold into apricot mixture. Spoon into individual serving dishes and chill. Makes 3 cups. Makes 6 servings.

Mrs. Thurgood Marshall, Wife of former Justice, U.S. Supreme Court

ELEANOR'S ONE-MINUTE CHOCOLATE MOUSSE

6 ozs. chocolate chips
¾ cup scalded milk
1 egg
2 tablespoons sugar
1 teaspoon either/or Amaretto, vanilla, or Bailey's Irish Creme

Blend all ingredients in blender for 1 minute. Pour into serving dishes. Cool in refrigerator. Makes 4 servings.

Valery J. Moorhead

Mrs. Carlos Moorhead, Wife of Representative (California)

WHITE CHOCOLATE MOUSSE WITH RASPBERRY SAUCE

6 ozs. white chocolate
6 tablespoons sweet butter, softened
3 large eggs, separated
¼ cup sugar
½ teaspoon vanilla

Raspberry Sauce:
2 cups fresh raspberries
2 tablespoons sugar
1 teaspoon fresh lemon juice
2 tablespoons Grand Marnier

Melt chocolate over hot water and beat with butter until creamy. Add egg yolks and continue beating until mixture gets creamy and thick. Beat egg whites until frothy, sprinkle on sugar and continue beating until soft peaks form. Stir half the egg whites and vanilla into the chocolate mixture, then fold in the rest. Spoon into demitasse cups, chill and serve with raspberry sauce.

Raspberry Sauce: Puree the berries and force them through a fine sieve to remove seeds. Mix in sugar, lemon juice and Grand Marnier. Chill before serving atop White Chocolate Mousse. Makes 4 to 6 servings.

Susan Dougher

Mrs. Jon Dougher, Daughter of Representative Gerald Solomon (New York)

FROZEN MOCHA SOUFFLE

8 eggs, separated
¾ cup granulated sugar
2 envelopes unflavored
   gelatin
½ cup cold strong coffee
¼ cup coffee liqueur
1½ teaspoons instant coffee
4 ozs. sweet cooking chocolate, melted
2 ozs. unsweetened choco-
   late, melted
2 cups heavy cream
2 tablespoons powdered
   sugar

Cut waxed paper long enough to go around a 1½ to 2 quart souffle dish (6½" to 7" in diameter). Fold the paper in half lengthwise and brush one side with vegetable oil. Wrap paper around the dish, extending it 2-3 inches above the rim. Tie paper on with string around dish. In a large mixing bowl, beat egg yolks until lemon colored and thick. Add the sugar slowly and beat until light and fluffy. In a small saucepan soften gelatin in the coffee. Place over low heat and stir until dissolved. And this gelatin to the egg mixture. Add liqueur, instant coffee and melted chocolates. Beat until well blended. In a separate bowl, beat egg whites until stiff and holds peaks. Combine egg whites with chocolate mixture by folding in with spatula. In a separate bowl, combine powdered sugar and heavy cream. Beat until it forms soft peaks. Fold whipped cream into chocolate mixture. Freeze 3—4 hours until set or overnight. When ready to serve, remove waxed paper. May be decorated with additional whipped cream and shaved chocolate. Makes 12 servings. May be frozen.

Nini Horn

Mrs. Steve Horn, Wife of Representative (California)

When fresh fruit is handy, but you don't have time to bake, just mix the filing as you normally would for pie. Line a pie pan with several layers of foil and place the filing in the pan. Wrap and freeze. When you're ready wih a pie crust the filling can be placed in the crust and baked. After filling is frozen solid it can be taken out of the pan so you will be able to use the pan and the fillings will stack neater in the freezer.

FROZEN SOUFFLE GRAND MARNIER

 5 eggs, separated
2/3 cup sugar
   grated rind of one orange
1/4 cup Grand Marnier (or
   Cointreau)
 2 cups whipping cream
16 Amaretti cookies, crushed
   (8 packets)

Beat egg yolks and sugar with electric mixer until thick and lemon-colored. Stir in orange rind and Grand Marnier. Beat cream until it barely forms peaks and fold into yolk mixture. In a separate bowl, beat egg whites until stiff then gently fold into egg yolk mixture. Pour 1/2 into a 2 quart souffle dish. Sprinkle with about half the crushed Amaretti cookies. Top with remaining mixture. Top with remainder of crushed Amaretti. Cover with saran wrap or put in plastic bag. Freeze at least 4 hours. Can be made a week in advance and kept in freezer. Remove from freezer and put in refrigerator 1/2 hour before serving. Makes 10 servings. May be frozen.

Audrey L. Hagen

Mrs. Harold Hagen, Wife of former Representative (Minnesota)

CYNTHIA'S HOT FUDGE SAUCE

1/2 cup sugar
1/4 cup butter
1/3 cup water
 2 tablespoons light corn
   syrup
 6 oz. pkg. (1 cup) semi-
   sweet chocolate chips
 1 teaspoon vanilla

In a medium saucepan, combine sugar, butter, water and corn syrup. Cook over medium heat, stirring constantly, until mixture comes to a full boil, about 5 to 8 minutes. Boil 3 minutes, remove from heat. Immediately add chocolate chips, beat with wire whisk or rotary heater until smooth. Stir in vanilla. Serve over ice cream or cake. Delicious. Makes 1 1/2 cups. May be frozen.

Julia Ann Shepard

Mrs. Tazewell Shepard, Daughter of former Senator, John Sparkman (Alabama)

PAVE AU CHOCOLAT

8 ozs. of Baker's semi-sweet chocolate
¼ cup of milk
2½ cups of powdered sugar
1¼ cups of butter at room temperature
4 egg yolks
6 to 7 pkgs. of plain lady fingers

Line a deep pyrex loaf pan with 1 piece of wax paper, running down one side, across bottom and up the other side leaving an excess of three inches at top edges. This excess paper will assist you in turning the pave upside down on a serving plate. Melt chocolate in a double boiler with ¼ cup milk. Beat sugar and butter until very smooth. When chocolate is cool, add the egg yolks and mix. Add this mixture to the creamed sugar and butter and beat until well blended. Put 1 teaspoon of the chocolate cream at the bottom of the lined dish. Tear the lady fingers apart and start to layer them on the bottom of dish placing very close together alternating each layer with a layer of chocolate cream. The top layer should be lady fingers and should be above the edge of dish to make a tall pave. Cover with wax paper and put a plate with some weight on it. I use soup cans. Refrigerate for at least 12 hours. You should have about 1 cup of the chocolate cream left over. Cover and refrigerate. Take this icing out 1 hour before you are to turn the pave onto a serving dish. Spread top and sides with this remainder of chocolate cream. Makes 10 servings.

Mrs. Glenn English, Wife of Representative (Oklahoma)

> *Be certain a meringue topping on a pie touches the edge of the crust; otherwise, it may shrink from the sides.*

LAYER DESSERT

1 cup flour
1 cup butter or margarine
1 cup chopped nuts
8 oz. cream cheese
1 cup powdered sugar
2 small containers Cool Whip
1 small pkg. instant vanilla
    pudding mix
1 small pkg. instant choco-
    late pudding mix
3½ cups milk
    Hershey bar

1st Layer: Mix together flour, butter and chopped nuts. Place in 13″ × 9″ pan. Bake at 350° for 15 minutes.

2nd Layer: Mix together cream cheese and powdered sugar. Add small container of Cool Whip and mix well. Spread on 1st layer.

3rd Layer: Mix vanilla pudding with 1¾ cup milk. Pour on 2nd layer. Let set.

4th Layer: Mix chocolate pudding with 1¾ cup milk. Pour on 3rd layer. Let set.

5th Layer: Spread Cool Whip on top of 4th layer. Top with chopped nuts and shredded Hershey bar.

Refrigerate overnight or several hours. Makes 20 servings.

Judy Istook

Mrs. Ernest Istook, Wife of Representative (Oklahoma)

JESSIE'S GINGER BREAD

1 cup white sugar
½ cup oleo margarine
2 eggs
1 cup molasses
2½ cups flour
2 teaspoons baking soda in 1
    cup hot water
½ teaspoon cinnamon
1 teaspoon ginger

Cream sugar and oleo margarine. Add eggs, 1 at a time, beating well. Combine molasses and baking soda water. Add alternately with flour to creamed mixture. Add spices, stirring until well mixed. Bake at 350° in greased and floured 9″ × 13″ pan for 35–40 minutes. Test for doneness in the middle of the cake with a toothpick. Serve warm. If cold, garnish with whipped cream. Makes 8 to 10 servings. May be frozen.

Bea Smith

Mrs. Neal Smith, Wife of Representative (Iowa)

JUST A TRIFLE

1 frozen pound cake (10¾
   ozs.), thawed
½ cup sherry, brandy, rum or
   orange juice
2 cans (17½ ozs.) vanilla
   pudding
1 can (21 ozs.) cherry pie
   filling
1 carton (4 ozs.) frozen
   whipped topping,
   thawed

Cut cake into ½ inch cubes. In pretty glass bowl, place a layer of cake cubes. Sprinkle with sherry or liquid of your choice. Spread about 1 cup pudding over cake, forming a thin layer. Top with a few spoonsful of cherry pie filling (doesn't need to make a complete layer). Continue layering until ingredients are used (except whipped topping). Make final layer of whipped topping. Refrigerate at least 2 hours before serving. Makes 6 to 8 servings.

Marion Giaimo

Mrs. Robert Giaimo, Wife of former Representative (Connecticut)

PUMPKIN ROLL

Cake Roll:
⅔ cup mashed pumpkin (may
   use canned)
¾ cup flour
1 cup sugar
3 eggs
1 teaspoon baking soda
1 teaspoon cinnamon

For Filling:
8 ozs. cream cheese
4 tablespoons butter
1 teaspoon vanilla
1 cup confectioners sugar

Cake Roll: Beat all ingredients together. Grease and flour jelly roll pan. Spread cake mixture evenly in pan. Bake at 400° 10–15 minutes. Remove from pan onto a tea towel while cake is still warm. Roll up cake and towel together and refrigerate for 1 hour.

Filling: Beat all ingredients together. Remove roll from refrigerator, unroll and remove from towel. Spread filling on cake, roll up as a jelly roll, wrap in foil and refrigerate. Spread whipped cream over top before slicing to serve. Makes 10 servings. May be frozen.

Carolyn Wolf

Mrs. Frank Wolf, Wife of Representative (Virginia)

PUMPKIN ROLL

Roll:
- 3 eggs
- 1 cup sugar
- 2/3 cup pumpkin
- 1 teaspoon lemon juice
- 3/4 cup flour
- 1 teaspoon baking powder
- 1 teaspoon cinnamon
- 1/2 teaspoon ginger
- 1/4 teaspoon nutmeg
- 1/2 teaspoon salt

Filling:
- 2 cups powdered sugar
- 8 oz. cream cheese
- 1/3 cup butter
- 1 teaspoon vanilla

Roll: Beat eggs on high for 5 minutes. Gradually add 1 cup sugar. Stir in pumpkin, flour, baking powder and spices. Line jelly roll with foil. Grease top of foil. Bake at 350° for 15–20 minutes. Cover the rough side of a terry cloth towel with powdered sugar. I use a sifter to make it even. Flip cake onto the towel and roll up. Cool completely.

Filling: Combine filling ingredients and beat until smooth. When cool, unroll cake and fill with filling. I sprinkle 1/2 cup chopped pecans on top of filling. Secure with toothpicks if needed. Makes 8 servings. May be frozen.

Mrs. Jim Slattery, Wife of Representative (Kansas)

DOROTHY'S CREAM PUFFS

- 2 pkgs. crescent rolls
- 2 8 oz. pkgs cream cheese
- 1 cup sugar
- 1 egg yolk
- 1 teaspoon vanilla
- 1 cup powdered sugar

Place 1 package of rolls on bottom of 9″ × 12″ pan. Beat cream cheese, sugar, egg yolk and vanilla. Pour over the rolls in pan, then top with other package of rolls. Bake at 350° for 30 minutes. Upon removing from oven, drizzle glaze of 1 cup of powdered sugar and 3–4 tablespoons water over top. Refrigerate. Makes 8 servings.

Mrs. Bob McEwen, Wife of former Representative (Ohio)

SWEET POTATO DESSERT

4 large sweet potatoes,
   cooked/baked
2 eggs
1 cup white sugar
1 teaspoon vanilla
⅓ cup butter, cut up in slices
½ cup plain flour
1 cup chopped pecans
1 cup brown sugar
⅓ cup butter, melted

Mash the sweet potatoes, beat the eggs and add to them the white sugar, vanilla and the butter. Mix all 5 of the first ingredients together. The last 4 ingredients make the topping. Mix flour, pecans, brown sugar and melted butter together and spread over the top of the sweet potato mixture. Bake at 350° for 30 minutes. Note: For a less rich topping, cut the flour, pecans and brown sugar portions in half. Makes 8 servings. May be frozen.

Mrs. Ted Strickland, Wife of Representative (Ohio)

GRAND MARNIER SOUFFLÉ

10 eggs, separated
⅔ cup sugar
½ cup Grand Marnier
¼ teaspoon cream of tartar
1 tablespoon butter

Beat 8 egg yolks with sugar in double boiler over hot water until mixture makes a ribbon when spoon is held up. Add the Grand Marnier. Transfer to a bowl and place over cracked ice in a dish, continue beating until mixture has cooled. Beat 10 egg whites until firm, but not dry. Add cream of tartar. Fold into mixture and blend thoroughly. Pour into buttered and sugared soufflé dish. Bake at 400° oven for 12 to 15 minutes (usually takes a little longer) or until risen and browned. Serve at once. Makes 4 servings.

Mrs. Fred Upton, Wife of Representative (Michigan)

> *When you buy cellophane-wrapped cupcakes and notice that the cellophane is somewhat stuck to the frosting, hold the package under the cold-water tap for a moment before you unwrap it. The cellophane will then come off clean.*

TIRAMISU DA ALFREDO

5 cups strong, cold Espresso
   coffee
32 Savoiardi (Italian Ladyfingers)
10 eggs yolks
10 tablespoons sugar
1 pound Mascarpone cheese
1 to 2 tablespoons Marsala
   wine
2 cups heavy cream
3 tablespoons unsweetened
   cocoa powder

Pour cold coffee into a large pie plate. Dip sixteen of the ladyfingers very quickly into the coffee. Line the bottom of a 12" × 9" × 2" oval dish with the ladyfingers. In a large mixing bowl, whisk the eggs and sugar until frothy. Add the Mascarpone and Marsala wine. Whisk until well-blended and smooth. In another bowl whisk or whip the cream until stiff and fold into the Mascarpone mixture, until well blended and smooth. Using a large pastry bag, pipe about ½ of the mixture over the ladyfingers. Dip the remaining ladyfingers quickly into the coffee. Arrange another layer of ladyfingers over the cheese mixture, and pipe remaining cheese mixture over this layer of ladyfingers. Cover with plastic wrap and chill at least 6 hours. When ready to serve, sprinkle the cocoa powder through a fine sieve over the entire surface of the Tiramisu. Spoon portions onto individual dessert plates. Makes 8 to 10 servings. May be frozen, (before cocoa powder is added—up to 2 weeks).

Carol Laxalt

Mrs. Paul Laxalt, Wife of former Senator (Nevada)

CHOCOLATE SAUCE FOR ICE CREAM

2 squares (1 oz.) Bakers unsweetened chocolate
1 can (5 oz.) Carnation evaporated milk
1 cup sugar
   dash salt
1 teaspoon butter
1 teaspoon vanilla

Melt chocolate in double boiler. Add milk, sugar and salt. Cook over low heat until thick (about 1 hour) stirring a few times. Add butter and vanilla. Serve over ice cream or store in glass jar in refrigerator and reheat in pan of water. Makes 8 to 10 servings.

Betty Adams

Mrs. Brock Adams, Wife of former Senator (Washington)

"HEAVEN" DESSERT

1 stick butter
1 cup flour
1 cup chopped pecans
8 oz. cream cheese
1 cup powdered sugar
1 large container Cool Whip
1 small pkg. instant vanilla pudding
1 small pkg. instant chocolate pudding
2 cups half and half chocolate Hershey bar if you want

Layer in 9″ × 14″ pan. Spray first with Pam.

1st Layer: Mix butter and flour. Add chopped pecans, press in pan. Bake 20 minutes at 350°. Cool.

2nd Layer: Mix cream cheese with powdered sugar. Fold in Cool Whip. Spread on 1st layer.

3rd Layer: Blend vanilla pudding and chocolate pudding with half and half. Spread. Top with remaining Cool Whip, sprinkle shaved Hershey bar over the top if you wish.

Mrs. Joyce Hubbard, Member of Congressional Club

MOTHER'S PEACH ICE CREAM

4 eggs
1½ cups sugar
2 teaspoons flour
pinch salt
1 quart milk, scalded
½ pint whipping cream
½ pint coffee cream
4 to 6 peeled peaches, mashed with sugar to taste
1 teaspoon almond extract

Beat together eggs, sugar, flour and salt, add to scalded milk. Cook, stirring constantly until coats spoon. Add ½ pint whipping cream and ½ pint coffee cream. Add peeled peaches mashed with sugar to taste and 1 teaspoon almond flavoring. Freeze. Makes 10 servings.

Mrs. Trent Lott, Wife of Senator (Mississippi)

Rinse a pan in cold water before scalding milk to prevent sticking.

CHOCOLATE MACAROON MUFFINS

Muffin:
- 2 cup all-purpose flour
- 1/2 cup sugar
- 3 tablespoons cocoa
- 1 tablespoon baking powder
- 1/4 teaspoon salt
- 1 egg, beaten
- 1 cup milk
- 1/3 cup vegetable oil

Macaroon Filling:
- 1 cup flaked coconut
- 1/4 cup sweetened condensed milk
- 1/4 teaspoon almond extract

Combine first 5 ingredients in a large bowl. Make a well in center of mixture. Combine egg, milk and oil, add to dry ingredients, stirring just until moistened. Spoon batter into greased muffin pans, filling 1/3 full. Combine all ingredients of macaroon filling together, spoon 2 teaspoons in center of each muffin cup. Spoon remaining batter over top, filling each muffin cup 2/3 full. Bake at 400° for 20 minutes. Serve warm. Makes 1 dozen.

Mae Guyer

Mrs. Tennyson Guyer, Wife of former Representative (Ohio)

FOURTH OF JULY TRIFLE

- 1 pint heavy cream (whipped and divided)
- 1 recipe Bird's custard (pudding section of store)
- 3 pkgs. of lady fingers (split)
- 1/2 cup cream sherry
- 1 pint strawberries (sliced and 3 left whole)
- 1 pint blueberries
- 1 pint raspberries

Whip the cream, divide into half and refrigerate. Prepare the custard according to package directions. When cool, fold in half of the whipped cream. Line the trifle dish with lady fingers. Sprinkle the cake with some of the sherry. Pour in 1/2 cup of custard/cream mixture and cover with a layer of berries. Put down another layer of cake and repeat the layering process twice more ending with a layer of cake. For the final layer, top the cake with the remaining whipped cream and arrange the blueberries and raspberries decoratively on top of the cream, place 3 whole strawberries in the center. Chill for at least 2 hours before serving.

Lucinda Florio

Mrs. James Florio, Wife of Governor (New Jersey)

GRAHAM CRACKER SURPRISE

1 box honey graham crackers
2 small boxes of instant vanilla pudding
3 cups cold milk
8 ozs. Cool Whip

Frosting:

6 tablespoons cocoa
2 tablespoons oil
6 tablespoons butter
2 tablespoons light Karo syrup
1 teaspoon vanilla
1½ cups confectioners sugar
3 tablespoons milk

Line bottom of 11″ × 13″ pan with whole crackers. Mix pudding and milk until thickened. Fold in Cool Whip. Layer half of pudding mix over crackers. Place another layer of whole crackers then another layer of pudding mix and top layer of remaining crackers. Melt cocoa, oil and butter over heat. Remove. Add syrup and vanilla, stir in sugar and milk until smooth. Spread over pudding and cracker mixture and refrigerate overnight. Makes 15 servings.

Virginia Bartlett

Mrs. Joe Bartlett, Daughter of former Senator George H. Bender (Ohio)

MOM'S CHOCOLATE DESSERT

Crust:

1 stick margarine
1 cup flour
1 cup chopped nuts

Filling:

8 oz. cream cheese
1 cup powdered sugar
1 large size container of Cool Whip (4 cups)
1 6 oz. pkg. of instant chocolate pudding
2½ cups milk

Melt margarine in 9″ × 13″ baking dish. Mix in flour and nuts. Pat out in baking pan to form a crust. Bake for 15 minutes at 350°. Cool. Mix cream cheese, powdered sugar and 2 cups of the Cool Whip. Spread this mixture over the cooled crust. Mix the chocolate pudding with the milk. When set and thick, spread over the cream cheese mixture. Top with the remaining Cool Whip. Makes 12 servings.

Gene Green

Gene Green, Representative (Texas)

CHOCOLATE DELIGHT

1 cup crushed vanilla wafers
1 stick butter, melted
½ to 1 cup chopped pecans
8 oz. cream cheese, softened
1 cup powdered sugar
1 cup whipped topping
2 pkgs. instant chocolate
    pudding
3 cups cold milk
1 teaspoon vanilla extract

Mix together vanilla wafers, butter and chopped pecans. Spread in 9″ × 13″ pan. Bake at 350° for about 10 minutes, let cool. Mix together cream cheese, powdered sugar and whipped topping. Carefully spread on wafer mix. Mix together chocolate pudding, cold milk and vanilla. Spread over cream cheese mix. Top with remaining whipped topping and sprinkle grated chocolate on top for decoration.

Mrs. Pat Roberts, Wife of Representative (Kansas)

SNOWBALLS

1 quart vanilla ice cream
1¼ cups coconut, flaked,
    toasted
1¼ cups nuts, chopped
1¼ cups peppermint candy,
    crushed
12 ozs. hot fudge topping,
    heated

Form 6 large ice cream balls and quickly roll in coconut, nuts and candy. Place snowballs in small baking pan and freeze until firm (1 to 2 hours). Before serving, place snowballs in dessert glasses. Serve immediately with hot fudge topping. For extended storage, wrap snowballs in foil and store in freezer for up to 5 days. Makes 6 servings. May be frozen.

Mrs. Howard Cannon, Wife of former Senator (Nevada)

When you are creaming butter and sugar together, it's a good idea to rinse the bowl with boiling water first. They'll cream faster.

VIENNA TARTS

3 sticks butter
1 8 oz. pkg. cream cheese
3 cups four
¾ cup tart jelly
3 egg yolks
6 tablespoons milk
¾ cup chopped walnuts

Cream butter and cheese until well blended and fluffy. Add flour and kneed to a smooth dough. Wrap and chill several hours. Roll dough ⅛ inch thick, into a rectangle. Cut into 2 inch squares. Place ¼ teaspoon jelly on each square in one corner. Beginning at this corner, fold edge over, completely covering jelly. Press down to seal and roll the squares diagonally. Turn into crescent shape. Brush with egg yolk mixed with milk. Sprinkle with nuts or dip brushed surface into nuts. Place on greased cookie sheet. Bake at 400° for 12 to 15 minutes. Cool on cake racks. Sprinkle with confectioners sugar. Makes 7½ dozen.

Mrs. Benjamin F. James, Wife of former Representative (Pennsylvania)

ORANGE PECANS

2 cups sugar
½ cup water
3 tablespoons white Karo
2 cups pecans
  juice and grated rind of 1 orange

Mix sugar, water, orange juice, rind and Karo. Boil to 230° or until soft ball stage. Stir until it begins to sugar. Add pecans and pour into buttered 9″ × 13″ × 2″ pan. Break apart when thoroughly cool and hardened. Makes 1½ pounds.

Kirk Fordice, Governor (Mississippi)

KAHLUA A LA KITTY HAWK

12 lady fingers, split in half
2 tablespoons instant coffee,
   dissolved in 1 tablespoon
   boiling water
2 tablespoons Kahlua
5 1⅛ oz. chocolate covered
   toffee candy bars frozen,
   then crushed
½ gallon vanilla ice cream,
   softened
½ cup whipping cream
2 tablespoons Kahlua

Line springform pan with lady fingers cutting to fit sides. Crush candy bars by pounding in wrappers. Combine all but 1 candy bar with ice cream, dissolved coffee, Kahlua and swirl together. Spoon into lady finger lined pan and freeze until firm. Whip cream with remaining Kahlua until stiff and spread over frozen ice cream. Sprinkle remaining candy bar over whipped cream and freeze again until firm. Release from springform pan and serve. Makes 8 to 10 servings. May be frozen.

W. G. (Bill) Hefner, Representative (North Carolina)

AMARETTO TORTE

2 pkgs. Almond Toast (Stella Dora) cookie section
½ cup Amaretto
½ cup warm water
1 3 oz. pkg. vanilla pudding (cooked type)
1 3 oz. pkg. chocolate pudding (cooked type)
Cool Whip or whipped cream

Place one package toast (broken pieces) in bottom of a spring form pan or glass bowl. Mix half of the Amaretto and water and dribble over the toast. Cook vanilla pudding and pour over toast. Add second package of toast (broken pieces) and dribble rest of Amaretto and water mixture on top of toast. Cook chocolate pudding and pour over second layer. Chill overnight. Cover with Cool Whip or whipped cream. May be garnished with chocolate curls. Keeps well in refrigerator for several days. Makes 12 servings. May be frozen.

Mrs. Jim Bunning, Wife of Representative (Kentucky)

PECAN TORTE

3 cups pecans
6 eggs, separated
1½ cups sugar
3 tablespoons flour
1 teaspoon salt
3 tablespoons Jamaican rum
½ cup heavy cream
2 tablespoons powdered sugar
1 cup semi-sweet chocolate bits
½ cup sour cream

Put pecans in the blender (1 cup at a time) and whirl until very fine. Beat egg yolks until very light, then beat in sugar, flour, salt, 2 tablespoons rum and nuts. Mix well. Fold in egg whites which have been beaten until stiff but not dry. Pour into three 8″ or two 10″ layer cake pans that have been lined with waxed paper and buttered. Bake in a preheated 350° oven until a gentle finger pressure fails to leave a mark—about 25 minutes. Cool and remove from pans. A few hours before serving, put together with filling of the cream whipped with the powdered sugar and 1 tablespoon Jamaican rum. For icing, melt the semi-sweet chocolate bits, fold in the sour cream and spread over the cake. Makes 6 to 10 servings.

Mrs. Thomas Petri, Wife of Representative (Wisconsin)

KEY LIME TORTE

Cake:
- 1 pkg. Butter Recipe cake mix
- 2 tablespoons lime juice plus water to equal 1 cup
- ½ cup butter, softened
- 3 eggs

Filling:
- 1 14 oz. can sweetened condensed milk
- ½ cup lime juice
- 2 cups whipping cream

Preheat oven to 350°. Grease and flour two 8″ round cake pans. In large bowl, combine all cake ingredients at low speed until moistened, beat 2 minutes on high speed until light and fluffy. Pour batter into greased and floured pans. Bake at 350° for 30 to 40 minutes. Cool 15 minutes, remove from pans and cool completely. In a small bowl, combine sweetened condensed milk and ½ cup lime juice, mix well. In large bowl, beat whipping cream until stiff peaks form. Reserve 1 cup of whipped cream. Fold condensed milk mixture into remaining whipped cream just until blended. To assemble cake, slice each cake layer in half horizontally to make 4 layers. Place one cake layer, cut side up, on serving plate, spread with ⅓ of whipped cream filling. Repeat with second and third cake layers. Top with remaining cake layer. Pipe in decorative pattern or spread reserved whipped cream over top of torte. Refrigerate 2 to 3 hours before serving. Garnish with lime slices. Store in refrigerator. Makes 10 to 12 servings. May be frozen.

Julia N. Doolittle

Mrs. John Doolittle, Wife of Representative (California)

Grated citrus rinds can be frozen.

ANGELIC STRAWBERRY DESSERT

3½ oz. pkg. instant vanilla
   pudding
1 cup sour cream
1 cup milk
1 teaspoon grated orange
   peel
1 pint whipped, whipping
   cream
½ 10 inch angel food cake,
   cut in cubes
2 pints fresh strawberries,
   sliced

In bowl, mix pudding, sour cream, milk and orange peel on low speed of electric mixer, 1-2 minutes. Fold in whipped cream. In serving bowl, layer cake, strawberries, pudding. Repeat these layers. Top with strawberries as garnish. Makes 8 servings.

Sharon S Vander Schel

Mrs. Kevin Vander Schel, Daughter of Representative Neal E. Smith (Iowa)

STRAWBERRIES A LA ELIZABETH

  fresh strawberries—if large,
    4 per person
4 tablespoons sour cream
4 tablespoons low calorie
   whip
2 tablespoons brown sugar
1 tablespoon Grand Mariner
2 tablespoons orange Curacao
½ tablespoon dark rum

Combine sour cream with whipping cream. Blend in brown sugar. Add Grand Mariner and whip. Add Curacao and whip. Add rum and whip. Serve in stem glass or strawberries can be dipped in cream sauce. Other fruits can be used. Makes 4 servings.

Shirley H. Wilson

Mrs. Bob Wilson, Wife of former Representative (California)

PRUNES IN RED WINE

1½ pounds extra large prunes,
      pitted
6 cups strong tea
1½ cups sugar
2½ cups red wine
1 large orange, peel only
1 3 inch stick cinnamon

Combine prunes with tea in pan. Bring to a simmer and cook, covered, over low heat for 15 minutes. Drain. Discard tea. Combine sugar, wine and orange peel in thin slices and cinnamon stick. Put in pan and bring to boil. Add prunes, bring to simmer and cook, covered over low heat for 20 minutes. Discard cinnamon. Cool and refrigerate. Serve with cream. Makes 6 servings.

Mrs. Emilio Daddario, Wife of former Representative (Connecticut)

RAISIN OR PRUNE FLAN

4 ozs. raisins or prunes
4 ozs. flour
1 pint milk
4 ozs. sugar
2 eggs
1 to 1½ tablespoons rum
3½ pint shallow baking dish

Set oven to 350°. Soak the raisins or prunes in a bowl of hot water for 2 hours, or until soft, then drain. Thoroughly butter the baking dish and spread the fruit over the bottom. Sift the flour into a bowl and make a well in the center, add the milk, whisk in the flour until just mixed. Strain if there are lumps. Add the sugar, eggs and rum and stir to make a smooth batter. Pour the batter over the fruit and bake in the heated oven for 1½ hours until well browned or when tested with a skewer it comes out clean and dry. Cut the flan into wedges or squares, serve warm. Makes 4 to 6 servings.

Mrs. John D. Rockefeller IV, Wife of Senator (West Virginia)

PINEAPPLE CRUNCH

2½ cups canned crushed pine-
    apple
  1 box yellow cake mix
  ½ cup flour
  1 cup chopped pecans
  1 cup butter

Heavily butter a 2 quart shallow casserole. Pour the pineapple over the bottom. Mix the cake mix with the flour and the pecans. Pour over the pineapple. Melt the butter and pour over all. Bake at 350° for 1 hour.

Ginny Hammerschmidt

Mrs. John Paul Hammerschmidt, Wife of former Representative (Arkansas)

PEACH COBBLER

   1 stick margarine or butter
1¼ cups Bisquick
   1 cup sugar
   1 cup milk
   2 cups fresh peaches

Melt margarine in baking dish. Add Bisquick, sugar, milk and peaches. Bake at 350° for 45 minutes. Makes 6 servings.

Christine Fountain

Mrs. L. H. Fountain, Wife of former Representative (North Carolina)

PEARS IN WINE

1 14 oz. can pear halves
2 teaspoons grated orange
   rind
1 3 inch cinnamon stick
1 tablespoon lemon juice
½ cup rose wine

Drain canned pears, reserve syrup. In a small saucepan, bring syrup, orange rind and cinnamon stick to a boil. Boil until liquid is reduced to ½ cup. Cool pear liquid sauce and add lemon juice and wine. Pour over pear halves and chill. Serve. Makes 2 servings.

Mildred Curtis

Mrs. Carl T. Curtis, Wife of former Senator (Nebraska)

BOU-BOU'S PEACH CRUMBLE

1 large can peaches, halved
¾ cup flour
¾ cup brown sugar
½ teaspoon nutmeg
1 stick margarine

Topping:
   peach juice (from peaches)
6 cloves
1 teaspoon lemon juice

Drain peaches and place cut side up in a baking dish, pie plate size. Mix other ingredients and spread over peaches. Bake at 350° for 1 hour or until brown.

Topping: Combine all ingredients in a saucepan and simmer for 15 minutes. Just before serving, strain and pour over peaches to moisten topping. Makes 6 servings.

Melanie Broyhill

Mrs. Edgar Broyhill, Daughter-in-law of former Senator James T. Broyhill (North Carolina)

LIZ'S PEACH COBBLER

1 cup sugar
1 cup self-rising flour
1 cup milk
1 stick butter
2 cups sliced peaches (fresh)
½ cup sugar (approximately)

Beat together sugar, flour and milk. Batter will be lumpy. Melt butter in casserole dish. Pour batter over butter. Sweeten peaches with sugar. Pour sweetened peaches over batter. Do not stir. Bake at 350° for 45 minutes. Makes 8 servings.

Libby Kingston

Mrs. Jack Kingston, Wife of Representative (Georgia)

> *Scalding tomatoes, peaches or pears in boiling water before peeling makes it easier on you and the fruit—skins slip right off.*

LAWING PEACH COBBLER SUPREME

8 cups sliced peaches (fresh)
2 cups sugar
3 tablespoons flour
½ teaspoon nutmeg
⅓ cup butter or margarine
1¼ teaspoon vanilla or almond extract or mixture of both
enough pastry for a double crust

Combine peaches, sugar, flour and nutmeg in a pot. When syrup forms, bring peach mixture to a boil. Reduce to low and cook 10 minutes. Remove from heat and add butter and extract. Spoon half of peach mixture into baking dish, top with ½ of pastry. Bake at 425° for 14 minutes. Remove from oven and add remaining peach mixture. Top with remaining pastry. Can make lattice design. Return to oven and bake at 425° or until brown. Makes 8 servings. May be frozen.

Louise Broyhill

Mrs. James Broyhill, Wife of former Senator (North Carolina)

MOM'S PEACH COBBLER

⅔ cup shortening (Crisco)
2½ cups sifted flour
1 teaspoon salt
4 to 6 tablespoons water
1 29 oz. can peaches or 2 pounds fresh ripe peaches (cooked)
½ stick butter
1 teaspoon lemon juice
1 teaspoon vanilla
2 tablespoons nutmeg
cornstarch to thicken

Cut shortening into flour and salt with pastry blender or fork until mixture consistency is that of corn meal. Sprinkle water over mixture. Blend lightly with fork. Use as little water as possible, but enough to absorb flour. Knead a few times and form into a ball. Cook peaches on medium heat. Add butter, lemon juice, vanilla and nutmeg (pinch of salt optional). Add enough cornstarch to thicken syrup. Pour peaches into baking dish lined with bottom crust. Place top crust on peaches and bake at 350° until nice and brown. Makes 10 to 12 servings. May be frozen.

Debra Horton Fields

Mrs. Cleo Fields, Wife of Representative (Louisiana)

PEACH COBBLER

1 stick butter
¾ cup all-purpose flour
2 teaspoons baking powder
1 teaspoon salt
¾ cup sugar
¾ cup milk
1 medium sized can peaches, drained

Melt 1 stick of butter in a deep baking dish. Mix together flour, baking powder, salt, sugar and milk. Pour over butter and stir. Dump in peaches. Bake at 350° for 45 minutes or until brown. Good served warm topped with vanilla ice cream. Makes 6 servings.

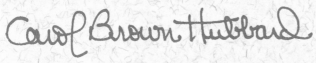

Mrs. Carroll Hubbard, Wife of former Representative (Kentucky)

PÊCHES BRÛLÉES

2 cups heavy cream
2 tablespoons sugar
¾ cup light brown sugar
5 egg yolks, well beaten
2 teaspoons vanilla, or to taste
8 canned peach halves
8 teaspoons butter
8 teaspoons brown sugar
8 teaspoons dark rum

To prepare sauce, heat cream in top of a double boiler. Add sugar, brown sugar and egg yolks, stirring constantly to avoid curdling. Cook over medium heat, reducing to low as necessary until mixture coats a spoon. Cover and refrigerate overnight. Just before serving, add vanilla.

Place peach halves, cut side up, in a 9″ × 13″ shallow baking dish. Into each peach, place 1 teaspoon butter, 1 teaspoon sugar and 1 teaspoon rum. Let set several hours, basting occasionally with the rum. Broil 4 to 5 minutes until brown and bubbly. Serve very cold sauce over very hot peaches. Makes 4 servings.

Mrs. Thomas H. Rhodes, Daughter-in-law of former Representative John J. Rhodes (Arizona)

LEMON PARFAIT

½ cup lemon juice
1 tablespoon lemon rind
3 large eggs, separated
1 cup sugar
   pinch creme of tartar
1 cup whipping cream or
   half and half
3 tablespoons powdered
   sugar

Thicken juice, rind, egg yolks and ½ of sugar in saucepan, stirring constantly. Make meringue with egg whites, remaining sugar and creme of tartar. Fold into lemon mixture. Beat cream and powdered sugar on moderate speed until stiff peaks form. Fold into lemon mixture. Spoon into parfait glasses. Freeze at least two hours before serving. Makes 6 servings. May be frozen.

Sally J Patterson

Mrs. *Jerry Patterson*, Wife of former Representative (California)

LEMON DESSERT

Crust:
1¼ cups flour
2 tablespoons sugar
1 stick margarine
½ cup chopped walnuts

Filling:
8 oz. pkg. cream cheese
   (room temperature)
1 cup confectioners sugar
1 cup Cool Whip
2 pkgs. instant lemon
   pudding
3 cups milk
   additional Cool Whip for
    garnish
   chopped walnuts or coco-
    nut for garnish

For crust, mix flour, sugar, and margarine until blended, using pastry blender or food processor. Stir in walnuts. Press into a 9″ × 13″ pan. Bake in preheated 350° oven 15 minutes or until light golden brown. Watch carefully so you don't let it get too brown.

Filling: While crust cooks, mix cream cheese and sugar. Fold in thawed Cool Whip, refrigerate. In another bowl, mix instant pudding with milk. Refrigerate. Spread cream cheese layer over cooled crust. Spread lemon pudding over cheese layer. Top with Cool Whip and chopped nuts or coconut. Refrigerate several hours or overnight. Makes 12 to 16 servings.

Kati Machtley

Mrs. *Ronald Machtley*, Wife of Representative (Rhode Island)

LEMON DELIGHT

1 cup flour
1 stick butter
1 tablespoon sugar
½ cup chopped pecans
1 cup confectioners sugar
8 oz. cream cheese
2 pkgs. instant pudding mix
3 cups milk
2 cups Cool Whip

Mix with a pastry cutter, flour, butter and sugar. Add nuts. Put mixture in a 9″ × 13″ pan and bake at 350° for 15 minutes. Blend confectioners sugar and cream cheese together. Spread this mixture over crust in pan. Beat pudding mix and milk. Pour over cheese mixture. Top with Cool Whip. Chill 2 hours. Makes 16 servings.

Scotty Baesler, Representative (Kentucky)

CRANBERRY SUPREME

1 cup graham cracker
    crumbs
¼ cup butter or margarine,
    melted
2 cups fresh cranberries
1 cup sugar
½ cup water
¾ cup chopped pecans
2 tablespoons orange mar-
    malade
1 8 oz. pkg. cream cheese,
    softened
⅓ cup sifted powdered sugar
1 tablespoon milk
1 teaspoon vanilla extract
1 cup whipping cream,
    whipped

Combine graham cracker crumbs and butter, stir well. Press mixture into a greased 8″ square dish. Chill. Combine cranberries, sugar and water in a saucepan, bring to a boil. Reduce heat, simmer 20 minutes. Stir in pecans and marmalade, chill. Combine cream cheese, powdered sugar, milk and vanilla, beat until light and fluffy. Fold in whipping cream, spread over crust. Top with cranberry mixture. Chill 8 hours. Makes 9 servings.

Mrs. Ralph Regula, Wife of Representative (Ohio)

CRANBERRY CRUNCH

1 cup quick cooking rolled
   oats
¾ cup brown sugar
½ cup all-purpose flour
½ cup moist coconut
⅓ cup butter or margarine
1 can whole cranberry sauce
1 tablespoon lemon juice

Mix oats, brown sugar, flour, coconut and butter. Place ½ of mixture in 8″ × 8″ × 2″ greased pan. Combine cranberry sauce and lemon juice. Spread on top of mixture in baking dish. Sprinkle remaining crumbs on top. Bake at 350° for 40 minutes. Cut in nine squares. Serve with ice cream. Makes 9 servings. May be frozen.

Mrs. John J. Rhodes, Wife of former Representative (Arizona)

CRANBERRY APPLE CRISP

½ cup butter, diced
3 cups diced apples
2 cups cranberries, fresh
1¼ cups sugar
1½ cups oatmeal, uncooked
½ cup brown sugar
⅓ cup flour
⅓ cup chopped pecans

Combine all ingredients. Put in buttered 13″ × 9″ pyrex dish. Bake at 350° for 1 hour. Makes 8 servings. May be frozen.

Mrs. Fran Symms, Member of The Congressional Club

Brushing frozen pies with melted butter before baking can eliminate dryness.

CHERRIES JUBILEE

1¼ cups cold 2% lowfat milk
½ teaspoon almond extract (optional)
1 pkg. (4 serving size) vanilla flavor sugar-free instant pudding and pie filling
1 cup thawed whipped topping, lite
2 tablespoons chopped toasted almonds
1 20 oz. can lite cherry pie filling

Pour milk and ¼ teaspoon of the extract into large bowl. Add pudding mix. Beat with wire whisk until well blended, 1 to 2 minutes. Stir in whipped topping and 1 tablespoon of the almonds. Mix pie filling with remaining ¼ teaspoon extract. Alternately spoon pudding mixture and cherries into dessert dishes. Refrigerate at least 1 hour. Garnish with remaining almonds. Makes 8 servings.

Shirley Volkmer

Mrs. Harold Volkmer, Wife of Representative (Missouri)

MARGARET'S ANGEL FRUIT DESSERT

1 angel food cake
2 boxes instant vanilla pudding
4 cups milk
1 pint sour cream
1 jar Musselmann's cherry pie filling

Break cake in bite size pieces and place evenly in bottom of 9″ × 13″ dish. Make pudding according to directions, let set 5 minutes, then beat in sour cream. Pour over cake. Chill until firm, then spoon fruit on top of pudding. Makes 12 servings.

Cecilia S. Marshall

Mrs. Thurgood Marshall, Wife of former Justice, U.S. Supreme Court

A pie crust will be more easily made and better if all the ingredients are cool.

BLUEBERRY-PEACH CRISP

¾ cup flour
   pinch salt
1 cup packed brown sugar
3 tablespoons soft butter
½ teaspoon cinnamon
2 cups fresh blueberries
6 fresh, ripe peaches (peeled
   and sliced)
   ice cream or whipped
   cream

Combine flour, salt and brown sugar. Cut in butter and cinnamon with fingers or in a processor, making a streusel topping. Place fruit in a quiche dish and sprinkle with topping. Bake at 325° for 30–35 minutes. Serve with ice cream or slightly sweetened whipped cream. Makes 8 servings.

Katie Lowery

Mrs. Bill Lowery, Wife of former Representative (California)

ZESTED SUMMER BERRIES

2 pints ripe strawberries,
   hulled and cut in half
1 cup ripe red raspberries
   zest of 1 lemon
   zest of ½ orange

Gently combine the strawberries and raspberries with citrus zests. Arrange on a platter. Makes 4 servings.

Michael Oxley, Representative (Ohio)

If the oven is turned off just when the meringue is brown, and the door is left slightly open, the pie cools slowly and prevents the meringue from splitting.

MOTHER'S APRICOT COCOONS

1 pound dried apricots
juice and grated rind of 1
   orange
1½ cups sugar
pecan halves
powdered sugar

Run dried apricots through the meat chopper or food processor. Add juice and rind of 1 orange and sugar. Cook for about 10 minutes, being careful not to scorch. Stir constantly. Cool slightly. Roll around pecan half and roll in powdered sugar. Good for the holidays. Makes 24 servings. May be frozen.

Tricia Lott

Mrs. Trent Lott, Wife of Senator (Mississippi)

SWEDISH BAKED APPLES WITH ALMOND FILLING

1 cup ground almonds
⅓ cup sugar
⅓ cup water
1 egg white
6 baking apples
3 tablespoons butter
⅓ cup bread crumbs

Blend almonds, sugar, water and egg white to a smooth paste. Peel and core apples. Brush apples with melted butter. Fill cores with almond paste. Place apples in a 8″ or 9″ baking dish. Sprinkle with bread crumbs. Bake at 350° for 30–40 minutes or until apple are tender. Serve at room temperature with sauce.

Vanilla Sauce:
3 egg yolks
¼ cup sugar
1½ cups heavy cream, divided
1 teaspoon vanilla extract

Vanilla Sauce: In a double boiler, beat egg yolks, sugar, 1 cup cream and vanilla together. Beat constantly and cook until thick. Remove from heat. Beat vigorously until custard is cool. Whip remaining ½ cup cream and gently fold into custard. Chill and serve on the baked apples. Makes 6 servings.

Elsie Barrett

Mrs. Bill Barrett, Wife of Representative (Nebraska)

OHIO'S BEST APPLE DUMPLINGS

3 cups flour
½ teaspoon salt
1 cup Crisco
¾ cup cold water
12 medium sized tart apples, peeled and cored
1 cup sugar
2 teaspoons cinnamon
⅓ cup minute tapioca
1 cup sugar
2 cups water
4 tablespoons butter
1 teaspoon cinnamon

To make pie crust: Mix flour and salt. Cut in Crisco until fine. Sprinkle with water. Mix gently. Shape into 3 balls. Roll out each ball about 14″ square. Cut each into 4 pieces 7″ square.

To make filling: Mix together sugar, cinnamon and minute tapioca. Onto each dough square, put 1 peeled and cored apple. Fill hole with filling mixture. Bring up corners over top of apple and moisten to make stick. Put in 10″ × 14″ pan (or 2 smaller pans). Bring to boil sugar, water, butter and cinnamon to make syrup. Pour syrup over apples and bake at 350° for 40-45 minutes. Can use 8 large apples. Divide dough into 2 balls, instead of 3. Makes 12 servings.

Fran DeWine

Mrs. Michael DeWine, Wife of former Representative (Ohio)

ENGLIGH ENGLISH

8 Granny Smith apples
1 cup granulated sugar
1 teaspoon cinnamon
½ cup water
1 cup brown sugar, packed
¾ cup flour
7 tablespoons melted butter

Peel and slice the apples as for pie. Put sugar on top and sprinkle with cinnamon. Pour water over the top. Mix brown sugar and flour together. Add melted butter. Put topping over apples (8″ × 12″ baking dish). Bake at 350° until apples are tender, approximately 1 hour. Makes 8 servings. May be frozen.

Chuck Grassley

Mrs. Charles E. Grassley, Wife of Senator (Iowa)

MICHIGAN APPLE CRISP

6 large Michigan apples
¾ cup dark brown sugar
½ cup white sugar
½ cup melted butter
½ tablespoon cinnamon
½ tablespoon nutmeg
1 tablespoon vanilla
1 cup flour
1 teaspoon baking powder
1 unbeaten egg
1 cup pecans

Peel and slice Michigan apples. Place in buttered baking dish and sprinkle with sugar and cinnamon. Mix all other ingredients, except pecans, until crumbly. Then, stir in pecans. Crumble mixture over apples and bake at 350° for 1 hour. Makes 6 to 8 servings. May be frozen.

Fred Upton, Representative (Michigan)

APPLE STRUDEL

5 sheets fillo dough leaves
½ cup melted butter or margarine
½ cup graham cracker crumbs
5 cooking apples, shredded and peeled
¼ cup white raisins
½ cup sugar
2 teaspoons cinnamon
2 tablespoons powdered sugar

First, with pastry brush, butter each fillo leaf, sprinkle with graham cracker crumbs and layer. Mix apples, raisins, sugar and cinnamon. Spread mixture down center of top fillo leaf. Roll jelly roll fashion sealing ends with water. Sprinkle top with sugar and melted butter. Bake at 350° for 25 to 30 minutes until top is brown. When cool, sift powdered sugar over top. Makes 6 servings.

Mrs. Marvin Esch, Wife of former Representative (Michigan)

APPLE BETTY

1 cup granulated sugar
1 teaspoon cinnamon
8 apples (average size, sliced)

Crust:
½ cup melted butter
½ cup packed brown sugar
1 cup flour

Mix sugar and cinnamon thoroughly. In a greased 9″ × 9″ baking dish, alternate apples and sugar mixture.

Crust: Mix all ingredients and then pat into pieces the size of a silver dollar. Star on the outside and lay the silver dollar pieces on top of the apples, having them overlap until all of the apples are covered. Bake at 375° for 45 minutes or until done. Makes 8 servings.

Shannon Payton, Daughter of Representative Elton Gallegly (California)

APPLE ORANGE COBBLER

5 good size baking apples (Staymen, Winesap or Granny Smith are great!)
¾ cup sugar (raw sugar also gives a nice flavor)
1 cup fresh squeezed orange juice
1 teaspoon grated orange rind (zest)
butter
1 Pillsbury All-Ready Pie Crust

Peel and slice apples into 2 quart casserole. Sprinkle sugar on top and pour orange juice over all. Sprinkle zest on top. Dot with butter. Lay pie crust on top of apples and flute around edges inside of casserole. Cut slit in top to let out steam. Bake at 350° for 30 minutes or until crust is browned. Serve in sauce dishes with vanilla or cinnamon ice cream. Makes 6 to 8 servings.

Mrs. Harry Johnston, Wife of Representative (Florida)

APPLE KUCHEN

½ cup margarine, softened
1 pkg. yellow cake mix
½ cup flaked coconut
2½ cups sliced, pared apples
½ cup sugar
1 teaspoon cinnamon
1 cup sour cream

Cut margarine into cake mix (dry) until crumbly. Mix in coconut. Pat mixture lightly into ungreased oblong pan, 13″ × 9″ × 2″, building up slight edges. Bake at 350° for 10 minutes. Arrange apples slices on warm crust. Mix sugar and cinnamon, sprinkle on apples. Blend sour cream and egg, drizzle over apples. Topping will not completely cover apples. Bake for 25 minutes or until edges are light brown. Do not over bake. Serve warm. Pears or peaches may also be used. Makes 12 to 15 servings.

Mrs. Joe Knollenberg, Wife of Representative (Michigan)

TONY'S APPLE CRISP

2 cans sliced apples, drained (not pie filling)
¾ teaspoon cinnamon
1 cup sugar
4 tablespoons water
2 teaspoons lemon juice
⅔ cup sifted flour
⅛ teaspoon salt
⅓ cup butter
1 carton whipping cream (8 ozs.), whipped

Place apples in a 10″ or 12″ round dish (do not grease). Combine cinnamon with ¼ cup of the sugar, sprinkle over apples. Add water and lemon juice. In a small bowl, combine remaining ¾ cup sugar, flour and salt. Work in the butter to form a crumbly mixture. Sprinkle over the top. Bake at 350° for 1 hour, or until apples are tender or topping brown. Serve with whipped cream. Makes 8 to 10 servings.

Anthony Beilenson, Representative (California)

PERSIMMON PUDDING

1 cup persimmon pulp
1 cup sugar
3 tablespoons melted butter
1 well beaten egg
½ cup sweet milk
1 cup sifted flour
2 teaspoons baking soda
¾ teaspoon baking powder
½ teaspoon salt
½ cup chopped nuts
1 tablespoon bourbon (optional)
½ teaspoon cinnamon

Use all skin except any black spots, remove stem and seeds (if any). I use blender to make pulp. Grease pudding mold. When filling pudding mold, allow at least 1″ space from the top and cover tightly. Place pudding mold on a rack in a large pot and add boiling water until it comes half way up the mold. Cover the pot, bring water to a boil, then reduce heat and simmer for 2 hours, adding boiling water as necessary to maintain level. Remove mold from pot and uncover pudding. The top should spring back when touched. Cool pudding for 1 hour, then run a sharp knife around the top edge of the pudding to loosen from the mold and invert carefully onto a serving platter. Serve with lemon sauce or hard sauce. Makes 8 servings.

Mary Kennedy

Mrs. Anthony Kennedy, Wife of Associate Justice, U.S. Supreme Court

CREAMY BANANA PUDDING

1 large pkg. instant vanilla pudding
3 cups milk
1 8 oz. carton whipped topping
1 can sweetened, condensed milk
1 12 oz. pkg. vanilla wafers
5 to 6 large bananas, sliced

Combine pudding and milk in bowl, beat 2 minutes. Fold in whipped topping. Add condensed milk and mix well. Stir sliced bananas into mixture. Layer half vanilla wafers, then pudding mixture. Repeat for a second layer. Chill for 1 hour. May sprinkle chopped pecans over top if desired. Makes 10 servings.

Suzie Brewster

Mrs. Bill Brewster, Wife of Representative (Oklahoma)

BREADFRUIT AND COCONUT PUDDING

1 coconut, grated
1½ cups coconut water or
    plain water
3 cups soft-ripe breadfruit
    pulp
½ cup sugar
½ teaspoon salt

Prepare coconut cream from coconut and water, following instructions for making. If it does not yield 1½ cups extracted milk, add water to make that amount. Combine with breadfruit pulp, sugar and salt. Place in oiled baking dish and bake at 350° for 1 hour. Serve warm with more coconut cream.

Coconut cream or milk: Put freshly grated coconut in a large bowl and pour in enough water to cover the coconut. Squeeze and knead the coconut until the water turns milky and white. Remove the coconut from the bowl one fist-full at a time, squeezing very hard to get out the last drops of the cream. (A little grated coconut will be left but don't bother about removing it). For thick coconut cream, use less water. For thin coconut cream, use more water. This is an indispensable ingredient for many tropical recipes. It is available canned in most local stores. Makes 6 servings. May be frozen.

Lorenzo I. De Leon Guerrero, Governor (Commonwealth of the Northern Mariana Islands)

LINDA'S LIME JELLO MOLD

1 large pkg. lime Jell-O
2 cups water
2 8 oz. pkg. cream cheese
2 cups 7-Up soda
1 cup walnuts
2 teaspoons vanilla
1 large can crushed pineapple, drained

Dissolve Jell-O in 2 cups boiling water (using drained pineapple juice as part of the 2 cups). Cool slightly. In large bowl, gradually mix cream cheese and 7-Up. Add remaining ingredients. Spoon mixture into a mold. Refrigerate overnight. May be a salad or dessert. Recipe may be cut in half. Makes 12 servings.

Mrs. Robert Giaimo, Wife of former Representative (Connecticut)

PLUM PUDDING

Pudding:
- 1 cup finely chopped suet
- 1 egg, beaten
- 1 cup buttermilk
- 1 cup molasses
- 1 cup raisins
- 1 teaspoon baking soda
- 3 cups flour
- 2 teaspoons baking powder

Sauce:
- 1½ cups sugar
- ½ cup butter
- 1 tablespoon vinegar
- 2 tablespoons flour
- 1 tablespoon brandy
  water to thin (about ½ cup)

Pudding: Combine ingredients thoroughly. Fill 4 pint jars ½ full. Grease jars prior to filling. Place jars in steamer. Steam 3½ hours.

Sauce: Blend sauce ingredients and boil until thick. Serve over sliced pudding. Makes 12 servings. May be frozen.

Janice H DeMeritte

Mrs. Fred DeMeritte, Daughter of former Associate Justice Hugo L. Black, U.S. Supreme Court

LEMON SNOW

- 2 pkgs. unflavored gelatin
- ½ cup sugar
- 1 quart buttermilk
- ⅓ cup lemon juice
- 1 teaspoon lemon rind
- 1 cup heavy cream

Heat, but do not boil buttermilk and dissolve gelatin in the buttermilk. Add sugar and beat with wire whisk, cool. Beat the heavy cream until stiff and add whipped cream, lemon rind and lemon juice to cool mixture and mix. Serve with fresh strawberries or raspberries and with vanilla wafers. This can be molded or served in sherbert glasses. Prepare ahead by at least 6 hours. Makes 10 servings.

Nancy Hughes

Mrs. William Hughes, Wife of Representative (New Jersey)

BOILED CUSTARD

2 cups milk
2 eggs
4 tablespoons sugar
⅛ teaspoon salt
½ teaspoon vanilla

Scald milk in double boiler. Beat eggs slightly, add sugar and salt. Mix well. Strain milk, add gradually to egg mixture stirring constantly. Cook and stir in double boiler over hot, not boiling water until mixture coats the spoon (about 7 minutes). Chill, flavor with the vanilla. Makes 4 servings.

Frances Hagan

Mrs. G. Elliott Hagan, Wife of former Representative (Georgia)

INDIVIDUAL CREAM CUSTARDS WITH RASPBERRY PUREE

6 cups sugar
6 envelopes unflavored gelatin
13½ cups heavy cream
12 cups plain yogurt or sour cream
6 teaspoons vanilla extract
30 ozs. frozen raspberries
6 ozs. raspberry jam

In a saucepan, mix the 6 cups of sugar with the gelatin. Stir in the cream and allow the mixture to stand for 5 minutes. Heat gently, stirring until the sugar and gelatin have completely dissolved. Chill for about 1 hour, or until slightly thickened. Fold in the yogurt or sour cream and the vanilla. Spray the custard cups with Pam. Pour in mixture to rim. Repeat. Place in refrigerator overnight. Heat raspberries and jam over medium heat for 5 minutes. Place in blender and blend until smooth. Cover dessert plate with raspberry puree and top with cream custard. Garnish with fresh raspberries and mint. Makes 50 servings.

The Congressional Club

A clean clothespin provides a cool handle to steady the cake tin when removing a hot cake.

OLD FASHION BANANA PUDDING

3 eggs
2 cups milk
1 cup sugar
⅓ cup flour or cornstarch
3 medium bananas
1 teaspoon vanilla extract
¼ cup butter
vanilla wafers

Mix flour and sugar together. Beat eggs and add to flour mixture. Add milk and vanilla extract. Place on medium heat and stir constantly until thick. Add butter. Take off heat and let cool. Line dish with vanilla wafers. Layer custard and sliced bananas on top. Repeat until dish is complete. Refrigerate and serve cold. Makes 8 to 10 servings.

Mrs. Cleo Fields, Wife of Representative (Louisiana)

BANANA PUDDING

bananas
¾ cup sugar
⅓ cup all purpose flour
dash salt
4 eggs, separated, at room temperature
2 cups milk
½ teaspoon vanilla extract
35 to 40 Nilla wafers

Combine ½ cup sugar, flour and salt in top of double boiler. Stir in 4 egg yolks and milk, blend well. Cook, uncovered over boiling water. Stir constantly until thickened. Reduce heat and cook, stirring occasionally for 5 minutes. Remove from heat, add vanilla. Spread small amount on bottom of 1½ quart casserole, cover with layer of Nilla wafers. Top with layers of sliced bananas, pour ⅓ of custard over bananas. Continue to layer wafers, bananas and custard to make 3 layers of each, ending with custard. Beat egg whites until stiff but not dry. Gradually add remaining ¼ cup sugar and beat until stiff peaks form. Spoon on top of pudding, spreading to edges. Bake at 425° for 5 minutes or until delicately brown. Cool slightly or chill.

Zell Miller, Governor (Georgia)

SOUR CREAM BANANA PUDDING

1 large (5 or 6 oz.) box instant pudding mix (vanilla, French vanilla or banana flavor)
3 cups whole milk
1 cup sour cream
8 ozs. Cool Whip topping
3 to 6 bananas
1 box Vanilla wafers

Combine pudding mix and milk. Set mixture aside for 5 minutes. Gently fold sour cream and Cool Whip into pudding. In a large trifle bowl, repeatedly layer ingredients as follows: wafers, pudding mixture, bananas sliced in circles ending with wafers. Refrigerate until served. Makes 15 servings.

Frances B. Hagan

Frances B. Hagan, Daughter of former Representative G. Elliott Hagan (Georgia)

CHOCOLATE NUGGET

6 ozs. Nestles chocolate chips
1 egg
½ teaspoon vanilla
dash of salt
¾ cup milk

Mix ingredients and microwave on high for 2 minutes. Put in blender for 1 minute. Pour in little cups and refrigerate until set. This is one of Governor Bob Miller's favorite recipes.

Bob Miller

Bob Miller, Governor (Nevada)

Ripen green fruits by placing in a perforated plastic bag The holes allow air movement, yet retain the odorless gas which fruits produce to promote ripening.

AMARETTO-CHOCOLATE SILK PUDDING

¾ cup granulated sugar
¼ cup unsweetened cocoa powder
¼ cup cornstarch
2 cups skim milk
¼ cup Amaretto liqueur
2 tablespoons margarine
¾ teaspoon pure vanilla extract
⅛ teaspoon almond extract
white chocolate shavings

Sift sugar, cocoa powder and cornstarch together in a heavy saucepan. Whisk together. Heat milk and Amaretto together until hot, but not boiling. As soon as little bubbles begin to appear on the surface, remove from heat. Slowly pour the hot milk over the dry ingredients. Whisk well and bring to a boil over medium low heat, whisking constantly, until pudding thickens and comes to a boil. Raise heat and boil for a minute more. Remove from heat. Stir in the margarine until it melts, then stir in the vanilla and almond extracts. Divide between 6 individual serving bowls. Place a piece of waxed paper over the top of each portion and chill for at least 2 hours before serving. Garnish with white chocolate shavings. Serve in crystal glasses. Makes 6 servings.

Kathleen Waters, Daughter of former Representative John R. Foley (Maryland)

SWEDISH RICE PUDDING

2 cups milk
dash of cinnamon
¼ cup butter
⅓ cup sugar
4 eggs, slightly beaten
¾ cup cooked rice

Scald milk with cinnamon. Add butter and sugar, stirring well. Add slowly to beaten eggs, mixing well. Add rice. Turn into buttered baking dish and bake at 300° for 45 minutes. Makes 6 servings.

Don Sundquist, Representative (Tennessee)

FOUR LAYER DELIGHT

1st layer:
 1 cup flour
 ½ cup margarine
 ½ cup chopped pecans

2nd layer:
 1 cup whipped topping
     (from 10 oz. carton) I
     use whipped cream
     sometimes
 1 cup powdered sugar
 1 8 oz. pkg. cream cheese

3rd layer:
 2 small pkgs. instant choco-
     late pudding
 3 cups cold milk

4th layer:
     grated chocolate

1st layer: Mix ingredients well and put into a 9″ × 13″ baking dish. Bake at 375° for 20 to 30 minutes. Cool.

2nd layer: Mix on low speed until fluffy. Spread on cooled crust.

3rd layer: Mix 2 minutes and spread on top of second layer.

4th layer: Spread remaining whipped topping on top. Refrigerate for 4 hours. If chocolate pudding is used, garnish 4th layer with grated chocolate. May be frozen.

Mrs. John S. Cross, Daughter of former Representative Claude Albert Fuller (Arkansas)

TOM'S FAVORITE SUGAR AND FAT FREE RICE PUDDING

 1 12 oz. can skimmed evapo-
     rated milk
 ⅓ cup rice
 ½ cup raisins
     brown sugar substitute,
     equal to 6 teaspoons of
     regular sugar
 1 teaspoon vanilla
 1 teaspoon cinnamon
 3 cups skim milk

Use 2½ or 3 quart baking dish, spray lightly with Pam. Pour canned milk into dish, add rice, raisins, brown sugar substitute, vanilla and cinnamon. Add 3 cups skim milk and stir. Put in preheated 350° oven for 45 minutes, stir to break up crust. Turn heat down to 300° and bake 1 more hour. Makes 6 to 8 servings.

Tom Lewis, Representative (Florida)

FARMERS RICE PUDDING (NO RICE INCLUDED)

1 cup flour
1 raw egg
1 quart boiling milk
⅔ cup sugar, a pinch of salt
   and nutmeg to taste

Into flour, cut up egg, using 2 knives, cutting criss cross until very fine (until it looks like rice). Slowly add this to the 1 quart boiling milk stirring constantly. Add sugar, a pinch of salt and nutmeg to taste. Thickens as it cooks. Remove from stove and serve warm. Thick when cold. Makes 6 servings.

Mrs. Thurgood Marshall, Wife of former Justice, U.S. Supreme Court

PARSI CUSTARD

4 eggs
1 12 oz. can evaporated milk
1 14 oz. can condensed milk
1 cup whipping cream
1 cup milk
⅓ cup slivered almonds
1 teaspoon vanilla
1 teaspoon nutmeg

Mix all ingredients together except for almonds and nutmeg. Bake at 350° for 1 hour. Add almonds after ½ hour. Chill before serving and sprinkle nutmeg on top. Makes 6 servings.

Folise Norwood

Mrs. David Norwood, Daughter of former Representative E. C. "Took" Gathings (Arkansas)

> *Before scalding milk, rinse pan with cold water for easy clean up.*

NOTES

NOTES

The Diplomatic Community

Organization of American States

The Diplomatic Community

The Diplomatic Community is an integral aspect of life in Washington, D.C. Traditional Congressional Club activities include a Diplomatic reception and luncheon for the wives of ambassadors.

We thank them for introducing us to foods of their culture and for the opportunity to share ideas.

White House "Blue Room"

DIPLOMATIC DISHES

GWEN TONGE'S BAKES OR JOHNNY CAKES AND SALT FISH

Ingredients:
1 cup flour
1 teaspoon baking powder
1 level tablespoon margarine
water to mix

Filling:
½ pound salt fish (cod)—soak
   to remove excess salt
1 teaspoon chopped onion
1 teaspoon chopped tomato
½ teaspoon finely chopped
   parsley
1 teaspoon chopped cu-
   cumber
lime juice and hot sauce to
   flavor

To make Bakes: Sift dry ingredients in a bowl. Mix lightly with the fingers. Add a small amount of water and press together to make a stiff dough. Knead. Cut into small pieces. Roll into balls. Flatten. Fry in hot oil until golden brown.

Filling: Mix all the ingredients together. Toss. Cut the bakes in half crosswise leaving attached to one side. Place a teaspoon of the fish mixture between each bake. Serve on decorated platter. Makes 12 servings.

H. E. Dr. Patrick Albert Lewis, Ambassador (Antigua and Barbuda)

SOMEN WITH SMOKED SALMON AND CHAMPAGNE SAUCE

8 oz. somen (Japanese noo-
    dles) or angel hair pasta
8 oz. Norwegian smoked
    salmon, cut into thin
    strips
    dill sprigs

Sauce:
1 oz. butter
1 leek, washed well and
    finely sliced
1 cup clam juice or fish
    stock
1 cup brut champagne
1 cup heavy cream
    pinch cayenne pepper
    salt and pepper to taste
1 small bunch fresh basil
    leaves, finely shredded

Sauce: Melt butter in skillet. Add leek, stir until limp. Add clam juice and champagne to pan. Bring to a boil and simmer gently until reduced by half. Add cream to pan, simmer sauce until reduced by half. Add cayenne pepper, salt and pepper. Just before serving, add basil to sauce.

Boil somen for 1-3 minutes, according to direction on packet. Drain. Place equal portions of somen and smoked salmon on 8 plates. Top with sauce, garnish with dill sprigs and serve at once. Makes 8 servings.

Catrina Cook

Mrs. Michael Cook, Wife of Ambassador (Australia)

SCOTTISH PÂTÉ

1 pound chicken liver,
    trimmed
1 pound pork sausage meat
1 large onion, cut in four
2 to 4 tablespoons Drambuie
1 teaspoon salt
3 whole bay leaves
    freshly ground pepper
¼ pound bacon

Grease a large loaf pan with bacon fat. Set remaining bacon and bay leaves aside. Blend all other ingredients together in a food processor until smooth. Pour into loaf pan. Seal top with bacon slices. Lay bay leaves on top. Cover with foil. Place an 8″ × 13″ pan of hot water (about 1 inch deep) in oven. Put loaf pan in this pan and bake for 1 hour, removing foil for last 20 minutes. Drain excess fat. Cool and serve with thinly sliced dark bread or homemade melba toast. Makes 12 servings. May be frozen.

Marghide Chastelain

Mrs. A. John de Chastelain, Wife of Ambassador (Canada)

SHRIMP CEBICHE

2 pounds shrimp or crawfish
½ pound onions
½ pound tomatoes
  juice of 10 lemons
1 orange
½ cup olive oil
1 teaspoon mustard
1 ground "aji"
  salt to taste
  parsley branches to ornament

Wash the shrimps and boil them for about 5 minutes in 3 cups of water, 1 cup of milk and salt to taste. Drain the water and take off the skin and the black vein in the back of the shrimp. Carefully rinse them a couple of times in cold water, then place them in a flat pyrex dish.

Cut the onion in thin slices, boil it and then transfer it to cold water; drain it in a deep dish and then sprinkle the juice of the lemons. As soon as the onions have changed color, add the orange juice and the juice of the tomatoes; mix them well and pour it over the shrimp. Immediately followed by the oil, the tomato sauce, salt, mustard and the "aji" to taste. Stir it thoroughly and leave the bowl in a fresh area for about 2 hours.

Hints for serving: Serve in small bowls or glasses using some parsley leaves to ornament the dish. This dish should be served with corn, fried peanuts and bread.

Mrs. Jenny Valdivieso, Cultural Office (Ecuador)

COOL CALAMARI SALAD

400 g (grammes) calamari
  tubes
  fresh salad greens for
    decoration
  paw paw or melon balls,
    7 per portion

Spicy fennel dressing:
  ½ cup (125 ml) crème
    fraîche
  1 tablespoon (15 ml)
    snipped chives
  ½ teaspoon (2 ml) ground
    cumin
  2 ml chopped fennel (or 1
    ml dried)
  1 ml salt
  ground black pepper

Clean calamari tubes, inside and out, in cold water. Slice into 7 mm rings and place in a large bowl. Pour over plenty of briskly boiling water, stirring calamari in the water. Allow to stand for 1 minute. Test calamari—it should be opaque right through, yet meltingly tender. Allow to stand in water for 30 to 60 seconds more if slightly undercooked, then tip into a colander to drain. Transfer calamari to a bowl. Mix together dressing ingredients, pour over calamari and toss. Makes 4 servings.

Hints for serving: Arrange salad greens prettily on 4 entrée plates. Pile calamari salad in the centre and garnish with paw paw or melon balls and sprigs of fresh fennel. Calamari may be dressed, covered and refrigerated for up to 2 days before serving. Arrange plates just before serving.

Mrs. Immo F. Stabreit, Wife of Ambassador (Federal Republic of Germany)

HONDURAN "CEVICHE"

2 pounds fish fillet (boneless)
2 cups lemon juice
1 pound tomatoes
1 pound green peppers
½ pound onions
16 oz. bottle catsup
16 oz. bottle Lea & Perrins
    sauce
salt and pepper to taste
Tabasco sauce to taste

Put your freshly squeezed lemon juice in a bowl. Use a wooden spoon to mix. Never use an aluminum or silver spoon when using raw fish and lemon. Cut raw fish in small pieces when it is half frozen. When finished, put it in the bowl and let it rest for 1 hour covered with the lemon juice, until fish becomes white. Add the finely chopped tomatoes, green peppers and onion to the fish and mix in the catsup, Lea & Perrins sauce, salt, pepper and Tabasco sauce. If necessary, you can add more catsup, if it is too acid. You can prepare it 2 or 3 days in advance and keep it in the refrigerator until the time of your party. Serve it with saltine crackers. It is ideal to freeze. When you want to serve it, let it defrost and taste it. Regularly you will need to add a little of catsup, salt and Tabasco to taste. Makes 10 servings. May be frozen.

Mrs. René Arturo Bendaña, Wife of Ambassador (Honduras)

CAVIAR MOUSSE

6 hardboiled eggs, riced
2 tablespoons lemon juice
2 tablespoons water
1 tablespoon (1 envelope) unflavored gelatin
1 8 oz. jar mayonnaise or 4
oz. mayonnaise and 4 oz.
sour cream
salt and pepper to taste,
but be careful with the
salt, because caviar is
salty
1/8 teaspoon onion salt
4 oz. jar red caviar
sour cream
chopped onion

In a small heat proof cup, mix lemon juice, water and gelatin until thoroughly mixed. Set in pan with 1″ water and bring to a boil. Cook until watery. Mix mayonnaise and eggs thoroughly. Add salt, pepper and onion salt. Add gelatin mixture, continue to blend. Fold in caviar, mixing well. Turn mixture into a ring mold that has been sprayed with vegetable oil. Cover with plastic wrap and chill overnight (at least 8 hours). Unmold by setting mold in hot water 30 seconds and then run knife around inside edges to loosen. Turn upside down on a serving platter. Serve with sour cream and chopped onion. Serve with crackers as an appetizer or as a first course with either buttered toast or pumpernickel bread. Note: I always use 2 jars of the caviar, since they usually come in 3 1/2 oz. sizes and the mousse is only better if more caviar is used. Makes 8 to 12 servings.

Mrs. Tomas A. Tomasson, Wife of Ambassador (Iceland)

BHAJIA (BATTER FRIED VEGETABLES)

1½ cup gram flour (available in Indian grocery stores)
1 teaspoon baking powder
¼ teaspoon tumeric powder
½ teaspoon salt or to taste
water
oil for deep frying
vegetables such as thinly sliced potatoes, small cauliflower florets or green beans could be used

Sift gram flour in bowl, add dry ingredients. Add enough water to make a "pancake-like" batter. Cover batter and let sit for at least 5 minutes. Heat oil in a deep pan. Dip vegetables one piece at a time and deep fry until golden. Drain on paper towels. Makes 6 servings.

Hints for serving: May be served with ketchup or mix hot sauce and ketchup.

Mrs. Chitmansing Jesseramsing, Wife of Ambassador (Mauritius)

ALOO ACHAR

4 medium size boiled, peeled potatoes
1 cup of sesame seeds
green chilies (optional)
½ teaspoon turmeric powder (Haldi)*
1 tablespoon corn oil
¼ teaspoon fenogreek (Methi)*
¼ cup lemon juice
salt to taste
sprig of parsley, chopped
*can be obtained at Indian grocery stores

Cut all boiled and peeled potatoes into bite size pieces. Set aside in a mixing bowl. Toast the sesame seeds until its deep brown in a frying pan. Let it cool. Grind the sesame seeds and mix it with the potatoes. Mix chopped green chilies (optional). Add turmeric powder to the above mixture. Heat the corn oil in a saucepan. Fry fenogreek until it becomes black. Then pour it over the turmeric in the bowl. Add lemon juice and salt to taste. Mix well. Add parsley. (Optional: add ½ cup water if you light a slight gravy. Add salt and lemon juice to adjust the taste). Serve with rice. Makes 5 servings.

Mrs. Yog Prasad Upadhyay, Wife of Ambassador (Nepal)

EGGPLANT PASTE (EGGPLANT CAVIAR)

1 large eggplant
½ cup olive or corn oil
1 tablespoon lemon juice
   salt
1 small onion, chopped
   pepper (optional)
   black olives
   crackers or bread

The eggplant is most popular in Romania and the visitors from foreign lands always love it very much. The eggplant paste is one of the most delicious of appetizers. Choose a large eggplant, firm and with a smooth skin. Broil it over the flame on a top burner (or in the ashes of an open fire), turning constantly until tender. After the skin is burned, let cool a little, then with fingers dipped in cold water, peel the burned skin, until the pulp is very clean. Now place on a wooden board and begin to chop it, while still warm, with a wooden knife (as the edge of any wooden utensil or board). Transfer the paste to a bowl, using a wooden spoon (metal blackens the eggplant). Stir constantly, the eggplant paste, with the spoon, adding at the same time about ½ cup of olive or corn oil, drop by drop, and also enough lemon juice, added drop by drop. Add salt and pepper to suit your taste. The stirring must continue until the seeds have disappeared and the paste is firm. Keep in dry, cool place. Just before serving, chop some onions very fine, place at the side of the plate holding the paste and garnish with ripe, black olives. Serve it on crackers or small pieces of bread. Makes 4 servings.

Ileana M. Munteanu

Mrs. Aurel-Dragos Munteanu, Wife of Ambassador (Romania)

RUM PUNCH

½ liter of rum
1 can concentrated orange
  juice
1 can concentrated grape-
  fruit juice
1 can concentrated passion
  fruit juice
1 can mango nectar
1 can guava nectar
1 can papaya nectar
1 can peach nectar
2 bottles of 7-Up or ginger
  ale
2 limes, juiced
2 tablespoons of grenadine
  liquor
½ cup of diced mango
½ cup of diced orange
½ cup of diced grapefruit
½ cup of diced pineapple
½ cup of diced peaches
1 bottle of maraschino cherries (small)

Mix rum, all concentrated and nectar juices, 7-Up, the juice of 2 limes and the grenadine liquor in a large bowl. Stir well until dissolved. Garnish with diced fruits and serve with cracked ice. Makes 20 servings. May be frozen.

Mercedes M. de Ariza

Mrs. Jose Ariza, Wife of Ambassador (Dominican Republic)

QAHWA ARABEYA

3 cups water
¾ an-Arab-coffee-cup of Arab
  coffee
1 Arab-coffee-cup of cardamom (coarsely ground)
¼ teaspoon saffron (optional)

Boil the water in a pan. Add the coffee to the water and boil over low heat for half an hour. Remove from the heat, let set 5 minutes to allow coffee to settle. Add cardamom to pot, strain the coffee into it and add the saffron. Place the pot over the heat and bring back to the boil once. Makes 6 to 8 servings.

H.R.H. Prince Bandar Bin Sultan, Ambassador (Saudi Arabia)

"CHAIRO" SOUP

½ pound of beef or lamb, lean meat
1 small piece of lamb jerky, if desired
8 cups water
½ cup peas
½ cup tender broad beans
½ cup carrots, cut lengthwise and very fine
6 potatoes cut lengthwise and very fine
½ cup "chuno" (dehydrated potatoes, soaked and cut in pieces)
½ cup wheat, whole kernel, cooked
½ cup hominy, cooked
1 teaspoon each, fresh oregano and parsley, finely chopped
¼ cup "Aji" sauce

Boil the beef or lamb meat and jerky in water for about 1½ hours. Remove from the stove and strain, leaving the broth. Cut the meat and jerky into fine pieces and return to the broth. Add peas, broad beans and carrots and cook until nearly tender. Half an hour before serving add the potatoes and "chuno" and cook until tender. Before removing from the stove, add the wheat, corn, "Aji" sauce and herbs.

Aji Sauce: Fry ⅓ cup finely chopped onion in 1 tablespoon of oil. Add chopped parsley and ground "Aji" (chili powder). Add a little water and cook until the onion is tender. Makes 6 servings. May be frozen.

Hints for serving: Garnish with chopped parsley and fried string potatoes.

Adela Crespo

Mrs. Jorge Crespo, Wife of Ambassador (Bolivia)

PEANUT SOUP

4 cups beef broth
1 medium sized onion, chopped
1 small tomato, chopped
1 tablespoon chopped parsley
1 tablespoon oil
½ cup cooked peas
1 carrot, cooked and chopped (optional)
½ cup raw peanuts, peeled and ground in a blender or food processor
fried string potatoes

Simmer together the onion, tomato and parsley in oil. Add broth and the other ingredients. Let cook without stirring for 30 minutes. Served with fried string potatoes on top as a garnish and pieces of beef used to make the broth. Makes 8 servings.

Mrs. Jorge Crespo, Wife of Ambassador (Bolivia)

SOPA MARINERA (SEAFOOD SOUP)

⅛ pound mussels
6 cups water
⅛ pound scallops (medium)
⅛ pound shrimp (small)
⅛ pound crabmeat
2 onions, finely chopped
1 cup oil
3 large tomatoes, peeled, seeded and crushed
salt to taste
¼ teaspoon oregano
¼ teaspoon cumin
¼ envelope of chopped saffron
⅛ pound haddock, cut in small pieces
1 cup of white wine
1 teaspoon of chopped parsley

Boil the mussels in water until cooked. Keep liquid to be used to cook the rest of the shellfish. After this is done, keep the liquid. Fry the finely chopped onions in 1 cup of oil until lightly brown. Add crushed tomatoes, salt, cumin, oregano and saffron and cook for 2 minutes. Add fish cut in small pieces. Add shellfish and boiling liquid in which the shellfish has already been cooked. Additional boiling water may be added as needed. Before serving, add 1 cup of white wine, bring to a boil for 15 seconds and cover with the chopped parsley. Makes 6 servings.

Mrs. Patricio Silva, Wife of Ambassador (Chile)

SEA URCHIN SOUP WITH ENOKIS

8 oz. enokis
4 oz. sweet butter (divided)
  salt and pepper
4 shallots
2 leeks
1 bottle dry white wine
1 quart fish stock
1 pound sea urchins
1 cup heavy cream

Saute enokis with a spoon of butter, salt and pepper for 1 minute, set aside for garnish. In the same pan, saute 4 shallots, 2 leeks (white part only). Add 1 bottle of dry white wine. Boil and reduce to 1 cup. Add 1 quart of fish stock made from dover sole, turbot or lobster. Reduce to 1 quart. When simmering, add 1 pound of sea urchins for 1 minute. Remove 10 urchins for garnish. Blend the remaining broth and urchins with 1 cup of heavy cream and 2 oz. sweet butter. Strain through cheesecloth or chinois. Return to stove, keep hot but without boiling. Taste for seasoning, salt and pepper before serving. Garnish with enokis and sea urchins. Makes 10 servings.

Mrs. Jacques Andréani, Wife of Ambassador (France)

CHILLED (OR HOT) CURRIED PEA SOUP

250 ml (millilitres) fresh or frozen peas
  1 onion, sliced
  1 carrot, sliced
  1 celery stalk, sliced
  1 potato, peeled and sliced
  1 clove of garlic, crushed
  5 ml curry powder
    Aromat or Fondor and pepper to taste
500 ml chicken stock
250 ml fresh cream
  mint sprigs

Combine vegetables and seasoning with half the stock and bring to boil. Simmer for about 15 minutes. Transfer to a blender and blend until smooth. Pour into a tureen and stir in remaining stock and fresh cream. Serve chilled in individual bowls and garnish with a sprig of mint. Tastes just as good, if heated. Makes 6 servings.

Mrs. Immo F. Stabreit, Wife of Ambassador (Federal Republic of Germany)

ONNO KOUSWE (MYANMAR COCONUT CHICKEN NOODLE SOUP)

Soup:

- 2 pounds egg noodles
- 1 pound of boneless chicken
  vegetable oil for simmering
- ½ cup of chopped onion
- 1 inch fresh ginger, chopped
- 1 clove garlic, chopped
- ½ teaspoon ground turmeric
- 2 teaspoons paprika
- 10 cups homemade chicken
  broth
- 1½ cups chick pea powder
  (bean)
- 2 cups coconut milk
- 4 tablespoons fish sauce

Garnishes:

- 1 cup onion, sliced
- 6 hard boiled eggs, sliced
- 2 cups crispy fried noodles
- ½ cup dried hot chili flakes
  lemon wedges
- 1 tablespoon ground hot red
  pepper
- ½ cup vegetable oil

Mrs. U Thaung Sein, Wife of Ambassador (Union of Myanmar)

Boil and drain noodles. Divide chicken into small ½" cubes. Heat oil in a large pan. Simmer the onion, ginger and garlic over moderate heat for 2 minutes with the lid on. Add turmeric and paprika and stir. Add chicken and stir fry for 10 minutes.

To make soup: Add the chicken to the homemade broth and boil over moderate heat. Add chick pea powder (bean) and cook for 20 minutes or until boiling while stirring continuously. The soup will begin to thicken. Add coconut milk and fish sauce and cook for 10 minutes stirring continuously.

Separately, simmer ground hot, red peppers and oil over light heat for about a minute. Add hot pepper onto soup at ratio of 1 tablespoon of hot pepper oil to one bowl of soup. Serve as follows: ½ cup cooked egg noodles, 1 tablespoon onion slices, ½ hard boiled egg (sliced), 1 cup of hot thick chicken coconut cream soup, 2 tablespoons crispy noodles, ½ teaspoon of chili flakes (optional) and squeeze 2 to 3 wedges of lemon. Makes 12 servings. May be frozen (soup only).

MUSHROOM SOUP WITH CREAM

8 cups water
1 oz. dried mushrooms
8 oz. mixed vegetables/cele-
　　riac and parsley root, car-
　　rots, leeks
6 pepper-corns
1 medium onion
½ to 1 cup sour cream
3 tablespoons flour
　　salt

Wash mushrooms thoroughly in warm water, rubbing with fingers. Prepare stock with mushrooms, vegetables and pepper. When mushrooms are tender, drain, cut into thin strips and place in tureen. Mix flour with sour cream. Pour into boiling stock, bring to boil, add salt to taste.

Hints for serving: Serve with large pearl barley, macaroni, dropped noodles, rolled pancakes, cut into strips or toast. Makes 6 servings.

Honorata Dziewanowska

Mrs. Kazimierz Dziewanowska, Wife of Ambassador (Poland)

CHICKEN SOUP WITH MATZO BALLS

Soup:
1 medium sized chicken
2 carrots
1 large onion
2 celery sticks
　　salt and pepper

Matzo Balls:
2 tablespoons oil or mar-
　　garine
2 large eggs
½ cup matzo meal
¼ teaspoon salt
2 tablespoons soup stock
　　parsley for garnish

Soup: Place chicken which has been washed, in pot containing 10–12 cups water. Scrub carrots, peel onion, wash celery. Dice and place in pot with chicken, salt and pepper to taste. Simmer gently (about 45 minutes) until chicken and vegetables are very soft. Strain. (I debone and flake the chicken and vegetables and give it to my dogs as a treat).

Matzo Balls: Blend eggs and oil/margarine together. Add matzo meal and salt to egg mixture and blend well. Add soup stock (2 tablespoons) and mix well. Cover and place in refrigerator for 15 minutes. Roll into small balls and cook in boiling salted water 10–15 minutes. Strain, throw away water and serve matzo balls in soup (if very small, five per person). Garnish with chopped parsley. Makes 8 servings. May be frozen (soup only).

Anette Schwarz

Mrs. Harry Schwarz, Wife of Ambassador (South Africa)

JOHNNY CAKE

2 cups flour
2 teaspoons baking powder
1 teaspoon salt
1 tablespoon sugar
1 tablespoon shortening
water to make a firm
    dough
additional shortening to
    grease fry pan

Place all ingredients, except water, in a mixing bowl and, using spoon or hands, mix thoroughly. Add just enough water to make a firm dough. Turn out on board and knead until smooth. Let stand 10 minutes. Place in hot fry pan which has been well greased. Fry at medium heat until brown and crusty turning several times. Then lower flame and finish cooking, about 15 minutes. Makes 5 to 7 servings.

H.E. Timothy B. Donaldson, Ambassador (Bahamas)

CHEESE ROLLS (PÃEZINHOS DE QUEIJO)

1 pkg. dry, granular yeast or
    1 cake compressed yeast
1 cup warm milk
2 tablespoons sugar
2 teaspoons salt
¼ pound butter
3 slightly beaten eggs
7 to 8½ cups all-purpose
    flour
¾ cup light beer
2 cups grated Muenster or
    Swiss cheese

Dissolve yeast in warm milk. Add sugar, salt, butter and slightly-beaten eggs. Let stand 10 minutes, then add the beer and 3 cups of sifted flour. Stir with a wooden spoon until bubbles appear. Add the cheese. Cover and set in a warm place to rise. When batter has doubled in bulk, cut it down with a knife and knead in another 3 cups sifted flour. Knead well and then add the extra sifted flour (from 1 to 2¼ cups) until you have a smooth, elastic dough which does not stick to the hands. Cover and let rise again. Shape into butterhorn rolls by dividing into portions which will roll out into rounds about 10 inches in diameter and ⅜ inch thick. Brush with melted butter and cut into 12 pie-shaped wedges. Roll up each piece beginning with the wide end, stretching dough slightly as you roll. Lay straight or in a crescent shape on a greased cookie sheet with tip underneath to keep from unrolling. Cover, set in a warm place again to rise. Brush with melted butter or an egg yolk slightly diluted with milk. Bake about 20 minutes in a preheated 375° oven. Makes approximately 48 rolls.

H.E. Rubens Ricupero, Ambassador (Brazil)

IRISH SODA BREAD

12 ozs. white flour
12 ozs. wholewheat flour
  (coarse grained if pos-
  sible)
2 ozs. bran
2 ozs. wheatgerm
1 tablespoon porridge oats
1 tablespoon pinhead
  oatmeal
1 heaped teaspoon baking
  soda
1 teaspoon salt
1 egg
1½ pints buttermilk
  sunflower seeds and sesame seeds (optional)

Mix grains together with baking soda and salt. Beat egg and buttermilk together. Add dry ingredients and gently mix. Place in 2 oiled loaf tins. Sprinkle the top with sunflower and sesame seeds if desired. Bake at 450° for 45–50 minutes. Makes 30 servings. May be frozen.

Mrs. Dermot Gallagher, Wife of Ambassador (Ireland)

CHEESE PUFFS

1 cup flour
1 cup grated cheese
2 teaspoons baking powder
  pinch salt
1 cup milk
  butter
  parsley sprigs

Mix dry ingredients together. Add milk and blend into dry ingredients. Spoon into and bake at 350°, in greased patty tins for 15 minutes. Cut open. Place small pat of butter or margarine in center of each cheese puff and serve immediately—hot. Decorate with sprigs of parsley. Makes 12 to 15 cheese puffs.

Mrs. Harry Schwarz, Wife of Ambassador (South Africa)

MAANDAZI (DONUTS)

2 cups wheat flour
2 tablespoons sugar
2 level teaspoons baking powder
½ teaspoon cardamon
1 litre oil for frying
1 egg
½ cup water or milk

Sieve flour with baking powder together and add sugar. Warm up 2 tablespoons oil, mix in the flour. Beat the egg and mix. Add water or milk and mix well. Roll ¼″ thickness and cut into required shapes (round, square, triangle, heart, etc.). Fry into medium heated oil until the color is golden; turn both sides and serve hot or cold. Makes 4 servings.

RACHEL NYIRABU

Mrs. Charles Nyirabu, Wife of Ambassador (Tanzania)

POTATOES WITH "HUANCAINA" SAUCE

1 large or 2 small cooked potatoes per person, peeled
3 yellow chili peppers, ground (dried hot chilies)
1 teaspoon "huakataya", chopped (optional)
1 cup milk
1 pound peanuts, roasted and ground
2 tablespoons oil
2 hard boiled eggs, sliced
1 tomato, sliced
   black olives
   fresh Farmers cheese

Fry "aji" chili peppers in the oil. Add milk, peanuts and the "huakataya". Simmer until the sauce thickens, about 15 minutes. To serve, on each plate, place lettuce leaves and the potatoes on top. Cover with a generous portion of the sauce. Garnish with hard boiled egg slices, black olives, tomato slices and a piece of fresh Farmers cheese on the side. This salad is a complete lunch. The sauce can also be used as an hors d'oeuvre dip for small potato balls or boiled new potatoes. Makes 6 servings. May be frozen (for 2 weeks).

Adela Crespo

Mrs. Jorge Crespo, Wife of Ambassador (Bolivia)

KYETTHA THOAT (MYANMAR CHICKEN SALAD)

½ clove garlic, diced
½ cup vegetable oil
8 ozs. ½ inch cubes of
    cooked chicken
8 ozs. cabbage, sliced ju-
    lienne
2 tablespoons ½ inch red
    bell pepper
6 small green Asian peppers,
    sliced julienne (optional)
1 large size onion, sliced thin
¼ cup of chopped cilantro
2 tablespoons lemon juice
2 tablespoons fish sauce
½ teaspoon ground red pep-
    pers (optional)
2 sliced ripe, red tomatoes
1 teaspoon roasted sesame
    (ground if possible)
1 tablespoon roasted peanuts
    (ground if possible)

Simmer the garlic in lightly heated oil for about a minute or until the garlic is brown. Pour oil and garlic over cooked chicken. Mix together all ingredients and toss salad. Makes 4 servings.

Mrs. U Thaung Sein, Wife of Ambassador (Union of Myanmar)

CHICK PEA (CHANNA) SALAD

Salad:
- 3 cans of chick peas
- 1 cucumber, chopped to small pieces
- 2 tomatoes, chopped to small pieces
- 1 small piece of ginger, chopped
- 2 onions, chopped to small pieces
- 1 bell pepper, chopped to small pieces
- 1 sprig of parsley, chopped
  green chilies, chopped (optional)

Dressing:
- ½ cup olive oil
- ¼ cup lemon juice or to taste
  salt to taste
  pepper to taste
- ½ teaspoon sesame seeds

Open the cans of chick peas, drain all the water. Add all the ingredients in a medium size bowl and mix well. To make the dressing: Mix the ingredients for the dressing in a small bowl and stir well. Add the dressing to the salad. Serve chilled. Makes 5 servings.

Bimala Upadhyay

Mrs. Yog Prasad Upadhyay, Wife of Ambassador (Nepal)

SALATA KHEYYAR BEL-LABBAN

- 2 cups yoghurt
- 2 cloves garlic (optional)
- 4 cucumbers
- 1 tablespoon dried mint
  salt

Wash and peel the cucumbers. Cut in two lengthwise. Chop in semi-circles. Put the yoghurt in a bowl and mix in the chopped cucumbers, salt and crushed garlic. Sprinkle the salad with dried mint and chill. Makes 2 to 4 servings.

H.R.H. Prince Bandar Bin Sultan, Ambassador (Saudi Arabia)

LOBSTER SALAD

1 Lobster
  salad lettuce
  salad dressing or mayon-
    naise sauce
  hard boiled egg
  tomato
  onions

Boil the lobster, break it up, pick out all the meat and cut in neat pieces. Arrange some lettuce leaves in a salad bowl, place the lobster on it and pour over the dressing. Garnish with slices of hard boiled egg, tomato and onion rings. Makes 1 serving.

Kamala Peiris

Mrs. Lal Peiris, Wife of Ambassador (Sri Lanka)

CHEF WILLY WYSSENBACH'S SUMMER SALAD WITH SALMON

4 portions of mixed greens
    for salad
1 oz. olive oil
1 oz. lemon juice
1 teaspoon of thin lemon
    peel strips
1 oz. butter
7 oz. salmon, diced in 1-inch
    cubes
  salt, pepper and paprika
16 tops of chives

Wash the greens and dry thoroughly. Blanch the lemon peel and pour through a sieve. Heat the butter in a pan, season the salmon pieces with salt and paprika and fry carefully on all sides, but let the inside be slightly raw, keep warm on a paper towel. Make dressing with lemon juice, oil, salt and pepper.

Hints for serving: Mix in the strips of lemon peel and toss the salmon with the dressing. Arrange artfully on 4 plates and place the warm salmon pieces on top. Decorate with chives.

Beate Vibe

Mrs. Kjeld Vibe, Wife of Ambassador (Norway)

TCHEKCHOUKA (RATATOUILLE)

green peppers
minced garlic
red pepper (ground)
tomatoes
salt
olive oil

Grill or roast the peppers (clean inside), peel and cut in small pieces. Clean the inside of the tomatoes and cut in pieces. Cook the garlic with the oil in a frying pan on low heat without browning, add the tomatoes, the peppers, a pinch of salt, and the red pepper. Cook for 5 to 10 minutes. Serve warm or cold.

Mrs. Nourredine Y. Zerbouni, Wife of Ambassador (Algeria)

ARGENTINE "HUMITA"

12 ears of corn (grated)
 1 cup of milk
100 grams of butter
 1 large onion (chopped)
 2 medium green peppers
    (chopped)
 2 large ripe tomatoes
    (peeled-chopped-seeded)
 1 tablespoon of paprika
 1 pinch of cinnamon
   salt and freshly ground
    pepper
   sugar

Soak grated corn in cup of milk. In a pot sauté the onions and green peppers in the butter. When onions are golden brown add tomatoes, cinnamon, paprika and corn. Season with salt and pepper. Simmer stirring occasionally until the corn is tender. If it dries out add a little milk. Pour mixture into small individual crocks, sprinkle with sugar and place in a hot oven (425°) for 10 minutes. The approximate preparation time is 25 minutes and the cooking time is about 20 minutes. Serve with dry white wine. Makes 6 servings.

Mrs. Carlos Ortiz de Rozas, Wife of Ambassador (Argentina)

PLANTAIN PIE

12 ripe plantains
1 cup oil
½ diced white onion
3 tomatoes (chopped and clean of seeds)
1 garlic (mashed)
1 tablespoon diced cilantro
½ pound smoked ham
1 tablespoon tomato paste
½ cup water
4 cups green beans
1 package mozzarella cheese, shredded
1 pinch salt
2 beaten eggs
⅛ teaspoon cinnamon powder

Cut ripe plantains in thin, lengthwise strips and fry until brown, drain the excess oil and reserve. Fry slightly, onions, tomatoes, mashed garlic, cilantro, smoked ham, tomato paste and add water until it makes a heavy sauce and then add the green beans. Reserve. Beat eggs and add the pinch of salt and the cinnamon powder. Reserve. In a pyrex 9″ × 11″ pan place one layer of fried plantains and then add one layer of green beans in sauce and sprinkle with the half of package of the mozzarella cheese, and pour half of the beaten eggs. Add one layer of plantain and then brush with the remaining beaten eggs and sprinkle with remaining mozzarella cheese. Cover up and place into the oven for 20 minutes at 350°. Makes 15 servings. May be frozen.

Mrs. Jose Ariza, Wife of Ambassador (Dominican Republic)

JANSSON'S TEMPTATION

6 medium-sized (about 1 pound) potatoes
2 large yellow onions
1 (4½-ounce) tin Swedish anchovy fillets (14 to 16 fillets)
1 to 1½ cups heavy (whipping) cream
2 tablespoons dry bread crumbs
1 tablespoon butter, melted

Preheat oven to 425°F. Butter a 2-quart shallow baking dish. Peel, rinse, and cut the potatoes into thin strips that are no thicker than ¼-inch. Peel the onions and discard the ends. Cut the onion in two, lengthwise. With the cut side face down, slice the onion lengthwise into ¼-inch strips. Spread the onions and anchovies into the prepared dish. Cover with the potato strips. Add just enough cream to cover the potatoes. Mix together the bread crumbs and melted butter, then sprinkle over the potato mixture. Bake for 45 to 50 minutes, until the potatoes are tender and the top is browned. Makes 6 servings.

Mrs. Jukka Valtasaari, Wife of Ambassador (Finland)

WILD MUSHROOMS IN CREAM SAUCE

1¼ pounds fresh mushrooms
(ceps, chanterelles, field
mushrooms or a
mixture)
1 tablespoon lemon juice
1 onion
1¼ ounces butter
1-2 tablespoons flour
a generous 8 fluid ounces
fresh cream
salt
freshly ground white
pepper
finely chopped herbs (parsley, chives, dill, chevril,
lovage)
4 fluid ounces sour cream

Clean and wash the mushrooms, cut them into small pieces and sprinkle with lemon juice. Dice the onion and sauté it in the butter. Add the mushrooms and, after 5 minutes, sprinkle with the flour and stir in the fresh cream. Cook gently for a few minutes. Season with salt and pepper. Add the herbs and complete the sauce with the sour cream. Potatoes, rice, pasta or bread are all good accompaniments.

Mrs. Jukka Valtasaari, Wife of Ambassador (Finland)

ASPARAGI AL FORNO (BAKED ASPARAGUS)

1 pound asparagus
1 tablespoon olive oil
salt and freshly ground
black pepper
1 oz. curls Parmigiano-
Reggiano cheese
1 teaspoon balsamic vinegar
1 tablespoon chopped
parsley

Preheat oven to 400°F. Snap off tough asparagus bottom and discard. Wash and pat spears dry. Place them in the bottom of a 9″ × 13″ baking dish. Pour olive oil over asparagus and roll spears until glistening with oil. Arrange spears in a large layer. Season with salt and pepper. Bake 12–15 minutes, until tender when pierced with the tip of a knife. Meanwhile, shave curls of cheese from a large piece of room-temperature Parmigiano-Reggiano using a vegetable parer. Scatter the curls over the asparagus. Drizzle with balsamic vinegar. Return dish to oven and bake just until cheese melts, about 2–3 minutes. Serve immediately on warm plates and sprinkle with chopped parsley, if desired. Makes 4 servings.

Mrs. Boris Biancheri, Wife of Ambassador (Italy)

CABBAGE & POTATO

1½ tablespoons oil
2 tablespoons finely sliced onion
2 cloves garlic finely crushed
1 small sprig thyme
½ medium tomato—sliced
1½ cups boiled potatoes—¾ inch cubed
4 cups finely shredded cabbage
salt to taste

Heat oil in pan, add onions and cook until soft, add garlic, thyme, tomato and potatoes, stir until all mix well. Add cabbage and salt, mix thoroughly, cover pot and turn off stove. Mix or stir 5 minutes later. Cabbage should be crisp. Serve as side dish with rice. Makes 6 servings.

Mrs. Chitmansing Jesseramsing, Wife of Ambassador (Mauritius)

BANANAS IN SPINACH

4 very green bananas
water
½ pound spinach
1 green pepper
1 bunch parsil
1 onion
salt to taste

Wash bananas. Peel them. Cut them into very small pieces (prism form). Boil them until very well cooked. Wash spinach. Add spinach to bananas and continue boiling until spinach is very tender. Drain the mixture. Cut pepper into small pieces. Mix green pepper to mashed parsil. Fry onion until brown. Add pepper and parsil. Add the mixture of bananas and spinach. Add salt. Cook lightly for about 5 minutes. Serve hot. Makes 4 servings.

Mrs. Vianney Mukandoli, Wife of Ambassador (Rwanda)

DEVILED MUSHROOMS

1 small tin black mushrooms
1 scant dessertspoonful
   butter
2 onions, chopped finely
   a pinch of red pepper/
   black pepper
¼ pint thick brown sauce
   rounds of fried bread

Melt the butter, and fry the onions in it until just browned. Then add the finely-chopped mushrooms and heat over low flame. Season strongly with the red pepper and black pepper, and add a little salt, if necessary. Then stir into the warm sauce and simmer for a few minutes. Pile up on fried bread, and place under a red-hot grill for about two minutes. Serve immediately. Makes 6 servings.

Kamala Peiris

Mrs. Lal Peiris, Wife of Ambassador (Sri Lanka)

BOILED BANANAS

12 big green bananas
 3 cups cold water
   juice of two lemons
 1 teaspoon salt
 4 tablespoons oil

Peel bananas and cut into required shapes. Wash into cold water which has lemon juice. If you are cooking green plantains instead of the ordinary green bananas, remove the blackish center part of the bananas. Place the bananas into a pot of water, add salt and oil—boil until the bananas are soft. Serve and eat with meat, fish and/or any type of vegetable. Makes 4 servings.

RACHEL NYIRABU

Mrs. Charles Nyirabu, Wife of Ambassador (Tanzania)

PEAS AND RICE

¼ lb. salt pork (bacon), diced
2 tablespoons cooking oil
1 onion, sliced
1 stalk celery, chopped
½ green pepper, sliced
2 teaspoons thyme
½ cup tomato paste
1½ tablespoons salt
¾ cups tinned pigeon peas
    water
    pepper to taste
2 cups uncooked rice

Fry salt pork (bacon) in frying pan. Add cooking oil. Saute the onion, celery and sweet pepper until translucent. Add thyme, tomato paste and salt. Allow to simmer for 5 minutes. Drain liquid from the pigeon peas reserving liquid. Add pigeon peas to vegetable mixture in pot and steam for a further 5 minutes. Pour mixture into large pot (pot should be large enough to allow for expansion of rice). Add water to pigeon peas liquid so that it measures 3 cups and add to mixture in pot. Season to taste. Bring to a boil. Add rice. Return to boil. Stir. Cover and cook on very low heat until dry (approx. 30 to 40 minutes). Makes 8 to 10 servings.

H.E. Timothy B. Donaldson, Ambassador (Bahamas)

SHRIMP IN GINGER SAUCE

2 pounds peeled shrimp
2 tablespoons garlic, finely
    chopped
2 onions, finely chopped
3 sweet peppers, finely
    chopped
    olive oil
4 cups peeled and chopped
    tomatoes
3 small ginger roots
½ cup soy sauce
4 tablespoons catsup
    Lea and Perrins sauce, salt
    and pepper, if necessary

Fry the garlic, onions and sweet peppers in olive oil, then add the already pealed tomatoes until making a sauce. Put in the shrimps already cleaned and peeled. Chop the ginger root in small pieces and add them to the sauce. Then, add the soy sauce, catsup, Lea & Perrins sauce and let it cook on a low fire from 20 to 30 minutes until cooked. Add salt and pepper to taste. Makes 6 servings. May be frozen.

Mrs. René Arturo Bendaña, Wife of Ambassador (Honduras)

ACARAJE (BLACK-EYED PEA FRITTERS)

2 cups black-eyed peas
¼ teaspoon red pepper flakes
¼ teaspoon hot pepper sauce
  salt and freshly ground
    black pepper
2 cups oil for frying

Wrap black-eyed peas in a dish cloth and coarsely crush by pounding with a hammer. Place peas in cold water to cover; soak for 3 to 4 hours. Skins should float to the surface. Pour off water and rinse beans two or three times to wash away skins. Purée the black-eyed peas in a blender, adding pepper flakes, hot sauce, salt and pepper to taste. Mixture should be highly seasoned. Heat ½-inch oil to 375 degrees. Drop spoonfuls of batter into the oil to form 2-inch pancakes. Fry the acarajes for 1 to 2 minutes per side, or until golden brown. Drain on paper towels and serve. Makes about 16 2-inch fritters.

H.E. Rubens Ricupero, Ambassador (Brazil)

PENNE AL SALMONE (PENNE WITH FRESH SALMON)

3 tablespoons unsalted butter
3 ounces best-cure smoked
    salmon finely chopped
1 tablespoon finely chopped
    shallots
  juice of a large lemon
½ pint heavy cream
2 ounces Scotch whiskey
  salt to taste
  a good amount of freshly
    ground white pepper
12 ounces penne (pen shaped
    pasta)
  freshly ground black
    pepper

Place the butter in a large skillet over low flame. When it has melted, add the salmon and shallot and cook for about 2 minutes. Add the lemon juice and mix well. Add cream and whiskey and cook long enough to let the alcohol evaporate. Add salt and pepper to taste. Mix well. Meanwhile cook the pasta very al dente. Drain well and add to the salmon mixture in the same large skillet. Mix gently so that the pasta is well coated. If the sauce is too dry, add some more cream. The texture should be smooth and creamy, but the pasta should not swim in it. Fresh black pepper atop each serving. Makes 6 servings.

Mrs. Boris Biancheri, Wife of Ambassador (Italy)

BAKED FISH—"A LA SPETSIOTA"

8 fish steaks or fish fillets
   from rockfish, red snapper or grouper (around
   3 pounds)
   salt and pepper to taste
   juice of 1 lemon
½ cup white wine
3 pounds onions
6 ounces olive oil
5-6 cloves garlic
1 cup water
2 bay leaves
10 ounces canned tomato
   paste
½ bunch of parsley, chopped

Wash fish, drain and place in medium-sized roasting pan, leaving space in between. Add salt, lemon juice and wine. Cover with plastic wrap and put in refrigerator overnight. Peel and slice onions. Put in a pot with oil, garlic, 1 cup water and the bay leaves. Boil for ½ hour on low heat. Add the tomato paste and continue boiling for 1 hour more or until sauce becomes thick and creamy. Remove from heat and mash through a potato puree machine. Add chopped parsley. Pour sauce over the fish, and place the fresh sliced tomatoes on the top. Place in preheated oven and bake for 15 minutes at 400 degrees. Makes 8 servings.

Baked fish "A la Spetsiota" can be served with any vegetables, such as boiled cauliflower, zucchini, broccoli, etc.

You can use a blender to mash the sauce mixture, or, if you prefer, you can use the mixture as is. The dish can be offered either as a first course or as a main family dish. It can be served hot or cold.

Naya Zacharakis

Mrs. Cristos Zacharakis, Wife of Ambassador (Greece)

LENTIL

1 cup lentils
3 cups water
1½ tablespoons oil
½ medium onion, finely
   sliced
½ teaspoon salt or to taste
1 small sprig thyme
1 medium clove garlic, finely
   crushed

Thoroughly rinse lentils, boil in water about 20 minutes skimming when necessary. Heat oil in small frying pan, add onions, stir until soft, add thyme and garlic, mix with onion, add to lentils, add salt and finish cooking on low heat until thick. Serve with rice. Makes 6 servings.

Mrs. Chitmansing Jesseramsing, Wife of Ambassador (Mauritius)

RAINBOW-TROUT IN HORSERADISH CREAM SAUCE

2 pounds trout (fillet)
1 oz. butter, melted
garlic powder
salt and ground pepper
lemon juice
melted butter

Sauce:
4 tablespoons mayonnaise
2 tablespoons heavy cream
1 tablespoon horseradish
lemon juice to taste
salt to taste

Trout fillets are cut in dinner size pieces and put in a buttered baking dish. Salt, pepper and garlic powder sprinkled over the trout. Lemon juice and melted butter (or margarine) mixed together and poured over the trout. Trout is baked in the oven for approximately 10 minutes at a preheated 375°F oven. Makes 6 servings. May be frozen.

Serve with horseradish sauce.
Serve with new potatoes.
ENJOY

Mrs. Tomas G. Tomasson, Wife of Ambassador (Iceland)

FISH CURRY

2 small onions
2 cooking apples
1 tablespoon butter
1 teaspoon mild curry powder
1 teaspoon plain flour
⅓ pint milk
1 pound cooked white fish
1 tablespoon lemon juice
salt and pepper

Peel and chop the onions and apples and fry them in the butter till golden; add the curry powder and the flour, stirring all the time. Cook for a few moments before gradually adding the milk. Simmer for 15 minutes and then add the flaked fish. Heat again, but do not boil. Add lemon juice and salt and pepper to taste. Makes 4 servings.

Mrs. Lal Peiris, Wife of Ambassador (Sri Lanka)

TEMPURA

Tempura is widely believed to be a typical Japanese dish. But as a matter of fact, it was introduced by Spanish and Portuguese missionaries who came to Japan in the late 16th century.

Now Tempura is not only one of my favorite dishes but also a favorite of everyone in the world.

Ingredients:

Shrimp (medium size)

Shell and devein shrimp leaving the tails on. Cut the edge of the tail and squeeze water out by pressing with the side of the knife.

Scallops

Slice in half

Squid (thick meat)

Cut into 1½ inch squares, then lightly cross-score the outer side of each piece.

Fish

Sole, flounder or any white meat fish. Cut into 1½ inch squares.

Onion (Bulb)

Peel onion and cut in half from top to bottom. Slice each half (cut-side down) into ⅓ inch thick semi-circular rings. Use toothpick to prevent the rings from separating.

Sweet potato

Cut crosswise into ⅓ inch thick rounds.

Pumpkin

Cut into ⅓ inch combo shapes.

Shiitake (Chinese black mushrooms)

Remove stem

Asparagus

Peel and cut each stalk into three pieces. Set together with a toothpick like a raft.

Eggplant

Cut into pieces ½ inch thick.

Green squash

Cut into pieces ½ inch thick.

Soft shell crab

Cut into two or four pieces after frying.

Nori (black seaweed sheets)

Use any combination of the ingredients listed above or try your own favorite vegetables and fish.

Shiso (Leaves of a beefsteak plant, "shiso"; green leaves with flavor.)

Prepare the batter:
Ingredients:

1 egg yolk and very cold water to equal 1 cup

1 cup flower

Mix egg yolk and water well. Add sifted flour all at once. Stir with chopsticks just until ingredients are loosely combined. Do not stir too much, as batter will become sticky and heavy.

Prepare the oil:

In a deep frying pan, put salad oil about half the depth of the pan. Add 3 tablespoons of sesame oil for flavor.

Oil temperature should be between 320 and 350 degrees. Test temperature by dropping a bit of batter into the oil. If it sinks halfway then comes up, it is within the correct temperature range. If the batter sinks to the bottom and then comes up, the temperature is still too low.

How to cook:

Dust raw fish, shrimp, scallops and squid with a thin coat of dry flour and then dip in batter. Fry in oil turning once or twice until they become golden and well-cooked. To prevent the oil temperature from going down, fry small amounts at a time. (Ingredients should not cover more than 60% of the total area of oil surface.)

Dip vegetables directly in the batter and fry. Place cooked pieces on a draining tray to remove excess oil. Fold absorbing paper into triangle and place on a serving dish. Arrange Tempura on the paper to keep crispy.

Prepare the sauce (4 services):
- 2 cups water
- ½ cup soy sauce
- ½ mirin (sweet rice wine)
- ½ cup dried bonito flakes (*Katsuo-bushi*)

Put ingredients together in a sauce pan, boil and then strain the flakes out of the broth.
Grate daikon (white radish) and drain excess water. Mix salt and curry powder and then heat in frying pan. Cut a lemon into small wedges.

How to eat: Dip Tempura into the sauce. Put small amounts of grated horse radish into the sauce, if desired. Dip Tempura into the salt mixture. Sprinkle lemon juice over tempura.

Variations:
Kakiage (mixed ingredients)
Frozen mixed vegetables, chopped shrimp, onion and green beans. Any combination of your favorite vegetables.
Ten-Don or *Kakiage-Don*
(Don is a shorten word of *donburi*, a large size bowl for rice)

Mix ingredients into the batter. Using a large spoon, drop small amounts into hot oil and fry in the same way as Tempura.

    cook Japanese rice
    prepare the sauce
- 1 cup water
- ½ cup soy sauce
- 3 tablespoons sugar
- ½ cup dried bonito flakes

Put all ingredients in a sauce pan, boil and then strain. Put rice in *donburi*. Dip Tempura into the sauce, and arrange pieces on the rice. Pour extra sauce on Tempura to taste.

Tempura (or Kakiage) Udon/
Tempura (or Kakiage) Soba
(Japanese style noodles)

Cook *udon* or *soba* according to the directions on package. Arrange Tempura (or *Kakiage*) on noodles. Pour hot soup over Tempura and noodles. Serves 4.

Soup:
½ cup water
½ cup soy sauce
½ cup *mirin*
½ cup dried bonito flakes

Mix ingredients together, boil and strain.

Ten-cha: Put rice in a bowl and arrange Tempura over the rice. Put a small amount of grated-green horseradish (*wasabi*) on top and sprinkle salt on Tempura. Pour very hot Japanese green-tea over the Tempura and rice (enough to cover).

Mrs. Takakazu Kuriyama, Wife of Ambassador (Japan)

CHICKEN WITH YOGURT AND MINT

1 chicken, cut in 8ths
1 onion, finely chopped
3 garlic cloves, minced
2 tablespoons lemon juice
½ tablespoon pepper
1 cup yogurt
¼ cup mint, minced
2 tablespoons green coriander, minced
½ cup mushrooms, sliced
½ tablespoon salt

Rub chicken with onion, garlic, lemon juice and pepper. Cover for ½ hour. Mix yogurt with mint, coriander and mushrooms and rub onto chicken. Place in ovenproof pan, cover with foil and place in preheated oven. Bake at 350° for 40 minutes. Remove foil, continue baking for 10 minutes, then broil 5 minutes and serve. Makes 4 servings.

Mrs. Abdul Al-Khalifa, Wife of Ambassador (Bahrain)

SPICY CHICKEN PICANTE OR "SAJTA"

1 medium size chicken, boiled
4 large onions, chopped and rinsed
3 medium tomatoes, peeled and chopped
1 to 2 tablespoons chopped, fresh parsley
1 teaspoon salt
2 cups seasoned chicken broth
6 to 8 yellow "aji" chili peppers, ground (use dried hot chilies)
2 to 3 tablespoons vegetable oil
1/2 teaspoon ground cumin
1/8 teaspoon black pepper
1 teaspoon oregano
1/4 teaspoon sugar

Raw Salad:
1 finely chopped tomato
1/2 cup finely sliced onion
2 finely sliced small green chili peppers
finely chopped parsley
salt to taste

Place onion, tomato, parsley, salt and 1 cup of broth in a large pot and boil for 10 minutes. Add peppers and oil to the tomato mixture and continue cooking for 20 minutes. Cut chicken into individual servings and add to the sauce along with cumin powder, pepper, oregano, sugar and the remaining cup of broth. Simmer for 5 minutes until the chicken is heated through. Serve with boiled peeled potatoes and top with Raw Salad.

Raw Salad: Combine all ingredients and cover each chicken serving. Makes 6 servings. May be frozen.

Mrs. Jorge Crespo, Wife of Ambassador (Bolivia)

CHICKEN VATAPÁ

1 onion, sliced
¼ cup parsley, chopped
   Malagueta peppers (op-
   tional)
2 or 3 chopped peeled to-
   matoes
2 tablespoons olive oil
1 chicken, cleaned and cut at
   joints
2 grated coconuts
½ pound ground dried
   shrimp
½ pound ground roasted
   peanuts
2 tablespoons dendê oil
   salt and black pepper

Saute onion, parsley and tomatoes in oil. If desired, add one or two chopped malagueta peppers. Cook the chicken in this *refogado*, adding
water as necessary until chicken is cooked and
falls away from bones. Remove chicken and separate it from the bones. Extract thick milk from
the coconuts and set aside. Add 5 cups water to
the residue and simmer gently until coconut is
soft. Add shrimp and peanuts and cook again,
then add the chicken gravy. Season with salt and
pepper and strain. Thicken with rice flour which
has been mixed with a little cold water. Add the
chicken and thick coconut milk and heat slowly.
Mixture should be of the consistency of a heavy
white sauce. Remove from heat, add the dendê
oil. Serve in a large deep platter surrounded by
individual molds of Corn Pirão which is a heavy,
salted, cornstarch pudding. Makes 8 to 10
servings.

H.E. Rubens Ricupero, Ambassador (Brazil)

HOT CHICKEN SALAD ON RICE, VERY SUIT
FOR MEN ONLY

8 chicken breast fillets, cut
  into squares
2 tablespoons (30 ml) lemon
  juice
¾ cup (190 ml) mayonnaise
1 teaspoon (5 ml) salt
2 cups (500 ml) chopped
  celery
1 small onion, chopped
2 tablespoons (30 ml) thinly
  sliced green or red
  sweet peppers
¾ cup (190 ml) chicken
  broth

Topping:
1 cup (250 ml) grated cheese
⅔ cup (170 ml) toasted almonds
2 cups (500 ml) crushed potato chips

Saute chicken fillets. Spoon into an ov
dish and mix all remaining salad ingredients together. Mix with chicken fillet squares. Sprinkle
cheese, almonds and chips over and heat in 200°
oven for 30 minutes. Serve with rice and a green
salad. Can be prepared 1 day ahead and kept in
refrigerator. If refrigerated, please heat in oven
for 40 minutes instead of 30! Makes 4 to 6 servings. May be frozen.

Mrs. Immo F. Stabreit, Wife of Ambassador (Federal Republic of Germany)

ALGERIAN COUSCOUS WITH VEGETABLES

2 pounds couscous grains
9 cups of water (divided)
1 teaspoon salt
   butter to coat cooked
   couscous
¼ lamb meat (shank or rump)
   cut in pieces
1 cup vegetable oil
2 onion, minced
½ hot chili peppers (if desired)
½ teaspoon cinnamon
1 teaspoon ground ginger
1 teaspoon black pepper
1 pinch of saffron or 1 teaspoon curry
2 tomato
2 turnips
2 zucchinis
2 potatoes
1 carrots
1 wedge of pumpkin
   pint dry chick peas
   (soaked overnight)

Put the couscous grains in a big bowl, sprinkle with 2 cups of water and wait until water is absorbed, steam cook about 10 minutes, put the grains in the bowl, add 1 teaspoon of salt and about 1½ cups of water, stir the grains to loosen them. Steam for 10 more minutes. Put the couscous in the bowl and coat with butter while you stir until fluffy. Keep warm (to reheat, steam again for a few minutes).

To cook the sauce: Put the meat in a pot with ¼ cup of oil, onions, hot peppers (if desired), the spices and the water, cook about 30 minutes on medium heat, covered. Add the vegetables and cook until done. To serve, put the couscous in the dish, garnish the top with chick peas, the meat and the vegetables and pour the sauce. Makes 8 to 10 servings. May be frozen.

Mrs. Nourredine Y. Zerhouni, Wife of Ambassador (Algeria)

SCALLOPINI "PORTEÑO"

Scallopini:
- 8 beef scallopini (same size, not too thin)
- 8 slices of gruyere cheese (thin)
- 100 grams bread crumbs
- 3 eggs
- salt and freshly ground pepper
- corn oil

Puree:
- 1 pound of carrots
- 1 pound of spinach
- cream, butter, salt and freshly ground pepper as needed

Sauce:
- 4 ripe tomatoes, chopped, peeled, seeded
- 1 glass of dry white wine
- 1½ teaspoons mustard
- 1 cup cream

Scallopini: With sharp knife, make a pocket in each scallopini and fill with a slice of gruyere cheese. Press down around edges of opening to close pocket. Beat the eggs and dip the scallopini in the egg and coat both sides with bread crumbs, pressing down firmly. Fry in hot corn oil until golden brown.

Puree: Mix carrot puree and spinach puree with cream, butter, salt and pepper.

Sauce: Cook tomatoes over low heat until tender, mash, add white wine and mustard. Simmer for a few more minutes. Remove from heat and add cream. Pour sauce on the bottom of serving dish, place scallopini on sauce and put carrot and spinach puree on either side. Preparation time, about 30 minutes and cooking time approximately 30 minutes. Makes 4 servings.

C. de Ortiz de Rozas

Mrs. Carlos Ortiz de Rozas, Wife of Ambassador (Argentina)

LAMB MEDALLIONS WITH BLUEBERRY SAUCE

2 racks of lamb, Frenched,
    boned (retain bones and
    pieces of fat)
10 oz. strong beef consommé
½ cup Port Wine
4 tablespoons unsalted butter
1 pint blueberries
2 tablespoons sugar
1 eggplant, peeled, sliced in
    ⅛″ slices and lightly fried

Heat oven to 425°. Place lamb bones in small pan and roast for 30 minutes. Transfer pan to stovetop, pour in beef consommé and bring to boil, scraping any browned bits off the bottom of the pan. Strain, discard bones. Set aside. Reduce oven temperature to 375°. Place lamb in same small pan, covering with reserved pieces of fat to prevent meat from drying out. Roast for 20 minutes, or until internal temperature of lamb reaches 120°. Remove lamb from pan, wrap in foil, discard the pieces of fat. Deglaze pan with Port, strain into reserved consommé mixture. In a medium saucepan, melt butter. Add blueberries, sprinkle with sugar and bring to boil, stirring for a few minutes, until some of the blueberries just begin to burst. Add strained consommé/port mixture to saucepan, as well as any juices from lamb. Slice lamb into 1″ thick medallions. Serve on fanned eggplant slices, topped with blueberry sauce. Makes 4 servings.

Catriona Cook

Mrs. Michael Cook, Wife of Ambassador (Australia)

SLOP BILLY

6 small potatoes, pared and
    diced
2 tablespoons cooking oil
2 onions, sliced
1 green pepper, sliced
2 stalks celery, chopped
½ cup tomato paste
1½ 16 oz. tins whole tomatoes
2 teaspoons thyme
1 bay leaf
    pepper to taste
2 tins corned beef

Peel potatoes and cut into bite size pieces. Boil until just tender and set aside. Meanwhile, heat oil in frying pan and saute onions, green pepper and celery until translucent. Add tomato paste and simmer for 10 minutes. Add whole tomatoes, thyme, bay leaf and pepper and simmer for another 10 minutes. Break corned beef up with spoon and add to corned beef mixture stirring to blend. Cook and simmer over low heat approximately 20 minutes, stirring occasionally. Remove cover and simmer over low heat, stirring occasionally, until most of the liquid has evaporated. Good served with white rice or johnny cake. Makes 5 to 7 servings.

H.E. Timothy B. Donaldson, Ambassador (Bahamas)

LAMB WITH RISOTTO "MASSLI AL-LAH'EM"

2½ pounds, lamb shoulder, cut
    in pieces
    water
    Peppercorns
4 seeds cardamon
1 clove garlic
1 onion
    spices of choice to rub on
    cooked meat
    salt and minced garlic
3 onions, coarsely chopped
3 potatoes, peeled and
    chopped
4 tablespoons margarine
1 green chili pepper, minced
2 teaspoons allspice
1 teaspoon salt
4 cups rice
1 stick cinnamon
    cardamon seeds
    saffron soaked in ¼ cup
    rose water

Remove all fat from meat, place in skillet. Cover with water, bring to boil, add peppercorns, cardamon, 1 garlic clove, 1 onion. Cover and simmer until meat is cooked. Remove meat to a plate, save water. Rub meat with spices of choice, salt and minced garlic. Boil water until reduced to ½ cup, remove from skillet and reserve. Saute onions and potatoes in margarine 5 minutes, stir in meat, garlic, allspice, salt and cook 3 minutes. Add tomatoes and ¼ cup boiling water, cover and simmer 10 minutes. Boil rice, 1 stick cinnamon, cardamon seeds in 6 cups boiling water and cook 10 minutes, add remaining boiled meat water, rose water, cover and simmer 30 minutes. On a platter, place rice, then meat, arrange potato and tomato pieces on top and serve. Makes 6 to 8 servings. May be frozen.

لطيفة سلمان آل خليفة

Mrs. Abdul Al-Khalifa, Wife of Ambassador (State of Bahrain)

CHICKEN REZALA (BANGLADESHI SWEET & SOUR CURRY)

½ cup butter oil
1 skinless medium chicken, cut into 8 pieces
½ cup chopped onion
½ cup sliced onion
2 teaspoons fresh chopped ginger
1 teaspoon fresh chopped garlic
5 to 6 pieces of cloves
5 to 6 pieces of cardamon
1 inch cinnamon stick
½ cup yogurt
½ teaspoon sugar
1 tablespoon lime juice
6 green chilies
½ teaspoon salt or according to taste

Put butter oil in a 4 quart pan, add sliced onions and cook on medium heat until onions are golden brown. Add chicken pieces, salt, cinnamon, cloves, cardamon, chopped ginger, onion and garlic and stir well with a spoon. Cover the pan and cook on medium heat for 20 minutes. Add sugar, lime juice and green chilies and simmer for 10 minutes. Serve with steamed rice. Makes 4 servings. May be frozen.

Mrs. Abul Ahsan, Wife of Ambassador (Bangladesh)

BELGIAN ENDIVES IN HAM WITH CHEESE SAUCE

8 heads of Belgian endives
    (not too thick)
1 cup white wine
8 slices boiled ham
    nutmeg, salt and pepper to
    taste

Sauce:
1 cup milk
¼ pound Emmentaler cheese,
    grated
2 tablespoons butter or mar-
    garine
    nutmeg, salt and pepper to
    taste
1 to 2 tablespoons flour

Wash the endives and hollow them out. Wrap each head with a slice of ham. Heat the wine, nutmeg, salt and pepper before pouring over the endives and ham. Place in a pre-heated oven (390°) in a covered pan, and cook for 20 minutes. In the meantime, melt the butter or margarine, add the flour and milk, stirring constantly to a boil. Taste when adding nutmeg, salt and pepper. Stir in the grated Emmentaler cheese. Pour the sauce over the endives and ham and return to the oven until the cheese is melted, approximately 10 minutes until the dish can be served quite hot.

Mrs. Juan Cassiers, Wife of Ambassador (Belgium)

FLEMISH BEEF STEW (CARBONNADES FLAMANDES)

2 pounds stewing beef, cut
    into pieces
3 large onions, thinly sliced
1 bottle of beer
8 oz. cubed lard
4 tablespoons butter
1 cup flour
1 teaspoon sugar
1 teaspoon vinegar
1 slice bread
1 tablespoon mustard
1 bay leaf
1 sprig thyme
1 parsley root

Coat beef with flour. Brown onion in heavy skillet in melted butter and lard. Set aside. In remaining fat, brown pieces of beef on all sides. Add onions, sugar and vinegar and top ingredients with slice of bread, spread with mustard. Pour beer over ingredients and season with pepper and salt. Let simmer for 1½ hours. Serve hot, with plain boiled potatoes. Makes 4 servings. May be frozen.

Mrs. Juan Cassiers, Wife of Ambassador (Belgium)

PASTEL DE CHOCLO (MEAT PIE)

3 cups chopped onions
4 tablespoons vegetable oil
6 tablespoons butter
1½ pounds lean round steak, cut into ¼-inch cubes
2 teaspoons salt
1 teaspoon paprika
1½ teaspoons oregano
½ to ¾ teaspoon Tabasco sauce
6 black olives, pitted
2 hard-cooked eggs, quartered
2 pounds chicken, cut into serving pieces
1 small onion, sliced
3 ear corn, grated (there should be 2½ cups)
2 teaspoons sugar, approximately
1 egg yolk

In a 3 quart heavy kettle, saute the chopped onions in 1 tablespoon of the oil and 2 tablespoons of the butter until golden. In a heavy skillet, heat 2 tablespoons of the oil and brown the beef. Season with 1 teaspoon salt, the paprika, ½ teaspoon oregano and the Tabasco. Cover and cook, stirring often, until the meat is tender. Transfer the beef to the kettle with the chopped onions. Arrange the olives and the quartered eggs over the beef. Heat 1 tablespoon of the oil and 2 tablespoons of the butter in the skillet and brown the chicken on all sides. Add the sliced onion, ½ teaspoon salt and 1 teaspoon oregano and saute until onion is golden brown. Transfer the chicken to the kettle, arranging it on top of the eggs. In the same skillet, combine the grated corn with 1 teaspoon of the sugar and the remaining ½ teaspoon salt and 2 tablespoons butter. Cook, stirring constantly, until the mixture boils and thickens. Transfer to the kettle and spoon over the chicken. Paint the corn with the egg yolk diluted with 1 teaspoon of water and sprinkle very lightly with sugar. Bake in a preheated 400° oven until top is golden brown, about 25 minutes. Makes 10 to 12 servings. May be frozen.

Mrs. Patricio Silva, Wife of Ambassador (Chile)

FRITADA

2 pounds of pork ribs or thick pork chops
½ cup of water
salt to taste
4 pieces of garlic, cut in two
1 white onion, cut in four

In a thick fry pan, place all the ingredients with exception of the onion. Cook everything in high heat, stirring the meat until the water evaporates. Turn the heat to medium and keep frying the thick pieces of pork for about 25 to 35 minutes or until they are brown. Add the onion in the last 15 minutes. The "fritada" must look very brownish (brown color). Makes 6 servings.

Mrs. Jenny Valdivieso, Cultural Officer (Ecuador)

AMETHA HIN (MYANMAR BEEF ENTREE)

1 pound boneless beef
    chunk
1 teaspoon salt
1 teaspoon paprika
1 teaspoon tamarind paste
1 medium-size onion, diced
2 cloves garlic, diced
1 inch fresh ginger, sliced
¼ teaspoon ground turmeric
2 tablespoons vegetable oil
2 teaspoons tamarind paste
1¾ cups water
1 pound steamed rice

Cut beef into 2-inch pieces. Marinate the beef in salt, paprika and tamarind and let it stand for 15 minutes. Put onion, garlic, ginger and turmeric in oil and simmer over light heat with lid on for 2 minutes. Separately cook the beef in 1¼ cups of water for 15 minutes. Add the beef in simmering oil and cook for 10 more minutes over moderate heat. Add tamarind paste dissolved in ½ cup of water, stir well and cook for 10 minutes. Bring to a boil or until beef is tender and cooked. Serve warm with steamed rice. Makes 4 servings. May be frozen.

Mrs. U. Thaung Sein, Wife of Ambassador (Union of Myanmar)

ROLLED BEEF STEAKS/ROLLED ZRAZY

2 pound round, rib, top sir-
    loin or chuck of beef
mustard
¼ pound of bacon
2 dill pickles
1 onion
3 tablespoon flour
½ cup sour cream
shortening
salt
pepper

Rinse meat, remove membrane, cut across the grain into flat steaks, pound with dampened meat hammer. Salt. Spread thinly with mustard. Cut bacon and dill pickles, lengthwise. Cut onion. Place a piece of bacon, dill pickle and onion on each steak, sprinkle with pepper, roll tightly, fasten with thread or toothpick. Dredge each steak with flour. Heat fat on skillet. Brown steaks on both sides. Place well-browned steaks with fat into saucepan, add a little water and stew covered until tender. Mix remaining flour with sour cream, add to meat, add salt to taste. Bring to the boil. Serve with fluffy buckwheat groat, parched or boiled potatoes and raw-vegetable relishes. Makes 6 servings.

Mrs. Kazimierz Dziewanowska, Wife of Ambassador (Poland)

MITITEI (SMALL SKINLESS SAUSAGES)

2 pound rump beef
1 pound pork (or breast beef)
3 or 4 cloves garlic
½ teaspoon bicarbonate of soda
  salt and pepper
  thyme or oregano
  powdered allspice
¼ teaspoon powdered cloves
1 cup seltzer water
  red or green peppers
  sour pickles

A favorite among the Romanian is MITITEI, home-made skinless sausages, which are usually broiled outdoors on charcoal. Buy two pounds of beef from the rump and 1 pound of pork or breast of beef, leaving some fat on the meat. Add 3 or 4 cloves of garlic and grind together. Place the meat in a bowl, add baking soda, powdered allspice, thyme (or oregano) powdered cloves. Salt and pepper to taste. Mix together with the hands, adding slowly seltzer water and continue mixing. When thoroughly mixed, take some in your palms and roll the meat into sausages about 3½ inches long and one inch thick. See that your palms are kept wetted, so the sausages will remain smooth surfaces. Place the sausages on a platter and keep them in a dry, cold place until the following day. This is necessary for the spices to penetrate deeply into the meat. You can keep them in the refrigerator for 2 or 3 days. Before you start to grill the sausages, keep them in the air for 1 or 2 hours. Wipe the grill with a damp cloth and grease with oil. When the grill is very hot, put the MITITEI on the broil over a quick fire, turning the sausages with flat tongs. Never use a fork or other sharp object, so as not to loose any of the juice. Serve very hot with red or green peppers and sour pickles. Makes 6 servings. May be frozen.

Ileana M. Munteanu

Mrs. Aurel-Dragos Munteanu, Wife of Ambassador (Romania)

SARMALE (CABBAGE STUFFED WITH MEAT AND RICE)

cabbage leaves
1 onion
oil
½ teaspoon thyme
1 teaspoon dill
salt and pepper
1 pound meat (chopped) it
    can be beef and pork,
    even chicken breast
¼ cup uncooked rice
sauerkraut
tomato juice (optional)
sour cream

SARMALE can be made either from pickled or from fresh cabbage. If you have a pickled head of cabbage, select equal-sized leaves. If you do not, buy a nice head of cabbage, place it in a large dish, scald it with salted boiling water, let it there for 30 minutes and select equal-sized leaves from it. Prepare the stuffing, mixing the minced meat and the finely chopped onion, and rice. Add thyme, dill, salt and pepper to taste. The cabbage rolls are prepared as follows, select a cabbage leaf and slice off with a sharp knife enough of the thickened border between segments, so that it will have about the same thickness as the rest of the leaf. Lay the leaf flat and put some stuffing in the center. Turn the right and left edges over towards the center, but not far enough that they will touch. Starting with the end in front of you, begin to roll and continue until the end. Now tuck in the loose side edges. Place the cabbage rolls in a pot, close together, until a layer is formed, leaving no empty spaces between rolls. Form layer on top of layer and between each, put a little sauerkraut, some dill, thyme and sprinkled over with some oil. On the top layer, place a little sauerkraut. Cover the rolls to the top with water (if you use fresh cabbage leaves, an alternative method permits adding tomato juice to the water). Heat slowly. As the liquid in the pot is reduced by evaporation and absorption, pour back some hot water as needed. Cook on a slow fire for 1½ hours. Place in a slow oven and bake for 1 hour longer. When finished, there should not remain more than 1 cup of liquid. Leave in pot and let stand until next day. Serve hot with sour cream. Makes 6 servings. May be frozen.

Ileana M. Munteanu

Mrs. Aurel-Dragos Munteanu, Wife of Ambassador (Romania)

EAGA'A BIL-TAMATEM

2¼ pounds mushrooms
3 tablespoons corn oil
1 teaspoon mixed spices
   (equal parts of cinna-
   mon, cardamom, cumin
   and black pepper)
1 pound tomatoes, chopped
   fine
1 pound cubed beef
2 medium onions
1 teaspoon salt

Wash mushrooms well, then put into a bowl filled with water for 2 hours. Remove and slice horizontally into round pieces (medium thickness). Wash again and pat dry. Chop onions and fry in 3 tablespoons corn oil until golden and somewhat transparent. Add the cubed beef to the onions and brown. Then add mixed spices and braise beef until tender on low heat, adding water as needed. Add chopped tomatoes and mushrooms and simmer on low heat until mushrooms are cooked through. Makes 6 to 8 servings.

H.R.H. Prince Bandar Bin Sultan, Ambassador (Saudi Arabia)

EASULIYA NASHEA

¾ pounds dried navy beans
½ teaspoon baking soda
1 to 1¼ pounds lamb or beef
   on the bone
¼ cup ground chervil
3 garlic cloves (optional)
3 minced onions
3 cups tomato juice
1 teaspoon salt
1 teaspoon black pepper
1 teaspoon ground cumin
4 tablespoons corn oil
1 teaspoon whole cumin
   seeds

Soak beans in water with baking soda for 12 hours. Saute onions in oil. Cut meat into medium-sized chunks and add to onions. Add pepper and tomato juice. Stir well. Add hot water as needed. Cook meat until half done, then add washed beans to broth and boil. Crush garlic and add to beans, along with ground chervil, cumin and salt. Stir well, then cover pot and let stew in small amount of broth until meat is tender. Makes 4 to 6 servings.

H.R.H. Prince Bandar Bin Sultan, Ambassador (Saudi Arabia)

GINGER BRISKET

4 pounds brisket
  salt and pepper to taste
2 garlic cloves
1 tablespoon vegetable oil
3 bay leaves
6 peppercorns
2 large onions, sliced
1 cup water

Sauce:
  liquid from cooked brisket
2 tablespoons cider vinegar
1 tablespoon brown sugar
1/4 packet ginger snaps
  parsley for garnish

Preheat oven to 325°. Rinse meat with water. Pat dry. Rub in salt, pepper and crushed garlic clove. Heat oil and brown meat on all sides. Add sliced onions, peppercorns, bay leaves and 1 cup of water. Cover and bake in oven for about 3 hours. Remove meat from pan and allow to cool (easier for slicing). Make sauce. Skim off any fat. Use liquid in pan that has remained. Add vinegar, brown sugar and a little more water. Add broken up ginger biscuits which flavour and thicken sauce. Stir well. Arrange slices of meat on platter. Pour over sauce. Taste and add more salt and pepper if necessary. Garnish with parsley. Serve with favourite vegetables of your choice. Makes 10 servings. May be frozen.

Mrs. Harry Schwarz, Wife of Ambassador (South Africa)

MEAT PILAU (SPICED RICE AND MEAT)

½ kilo meat
1 teaspoon salt
1 big onion
5 small potatoes
8 grains fresh garlic
4 big pieces cinnamon
1 teaspoon cardamon
1 teaspoon coriander seeds
2 tablespoons raisins
8 pieces cloves
6 tablespoons oil
½ kilo rice
14 cups water or soup

Wash and cut meat into required sizes. Place the meat in a cooking pot and add 7 cups of water and salt. Cook until the meat is cooked. Wash and cut the onions, peel the potatoes and place the peeled potatoes into a bowl of cold water. Peel garlic. Crush the cinnamon, garlic, cardamon and coriander seeds until they are all very soft. Wash raisins and cloves and dry them. Remove meat from the heat, leaving enough gravy which will be used to cook the rice. Using 6 tablespoons of oil, fry the onion, spices, potatoes and the cook meat. Add the meat soup and 4 cups of water. Boil the meat, potatoes and spices. Wash rice and spread it over the meat. Boil until the rice is cooked. Remember: You measured 14 cups of water, you used 7 cups to cook meat and 4 cups of water and soup to cook rice. If the rice is not cooked, you can use the remaining water, but the water or soup used to cook rice must be boiled. When the water is dry, cover and simmer or keep in the oven at 200° for 15 minutes. Serve. Makes 4 servings.

RACHEL NYIRABU

Mrs. Charles Nyirabu, Wife of Ambassador (Tanzania)

MEHELBI (RICE PUDDING)

4½ pints milk
1 cup rice
½ cup sugar
1 whole egg
1 vanilla stick
1 tablespoon orange extract
1 tablespoon cornstarch
ground cinnamon

Put the milk and the rice in a pressure cooker and cook about 10 minutes. While they cook, mix the rest of the ingredients. Open the pressure cooker and add the mixture while stirring and cook on low heat for 5 minutes. Pour in dessert dishes and decorate with ground cinnamon. Makes 8 to 10 servings.

Mrs. Nourredine Y. Zerhouni, Wife of Ambassador (Algeria)

GWEN TONGE'S ANTIGUA AND BARBUDA FRUIT STICKS

1 cup diced Antigua black pineapple (medium size)
1 cup diced mangoes
1 cup bananas sliced cross-wise (sprinkle with lime juice)
1 cup diced papaw (papaya, hard ripe)
1 cup springs of grapefruit (cut crosswise in pieces)
1 cup springs of orange (cut crosswise in pieces)
The midrib or center stick of coconut leaves (wash, smooth with a sharp knife and dry)
1 teaspoon grated lime rind

Place all fruit cubes on separate plates. Sprinkle with lime rind. Place the fruit cubes attractively on each stick. Arrange on a platter decorated with lettuce leaves. Served chilled. Makes 12 servings.

H.E. Dr. Patrick Albert Lewis, Ambassador (Antigua and Barbuda)

"QUIMBO" EGGS

Quimbo Eggs:
12 egg yolks
3 egg whites
1 teaspoon vanilla extract
2 tablespoons flour (all-purpose)

Syrup:
300 grams sugar
1 cup sweet wine
1 vanilla bean
½ cup of cognac

Quimbo eggs: In a bowl, beat the egg yolks, egg whites, vanilla extract until frothy. Fold in the flour. Pour mixture into small individual bowls previously coated in butter and cook in a medium oven (300°). When done (spongy and moist) take out of the mold and place in a deep serving dish.

Syrup: Combine sugar, wine and vanilla bean in a pot and bring to a boil over low heat. Once it starts thickening turn the heat off and stir in cognac. Pour syrup over the "Quimbo" eggs and let cool. Makes 4 servings.

Mrs. Carlos Ortiz de Rozas, Wife of Ambassador (Argentina)

COCONUT ICE-CREAM

2 cups heavy cream
1 cup whole milk
2 cups shredded or desic-
    cated coconut
4 egg yolks
⅓ cup sugar
¼ cup flaked coconut,
    toasted, plus extra for
    garnish

Place cream, milk and shredded coconut in a medium saucepan over medium heat and bring just to the boil. Cover and set aside for 1 hour. Strain into a bowl, pressing on coconut to remove all liquid. Discard coconut (or save for other use). Using electric mixer, whisk yolks and sugar until very pale and fluffy. Gradually whisk in strained coconut liquid. Transfer to a medium saucepan and cook over low heat, stirring constantly, until mixture thickens slightly and coats the back of a spoon. Pour mixture into a bowl, add toasted flaked coconut, and cool to room temperature. Cover and refrigerate until well chilled. Pour into ice-cream maker, churn until frozen. Delicious with bananas that have been sprinkled with coconut milk and raw sugar, and baked or grilled. Garnish with extra toasted flaked coconut. Makes 6 servings. May be frozen.

Mrs. Michael Cook, Wife of Ambassador (Australia)

BRUSSELS WAFFLES

1¾ cup flour
1 tablespoon sugar
1 egg
1½ cup light beer
¼ cup salad oil
    vanilla extract to taste

Blend all ingredients in a mixing bowl to a smooth paste. Allow to stand at room temperature for at least 2 hours or overnight in refrigerator. Grease the waffle iron generously, warm it and spread a thin layer of dough. Bake until golden brown. Serve with sprinkled confectionary sugar or serve with whipped cream and confectionary sugar sprinkled on top. Makes 8 waffles.

Mrs. Juan Cassiers, Wife of Ambassador (Belgium)

GUAVA DUFF WITH HARD SAUCE

4 tablespoons butter or margarine
1 cup sugar
3 eggs, beaten
2 cups guava pulp, unseeded
½ teaspoon nutmeg
½ teaspoon cinnamon
½ teaspoon ground clove (optional)
3 cups flour
2 teaspoon baking powder

Hard Sauce:

½ cup butter or margarine,
   softened to room temperature
1 cup confectioners' or
   lightly packed light
   brown sugar
1 teaspoon vanilla or almond
   extract
   rum, brandy or sherry to
   taste

Cream butter or margarine with sugar, add eggs, guava and spices. Beat until smooth. Sift flour and baking powder and add to mixture. The dough will be stiff. Place mixture in greased top of boiler and cook over boiling water. Steam for 3 hours. Slice and serve with Hard Sauce.

Hard Sauce: Cream butter or margarine and gradually add sugar, beating until creamy. Gradually beat in flavoring and rum, brandy or sherry. Makes approximately 1 cup. Makes 8 to 10 servings.

H.E. Timothy B. Donaldson, Ambassador (Bahamas)

PAPAS DE NUECES (WALNUT BALLS)

1 can of Borden's ("Eagle
   Brand") sweetened, condensed milk
   about 20 "wine" biscuits
1 medium size bag of ground
   walnuts

Boil the unopened can of sweetened, condensed milk, for 1 hour in a covered saucepan, being careful to maintain sufficient water to keep the can covered. Allow the can to cool before opening. Grind the biscuits. Remove the milk from the can. Mix the cooked condensed milk and the biscuits in a bowl. The mixture should be of a medium consistency, so as to form small balls. Roll each ball in the crushed walnuts (or an alternative is to roll them in unsweetened chocolate powder). Serve in decorative paper cups. Makes 15 to 20 servings. May be frozen.

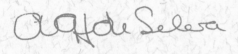

Mrs. Patricio Silva, Wife of Ambassador (Chile)

CELEBRATION CAKE—DANISH STYLE

1½ pounds almond paste
1½ cups sugar
  3 egg whites, slightly beaten

Frosting:
  1 egg white, beaten frothy
  4 drops vinegar
    enough powdered sugar to
    make a thin icing

To prepare cake: Crumble almond paste and mix thoroughly with sugar and egg whites. Shape dough into 1-inch diameter rolls. Form into rings of decreasing size and place on well buttered and floured baking sheet. There should be approximately 18 rings. Bake at 300° for 20 minutes or until light brown.

To assemble: Place icing in a decorating tube. Use tube to make scallops on top and the sides of each ring as you build a cake tower. The final product should appear cone-shaped. Traditionally, the cake is trimmed with Danish flags. For a wedding, there would be white doves or figures representing the bride and groom. Makes 24 servings. May be frozen.

Mrs. Peter Dyvig, Wife of Ambassador (Denmark)

TORTA DE MAQUEÑO CON REQUESÓN

First coating:

- 4 large sized bananas, shredded (maqueño)
- 2 ozs. diluted butter
- 2 eggs
- 6 ozs. sugar
- ½ teaspoon of lemon skin, shredded

Second coating:

- 12 ozs. cottage cheese (requesón)
- 8 ozs. sugar
- 1 oz. cornstarch
- 3 eggs
- 2 ozs. seedless raisins
- 1 teaspoon vanilla essence

In a small container, place the shredded large sized bananas with the butter, sugar and lemon skin. Mix all these ingredients and then add the eggs followed by a strong whip. In a fry pan, place the cottage cheese, sugar, cornstarch and the eggs. Keep on slow heat stirring the whole time until it boils. Add the seedless raisins and the vanilla essence and leave at slow heat for about 3 minutes and then place it away from the burner. In a butter mold, pour the preparation of the maqueño covered by the cottage cheese and place it in the hot oven until it browns. Makes 6 servings.

Jenny Valdivieso

Mrs. Jenny Valdivieso, Cultural Officer (Ecuador)

KISSEL

- sugar (according to taste and the sweetness of the fruit juices)
- 1¼ pints berry juice
- 3 tablespoons cornstarch or potato starch
- 4 tablespoons water
- juice of ½ lemon
- 7 ozs. fresh soft fruit
- 8 fluid ozs. fresh cream

Bring the juice and sugar to the boil. Mix the corn starch with the water and add to the juice. Bring to the boil, then remove from the stove immediately. Add the lemon juice and fresh fruit. Chill in the refrigerator until very cold. Serve with lightly whipped cream.

Jukka Valtasaari

Mrs. Jukka Valtasaari, Wife of Ambassador (Finland)

TARTE AU CITRON

Pastry dough:
5 oz. sweet butter
2 eggs
2 tablespoons sugar
9 oz. flour

Filling:
6 oz. sugar
6 lemon
4 whole eggs
4 egg yolks
2 cups heavy cream

Dough: Mix eggs, sugar and sweet butter in a mixer at low speed for 5 minutes. Add the flour and knead by hand. Cut in half to make 2 tarts. Cover with plastic wrap. Keep the dough and refrigerate for 1 hour. Roll dough, back to refrigerator. Remove dough and prick surface with a fork. Bake at 400° until lightly brown, 10 minutes approximately.

Filling: Remove all peel from lemon including white part. Chop lemon coarsely, put in the blender with sugar, eggs and cream. Blend thoroughly, approximately 10 seconds. Strain contents directly into tart shells. Bake until set at 300° approximately 20 minutes. Makes 10 servings.

Mrs. Jacques Andréani, Wife of Ambassador (France)

FABULOUS CHOCKOLATE DESSERT

6 egg whites
1 tablespoon sugar
4 ozs. chopped chockolate
2 ozs. chopped hazelnuts
1 pkg. chopped dates, finely
orange juice
4 ozs. strawberry jam
1 cup whipping cream
melted chockolate for top
butter or cream

Preheat oven to 400°. Whip egg whites with sugar until stiff. Mix the chockolate, nuts and dates (all chopped) with the eggs. Divide onto 2 well buttered cake pans and bake in oven 10–12 minutes. Let cool. Sprinkle orange juice on them to moisten. Then the jam. Spread whipped cream on top of the jam and assemble the layers so that the whipped cream is together. Melt chockolate in a double boiler with a little butter or cream and pour on top of the cake. Decorate the sides of the cake with whipped cream. Truly delicious. Makes 8 servings.

Mrs. Tomas A. Tomasson, Wife of Ambassador (Iceland)

GALATOBOUREKO

For Galatoboureko:
lemon peel
45 ozs. milk
9 eggs
10 ozs. sugar
3 ozs. rice flour
2 ozs. fine semolina
9 ozs. heavy cream
1 teaspoon vanilla extract
1 pound phyllo pastry sheets
12 ozs. unsalted butter

For Syrup:
18 ozs. sugar
9 ozs. water
1 cinnamon sick
2 to 3 cloves
lemon peel
juice of ½ lemon

Galatoboureko: Place lemon peel in milk and bring to boil. Beat eggs with sugar. Add rice flour and semolina. Add boiling milk in mixture and stir over low heat. When thickened, remove from heat. Add the heavy cream (unwhipped) and the vanilla extract. Grease a large baking pan about 2 inches deep. Lay one by one the pastry sheets, while brushing with melted butter. Use ⅔ of the sheets, making sure the edges hang over the sides of the pan. Add the mixture and turn the edges of the phyllo over the mixture. Cover the mixture with the remaining sheets, one at a time, brushed with butter. With a sharp knife, cut strips lengthwise through the top layer only. Bake in a preheated oven at 350° for 90 minutes. Remove from oven. Add the syrup (cold) immediately.

Syrup: In a saucepan, combine sugar, water, lemon juice, cinnamon and cloves. Boil for 10 minutes. Let cool. Add the syrup, when cool, over the galatoboureko while it is still hot from the oven. Slice the pie when cold in squares or diamond shaped pieces. Makes 1 large pan.

Naya Zacharakis

Mrs. Cristos Zacharakis, Wife of Ambassador (Greece)

PORTER CAKE

2 sticks butter
1½ cups brown sugar
1¼ cups Guinness
   zest of 1 orange
1 cup sultanas
1 cup raisins
½ cup mixed peel
4 cups plain flour
½ teaspoon baking soda
2 teaspoons mixed spice
½ cup glace cherries
3 eggs

Melt butter and sugar with Guinness. Add zest of orange and all the fruit except cherries. Bring to the boil for 3–4 minutes, stirring frequently. Remove from heat and cool until lukewarm. Sieve flour, soda and spice into a mixing bowl. Add the fruit mixture to the flour and add the cherries. Whisk eggs and add gradually, mixing well. Spoon mixture into a prepared 9″ round tin and bake in the middle of a preheated 350° oven for about 1½ hours. If you wish you may pour 4 tablespoons of stout over the cake when it is cooked (prick the cake with a skewer first). Keep a day before cutting. Keeps several weeks. Makes 20 servings. May be frozen.

Mrs. Dermot Gallagher, Wife of Ambassador (Ireland)

CROSTATA DI FRUTTA (FRUIT TART)

1 whole egg
5½ oz. butter, softened
3½ oz. sugar
9 oz. flour
2 oz. grated hazel-nuts

Mix egg, butter and sugar with fingertips, add flour and hazel-nuts and mix kneading delicately. Shape into a ball. Allow to rest. Line a 10″ fluted flan tin pan with dough, pierce with a fork, bake in a preheated oven at 400° for 20 minutes.

Zabaglione Cream:
4½ oz. sugar
3 egg yolks
1 oz. flour
¾ cup dry Marsala wine, heated
   selection of fresh fruit and jam for glazing

Zabaglione cream: Whip sugar and egg yolk with a wire-whisk, add flour and, *when well amalgamated,* start adding the heated Marsala a little at the time. Keep whisking until smooth and creamy. When cool, fill the tart and decorate with fresh fruit. Glaze with diluted jam. Makes 6 to 8 servings.

Mrs. Boris Biancheri, Wife of Ambassador (Italy)

RICE PUDDING

½ gallon whole milk
½ cup uncooked rice
1 can condensed milk
¼ cup chopped almond
¼ cup chopped cashews
¼ cup raisins

Boil whole milk in a deep sauce pan. After it boils, turn the heat to medium. Add rice and let it cook until the rice is done. Keep stirring all the time. When the rice is done, add condensed milk. Keep stirring. When the mixture is thick and done, add all the nuts and raisins. Let it simmer for 3 minutes and then serve hot or cold. Makes 5 servings.

Bimala Upadhyay

Mrs. Yog Prasad Upadhyay, Wife of Ambassador (Nepal)

MAZUREK WITH CHOCOLATE FROSTING/ EASTER CAKE

Dough:
2¼ cups flour
9 tablespoons butter
½ cup powdered sugar
2 egg yolks
2 teaspoons baking powder
2 to 3 tablespoons sour cream
2 egg whites

Frosting:
1 cup light cream
pinch of soda
1 cup sugar
2½ tablespoons butter
2½ tablespoons cocoa

Decorations:
preserved cherries
preserved orange peel
almonds

Cut butter into flour, combine with sugar, add egg yolks, baking powder. Knead with sour cream into rather thick dough. Divide dough into 3 parts. Roll out ⅔ dough into rectangular shape. Spread evenly in greased pan 9″ × 12″. Shape remaining ⅓ dough into uniform rolls, cut up to the exact size of the sides of the rectangularly-shaped dough. Brush the edges of the dough with egg white, place the rolls of dough on top, press lightly so that they adhere. Bake at 375° to a golden color, about 20 minutes. Prepare frosting. Heat cream, add soda, sugar, mix and cook in low temperature. Brown while stirring to avoid burning. When the syrup is very thick, when dropped on plate, it maintains a round shape and does not spread. Add butter, heat for a bit, add cocoa, mix, boil. If the frosting is too thick, add a few drops of boiling water, mix. Pour the frosting over the mazurek immediately, spread evenly, cool. Decorate with preserved cherries, preserved orange peel and almonds. Makes 6 servings.

Honorata Dziewanowska

Mrs. Kazimierz Dziewanowska, Wife of Ambassador (Poland)

CHEESE BLINTZES

Crepe:
- 3 eggs
- 1½ cups flour
- 2 cups water (or ½ water, ½ milk)
- ¼ teaspoon salt

Filling:
- 1 pound cream cheese
  pinch of salt
- 1 teaspoon sugar (more if desired)
- 2 egg yolks
- 2 tablespoons cream

Crepe: Beat eggs well, add flour, salt and water or milk gradually to make smooth mixture. Grease pan and when hot, spoon one or more tablespoons of mixture to thinly cover base of pan. Fry lightly on one side. Turn crepe out onto a plate. Repeat making crepes until batter is finished.

Filling: Mix all ingredients together until smooth. Place a tablespoon of cheese mixture onto the cooked side of each crepe. (Middle) Fold up to form a parcel. Add a little oil to pan and fry each little parcel (Blintz) on each side until golden brown. Serve hot with sprinkling of sugar and cinnamon. Makes 15 to 20 servings. May be frozen.

Mrs. Harry Schwarz, Wife of Ambassador (South Africa)

CHEF HARRY SIMPSON'S SUMMER PUDDING

- 2 pounds black currants, raspberries or a mixture of red currants and blackberries
  white bread, one day old
- 1½ cups sugar
- 1 cup whipping cream
  Grand Marnier or cherry brandy

Mix fruit and 1 cup sugar. Leave overnight. Next day, bring mixture to the boil and simmer for 1 minute. Strain liquid from fruit and reduce liquid by ⅓. Return ½ the remaining liquid to the fruit. Set other half to 1 side. Remove crusts from bread. Very carefully line 2½ pint pudding basin. Cut a circle from one slice of bread to fit base of the bowl. Leave no gaps. Pour in fruit. Cover top with layer of bread. Put a plate on top and use a tin as a weight. Leave overnight in the refrigerator. Turn out onto serving dish and pour remaining liquid over the pudding. Whip cream. Add ½ cup sugar and brandy. Decorate pudding with rosettes of cream. Serve remaining cream in sauce boat. Makes 8 to 10 servings.

H.E. Sir Robin Renwick, Ambassador (United Kingdom)

NOTES

The Congressional Club

Menus

We recognize entertaining is a personal matter. When friends join you for food or drink, whether it be a black-tie affair or simply a fourth of July barbeque, the dishes you prepare, the location of the party and the atmosphere all reflect your individual style.

Over the years, your family and friends have come to look forward to a particular warmth and welcome in the way you entertain.

It is our pleasure to offer you menus and recipes both created and borrowed from those submitted for this Twelfth Edition of The Congressional Club Cookbook.

We hope you will find them successful and your guests will find them enjoyable.

MENUS

PRE-INAUGURAL DINNER

Caviar Pie

Vichyssoise Made Easy

Raspberry Radicchio

Beef Tenderloin au Poivre

Nutty Wild Rice

Stuffed Tomato with Broccoli Purée

Congressional Club Crescents

Famous California Toffee Pie

Suggested wines:

Soup & Salad course:
Chardonnay or Sauvignon Blanc

Main Course: Merlot or
Cabernet Sauvignon

Dessert:
Champagne

PRE-INAUGURAL DINNER

The keys to gracious formal dining are planning, preparation and caring. With forethought, sensitivity - and with the consideration of the comfort of your guests at the basis of each decision - an elegant dining experience will be rewarding for guests and hostess alike.

Too much fuss can result in a self-conscious, even pretentious "presentation." Co-ordination and timing, leaving room for flexibility, produces a smoothly flowing affair.

Every hostess loves the opportunity to pamper her special guests by using her finest table settings and most delectable menus.

We have chosen to use formal handmade linen and lace placemats and napkins, which compliment the beautifully gleaming cherry dining table. What could be more appropriate for a formal dinner than to grace the center of your table with the elegance of roses? (Be sure to keep the flowers at a suitable "conversational level.") Complete the intimacy with twinkling votive candles... and don't forget the Mozart!

CAVIAR PIE

8 oz. softened cream cheese
1 small jar red or black
  caviar
3 hard boiled eggs
  (chopped)
3-4 chopped green onions
  lemon slices
  thinly sliced pumpernickel
  bread

Spread cream cheese onto medium sized plate. Spread caviar in ring 1″ from edge of cream cheese. Third ring of chopped eggs with chopped onions piled in the middle. Garnish with sliced lemon and parsley sprigs. Serve with pumpernickel bread slices.

Serves 8

Lauri Bellamy

Mrs. Al Bellamy, Daughter of Representative Al Swift (Washington)

VICHYSOISSE MADE EASY

Vichysoisse is the most elegant of cold soups, but it is a pain to make. With this recipe you do the time-consuming work once a year or so and can then whip out great bowls of the soup very quickly (if you have a micro-wave, on a moments notice). The secret is to make up a large quantity of what we call a BASE, freeze that in convenient quantities and then thaw it and do the simple final touches just before serving.

The Base
(This can be made in almost any quantity,
but the following is convenient.)

3 cups leek whites, cleaned and sliced

3-4 cups potatoes, peeled and diced large

2 quarts water or mixture of water and chicken broth (The more broth, the richer the soup)

1 tablespoon salt

BRING the liquid to a boil. ADD the leeks and potatoes. LET SIMMER until the potatoes are soft. Let cool enough that the next step is convenient.

With a slotted spoon, TRANSFER the solids to a blender. ADD enough liquid for blending and PUREE the mixture. If necessary, ADD more liquid to obtain the consistency of thick pea soup. This is the BASE.

At this point you can do one of two things:

A: Let base cool, add rest of ingredients, cool and serve.

B: Put the BASE in freezer containers in appropriate quantities.

ONE CUP OF BASE WILL MAKE TWO SERVINGS OF FINISHED VICHYSOISSE.

Final Preparation. (for 6 servings)

3 cups BASE.

1½ cups sour cream

¾ cup buttermilk or a variation of these, milk, yogurt, etc.

1 cup heavy cream
salt to taste
white pepper to taste

THAW the base until it is sufficiently soft that it will smooth out in the blender. If you have a microwave, this only takes a couple of minutes.

PUT it in the blender and BLEND ON SLOW. ADD gradually the other ingredients, TASTING as you go.

SERVE chilled. GARNISH with chopped chives, nutmeg, slivered snow peas or anything else that fits your fancy.

Al Swift, Representative (Washington)

RASPBERRY RADDICHIO

1 head raddichio
1 bunch watercress
1 cup pine nuts
4-6 oz. goat cheese
   raspberry vinàigrette

Wash and separate raddichio and watercress. Line each salad plate with 2 raddichio leaves. Lay springs of watercress in between raddichio. Adorn with 2 round medallions of goat cheese. Sprinkle each salad with pine nuts and drizzle with raspberry vinàigrette. Makes 8 servings.

Mrs. John W. Bryant, Wife of Representative (Texas)

BEEF TENDERLOIN AU POIVRE

3 to 3½ pound beef tenderloin roast
⅔ cup Rhine wine
⅓ cup vegetable oil
1 small onion, chopped
1 clove garlic, minced
1½ teaspoons salt
1 to 2 tablespoons cracked
   black pepper

Combine wine, oil, onion, garlic and salt. Place tenderloin in plastic bag. Add marinade, turning to coat. Tie bag securely and marinate in refrigerator 8 hours or overnight. Remove tenderloin from marinade; pat dry with absorbent paper. Roll roast in cracked pepper, lightly pressing into surface of beef. Place tenderloin on rack in open roasting pan. Do not cover or add water. Roast in preheated 425°F oven until thickest part of roast registers 135°F (approximately 50 minutes). Let stand 15 minutes. Carve into slices. Makes 8 servings.

Mrs. Craig James, Wife of former Representative (Florida)

NUTTY WILD RICE

¾ cup golden raisins
½ cup dry sherry
1 cup wild rice
1 cup white or brown rice
4½ cups chicken stock or
    broth
8 tablespoons unsalted butter
1 cup slivered almonds
½ cup chopped parsley
    salt & pepper to taste

Heat the raisins and sherry in a small saucepan to boil. Reduce heat and simmer 5 minutes. Set aside. Boil the chicken stock and pour into large saucepan containing rice. Cover and cook in oven at 350° for 25 minutes. Add butter, stir rice, re-cover and cook for an additional 25 to 30 minutes. Uncover rice, stir in raisin mixture. Add almonds and parsley before serving. Makes 8 servings.

Mrs. Martin Sabo, Wife of Representative (Minnesota)

STUFFED TOMATO WITH BROCCOLI PURÉE

1 large bunch broccoli
½ cup butter
½-1 teaspoon salt
½ teaspoon pepper
1-2 teaspoons nutmeg
8 large, firm tomatoes
    Parmesan cheese

Steam cut up broccoli until tender. Add small amounts of broccoli to blender and purée adding bits of butter, salt, pepper and nutmeg until all broccoli is a smooth purée. Hollow out tomatoes, salt and pepper insides and drain upside down on paper towels. When drained, fill each tomato with broccoli purée and bake in oven about 30 minutes or until warmed. Sprinkle with Parmesan cheese and run back under broiler until lightly browned. Makes 8 servings.

Mrs. John W. Bryant, Wife of Representative (Texas)

CONGRESSIONAL CLUB CRESCENTS

4 packages dry yeast
1½ cups warm water (180°)
1 cup sugar
1 cup shortening
1 teaspoon salt
8 eggs
8 cups all purpose flour
¼ cup heavy cream
1 cup butter

Mix first 6 ingredients plus 4 cups of flour together. Beat until smooth. Add additional 4 cups of flour. Knead for 5 minutes on a floured board. Place in bowl, brush top with oil, cover with foil and let rise for 1 hour in a warm place.

Cut mixture into 4 equal amounts. On a greased surface roll into a 12 inch circle. Cut circle into 16 even triangles. Roll, starting with wide end into a crescent shape. Place crescent on to a greased cookie sheet. Brush with heavy cream, repeat until all dough is used, let rise an additional hour.

Bake at 400° for 8-10 minutes. Brush immediately with melted butter. May be frozen for up to 1 month. Makes 62 rolls.

The Congressional Club

FAMOUS CALIFORNIA TOFFEE PIE

Step 1
- ¾ cup chopped nuts
- 1 square grated unsweetened chocolate
- ¼ cup brown sugar
- 1 teaspoon vanilla
- 1 tablespoon water

Press into well-buttered 9″ pie pan. Bake at 375 for 15 minutes. Cool completely.

Step 2
- 1 cube softened butter
- ¾ cup sugar
- 1 square chocolate, melted
- 2 tablespoons coffee
- 2 eggs

At medium speed beat 1 cube butter, softened, and ¾ cup sugar.

Blend in 1 square chocolate, melted, 2 teaspoons coffee (1 tablespoon crystals dissolved in 2, tablespoons water).

Add and beat 5 minutes, 1 egg.

Add and beat 5 minutes, 1 egg.

Pour into crust and refrigerate overnight.

Step 3
- 1½ pints whipping cream
- ½ cup powdered sugar
- 1 tablespoon coffee crystals

10 hours before serving:

Combine 1½ pints whipping cream, ½ cup powdered sugar, 1 tablespoon coffee crystals.

Day Before
Combine:
- ¾ cup chopped nuts
- 1 square grated, unsweetened chocolate
- ¼ cup brown sugar
- 1 teaspoon vanilla
- 1 tablespoon water

Refrigerate 60 minutes. Beat cream mixture until stiff. Swirl on top of pie. Garnish with chocolate curls. Refrigerate 8 more hours. Makes 8 servings.

Doris O. Matsui

Mrs. Robert Matsui, Wife of Representative (California)

KIDS' KAPER

Pizza Faces

Soda Fountain Jell-O Molds

Banana Strawberry Sandwiches

Ice Cream Bites

Popcorn

Flemming's Ice Cream Cone Cupcakes

KIDS' KAPER

Birthdays, Halloween, Presidents', Valentines or May Day. Whatever the celebration here are some ideas. Use your imagination; your child's party needn't cost a fortune.

Turn your family room, basement or backyard into a theme to fit the occassion.

Various colored balloons, streamers and decorations will make your kids' fantasy come true.

Old faithful games never go out of style; pin the tail on the donkey, piñatas, musical chairs, bobbing for apples, Simon says and hide and seek.

As children arrive, give each one a paper bag and send them on a peanut hunt in your backyard. If weather is inclement, move the treasure hunt inside winding individual strings throughout the house with a special prize at the end of each.

A different thought for favors might be trial samples; a toothbrush, toothpaste, nail polish, shampoo, creme rinse, hand lotion and shaving creme all tucked into a small travel bag. Use these as the centerpiece with all sorts of balloons.

PIZZA FACES

1 large or 2 medium toma-
toes, halved
5 english muffins, halved
softened butter
225 g (8 oz) mild cheese,
grated
4 tablespoons mayonnaise
salt
freshly ground black
pepper
4 tablespoons finely chopped
fresh parsley
5 small gherkins, halved
crossways
20 slices of stuffed olives

Preparation time: 10–15 minutes
Cooking time: 3–4 minutes

You can use crumpets as a base for the cheese topping in place of English muffins.

1. Scoop the centre seeds from the tomato halves, leaving just a thin layer of flesh under the tomato skin (use this centre tomato for a soup or sauce). Cut 10 half moon shapes from the tomato skin, to use as 'mouths'.
2. Lightly toast the halved muffins on the cut surface. Spread lightly with butter.
3. Mix the grated cheese with the mayonnaise, and season to taste with a little salt and pepper.
4. Spread the cheese mixture evenly over each muffin half.
5. Place the English muffins under a preheated moderately hot grill until bubbling and lightly golden.
6. Sprinkle the parsley round the top edge of the muffins to represent hair. Garnish each half toasted muffin with a tomato 'mouth', a gherkin 'nose' and two olive 'eyes'.

Rodolfo Franco, A Member of The Congressional Club Staff

SODA FOUNTAIN JELL-O MOLDS

This idea suits kids of all ages. For large informal buffets, make one giant soda in a brandy snifter. Vary fruits, nuts and flavors to your liking.

3-ounce package lime gelatin
3-ounce package strawberry gelatin
8-ounce container frozen dessert topping
2 bananas, coarsely chopped
whipped cream or frozen dessert topping
12 to 14 maraschino cherries with stems

In separate bowls, make lime and strawberry gelatin according to package directions. Chill each until almost jelled, or thick enough to "plop" when dropped from a spoon. Add 4 ounces of dessert topping to each flavor and mix with rotary or electric mixer until frothy. Fill 8 to 10 six-ounce glasses half full with lime gelatin. Place a few pieces of banana over top and cover with strawberry gelatin. Cover with plastic wrap and refrigerate.

May be refrigerated overnight.

Before serving, pipe or dollop a rosette of whipped cream or topping in the center of each glass. Top with a maraschino cherry. Cut drinking straws in half and place two at an angle next to the cream in each glass. Makes 8 to 10 servings.

choi Lin Phua

Choi Lin Phua, A Member of The Congressional Club Staff

BANANA AND STRAWBERRY SANDWICHES

2 large ripe bananas, thinly
   sliced
juice of 1 lemon
caster sugar
6 large slices of wholemeal
   bread
butter, softened
3 tablespoons strawberry jam

Preparation time: 15–20 minutes

1. Toss the banana slices in the lemon juice and sprinkle with a little caster sugar to taste.
2. Spread one side of each slice of bread with softened butter.
3. Spread half the slices with strawberry jam and top with a layer of banana slices.
4. Sandwich together with the remaining slices of bread.
5. Cut off the crusts and cut each sandwich either into triangles, or into small shapes using cookie cutters. Remember to wrap sandwiches carefully and tightly when preparing them in advance. Makes 12 small sandwiches.

GLORIA CHAVEZ

Mrs. Gloria Chavez, A Member of The Congressional Club Staff

ICE CREAM BITES

10 heaped tablespoons or
   scoops of 'soft scoop'
   strawberry or chocolate
   ice cream
20 chocolate-covered wafers

Preparation time: 3 minutes, plus freezing

1. Spread a tablespoon or scoop of ice cream on the plain side of 10 of the wafers—work quickly so that the ice cream does not melt.
2. Sandwich together with the remaining wafers, so that the plain sides touch the ice cream.
3. 'Open-freeze' for 1 hour, then wrap each ice cream and wafer sandwich in freezer film and return to the freezer until needed.
4. Allow the bites to soften for 3–4 minutes at room temperature before serving.

Susan Keenan, Manager of The Congressional Club

POPCORN BALLS

2 cups light corn syrup
1 cup sugar
1 package (6 ounces) Jello
   (any flavor)
18 cups popped corn

Pop enough corn to make eighteen cups and allow to cool. Set aside. Bring syrup and sugar to a boil until dissolved. Add Jello, stirring well until Jello is dissolved. Pour over popcorn, mixing well. Allow to cool and shape into balls. The secret to shaping popcorn balls is to keep your hands moist with warm water and cooking oil. Makes 18 servings.

Mrs. George Hansen, Wife of former Representative (Idaho)

FLEMMING'S ICE CREAM CONE CUPCAKES

1 18½ ounce box cake mix
24 to 28 flat bottomed ice
   cream cones
   Frosting:
1 16 ounce box powdered
   sugar
½ cup shortening
1 teaspoon vanilla
1 teaspoon almond flavoring
¼ cup milk
   food coloring, optional

Prepare batter according to directions on box. Fill cones ¾ full with batter. To bake, place cones in muffin tins to prevent toppling. Cook 20 minutes at 350 degrees. Remove from oven and cool.

Frosting: Cream together all ingredients until frosting is smooth. Decorate cooled cupcakes. Makes 24-28 servings.

Mrs. Mark White, Daughter of former Representative Richard H. Ichord (Missouri)

NORTHWEST PATIO DINNER

All American Clam Chowder

Green Salad With Raspberry Vinaigrette

Perfect Barbequed Pacific Northwest Salmon

Potatoes, Bakery Style

Fresh Asparagus With Lemon Butter

Fresh Bread With Garlic Spread

Fresh Nectarines and Raspberries With
Creme de Cassis Liquer

NORTHWEST PATIO DINNER

The cuisine of the Pacific Northwest boasts simplicity. Fresh food chosen for natural aromas and flavors will highlight this typical summer patio dinner.

Flowers, fresh from the garden or the local farmers' market decorate the table which can be softly lighted with candles in small hurricane globes.

The entire menu, except the asparagus which is steamed for 6 to 8 minutes just before sitting down, and the salmon which grills while the arriving guests have a pre-dinner cocktail, may be prepared ahead of time. This leaves the hosts free to enjoy their guests and the lovely summer evening.

ALL AMERICAN CLAM CHOWDER

3 slices bacon
½ cup minced onions
1 7½ oz. can minced clams
   (save clam liquor)
1 cup cubed potatoes
1 can cream of celery soup
1½ cups milk
   dash of pepper

Cook bacon in frying pan until crisp. Remove and break into one inch pieces. Brown onion in bacon fat. Add clam liquor and potatoes. Cover and cook over low heat until potatoes are done (about 15 minutes). Blend in bacon pieces, minced clams, and other ingredients. Heat, but do <u>not</u> boil. Bacon may be used for garnish.

Barbara Bush

Mrs. George Bush, Wife of former President of the United States

RASPBERRY VINAIGRETTE

¼ cup oil
5 tablespoons red raspberry
   vinegar
¼ cup water
2 tablespoons fresh or
   thawed raspberries
1 tablespoon lime juice
1 tablespoon finely chopped
   onion
1½ teaspoon sesame oil
   dash Tabasco

Mix all ingredients and refrigerate in jar at least 2 hours before serving. About 38 calories per tablespoon. Makes 1 cup.

Jean M. Cole

Mrs. Thomas Cole, Daughter-in-law of former Representative Sterling Cole (New York)

PERFECT BARBEQUED PACIFIC NORTHWEST SALMON

One fileted salmon, cut down center into 2 pieces. Skin remains on.

Sauce:
butter or margarine
Worcestershire sauce
onion diced
seasoning as desired
lemon juice
soy sauce to taste

Combine sauce ingredients and simmer together. Lay salmon skin side down on foil, allowing enough foil to cover salmon, if necessary later. Place foil with salmon on top of the grill. Baste salmon with sauce. Barbeque salmon until it loses its red color, but is still tender. Do not turn salmon. If you are barbequeing a thick salmon you may have to tent the foil over salmon briefly to cook through the thickest part. The trick is not to overcook!

Norm Dicks, Representative (Washington)

POTATOES, BAKERY STYLE

green onions
bacon
white potatoes
salt
pepper
whipping Cream or Half and
   Half
parsley

Lightly saute chopped green onions and thinly sliced bacon. Drain and set aside. Thinly slice potatoes. Arrange in overlapping rows in well-greased au gratin pan. Sprinkle with salt and pepper. Cover with cream. Sprinkle bacon and onions between rows. Bake 45 minutes or until done in 350° oven. Garnish with finely minced parsley. Serve.

Mrs. Al Swift, Wife of Representative (Washington)

GARLIC SPREAD

2 sticks of favorite butter or
   margarine, one cup
8 cloves of garlic

Soften at room temperature (do not heat) 2 sticks, one cup, or butter or margarine. With garlic press add 8 cloves of garlic, more if desired, and stir until thoroughly mixed. Refrigerate and use as needed for quick and easy garlic bread.

Jerry Solomon

Gerald Solomon, Representative (New York)

FRESH NECTARINES AND RASPBERRIES WITH CREME DE CASSIS

fresh nectarines
fresh raspberries
Creme de Cassis liquer
mint sprigs

Slice fresh nectarines and toss with fresh raspberries and Creme de Cassis liquer. Chill and serve with sprigs of fresh mint.

Carol Williams

Mrs. Pat Williams, Wife of Representative (Montana)

NEW ENGLAND CLAM BAKE

Clam Chowder

Steamed Clams

Boiled Maine Lobster

Corn on the Cob

Baked Beans

Cole Slaw

Biscuits

Blueberry Cake

NEW ENGLAND CLAM BAKE

If you have access to a lobster pot, that's great, but if you are landlocked here are some ideas to give the feel of the seashore to your party.

Our clam bake can be served outside after preparation is completed inside. Cover your tables with colors of the sea and creatively drape with a fishnet. Sand, seashells and driftwood can be scattered on tabletops with an array of beautiful fresh or dried grasses and flowers. To finish off the table why not use some of the small clam shells for place cards?

Your entire meal can be served in buckets and don't forget the bib to catch the drips. Top off the evening with the delicious blueberry cake served in individual scallop shells.

CHASE CLAM CHOWDER

2 quarts clams (steamers) raw in shell or 2 cups chopped clams
4 oz. salt pork (or bacon) diced very fine
1 tablespoon flour
2 med. onions chopped fine
4 med. potatoes, peeled and diced
2 cups water
2 cups clam broth (fresh or canned)
1 qt. milk or half & half
2 teaspoons Worcestershire sauce
½ teaspoon garlic powder
salt and pepper to taste

To cook clams, place washed clams in a pot with 2 cups water. Cover and bring to a boil. Cook for 5 to 10 minutes, or until the shells open. Let cool and remove the clams from the shells, reserving the cooking liquid. Remove the "beard" from the clams (the brownish membrane that surrounds the black neck of the clam). Chop the clams into bite size pieces.

Fry the pork until golden brown. Add the onions and cook until they are tender. Add in the flour and stir well. Stir in the water and bring to a boil. Add the clam broth and potatoes. When the potatoes are cooked, add the chopped clams. Bring back to a boil and add the milk. Season, and heat to serve. Makes 12 servings.

Mrs. Jay Rhodes, Wife of former Representative (Arizona)

STEAMED CLAMS

6-7 lb. clams "steamers" or softshell
1 cup water
1 teaspoon salt
2 lb butter

Wash the clams by placing them in enough water to cover them at least 2 inches. Lightly toss them around removing any dirt or mud from the clams. Discard any broken, open or floating clams. Repeat.

In a large pot, place the water, clams and salt. The clams should only half fill the pot. Cover and cook on high heat until all of the clams open up (15-20 minutes). In a separate pot, heat the butter until melted and warm. Ladle the clams into a bowl, top with broth, and serve with a side of the melted butter. Makes 12 servings.

Mrs. Bill Barrett, Wife of Representative (Nebraska)

BOILED MAINE LOBSTER

1 each 1½ lb lobster
2 each lemon wedges
¼ cup melted butter
1 tablespoon salt per quart
    of water

Lightly rinse the lobsters under a faucet and make sure they are good and lively, (the tail should snap back after it is stretched out flat). Place the lobsters in enough boiling salted water to cover them completely. Cover the pot and bring back to a boil. Simmer the lobsters for 8 to 10 minutes per pound or until the lobsters turn a bright red. Serve hot with melted butter and lemon on the side.

Tom Andrews, Representative (Maine)

CORN ON THE COB

Remove the husks and silk from the ears and place in enough boiling water to cover the corn completely. Bring the water back to a boil and simmer approximately 5 minutes or until the corn is tender. Serve with butter, salt and pepper.
Note: If the corn is not in peak season, you may want to add ¼ cup sugar per quart of water.

Mrs. Dale Kildee, Wife of Representative (Michigan)

BAKED BEANS

1 quart beans
¼ teaspoon soda
3 tablespoons olive oil
   small square salt pork
2 teaspoons salt
½ teaspoon ginger
   pinch—mustard
   pinch—red pepper
1 tablespoon molasses
1 peeled onion

Soak 1 quart of beans overnight. Drain off water through a strainer. Cover with cold water to which ¼ teaspoon soda has been added. Parboil until the skin of the beans breaks, not too much. Let set a few minutes, then drain off water. Rinse with cold water. Add 3 tablespoons olive oil, a small square of salt pork, 2 teaspoons of salt, ½ teaspoon ginger, a pinch of mustard and of red pepper, 1 tablespoon molasses and 1 peeled onion. Cover with hot water. Let stand on top of warm stove a few minutes. Place in oven and bake slowly for 8 hours, keeping covered with water as needed.

Margaret Chase Smith, former Senator (Maine)

COLE SLAW

1 medium head of cabbage,
   shredded
1 lb carrots, peeled and
   shredded
4 apples, cored and diced
2 cups mayonnaise
¼ cup sugar
1 teaspoon celery salt
¼ teaspoon celery seed
2 teaspoons Worcestershire
   sauce
¼ teaspoon garlic powder
½ teaspoon black pepper

Mix all of the ingredients in a large bowl and refrigerate for at least one hour. Stir well and serve.

Mrs. Bob Filner, Wife of Representative (California)

ALABAMA BUTTERMILK BISCUITS

2 cups flour
4 teaspoons baking powder
½ teaspoon salt
½ teaspoon baking soda
4 tablespoons (¼ cup) Crisco
1 cup buttermilk

Sift together the dry ingredients into a large bowl, add shortening and mix well until blended. Gradually add the buttermilk, mixing until dough is soft.

Preheat oven to 475°. Turn the dough onto a lightly floured surface and toss lightly with hands till outside looks smooth. With fingers pat the dough out about half-inch thick, cut out biscuits with floured biscuit cutter, and place on baking sheet about 1 inch apart. Bake the biscuits for about 12 minutes—or until lightly brown on top. Yields 16 biscuits.

Julia Ann Shepard

Mrs. Tazewell Shepard, Daughter of former Senator John Sparkman (Alabama)

BLUEBERRY CAKE

1 9 x 13 baking dish
1½ cup sugar
½ cup margarine
3 eggs
1 cup milk
4 cups flour
1 teaspoon salt
4 teaspoons baking powder
4 cups blueberries

Cream together the sugar and margarine. Add the eggs and the milk. Sift together the flour, salt and baking powder and add to the mixture. Gently fold in the blueberries. Pour into the greased baking dish and spread evenly (will be thick). Dust the top with ⅓ cup of cinnamon sugar and bake at 350° until a knife comes out clean. Cool and serve with whipped cream.

WHIPPED CREAM

2 cups heavy or whipping cream
1 teaspoon vanilla
½ cup powdered sugar

Combine and whip until stiff.

Sydna Zeliff

Mrs. Bill Zeliff, Wife of Representative (New Hampshire)

SOUPER—SUNDAE
SUPER BOWL PARTY

Soups
Tortellini Soup
Zucchini Soup
Potato Soup

Sundaes
Victory Vanilla Ice Cream
Scrumptious Strawberry Ice Cream
Mint Ice Cream
Chocolate Sauce
Raspberry Grand Marnier Sauce

Assorted crackers and rolls

SOUPER-SUNDAE
SUPER BOWL SUNDAY

Over the past several years Super Bowl Sunday has rapidly emerged as a new American tradition.

The menu for our Super Bowl Sunday celebration is a play on words, with soups and sundaes providing the fare of the day.

Color coordinate your decorations with the team colors.

As guests arrive, provide a basket of mums decorated in appropriate colors as favors—and don't forget the football pool!

Crock-pot soups, rolls and crackers can be self-served as desired, with sundaes provided with half-time entertainment.

TORTELLINI SOUP

1 tablespoon butter
4 garlic cloves, minced
2 14½ ounce cans of
    chicken broth
10 ounce package cheese
    tortellini
¼ cup grated Parmesan
    cheese
1 14½ ounce can stewed
    tomatoes
½ bunch spinach, stemmed
    and chopped
6 fresh basil leaves, chopped
    salt and pepper to taste

Melt butter in heavy large pan. Add garlic and sauté for 2 minutes. Stir in broth, tortellini. Bring to a boil. Reduce heat and season with salt and pepper. Simmer until tortellini are just tender, about 5 minutes. Stir in tomatoes, spinach and basil. Add ¼ cup Parmesan cheese and simmer for 2 minutes. Serve, passing extra Parmesan cheese separately. Makes 8 servings.

Jim Bunning, Representative (Kentucky)

ZUCHINNI SOUP

2 medium onions, chopped
1 cup butter
6 small zuchinni, sliced
1 teaspoon salt
3 cups chicken stock
    juice of ½ lemon
    salt and pepper to taste

Sauté onions in butter till transluscent. Add zuchinni. Stir. Add salt and sauté one minute. Add stock. Simmer covered for 15 minutes. Put in blender or food processor and puree till smooth. Add lemon juice and salt and pepper. Serve hot or cold. Will freeze very well.

Mrs. Robert Matsui, Wife of Representative (California)

POTATO SOUP

7 slices bacon
4 onions, chopped
3 mushrooms, chopped
4 tablespoons flour
9 cups beef bouillon
6 large potatoes, peeled and
   sliced
3 egg yolks
1½ cups sour cream
2 tablespoons fresh parsley,
   minced
2 tablespoons dried basil
1 bay leaf
  pepper to taste

Dice bacon and sauté in deep kettle; stir in onions and mushrooms, sauté until soft. Stir in flour and gradually add bouillon, stirring constantly. Add potatoes and cook (simmer) for one hour.
Beat egg yolks and mix with sour cream. Stir one half cup of the hot soup into egg and cream mixture, then add to soup and simmer for 10 minutes. Add pepper to taste. Serve hot, sprinkled with basil and parsley. Makes 8 servings.

Jay Rhodes, former Representative (Arizona)

VICTORY VANILLA ICE CREAM

5 pints whipping cream
1 13-ounce can evaporated
   milk
5 large eggs
2½ cups sugar
   half and half cream and
   milk to fill electric ice
   cream freezer ⅔ full
2 teaspoons vanilla

Scald whipping cream and evaporated milk in double boiler. Beat eggs with sugar and slowly add to custard. Continue to heat until mixture coats spoon. Chill thoroughly. When ready to freeze, add enough milk and half and half to fill electric ice cream freezer only two thirds full, leaving room for ice cream to expand. Add vanilla. Add equal layers of chipped ice and ice cream salt, packing ice cream freezer well to start and then adding as needed until motor shuts off. Makes 20 servings.

Mrs. Peter Smith, Wife of former Representative (Vermont)

SCRUMPTIOUS STRAWBERRY ICE CREAM

3 pints fresh strawberries or 3 16-ounce packages frozen strawberries, thawed and drained
2½ cups sugar
   juice of 3 lemons
½ pint whipping cream
1 12 ounce can Carnation milk (whole)

Put strawberries in blender and add remaining ingredients. Fill ice cream freezer and freeze. Makes 25 servings.

Mrs. Trent Lott, Wife of Senator (Mississippi)

MINT ICE CREAM

1½ cups sugar
1 cup freshly crushed pineapple
2 cups finely crushed mint leaves
1 cup light corn syrup
1 cup canned unsweetened pineapple juice
2 cups milk
2 cups cream
¼ cup creme de menthe
1½ cups water

Combine sugar and water. Cook and stir until mixture boils. Cook to soft ball stage (236°). Add mint leaves. Cook 10 minutes longer, or just put all sugar and water together with leaves in pan and cook until it looks right—about 15 minutes. Remove from heat, strain. Add corn syrup. Let cool. Add remaining ingredients. Freeze. Let ripen. Makes 2 quarts.

Kirk Fordice, Governor (Mississippi)

CHOCOLATE SAUCE

2 squares (1 oz.) Bakers unsweetened chocolate
1 can (5 oz.) Carnation evaporated milk
1 cup sugar
   dash salt
1 teaspoon butter
1 teaspoon vanilla

Melt chocolate in double boiler. Add milk, sugar, and salt. Cook over low heat until thick (about 1 hour) stirring a few times.
Add butter and vanilla. Makes 8-10 servings.

Hints for serving: Serve over ice cream or store in glass jar in refrigerator and reheat in pan of water.

Betty Adams

Mrs. Brock Adams, Wife of former Senator (Washington)

RASPBERRY GRAND MARNIER SAUCE

2 12 ounce packages frozen
   raspberries, thawed or 1
   quart fresh raspberries
¾ cup sugar
3 tablespoons Grand Marnier

Press the berries through a fine sieve. Add the sugar and stir until completely dissolved. Add the liqueur and chill until ready to use.

Lydia de La Viña de Foley

Mrs. John Foley, III, Daughter-in-law of former Representative (Maryland)

SPRINGTIME GARDEN TEA

Hot Cheese Puffs

Cucumber Sandwiches

Tea Time Tassies

Chicken-Almond Sandwiches

Fresh Fruit Bowl

Al's Brownies

Spiced Lemon Tea

Isle of Wight Punch

SPRINGTIME GARDEN TEA

An afternoon tea table draped in delicate lace linens, adorned with the fragrant springtime blossoms of your region, and an array of sweets and savories. This is the epitome of graciousness and a tribute to your special guests.

While a tea is more often held in the afternoon and a coffee in the morning, they are actually interchangeable.

With flowers as the theme, your garnishes are as close and varied as your springtime garden—and creativity is unlimited!

HOT CHEESE PUFFS

8 oz sharp cheese, grated
½ cup mayonnaise
1 egg
½ teaspoon cayenne
1 loaf thinly sliced sandwich bread

Grate cheese. Set aside to soften. Beat egg with electric mixer; add mayonnaise and continue beating. Stir the egg mixture into the grated cheese. Cut small rounds from bread (about the size of large quarter). Spread cheese mixture on rounds and place on ungreased cookie sheet.

Bake at 375° until cheese bubbles and begins to brown—about 10-12 minutes.

These freeze nicely before baking.

Mrs. Herbert Bateman, Wife of Representative (Virginia)

CUCUMBER SANDWICHES

white sandwich bread (one loaf)
2 8 oz. pkgs. cream cheese
mixed herb salt to taste
2 large cucumbers sliced

Soften cheese to room temperature, and cream. Use a round cookie cutter to cut out slices. Spread each slice with cream cheese, top with cucumber and sprinkle with herb salt. Makes 20 servings.

Susan Keenan, Manager, The Congressional Club

TEA TIME TASSIES

3 ounces cream cheese
½ cup butter
1 cup sifted flour

Let cream cheese and butter soften to room temperature. Blend. Stir in flour. Chill about 1 hour. Shape into 24 1 inch balls; place in tiny ungreased 1¾ inch muffin tins. Press dough on bottom and sides of cups.

Pecan Filling:
1 egg
¾ cup brown sugar
1 tablespoon margarine, softened
1 teaspoon vanilla
dash of salt
⅔ cup pecans, chopped

Preheat oven to 325°. Beat together egg, sugar, margarine, vanilla and salt until smooth. Divide half the pecans among pastry-lined cups; add egg mixture and top with remaining pecans. Bake for 25 minutes or until filling sets. Cool before removing from pan. Makes 24 servings.

Mrs. John Heins, Daughter of Representative Tom Lewis (Florida)

CHICKEN-ALMOND SANDWICHES

4 cups cooked minced chicken
½ cup heavy cream, whipped
1 cup mayonnaise
2 cups minced celery
1 cup slivered almonds, chopped
1 large loaf of thinly sliced white sandwich bread with crusts removed

Combine whipped cream and mayonnaise, then blend all ingredients together. Spread on bread and top with bread slice. Cut each sandwich into quarters.

Mrs. Richard Bowman, Daughter of Representative Tom Lewis (Florida)

FRUIT SALAD

3 tablespoon lemonade concentrate
1 medium cored diced apple
1 medium orange peeled, sectioned
1 medium peach pitted, peeled & diced
1 medium banana peeled & sliced
½ cup seedless grapes, halved
½ cup blueberries (added last) (may use frozen berries and use other kinds for variety)
1 tablespoon walnuts finely chopped, optional

Put lemon concentrate in large bowl mix lightly with fruit. Chill. Garnish with walnuts if using as fruit cup. Makes 6 servings, ⅔ cup each.

Mrs. Neal Smith, Wife of Representative (Iowa)

AL'S BROWNIES

2 squares unsweetened chocolate
1 cup sugar
¼ pound margarine
2 eggs
½ cup flour
1 tablespoon vanilla extract
1 cup chopped pecans

Melt chocolate in top of double boiler. Cream sugar and margarine in mixing bowl until smooth. Add eggs and blend well, then slowly add flour. Add melted chocolate and vanilla. Stir in chopped nuts. Pour into buttered and floured 9″ × 13″ pan and bake for about 30 minutes at 350°. Cool brownies before cutting.

Frosting

1 stick margarine
¼ cup milk
2 squares unsweetened chocolate
1 pound confectioners sugar
1 teaspoon vanilla

For frosting: combine margarine, milk and chocolate. Heat to boiling, and stir well. Mix in sifted sugar and vanilla and stir until smooth. Frost while brownies are warm. Makes 2½ dozen servings.

Elford Cederberg, former Representative (Michigan)

ISLE OF WIGHT PUNCH

1 small Kool Aid (any flavor)
1 6 oz. can frozen orange juice
1 46 oz. can unsweetened pineapple juice
1¼ cups sugar
1 qt. water
3 qts. ginger ale (chilled)

Mix and chill first five ingredients. Add the chilled ginger ale when putting the punch in the punch bowl. Makes 1½ gallons.

Mary Bateman

Mrs. Herbert Bateman, Jr., Daughter-in-law of Representative Herbert Bateman, Sr. (Virginia)

SPICED LEMON TEA

2 cups sugar
2 cups Tang
1 small jar lemon-flavored tea (10 oz.)
1 heaping teaspoon cinnamon
1 level teaspoon ground cloves

Put all ingredients in a large bowl, and mix well. Store in a jar. For 1 cup of hot spiced tea, put 2 teaspoons of mixture in a cup, fill with boiling water and stir. Makes 40 servings.

Elsie Barrett

Mrs. Bill Barrett, Wife of Representative (Nebraska)

FIESTA
de AÑO NUEVO

Margaritas and Sangria
Chips and Salsa

Gazpacho

Jicama-Citrus Salad

Mexican Quiche or Breakfast Casserole

Mexican Cornbread

Biscochitos and Pralines

Coffee

FIESTA DE AÑO NUEVO

Start the New Year with a Southwestern Brunch served casually during the annual parades.

Greet your guests with frosty Margaritas or tangy Sangria.

Dare to be different! Tie-dye white tablecloths in bright Mexican colors. Use plastic terra cotta plant saucers as plates. Wrap the silverware in colorful bandanas tied with raffia.

Decorate throughout the party area using clay pots filled with cheery sunflowers.

For a fiesta finale serve steaming mugs of cinnamon coffee and pass the pralines.

EASY MARGARITAS

1 6 oz. can limeade
1 6 oz. can 7-up or Sprite
1 6 oz. can Tequila (gold)
  Ice

In blender, empty limeade, fill can with 7-up or Sprite, add to blender. Add 1 can of Tequila. Fill blender with ice and blend until slush consistency. Serve in chilled glasses rimmed with salt. Makes 4–5 servings. May be frozen.

Janet Bryant

Mrs. John Bryant, Wife of Representative (Texas)

MENDOCINO SANGRIA

1 bottle Scharggenberger
    Champagne or the best
    quality Brut or extra-dry
2 very ripe peaches
4 strawberries
1 handful raspberries

Cut each peach into 5 to 6 wedges. Cut strawberries in half (if you slice them they become too overpowering). Blend the raspberries in your blender. Pour the *ice cold* champagne over the cut fruit. Gently mix in the blended raspberries. Makes 6 servings.

Carrie Hamburg

Mrs. Dan Hamburg, Wife of Representative (California)

SALSA

Tomato Salsa:

- 3 medium ripe tomatoes, chopped
- 2 green onions, finely sliced
- 1 tablespoon balsamic vinegar
- 1 teaspoon olive oil
- ½ teaspoon salt
- ¼ teaspoon pepper
- ¼ cup chopped fresh coriander

Prepare tomato salsa: mix together ingredients. Let set at least 6 hours. Take out 1 hour before serving. Serve with tortilla chips. Makes 4 servings.

Mrs. Daniel Donovan, Daughter of Representative Al Swift (Washington)

GAZPACHO

- 6 large ripe tomatoes
- 2 sweet red peppers
- 2 medium-size yellow onions
- 2 large shallots
- 2 large cucumbers
- ½ cup red wine vinegar
- ½ cup olive oil
- 1½ cups canned tomato juice
- 3 eggs, lightly beaten
  Pinch of cayenne pepper
  Salt and freshly ground black pepper
- ½ cup chopped fresh dill
- 2 teaspoons minced garlic

Core and coarsely chop tomatoes; save the juice. Core, seed and coarsely chop peppers. Peel and coarsely chop onions and shallots. Peel, seed and coarsely chop cucumbers. In a bowl, whisk together vinegar, olive oil, reserved tomato juice, canned tomato juice and eggs. In a blender or food processor fitted with steel blades, puree the vegetables in small batches, adding tomato juice mixture as necessary to keep blades from clogging. Do not puree completely; the gazpacho should retain some of its crunch. Stir in cayenne, salt and pepper to taste, dill and garlic. Cover and chill at least 4 hours. To serve, stir, taste and correct seasonings, and ladle into chilled bowls or mugs. Garnish with crisp fresh scallion. Makes 8-10 servings.

Mrs. Bob Filner, Wife of Representative (California)

JICAMA-CITRUS SALAD

2 bunches red leaf lettuce, torn
3 to 4 peeled and sectioned oranges
1 large jicama, peeled and cubed
1 small red onion, sliced in rings
oil and vinegar dressing

Combine all ingredients in large glass salad bowl and toss with dressing. Makes 12 servings.

Betty Chapman

Mrs. Jim Chapman, Wife of Representative (Texas)

MEXICAN QUICHE

⅔ pound sausage
4 tart shells, baked
4 ounces canned green chiles
4 eggs, lightly beaten
1⅓ cups milk
⅓ cup grated Swiss cheese
¼ cup grated Parmesan cheese
¼ teaspoon salt
Dash of pepper

Crumble and brown the sausage until well browned. Drain well. Line shells with chiles and sausage. Combine eggs, milk, cheeses and seasonings; pour over sausage. Bake at 350°F for 20 to 30 minutes until golden brown and custard is set half-way between edge and center. Let stand for 5 minutes to finish setting before serving. Makes 4 servings.

Tyler Lott

Miss Tyler Lott, Daughter of Senator Trent Lott (Mississippi)

BREAKFAST CASSEROLE

2 pounds sausage
1 can chopped chili
1 pound Monterey Jack
   cheese
8 eggs
½ teaspoon salt
½ teaspoon pepper

Fry, drain, and put 16 sausage patties into a 13 × 9 × 2 pan. Layer chili and Monterey Jack over sausage. Cover with foil and refrigerate over night. (Or make days ahead of time and freeze.) When ready to serve, pour beaten eggs, salt and pepper over top of sausage, chili and cheese. Bake until eggs are set—approximately 45 minutes. Serve with fruit, bread and jelly. Makes 8 servings. Oven temperature 350°F—preheated.

Mrs. Joe Skeen, Wife of Representative (New Mexico)

MEXICAN CORN BREAD

2 eggs
⅔ cup cooking oil
1 cup sour cream
1 cup yellow cornmeal
1 cup yellow creamed corn
1 tablespoon baking powder
1½ tablespoons salt
4 jalapeno peppers, seeded
   and finely chopped
1 cup grated sharp cheese

Combine eggs, oil, sour cream, cornmeal, corn, baking powder and salt. Add chopped peppers and half of the cheese. Spread in well-greased baking pan (12″ × 8″ × 2″) and cover with remaining cheese. Bake at 425° for 20–25 minutes. Makes 8–10 servings.

Mrs. Lloyd Bentsen, Wife of Secretary of the Treasury

GOVERNOR'S MANSION BISCOCHITOS

2 cups Morrell lard
1 cup sugar
3 eggs
3 teaspoons baking powder
½ teaspoon salt
1 teaspoon vanilla
¼ cup orange juice
5 cups flour

Cream lard, sugar and eggs.
Add vanilla and orange juice. Then mix in baking powder, salt and flour.

Can be put in refrigerator over night or made right away. Can be made with cookie cutter or with pastry gun. If made with gun dip them in sugar and cinnamon after they are baked. If cut with cookie cutters dip them before baking. Bake at 400 degrees for 12 to 15 minutes.

Bruce King, Governor (New Mexico)

PECAN PRALINES

2 cups brown sugar
1 cup white sugar
¾ can condensed milk
  (not evaporated)
½ cup water
2 teaspoons white corn
  syrup
  pinch of soda
15 large marshmallows
1 quart small to medium
  pecan halves

Mix all ingredients except pecans and marshmallows. Bring to a boil and cook until soft ball stage (235°F), stirring constantly. Remove from heat, add marshmallows. Return to heat and cook until soft ball stage again. Remove from heat, add pecans, and beat until mixture thickens. Spoon out quickly onto waxed paper and let set until firm. Yield: 36 pralines.

Mrs. John Breaux, Wife of Senator (Louisiana)

SOUTHERN THANKSGIVING DINNER

Roast Turkey (Traditional)
or Deep Fried Turkey

Mother's Cornbread Dressing
Giblet Gravy

Southern Sweet Potato Ring
Green Beans in Tomato Vinaigrette
Mom's White Salad

Grandpa Yacobi's Pickled Pumpkin
Fresh Cranberry Relish

Catherine's Applespice Muffins
Grandma's Dinner Rolls

Georgia Pecan Pie
Pumpkin Chiffon Pie

SOUTHERN THANKSGIVING DINNER

Thanksgiving . . . a time for reflection about all that is good in this life. A time for southern hospitality to express its abundance, generosity and warmth. A time for grateful hearts to gather and enjoy the fruits of a blessed, productive land on an especially American day.

When decorating your home and table, the rich, warm colors of fall mums and gourds reflect the spirit of the occasion which abounds with tradition.

As family and friends relax and indulge, some recipes which include fresh surprises to the otherwise familiar can add interest. A few are offered here . . .

CAJUN DEEP FRIED TURKEY

4 oz. liquid garlic
4 oz. liquid onion
4 oz. liquid celery
1 tablespoon red pepper
2 tablespoons salt
2 tablespoons Tabasco
1 oz. liquid crab boil or 1
    tablespoon Old Bay
    Seasoning
1 poultry or meat injector
  one defrosted 10-12
    pound turkey
5 gallons peanut oil

Saute first seven ingredients until salt and pepper are dissolved. Fill injector and inject turkey at breast, wings, drumsticks, thighs and back.

Allow to marinate 24 hours in refrigerator or ice chest.

Use a 10 gallon pot for frying.

Bring peanut oil to 350 degree temperature and fry turkey for 38-42 minutes. Turkey should float to surface after 35 minutes and you should cook an additional 5-7 minutes.

***You may want to tie turkey legs with ½" cotton ropes to be able to remove from frying pot when done.

Cooking of fried turkey should be done outdoors. Extreme caution should be taken when placing cold turkey into hot oil.

Lois Breaux

Mrs. John Breaux, Wife of Senator (Louisiana)

MOTHER'S CORNBREAD DRESSING AND GIBLET GRAVY

Dressing:

- 2 cups homemade chicken or turkey broth
- 3 tablespoons butter or margarine
- 12 cups crumbled cornbread (bake 4 packets of cornbread mix)
- 6 cups torn toast (may use biscuits)
- 3 cups chopped celery
- 1 cup onion, chopped
- 1 teaspoon sage
- 1½ teaspoons poultry seasoning
- 2 cans chicken broth (in addition to homemade broth)
- 2 eggs slightly beaten
  salt and pepper to taste

Gravy:

- 2 cups broth reserved from cooking giblets
- 2 tablespoons flour mixed with ¼ cup water
- 2 boiled eggs
  salt and pepper to taste

The day before: Make homemade broth by boiling turkey or chicken breasts . (I use the cooked poultry in a casserole at a later date.) Also, the day before, cook 4 packets of cornbread according to packet directions.

To prepare dressing: Sauté onions and celery in a little broth and butter. In a very large mixing bowl combine the onions and celery, 12 cups crumbled cornbread, 6 cups torn toast, sage, poultry seasoning, canned chicken broth, the remainder of the freshly cooked broth, 2 slightly beaten eggs and salt and pepper to taste. (You may add extra hot water to be sure the mixture is moist, but it should hold its shape in the bowl.) Place in 2 large casserole dishes. (Some may be placed in the turkey cavity, but we prefer ours cooked separately.) You may make the mixture the night before serving and keep in the refrigerator before baking the next day. Bake at 350° for 45 minutes or until lightly browned.

To prepare gravy: Place giblets in saucepan, cover with water and boil for 2 hours. Remove giblets from broth and chop. To boiling broth, add the flour and water mixture. Continue boiling, stirring constantly, until sauce thickens to desired consistency. Add 2 chopped, boiled eggs, chopped giblets and salt and pepper to taste. Serve in gravy bowl with turkey and dressing.

Betty Chapman

Mrs. Jim Chapman, Wife of Representative (Texas)

SOUTHERN SWEET POTATO RING

8 medium sweet potatoes or
   1 large can
9 tablespoons butter
   (softened)
½ cup light brown sugar
1 5-ounce can evaporated
   milk
1 teaspoon nutmeg
1 teaspoon cinnamon
1 teaspoon vanilla
1 egg
½ cup dark brown sugar
1½ cups pecan halves

Bake sweet potatoes, remove peeling. In a large bowl, mash potatoes with a fork or put in food processor. Add butter, light brown sugar, milk, nutmeg, cinnamon, vanilla and egg. Mix well. Generously spray a bundt pan with cooking spray or butter. Sprinkle dark brown sugar in bottom of pan, follow with pecan halves, then spoon in the sweet potato mixture. Bake at 350° for 1 hour. Let cool 15 minutes before removing from the mold. Great for the holidays! Makes 8-10 servings.

Mrs. John Breaux, Wife of Senator (Louisiana)

STEAMED GREEN BEANS IN TOMATO VINAIGRETTE

3 pounds green beans,
   trimmed
⅓ cup olive oil
1 medium onion, chopped
1 large garlic clove, finely
   chopped
3 plum tomatoes, seeded and
   coarsely chopped
4 bay leaves
1 teaspoon capers
1 tablespoon lemon juice
   salt and freshly ground
   black pepper

Steam the beans until just tender, but no longer crunchy, about 12 minutes. Plunge into cold water or ice to stop cooking process. Drain. Combine the oil, onion and garlic in a medium skillet and sauté over medium heat until the vegetables are transparent, about 5 minutes. Stir in the tomatoes, bay leaves, capers and lemon juice; bring to a simmer and cook 5 minutes longer. Season to taste with salt and pepper.
Pour the dressing over the green beans and toss. Cover and let stand for a few hours before serving. *Can be made up to 2 days in advance and refrigerated; return to room temperature before serving.* Serves 20.

Mrs. Martin Sabo, Wife of Representative (Minnesota)

MOM'S WHITE SALAD

2 eggs beaten
2 tablespoons sugar
2 tablespoons vinegar
1 tablespoon butter
¼ teaspoon salt
1 pint whipping cream, whipped
1 large can pears, cut into pieces
1 large can pineapple, diced
2 8-ounce cans white seedless grapes
¼ pound small marshmallows
6 maraschino cherries chopped (for color)

Combine eggs, sugar, vinegar, salt, butter and cook over low heat until thick. Remove from heat and let cool. Fold whipped cream into cooled mixture. Drain all fruit well. Fold fruit into mixture. Chill 24 hours. Makes 10 servings.

Nancy Beall

Mrs. J. Glenn Beall, Jr., Wife of former Senator (Maryland)

GRANDPA YACOBI'S PICKLED PUMPKIN

6 lbs pumpkin (weigh before preparing)
5 lbs sugar
2 cups white vinegar
2 tablespoons whole cloves
6 sticks cinnamon

Peel pumpkin and scrape away all seeds and stringy matter from the center. Cut into slices about ¼ inch thick and 1½ inches to 2 inches long. Cover with sugar and let stand overnight. Next morning add vinegar, cloves and cinnamon to sugared pumpkin and cook over medium heat until pumpkin is transparent and syrup is thick— about 1 to 1½ hours. Pour into sterilized pint jars (6). Pour remaining syrup over them and seal. Makes 6 pint jars.

Laura Hehner

Mrs. H. Dee Hehner, Daughter of Representative Herbert Bateman (Virginia)

FRESH CRANBERRY RELISH

2 12 ounce bags of fresh
   cranberries
1½ cup sugar
1 cup orange juice
1 tablespoon grated orange
   peel
1 teaspoon cinnamon
1 teaspoon ground ginger
1 cup golden raisins
1 cup water
1 cup coarsely chopped walnuts or pecans
½ cup finely chopped crystallized ginger (found in
   the oriental food section
   of your grocery store)

Combine first seven ingredients with water and boil for about 5 minutes, stirring occasionally until cranberries finish popping. Remove from heat. Mix in nuts and crystallized ginger. Serve while warm or pour into clean jar and store in refrigerator until used. Will keep up to 30 days. May be frozen in plastic container. Makes 10 servings.

Mrs. David S. King, Wife of former Representative (Utah)

CATHERINE'S APPLESPICE MUFFINS

1 cup or 2 sticks soft
   margarine
2 cups sugar
2 eggs
4 cups plain flour
⅓ to 1 cup chopped pecans
3 teaspoons cinnamon
3 cups hot applesauce
2 teaspoons allspice
1 teaspoon cloves
2 teaspoons soda

Cream sugar and margarine. Add eggs and flour. Mix well then add other ingredients. Bake in small greased muffin tins at 350° for 12 minutes or until muffins spring back at center. Batter can be refrigerated for up to two weeks. Muffins can be frozen. Makes 84 muffins.

Mrs. Trent Lott, Wife of Senator (Mississippi)

GRANDMA'S DINNER ROLLS

1 cup milk, scalded
2 tablespoons sugar
1 teaspoon salt
2 tablespoons melted
    shortening
3 to 4 cups sifted flour
1 yeast cake or 1 package
    dry yeast, dissolved in
    ¼ cup warm water
2 eggs, beaten

To scalded milk, add sugar, salt and shortening. Cool to lukewarm. Add 1½ to 2 cups of the flour. Add dissolved yeast and beat until smooth. Add eggs and remaining flour, a small amount at a time until dough is moderately firm. Knead lightly, using as little flour as possible.

Place dough in a well-greased bowl. Cover and place in a warm spot and allow to rise until doubled, about 1 to 2 hours.

Shape into rolls. Place in well-greased muffin tins. Cover again and allow to rise until double, about 40 minutes. Brush tops with melted butter. Bake at 450° for 10 minutes or until brown. Makes 1–2 dozen rolls.

Mrs. Jay Rhodes, Wife of former Representative (Arizona)

GEORGIA PECAN PIE

½ cup granulated sugar
1 cup white corn syrup
3 eggs
4 tablespoons margarine
    dash salt
1 tablespoon vanilla extract
1 cup broken pecan meats
    unbaked 9-inch piecrust

Cook sugar and syrup until it thickens. Beat eggs; slowly add hot syrup to eggs, beating constantly. Add margarine, salt, vanilla and pecans and pour into unbaked piecrust. Bake in a preheated 450° oven for 10 minutes. Lower temperature to 300°; bake 35 minutes.

Zell Miller, Governor (Georgia)

PUMPKIN CHIFFON PIE

½ cup brown sugar
2 envelopes gelatin
½ teaspoon salt
½ teaspoon cinnamon
¼ teaspoon nutmeg
¼ teaspoon ginger
1 cup milk
4 eggs, separated
1¼ cups canned pumpkins
⅓ cup rum
½ cup sugar
9 inch gingersnap pie crust
(recipe below)
½ cup coconut flakes

Pie Crust:
½ pound gingersnaps
¼ cup butter, melted

Thoroughly mix brown sugar, gelatin, salt and spices in a saucepan. Stir in milk, egg yolks and pumpkin. Cook, stirring frequently, over low heat for 10 minutes or until the gelatin is completely dissolved. Let it cool, then stir in the rum. Chill in the refrigerator until the mixture thickens enough to mound slightly when dropped from a spoon. It must be about the consistency of mayonnaise. Beat egg whites until stiff. Beat in the sugar, a little at a time, then continue beating until smooth. Fold the egg whites into the pumpkin mixture, ladle into the prepared crust and *chill until firm at least two hours.* Meanwhile toast the coconut flakes. Spread them on a baking sheet and brown them in a 350° oven for five to 10 minutes. To serve, sprinkle toasted coconut over pie.

Gingersnap Crust:
Make crumbs of the gingersnaps by whirling them in a blender a few at a time, or by crushing them with a rolling pin. Measure out the crumbs— there may be some left over. Mix the crumbs with the butter in a nine-inch pie plate, using your fingers to blend thoroughly. Press and pat the mixture firmly to make a smooth coating on the bottom and around the sides of the pie plate.

Mrs. Dan Donovan, Daughter of Representative Al Swift (Washington)

4TH OF JULY

Fried Chicken

Louise's Best Ever Bar-B-Q Brisket

Ben's Baked Beans

New Potato Salad in Red Onion Dressing

4 Bean Salad

Mom's Pickled Beets

Crusty White Braided Bread

Billie's Peach Ice Cream

Triple Chocolate Cake

4TH OF JULY

Whether your Independence Day celebration occurs at the beach, the park, the urban roof top, or on a boat, the traditional All-American menu can be presented in gala fashion.

Red, white and blue, stars and stripes forever can embellish the most casual or elegant of presentations.

This is a time for fun with flags and flowers, paper and fabric. Cover your table with bunting or ticking. Red, white and/or blue pots or pails can be sand-filled flag holders. Small flags with wood or plastic stems can be mounted to "fly" over your potato salad or anywhere you choose. A watermelon can serve as a "vase" by cutting the ends, setting the melon upright and "planting" sunflowers, or red, white and blue bachelor buttons, delphinium, larkspur or pansies. Ribbons and bows with stars or stripes can complete your centerpiece. The 4th of July—"sky is the limit"—do whatever appeals to your festive fancy!

FRIED CHICKEN

6–8 pieces chicken
    milk
    flour
    salt and pepper
2 cups vegetable oil

Dip chicken in milk and roll in salt and pepper flavored flour. Chicken should stand for one hour. Heat vegetable oil in frying pan. Add the chicken and brown until golden on all sides. Place on rack in broiling pan to keep chicken from getting soggy. Cover.

Bake at 375° for ½ hour. Makes 4 servings.

Mrs. Jimmy Hayes, Wife of Representative (Louisiana)

LOUISE'S BEST EVER BAR-B-Q BRISKET

1 large beef brisket
⅓ bottle of liquid smoke
    garlic salt and freshly
      ground pepper to taste
1 large can tomato sauce
1 generous cup brown sugar
    juice of ½ lemon
    Worchestershire sauce to
      taste

Place brisket in heavy foil lined roasting pan, fat side up, with foil long enough to close over top. Pour ⅓ bottle of liquid smoke over meat. Add a little water to pan, sprinkle with garlic salt and grind fresh pepper over top. Bake, covered with foil, at 300° to 325° for 2 hours.

After the two hours, remove roasting pan, open foil and pour tomato sauce over meat. Sprinkle with the brown sugar and juice of the lemon. Add Worchestershire sauce and continue roasting uncovered until tender (time depends on size of the brisket). This can be cooked the day before, refrigerated, sliced, covered with the sauce and reheated in foil covered pan. Makes 8-10 servings.

Mrs. John W. Bryant, Wife of Representative (Texas)

BEN'S BAKED BEANS

3 pounds Italian sausage
2 large onions, chopped
3 large cans pork & beans, drained
2 teaspoons liquid smoke
3 12-ounce bottles of chili sauce
  32-ounce jar of molasses (use ⅔ of it)
4 teaspoons horseradish
3 teaspoons prepared mustard
2 large green peppers, cut into rings

Cut up the sausage into small chunks and cook until brown. Remove from pan and add chopped onion. Cook onion until transparent. Mix sausage and onion with remaining ingredients with the exception of green pepper rings. Pour mixture into a 3-quart casserole dish. Arrange green pepper rings on top. Bake at 350° for 1½ hours. Makes 20 servings.

E. Benjamin Nelson, Governor (Nebraska)

NEW POTATO SALAD IN RED ONION DRESSING

2 lbs. new small potatoes
  salt
  fresh ground black pepper
¾ cup mayonnaise
¾ cup yogurt or sour cream
½ cup chopped sweet red onion
½ cup minced fresh dill or parsley
  fresh dill or parsley sprigs to garnish
  optional: 1 cup cooked fresh peas

Cook clean potatoes. In a large bowl cut potatoes into quarters or slices. Season to taste with salt and pepper. Cool slightly.

In a separate bowl, combine remaining ingredients. Blend well. Pour over warm potatoes. Toss gently. Garnish with herb sprigs. Serve at room temperature or chilled. For a dash of color, add 1 cup cooked fresh peas. Makes 6 servings.

Mrs. Dale Kildee, Wife of Representative (Michigan)

BEAN SALAD

This is a very easy recipe, popular in New Jersey for picnics and barbeques.

Drain and mix together:
1 can (15 oz.) yellow
    wax beans
1 can (15 oz.) red kidney
    beans
1 can (15 oz.) cut green
    beans
1 can (15 oz.) chick peas

Add:
1 onion, chopped
1 green pepper, chopped
1 red pepper, chopped

Mix and pour over bean mixture:
½ cup vegetable oil
½ cup sugar
⅔ cup vinegar (wine or
    balsamic)
½ teaspoon Worchestershire
    salt and pepper

Allow to marinate in refrigerator a day or more, mixing occasionally. Drain and serve. Makes a lot.

Jacqueline Klein

Mrs. Herbert C. Klein, Wife of Representative (New Jersey)

MOM'S PICKLED BEETS

12 cloves
12 all spice
2 dashes cinnamon
4 tablespoons sugar
1/2 cup apple cider vinegar
1/4 cup water
1 large can beets, drained

Combine the first six ingredients and boil for several minutes. Put drained beets in jar and pour hot liquid over beets. Cool and then refrigerate. Please note that this is very spicy and can be made milder by decreasing the amounts of spices. Makes 10-12 servings.

David L. Hobson, Representative (Ohio)

CRUSTY WHITE BRAIDED BREAD

4 to 4 1/2 cups unbleached flour
2 pkgs. dry yeast
2 cups warm water
1/2 cup cooking oil
2 tablespoons sugar
1 tablespoon salt

In large mixing bowl, combine 2 cups unbleached flour and the yeast. Add water, oil, sugar and salt to dry mixture. Beat at low speed with an electric mixer 1/2 minute until moistened. Beat 3 minutes. on high. By hand, stir in enough of the remaining mixture to make a moderately stiff dough. Turn out onto a lightly floured surface and knead until smooth and elastic, about 8-10 minutes.
Shape dough into a ball. Place dough into a greased bowl, turning once to grease surface. Cover. Let rise until doubled in size—about 1 to 1 1/2 hrs.
Punch dough down. Shape into 6 equal sized balls. Let rest 10 minutes (covered). Roll each ball into a 16 inch rope. Line up 3 ropes and braid loosely, beginning in the middle. Repeat with other 3 ropes. Place both loaves on lightly greased cookie sheet. Let rise until double—30-45 minutes.
Bake at 375°F. for 30 minutes until golden brown. Makes 2 loaves.

Mrs. Terry Bruce, Wife of former Representative (Illinois)

BILLIE'S PEACH ICE CREAM

1 pint whipping cream
2 quarts milk
2 cans Eagle Brand condensed milk
½ cup sugar
1 tablespoon vanilla
5-8 very ripe peaches sweetened with sugar

Peel and partially mash peaches with sugar to sweeten. This may be done in a blender or with potato masher.

In ice cream freezer, put cream, condensed milk, sugar and vanilla. Add sweetened peaches and fill to the line of freezer with the milk. This is good eaten right after freezing but the flavors tend to blend if it sits for a while.

John W. Bryant, Representative (Texas)

TRIPLE CHOCOLATE CAKE

cocoa
1 (18½ oz.) deep chocolate cake mix
1 (4 oz.) instant chocolate pudding mix
¾ cup sour cream
½ cup vegetable oil
½ cup water
½ cup toasted chopped slivered almonds
¼ cup mayonnaise
4 eggs
3 tablespoons almond liqueur
1 teaspoon almond extract
1 cup chocolate chips

Preheat oven to 350°. Grease 10 inch bundt pan; dust with cocoa. Place all ingredients except chocolate chips in large bowl. Stir to dust almonds. Beat 2 minutes with electric mixer, medium speed. Fold in chocolate chips. Pour batter into prepared pan. Bake 50-55 minutes. Cool on rack 10 minutes before removing from pan. Place warm cake on cake plate and drizzle with glaze. Makes 12 servings.

Glaze:
1 cup powdered sugar
3 tablespoons milk
1 teaspoon almond extract

Mix all ingredients thoroughly in small bowl. Let stand at room temperature until ready to glaze cake.

Mrs. Ike Skelton, Wife of Representative (Missouri)

COCKTAIL BUFFET

Skewered Tortellini with Basil-Ginger
Dressing

Miniature Tenderloin Crescents

Festive Party Meatballs

Sesame Chicken Fingers with
Roasted Garlic Mayonnaise

Smoked Chicken Salad with Basil
Parmesan Mayonnaise

Stone Crab Claws with Four Pepper
Dipping Sauce

Chicken-Pistachio Paté

Puff Pastry Straws

Baked Brie

Crudite Basket served with fresh Herb Dip

Cocktail Buffet

Members of the Congressional Club often use the elegant ballroom of the historic Congressional Club to introduce newly engaged family members to their friends and family.

In honor of this formal occasion a beautiful, antique, Italian, lace banquet cloth covers the buffet table.

Centering the table, is an ornate silver and crystal epergne filled with multi colored peonies and slender tapers. The table is set with china, silver and linen napkins.

Waiters circulate with an assortment of beverages and canapés on silver trays.

SKEWERED TORTELLINI WITH BASIL-GINGER DRESSING

2 cups light sesame oil
2 cups white wine vinegar
2 cups chopped sun-dried
    tomatoes
2 teaspoons dried red
    pepper flakes
4 tablespoons ginger root,
    chopped
1 cup fresh basil, chopped
8 pounds cheese/meat filled
    fresh or frozen tortellini

In a large bowl, combine first 6 ingredients and whisk. Cook tortellini until al dente; drain. Toss tortellini in marinade. Cover, refrigerate and let marinate from 2-6 hours (no longer or it may become soggy). Two hours before serving, skewer 2 tortelini onto bamboo skewers. Serve at room temperature. Makes 100 servings

Hints for serving: Use alternating colored tortellini for a nicer presentation. Serve on wicker trays lined with green leaf.

The Congressional Club

MINIATURE TENDERLOIN CRESCENTS

3 whole beef tenderloins
    salt and pepper to taste
3 tablespoons rosemary

for Horseradish Cream:
1 jar horseradish
2 cups whipping cream
300 Congressional Club
    crescent rolls

Season tenderloin with salt and pepper. Sprinkle 1 tablespoon of rosemary on to each tenderloin. Bake uncovered for 30 minutes at 425°. Sprinkle with water, reduce temperature to 350° and bake an additional 60 minutes. Let stand to room temperature. Beat horseradish with the whipping cream. Place in refrigerator for 3 hours. Slice tenderloin to 1/4 inch thickness. Slice crescents horizontally and place on each a piece of the tenderloin along with 1/2 teaspoon of the horseradish sauce. Makes 100 servings

Hints for serving: Stack filled crescents on a wicker tray lined with redleaf lettuce.

The Congressional Club

FESTIVE PARTY MEATBALLS

14 pounds ground beef
5 bunches green onion,
    finely chopped
4½ fresh soft bread crumbs
9 eggs
9 tablespoons paprika
1 large bunch fresh dill;
    snipped
3 tablespoons dry mustard
    salt and fresh ground
    pepper
for sauce:
4½ sticks butter
13½ cups beef stock or broth
54 ounces tomato paste
¾ cups Worchestershire
    sauce
5 pounds sour cream
    fresh dill, snipped

Mix first 8 ingredients together. Roll mixture into 1 inch balls and place on broiler pan. Broil meatballs directly under heat for 5 minutes or until brown. Turn balls over and cook an additional 2-3 minutes. Melt butter in saucepan. Add beef stock, tomato paste and Worchestershire sauce, bring to a boil. Remove from heat and add sour cream. Prior to serving add meatballs to sauce and heat. Makes 100 servings

Hints for serving: Place meatballs in a chafing dish and garnish with fresh snipped dill. Place a decorative glass, filled with colored frilly toothpicks, next to the chafing dish to eliminate the need for forks.

The Congressional Club

SESAME CHICKEN FINGERS WITH ROASTED GARLIC MAYONNAISE

25 chicken breasts, skinned and boned
¾ cup light soy sauce
¾ cup dry white wine
¾ cup light sesame or peanut oil
2½ tablespoons ginger root; finely chopped
3 large garlic cloves, finely chopped
2½ teaspoons salt
1¼ cup sesame seeds; mix black and white seeds for nicer presentation
for mayonnaise:
3 large heads of garlic
3 cups mayonnaise
3 teaspoons lemon juice

Pound each chicken breast to flatten. Cut the chicken diagonally into "fingers" approx. ½ inch wide by 2½-3 inches long. In a shallow dish mix together the soy, wine, oil, gingerroot, garlic and salt. Add the chicken, toss, cover and refrigerate overnight, turning twice. Preheat the broiler, lightly grease a large baking sheet. Spread the sesame seeds out in a large bowl. Toss the chicken in the seeds until lightly coated. Repeat until all the chicken is used. Broil approx. 10 minutes, turning once, until lightly browned and cooked through, serve immediately.

Hint: For a large crowd make hors d'oeuvres in advance, cover tightly and refrigerate. Heat in a moderate oven and let cool to room temperature before serving.

For Mayonnaise:

Heat oven to 375°. Peel away outer layers of garlic while keeping head intact. Wrap in foil and roast 1 hour and 15 minutes. Allow to cool. Separate garlic heads and squeeze clove into a sieve placed over a bowl. Discard skin. With the back of a spoon, press the garlic through the sieve into the bowl. Add the mayonnaise and the lemon juice and whisk, may be stored in refrigerator for up to 3 weeks. Makes 100 servings

Hints for Serving: Serve chicken on a serving tray lined with red leaf lettuce. Carve out the center of a purple cabbage and use it to hold the sauce; place in the center of the tray.

The Congressional Club

SMOKED CHICKEN SALAD WITH BASIL-PARMESAN MAYONNAISE

15 smoked chicken breasts cut into julienne
1 pound prosciutto cut julienne
2 pounds Gruyer cheese cut julienne
2 jars sun-dried tomatoes (packed in oil) drained and cut julienne
3 bunches scallion (whites only) cut julienne
1½ pounds mushrooms, sliced
4½ cups olive oil
2 cups fresh lemon juice
10 egg yolks
1¾ cups Parmesan cheese
1 cup fresh basil
¼ cup grainy Dijon style mustard
5 cups vegetable oil

Combine the chicken, prosciuto, Gruyer, tomatoes, scallions and mushrooms. Toss with olive oil and ¾ cup of the lemon juice. Process the egg yolks, Parmesan, basil, mustard and remaining lemon juice in a food processor fitted with a steel blade for 30 seconds. With the machine running, pour in the olive oil and then the vegetable oil in a thin steady stream through the feed tube to make a thick mayonnaise. Season with salt and pepper. Toss chicken with mayonnaise mixture. Makes 100 servings

Hints for serving: Serve small amounts of the salad on the tips of the Belgin endive. Place the filled tips on an alfalfa sprout lined round serving tray; place a flower that is in full bloom in the center of the tray.

The Congressional Club

STONE CRAB CLAWS WITH FOUR PEPPER DIPPING SAUCE

300 stone crab claws; can be purchased fully cooked and frozen.

for sauce:

6 red peppers, seeded and finely chopped

6 yellow peppers, seeded and finely chopped

6 long green chili peppers, seeded and finely chopped

7 jalapeno peppers, seeded and finely chopped

1½ cups wine vinegar

2¼ cups olive oil

salt and fresh ground pepper

3 cups cilantro, finely chopped

3 cups Italian parsley, finely chopped

Combine all ingredients for sauce, cover and refrigerate 1-2 hours. Thaw and crack claws with a nut cracker or hammer. Peel away most of the shell but leave the bottom tips intact. Makes 100 servings

Hints for serving: Place crab claws in a silver punch bowl filled with crushed ice. Pour sauce in a colorful bowl and place in the center of the claws. Garnish with lemon twists.

The Congressional Club

CHICKEN-PISTACHIO PATÉ

4 cups chicken livers
2 cups water
4 cups + 10 tablespoons
    butter or margarine
3 large onions, chopped
6 garlic cloves, chopped
1 cup cognac
1 cup whipping cream
5 cups pistachio nuts,
    chopped slightly
warm toast points

Clean livers of all dark spots and veins; pat dry. Bring pot of water to a boil, add livers, reduce heat and simmer 5 minutes. Drain and set aside. Melt 2 cups of butter in a skillet over medium/low heat. Sauté garlic and onions till tender. Add livers, stirring until cooked through. Remove from heat and cool 10 minutes. In a food processor fitted with a metal blade, process until smooth. Melt 2 cups of butter, add to pureed liver mixture with cognac and cream. Process until blended. Stir in 2 cups of pistachios. Pour into two-1½ quart souffle dishes, refrigerate until cold. Sprinkle remaining pistachios on top. Refrigerate until ready to use. Makes 100 servings

Hints for serving: Place souffle dish in the center of a silver tray, surround with warm toast points. Garnish pate with tomato rose and fresh parsley sprigs.

The Congressional Club

PUFF PASTRY STRAWS

5 puff pastry dough sheets;
   can be purchased from
   the frozen section
4 eggs, lightly beaten
4 teaspoons water
2 pounds Parmesan cheese

Add the water to the eggs and beat. Brush egg over the tops of each sheet of puff pastry. Sprinkle with Parmesan. Fold pastry sheet in half. Cut each sheet vertically into 8 equal strips, then cut horizontally into 5 equal strips. Brush tops with egg and sprinkle with the remaining Parmesan. Pull each strip to approximately 4-5 inches while twisting at the same time. Place on a parchment lined cookie sheet. Bake for 8-10 minutes or until golden brown. Wrap well if straws are to be frozen. Can be frozen for up to 1 month. Makes 100 servings

Hints for serving: Line a wicker basket with pretty linen napkins and place the straws vertically in the basket.

The Congressional Club

BAKED BRIE

2 whole wheels of Brie
   cheese (2.5 pounds
   each)
4 tablespoons butter or margarine
½ cup brown sugar
¾ cup sliced almonds, toasted
8 boxes Bremner Wafers

Slice Brie horizontally with a warm knife. Spread a thin layer of butter or margarine over the inside half. Sprinkle with brown sugar and almonds. Bake at 350° for 10-15 minutes or until cheese is soft. Serve warm with Bremner Wafers. Makes 100 servings.

Hints for serving: Place brie in the center of a silver tray, surround with fresh grapes. Place the Bremners in a wicker, linen lined basket.

The Congressional Club

CRUDITE BASKET SERVED WITH FRESH HERB DIP

10 pounds fresh asparagus
    spears, medium
5 pounds carrots, cut into
    3½ inch strips
2 pounds zucchini, cut into
    3½ inch strips
4 pounds broccoli, flower
    only
2 pounds medium size
    mushrooms
4 cups black olives
1 whole red pepper
    kale leaves for garnish
1 package ranch dressing
    mix
2 cups sour cream

Cut asparagus to 3½ inches. Blanch in boiling water for 4 minutes, run under cold water to stop the cooking. Blanch the carrots for 5 minutes and the broccoli for 2 minutes. Line a wicker basket with kale leaves and arrange the vegetables in an attractive way. Mix together the ranch mix and sour cream, refrigerate overnight. Core a red pepper and pour the dip into it, place in the center of the vegetable basket. Makes 100 servings.

The Congressional Club

NOTES

NOTES

Special Friends

Special Friends

The members of The Congressional Club wish to thank those organizations, companies and individuals listed on the following pages for their generosity and continued support.

SPECIAL SELECTIONS

GOLDEN CHEFS

Connell Company
Kraft General Foods
The NutraSweet Company
StarKist Seafood

GOLDEN CHEF

CONNELL
SPECIAL DINNER

Greek Salad

Baked Cornish Hen
Mom's Rice Dressing
Red Cabbage and Apples

Pineapple Delight

Connell Company

GOLDEN CHEF

GREEK SALAD

red leaf lettuce
curly Escarole
fresh spinach
cherry tomatoes
black olives
cucumbers, sliced
Spanish red onion, sliced
1 lb. crumbled Feta cheese

DRESSING

½ cup olive oil
¼ cup red wine vinegar
1 teaspoon oregano
1 teaspoon sugar
2 teaspoon Cavender's Greek
    seasoning

Connell Company

Mix lettuce, escarole, spinach, tomatoes, olives, and cucumbers. Spread onion and crumble Feta cheese over top. Mix dressing well and pour over salad.

BAKED CORNISH HEN

1 Cornish hen per person
¼ onion, peeled and chopped
½ stalk celery, chopped
    salt and pepper

Preheat the oven to 350°. Clean the inside of the hen and rub with salt and pepper. Add the onion and celery to the cavity. Place in roasting pan. Bake 20 minutes per pound. Baste with its own juices. Hen is done when leg moves up and down easily.

Connell Company

MOM'S RICE DRESSING MIX

1 lb. ground meat
3 tbsp. cooking oil
1 cup chopped onion
1 cup chopped celery
1 large chopped bell pepper
3 cups cooked rice
½ cup chopped green onion
    tops
½ cup chopped parsley
    salt and pepper to taste
1 cup water
2 tbsp. kitchen bouquet
    (optional)

Connell Company

Cook meat in oil in large pot until brown; add onions, celery, bell pepper. Reduce heat and cook until wilted. Add water and all other ingredients, except rice. Simmer for about 45 minutes; add more water if needed to keep about the same amount of juice started with. Add to cooked rice and keep warm until ready to serve. Serves 10 to 12.

RED CABBAGE AND APPLES

3 tablespoons bacon drip-
    pings
4 cups shredded red cabbage
2 cups cubed, unpeeled
    apples
¼ cup brown sugar
¼ cup vinegar
1¼ teaspoons salt
    pepper to taste
¼ cup water

In a large skillet, heat bacon drippings. Add the cabbage, apples, brown sugar, vinegar, salt and pepper. Add water and cover tightly to steam for 5 minutes. Simmer until cabbage and apples are crisp and tender.

Yield: 6 servings.

Connell Company

TROPICAL PINEAPPLE DELIGHT

1 package pie crust stick or
    1 frozen pie crust
1 8-ounce can crushed
    pineapple, drained
1 tablespoon flour
½ cup margarine, softened
1 8-ounce package cream
    cheese, softened
½ cup sugar
½ cup brown sugar
2 teaspoons vanilla
¼ teaspoon salt
¼ teaspoon cinnamon
¼ teaspoon nutmeg
3 eggs
1 cup whipping cream,
    whipped

Preheat oven to 350°. Make a 9-inch pie crust according to package directions. In a bowl, toss pineapple and flour. In another bowl, cream margarine and cream cheese. Slowly add sugars, continuing to beat until mixture is light and fluffy. Add vanilla, salt, cinnamon and nutmeg. Beat in eggs, one at a time. Fold in pineapple. Pour into pastry shell. Bake 40 minutes. Cool and serve with whipped cream.

Yield: 8 servings.

Connell Company

GOLDEN CHEF

SPECIAL CONGRESSIONAL CLUB DINNER

Creamy Rice and Broccoli Soup

Honey Mustard Chicken Appetizers
with Raspberry Marinated Onions

Dried Cherry Pork Tenderloin
with
Mango Barbecue Sauce

Swiss Asparagus Au Gratin

Philly 3-Step Tiramisu Cheesecake

Kraft USA • Kraft General Foods

CREAMY RICE AND BROCCOLI SOUP

1 small onion, chopped
1 tablespoon PARKAY Margarine
1 tablespoon flour
2 cups milk
1 cup water
2 cups BIRDS EYE Broccoli Cuts
2 chicken bouillon cubes
1/3 teaspoon dried thyme leaves
1/8 teaspoon garlic powder
1 cup MINUTE Original Rice Pepper

Cook and stir onion in margarine in skillet on medium heat until tender but not browned. Blend in flour. Add milk, water, broccoli, bouillon cubes, thyme and garlic powder. Bring to boil; reduce heat to low. Simmer 5 minutes. Stir in rice; simmer 5 minutes longer. Sprinkle with pepper. Serve immediately. Makes 4 to 6 servings.

Prep time: 10 minutes
Cooking time: 20 minutes

Kraft USA, Kraft General Foods

HONEY MUSTARD CHICKEN APPETIZERS WITH RASPBERRY MARINATED ONIONS

1/2 cup MIRACLE WHIP Salad Dressing
2 tablespoons Dijon mustard
2 tablespoons honey
2 tablespoons freshly squeezed lime juice
1 garlic clove, minced
1/8 teaspoon ground red pepper
4 boneless skinless chicken breast halves (about 1 1/4 pounds)
Raspberry Marinated Onions
28 Belgian endive leaves
1/2 cup chopped toasted macadamia nuts

Heat grill. Mix salad dressing, mustard, honey, juice, garlic and red pepper. Place chicken on grill over medium coals. Brush with half of the salad dressing mixture. Grill 4 to 6 minutes. Turn; brush with remaining salad dressing mixture. Continue grilling 4 to 6 minutes or until chicken is cooked through. Slice each chicken breast half into 6 to 8 (1/2-inch) strips. For each appetizer, place 1 tablespoon Raspberry Marinated Onions on 1 Belgian endive leaf. Top with chicken strip; sprinkle with macadamia nuts. Makes about 28.

Prep time: 20 minutes
Cooking time: 12 minutes

Kraft USA, Kraft General Foods

RASPBERRY MARINATED ONIONS

¼ cup raspberry vinegar
2 tablespoons chopped fresh
   Italian parsley
1 teaspoon sugar
⅛ teaspoon salt
½ cup olive oil
1 red onion, very thinly
   sliced

Mix vinegar, parlsey, sugar and salt in medium bowl. Gradually add oil, beating until smooth and well blended. Add onion to dressing mixture. Refrigerate 30 minutes; drain. Makes about 1 cup.

Kraft USA, Kraft General Foods

DRIED CHERRY PORK TENDERLOIN WITH MANGO BARBECUE SAUCE

½ cup KRAFT Original Barbecue Sauce
¼ cup freshly squeezed lime
   juice
1 tablespoon grated orange
   peel
1½ pounds pork tenderloin
1 cup finely chopped dried
   cherries
1 cup Italian seasoning
   Mango Barbecue Sauce

Heat oven to 425°F. Mix barbecue sauce, juice and peel; brush on meat. Mix cherries and seasoning; pat evenly over meat. Place meat on rack in baking pan. Insert meat thermometer into thickest part of meat. Roast 25 to 30 minutes or until meat thermometer registers 160°F. (Temperature will rise 5° to 10° during standing.) Serve with Mango Barbecue Sauce. Makes 6 servings.

Prep time: 20 minutes
Cooking time: 35 minutes

Kraft USA, Kraft General Foods

MANGO BARBECUE SAUCE

1 cup white vinegar
½ cup sugar
   Peel from 2 oranges
1 tablespoon minced peeled
   ginger root
1 tablespoon fresh thyme
   leaves
¾ cup freshly squeezed
   orange juice
¼ cup KRAFT Original Barbecue Sauce
1 mango, peeled, seeded,
   chopped

Boil vinegar and sugar in small saucepan. Stir in peel, ginger and thyme. Cook on medium heat until mixture is reduced by half. Strain, reserving sauce. Return sauce to small saucepan. Stir in remaining ingredients. Cook on medium heat until mixture is reduced by half. Cool. Place sauce in blender or food processor container fitted with steel blade; cover. Blend until smooth. Serve with Dried Cherry Pork Tenderloin. Makes ¾ cup.

Prep time: 10 minutes plus cooling
Cooking time: 20 minutes

Kraft USA, Kraft General Foods

SWISS ASPARAGUS AU GRATIN

½ cup water
1½ pounds asparagus spears, trimmed
½ cup (2 ounces) KRAFT Toppings Finely Shredded Natural Swiss Cheese
¼ cup dry bread crumbs
2 tablespoons (¼ stick) TOUCH OF BUTTER Spread, melted
½ teaspoon dry mustard
⅛ teaspoon pepper

Heat oven to 400°F. Bring water to boil in 10-inch skillet; add asparagus. Cook 2 minutes; drain. (Asparagus will still be crisp.) Place in 10 × 6-inch baking dish. Mix remaining ingredients; sprinkle over asparagus. Bake 8 to 10 minutes or until cheese mixture is lightly browned. Makes 4 servings.

MICROWAVE TIP: Place asparagus and ¼ cup water in 10 × 6-inch microwavable baking dish; cover. Microwave on HIGH 2 minutes; drain. (Asparagus will still be crisp.) Continue as directed.

Prep time: 10 minutes
Cooking time: 10 minutes

Kraft USA, Kraft General Foods

PHILLY® 3-STEP TIRAMISU CHEESECAKE

2 (8 oz.) pkgs. PHILADELPHIA BRAND Cream Cheese, softened
½ cup sugar
½ teaspoon vanilla
2 eggs
2 tablespoons brandy
12 ladyfingers, split
½ cup strong black coffee
1 cup thawed COOL WHIP Whipped Topping
1 square BAKER'S Semi-Sweet Chocolate, shaved

1. MIX cream cheese, sugar and vanilla with electric mixer on medium speed until well blended. Add eggs; mix until blended. Stir in brandy. Arrange ladyfingers on bottom and sides of 9-inch pie plate; drizzle with coffee.
2. POUR cream cheese mixture into prepared pie plate.
3. BAKE at 350°F, 40 minutes or until center is almost set. Cool. Refrigerate 3 hours or overnight. Top with whipped topping and shaved chocolate just before serving.

Makes 8 servings.

Our takeoff on a classic Italian treat.

Prep time: 10 minutes
Cooking time: 40 minutes

Kraft USA, Kraft General Foods

GOLDEN CHEF

HEALTHY OUTDOOR BARBECUE

Orange Lemonade

Steak with Papaya Salsa

Zucchini-Cauliflower Toss

Whole Wheat Breadsticks

Summer Fruit Tart

The Nutrasweet Company

ORANGE LEMONADE

1 cup freshly squeezed
   lemon juice (4 to 5
   lemons)
1 cup freshly squeezed
   orange juice (3 to 4
   oranges)
12 packets Equal® or 3½ teaspoons Equal® Measure™
3 cups water
   Ice cubes
   Lemon slices (optional)
   Mint sprigs (optional)

The NutraSweet Company

In a large pitcher combine juices and Equal®; stir to dissolve. Stir in water. Cover and chill. Serve over ice. Garnish each serving with a lemon slice and mint sprig, if desired. Makes 5 (8-ounce) servings.

Nutrition Information per serving: 44 calories, 1 g protein, 12 g carbohydrate, 0 g fat, 0 mg cholesterol, 5 mg sodium

Diabetic Food Exchanges: ½ Fruit

ZUCCHINI-CAULIFLOWER TOSS

½ cup water
¼ cup vinegar
1 tablespoon cornstarch
1 tablespoon olive oil or
   cooking oil
2 teaspoons prepared
   mustard
½ teaspoon garlic salt
¼ teaspoon celery seed
⅛ teaspoon pepper
2 packets Equal® or ¾ teaspoon Equal® Measure™
3 cups cauliflower slices
2 cups halved and thinly
   sliced zucchini
1 red sweet pepper, cut in
   thin strips
2 green onions, sliced

The NutraSweet Company

In a small saucepan combine water, vinegar, cornstarch, oil, mustard, garlic salt, celery seed and pepper. Cook and stir till thickened and bubbly. Cook and stir for 2 minutes more. Remove from heat; stir in Equal®. In large bowl combine vegetables; toss with dressing. Cover and chill 2 to 24 hours or till serving time, stirring occasionally. Makes 6 servings.

Nutrition Information per serving: 51 calories, 2 g protein, 7 g carbohydrate, 2 g fat, 0 mg cholesterol, 203 mg sodium

Diabetic Food Exchanges: 1 Vegetable, ½ Fat

STEAK WITH PAPAYA SALSA

1 medium papaya, peeled, seeded and chopped (2 cups)
1 medium cucumber, seeded and chopped (1½ cups)
½ cup chopped onion
¼ cup snipped cilantro
¼ cup cooking oil
¼ cup vinegar
2 packets Equal® or ¾ teaspoon Equal® Measure™
¼ teaspoon salt
¼ teaspoon pepper
½ cup reduced-calorie clear Italian salad dressing
2 tablespoons reduced-sodium soy sauce
½ teaspoon dry mustard
½ teaspoon lemon-pepper seasoning
1¼ to 1½-pound beef flank steak

To make salsa, in a bowl combine papaya, cucumber, onion and cilantro. In a small screw-top jar combine oil, vinegar, Equal®, salt and pepper; shake to mix well. Pour over papaya mixture; toss to coat. Cover and chill. Meanwhile, stir together salad dressing, soy sauce, mustard and lemon-pepper seasoning. Score steak on both sides, making shallow cuts at 1-inch intervals diagonally across meat in a diamond pattern. Place steak in a plastic bag set in a shallow dish; pour in dressing mixture. Close bag. Marinate in the refrigerator for 6 to 24 hours, turning the bag several times. Drain steak, reserving the marinade. Grill steak on an uncovered grill directly over medium coals for 12 to 14 minutes or till medium-rare, turning once and brushing frequently with reserved marinade during first 8 minutes. To serve, diagonally slice meat across the grain into very thin slices. Serve with salsa. Makes 6 servings.

Nutrition Information per serving: 273 calories, 19 g protein, 9 g carbohydrate, 18 g fat, 46 mg cholesterol, 535 mg sodium

Diabetic Food Exchanges: ½ Vegetable, ½ Fruit, 2½ Meat, 2 Fat

The NutraSweet Company

SUMMER FRUIT TART

1¼ cups all-purpose flour
¼ teaspoon salt
⅓ cup shortening
¼ cup plain nonfat yogurt
¼ cup reduced-fat dairy sour
  cream
¼ teaspoon almond extract
5 packets Equal® or 1½ teaspoons Equal® Measure™
4 cups fresh fruits
¾ cup pineapple juice
1 tablespoon lemon juice
2 teaspoons cornstarch

Combine flour and salt. Cut in shortening till well combined. Sprinkle 3–4 tablespoons cold water over mixture; toss with fork until moistened. Divide dough into 5 equal portions; roll each portion out into a ball. On a lightly floured surface roll each ball into a 5-inch circle. Ease pastry into 4½-inch tart pans with removable bottoms. Press pastry up sides; trim and remove excess. Prick bottom and sides with a fork. Line with foil. Bake in a 450° oven for 8 minutes. Remove foil. Bake till golden (5 to 6 minutes). Cool on wire rack. Combine yogurt, sour cream, almond extract and 2 packets Equal® or ½ teaspoon Equal® Measure™. Spread in cooled crust. Arrange fruits on top. In a small saucepan combine pineapple juice, lemon juice and cornstarch. Cook and stir till thickened and bubbly. Cook and stir 2 minutes more. Remove from heat; stir in 3 packets Equal® or 1 teaspoon Equal® Measure™. Cool. Spoon over fruit; cover and chill. Makes 10 servings. (Each individual tart serves two.)

Nutrition Information per serving: 166 calories, 3 g protein, 22 g carbohydrate, 8 g fat, 1 mg cholesterol, 65 mg sodium

Diabetic Food Exchanges: ½ Fruit, 1 Bread, 1½ Fat

The NutraSweet Company

STARKIST
CONGRESSIONAL
CLUB DINNER

Albacore Fettucine

"White" House Salad

Capitol-Hill Tomato Cups

White Chocolate Decadence

GOLDEN CHEF

STARKIST CONGRESSIONAL COOKBOOK RECIPES

This special menu was created around a centerpiece dish—Albacore Fettucini—which features the StarKist Seafood showpiece, solid white albacore tuna. Versatile and delicious, white albacore fillets make an appetizing low-fat alternative to other white meats. Appealing to the eye and tantalizing to the taste buds, this three-course meal will satisfy even the hungriest appetites.

ALBACORE FETTUCINE

4 cups broccoli florets or 10 oz. package frozen broccoli cuts
½ lb. fettucine
1 can 12½ oz. STARKIST SOLID WHITE ALBACORE in spring water, drained
1 cup part skim ricotta cheese
⅓ cup grated Parmesan cheese
½ cup low fat milk
½ tsp. garlic salt
½ tsp. dried Italian seasoning
salt and pepper to taste

StarKist

In a large pot of boiling water, cook broccoli until crisp-tender. Remove with a slotted spoon to serving bowl. Add fettucine to same pot of boiling water, and cook until tender. Drain and add to broccoli. Stir in StarKist Albacore. In same pot, combine remaining ingredients, stirring until sauce is smooth and heated through. Season to taste with salt and pepper. Pour sauce over pasta mixture and toss.

Yield: 4 very large servings

Recommended wine choice: Grgich Hills '92 Chardonnay

"WHITE" HOUSE SALAD

2 tbsp. fresh lemon juice
3 tbsp. fresh orange juice
1½ tsp. prepared dijon mustard
⅔ cup canola or safflower oil
½ tsp. grated fresh orange peel
12 medium white asparagus spears*
8 large red leaf or butter lettuce leaves
12 large belgian endive leaves (from outside of head)
1 small package (about 3 oz.) enoki mushrooms
12 orange zest strips

StarKist

Combine lemon and orange juice with mustard in small bowl. Slowly whisk in oil until emulsified. Stir in orange peel. Cover and chill. Trim asparagus, removing tough, woody stocks. Steam until barely crisp-tender. Plunge immediately in ice water chill. Pat dry. Arrange lettuce leaves on four salad plates. Place one asparagus spear on each endive leaf, trimming asparagus, as necessary. Divide mushrooms between plates, creating a cluster at base of each endive fan. Drizzle lightly with reserved dressing. Garnish with orange zest strips.

Yield: 4 servings

* Substitute one 12-ounce jar imported white asparagus spears, or use fresh green asparagus spears.

Recommended wine choice: Spottswoode '92 Sauvignon Blanc

CAPITOL-HILL TOMATO CUPS

4 large tomato cups
1 medium onion, chopped
1 tbsp. butter
3 cups fresh cauliflower
   florets
3 cups broccoli florets
3/4 cup lowfat sour cream
1/4 tsp. freshly grated nutmeg
1/8 tsp. white pepper
3 tbsp. freshly grated Parmesan cheese
4 tbsp. grated white cheddar
   or jack cheese
   salt to taste

Cut top 1/4 off each tomato, discard. Remove pulp, seeds and ribs with small spoon. Rinse thoroughly, invert on paper towels to drain. Sauté onion in butter until tender; set aside. Steam cauliflower and broccoli, separately, until tender. Plunge both in separate bowls of ice water. Place cauliflower, 1/2 of onion mixture, 1/2 of sour cream, nutmeg and salt in food processor or blender, process until smooth. Scrape into clean bowl; set aside. Repeat process with broccoli, remaining 1/2 of onion mixture, 1/2 of sour cream, white pepper, Parmesan and salt; set aside. Place tomato cups in microwave-safe dish. Divide broccoli puree evenly between cups. Top with cauliflower puree. Microwave on high 2 to 4 minutes, rotating once, until evenly heated. Sprinkle with grated cheddar, microwave on high 30 to 40 seconds, to melt cheese.

Yield: 4 servings

* Serve as an accompaniment to Albacore Fettucine

StarKist

WHITE CHOCOLATE DECADENCE

9-inch round chocolate cake base*
3 tbsp. seedless strawberry preserves, melted
1 pint whole strawberries, rinsed and hulled
1 recipe Strawberry Truffle filling
1 recipe White Chocolate Mousse
Recipes for Chocolate Cake Base, Strawberry Truffle Filling and White Chocolate Mousse follow.

StarKist

Cut top from cake layer so it is ¾-inch thick. Fit cake layer into 9-inch springform pan, pressing gently with hand to fit snugly. Brush lightly with preserves. Cut 10 to 12 uniform size strawberries in half vertically. Arrange, pointed end up, around circumference of pan, placing cut sizes firmly against inside of pan. Carefully pour Strawberry Truffle filling in pan, spreading evenly to touch base of strawberries, holding them in place. Chill until firm. Pour White Chocolate Mousse over truffle mixture, covering strawberries completely. Smooth top of mousse with broad spatula. Refrigerate in covered container for 4 to 6 hours, until set.

Yield: 12 to 16 servings

* Substitute one 9-inch round cake base made from packaged chocolate cake mix, if desired.

Recommended wine choice: Fonseca '77 Vintage Port

CHOCOLATE CAKE BASE

1¼ cup cake flour
1 cup granulated sugar
½ tsp. baking soda
½ tsp. baking powder
¼ tsp. salt
⅓ cup water
½ cup lowfat sour cream
1 tsp. vanilla
1 egg, lightly whisked
3 tbsp. unsalted butter, softened
3 oz. unsweetened chocolate, melted and cooled

StarKist

Grease and flour bottom of 9-inch round cake pan, tapping out excess flour. Combine dry ingredients in small bowl. Mix water, sour cream, vanilla and egg in large mixing bowl. Stir in butter and chocolate. Add dry ingredients and beat gently, on low speed of electric mixer, until just combined. Beat on high speed, scraping bowl frequently, for 3 minutes. Pour into prepared pan. Bake in preheated 350° oven 30 to 35 minutes, or until tester inserted in center comes out clean. Cool on wire rack.

STRAWBERRY TRUFFLE FILLING

¼ cup heavy cream
4 oz. bittersweet chocolate, finely chopped
2 tbsp. seedless strawberry preserves
¼ tsp. vanilla

Heat cream over medium low heat. Place chocolate in double boiler over hot, not simmering, water. Pour heated cream over chocolate, stirring gently until melted and smooth. Stir in strawberry preserves and vanilla. Cover and chill to thicken.

StarKist

WHITE CHOCOLATE MOUSSE

12 oz. white chocolate, finely chopped*
4 tbsp. water
1 tbsp. vanilla
2 cups heavy cream, chilled

Place chocolate, water and vanilla in double boiler over hot, not simmering, water. Stir constantly until chocolate is melted and smooth. (White chocolate is delicate, and burns easily. Do not increase heat.) Remove pan and cool to lukewarm (about 85°). Whip cream until soft (not stiff) peaks form. Carefully fold cream into chocolate mixture so that it is just barely combined. (Do not stir or cream will deflate. Mousse will appear soft, but sets quickly.) Use immediately.

* Use a high quality brand like Tobler, Lindt or Nestle's, made with cocoa butter. Do not use white compound, white coating or vanilla milk chips.

StarKist

SILVER CHEFS

Amway Corporation

Archer Daniels Midland Company

Catfish Farmers of America

CSX Corporation

Decorating Den Systems, Inc.

Fluor Corporation

Hecht's

Holland America Line Westours Inc.

m & m Mars

National Association of Broadcasters

Pacific Telesis

South Central Bell

T.G.I. Friday's

Uncle Ben's, Inc.

CHARRED VEAL T-BONE WITH MORELS, COGNAC AND GLAZED PEARL ONIONS

Winner—1992 Best Veal Entree in State of Michigan, Awarded by Michigan Veal Council

4 1 in. thick veal t-bone
    salt and white pepper, to
    taste
½ cup olive oil
16 pearl onions, peeled
16 morels, cleaned and
    trimmed
¼ cup cognac
1½ cups heavy cream
2 oz. veal brown sauce
1 teaspoon thyme, chopped

Season veal with oil, salt and white pepper. Grill to doneness desired. In a hot pan with remaining olive oil, saute pearl onions for 3 minutes until brown. Add morels and deglaze with cognac. Add cream reduce by half. Add veal glaze. Place veal on 4 plates, spoon sauce over. Makes 4, 6½ oz. servings.

Chef Scott Gilbert, C.E.C., Amway Grand Plaza Hotel, Grand Rapids, Michigan
Amway Corporation

SILVER CHEF
PASTITSIO
(Baked Macaroni and Cheese Casserole with Midland Harvest Burger N' Loaf and Cream Sauce)

1 tbsp. salt
1 pound ziti or elbow macaroni
7 tablespoons olive oil
1 cup chopped onions
1 6 oz. package Midland Har-
   vest Original Burger N'
   Loaf
6 medium tomatoes, peeled
   and finely chopped or 1
   16 oz. can canned tomatoes, chopped and
   drained
1 cup canned tomato puree
1 clove garlic, minced
1 tsp. oregano
1/4 tsp. ground cinnamon
   freshly ground black
   pepper
1/2 cup fresh bread crumbs
   from white bread
1 egg lightly beaten
3/4 cup grated Parmesan
   cheese

Sauce:
4 cups milk
2 tablespoons butter
6 eggs
1 tsp. salt
1/2 cup flour

1. Cook ziti in 6–8 quarts salted boiling water until soft but still resistant. Drain pasta and set aside.
2. Heat 6 tablespoons olive oil in skillet and add onions. Cook for 5 minutes or until soft.
3. Prepare Burger N' Loaf according to package instructions and brown in skillet in the same manner as loose ground meat.
4. When Burger N' Loaf is cooked, add tomatoes, tomato puree, garlic, oregano, cinnamon, a dash of salt and freshly ground black pepper and bring to a boil. Reduce heat, cover, and simmer for 15 minutes.
5. Remove skillet from heat and stir in 1/4 cup bread crumbs and the egg.
6. Make the cream sauce by combining 3 cups of milk and the butter in a pan until butter is melted over very low heat. Remove from the heat. Do not boil.
7. Beat the eggs with a whisk until frothy in a separate 2–3 quart saucepan. Add remaining 1 cup of milk and 1 tsp. salt, beating constantly, add the flour, 1 tablespoon at a time.
8. Stirring constantly, slowly stir in heated milk over very low heat. Continue to stir constantly over low heat until sauce is smooth and thickens. Do not apply heat too quickly or eggs will curdle.
9. Preheat oven to 350 degrees.
10. Assemble the Pastisio by greasing a 9 × 15 × 2.5 inch baking dish with olive oil. Sprinkle remaining bread crumbs on bottom of dish. Then spread half of pasta, followed by the meat mixture. Then pour 2 cups of cream sauce evenly over top. Sprinkle with half of grated cheese. Make another layer with remaining pasta and pour remaining cream sauce over it. Sprinkle remaining cheese over the top.
11. Bake in oven for 45 minutes or until top is golden brown.
12. Cut in squares and serve hot.
    Serves 12

Archer Daniels Midland Company

PARMESAN CATFISH

1/3 cup Parmesan cheese
2/3 cup Italian bread crumbs
4 farm-raised catfish fillets
  margarine
  salt and pepper to taste
  paprika

Preheat oven to 350°. Rinse the catfish fillets with water and pat dry. Mix the Parmesan cheese and Italian bread crumbs together in a bowl. Dip the fillets in melted margarine to coat. Bread the fillets in cheese and crumb mixture, coating both sides well. Place the fillets in one layer in a lightly buttered, glass baking dish. Do not crowd the fish. Any left over breading may be sprinkled over the top of the fillets before baking. Bake fish 45 minutes or until well done and crunchy around the sides. Sprinkle with paprika and garnish with parsley if desired.

CATFISH FARMERS OF AMERICA

CLASSIC FRIED CATFISH

3/4 cup yellow cornmeal
1/4 cup flour
2 teaspoons salt
1 teaspoon cayenne pepper
1/4 teaspoon garlic powder
4 farm-raised catfish fillets
  vegetable oil

Combine cornmeal, flour, salt, cayenne pepper and garlic powder. Coat catfish with mixture, shaking off excess. Fill deep pot or 12-inch skillet half full with vegetable oil. Heat to 350°F. Add catfish in a single layer and fry until golden brown, about 2-3 minutes on each side. Remove and drain on paper towels.

CATFISH FARMERS OF AMERICA

RACK OF LAMB GREENBRIER

The Greenbrier Cookbook
Tender young lamb from neighboring Monroe County gets regal treatment in this classic roast lamb preparation.

1 cup fresh bread crumbs
1 cup loosely-packed fresh
   parsley sprigs
1 medium clove garlic,
   crushed
1 tablespoon chopped fresh
   rosemary or 1 teaspoon
   dried
   salt and freshly ground
   black pepper, to taste
3 trimmed lamb racks (6
   chops each, about 2 per
   person)
1 tablespoon oil (such as
   olive, canola or soy)
1 egg
2 tablespoons prepared
   mustard
2 tablespoons unsalted
   butter, melted

1. Combine the bread crumbs, parsley, garlic, rosemary, salt and pepper in a food processor and work until thoroughly mixed. (Alternatively, finely chop all ingredients by hand and stir to combine.)

2. Preheat the oven to 400F. Season the lamb racks with salt and pepper. Heat the oil in a large sauté pan until quite hot and *sear* the racks on all sides until thoroughly and evenly browned. (Do this in batches if necessary.) Remove the lamb from the pan and leave until cool enough to handle.

3. Mix the egg and mustard together until smooth. Spread over the fat sides of the cooled lamb. Coat the same sides with a thick layer of the crumb mixture, patting to help the crumbs adhere. Drizzle the melted butter over the crumb coating. Set the lamb on a roasting pan, coating side up, and roast in the preheated oven 20 minutes for medium rare. (The internal temperature should be 125°F.)

4. Remove the lamb from the oven, cover loosely with aluminum foil and leave in a warm place for 5-7 minutes to let the juices redistribute for better texture. Cut the racks into individual chops and arrange on a warmed platter or plates, or present the racks of lamb whole on a warmed serving platter and carve at the table. Serves 8.

CSX Corporation

DOVES IN CREAM GRAVY

8 doves
6 slices of bacon
salt and pepper
flour
¼ cup chopped onion
1½ cups milk

Prepare whole doves by cutting them down the back from neck to tail, then spread out the doves, salt and pepper and flour both sides of the birds, shaking off excess. Fry bacon over moderate heat until fat is rendered. Remove bacon, drain on paper towels, crumble into bits and reserve. Brown doves in hot bacon fat for 5 minutes, reduce heat to low, cover and cook for about twenty minutes, turning birds once or twice. Set doves aside on a heated platter, and cover loosely with foil. To make gravy, pour off all but a thin film of fat, cook onions till soft, stir in any brown bits that cling to pan, remove skillet from heat, stir in two tablespoons of flour until a thick paste forms, rewisk until sauce thickens slightly, add salt and pepper to taste, stir in bacon bits, simmer for a minute. Serve doves with cream gravy and hot biscuits. This marvelous gravy recipe can also be used with rabbit, pheasant quail or cornish game hen. During the Fall, this is our favorite Sunday morning brunch at "Poverty Point", our Eastern Shore hunting lodge. Serves 4.

Carol Bugg

Carol Donayre Bugg, ASID
Decorating Den Systems, Inc.

HAM AND BEAN SOUP

Take a big ham bone with meat still on it. Put it in a big pot. Cover the ham bone with water and boil it for two hours or so. Put the pot in the refrigerator (or outside if it's cold) and let it cool until the fat can be skimmed off. Skim off the fat, pick out the pieces of lean meat, and save them. Pour the remaining stuff into a strainer. Save the broth that goes through the strainer.

Go to the store—get a six pack of St. Pauli Girl and a small bag of every kind of dried bean on the shelf (Navy, Great Northern, Lima, Pinto, Garbanzo, Split Pea, Lentil, Black Eyed Pea, Kidney, etc.).

Go home—drink a St. Pauli Girl and mix all of the beans in a big container.

Put two cups of beans and four cups of water in a large pot. Cover the pot and boil the beans real hard for five minutes. Turn off the burner and let the pot sit for one hour. *DO NOT LIFT THE LID.*

While the beans are "under the lid," have another St. Pauli and saute some onion and some celery in olive oil and butter.

When the beans have had their hour, take off the lid, add the sauted onions and celery and add to the pot:

Some chopped tomatoes (2 or 3 cans—wash out the seeds).

Spices—basil, marjoram, thyme, rosemary, salt, pepper, parsley.

A couple of shots of Worchestershire sauce.

Some garlic cloves (about 4 or 5) peeled but not cut or crushed. (Don't worry, by not cutting or crushing them, you will get a very subtle flavor when the cloves have cooked tender—not the harsh flavor of crushed garlic. You can pick out the cooked cloves, if you want, but they are really quite mild and tasty.)

One package of fresh spinach—cooked and chopped.

The ham and ham broth saved from step 1.

Let this all cook for an hour or so—clean up the kitchen—fix some cornbread— have another Pauli.

Enjoy.
Fluor Corporation

ROAST DUCK WITH CHAMBORD SAUCE

1 duck, 4-5 pounds
1 carrot, chopped
1 onion, chopped
1 tomato, chopped
1 cup brown stock or beef broth
3 tablespoons sugar
⅓ cup cider vinegar
1 10-ounce package frozen raspberries
⅓ cup Chambord liqueur

Trim excess fat from duck. Prick skin and season with salt and pepper. Roast duck with chopped giblets for 1½ hours at 450° or until done. Pour off all but 2 tablespoons of fat from roasting pan. Add carrot, onion and tomato and sauté for 10 minutes. Add stock and scrape pan to loosen brown bits. Strain into a container. Melt sugar in butter in a saucepan. Cook until brown. Add vinegar and cook until reduced by half. Pour in duck sauce and reduce heat to simmer. Add raspberries and Chambord. Simmer 10 minutes. Serve over duck.

Judy Zazulia
Irwin Zazulia, **President & C.E.O., Hecht's**

SILVER CHEF

On behalf of Holland America Line's First Lady, the ss Rotterdam, Executive Chef Wolfgang Wasshausen submits his Dutch Green Pea Soup recipe. This is one of the soups served on board the new ms Statendam's 1994 World Cruise which continues the Tradition of Excellence.

HOLLAND AMERICA'S DUTCH GREEN PEA SOUP

1 pound dried split green peas
2 quarts of water
¼ cup diced pork belly
1 smoked sausage ring, sliced
1 chopped leek
1 medium size onion, chopped
1 stalk celery
1 chopped celery root
1 bay leaf
1 pigs knuckle

Place the peas in a kettle, add cold water and let stand over night. In a saute pan cook the diced pork and vegetables for 5 minutes until tender. Add the salt pork and vegetable mixture along with the bay leaf and pig's knuckle to the peas. Cover and bring to a slow boil. Reduce the heat, skim foam from top and simmer for two hours, or until meat from the pig's knuckle separates from the bone. Remove pig's knuckle, shred the meat and reserve. Discard knuckle and bay leaf. Strain the soup and press vegetables through a sieve. Return the meat and sieved vegetables to the soup kettle and adjust seasoning to your taste. Add the sliced smoked sausage and serve.

Holland America Line Westours Inc.

HEAVENLY NO BAKE CHEESECAKE

1½ cups chocolate wafer
   crumbs (about ¾-8 oz.
   pkg.)
4 tablespoons butter or
   margarine, melted
1 envelope unflavored
   gelatine
1 cup milk
4 MILKY WAY Bars (2.23 oz.
   ea.), sliced
2 pkgs. (8 oz. ea.)
   cream cheese, softened
2 tablespoons sugar
1 teaspoon vanilla extract
1 cup (½ pt.) heavy or whipping cream

Combine chocolate crumbs and butter and press into bottom and 2 inches up the sides of an 8-inch springform pan; chill. Sprinkle gelatine over milk in a medium saucepan. Stir over low heat until gelatine is dissolved. Add MILKY WAY Bars and continue to stir over low heat until mixture is smooth; cool slightly. Meanwhile, beat cream cheese and sugar until smooth. Beat in MILKY WAY Bar mixture and vanilla. Add cream and beat at high speed 4 minutes. Pour mixture into prepared crust. Chill until firm, about 4 hours. If desired, garnish with additional whipped cream and sliced MILKY WAY Bars. Makes about 12 servings.

NOTE: *This cheesecake is also good when served with a Fresh Strawberry Sauce; puree 2 cups strawberries with 1 tablespoon sugar in a blender.*

Preparation Time: About 30 minutes
Chilling Time: 4 hours

m & m and Mars

DELTA MINT TEA

7 tea bags
12 sprigs mint
   rind of 3 lemons
8 cups boiling water
   juice of 7 lemons
2 cups sugar
8 cups water

Steep tea, mint and lemon rind in boiling water for 12 minutes. Remove from water. Add juice and sugar. Strain. Add water. Makes 1 gallon.

Eddie and Martha Dale Fritts
National Association of Broadcasters

ARTICHOKE SOUP

2 cans artichoke bottoms
4 egg yolks
2 cans of undiluted chicken broth
  salt and pepper to taste
8 tablespoons flour
8 tablespoons butter
2 cartons whipping cream (1 pint)
2 cans artichoke hearts, mashed

In a blender combine the artichoke bottoms, egg yolks, chicken broth and seasonings using a medium speed until smooth. Leave this mixture in the blender for later use. In a pan, heat the butter, flour and whipping cream until very hot, but not boiling. Add this mixture to the blender and mix well. Pour the entire contents of the blender in the saucepan and reheat. When hot, add the mashed artichoke hearts and serve. May be made the day ahead. Serves 8.

Pacific Telesis Group

TROUT MEUNIERE

6 trout fillets
  flour, salt and pepper

Sauce:
½ cup butter
3 green onions, chopped fine
2 tbsp. Worcestershire
4–5 drops Tabasco
2 tbsp. chopped parsley
1 tsp. salt
3 tbsp. lemon juice

Coat fillets with seasoned flour. Fry in hot oil. Drain and arrange in oven-proof platter. Top with Sauce Meuniere. (This much may be prepared ahead.) Continue just before serving, bake at 400 degrees about 10 minutes or until warm and bubbly. Garnish with lemon slices and parsley.

Simmer until onion and parsley are wilted and flavors are well mingled.

Nancy Allgood

Mrs. Kelly Allgood, *Wife of J. Kelly Allgood, President*
South Central Bell

FRIDAY'S CARROT CAKE

STEP 1—CAKE

1½ cups white flour
   (all-purpose)
1½ teaspoons baking soda
1½ teaspoons cinnamon
¼ teaspoon salt
2 eggs
½ cup vegetable oil
⅔ cup buttermilk
½ cup sugar
1½ teaspoon vanilla extract
¼ cup crushed pineapple
   (drained)
2 cups shredded carrots
   (unpeeled; shredded
   with ³/₁₆" blade)
¾ cup chopped pecans
   (chopped coarse)

Mix flour, baking soda, cinnamon, and salt in a large mixing bowl. Beat eggs, oil, buttermilk, sugar, and vanilla in a separate bowl. Add the flour mixture, pineapple, carrots, coconut, and pecans. Stir well. Grease a 9½" × 13½" pan. Pour in batter and bake at 350°F for 50–55 minutes, or until a toothpick inserted in the center comes out clean.

STEP 2—GLAZE

¾ cup sugar
⅜ teaspoon baking soda
⅓ cup buttermilk
6 tablespoons margarine
2 teaspoons corn syrup
¾ teaspoon vanilla extract

Combine sugar, baking soda, buttermilk, margarine, and corn syrup in a sauce pan and bring to a boil. Cook 5 minutes, stirring often. Remove from heat and stir in vanilla. Prick warm cake surface with a skewer every 2 inches. Slowly pour glaze over the cake. Allow cake to cool until glaze is absorbed (approximately 15 minutes). Do not refrigerate.

STEP 3—FROSTING

¼ pound margarine
½ pound cream cheese
2 teaspoons vanilla extract
1½ cups confectioners' sugar

Combine margarine and cream cheese in a mixing bowl and beat until fluffy. Add vanilla and confectioners' sugar and continue to beat until smooth. Hold at room temperature for easier spreading. Frost cake in pan, spreading room temperature icing smoothly and evenly over the cake. Refrigerate cake until frosting sets (approximately 30 minutes). Serve directly from the pan. Serves 8 to 12.

T.G.I. Friday's

WILD RICE CHICKEN SUPREME

1 package (6 ounces) UNCLE
  BEN'S Long Grain &
  Wild Rice Original
  Recipe
¼ cup butter or margarine
⅓ cup chopped onion
⅓ cup flour
1 teaspoon salt
  dash black pepper
1 cup half & half
1 cup chicken broth
2 cups cubed cooked
  chicken
⅓ cup diced pimiento
⅓ cup chopped fresh parsley
¼ cup chopped slivered
  almonds

Uncle Ben's, Inc.

Cook contents of one 6-ounce package UNCLE BEN'S Long Grain & Wild Rice as directed on package. While rice is cooking, melt butter in a large saucepan. Add onion and cook over low heat until tender. Stir in flour, salt and pepper. Gradually stir in half & half and chicken broth. Cook, stirring constantly, until thickened. Stir in chicken, pimiento, parsley, almonds and cooked rice. Pour into a greased 2-quart casserole. Bake, uncovered, in 400°F oven for 30 minutes. Makes 6-8 servings.

BRONZE CHEFS

Anheuser-Busch

AT&T

Bristol-Myers Squibb Company

CBS Inc.

Coca-Cola, Inc.

Conagra, Poultry Companies

Domino's Pizza Team Washington

Domino's Sugar

Dow Chemical

Ebasco Services Incorporated

ENSERCH Corporation

Food Marketing Institute

General Mills Inc.

General Motors Corporation

Grocery Manufacturers of America, Inc.

Hallmark Cards, Inc.

Hotel Employees and Restaurant Employees International Union

International Paper

Massachusetts Mutual Life Insurance Company

National Potato Council

NYNEX

Ocean Spray Cranberries, Inc.

Riceland Rice

RJR Nabisco

The Tobacco Institute

Turner Broadcasting System, Inc.

Tyson's Foods

United Parcel Service

Appendix

After Thoughts

We have tried to make each recipe as clear and concise as possible. We hope in the following section your questions are answered and your problems solved, so both novice and experienced cooks will enjoy using this Congressional Club Cookbook.

APPENDIX

After Thoughts

Entertaining

Napkin folding

Garnishes

Food quantities for 25, 50, 100

Terms used in cooking

Steak cooking chart

Buying guide for fresh fruit & vegetables

Vegetable time table

Cheese guide

Herbs and spices

Baking perfect breads

Microwave hints

Calorie counter

Substitutions

Metric conversion charts

ENTERTAINING

TABLE SETTINGS

As any gracious hostess will tell you, half the fun of planning a meal is the creative table setting. Where to begin? Your table setting should reflect the theme of the occasion. Is it casual, elegant, a tea, shower or a simple barbecue? Your goal is to make the table setting an attractive background for the food.

Traditional table linens have been replaced by every fabric imaginable. Feel free to use burlap or linen—whatever suits the mood and your lifestyle and don't forget the disposable variety. It you entertain often you may want a wide selection of colors and patterns, materials and cloths, mats and runners. They can be used interchangeably which seems to make the food taste better. Creativity is the key, and don't be timid—it's fun.

TABLECLOTHS: Buy them in the size of your table. Allow an overhang of 16 to 24 inches. If they are too long tie them up with bows or raffia. If your table is precious be sure to place a pad or sheet underneath to protect the antique. When you store your grandmother's tablecloths, they keep best on a cylinder roll or a clothes hanger.

PLACEMATS: Come in every imaginable fabric and color. Again, be creative, use different textures and colors depending on your goal, just remember, placemats should not be used for teas.

TABLE RUNNERS: Used for buffets or as place settings. Any material from linen to burlap. A shawl, or hemmed sheet, a quilt, or material you find on sale at your local fabric store. It's easy to get the length—crisscross for an added effect.

NAPKINS: Have fun—for a barbecue use blue jean material—a breakfast, sunny yellow, it will brighten any room. Add napkin rings: paper mache, or terra cotta, shower rings or bows. Have fun, keep your theme in mind and tuck a fresh flower in to compliment the centerpiece.

CENTERPIECES: Flowers are a favorite but bunnies at Easter or Santa Claus at Christmas, shells for seafood, the skull of a steer for a barbecue can be real conversation pieces as your guests make their way around the table. You will be surprised how many centerpieces sit on your mantle or act as a door stop, your child's goldfish, a miniature greenhouse, dried flowers and even family pictures for graduations or birthdays. Let your imagination run wild. And, don't forget candles. Use silver or pewter, glass or clay, use them together for informal or alone for formal. Or, use them all together and be surprised at the effect.

TABLEWARE: When choosing your dinnerware the size of your family and lifestyle should play a major role. Colors, patterns and styles of dinnerware range from bold to traditional. In today's world it's fun to mix and match. Different textures and colors add to the decor.
Glassware: Adds the dimension of height to your table setting. For buffet service use sturdy glassware, for formal dinners taller goblets. You will find all sorts of colors to choose from that will compliment any table.
Flatware: Your choices are numerous, sterling silver, silverplate, gold electroplate, or stainless steel. Be sure you will be happy using it for many years.

SETTING THE TABLE:

Drawings show how to set the table for each course. Appetizer course: Provide seafood fork, if needed, napkin, and silverware and glassware for the rest of the meal. Serve the appetizer on an underliner plate. (2) Soup course: Provide a soup spoon. Place soup bowl on an underliner plate. This course is often omitted, especially if an appetizer is served. (3) Main course: Provide dinner plate, salad plate (optional), bread-and-

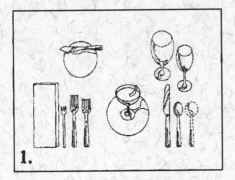

3.

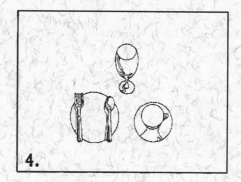

4.

butter plate and knife (optional), dinner fork, salad fork (optional), knife and spoon. Provide a glass for each beverage. Include a napkin if no previous courses have been served. (4) Dessert course: Serve dessert from the kitchen with the necessary silverware.

Serve coffee with dessert at the table or later in the living room.

If bread-and-butter plate is used, place it above the forks, with the bread-and-butter knife straight across the top of the plate. (This plate may be omitted if table space is limited.)

The salad plate may take several placements. If a bread-and-butter plate is used, place the salad plate to the left and below the bread-and-butter plate. When no bread-and-butter plate is used, place the salad plate at the tip of the forks.

Place napkins to the left of the forks with the open corners at the lower right. The napkin is placed on the dinner plate or in the center of the place setting when both salad and bread-and-butter plates are on the table.

The water glass or goblet belongs at the tip of the knife. If wine is served, set the wine glass above the spoons, below and to the right of the water glass.

STYLES OF SERVICE

You may use several styles of food service when entertaining.

Continental service requires servants to serve the food. With today's informal life-style, this service is rarely used.

When English service is used, dinner plates are stacked in front of the host, who serves the meat. The hostess serves the vegetables, then the plates are passed to guests. A variation of this style is family-style service. All food for the entrée is served by one person, then the filled plates are passed to the guests.

Other popular styles include country-style service and blue-plate service. For country-style service, filled serving dishes are placed on the table at the beginning of the meal. The person closest to the dish helps himself and passes the dish to the person on his right. For blue-plate service, plates are filled in the kitchen, then placed on the table just before guests sit down at the table.

Buffet-style is another service style. Containers of food are placed on a table, counter or side buffet. Guests help themselves to the food, then sit down at set tables or small tray tables placed around the room, or balance plates or trays on their laps.

TEAS AND RECEPTIONS

One of the most delightful traditions in entertaining is the afternoon tea or reception. When the tea is small, the beverage and food may be placed on a tray or small table. Arrange a teapot, hot water pot, sugar, and

Table set for family-style service

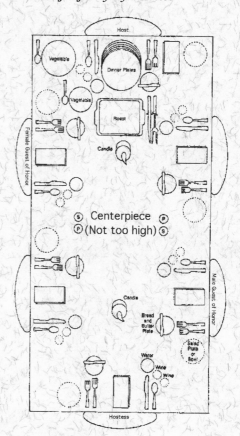

899

creamer to the right of the hostess for easy serving. Cups and saucers, stacked plates, silverware and napkins are placed to her left.

A formal tea or reception usually is given in honor of a person or a special occasion. It is customary to serve two beverages. The tea service sits at one end of a large table. The other beverage, coffee or a light punch, is at the other end. Set cups and saucers on the left, teaspoons and napkins on the right and food platters in easy reach along the length of the table.

Buffet Tables

A successful buffet always looks delightfully easy to the guests—but, as every hostess knows, it does require special planning. If space allows, place the buffet table in the middle of the room so guests can circulate around it. Or, you may choose to place the table just far enough away from the wall for the hostess to work comfortably behind it. Use a cart of small table nearby for beverage.

When setting the buffet table, it is important that guests can serve themselves in a logical sequence. At one end of the table, place the dinner plates and the main dish. Other foods, along with serving pieces, are placed near the edge of the table within easy reach of guests. Leave enough space near serving dishes for guests to set the plates.

Set the table attractively. Arrange silver and napkins so they can be picked up last. Carefully go over every item on the menu to see that everything is in order.

When the group is quite large, set up twin arrangements of plates, food, silver and napkins on each side of the table. Suggest that guests form two lines to help themselves to the food.

If a sit-down buffet is possible, arrange small tables in another room with silver, napkins and water glasses. Provide beverage cups, cream, and sugar at each table. Place beverage containers on the tables or have the beverage served, if desired.

Buffet with beverage cart

One-line buffet

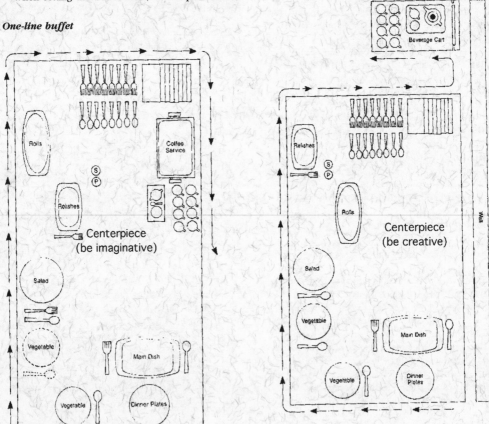

NAPKIN FOLDING

General Tips:
Use linen napkins if possible, well starched.
Add a final "party" touch to your table by folding napkins into decorative shapes.
For the more complicated folds, 24 inch napkins work best.
Practice the folds with newspapers.
Children can help. Once they learn the folds, they will have fun!

SHIELD
This fold is easy. Elegant with monogram in corner

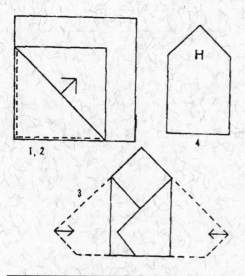

1. Fold into quarter size. If monogrammed, ornate corner should face down.
2. Turn up folded corner three-quarters.
3. Overlap right and left side points.
4. Turn over; adjust sides so that they are even, single point in center.
5. Place point up or down on plate, or left of plate.

ROSETTE
Elegant on Plate.

1. Fold top and bottom edges to the center, leaving 1/2″ opening along the center.
2. Pleat firmly from the left edge. Sharpen edges with hot iron.
3. Pinch center together. If necessary, use small piece of pipe cleaner to secure and top with single flower.
4. Spread out rosette

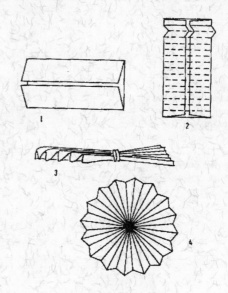

FAN

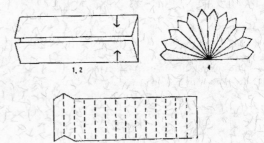

1. Fold top and bottom edges to the center.
2. Fold top and bottom edges to center a second time.
3. Pleat firmly from the left edge. Sharpen edges with a hot iron.
4. Spread out fan. Balance flat folds on each side on table. Well starched napkins will hold the shape.

CANDLE
Easy to do, can be decorated.

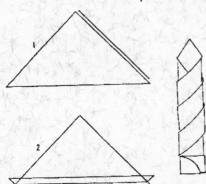

1. Fold into triangle, point at top.
2. Turn lower edge up 1″.
3. Turn over, folded edge down.
4. Roll tightly from left to right.
5. Tuck in corner. Stand upright.

LILY
Effective and Pretty on Table.

1. Fold napkin into quarters.
2. Fold into triangle, closed corner to open points.
3. Turn two points over to other side. (Two points are on either side of closed point.) Pleat.
4. Place closed end in glass. Pull down two points on each side and shape.

BUTTERFLY
For A Different Look

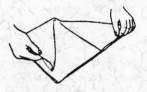  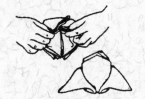

1. Form a triangle from an open napkin. 2. Fold the right corner to the center.

3. Take the left corner up to center, making a diamond. Keeping the loose points at the top, turn the napkin over, then fold upward, to form a triangle.

4. Tuck the left corner into the right. 5. Stand up napkin; turn it round, then turn the petals down; it's now a butterfly.

ARTICHOKE
Easier Than It Looks

1. Place all 4 points to the center of an opened napkin.

2. Fold the 4 points to the center of the napkin once more.

3. Repeat a third time; turn napkin over and fold points to the center once more.

  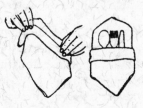

4. Holding finger firmly at center, unfold 1 petal first from underneath each corner.

5. Pull out 4 more from between the petals. Then pull out the next 4 under the petals.

6. The artichoke now has 12 points.

SILVER BUFFET
For Quick Service

  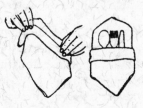

1. Fold the napkin over twice to form a square. 2. Hold the square in a diamond shape.

3. Take the top 2 flaps and roll them halfway down the napkin.

4. Fold under the right and left points at the sides. 5. There is now a pocket into which you can place the knife, fork and spoon.

GARNISHES

VEGETABLE GARNISHES

Artichoke Cup: Cut off stem so that artichoke will sit level. Snip tips of leaves off artichoke. Steam until tender about 45 minutes. Drain and chill. Hollow out inside of artichoke. Place a bowl inside cavity. Fill with dip and place in center of tray. Place crackers, vegetables, etc. to be dipped around artichoke.

Cabbage Container: Select a red or green cabbage that has large outer leaves. Carefully curl back outer leaves. Cut so cabbage will sit flat. Cut a cavity in center. Place a small glass or bowl in cavity. Fill with dip. Surround with fresh vegetables or boiled shrimp.

Carrot Curls: With a swivel vegetable peeler, cut long strips of carrot pushing peeler away from body. Roll up strips and secure with toothpicks. Drop in ice water and chill for several hours. Remove toothpicks for serving.

Stuffed Celery: Use 2 ribs of celery approximately the same size. Cut off leaves and tough end. Fill each with favorite cheese spread. Place 1 celery rib on top of other. Tie ribs together at each end. Refrigerate. When ready to serve, remove string and cut crosswise into small slices. Serve with sandwiches or on relish trays.

Cucumber Pinwheels and Twists: Using fork or citrus stripper, score cucumber lengthwise all the way around. Cut in thin slices to form pinwheel. Use as a garnish for meat trays, for relish trays, or for salads. To form a twist, cut from center of cucumber slice through outside edge. Gently twist to form an "S" shape. Chill in ice water to set.

Cucumber or Turnip Lily: Cut 2 thin cucumber circles. Carefully curl 1 circle into a cone shape. Wrap the other cucumber circle in opposite direction around cone shape. Secure base with toothpick. Use a small strip of carrot in center of lily for stamen. Chill in ice water until serving time. The same method may be used with turnip slices.

Cucumber Tulip: Cut a 2-inch piece off end of cucumber. Cut 6 triangular sections down from cut edge evenly around cucumber to make tulip petals. Scoop seeds and some pulp out of center. Push a small circle of carrot into cavity to form center of flower. Chill in ice water.

Green Onion Fans: Cut root off thick green onion. Cut again making a 2 to 3-inch length piece. With the point of a small knife, starting 1/4 of the way from stem end, cut into center and down to root end. Continue to make cuts around onion, keeping cuts as close together as possible. Chill in ice water to make onion curl.

Onion Mums: Choose a medium-sized, well-rounded white onion. Do not use onions with a double growth inside. Remove skin and cut off roots but leave root end intact. Use a small sharp knife and start cutting at top of onion through center towards root end. Do not cut all the way through. Stop 1/2-inch from root end. Continue making cuts all the way around onion. Place onion in hot water for 5 minutes. Then chill in ice water until time to serve.

Parsley Wreath: Cover a small, green florist's wreath with parsley sprigs, using wire florist picks to secure parsley. Decorate wreath with broccoli and cauliflower florets, fluted mushrooms, celery fans, radish roses, carrot curls and boiled shrimp. Use toothpicks to secure these decorations. Place bowl of vegetable dip in center of wreath.

Pepper Cups: Use large green, red, or yellow peppers that will sit flat. Cut stem end off peppers and remove seeds. Fill with mustard and mayonnaise and place on meat trays or fill with vegetables or relishes.

Pumpkin Bowl: Cut top off pumpkin and remove seeds. Place a bowl inside pumpkin. Use as a container to serve fresh fruit, vegetables, or punch.

Radish or Pickle Fan: Cut root and stem off a long oval radish with a small knife. Make crosswise cuts in accordion fashion almost through radish. Keep cuts as close together and as even as possible. Chill in ice water to open into fan shape. Small pickles may be used, also.

Radish Rose: Cut root and stem off a well-rounded radish. Starting halfway down radish, make a downward cut in red skin parallel to side of radish, stopping ¼-inch from end of radish to make petal. Repeat evenly around radish making 4 cuts. Turn radish ¼ turn. Starting further toward center, make 4 more downward cuts around radish, stopping at top of first row of cuts. Hollow out center. Push a small circle of carrot into cavity to form center. Chill in ice water to make petals open.

Tomato Rose: Choose a firm tomato. Start at bottom of tomato and peel in a 1-inch wide continuous spiral slightly scalloping edge. Be careful not to break spiral. Coil spiral skin-side out to form rose bloom. Secure with toothpick, if necessary. Place rose on small lettuce leaf or bed of parsley to garnish. This process can be used with lemons and oranges.

Turnip Flowers: Cut thin slices of turnips. Use flower-shaped canapé cutters to cut flower shapes out of turnip slices or cut flower shapes with small, sharp knife. Cut small circles out of carrots or turnips. Place circles in middle of flowers. Secure with toothpick. Flowers may be tinted by soaking in water colored with food coloring. A stem may be added by slipping tops of green onions over toothpicks. Use without stem to garnish molds. Fill an orange or grapefruit cup with turnip flowers with stems and parsley or curly leaf lettuce to make a small flower arrangement to be used in center of tray.

FRUIT GARNISHES

Citrus Bows: With a citrus stripper or mushroom fluter, cut around lemon, lime, or orange making 1 continuous thin strip at least 8 inches long. Tie strip in a bow or use as a curlicue to garnish seafood, vegetables, salads, or desserts.

Citrus or Melon Crowns: Slice off stem ends of lemon or other citrus fruit. Holding fruit on its side, make a diagonal cut into core. Continue making cuts in a zigzag fashion all the way around center of fruit. Make sure each cut goes all the way into core and that first and last cuts will meet evenly. Gently twist halves and pull apart. Place sprig of parsley, cherry, or olive slice in center of crown. Cut melons in the same manner. Scoop out seeds and fill with melon balls, cottage cheese, chicken salad, etc.

Citrus Twists: Using a citrus stripper score fruit lengthwise at regular intervals. Slice the fruit ¼-inch thick. Cut from center of fruit through outer edge at 1 of scored spaces. Gently twist into "S" shape. Use to garnish food or beverages. For extra color, dip a cotton swab in food coloring and paint the scored spaces in either same or alternating colors.

Cranberry Garlands: With needle and thread, string fresh cranberries. Use to garnish turkey or some other meat trays at holiday time.

Cranberry Cut Outs: Slice canned jellied cranberry sauce ¼-inch thick. Cut into shapes with cookie cutters. Place on orange slices and use to garnish meat or seafood.

Sugared Grapes: Wash and dry grapes. Break into clusters. Bring to boil ½ cup water and 1 cup sugar. Simmer about 5 minutes. Dip each cluster into sugar syrup. Let excess syrup drip off and immediately sprinkle with additional sugar. Place on waxed paper to harden. Do not refrigerate. Use to garnish cheese boards, sandwich and dessert trays or cakes. Other small fruit may be sugared in same manner.

Grapefruit or Orange Baskets: Use a thick skinned fruit. With stem down, cut away a wedge on each side of center leaving a ½ to ¾-inch wide strip to form handle. If desired, zigzag or scallop around sides of basket. Carefully scoop out fruit pulp. A grapefruit spoon is helpful for this. Fill basket with sugared grapes, fresh flowers, greenery, or flowers made from vegetables.

Pineapple Boats: Slice large pineapple in half lengthwise. Scoop out fruit. Fill halves with fresh fruit, chicken or shrimp salad. Pineapple may also be cut in quarters. Then cut fruit away from skin in 1 piece. Leaving the fruit in the skin, remove core and cut into bite-size pieces. (Leave core whole.) Place a maraschino cherry on top of each pineapple piece and secure each with a toothpick. This makes a beautiful as well as delicious garnish.

Strawberry Fan: Leave stem on strawberry. Turn strawberry stem-side down. Make 5 to 6 parallel, verticle cuts through bottom of strawberry almost to stem.

BEVERAGE GARNISHES

Ice Bowl: Fill a large bowl ¾ to 1 inch deep with water and freeze. Place another bowl (of similar shape but 2 inches smaller) inside large bowl. Secure bowls with masking tape and place a weight, such as a heavy can, inside smaller bowl. Place citrus slices or fresh flowers and greenery around insides of larger bowl; fill with water and freeze at least 24 hours. To unmold, let stand until bowls come loose. Place ice bowl on tray. Surround with greenery and fill with cold beverage. Bowl may also be lined with plastic wrap or a clear plastic bowl and used as a container for boiled seafood or melon balls.

Ice Ring: Fill a metal ring mold with water. Pour this water into a bowl. Let this water sit 10 to 15 minutes, stirring water 4 or 5 times. This process expels the air bubbles. Pour ¼ to ⅓ water back into mold. Place mold in freezer and refrigerate remaining water to chill. When water in mold is slushy, remove and add a wreath of fruit, flowers, and greenery. Holly is attractive at Christmas time. Pour cold water just to top of decorations. Freeze until firm. Pour over another layer of cold water to fill mold. Freeze. To unmold, wrap a hot towel around mold. Float ring in punch bowl.

Garnishes by the Glass: (1) Cut a slit in citrus slices to garnish rim of glasses. (2) Garnish a red wine glass with a small cluster of red grapes and white wine glass with green grapes. (3) Cut a small piece from a ring of pineapple and place over rim of a glass of fruit drink. (4) Garnish the rim of a glass of sangria with a wedge of apple dipped in lemon juice. (5) Float a strawberry in a glass of champagne. (6) Cut a slit in a strawberry and place it on the rim of a glass of strawberry daiquiri. (7) Make a fruit kabob for fruit drinks by placing a cherry, a pineapple chunk, and a small orange wedge on a toothpick. (8) Garnish a Bloody Mary with a carrot stick or a small celery rib. (9) Float a lemon or orange slice studded with whole cloves in hot spiced cider or tea. (10) Garnish hot chocolate with a cinnamon stick, a cinnamon candy stick, or peppermint stick. (11) Place a long sprig of mint in ice tea.

MISCELLANEOUS GARNISHES

Bacon Curls: Fry bacon until almost crisp. Press bacon flat as it cooks. Immediately upon removing from skillet, roll into coil. As bacon cools, it will hold the shape. Use as a garnish for egg dishes or quiches.

Bread Baskets: Hollow out center of large round, rectangular, or oval bread leaving a ¾-inch shell. Fill with dip and use bread pieces for dipping. A rectangular bread can be used as a container for finger sandwiches. The bread can also be cut with a sharp knife to make a basket with a handle.

Butter Balls and Curls: Dip a melon ball scoop in hot water for a few minutes; then scoop out butter. Drop butter balls into ice water. Refrigerate until time to serve. To make butter curls, place butter curler in hot water. Pull curler lightly across top of a firm, but not too cold, stick of butter. Drop curls into ice water. Refrigerate. To serve butter balls or curls, drain and serve piled in a pyramid on a dish of cracked ice.

Chocolate Curls: Warm slightly the blade of a vegetable peeler. Hold a wrapped chunk or bar of chocolate in hand to warm. Pull blade across chocolate to make curls. Use a toothpick to pick up curls and place on dessert.

Chocolate Cutouts: Melt 6 ounces semisweet chocolate over low heat. When slightly cooled, pour chocolate onto a cookie sheet covered with foil. Spread over pan until chocolate is smooth and about ⅛ to ¼ inch thick. When chocolate is almost set, cut firmly with cookie cutters. Lift with spatula when firm. Cover and store in refrigerator.

FOOD QUANTITIES FOR SERVING
25, 50, AND 100 PEOPLE

Food	25 Servings	50 Servings	100 Servings
Sandwiches:			
Bread	50 slices or 3 1-lb. loaves	100 slices or 6 1-lb. loaves	200 slices or 12 1-lb. loaves
Butter	½ pound	¾ to 1 pound	1½ pounds
Mayonnaise	1 cup	2 to 3 cups	4 to 6 cups
Mixed Filling (meat, eggs, fish)	1½ quarts	2½ to 3 quarts	5 to 6 quarts
Mixed Filling jams, etc.	1 quart	1¾ to 2 quarts	2½ to 4 quarts
Lettuce	1½ heads	2½ to 3 heads	5 to 6 heads
Soup:	1¼ gallons	2½ gallons	5 gallons
Meat, Poultry, or Fish:			
Wieners	6½ pounds	13 pounds	25 pounds
Hamburger	9 pounds	18 pounds	35 pounds
Turkey or Chicken	13 pounds	25 to 35 pounds	50 to 75 pounds
Fish, large whole	13 pounds	25 pounds	50 pounds
Fish fillets or steak	7½ pounds	15 pounds	30 pounds
Oysters	4½ quarts	9 quarts	18 quarts
Salads, Casseroles:			
Potato Salad	4¼ quarts	1¼ gallons	4½ gallons
Scalloped Potatoes	4½ quarts or 1 12 × 20″ pan	8½ quarts	17 quarts
Spaghetti	1¼ gallons	2½ gallons	5 gallons
Baked Beans	¾ gallon	1¼ gallons	2½ gallons
Jello Salad	¾ gallon	1¼ gallons	2½ gallons
Cabbage for slaw	5 lbs.	10 lbs.	20 lbs.
Ice Cream:			
Brick	3¼ quarts	6½ quarts	12½ quarts
Bulk	2¼ quarts	4½ quarts or 1¼ gallons	9 quarts or 2½ gallons
Beverages:			
Coffee	½ pound and 1½ gal. water	1 pound and 3 gal. water	2 pounds and 6 gal. water
Tea	¹⁄₁₂ pound and 1½ gal. water	⅙ pound and 3 gal. water	⅓ pound and 6 gal. water
Lemonade	10 to 15 lemons, 1½ gal. water	20 to 30 lemons, 3 gal. water	40 to 60 lemons, 6 gal. water
Desserts:			
Watermelon	37½ pounds	75 pounds	150 pounds
Cake	1 10 × 12″ sheet cake 1½ 10″ layer cakes	1 12 × 20″ sheet cake 3 10″ layer cakes	2 12 × 20″ sheet cakes 6 10″ layer cakes
Whipping Cream	¾ pint	1½ to 2 pints	3 pints

TERMS USED IN COOKING

Au gratin — Topped with crumbs and/or cheese and browned in the oven or under the broiler.

Au jus — Served in its own juices.

Bake — To cook covered or uncovered in an oven or oven type appliance. For meats cooked uncovered, it's called roasting.

Baste — To moisten foods during cooking with pan dripings or special sauce to add flavor and prevent drying.

Beat — To make mixture smooth by adding air with a brisk whipping or stirring motion using spoon or electric mixer.

Blanch — To immerse in rapidly boiling water and allow to cook slightly.

Blend — To thoroughly mix two or more ingredients until smooth and uniform.

Boil — To cook in liquid at boiling temperature (212° at sea level) where bubbles rise to the surface and break. For a full rolling boil, bubbles form rapidly throughout the mixture.

Braise — To cook slowly with a small amount of liquid in tightly covered pan on top of range or in oven.

Broil — To cook by direct heat, usually in broiler or over coals.

Candied — To cook in sugar or syrup when applied to sweet potatoes and carrots. For fruit or fruit peel, to cook in heavy syrup till transparent and well coated.

Chill — To place in refrigerator to reduce temperature.

Chop — To cut in pieces about the size of peas with knife, chopper or blender.

Cool — To remove from heat and let stand at room temperature.

Cream — To beat spoon or electric mixer till mixture is soft and smooth. When applied to blending shortening and sugar, mixture is beaten till light and fluffy.

Cut In — To mix shortening with dry ingredients using pastry blender or knives.

Degrease — To remove fat from the surface of stews, soups or stock. Usually cooled in the refrigerator so that fat hardens and is easily removed.

Dice — To cut food in small cubes of uniform size and shape.

Dissolve — To disperse a dry substance in a liquid to form a solution.

Dredge — To coat lightly with flour, cornmeal, etc.

Fold — To incorporate a delicate substance, such as whipped cream or beaten egg whites, into another subtance without releasing air bubbles. A spatula is used to gently bring part of the mixture from the bottom of the bowl to the top. The process is repeated, while slowly rotating the bowl, until the ingredients are blended.

Glaze — A mixture applied to food which hardens or becomes firm and adds flavor and a glossy appearance.

Grate — To rub on a grater that separates the food into very fine particles.

Julienne — To cut vegetables, fruits or cheeses into match-shaped slivers.

Marinate —To allow food to stand in a liquid to tenderize or to add flavor.

Mince — To cut or finely chop food into very small pieces.

Mix — To combine ingredients, usually by stirring, till evenly distributed.

Parboil — To boil until partially cooked; to blanch. Usually this procedure is followed by final cooking in a seasoned sauce.

Pare — To remove the outer most skin of a fruit or vegetable.

Poach — To cook in hot liquid, being careful that food holds its shape while cooking.

Precook — To cook food partially or completely before final cooking or reheating.

Puree — To mash foods until perfectly smooth by hand, rubbing through a sieve, or whirling in a blender or food processor.

Roast — To cook uncovered without water added, usually in an oven.

Saute — To cook brown or cook in a small amount of hot shortening.

Scald — To bring to a temperature just below the boiling point where tiny bubbles form at the edge of the pan.

Scallop — To bake food, usually in a casserole, with sauce or other liquid. Crumbs are often sprinkled atop.

Simmer — To cook in liquid just below the boiling point. The surface of the liquid should be barely moving, broken only by slowly rising bubbles.

Steam — To cook in steam with or without pressure. A small amount of boiling water is used, more water being added during steaming process if necessary.

Stir — To mix ingredients with a circular motion until well blended or of uniform consistency.

Toss — To mix ingredients lightly.

Truss — To secure fowl or other meat with skewers to hold its shape during cooking.

Whip — To beat rapidly to incorporate air and produce expansion, as in heavy cream or egg whites.

TO PREPARE STEAKS

Thaw in refrigerator, bring meat to room temperature before cooking. You can successfully cook frozen steaks. Start by searing both sides to seal in juices. Then reduce heat for slow cooking to allow the inside to thaw. Follow the chart below, but allow about twice the cooking time for frozen steaks.

For juicier and more flavorful steaks, tongs should be used when handling or turning. Cooking units vary of course and it is always advisable to run your own tests when cooking steaks. The chart below is a guide.

The cooking times below are for fully thawed steaks.
Filet Mignons take one to two minutes less total time to cook.

		Red-Hot Charcoal 2¾" from heat source		Pre-heated oven broiler 2" from heat source	
Cooking Instructions					
Thickness	Doneness	First side	After turning	First side	After turning
¾"	Rare	4 Minutes	2 Minutes	5 Minutes	4 Minutes
	Medium	5 Minutes	3 Minutes	7 Minutes	5 Minutes
	Well	7 Minutes	5 Minutes	10 Minutes	8 Minutes
1"	Rare	5 Minutes	3 Minutes	6 Minutes	5 Minutes
	Medium	6 Minutes	4 Minutes	8 Minutes	6 Minutes
	Well	8 Minutes	6 Minutes	11 Minutes	9 Minutes
1¼"	Rare	5 Minutes	4 Minutes	7 Minutes	5 Minutes
	Medium	7 Minutes	5 Minutes	8 Minutes	7 Minutes
	Well	9 Minutes	7 Minutes	12 Minutes	10 Minutes
1½"	Rare	6 Minutes	4 Minutes	7 Minutes	6 Minutes
	Medium	7 Minutes	6 Minutes	9 Minutes	7 Minutes
	Well	10 Minutes	8 Minutes	13 Minutes	11 Minutes
1¾"	Rare	7 Minutes	5 Minutes	8 Minutes	7 Minutes
	Medium	8 Minutes	7 Minutes	9 Minutes	8 Minutes
	Well	11 Minutes	9 Minutes	14 Minutes	12 Minutes

If you prefer to cook your steaks in your conventional oven, do not thaw, and preheat oven to 450°. As a guide for medium-rare steaks allow approximately:
10–11 minutes per side for an 8 oz. Filet of Prime Rib
12–13 minutes per side for an 8 oz. Top Sirloin
9 minutes per side for an 11 or 12 oz. Boneless Strip Sirloin
10–11 minutes per side for a 6 oz. Filet Mignon

Because ovens may vary in the amount of heat produced and the best distance to place the meat from the burners, tests on your equipment are valuable.

BUYING GUIDE

Fresh Vegetables and Fruits

Experience is the best teacher in choosing quality, but here are
a few pointers on buying some of the fruits and vegetables.

Asparagus: Stalks should be tender and firm, tips should be close and compact. Choose the stalks with very little white—they are more tender. Use asparagus soon—it toughens rapidly.

Beans, Snap: Those with small seeds inside the pods are best. Avoid beans with dry-looking pods.

Berries: Select plump, solid berries with good color. Avoid stained containers, indicating wet or leaky berries. Berries such as blackberries and raspberries with clinging caps may be under-ripe. Strawberries without caps may be too ripe.

Broccoli, Brussel Sprouts, and Cauliflower: Flower clusters on broccoli and cauliflower should be tight and close together. Avoid yellow flowers. Brussel sprouts should be firm and compact. Smudgy, dirty spots may indicate insects.

Cabbage and Head Lettuce: Choose heads heavy for size. Avoid cabbage with worm holes, lettuce with discoloration or soft rot.

Cucumbers: Choose long, slender cucumbers for best quality. May be dark or medium green but yellowed ones are undesirable.

Melons: In cantaloupes, thick close netting on the rind indicates best quality. Cantaloupes are ripe when the stem scar is smooth and space between the netting is yellow or yellow-green. They are best when fully ripe with fruity odor.

Honeydews are ripe when rind has creamy to yellowish color and velvety texture. Immature honeydews are whitish-green.

Ripe watermelons have some yellow color in one side. If melons are white or pale green on one side, they are not ripe.

Oranges, Grapefruit, and Lemons: Choose those heavy for their size. Smoother, thinner skins usually indicate more juice. Most skin markings do not affect quality. Oranges with a slight greenish tinge may be just as ripe as fully colored ones. Light or greenish-yellow lemons are more tart than deep yellow ones. Avoid citrus fruits showing withered, sunken, or soft areas.

Peas and Lima Beans: Select pods that are well-filled but no bulging. Avoid dried, spotted, yellowed, or flabby pods.

TABLE FOR DRIED FRUITS		
Fruit	**Cooking Time**	**Amount of Sugar or Honey**
Apricots	About 40 minutes	1/4 cup for each cup of fruit
Figs	About 30 minutes	1 tablespoon for each cup of fruit
Peaches	About 45 minutes	1/4 cup for each cup of fruit
Prunes	About 45 minutes	2 tablespoons for each cup of fruit

VEGETABLE TIME TABLE

Vegetable	Cooking Method	Time
Asparagus Tips	Boiled	5-10 minutes
Artichokes, French	Boiled	40 minutes
	Steamed	45-60 minutes
Beans, Lima	Boiled	20-40 minutes
	Steamed	60 minutes
Beans, String	Boiled	15-35 minutes
	Steamed	60 minutes
Beets, young with skin	Boiled	30 minutes
	Steamed	60 minutes
	Baked	70-90 minutes
Beets, old	Boiled or Steamed	1-2 hours
Broccoli, flowerets	Boiled	5-10 minutes
Broccoli, stems	Boiled	20-30 minutes
Brussel Sprouts	Boiled	20-30 minutes
Cabbage, chopped	Boiled	10-20 minutes
	Steamed	25 minutes
Cauliflower, stem down	Boiled	20-30 minutes
Cauliflower, flowerets	Boiled	8-10 minutes
Carrots, cut across	Boiled	8-10 minutes
	Steamed	40 minutes
Corn, green, tender	Boiled	5-10 minutes
	Steamed	15 minutes
	Baked	20 minutes
Corn on the cob	Boiled	8-10 minutes
	Steamed	15 minutes
Eggplant, whole	Boiled	30 minutes
	Steamed	40 minutes
	Baked	45 minutes
Parsnips	Boiled	25-40 minutes
	Steamed	60 minutes
	Baked	60-75 minutes
Peas, green	Boiled or Steamed	5-15 minutes
Potatoes	Boiled	20-40 minutes
	Steamed	60 minutes
	Baked	45-60 minutes
Pumpkin or Squash	Boiled	20-40 minutes
	Steamed	45 minutes
	Baked	60 minutes
Tomatoes	Boiled	5-15 minutes
Turnips	Boiled	25-40 minutes

CHEESE GUIDE

Cheese	How it looks and tastes	How to serve
American, Cheddar	Favorite all-around cheeses. Flavor varies from mild to sharp. Color ranges from natural to yellow-orange; texture firm to crumbly.	In sandwiches, casseroles, souf-fles, and creamy sauces. With fruit pie or crisp crackers; on a snack or dessert tray with fruit.
Blue, Gorgonzola, Roquefort	Compact, creamy cheeses veined with blue or blue-green mold. Sometimes crumbly. Mild to sharp salty flavor. (Stilton is similar, but like a blue-veined Cheddar.)	Crumble in salads, salad dressings, dips. Delicious with fresh pears or apples for dessert. Blend with butter for steak topper. Spread on crackers or crusty French or Italian bread.
Brick	Medium firm; creamy yellow color, tiny holes. Flavor very mild to medium sharp.	Good for appetizers, sandwiches, or desserts. Great with fresh peaches, cherries or melons.
Brie *(bree)*	Similar to Camembert, but slightly firmer. Distinctive sharp flavor, pronounced odor.	Serve as dessert with fresh fruit. Be sure to eat the thin brown and white crust.
Camembert *(kam' em bear)*	Creamy yellow with thin gray-white crust. When ripe, it softens to the consistency of thick cream. Full, rich, mildly pungent.	Classic dessert cheese—serve at room temperature with fresh peaches, pears, or apples, or with toasted walnuts and crackers.
Cottage	Soft, mild, unripened cheese; large or small curd. May have cream added.	Used in salads, dips, main dishes. Popular with fresh and canned fruits.
Cream	Very mild-flavored soft cheese with buttery texture. Rich and smooth. Available whipped and in flavored spreads.	Adds richness and body to molded and frozen salads, cheesecake, dips, frostings, sandwich spreads. Serve whipped with dessert.
Edam, Gouda	Round, red-coated cheeses; creamy yellow to yellow-orange inside; firm and smooth. Mild nut-like flavor.	Bright hub for dessert or snack tray. Good in sandwiches or crunchy salads, or with crackers. Great with grapes and oranges.
Liederkranz, Limburger	Robust flavor and highly aromatic. Soft and smooth when ripe. Lie-derkranz is milder in flavor and golden yellow in color. Limburger is creamy white.	Spread on pumpernickel, rye, or crackers. Team with apples, pears, and Tokay grapes. Serve as snack with salty pretzels and coffee.
Mozzarella, Scamorze	Unripened. Mild-flavored and slightly firm. Creamy white to pale yellow.	Cook cheese. A "must" for pizza, lasagne; good in toasted sandwiches, hot snacks.
Muenster *(mun' stir)*	Mild to mellow flavor, creamy white. Medium hard, tiny holes.	Use in sandwiches or on snack or dessert tray. Good with fresh sweet cherries and melon wedges.

Cheese	How it looks and tastes	How to serve
Parmesan, Romano	Sharp, piquant, very hard cheese. Comes grated in shakers. (Parmesan is also available shredded.) Or grate your own.	Sprinkle on pizza, main dishes, breads, salads, soups. Shake over buttered popcorn!
Port du Salut (*por du sa lu'*)	Semisoft, smooth, and buttery. Mellow to robust flavor between Cheddar and Limburger.	Dessert cheese—delicious with fresh fruit; great with apple pie. Good for snack tray.
Provolone (*pro vo lo' nee*)	Usually smoked; mild to sharp flavor. Hard, compact and flaky. Pear or sausage shaped.	Use in Italian dishes, in sandwiches, on snack and appetizer trays.
Swiss	Firm pale yellow cheese, with large round holes. Sweet nutlike flavor.	First choice for ham-cheese sandwiches, fondue. Good in salads, sauces, as a snack.
Process cheeses	A blend of fresh and aged natural cheeses, pasteurized and packaged. Smooth and creamy, melts easily. May be flavored.	Ideal for cheese sauces, souffles, grilled cheese sandwiches, in casseroles. Handy for the snack tray, too.

HERBS AND SPICES

When substituting fresh herbs for dried, use three times more fresh herbs.

Basil Sweet warm flavor with an aromatic odor, used whole or ground. Good with lamb, fish, roast, stews, ground beef, vegetables, dressing and omelets.

Bay Leaves A pungent flavor, use whole leaf but remove before serving. Good in vegetable dishes, soups, fish and seafood, stews and pickles.

Caraway Has a spicy smell and aromatic taste. Use in cakes, breads, soups, cheese and sauerkraut.

Cayenne Pepper Pepper very hot ground spice from dried cayenne chili pepper. Use on pizza, spaghetti and clam sauce. Add to stews and chili.

Chives Sweet mild flavor of onion, this herb is excellent in salads, fish, soups and potatoes.

Cilantro Also known as Chinese or Italian parsley is the leaf of the coriander plant. Use in fillings for burritos, tacos and enchiladas. Add to Mexican salsas, guacamole, gazpacho, pea and chicken soup.

Curry Powder A number of spices combined to proper proportions to give a distinct flavor to such dishes as meat, poultry, fish and vegetables.

Dill Both seeds and leaves of dill are flavorful. Leaves may be used as a garnish or cook with fish, soup, dressings, potatoes and beans. Leaves or the whole plant may be used to spice dill pickles.

Fennel Both seeds and leaves are used. Has a sweet hot flavor. Use in small quantities in pies and baked goods. Leaves can be boiled with fish.

Ginger A pungent root, this aromatic spice is sold fresh, dried, or ground. Used in pickles, preserves, cakes, cookies, soups, meat dishes and many Asian dishes.

Marjoram May be used both dry or green. Used to flavor fish, poultry, omelets, lamb, stew, stuffing and tomato juice. Also good on some vegetables.

Mint Leaves are aromatic with a cool flavor. Excellent in beverages, fish, cheese, lamb, soup, peas, carrots and fruit desserts.

Oregano Strong aromatic odor, use whole or ground to spice tomato juice, fish, eggs, pizza, omelets, chili, stew, gravy, poultry, salads and vegetables.

Paprika

A bright red pepper, this spice is used in meat, vegetables and soups. Can be used as a garnish for potatoes, salads or eggs.

Parsley

Best when used fresh but can be used dry, use as garnish or seasoning. Try in fish, omelets, soup, meat, stuffing and mixed greens.

Rosemary

Very aromatic, used fresh or dried. Season fish, stuffing, beef, lamb, poultry, onions, eggs and bread.

Saffron

Orange yellow in color, this spice is used to flavor or color foods. Use in soup, chicken, rice and fancy breads.

Sage

Use fresh or dried. The flowers are sometimes used in salads. May be used in tomato juice, fish, fondue, omelets, beef, poultry, stuffing, cheese spreads, cornbread and biscuits.

Tarragon

Leaves have a pungent, hot taste. Use to flavor sauces, salads, meat, poultry, tomatoes and dressings.

BAKING PERFECT BREADS

Proportions

Biscuits	To 1 cup flour use 1¼ teaspoon Baking Powder
Muffins	To 1 cup flour use 1½ teaspoon Baking Powder
Popovers	To 1 cup flour use 1¼ teaspoon Baking Powder
Waffles	To 1 cup flour use 1¼ teaspoon Baking Powder
Cake with oil	To 1 cup flour use 1 teaspoon Baking Powder

Rules for Use of Leavening Agents

1. To 1 teaspoon soda use 2¼ teaspoons cream of tartar, or 2 cups freshly soured milk, or 1 cup molasses.

2. In simple flour mixtures, use 2 teaspoons baking powder to leaven 1 cup flour. Reduce this amount ½ teaspoon for each egg used.

3. To substitute soda and an acid for baking powder, divide the amount of baking powder by 4. Take that as your measure of and add the acid according to rule 1 above.

Proportions for Batters and Dough

Pour Batter	To 1 cup liquid use 1 cup flour
Drop Batter	To 1 cup liquid use 2 to 2½ cups flour
Soft Dough	To 1 cup liquid use 3 to 3½ cups flour
Stiff Dough	To 1 cup liquid use 4 cups flour.

Hints for Baking Breads

Kneading the dough for a half minute after mixing improves the texture of baking powder biscuits.

Use cooking or salad oil in waffles and hot cakes in the place of shortening. No extra pan or bowl to melt the shortening and no waiting.

When bread is baking, a small dish of water in the oven will help to keep the crust from getting hard.

Dip the spoon in hot water to measure shortening, butter, etc., the fat will slip out more easily.

Small amounts of leftover corn may be added to pancake batter for variety.

To make bread crumbs, use fine cutter of the food grinder and tie a large paper bag over the spout to prevent flying crumbs.

MICROWAVE HINTS

1. Place an open box of hardened brown sugar in the microwave oven with 1 cup hot water. Microwave at high for 1½ to 2 minutes for ½ pound or 2 to 3 minutes for 1 pound.

2. Soften hard ice cream by microwaving at 30% power. One pint will take 15 to 30 seconds; one quart, 30-45 seconds; and one-half gallon 45-60 seconds.

3. One stick of butter or margarine will soften in 1 minute when microwaved at 20% power.

4. Soften one 8-ounce package of cream cheese by microwaving at 30% power for 2 to 2½ minutes. One 3-ounce package of cream cheese will soften in 1½ to 2 minutes.

5. Thaw frozen orange juice right in the container. Remove the top metal lid. Place the opened container in the microwave and heat on high power 30 seconds for 6 ounces and 45 seconds for 12 ounces.

6. Thaw whipped topping... a 4½ ounce carton will thaw in 1 minute on the defrost setting. Whipped topping should be slightly firm in the center but it will blend well when stirred. Do not overthaw!

7. Soften Jello that has set up too hard—perhaps you were to chill it until slightly thickened and forgot it. Heat on a low power setting for a very short time.

8. Heat hot packs in a microwave oven. A wet finger tip towel will take about 25 seconds. It depends on the temperature of the water used to wet the towel.

9. To scald milk, cook 1 cup for 2 to 2½ minutes, stirring once each minute.

10. To make dry bread crumbs, cut 6 slices bread into ½-inch cubes. Microwave in 3-quart casserole 6-7 minutes, or until dry, stirring after 3 minutes. Crush in blender.

11. Refresh stale potato chips, crackers or other snacks of such type by putting a plateful in the microwave oven for about 30-45 seconds. Let stand for 1 minute to crisp. Cereals can also be crisped.

12. Nuts will be easier to shell if you place 2 cups of nuts in a 1-quart casserole with 1 cup of water. Cook for 4 to 5 minutes and the nutmeats will slip out whole after cracking the shell.

13. For stamp collectors: place a few drops of water on stamp to be removed from envelope. Heat in the microwave for 20 seconds and the stamp will come right off.

14. Using a round dish instead of a square one eliminates overcooked corners in baking cakes.

15. A crusty coating of chopped walnuts surrounding many microwaved-cooked cakes and quick breads enhances the looks and eating quality. Sprinkle a layer of medium, finely chopped walnuts evenly onto the bottom and side of a ring pan or bundt cake pan. Pour in batter and microwave as recipe directs.

16. Heat left-over custard and use it as frosting for a cake.

17. Melt marshmallow cream in the microwave oven. Half of a 7-ounce jar will melt in 35-40 seconds on high. Stir to blend.

18. Toast coconut in the microwave. Watch closely as it browns quickly once it begins to brown. Spread ½ cup coconut in a pie plate and cook for 3-4 minutes, stirring every 30 seconds after 2 minutes.

Beverages

Apple juice, 6 oz. 90
Coffee (black/unsw.) 0
Cola type, 12 oz. 115
Cranberry juice, 6 oz. 115
Ginger ale, 12 oz. 115
Grape juice, (prepared from
   frozen concentrate), 6 oz. 142
Lemonade (prepared from
   frozen concentrate), 6 oz. 85
Milk
   protein fortified, 1 cup 105
   skim, 1 cup 90
   whole, 1 cup 160
Orange juice, 6 oz. 85
Pineapple juice, unsweetened, 6 oz. 95
Root beer, 12 oz. 150
Tonic (quinine water), 12 oz. 132

Breads

Corn Bread, 1 small square 130
Dumplings, 1 med. 70
French Toast, 1 slice 135
Muffins
   bran, 1 muffin 106
   blueberry, 1 muffin 110
   corn, 1 muffin 125
   English, 1 muffin 280
Melba Toast, 1 slice 25
Pancakes, 1 4 in. 60
Pumpernickel, 1 slice 75
Rye, 1 slice 60
Waffles, 1 216
White, 1 slice 60-70
Whole wheat, 1 slice 55-65

Cereals

Corn Flakes, 1 cup 105
Cream of Wheat, 1 cup 120
Oatmeal, 1 cup 148
Rice Flakes, 1 cup 105
Shredded Wheat, 1 biscuit 100
Sugar Krisps, ¾ cup 110

Crackers

Graham, 1 cracker 15-30
Rye Crisp, 1 cracker 35
Saltine, 1 cracker 17-20
Wheat Thins, 1 cracker 9

Dairy Products

Butter or Margarine, 1 tablespoon 100
Cheese
   American Cheese, 1 oz. 100
   Camembert, 1 oz. 85
   Cheddar, 1 oz. 115
   Cottage Cheese, 1 oz. 30
   Mozzarella, 1 oz. 90
   Parmesan, 1 oz. 130
   Ricotta, 1 oz. 50
   Roquefort, 1 oz. 105
   Swiss, 1 oz. 105
Cream
   Light, 1 tablespoon 30
   Heavy, 1 tablespoon 55
   Sour, 1 tablespoon 45
Hot chocolate, with milk, 1 cup 277
Milk chocolate, 1 oz. 145-155
Yogurt
   made w/whole milk, 1 cup 150-165
   make w/skimmed milk, 1 cup 125

Eggs

Fried, 1 large 100
Poached or boiled, 1 large 75-80
Scrambled or in omelet, 1 large 110-130

Fish and Seafood

Bass. 4 oz. 105
Salmon, broiled or baked, 3 oz. 155
Sardines canned in oil, 3 oz. 170
Trout, fried, 3½ oz. 220
Tuna, in oil, 3 oz. 170
Tuna, in water, 3 oz. 110

Fruits

Apple, 1 medium 80-100
Applesauce, sweetened, ½ cup 90-115
Applesauce, unsweetened, ½ cup 50
Banana, 1 medium 85
Blueberries, ½ cup 45
Cantaloupe melon, ½ cup 24
Cherries (pitted), raw, ½ cup 40
Grapefruit, ½ medium 55
Grapes, ½ cup 35-55
Honeydew melon, ½ cup. 55
Mango, 1 medium 90
Orange, 1 medium 65-75
Peach, 1 medium 35
Pear, 1 medium 60-100

Pineapple, fresh, ½ cup 40
Pineapple canned in syrup, ½ cup 95
Plum, 1 medium 30
Strawberries, fresh, ½ cup 30
Strawberries, frozen
   and sweetened, ½ cup 120-140
Tangerine, 1 large 39
Watermelon, ½ cup 42

Meat and Poultry

Beef, ground (lean), 3 oz. 185
Beef, roast, 3 oz. 185
Chicken, broiled, 3 oz. 115
Lamb chop (lean), 3 oz. 175-200
Sirloin steak, 3 oz. 175
Tenderloin steak, 3 oz. 174
Top round steak, 3 oz. 162
Turkey, dark meat, 3 oz. 175
Turkey, white meat, 3 oz. 150
Veal cutlet, 3 oz. 156
Veal, roast, 3 oz. 176

Nuts

Almonds, 2 tablespoons 105
Cashews, 2 tablespoons 100
Peanuts, 2 tablespoons 105
Peanut butter, 1 tablespoon 95
Pecans, 2 tablespoons 95
Pistachios, 2 tablespoons...92
Walnuts, 2 tablespoons 80

Pasta

Macaroni or spaghetti,
   ¾ cup cooked 115

Salad Dressings

Blue Cheese, 1 tablespoon 70

French, 1 tablespoon 65
Italian, 1 tablespoon 80
Mayonnaise, 1 tablespoon 100
Olive oil, 1 tablespoon 124
Russian, 1 tablespoon 70
Salad oil, 1 tablespoon...120

Soups

Bean, 1 cup 130-180
Beef noodle, 1 cup 70
Bouillon and consomme, 1 cup 30
Chicken noodle, 1 cup 65
Chicken with rice, 1 cup 50
Minestrone, 1 cup 80-150
Split pea, 1 cup 145-170
Tomato with milk, 1 cup 170
Vegetable, 1 cup 80-100

Vegetables

Asparagus, 1 cup 35
Broccoli, cooked, ½ cup 25
Cabbage, cooked, ½ cup 15-20
Carrots, cooked, ½ cup 25-30
Cauliflower, ½ cup 10-15
Corn (kernels), ½ cup 70
Green Beans, 1 cup 30
Lettuce, shredded, ½ cup 5
Mushrooms, canned, ½ cup 20
Onions, cooked, ½ cup 30
Peas, green, cooked, ½ cup 60
Potato
   baked, 1 medium 90
   chips, 8-10...100
   mashed, with milk
   and butter, 1 cup 200-300
Spinach, 1 cup 40
Tomato
   raw, 1 medium 25
   cooked, ½ cup 30

SUBSTITUTIONS

1 cup self rising flour	*1 cup all-purpose flour, 1/2 tsp. salt, and 1 tsp. baking powder*
1 tablespoon cornstarch	*2 tablespoons flour or 2 tsp. quick-cooking tapioca*
1 teaspoon baking powder	*1/4 tsp. baking soda plus 1/2 tsp. cream of tartar*
1 cup powdered sugar	*1 cup granulated sugar plus 1 tsp. cornstarch*
1/2 cup brown sugar	*2 tablespoons molasses in 1/2 cup granulated sugar*
1 cup sour milk	*1 tablespoon lemon juice or vinegar plus sweet milk to make 1 cup (let stand 5 minutes).*
1 cup whole milk	*1/2 cup evaporated milk plus 1/2 cup water*
3/4 cup cracker crumbs	*1 cup bread crumbs*
1 square chocolate	*3 or 4 tablespoons cocoa plus 1 tablespoon butter*
1 tablespoon fresh herbs	*1 tsp. dried herbs*
1 small fresh onion	*1 tablespoon instant minced onion, rehydrated*
1 teaspoon dry mustard	*1 tablespoon prepared mustard*
1 cup tomato juice	*1/2 cup tomato sauce plus 1/2 cup water*
1 cup catsup or chili sauce	*1 cup tomato sauce plus 1/2 cup sugar and 2 tablespoons vinegar (for use in cooking).*
1 pound dates	*1 1/2 cup dates, pitted and cut*
3 medium bananas	*1 cup mashed*
10 minature marshmallows	*1 large marshmallow*
2 large eggs	*3 small eggs*
1 cup sour cream	*1 tablespoon lemon juice plus evaporated milk to equal 1 cup*
1 cup all purpose flour	*1 cup plus 2 tablespoons cake flour*
1 cup cake flour	*1 cup minus 2 tablespoons all purpose flour*
1 pound fresh mushrooms	*6 ounces canned mushrooms*
1 clove fresh garlic	*1 teaspoon garlic salt or 1/8 teaspoon garlic powder*
1 tablespoon fresh herbs	*1 teaspoon dried herbs or 1/4 teaspoon powered herbs*

In substituting cocoa for chocolate in cakes, the amount of flour must be reduced. Brown and White Sugars: Usually may be used interchangeably.

METRIC CONVERSION CHARTS

TABLESPOONS AND OUNCES
(U.S. Customary System)

GRAMS
(Metric System)

1 pinch = less than ⅛ teaspoon (dry)	0.5 gram
1 dash = 3 drops to ¼ teaspoon (liquid)	1.25 grams
1 teaspoon liquid	5.0 grams
3 teaspoons = 1 tablespoon = ½ ounce	14.3 grams
2 tablespoons = 1 ounce	28.35 grams
4 tablespoons = 2 ounces = ¼ cup	56.7 grams
8 tablespoons = 4 ounces = ½ cup (1 stick of butter)	113.4 grams
8 tablespoons (flour) = about 2 ounces	72.0 grams
16 tablespoons = 8 ounces = 1 cup = ½ pound	226.8 grams
32 tablespoons = 16 ounces = 2 cups = 1 pound	453.6 grams or 0.4536 kilograms
64 tablespoons = 32 ounces = 1 quart = 2 pounds	907.0 grams or 0.907 kilogram
1 quart = (roughly 1 liter)	

CONVERSION FACTORS

ounces to grams: multiply ounce figure by 28.3 to get number of grams

grams to ounces: multiply gram figure by .0353 to get number of ounces

pounds to grams: multiply pound figure by 453.59 to get number of grams

pounds to kilograms: multiply pound figure by 0.45 to get number of kilograms

ounces to milliliters: multiply ounce figure by 30 to get number of milliliters

cups to liters: multiply cup figure by 0.24 to get number of liters

Fahrenheit to Celsius: subtract 32 from the Fahrenheit figure, multiply by 5, then divide by 9 to get Celsius figure

Celsius to Fahrenheit: multiply Celsius figure by 9, divide by 5, then add 32 to get Fahrenheit figure

inches to centimeters: multiply inch figure by 2.54 to get number of centimeters

centimeters to inches: multiply centimeter figure by .39 to get number of inches

NOTES

Index to Contributors

A

Adair, Mrs. E. Ross, Wife of former Representative (Indiana), 467, 513

Adams, Abigail Smith, Wife of the President of the United States (1797–1801), 2

Adams, Mrs. Brock, Wife of former Senator (Washington), 368, 676, 812

Adams, Louisa Catherine Johnson, Wife of the President of the United States (1825–1829), 6

Ahsan, Mrs. Abul, Wife of Ambassador (Bangladesh), 757

Albert, Mrs. David, Daughter-in-law of former Representative Carl Albert (Oklahoma), 451, 666

Al-Khalifa, Mrs. Abdul, Wife of Ambassador (Bahrain), 748, 756

Allard, Mrs. Wayne, Wife of Representative (Colorado), 213, 498

Amway Corporation, Gilbert, Chef Scott, C.E.C., 882

Andréani, Mrs. Jacques, Wife of Ambassador (France), 728, 772

Andrews, Mrs. Thomas, Wife of Representative (Maine), 129, 186

Andrews, Tom, Representative (Maine), 410, 804

Andrus, Mrs. Cecil, Wife of Governor (Idaho), 232, 392, 529

Applegate, Doug, Representative (Ohio), 278

Applegate, Mrs. Doug, Wife of Representative (Ohio), 72, 539, 640

Archer, Mrs. Bill, Wife of Representative (Texas), 47, 327, 346, 482

Archer Daniels Midland Company, 883

Ariza, Mrs. Jose, Wife of Ambassador (Dominican Republic), 725, 738

Arthur, Ellen Lewis Herndon, Wife of the President of the United States (1881–1885), 21

Ayres, Mrs. William H., Wife of former Representative (Ohio), 447

B

Baesler, Scotty, Representative (Kentucky), 692

Baesler, Mrs. Scotty, Wife of Representative (Kentucky), 39, 135, 317

Baker, William, Representative (California), 161

Baker, Mrs. William, Wife of Representative (California), 318, 592

Barlow, Mrs. Thomas, Wife of Representative (Kentucky), 312, 469, 572

Barrett, Bill, Representative (Nebraska), 203

Barrett, Mrs. Bill, Wife of Representative (Nebraska), 509, 696, 803, 818

Bartlett, Mrs. Joe, Daughter of former Senator George H. Bender (Ohio), 679

Bateman, Herbert H., Representative (Virginia), 516

Bateman, Mrs. Herbert, Daughter-in-law of Representative Herb Bateman, Sr. (Virginia), 262, 818

Bateman, Mrs. Herbert, Wife of Representative (Virginia), 403, 514, 656, 815

Battle, Mrs. James, Daughter-in-law of former Representative Laurie C. Battle (Alabama), 162, 448, 635

Battle, Laurie C., former Representative (Alabama), 661

Battle, Mrs. Laurie C., Wife of former Representative (Alabama), 163, 211, 467

Battle, Mrs. L. Hunt, Daughter-in-law of former Representative Laurie C. Battle (Alabama), 97, 494

Bayh, Evan, Governor (Indiana), 158, 619

Beach, Mrs. Robert, Daughter of former Senator James T. Broyhill (North Carolina), 81, 92, 266, 324

Beall, Mrs. J. Glenn, Jr., Wife of former Senator (Maryland), 187, 411, 832

Beilenson, Anthony, Representative (California), 700

Beilenson, Mrs. Anthony, Wife of Representative (California), 270, 449, 547

Bellamy, Mrs. Al, Daughter of Representative Al Swift (Washington), 530, 783

Bendaña, Mrs. René Arturo, Wife of Ambassador (Honduras), 721, 742

Bennett, Lucinda, Daughter of former Representative Charles Bennett (Florida), 164, 286

Bentsen, Mrs. Lloyd, Wife of Secretary of the Treasury, 824

Bethune, Ed, former Representative (Arkansas), 301

Bethune, Mrs. Ed, Wife of former Representative (Arkansas), 160, 432

Bevill, Mrs. Tom, Wife of Representative (Alabama), 50, 143, 170, 661

Biancheri, Mrs. Boris, Wife of Ambassador (Italy), 739, 743, 774

Bilbray, Jim, Representative (Nevada), 442

Bilbray, Mrs. Jim, Wife of Representative (Nevada), 209, 582

Bilirakis, Michael, Representative (Florida), 94

Bilirakis, Mrs. Michael, Wife of Representative (Florida), 108, 458, 519

Filner, Mrs. Bob, Wife of Representative (California), 148, 594, 805, 822

Finney, Joan, Governor (Kansas), 659, 667

Fish, Hamilton, Jr., Representative (New York), 229

Flippo, Ronnie, former Representative (Alabama), 360

Flippo, Mrs. Ronnie, Wife of former Representative (Alabama), 53, 174, 345

Florio, Mrs. James, Wife of Governor (New Jersey), 505, 678

Fluor Corporation, 887

Foley, John R., former Representative (Maryland), 297

Foley, Mrs. John R., Wife of former Representative (Maryland), 327, 376, 633

Foley, John R., III, Son of former Representative John R. Foley (Maryland), 618

Foley, Mrs. John R., III, Daughter-in-law of former Representative John R. Foley (Maryland), 109, 112, 154, 812

Ford, Mrs. Gerald R., Jr., Wife of former President of the United States, 102

Fordice, Kirk, Governor (Mississippi), 306, 681, 811

Fountain, Mrs. L.H., Wife of former Representative (North Carolina), 223, 366, 620, 687

Franco, Rodolfo, A Member of the Congressional Club Staff, 791

Friedman, Hugh, Husband of Representative Lynn Schenk (California), 506

Fuqua, Mrs. Don, Wife of former Representative (Florida), 510

G

Gallagher, Mrs. Dermot, Wife of Ambassador (Ireland), 732, 774

Gallegly, Elton, Representative (California), 421, 515

Gallegly, Mrs. Elton, Wife of Representative (California), 217, 431

Garfield, Lucretia Rudolph, Wife of the President of the United States, (1881), 20

Gavin, Mrs. Stephen, Daughter of Representative Jon Kyl (Arizona), 84, 131, 288, 432

Giaimo, Mrs. Robert, Wife of former Representative (Connecticut), 548, 639, 673, 702

Gibbons, Mrs. Sam, Wife of Representative (Florida), 331, 347, 470, 471

Gillmor, Paul, Representative (Ohio), 633

Gillmor, Mrs. Paul, Wife of Representative (Ohio), 334, 569, 595

Glickman, Dan, Representative (Kansas), 500

Glickman, Mrs. Dan, Wife of Representative (Kansas), 70, 443, 591

Goss, Mrs. Porter, Wife of Representative (Florida), 125, 414, 631

Grant, Julia Dent, Wife of the President of the United States (1869-1877), 18

Grant, Mrs. Robert A., Wife of former Representative (Indiana), 332, 535, 589, 636

Grassley, Mrs. Charles E., Wife of Senator (Iowa), 108, 227, 315, 697

Green, Gene, Representative (Texas), 679

Green, Mrs. Gene, Wife of Representative (Texas), 463, 586, 627

Grotberg, Mrs. John, Wife of former Representative (Illinois), 177, 393, 420

Guyer, Mrs. Tennyson, Wife of former Representative (Ohio), 657, 678

H

Hagan, Frances B., Daughter of former Representative G. Elliott Hagan (Georgia), 448, 543, 706

Hagan, Mrs. G. Elliott, Wife of former Representative (Georgia), 316, 593, 704

Hagen, Mrs. Harold, Wife of former Representative (Minnesota), 469, 625, 662, 670

Hall, Mrs. Tony, Wife of Representative (Ohio), 559

Hamburg, Mrs. Dan, Wife of Representative (California), 821

Hamilton, Mrs. Lee, Wife of Representative (Indiana), 464, 588, 600

Hammerschmidt, John Paul, former Representative (Arkansas), 640

Hammerschmidt, Mrs. John Paul, Wife of former Representative (Arkansas), 49, 110, 687

Hancock, Mrs. Mel, Wife of Representative (Missouri), 141, 355, 643

Hanley, Mrs. James, Wife of former Representative (New York), 230, 260, 614, 665

Hansen, Mrs. George, Wife of former Representative (Idaho), 156, 167, 632, 794

Harding, Florence Kling DeWolfe, Wife of the President of the United States (1921-1923), 28

Harkin, Mrs. Tom, Wife of Senator (Iowa), 543

Harris, Claude, former Representative (Alabama), 133

Harris, Mrs. Claude, Wife of former Representative (Alabama), 208, 464, 650

Harrison, Anna Tuthill Symmes, Wife of the President of the United States (1841), 9

Harrison, Caroline Lavinia Scott, Wife of the President of the United States (1889-1893), 23

Harvey, Mrs. James, Wife of former Representative (Michigan), 74, 280, 603

Hastert, Mrs. Dennis, Wife of Representative (Illinois), 152, 579, 606

Hatfield, Mrs. Mark, Wife of Senator (Oregon), 74, 393

Hayes, Mrs. Jimmy, Wife of Representative (Louisiana), 495, 511, 839

Hayes, Lucy Ware Webb, Wife of the President of the United States (1877-1881), 19

Hecht's, Judy Zazulia, Irwin Zazulia, President & C.E.O., 888

Hefley, Joel, Representative (Colorado), 80

Hefley, Mrs. Joel, Wife of Representative (Colorado), 198, 567

Heflin, Mrs. Howell, Wife of Senator (Alabama), 134, 273, 527

Hefner, Shelly, Daughter of Representative Bill Hefner (North Carolina), 46, 564

Hefner, W.G. (Bill), Representative (North Carolina), 682

Hefner, Mrs. W.G. (Bill), Wife of Representative (North Carolina), 117, 270, 314

Hehner, Mrs. H. Dee, Daughter of Representative Herbert Bateman (Virginia), 255, 658, 832

Heins, Mrs. John, Daughter of Representative Tom Lewis (Florida), 816

Herger, Mrs. Wally, Wife of Representative (California), 63, 76, 155

M

R

Racicot, Marc, Governor (Montana), 530, 660

Randolph, Martha Jefferson, Daughter and Official Hostess of the Widower President, Thomas Jefferson (1801–1809), 3

Ratcliffe, Mrs. Brian, Daughter of Representative Bill Brewster (Oklahoma), 104

Reagan, Mrs. Ronald, Wife of former President of the United States, 132, 429

Reeves, Mrs. Eric, Daughter of former Senator Robert B. Morgan (North Carolina), 207, 615, 626

Regula, Martha, Daughter of Representative Ralph Regula (Ohio), 43, 284, 301

Regula, Ralph, Representative (Ohio), 294

Regula, Mrs. Ralph, Wife of Representative (Ohio), 220, 415, 692

Reich, Frank J., Son-in-law of former Representative John J. Rhodes (Arizona), 534

Reich, Mrs. Frank, Daughter of former Representative John J. Rhodes (Arizona), 235, 479, 516

Renwick, H.E. Sir Robin, Ambassador (United Kingdom), 776

Rhodes, Jay, former Representative (Arizona), 810

Rhodes, Mrs. Jay, Wife of former Representative (Arizona), 186, 228, 371, 562, 803, 834

Rhodes, John J., former Representative (Arizona), 630

Rhodes, Mrs. John, Wife of former Representative (Arizona), 181, 343, 693

Rhodes, Scott, Son of former Representative John J. Rhodes (Arizona), 533

Rhodes, Mrs. Scott, Daughter-in-law of former Representative John J. Rhodes (Arizona), 399, 568, 576

Rhodes, Thomas H., Son of former Representative John J. Rhodes (Arizona), 497

Rhodes, Mrs. Thomas H., Daughter-in-law of former Representative John J. Rhodes (Arizona), 47, 247, 690

Rice, Mrs. Christopher, Daughter of former Representative Laurie C. Battle (Alabama), 329, 465, 629, 646

Richards, Ann, Governor (Texas), 610

Ricupero, H.E. Rubens, Ambassador (Brazil), 731, 743, 750

Robb, Mrs. Charles S., Wife of Senator (Virginia), 324, 606

Roberts, Barbara, Governor (Oregon), 159

Roberts, Pat, Representative (Kansas), 441

Roberts, Mrs. Pat, Wife of Representative (Kansas), 111, 265, 680

Robinson, Mrs. J. Kenneth, Wife of former Representative (Virginia), 123, 588, 601

Rockefeller, Mrs. John D., IV, Wife of Senator (West Virginia), 686

Roemer, Mrs. Tim, Wife of Representative (Indiana), 153, 365, 590

Rogers, Paul, former Representative (Florida), 73

Rogers, Mrs. Paul, Wife of former Representative (Florida), 113, 400, 614

Roosevelt, Anna Eleanor, Wife of the President of the United States (1933–1945), 31

Roosevelt, Edith Kermit Carow, Wife of the President of the United States (1901–1909), 25

Rowland, J. Roy, Representative (Georgia), 406

Rowland, Mrs. J. Roy, Wife of Representative (Georgia), 201, 298, 472

Royce, Mrs. Ed, Wife of Representative (California), 133, 146, 569

Runnels, Mrs. Harold, Wife of former Representative (New Mexico), 215, 313, 332

S

Sabo, Mrs. Martin, Wife of Representative (Minnesota), 102, 137, 446, 786, 831

Sanders, Mrs. John, Daughter of former Representative John E. Rankin (Mississippi), 236, 412, 456

Sangmeister, George E., Representative (Illinois), 375

Sangmeister, Mrs. George, Wife of Representative (Illinois), 201, 512, 616

Santini, Mrs. Jim, Wife of former Representative (Nevada), 68

Sasser, Mrs. Jim, Wife of Senator (Tennessee), 107, 355, 356, 649

Sawyer, Harold S., former Representative (Michigan), 98

Sawyer, Mrs. Harold S., Wife of former Representative (Michigan), 214, 341, 445

Schaefer, William Donald, Governor (Maryland), 403

Schermer, Beth, Wife of Representative Sam Coppersmith (Arizona), 354

Scheuer, Mrs. James H., Wife of former Representative (New York), 525

Schiff, Mrs. Steven, Wife of Representative (New Mexico), 578

Schulze, Mrs. Richard T., Wife of former Representative (Pennsylvania), 220, 272, 634

Schwarz, Mrs. Harry, Wife of Ambassador (South Africa), 730, 732, 765, 776

Schweiker, Richard S., former Senator (Pennsylvania), 605

Schweiker, Mrs. Richard S., Wife of former Senator (Pennsylvania), 162, 205, 407

Schwengel, Mrs. Fred, Wife of former Representative (Iowa), 176, 230, 238

Sein, Mrs. U. Thaung, Wife of Ambassador (Union of Myanmar), 729, 734, 761

Shaw, E. Clay, Representative (Florida), 104

Shaw, Mrs. E. Clay, Wife of Representative (Florida), 187, 397, 520

Shepard, Mrs. Tazewell, Daughter of former Senator John Sparkman (Alabama), 249, 319, 670, 806

Shoup, Mrs. Richard, Wife of former Representative (Montana), 358, 459, 636

Shriver, Mrs. Garner E., Wife of former Representative (Kansas), 496, 584, 642

Silva, Mrs. Patricio, Wife of Ambassador (Chile), 727, 760, 770

Simpson, Mrs. Alan, Wife of Senator (Wyoming), 53, 521, 611

Simpson, Mrs. Richard, Wife of former Representative (Pennsylvania), 392, 601

Sinovic, Ms. Gina, Daughter of Representative Jerry F. Costello (Illinois), 245

Skeen, Mrs. Joe, Wife of Representative (New Mexico), 80, 824

Skelton, Ike, Representative (Missouri), 266

Skelton, Mrs. Ike, Wife of Representative (Missouri), 250, 451, 843

Skelton, Mrs. Ike, IV, Daughter-in-law of Representative Ike Skelton (Missouri), 457

Volkmer, Mrs. Harold, Wife of Representative (Missouri), 221, 628, 694

Vucanovich, Barbara, Representative (Nevada), 45, 439

W

Walker, Mrs. Robert, Wife of Representative (Pennsylvania), 233

Wampler, Mrs. William, Wife of former Representative (Virginia), 64, 349

Washington, Martha Dandridge Custis, Wife of the President of the United States (1789–1797), 1

Waters, Mrs. Kathleen, Daughter of former Representative John R. Foley (Maryland.), 199, 458, 707

Watson, John, Son-in-law of former Representative Glenard P. Lipscomb (California), 367

Watson, Mrs. John, Daughter of former Representative Glenard P. Lipscomb (California), 234, 253

Watt, Mrs. Mel, Wife of Representative (North Carolina), 132, 634, 664

Waxman, Mrs. Henry A., Wife of Representative (California), 216, 240

Weaver, Mrs. George Arthur, Daughter of former Representative M.G. Burnside (West Virginia), 42, 206, 471, 659

Weicker, Lowell P., Jr., Governor (Connecticut), 417, 538

Weld, Bill, Governor (Massachusetts), 185

Wellstone, Mrs. Paul, Wife of Senator (Minnesota), 365, 435, 478

White, Mark, Son-in-law of former Representative Richard H. Ichord (Missouri), 637

White, Mrs. Mark, Daughter of former Representative Richard H. Ichord (Missouri), 282, 304, 794

Whitten, Mrs. Jamie L., Wife of Representative (Mississippi), 145, 203, 262, 629

Williams, Erin, Daughter of Representative Pat Williams (Montana), 96

Williams, Pat, Representative (Montana), 166

Williams, Mrs. Pat, Wife of Representative (Montana), 371, 501, 799

Williams, Whitney, Daughter of Representative Pat Williams (Montana), 48

Wilson, Mrs. Bob, Wife of former Representative (California), 348, 450, 685

Wilson, Edith Bolling Galt, Wife of the President of the United States (1915–1921), 27

Wilson, Ellen Louise Axson, Wife of the President of the United States (1913–1914), 27

Wilson, Mrs. Pete, Wife of Governor (California), 433

Wolf, Frank R., Representative (Virginia), 652

Wolf, Mrs. Frank, Wife of Representative (Virginia), 310, 482, 673

Worby, Ms. Rachael, Wife of Governor Gaston Caperton (West Virginia), 119, 136, 662

Wylie, Chalmers, former Representative (Ohio), 527

Wylie, Mrs. Chalmers, Wife of former Representative (Ohio), 210, 383, 531

Z

Zacharakis, Mrs. Cristos, Wife of Ambassador (Greece), 744, 773

Zeliff, Mrs. William H. (Bill), Wife of Representative (New Hampshire), 92, 546, 570, 806

Zerhouni, Mrs. Nourredine Y., Wife of Ambassador (Algeria), 737, 752, 766

Zorinsky-White, Mrs. Cece, Wife of former Senator Edward Zorinsky (Nebraska), 38, 85, 258, 617

Zschau, Mrs. Ed, Wife of former Representative (California), 61, 303, 333

Index to Recipes

P

NOTES

NOTES

NOTES

NOTES

Reprinted from
"First Lady's Tribute" Fabric.
Specially designed
by Decorating Den Systems, Inc.